A

POLITICAL
ECONOMY
OF THE
MIDDLE EAST

SECOND EDITION

A
POLITICAL
ECONOMY
OF THE
MIDDLE EAST

Alan Richards
UNIVERSITY OF CALIFORNIA–SANTA CRUZ

John Waterbury
PRINCETON UNIVERSITY

WestviewPress

A Division of HarperCollins*Publishers*

Table 10.10 is reproduced by permission from Ronnie Margulies and Ergin Yildizoğlu, "Trade Unions and Turkey's Working Class," *Middle East Reports* 14, no. 2 (Feb. 1984), p. 18, Table VII. MERIP/Middle East Reports, 1500 Massachusetts Ave. NW, #119, Washington, DC 20005.

Published in 1996 in the United States of America by Westview Press, 5500 Central Avenue, Boulder, Colorado 80301, and in the United Kingdom by Westview Press, 12 Hid's Copse Road, Cumnor Hill, Oxford OX2 9JJ

Library of Congress Cataloging-in-Publication Data
Richards, Alan, 1946–
   A political economy of the Middle East / Alan Richards, John Waterbury.—2nd ed.
      p.   cm.
   Includes bibliographical references and index.
   ISBN 0-8133-2410-6 (hc). — ISBN 0-8133-2411-4 (pbk.)
      1. Middle East—Economic conditions—1979–   2. Middle East—Economic policy.   3. Working class—Middle East.   4. Middle East—Politics and government—1979–   I. Waterbury, John. II. Title.
HC415.15.R53   1996
338.956—dc20   96-24374
                                                                             CIP

The paper used in this publication meets the requirements of the American National Standard for Permanence of Paper for Printed Library Materials Z39.48-1984.

10   9   8   7   6   5   4   3   2   1

CONTENTS

ILLUSTRATIONS

Figures

Maps

ACKNOWLEDGMENTS

This book is the distillation of over fifty years of the authors' combined experience of living in and studying the Middle East. In that respect it would be impossible to single out individuals who influenced us and helped with this text. Nonetheless, during a five-year period both authors were members of the Joint Committee for the Near and Middle East of the Social Science Research Council, and in the course of our regular meetings we drew on the collective wisdom of that committee's members.

We wish to thank As'ad Abu Khalil and Shahrough Ahkavi, who pointed out to us a number of errors in the first edition. We are grateful to Fareed Mohamedi of Petroleum Finance Corporation for timely data on oil revenues used in Chapter 3 and to Dennis Winstead of the U.S. Arms Control and Disarmament Agency for current data on military expenditures and arms transfers used in Chapter 13. Peter Barsoom, Eduardo Guerra, and Hui Miao provided crucial and expert research assistance in the preparation of the second edition. Alisa Richards provided excellent hospitality in July 1995. (Alan Richards would add: and constant support in myriad other ways, as always.) We pay special homage to Fred Praeger, who founded Westview Press and to whom the idea of this book owes its inception. Fred Praeger passed away in 1994, after a long and distinguished career as a publisher as well as an indefatigable devotee of track and field. We dedicate the second edition to his memory.

Alan Richards
Santa Cruz

John Waterbury
Princeton

ACRONYMS AND ABBREVIATIONS

AAAID	Arab Authority for Agricultural Investment and Development
AMIO	Arab Military Industrialization Organization
ANM	Arab National Movement
ASU	Arab Socialist Union
BNDE	National Economic Development Bank
BP	British Petroleum
CBR	crude birthrate
CIA	Central Intelligence Agency
CNRA	National Council of the Algerian Revolution
DC	developed country
DISK	Confederation of Progressive Trade Unions
DOP	Declaration of Principles
EC or EEC	European Community or European Economic Community
FAO	Food and Agriculture Organization
FDI	foreign direct investment
FDIC	Front for the Defense of Constitutional Institutions
FIS	Islamic Salvation Front
FLN	National Liberation Front
GATT	General Agreement on Tariffs and Trade
GDI	gross domestic investment
GDP	gross domestic product
GDS	gross domestic savings
GNP	gross national product
HAMAS	Islamic Resistance Movement
IBRD	International Bank for Reconstruction and Development
ICOR	incremental capital-to-output ratio
ICP	Iraqi Communist party
IFAD	International Fund for Agricultural Development
ILO	International Labour Organisation
IMF	International Monetary Fund
IPC	Iraq Petroleum Company
ISI	import-substituting industrialization
JI	Ja'amat-i-Islami

LDC	less-developed country
LEB	life expectancy at birth
MAPAI	Israel Labor party
MEB	Military Economic Board
MENA	Middle East and North Africa
MVA	manufacturing value added
NATO	North Atlantic Treaty Organization
NIC	newly industrializing country
NIF	National Islamic Front
NLF	National Liberation Front
NPC	nominal protection coefficient
OCE	Cherifian Foreign Trade Office
OCP	Cherifian Phosphates Office
OECD	Organization for Economic Cooperation and Development
OPEC	Organization of Petroleum Exporting Countries
ORT	oral rehydration therapy
ÖYAK	Armed Forces Mutual Assistance Fund
PDRY	People's Democratic Republic of Yemen
PKK	Kurdish Workers' party
PLO	Palestine Liberation Organization
PPA	Algerian People's party
PPP	purchasing-power-parity
PRC	People's Republic of China
RCC	Revolutionary Command Council (Iraq, Egypt)
RCD	Democratic Constitutional Rally
ROK	Republic of Korea
RPP	Republican People's party
SAVAK	Iranian Security and Intelligence Organization
SNS	National Steel Corporation
SPLA	Southern People's Liberation Army
SSU	Sudanese Socialist Union
TFR	total fertility rate
UAE	United Arab Emirates
UAR	United Arab Republic
UGTA	General Confederation of Algerian Workers
UGTT	General Confederation of Tunisian Workers
UK	United Kingdom
UNESCO	United Nations Economic, Scientific, and Cultural Organization
UNICEF	United Nations International Children's Emergency Fund
USAID	United States Agency for International Development
VAT	value-added tax
WHO	World Health Organization
WTO	World Trade Organization
YAR	Yemen Arab Republic
YSP	Yemen Socialist party

1

INTRODUCTION

Two great games are being played out in the Middle East today. One, upon which this book is focused, is a quiet game that seldom makes headlines. It is the game of peoples and governments, states and societies, sometimes in cooperation but more often at odds, trying to advance the prosperity and overall development of the region's nations. The other is the more conventional great game (see Brown 1984; Walt 1987) in which regional and superpower politics intersect. It has been the unhappy fate of the Middle East to be the stage for an extraordinary amount of conflict, much of it generated within the region itself and the rest provoked from without. In this century alone, it has been a major theater in two world wars and has witnessed a war for liberation in Turkey and seven years of colonial war in Algeria. There have been four wars between Israel and several of its Arab neighbors, prolonged civil wars in Lebanon and the Sudan, major long-term insurrections in Iraq and the former Spanish Sahara, prolonged violence between Israelis and Palestinians, and, until the fall of 1988, one of the two longest conventional wars of this century, between Iraq and Iran (the other being that between Japan and China, 1937–1945).

Since the first edition of this book, Iraq has invaded Kuwait and then been deprived of its prize by an international force led by the United States. Since 1992 Turkey has been conducting a costly and so far unsuccessful campaign, mostly on its own territory but sometimes in neighboring northern Iraq, to snuff out a Kurdish insurrection. In the summer of 1994 southern and northern Yemen, nominally united since 1991, fought a brief but bloody civil war in which the north defeated the south. Finally, in Algeria near–civil war has developed since 1991 between the central government and militant Islamic groups.

Against this backdrop of continued military tension have been two fragile breakthroughs to less belligerent behavior: the end of the Lebanese civil war in 1989 and the establishment of peaceful relations between Israel, on the one hand, and the Palestine Liberation Organization and the Kingdom of Jordan, on the other, in 1993 and 1994.

The Middle East throughout history has been center stage in world politics. It has been endlessly fought over, coveted as strategic real estate on the world's major trade routes, and occasionally used as the launchpad for homegrown expansionist powers, the latest of which was the Ottoman Empire. The Middle East will not be left alone; that is its curse and its blessing. Geopolitical significance draws resources and special treatment from outside powers, but it also draws interference, meddling, and occasionally invasion. Notwithstanding, much of our argument is premised on the assumption that the game of development, no less painful and destructive in some ways than the game of conflict, is of equal if not greater importance. But the two are closely interrelated, as conflict obviously influences the course of development and vice versa.

History has made clear, for instance, that regional conflict, even single events, can set in motion processes that destroy resources and disrupt societies, thereby irreversibly altering the political economies of large populations. One need think only of the assassination of the Archduke Franz Ferdinand in Sarajevo, which triggered the events leading to World War I, to realize what extraordinary consequences small incidents may have. The June War of 1967 in the Middle East could have been avoided—in fact, it took some colossal bungling on the part of all parties to launch it. Once launched, however, it changed not only the military and political landscape of the region but its economic landscape as well. Much the same could be said of the long war between Iraq and Iran.

That said, the sheer scale of military conflict in the region cannot be passed off as a series of unfortunate accidents. The Middle East, more than any other developing area, was crucial turf in the playing out of the cold war and superpower rivalry. Lying on top of two-thirds of the world's known petroleum reserves and astride the main sea and overland links between Asia and the Mediterranean, it was an area in which no local conflict could be conducted without great-power involvement, if not direct then through local proxies. In addition, preparation for war has been continuous. In Chapter 13 we look at the economic costs of mobilization for and the actual conduct of war and internal conflict; it is harder to assess the social and political costs. We do know that two or three generations in several Middle Eastern countries have known little but military rule, preparation for war, and, all too frequently, the reality of conflict.

In the midst of these tensions and conflicts, rapidly growing populations must be fed, educated, and employed, water conserved, agricultural productivity increased, industrialization promoted, universities founded and expanded, technology acquired, armed forces trained and equipped, and some semblance of political order maintained. These are the issues with which we are concerned, and we address them through the lenses of political economy. What we have in mind is the formulation of public policies that determine the allocation of resources within societies and their political consequences. Public policy is about choice, alternatives, and opportunity costs. Sometimes it is small groups of leaders who make public policy choices and then impose them on their societies. Sometimes choices reflect the aspirations of major sectors of society, and sometimes they are made through the society's elected representatives. However they are made, choices always produce relative losses and gains for various sectors of society. Normally we expect those who benefit to try to consolidate their advantages and privileges and those who have fared poorly to try to alter the status quo. Contending groups have various means at their disposal, some legal and some illegal, to try to influence public authorities and public policy in their favor. And, as we shall show repeatedly, those authorities—the people who make up the governments and staff the upper echelons of the bureaucracies and public enterprises—frequently constitute an autonomous set of actors and interests in their own right.

Middle Eastern societies range from the very poor, such as Yemen and the Sudan, to the very rich, such as Kuwait and Saudi Arabia. The highest generalized standards of living are probably to be found in Israel. Similarly, in political terms these societies run the gamut from authoritarian rule by cliques and juntas to the qualified democracies of Israel,[1] Turkey, and, until the outbreak of civil war in 1975, Lebanon. No simple generalizations can be made about the economic resources available to Middle Eastern nations or about the permissible channels through which Middle Easterners may seek to influence the allocation of those resources. What can be said is that there is a constant dialectic between state actors and various segments of their societies and that in this century the dialectic has yielded dynamic, constantly changing equilibria. Like the unicorn, the status quo in the Middle East is a figment of fertile imaginations. Nonetheless, as we shall see, several military authoritarian regimes in the region have fought stubbornly to contain the consequences of socioeconomic change.

When we first conceived of this book in the early 1980s, the analytic issues facing economists and political scientists interested in political economy were still shaped by debates the terms of which had been set in the 1960s and 1970s. They were debates over the dynamics of the distribution and utilization of resources on a global scale (so-called world-order or world-system studies) and within societies. Real events such as the Vietnam War and the civil rights movement fed into the analyses and all too often imparted to them a strong ideological if not polemical cast. One either advanced propositions stemming from a neomarxist understanding of the dynamics of advanced capitalist economies and how they shaped the world economy or sought to debunk these propositions. It is no exaggeration to state that until the advent of Margaret Thatcher in the UK the debates were framed by neomarxist analysts, whether in the dependency school or in world-order studies. Thatcherism, Reaganism, and then the collapse of the Soviet Union left the definitional task of the debates of the late 1980s and the 1990s to the neoconservatives.

We have lived through this paradigmatic shift and the events that gave rise to it, and it would be foolish to suggest that we have not been deeply affected by it. In the first edition we expressed dissatisfaction with dependency and world-systems analysis but hewed to a class-analytic line that now seems inappropriate. We have broadened our approach to encompass not only economic interests, whether class-based or more narrowly defined, but also groups driven, ostensibly, by nonmaterial concerns as manifested in religious or ethnic movements. We have not become so revisionist as to abandon our long-held premise that, at one or two removes, such movements are rooted in competition for political and economic rewards or, more negatively, in the defense of material and power assets that group leaders perceive as in jeopardy.

This edition differs in a second respect from the first. The international environment has impinged decisively on the domestic economic and political structures of the region's nations. The collapse of the oil economy in the mid-1980s, already signaled in the first edition, the end of the cold war and the superpower rivalries that had sustained a flow of resources and arms to client states in the region, and the devastating expulsion of Iraq from Kuwait in 1992 were the defining events of a structural transformation—both economic and political—still under way in the region. More than we were willing to concede in the first edition, it is clear that since the late 1980s the political economy of the Middle East has been shaped by global changes, especially the end of the Cold War, over which it has had little influence. We attempt in this edition to give the influence of the international environment its due weight.

Finally, the strengthening of movements throughout the region that we refer to as "political Islam" has obliged us to pay more explicit attention than in the first edition to their implications for the economies and polities of the Middle East. The establishment of an Islamic republic in the Sudan, the near electoral victory of an Islamic front in Algeria, the strong electoral showing of the Islamic Welfare party in Turkey, and the growing visibility of Islamic parties in Egypt, Tunisia, Yemen, and the West Bank and Gaza raise the possibility of the spread of Islamic governance in the region. We seek, especially in Chapter 14, to assess the political and economic impact of such transitions.

In many respects our endeavor in these pages is unique, but it has many forerunners and sources of inspiration. We have tried to write an integrated, analytic text covering all of the contemporary Middle East. We believe that we are the first to have tried to do this in the political-economy mode, although Samir Amin's *The Arab Economy Today* (1982) might be seen as a cursory and polemical antecedent. Galal Amin's *The Modernization of Poverty* (1980) is richer and analytically more satisfying. Generally one encounters anthologies of country case studies, often descriptive and not necessarily related to any set of analytic themes. Some of these, such as Reich and Long (1986), Harik and Sullivan (1992), and Barkey (1992), are highly useful and could nicely accompany the present study.

There have been some notable attempts at synthetic analysis, although, with two exceptions, none has adopted a political-economic approach. Halpern's *The Politics of Social Change in the Middle East and North Africa* (1963) is a landmark work and, although dated, still of great value. Hudson's *Arab Politics* (1977) is also highly recommended, as is Bill and Springborg's *Politics in the Middle East* (1994). Limited to the Maghreb are Moore's now-dated *Politics in North Africa* (1970) and Entelis's *Comparative Politics of North Africa* (1980). In other disciplines there have been illustrious forerunners: in sociology, for example, Berger's *The Arab World Today* (1964) and Lerner's *The Passing of Traditional Society* (1959). The study of North Africa by

Hermassi (1972) is one of the rare contemporary contributions to sociological synthesis. Two economic historians have unquestionably been a source of inspiration for us in that their writings have been explicitly in the political-economy vein: Issawi, for his *Economic History of the Middle East and North Africa* (1982) and his pioneering article "Economic and Social Foundations of Democracy in the Middle East" (1956), and Owen, for *The Middle East in the World Economy* (1981).

A number of writers have used political economy, implicitly or explicitly, in single-country studies. It is no surprise that studies in the French tradition of marxist political economy have played a major role here: Hassan Riad's (Samir Amin's) *L'Egypte nassérienne* (1964), Abdel-Malek's *Egypt: Military Society* (1968), and Raffinot and Jacquemot's *Le capitalisme d'état algérien* (1977) are all important. But Anglo-Saxons and anglophones have also made important contributions: O'Brien's *The Revolution in Egypt's Economic System* (1966), Hudson's *The Precarious Republic* (1968), Abdel-Fadil's *The Political Economy of Nasserism* (1980), Bennoune's *The Making of Contemporary Algeria* (1988), Hale's *The Political and Economic Development of Modern Turkey* (1981), Keyder's *State and Class in Turkey* (1987), Waterbury's *The Egypt of Nasser and Sadat* (1983), Hansen's *The Political Economy of Poverty, Equity, and Growth: Egypt and Turkey* (1992), and Galal Amin's *Egypt's Economic Predicament* (1995). Michael Barnett assesses the influence of military mobilization on the domestic policies of Israel and Egypt (1992). In addition to Beblawi (1984) and Islami and Kavoussi (1984), there are more recent political-economic studies of the Gulf States: Crystal (1990), Chaudhry (n.d.), Gause (1994), and Krimly (1993). In Arabic, works by Khafaji (1983), 'Adil Hussein (1982), and Ayubi (1989 and 1991a) are noteworthy.

Finally, in much the same spirit as this book, Elias Tuma (1987) and Roger Owen (1992) attempt synthetic analyses of the political economy of the entire region, while Sadowski (1993) examines the impact of military expenditures on its political economy.

There is much that we do not attempt to do in this text, and some analytic approaches that we leave aside are admittedly important. We shall not, for instance, dwell much on psychological variables in explaining political and economic outcomes. We do not deny their importance, and there is a significant literature now that examines psychological factors affecting Middle Eastern leaders and elites: see, inter alia, Brown and Itzkowitz, *Psychological Dimensions of Near Eastern Studies* (1977), Volkan and Itzkowitz, *The Immortal Atatürk* (1984), and Zonis, *Majestic Failure* (1991).

Political culture is another important tool in understanding the Middle East but, again, one that we shall largely pass over. Much has been written about the cultural attributes, political predispositions, and styles of governance in the Middle East. We hear of the quest for martyrdom among Shi'ite Muslims as explaining in part the way in which the Iranian revolution unfolded and the course of the war with Iraq. Israel's "Masada Complex" is said to determine the country's outlook toward its adversaries.

The docile, wily peasant society of Egypt has been credited with that country's style of government since the pharaohs, and Morocco's tribal past has been invoked to explain contemporary elite behavior (Waterbury 1970).

The enormous journalistic and scholarly concern lavished in recent years on political Islam and contemporary Islamism in general frequently takes the form of political-culture analysis. Various writers have tried to discern the values and ideals that inspire those Muslims who seek the political kingdom and to describe the socioeconomic contexts that purportedly give rise to the movements. We shall have a great deal more to say about these movements and their professed ideals in Chapters 11, 12 and, above all, 14, and we shall save reference to the relevant studies until then.

In general, we view political-culture analysis as potentially a more powerful tool than the psychological analysis of leaders, and we shall refer to political-cultural variables with some frequency. Still, how much they can explain is seldom clear. Let us hypothetically compare Egypt and Iran in terms of tax delinquency. We could hypothesize in political-cultural terms that those in Iran who failed to pay their taxes during the time of the shah did so with a relatively clear conscience, because to Shi'ites awaiting the return of the true Imam all secular authorities are in some way interlopers and usurpers and hence without legitimacy. In Egypt, by contrast, the tax dodger may be seen as playing an age-old game of manipulating or evading a large, tentacular state whose legitimacy, however, is not at stake. But whatever the cultural explanation of the phenomenon, the end result is the same: tax evasion and decreased government revenues. More important, the means by which to extract more taxes may not vary much from one culture to another. Even in those rare instances when we can assess the independent effect of culture on politics and economic life, we must remember that cultures change rapidly too, as the patterns of employment, residence, and lifestyle themselves change.

In sum, our approach is to focus on major problems in the social and economic transformation of the Middle East, not on specific countries. All the societies of the region face similar problems in extracting and investing resources, building an industrial sector while modernizing agriculture, and absorbing an ever-larger proportion of a growing population into cities, all the while trying to maintain political order and to build a credible military establishment. This set of problems confronts all developing countries. What differs is the human and material resources available to the twenty-three countries in the region, and those differences determine in an important way the strategies of resource allocation, the process of class formation, and the political process in each.

We are convinced that in general the process of economic and social change in the Middle East and North Africa (MENA) is not qualitatively different from that in most of the less-developed countries (LDCs). We hasten to add that the differences in levels of overall development, including industrialization, and in standards of living and welfare are as great among the LDCs (compare Brazil, for example, with Rwanda or Nepal) as between the developing and the advanced industrial nations. As we shall see, the variance among Middle Eastern nations is also very great (see especially Chapter 3). Thus we hope that our detailed examination of Middle Eastern experience will contribute to a more general understanding of the development process.

At the same time there are facets of the development process in the Middle East, flowing from its long history of intense and generally adversarial interaction with Europe, that do set this region apart. We try to be attentive to these distinguishing traits and to signal to the reader where and when we think they make a qualitative difference in the processes under scrutiny.

In Chapter 2 we set forth the premises of our analysis, which centers on three vertices: strategies of economic transformation, the state agencies and actors that seek to implement them, and the social actors such as interest groups that react to and are shaped by them. Each of the three vertices entails questions about the nature of the state, the emergence of economic interests, and the effects of various development strategies—questions that should be asked in any developing country. We do not pretend to have definitive answers to any of them, but we do have some strongly held views and, we think, solid evidence to back them.

NOTES

1. Israeli democracy is the real thing but only for the country's Jewish citizens. Non-Jews, although enjoying a range of political rights, are second-class citizens.

2

THE FRAMEWORK OF THE STUDY

Many of the major problems and questions facing the Middle East today can and should be approached in much the same way as one would approach the problems of any set of LDCs. Accordingly, we shall begin by presenting a broad-brush model of LDC political economy.

Outcomes in LDC political economy can best be conceptualized as the product of the interaction of three variables: (1) economic growth and structural transformation, (2) state structure and policy, and (3) social actors, whether groups or individuals. We shall start with fairly conventional definitions of each of these concepts, discussing major conceptual difficulties, disputes, and so forth, surrounding each as we proceed.

Economic growth means simply the increase over time in total output in the economy. Since the concept is often also associated with some idea of increasing welfare for the population, per capita growth is usually also implied. Such growth is almost always quite uneven, however. Some sectors grow faster than others, some groups' wealth and power may increase faster than those of other groups, and in some extreme cases the absolute standard of living of some (usually poor) individuals and groups may actually decline in some phases of the process. Although the ubiquity or necessity of these outcomes is much disputed, several other features of unevenness do appear to be universals: the decline of the percentage of both national output and employment accounted for by the agricultural sector and the increasing proportion of the population that is urban rather than rural. The process of unbalanced sectoral growth just characterized is called *structural transformation*. By *state structure and policy* we mean the organization of the monopoly of coercive means within society, the interventions into the economy that such a monopoly makes possible, and the institutions through which intervention is carried out. Finally, by *social actors* we mean any and all interests, groups, and classes that interact with the state, seek to shape its policies, and are affected by the state's growth strategies.

Each of these definitions can be questioned, of course. As noted, economic growth may not be associated with increasing welfare for some groups and/or inequality among social groups may increase. Similarly, there is little agreement on the role of the state in the development process—on its freedom of choice of policy with respect to powerful domestic classes and international actors such as the International Monetary Fund (IMF) or the World Bank. And finally, what drives groups— material interests, shared values, or shared blood—is at the heart of a debate in the social sciences that ranges far beyond the scope of this book.

We do not suffer from the delusion that we can settle such debates or persuade all potential critics. We believe that each of the major variables is vital for an understanding of outcomes in the political economy of the region, as we hope to show through the concrete analysis of specific development problems in subsequent chapters. The proof of the pudding will certainly be in the eating. Before proceeding to a more detailed discussion of each of our three variables in the context of the Middle East, it is worth emphasizing that they are interdependent. Each one influences and shapes the others; each is therefore both cause and effect, both starting point and outcome. Our model is one of reciprocal causation (Figure 2.1).

We stress that we do not imply any rank ordering of the arrows of Figure 2.1; this is a fully simultaneous model. The meaning of the interconnections may be illustrated as follows:

1. Economic growth and structural transformation have unintended outcomes to which state actors must respond. For example, if the pattern of industrialization is highly capital-intensive, the state may need to respond to a growing employment problem.

2. Although there is much debate on the precise effect of specific policies, few deny that state structure and fiscal, monetary, and trade policy affect the rate and form of economic growth.

3. Social actors mold state policy. Interest and pressure groups and, most broadly, proprietary classes seek to protect and promote their own interests through the state. In some cases, the influence of a particular social actor may be so strong that the state becomes its "instrument."

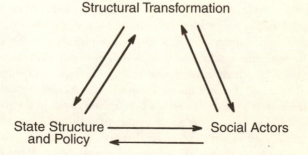

Structural Transformation

State Structure and Policy → Social Actors

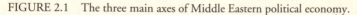

FIGURE 2.1   The three main axes of Middle Eastern political economy.

4. The state shapes, even creates, social actors, including classes. If, for example, classes are defined primarily with respect to property rights and if property rights always require enforcement, then it is difficult to see how the concepts of "state" and "class" could *not* be closely linked. In the context of LDCs, the impact of the state on class is especially striking, as the state redistributes property through nationalizations, land reforms, and privatizations.

5. Economic growth and structural transformation shape social actors. A "manufacturing bourgeoisie" emerges only as the result of the growth of industry; the more rapidly industry develops, the stronger that bourgeoisie becomes. The rise of militant Islamic groups is in part attributed to high rates of unemployment among educated youth. That unemployment is the result in turn of the slow growth of the nonagricultural sector combined with rapid growth of the educational system.

6. Finally, social actors affect the rate and form of economic growth not only indirectly, through their impact on state policy, but also directly. For example, an initial concentration of landownership will probably favor a capital-intensive pattern of agricultural growth, with consequences for employment, income distribution, and the growth of different industrial sectors. Similarly, the concentration of rural assets may retard the emergence of a rural domestic market. A highly concentrated distribution of urban income may favor the rapid growth of certain sectors (e.g., consumer durables) rather than of others. We now turn to a more detailed discussion of each vertex of our triangle and of the interactions among these variables.

ECONOMIC GROWTH AND STRUCTURAL TRANSFORMATION

Economic growth is usually measured by gross domestic product (GDP) in a unit of common currency, usually dollars, in order to facilitate international comparisons. GDP is obtained by weighing all outputs by their prices and adding them up. Since output and income are closely related concepts, the measure also serves as a kind of summary statistic for the level of income in the country. When expressed in per capita terms, the GDP is often employed as a crude indicator of average social welfare.

Several criticisms have been made of this concept. First, GDP per capita offers no evidence on distribution. Therefore one can use increases in GDP as an indicator of increasing social welfare only with great caution. Second, the measure explicitly excludes nonmarketed output; this is a problem especially for the evaluation of changes in the agricultural sector over time. A shift from home production to market production could, in principle, leave total output unaffected while the measure of output, GDP, increased. Further, the exclusion of nonmarketed output from the calculation systematically neglects household production; much of the contribution of women to production thus escapes notice. A variant of this problem is that the value of production and services in the "informal sector" goes unmeasured or is at best crudely estimated. As we shall see in subsequent chapters, the informal sector plays an important but poorly understood role in Middle Eastern economies.

Third, the use of official exchange rates as the common denominator for international GDP comparisons introduces further distortions. To say that the average annual income in Egypt is US$640 evokes the image of an American buying only US$640 worth of goods in a year. In fact, however, an Egyptian with the equivalent of this dollar sum, when converted at the official exchange rate, would be able to buy more goods and services than the American. This is because the price of nontradable goods (e.g., housing and haircuts) in relation to that of tradable goods (e.g., wheat, cars, textiles) is typically much lower in LDCs than in developed countries (DCs). Using official exchange rates to compare incomes across countries ignores this difference (Box 2.1). Even if Egyptians spent the same percentage of their income on nontradable goods as Americans (which is unlikely, given the relative prices), the Egyptians' purchasing power relative to the Americans' would be understated by using

---

BOX 2.1
PURCHASING-POWER-PARITY

To say that the average annual income in Egypt is US$640 evokes the image of an American buying only US$640 worth of goods in a year. In fact, however, an Egyptian with the equivalent of this dollar sum, when converted at the official exchange rate, would be able to buy more goods and services than would the American. This is because the price of nontradable goods (e.g., housing and haircuts) in relation to that of tradable goods (e.g., wheat, cars, textiles) is typically much lower in LDCs than in DCs. As an economy grows, productivity in tradable goods production (agriculture and industry) increases much faster than in nontradable goods: It is much easier to raise the productivity of auto workers than of barbers. Competitive pressures in labor markets (combined with the fact that goods are far more mobile internationally than is labor) will drag up the wages of workers (and therefore, of costs) in nontradable goods production behind the increasing wages in tradable goods. But since productivity doesn't change much in nontradable goods, relative costs rise. Hence the conclusion: The price of nontradable goods relative to tradable goods is higher in rich countries than in poor ones.

Using official exchange rates to compare incomes across countries ignores this difference. Even if Egyptians spent the same percentage of their income on nontradable goods as Americans (which is unlikely, given the relative prices), the Egyptians' purchasing power relative to the Americans' would be understated by using official exchange rates to compare them (Kravis, Heston, and Summers 1978). Figure 2.2 shows the disparity between the two measures for some selected MENA countries.

---

official exchange rates to compare them (Kravis, Heston, and Summers 1978). Figure 2.2 shows the disparity between the two measures for some selected MENA countries.

Finally, the concept of GDP faces a special difficulty in those countries that derive much revenue from the sale of exhaustible natural resources. Most of this revenue is not income that can be sustained over time. Stauffer (1984) has estimated that the "reproducible" component of GDP of Saudi Arabia may be as little as one-quarter to one-half of reported GDP. Another way to put it is that some, often most, of GDP in the Gulf is not "income" but "liquidation of capital."

Despite these problems and issues, the GDP, employed with caution, offers us the most comprehensive available set of statistics on national income. The above problems will be taken here as cautionary notes about rather than devastating criticisms of the concept.

Economic growth invariably involves unevenness across sectors, or structural transformation. Despite the wide variation in the patterns of economic growth, in virtually all countries rising per capita income is accompanied by a decline in agriculture's share of output and employment and a corresponding increase in the share of industry and services.

There are numerous interactions among sectors as development proceeds. Since labor productivity and therefore incomes are much higher in industry than in agriculture, the transfer of population to industry raises national income. Furthermore, the rate of technological change that raises income per person is typically faster in industry. Consequently, many have thought of industry as the leading sector of development, a sort of engine that pulls the rest of the train behind it. There is much truth to this picture, but neglect of the agricultural sector can be disastrous. The agricultural sector provides not only labor but also food, raw materials for process-

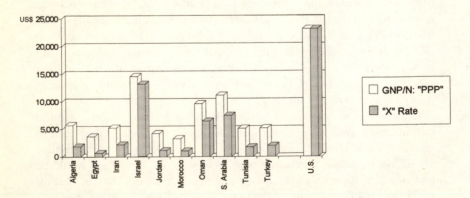

FIGURE 2.2   Purchasing-power-parity versus exchange-rate measures of per capita income, 1992. N = population. *Source:* World Bank (1994g, 220–221).

ing, exports, needed foreign exchange, a domestic market for local industry, and an investable surplus that may be used to construct industrial facilities. As we shall see, Middle Eastern states, like many LDCs, have neglected or mismanaged the linkages between agriculture and industry. As a result, bottlenecks such as inadequate food supplies, stagnant exports, and feeble domestic markets have undermined economic growth and structural transformation.

The concept of "services" is something of a residual category. It contains activities as diverse as government service and street peddling. Moreover, the mix within the service sector also changes over time, with the proportion of self-employed, typically very poor service-sector workers declining as national income rises beyond a certain level. The increase in the proportion of the population employed in services may be as much an indicator of economic weakness as of strength, as large numbers of unskilled rural migrants arrive in the cities and engage in a host of small-scale activities that are carried out at low technological levels and generate paltry incomes. In most cases, however, it seems clear that these people believe that they have improved their lot by migrating, and the available evidence suggests that they know what they are talking about. After all, productivity, technology, and incomes for some agricultural workers may be and often are even lower than those obtainable in the urban informal sector (see Chapter 10).

The process of economic growth and structural transformation is typically characterized by a variety of distortions and unintended outcomes. Such distortions are both the consequence and the cause of state economic policies. The first distortion is really a final cautionary note on the definition of economic growth and its links to welfare. It is clear that "economic growth" as measured by changes in per capita GDP is not the same as the usual notion of "economic development." The latter concept includes some recognition that improvement in living standards includes especially the meeting of the basic needs (e.g., food, housing, safe drinking water, and education) of all members of a society. It is equally clear that there is only a loose correlation between improvement in the satisfaction of basic needs and increase in GDP. Some countries with relatively high per capita incomes have quite poor records on meeting basic needs (e.g., Brazil), while some with very low per capita incomes appear to have gone very far toward doing so (e.g., Sri Lanka and the People's Republic of China [PRC]).

There is a particular connection between economic development and the development of skills, or "human-capital formation." Indeed, by some accounts (e.g., T. W. Schultz 1981) growth is inconceivable without the improvement of human skills; in this view, education and other types of skill formation are the core of the development process. Technological change, which lies at the core of the process of economic growth, is impossible without an increasingly skilled population. In addition, the very unevenness of economic growth and structural transformation creates numerous disequilibria. Schultz hypothesized that the more educated and trained the population, the more rapidly it can respond to such imbalances and therefore the more quickly they are eliminated. Unfortunately, however, the educational standards in many Middle Eastern countries have lagged behind what we might expect from the growth rates of incomes.

A second blockage or distortion to the process of economic growth and structural transformation is the problem of foreign exchange. For a variety of reasons, some Middle Eastern governments, for example, the Sudan, where growth has collapsed, and Tunisia, Morocco, and Turkey in the late 1970s and early 1980s, have found their growth process interrupted by the inadequacy of foreign exchange. Turkey's growth in the late 1970s was likewise slowed by the steadily increasing demand for imports at the same time as export revenues lagged. Both external factors (falling terms of trade) and internal policies that encourage imports and discourage exports (overvalued exchange rates, the need to import machinery for industries producing industrial goods for local consumers) created these problems.

These difficulties are endemic in LDCs and are especially associated with import-substituting industrialization (ISI)—many Middle Eastern countries have been spared this squeeze, largely because of oil revenues, their regional multipliers (such as investment), and, especially, workers' remittances. However, the experience with such revenues shows that ample foreign exchange is not a panacea for the problems of economic growth and structural transformation. Indeed, the influx of large amounts of foreign exchange can itself cause problems.

The sudden increase in revenues from abroad leads to a phenomenon known as the "Dutch Disease," so called because of the experience of the Dutch economy with the large influx of North Sea gas revenues in the 1970s. Government spending of oil revenues induces labor and capital to shift from tradable goods (industry and agriculture) to nontradable goods (services). There are two proposed causal sequences. A monetary version holds that the spending of oil revenues stimulates a rate of inflation that is higher than that of the major (typically Western) trading partners of the oil-exporting country. Since LDC nominal exchange rates are usually fixed, the differential inflation leads to overvaluation of the real exchange rate. Since tradable goods' prices may be denominated in Organization for Economic Cooperation and Development (OECD) currencies (say, the dollar) while nontradable-goods prices are, of course, in local currency, such revaluation of the real exchange rate is the same thing as an increase in the relative price of nontradable goods relative to tradable goods.

An alternative version arrives at this same conclusion by a nonmonetary ("real-economy") route. In that version, the spending of government revenue increases demand for both tradable and nontradable goods. For most small countries the supply of tradable goods is perfectly elastic; that of nontradable goods is not. Therefore, the increased spending will bid up the price of nontradable goods more than that of tradable goods (Figure 2.3). This effect will be compounded if government spending is concentrated in nontradables, such as services and construction, as happened in the oil-exporting countries during the 1970s. Once again, the prices of nontradable relative to tradable goods will increase. The advantage of this latter formulation is that it can allow for the fact that some so-called nontradables actually do move in in-

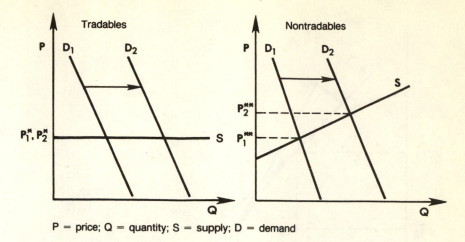

P = price; Q = quantity; S = supply; D = demand

FIGURE 2.3   Changes in the relative price of tradable and nontradable goods. (Assume that both sectors face the same shift in the demand function. The price of tradable goods remains the same; the price of nontradable goods rises, and their relative price [P*/P**] falls.)

ternational trade. There are international construction firms, financial and insurance services have international markets, foreign teachers may be hired, and so forth. The only question becomes differential supply elasticities, which can in principle be determined empirically rather than simply assumed.

Whatever the causes, these relative-price changes reallocate capital and labor and shift resources out of the production of tradable goods into nontradable-goods production (Figure 2.4). This allegedly leads to stagnation of the agricultural and manufacturing sectors while government and the building industry boom. International competition holds down the prices of, say, food and manufactures, whereas wages and costs in domestic agriculture and industry rise, catching local producers in a profit squeeze. The Dutch Disease contributes to the rural exodus, as farm workers abandon the countryside in search of construction jobs in the cities. The increase in wage levels thus combines with the overvalued real exchange rate to diminish international competitiveness in agriculture and industry.

There is evidence for such effects in the Middle East and elsewhere, most notably in agriculture. As with any growth-rate comparison, one can obtain quite different results for slightly different time periods. For example, according to the World Bank, Tunisian agriculture grew at a 4.1% average annual rate from 1970 to 1981 but at only 1.6% from 1973 to 1983. For some oil exporters such as Algeria, growth rates of manufacturing and agriculture were greater during the 1973–1983 period than they had been during the previous "cheap oil" decade. The reason for the discrepancy between this evidence and the predictions of the theory was that Middle Eastern and other oil-exporting governments often intervened directly to counteract

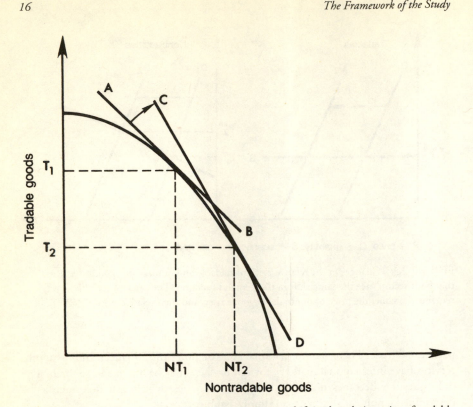

FIGURE 2.4   Reallocation of resources in response to a shift in the relative price of tradable and nontradable goods. (The shift in relative prices is shown by the change in the price line from AB to CD. Resulting reallocations of labor and capital reduce the equilibrium output of tradables [$T_2 < T_1$] and increase that of nontradables [$NT_2 > NT_1$].)

these relative-price shifts, usually by subsidizing their tradable-goods sector. Such subsidies, of course, create problems of their own, and no country has fully met the challenges posed by rural emigration. In addition, both the seriousness of the disease and the cure have varied considerably from one country to another. The case of the Dutch Disease illustrates the argument that state policy both shapes development and responds to the unintended outcomes of that same process.

The inflow of oil revenues also has important direct political consequences. Oil revenues are rents. Economic rent is the difference between the market price of a good or a factor of production and its opportunity cost (the price needed to produce the good or to keep the factor of production in its current use) (see Box 2.2). For example, oil rents in the Gulf are the difference between the market price (say, US$14.50 per barrel) and the cost of producing oil there (about US$1.50). Furthermore, these rents are collected directly by governments, increasing their freedom of maneuver. Oil rents are politically centralizing. However, as the revenues are spent, new domestic actors emerge (as contractors, agents, recipients of subsidies) who, in

BOX 2.2
ECONOMIC RENT

Economists define rent as the difference between the market price of a good or factor of production and its opportunity cost. Owners of certain assets or providers of certain services enjoy strategic positions in markets that allow them to set prices well above the opportunity cost for what they are providing. The revenue stream that is generated is not directly related to greater efficiency in production or to new investment. When oil prices were quadrupled by the Organization of Petroleum Exporting Countries in 1973 (see Chapter 3), the new market price reflected neither increases in the cost of production nor new investment. Rather, consumers of petroleum had to accept the new price, and only with the passage of considerable time could they reduce consumption through improved efficiency in energy use. In the interim the oil-exporting states of the MENA region reaped enormous rent streams.

These rents may be referred to as "external," and to them analysts of the Middle East have attributed a host of ills. Access to rents has allowed several states to avoid improving the efficiency with which their economies produce anything and has particularly hurt those sectors producing tradable goods. Rents have allowed governments to avoid taxing their own citizenries heavily, thereby breaking that vital, often adversarial link between governments and the people they tax. Out of such links governmental accountability may flow; in their absence governments may ignore their citizens.

External rents are not confined to petroleum revenues. Several Middle Eastern nations have, throughout the cold-war era, had continuous access to "strategic rents." Countries enjoying peculiar geostrategic value in the confrontation between the two superpowers could count on financial flows and aid designed quite openly to buy their allegiance to one side or the other. Israel has been by far the greatest regional beneficiary of strategic rents: Development assistance to Israel averaged US$338 per capita per year for the period 1971–1980, US$695 for 1981–1990, and US$812 for 1991–1993. Its nearest competitor was Jordan with US$246, US$336, and US$138 for the same three periods. Egypt lagged far behind in per capita terms: US$35, US$29, and US$57. Although these figures from the World Bank are classified as development assistance, it is indicative of the noneconomic rationale behind these transfers that Israel in the early 1990s registered per capita GDP of US$12,000 compared with Egypt's US$650.

Not all economic rents are external. The notion of "rent-seeking behavior" refers primarily to the search for strategic privilege in domestic markets. Such privilege is usually bestowed by public authorities through the issuance of import licenses, targeted tariff protection, franchises, and the like. When the privileged are protected from competition in specific markets, revenues and profits are generated without changes in productive efficiency or new investment (beyond the cost of acquiring the privilege).

turn, begin to limit the freedom of maneuver of the state. This is a very typical pattern; state autonomy may rise in a particular conjuncture but then typically will decline with its exercise over time.

A further effect of oil rents is that they permit the evasion of hard development choices. This is not a problem if the rents are very large or are assumed to be very stable. For many middle-income oil exporters, neither condition holds. Consider the case of Egypt in the early 1980s: With annual oil receipts of some US$2.8 billion, along with ample foreign-exchange revenues from workers' remittances (about US$3 billion) and from other "locational rents" (tourism, the Suez Canal, and U.S. aid), the country could avoid a thorough reform of both its highly distorted pricing system and its structurally imbalanced labor market. By the time the rents declined and the day of reckoning arrived, the problems and their potential solutions were all the more painful.

Rents also contribute to a further set of difficulties and disequilibria in the process of economic growth and structural transformation: the problem of lagging food supply. The Middle East is now the least food-self-sufficient area in the world. Demand for food rose by 4–5% per year during the 1970s, driven by rapidly rising per capita incomes and by population growth rates that were surprisingly high given national incomes. Supply was constrained by nature and by political economy. Scarce water resources, urban bias, unequal land-tenure systems, and the Dutch Disease all contributed to the relatively sluggish supply response. The 1980s saw a deceleration in demand growth as incomes fell, as well as some modest improvements in supply due to improved policies. The range of agricultural outcomes in the region is extremely wide, however, extending from the Sudanese famine of 1984 to Turkish net grain exports (see Chapter 6).

Such agricultural problems impede economic development and create problems for policymakers. Food imports accounted for some 29% of all Egyptian imports and 14% of Moroccan imports in 1992. This is perhaps acceptable, provided that the states in question can find other things to sell. The difficulties of agricultural transformation, such as the rural exodus toward already bulging cities and the provision of adequate food supplies, are among the most pressing of the disequilibria of economic growth and structural transformation facing the region today.

The pattern of industrial growth has exacerbated the employment problems fostered by rural neglect. The form of industrialization characteristic of the Middle East has also created some additional and unique problems. Partly because of a desire to have the most modern technology available and partly because of distorted price signals, much of the industry installed in the Middle East during the past generation has been capital-intensive. Consequently, the amount of investment required to create a job has been very high. Because of managerial inefficiencies and foreign-exchange bottlenecks, these same industrial facilities have been plagued by idle capacity, driving up the amount of investment needed to add to output. Only a few Middle Eastern countries have internationally competitive industries.

Finally, the state itself has often become a drain on resources in the Middle East. This is not to say that the state should not (still less could not) intervene in the development process. In certain conjunctures, however, the state can inhibit the very process that at least officially it seeks to promote. Not only do its interventions often generate misleading price signals for private actors (e.g., undervaluing foreign exchange and local capital) but also its bloated bureaucracies and inefficient state-owned enterprises often absorb resources. State borrowing to finance its own activities may crowd out private investors from credit markets. One might be tempted to include military spending and the maintenance of large, lethal arsenals and standing armies among the burdens that the state itself creates for the growth process (see Chapter 13).

In summary, the course of economic growth and structural change is far from smooth. It is characterized by extensive state intervention, numerous bottlenecks, and serious macro- and microeconomic problems. Many of these problems have their origins in state policy; each generates a policy response. It is important to remember, however, that these distortions and problems have rarely been the result of obvious error or stupidity. Hindsight is always 20/20, while future outcomes and unintended consequences are always opaque. Many of the price and other distortions generated by state policy originated in states' attempts to mobilize savings. Agriculture had to be taxed because, for countries like Egypt in the 1950s, there was no alternative source of investable funds. Industry tended to be capital-intensive because planners believed this was necessary to create a modern industrial core. Growth and modernization of production were to take precedence over employment generation and agricultural development because growth itself was expected automatically to provide the latter two. Rapid industrial development under state auspices was also held to be essential to national security. State-led growth was designed to weaken or destroy internal and external enemies. States intervened to accelerate the process of economic growth and to forge a powerful modern nation. Their leaders held certain images of the future that explicitly included industrialization, but the reality often turned out to be different from the image.

Perhaps no state in the Middle East had formulated a more detailed image of its future than Algeria. By 1969, seven years after independence and a bloody colonial war, Algeria launched a four-year plan that was intended to be the first of several. It was premised on a "big-push" strategy of heavy industrialization entirely within the state sector. The crucial element in the strategy was the country's hydrocarbon riches: petroleum and natural gas. Those were to provide, as was to be expected, exports to generate foreign exchange to pay for imported technology, capital goods, and turnkey industries. More important, they were to be the source of energy and basic feedstock for large industrial undertakings in petrochemicals and basic metals.

These industries were in turn to provide a wide range of intermediate and finished goods: fertilizers, butane gas, plastic sheeting and sacking, irrigation pipes, tractors, motors, and consumer durables. It was assumed that the rural sector, under socialist management in the most favored areas, would become the principal consumer of these products, but little attention was paid to issues of agricultural productivity. It was also assumed that, given the state-of-the-art technology imported (for instance, gas liquefaction plants), many of these industries would be able to compete in international markets.

In terms of structural transformation, Algeria's technocrats saw the agrarian sector primarily as a customer for the industrial sector, one whose workforce would continue to dwindle and whose per capita productivity would rise. The regime was prepared during the big-push phase to tolerate high rates of urban unemployment and high levels of worker migration to France. Eventually rising incomes in agriculture and in the new industrial sector would generate substantial demand for goods and services, which would create the jobs necessary to absorb the unemployed. President Houari Boumedienne (1965–1978) saw no reason to worry about Algeria's 3.5% annual population growth rate because he expected the economic growth that his plan would provide to yield the prosperity necessary to lower fertility.

The whole strategy came to be known by the label "industrializing industries" affixed to it by its major foreign architect, G. Destanne de Bernis (1971) of the University of Grenoble. It was an integrated plan, and, for that very reason, when one of its parts failed to conform to the overall strategy the whole process rather quickly collapsed. Mismanagement in the socialist agrarian sector and production declines throughout the agricultural sector meant that the latter could not become a reliable customer for industry. The new industries soon faced problems of idle capacity, compounded by the sophistication of their imported technology and inadequate management skills. Except for some petroleum products, seeking external markets was not a feasible alternative. Unemployment and underemployment mounted while the rural exodus continued. The population continued to grow as broad-based prosperity remained a distant goal. Increasingly large amounts of foreign exchange had to be used to import food and sustain urban standards of living.

By 1976 it had become clear that the big push was in trouble, and after Boumedienne's death in 1978 Algeria's new president, Chadli Benjadid, moved to break up the large state industrial sector into smaller, decentralized units, stimulate the agricultural sector through more favorable prices, and encourage the long-maligned private sector to play a more active role in the country's development (Lawless 1984). In the 1980s Algeria's earnings from petroleum exports fell from US$11 to US$4 billion. Not only was any further big-push development out of the question but the decline in rents made even downsizing the state extremely difficult. By the end of the decade Algeria was in economic crisis and political turmoil.

One may contrast with Algeria's experience that of another oil-rich country, Iraq, at a much earlier period. In 1950 Iraq was still a monarchy, nominally independent but closely allied to its former imperial master, the UK. In that year royalties paid the Iraqi government on the production and sale of oil increased by 30%, and by 1958 the royalties had grown nearly sixfold to over US$200 million. The government, not unwisely, wanted to use these revenues for long-term development purposes. Toward this end an autonomous Development Board was established and 70% of oil royalties were earmarked for it. The board had the authority and the finances to set Iraq's growth course (Penrose and Penrose 1978, 167–177).

Unlike Algeria, Iraq aimed its big push at agriculture. The Development Board began large hydraulic projects to master floods in the Tigris-Euphrates system, store water, irrigate new lands, improve drainage, and cope with soil salinity. Whereas Algeria's slogan was "Sow oil to reap industry," Iraq's was "Sow oil to reap agriculture," and that sector was to be the engine of long-term growth. The flaws in this farsighted strategy were that it neglected immediate problems of agricultural production, had no particular industrialization program, and devoted no resources to social infrastructure (such as housing and health). The hydraulic projects were not likely to contribute to the economy for years if not decades. In the meantime, peasants continued to pour into Baghdad and other cities as floods, salinity, and grossly inequitable land distribution impeded increased production. In the cities, neither the urban job market nor the network of social services was adequate to provide a decent standard of living to the hundreds of thousands of Iraqis crowded into slums and shantytowns. When elements of the Iraqi armed forces moved to overthrow the monarchy on July 14, 1958, their advancing tank columns were accompanied by masses of denizens of the shantytowns who wanted to assist in bringing down the regime. With its demise came also that of the Development Board's strategy. The military and its Ba'ath party successors elaborated an entirely new image of the future not unlike that of Algeria.

STATE STRUCTURE AND DEVELOPMENT POLICY

The interaction of state policy and the process of economic growth and structural transformation is not merely one of images of the future. Most states of the region have had visions of where they would like to go—how they hoped their societies would appear in the future. The problem, of course, has been getting there. What strategy would be employed, and who would implement which parts of it? We shall now examine these questions of strategies and agencies.

Without prejudging whether economic-development strategies are "choices" or "sequences" or whether they are politically imposed from within (e.g., by domestic proprietary classes) or from without (e.g., by international financial agencies), we can identify five major routes from predominantly rural, agricultural political economies to urban, industrial ones. These are the paths of agro-exports, mineral exports, import-substituting industrialization, manufactured exports, and agricultural-development–led industrialization. Let us examine these in turn.

Economic-Development Strategies

Agro-export–led growth. The usual justification for the agro-export strategy is as follows: At the beginning of the process of structural transformation, most people are by definition rural and agricultural. If there are underexploited land and/or labor resources, these could be used to produce more crops for sale, but because of the poverty of the local population and (perhaps) the relatively small number of people, the domestic market is quite limited. Exports provide the exit from this impasse. The incomes of the farmers may rise, and if some of the profits from such activities are reinvested in increasing productivity and expanding the productive base of the economy (e.g., by investing in industry), a process of self-sustaining growth may be launched (Lewis 1954; Myint 1959). Further, the process of industrialization requires imports; in the long run, such imports can be financed only by exports. Since such countries may have little to sell except agricultural commodities, developing such exports then provides the foreign exchange needed for structural transformation. Finally, the country may have a strong international comparative advantage in the production of a particular crop, such as cotton in the Nile Valley or wine grapes in Algeria.

However, for better or for worse, reliance on agro-exports is commonly associated with colonialism. Historically, of course, the two were closely linked all over the world. The Middle East was no exception; cotton cultivation for export to Europe was expanded under colonial rule in Egypt and the Sudan, while wine production was introduced and flourished in the settler areas of North Africa. A division of labor between metropole and colony was an integral part of colonial ideology. The agro-export strategy faces several problems besides its historical associations, among them declining terms of trade for agricultural-export products, the favoring of certain classes, and excessive taxation.

Critics of agro-export–led growth strategies have long maintained that there is a long-run necessary tendency for a unit of agro-exports to buy progressively fewer manufactured products. Although one might reject the more extreme forms of this proposition, it is nevertheless clear that countries can and have experienced uncomfortably long periods of declining terms of trade (e.g., the Sudan, 1978–1985). Third, price fluctuations cause problems in their own right, independently of longer-run trends. If commodity-export prices fluctuate greatly from year to year, so also will export revenues. Since the point of any agro-export–led growth strategy is to acquire funds for industrialization and since industrial planning often involves fairly long lead times, such fluctuations can seriously disrupt industrialization efforts.

A second problem with this strategy is that (as with any strategy) certain domestic classes are more favored than others. In particular, many critics of the agro-export approach argue that it strengthens powerful urban commodity-trading interests, which may block further development. If such classes' power derives from the unchallenged economic dominance of their sector, they may especially resent any attempt to impose tariffs on imported domestic goods or taxes to finance infrastructure for industry.

It is not clear from the historical record of the Middle East that agro-exporters failed to invest, eschewed industrial projects, and generally blocked the rise of "infant industry." The Egyptian case is particularly instructive. Wealthy indigenous Egyptian cotton producers often invested in the agricultural sector and provided the bulk of the capital for the initial industrial endeavors of the Bank Misr in the 1920s (Davis 1983; Tignor 1984). Their loyalty to the nation also seems never to have been seriously in doubt. But it is true that such groups ultimately failed to solve the many pressing domestic political, economic, and social problems facing the country and could not rid the country of the British imperial presence. Their demise as agents of development also spelled the demise of the agro-export–led strategy.

A final problem that often arises with agro-exports is the temptation of the government to tax the sector excessively. This problem is the reverse of the previous one. Whereas the argument against compradors and oligarchs is based on the political *power* of these classes, the problem of excessive taxation is a result of the political *weakness* of export-crop producers. This situation usually arises if the producers are small peasants whose number, poverty, and geographical dispersion render collective action difficult. Governments are then often tempted to place the burden of growth on such classes, usually through establishing government control over marketing, input supply, or both. Such an approach is usually self-defeating, however; small peasants shift land, labor, and other inputs out of the controlled-export crops into other noncontrolled ones or resort to smuggling.

Mineral-export–led growth.   The second principal strategy is also based on the export of natural resources: mineral-export–led growth. In the Middle East, petroleum and phosphates are the major exports of this type. Jordan and, above all, Morocco, have substantial phosphate reserves and large exports. Moroccan phosphate exports are the largest in the world, and reserves (including those of the western Sahara) are 40% of the world's total. Petroleum, of course, is by far the most valuable and significant natural resource in the region.

One should distinguish between those oil and mineral exporters that have other resources, for example, substantial populations and considerable agricultural potential, and those whose economies are entirely dominated by mineral exports. The first group includes Algeria, Morocco, Tunisia, Iraq, and Iran, while the second set consists of Libya and the Gulf States. Saudi Arabia is a unique case because of the size of its petroleum reserves. The officially stated goals of the mineral-based export strategy are quite similar to those of agro-exporters: to acquire revenue from mineral exports to create an industrial base for sustained development after the natural resource is exhausted. This strategy is distinguished from the agro-export–led strategy by the very different pattern of international price developments (for oil but not for phosphates) and by the exhaustibility of the exported natural resource. By using the receipts from a depleting asset, a future without oil can be built.

This is a perfectly reasonable approach for countries that have significant nonpetroleum resources, but it is much more difficult to see what economic future is in store for Libya and the Gulf States after their oil runs out. Perhaps sufficient financial assets can be accumulated that can then serve as a reliable source of income. Before the Iraqi invasion, Kuwait reached this "pure-rentier-state" stage, with income from foreign investments exceeding that from petroleum exports. But such rentier activity leaves a nation very much at the mercy of international political developments; financial assets are fairly easy to seize or impound. Kuwait had to spend them during the Iraqi occupation for military, diplomatic, and political purposes related to regaining its independence. But the absence of arable land, water, and nonoil mineral resources and the presence of a small, poorly educated population suggest that the future without oil may be bleak.

The Saudis, for example, have about one-fifth of the world's petroleum reserves, with new discoveries announced nearly annually. These reserves can be expected to last 50 to 250 years depending on the rate of production. The Saudi strategy of oil-based development has had three major components. First, funds have been used to expand infrastructure, leading to one of the most massive construction booms in economic history. Despite numerous bottlenecks (inevitable given the low level of infrastructure and the size of the projects), roads, schools, hospitals, shopping centers, offices, and other buildings have mushroomed throughout the kingdom. Second, surplus funds—funds that could not be spent immediately—were placed in Western financial institutions. The Saudis thereby gained the benefit of those institutions' expertise in investment. Finally, the Saudis have invested in petroleum-based industry. They have selected industries for expansion that are highly capital- and energy-intensive and/or use oil or gas as a feedstock. The principal investments have been in petrochemical complexes, fertilizer plants, aluminum smelting, and steel production, using natural gas in a direct reduction process to convert imported iron ore.

None of these industrial schemes would be viable without oil; they are in no sense, then, "creating a future without oil." Instead, they are increasing the percentage that remains in Saudi Arabia of the value added that is embodied in the final output of petroleum- or energy-intensive industries. Saudi petrochemicals are now so highly competitive internationally that there have been protectionist moves against them in Western Europe and the United States. Despite such problems, the strategy of stretching out the life of its already massive reserves of petroleum makes good sense for Saudi Arabia. It is not really a viable strategy for other oil exporters, none of which enjoys reserves on the Saudi scale.

Any mineral-export–led growth strategy faces two major problems. First, most countries are likely to have only one significant mineral for export. Consequently, their export revenues are highly dependent on price developments for that product or products. This subjects their economies to the problems and difficulties of a sudden fall—or a sudden rise—in the price of their export. Second, the existence of large oil revenues combines with political structures and imperatives to create cradle-to-the-grave welfare systems. Although potential human capital is the only nonoil resource that many of these countries have, the incentives to develop it are limited. Why should a Saudi become an engineer if he can more easily become a joint director of a company whose head must always be Saudi? Why should a woman pursue higher education if there will be only a very few interesting job opportunities open for her? Although these problems may be overcome with time and although the ease of life for the poorer classes of Saudi society may be readily exaggerated, the presence of large oil rents poses problems for the accumulation of human capital.

The situation of these oil exporters is in many ways highly special. The combination of massive reserves, small populations, and few additional resources makes their development strategies and prospects sui generis. Oil exporters of the first group, however, are in a rather different situation. Only Iraq was a capital-surplus nation before its invasion of Iran. Countries such as Iran, Algeria, and Iraq faced a problem rather similar to that of Egypt after its period of agro-export–led growth: how best to foster the rise of industry. All of these countries adopted an import-substituting-industrialization approach and because of their petroleum rents have been able to sustain it longer than countries that do not export oil.

Import-substituting industrialization.   Import-substituting industrialization (ISI) is one of the LDCs' most tested development strategies. Its logic is compelling. It is designed to move economies traditionally dependent on the export of primary commodities and raw materials to an industrial footing. The new industries are expected both to produce goods that were previously imported (everything from textiles and shoes to fertilizers and refined sugar) *and* process domestic raw materials (e.g., cotton, minerals, sugarcane, petroleum). The result would be economic diversification and reduced dependency on volatile external markets for primary products and on high-priced imports.

Through ISI, it was hoped, developing countries could escape the agrarian trap into which imperialist powers or, more anonymously, the international division of labor had thrust them. The place to begin was with known domestic markets. As the process gathered steam and raised revenues for the new workers and managers as well as for the producers of agricultural commodities destined for processing, new markets would develop, and infant industries would achieve economies of scale that would make them profitable and competitive. Eventually the first industries would produce backward linkages, stimulating new enterprises in capital goods, basic metals, machine tools, and the like. In Egypt in the 1960–1965 period, when this strategy was pursued with vigor, it was envisaged that the textile sector, using Egyptian cotton and replacing foreign imports, would "link back" to the setting up of an industry to manufacture spinning and weaving machinery, itself utilizing steel from the new iron-and-steel complex.

Before these linkages could be firmly established and economies of scale achieved, the new industries would have to be protected from foreign competition by high tariff walls. Moreover, given the narrowness of domestic markets, any industry might enjoy, de facto or de jure, a monopoly in its particular sector. Thus, although seen as a temporary phenomenon, ISI implied and frequently meant monopolistic production and marketing at costs higher than for similar imports. It also frequently meant lower-quality goods than those that could be imported.

Turkey pioneered among Middle Eastern states in pursuing an ISI strategy. Atatürk's republic, founded at the end of World War I amid the debris of the Ottoman Empire, was the first fully independent country in the region, and its leader was determined to transform it into an industrial and "Western" nation. During the 1930s, in the absence of a formulated strategy and without any socialist justification, the Turkish state began to launch industries in textiles, cement, and basic metals. With the impact of the Great Depression, Turkey in 1933 launched its first five-year industrial plan and, with some advice from Soviet planners, entered a phase of concerted state-led growth. Next door in Iran, Reza Khan, the founder of the Pahlavi dynasty, was moving in a similar direction, and throughout the Arab world young men who would lead their countries in the 1950s observed Turkey's experiment closely.

With Algeria's independence in 1962, all major states in the Middle East had won formal sovereignty (the one exception was the former Aden Protectorate, which became the People's Democratic Republic of Yemen [PDRY] in 1969). With rare exceptions, these states pursued, to varying degrees and with different ideological underpinnings, ISI strategies. These made good sense for the larger, more differentiated economies in the region, those with important domestic markets that could sustain large industrial units. They made less sense for the small, undiversified economies of the not-yet-rich oil-exporting countries and for some without oil, such as Lebanon and Jordan. We should note, however, that one large country, the Sudan, only briefly toyed with an ISI strategy, while three large oil-exporting countries, Algeria, Iraq, and Iran, pursued it resolutely.

The most determined efforts to follow in Turkey's footsteps were undertaken by Egypt, Iran, Tunisia, Algeria, Syria, and Iraq. Israel followed the policy mainly with respect to military industries, but given its small population and economic isolation within the Arab world it could not afford a broad-based ISI strategy. ISI projects tended to fall within the following categories:

1. Consumer durables destined for established middle- and upper-income markets.
2. Textiles, shoes, and other apparel for mass markets.
3. Soft drinks and tobacco products for mass markets.
4. Processing of local agricultural produce: canning, sugar refining, spinning and weaving, alcohol, beer, etc.
5. Processing local raw materials: petroleum to fertilizers and plastics, iron ore to iron and steel.

ISI strategies led several states to ignore what neoclassical economists saw as their comparative advantage in world trade: the export of raw materials and unprocessed agricultural produce. But the states' object was precisely to promote economic diversification by building new skills within the workforce, to capture for national purposes the value added in processing that had heretofore accrued to the advanced industrial nations, and to reduce the states' dependency upon unstable world markets for primary produce. ISI has experienced widespread setbacks in the Middle East and elsewhere, but that does not mean that it was conceptually wrong at its inception.

The setbacks in the ISI strategy stemmed primarily from the degree of protection granted to the infant industries and the proportion of public resources devoted to them at the expense of the agricultural sector. The agricultural sector was taxed through various devices to provide an investable surplus for the new industrial undertakings, while the foreign exchange earned from agricultural exports went to pay for the technologies, capital goods, and raw materials required by the industrial sector. The price paid for these income transfers was frequently slow or nonexistent agricultural growth. This in turn meant, as we have seen in the Algerian case, that the large rural populations could not generate the demand to keep the new industries operating at full capacity. Consequently, idle capacity and production costs rose, but because the industries were protected against cheaper imports by high tariffs and enjoyed sectoral monopolies in domestic markets they had no incentive to keep costs down. The industries were in general capital-intensive and under the best of circumstances not providers of large numbers of jobs. When operating below capacity, they could only either lay off workers (a rare occurrence) or increase operating costs further by carrying redundant labor. In no way could they meet the challenge of providing jobs for rural workers abandoning a depressed agricultural sector for life and livelihood in the cities.

The net result in many instances was high-cost production destined either for upper-income luxury markets (such as automobiles and refrigerators) or for mass markets in which retail prices were subsidized by the government (everything from fertilizers to sugar). The new industries could not, because of their high costs, export their products and earn the foreign exchange needed to pay for imported raw materials and equipment. Thus they contributed to the growing balance-of-payments crises that plagued several ISI experiments. Clearly this was more a problem for the oil-poor, such as Turkey, Egypt, Syria, and Tunisia, than for the oil-rich, such as Iran, Iraq, and Algeria.

In order to lower the price of goods imported for the new industries, most governments maintained overvalued exchange rates for their currencies. These in combination with foreign-exchange-rationing systems that favored the new industries put no pressure upon those industries to reduce the import content of their operations. By contrast, traditional exporters in the agricultural sector in some instances lost their competitive edge in foreign markets because the artificially high exchange rate dampened demand for their commodities.

The need for the government to subsidize the price at which the products of the new industries were sold to consumers, be they other industrial users or buyers at the retail level, contributed significantly to the mounting public deficits and thereby to increasing rates of domestic inflation. Faced with sluggish agricultural performance, industries operating at a loss, large domestic deficits, and growing balance-of-payments difficulties, Middle Eastern governments turned to borrowing abroad to fill these gaps, incurring large foreign debts and heavy servicing requirements (payments of interest and principal).

Not all Middle Eastern countries adopted this strategy, but for many that did the 1970s brought a far-reaching reappraisal of what they had undertaken. For some, the moment of truth was brought about by the huge increase in their petroleum-import bill after 1973; for countries with abundant oil (for example, Algeria after 1976), the issue seemed to be more one of overheating and structural inefficiencies. The collapse of oil prices in the mid-1980s sounded the death knell of ISI in the region.

Manufactured-export–led growth.   For Western creditors of heavily indebted Middle Eastern economies, a way out seemed to lie in dramatically increasing manufactured exports to the markets of the OECD countries. South Korea, Taiwan, Singapore, India, and Brazil, among others, had to varying degrees succeeded in this, earning themselves the epithet of "newly industrializing countries" (NICs). What recommends this strategy is that it addresses two of the main problems arising from ISI. First, it earns the country foreign exchange without sacrificing the goal of industrialization. Second, if it is to have any chance of success, it requires the reduction of production costs so that the exporting industries can compete abroad, and therefore the problems of idle capacity, operating losses, and redundant labor have to be overcome. With world markets as their target, economies of scale can be achieved even for countries with relatively small domestic markets (Hong Kong, Singapore, Honduras, and Costa Rica demonstrate the possibilities).

There are daunting domestic challenges to this strategy. "Bad habits" that may have developed during the ISI phase may be dealt with only at high political cost. Some analysts, such as Lipton (1977) and Bates (1981), have suggested the existence in LDCs of an urban or at least nonagrarian alliance consisting of industrial management and capitalists in protected industries, the organized industrial workforce, civil servants, and virtually all urban consumers. All have become accustomed to protection of inefficient management, redundant labor, and consumer and input subsidies. None of this protection can be allowed to endure if export-led growth is to gain momentum. Moreover, devaluation may have a particularly sharp impact on urban consumers, who will see the price of many imported items skyrocket.

A government contemplating this strategy must think carefully of the constituencies it will alienate, some of which are part of the state apparatus itself. The owners and managers of import-substituting industries may try to sabotage the new experiment, and they will find tacit allies among the workers who risk being laid off as enterprises streamline or who may face relative reductions in salary. All urban constituents may see a sharp rise in the cost of living. It is important to remember that the negative effects of the new strategy will be felt immediately, whereas the economic payoffs may be years in coming. No politician likes that sort of bargain.

Despite the risks, some Middle Eastern countries have moved in this direction. Two of the earliest experiments involve Morocco and Tunisia, both of which negotiated preferential trade agreements with the European Union in the late 1960s. Tunisia was moving away from a period of concerted ISI under state auspices, while Morocco was seeking to diversify its exports beyond its traditional combination of phosphates and citrus. Both hoped to attract light industry from Europe in ready-made apparel, electronics, consumer-durable assembly, and so forth, or to stimulate their own private sectors to move into similar fields. They accelerated these efforts after the mid-1980s (Chapter 9).

For nearly two decades Turkey, already a member of the North Atlantic Treaty Organization (NATO), has aspired to full membership in the European Economic Community (EEC). Since the early 1970s it has been trying to restructure its economy (after the experiment in ISI launched by Atatürk) so as to be able to compete in European markets. The process took on added urgency in the late 1970s as Turkey, without petroleum deposits, absorbed the full impact of rising international prices for fossil fuels at the same time that European labor markets were closing themselves off to migrant Turkish workers. Balance-of-payments crises, growing external debt, mounting domestic deficits, and inflation produced a situation of political instability and eventual military intervention in 1980. Since then a return to civilian rule has been accompanied by a concerted and partially successful export drive for Turkish manufactures and construction services.

Israel's economy has always been aid- and trade-dependent. As did Tunisia and Morocco, and well before them, it negotiated a preferential trade agreement with the EEC, and it has had great success in marketing avocados, citrus, and vegetables in Europe. Its major manufactured export has traditionally been finished industrial diamonds. In the past decade, however, diamonds have been eclipsed by manufactured metal products and high-tech electronics. Equally important is Israel's having become a major actor in the international arms trade, supporting the scale and sophistication of its own armaments industry by developing foreign markets for its weaponry. Despite its relative success in all export sectors, Israel found itself in the early 1980s facing huge domestic deficits, high labor costs for Israeli workers that limited the areas in which Israel could be competitive internationally, the largest per capita external debt in the world, and a domestic inflation rate in 1985 second only to Bolivia's. Since 1985, however, Israel has simultaneously pursued economic reforms at home and export promotion abroad. By 1995 it had earned from London's *Economist* the epithet of "tiger" reserved mainly for the export dynamos of East Asia.

Agricultural-development—led growth. A final strategy that has received emphasis among political economists is agricultural-development—led growth (e.g., Adelman 1984; Mellor 1976). The strategy is especially aimed at very poor countries with most of their population still in agriculture, without vast mineral resources, and with little prospect of penetrating foreign markets for manufactured goods. It is particularly designed to minimize any conflict between growth and equity in development. The strategy draws on the "basic-needs" approach popular with international agencies during the 1970s, which focused on providing adequate nutrition, health, and education to all people. However, the agricultural-development—led growth approach places more stress on sustaining such human-capital investments by raising productivity and on realistic price signals for achieving growth-with-equity. Although no Middle Eastern countries have adopted this strategy, if austerity and sluggish international markets persist, poorer countries like Yemen and Sudan could do worse than to try to implement it.

The strategy relies heavily on the linkages between the growth of small-farmer agriculture and the labor market. Empirical evidence suggests that agriculture is the most labor-intensive of any industry; increasing output per unit of land also raises the demand for agricultural laborers, usually the poorest people in any country. Furthermore, farmers spend a high proportion of their increased incomes on labor-intensive manufactured goods such as housing, furniture, and bicycles. Consequently, agricultural productivity growth, which augments farmers' incomes, raises the demand for industrial labor. Increases in agricultural output can be obtained at a relatively low cost in imported goods (unlike, say, automobile manufacturing, where all of the parts may be imported, as was true in Iran under the shah). Finally, activities that improve agricultural infrastructure (roads, irrigation and drainage systems) are also typically very labor-intensive. The strategy tries to take advantage of the agricultural production function and farmers' tastes to create "virtuous circles" of increased food production, improved health, steadily growing labor absorption, and relatively equitably rising incomes.

The choice of strategies.   Countries in the region will most probably select and combine some or all of the elements of these strategies. For example, ISI and manufactured-export–led growth strategies are not mutually exclusive. It is in fact likely that most of the more developed countries will try to combine elements of both, just as poorer countries may combine agricultural-development–led growth with agro-exports or some modest import substitution. We may find two sectors side by side, one following the ISI pattern perhaps in metals, automobile assembly, fertilizers, and the like, and the other oriented toward external markets in finished textiles, electronic appliances, and instruments. Turkey in the 1980s was pursuing an export-led strategy without totally renouncing its heritage from the years 1930 to 1970 of protected, domestically oriented industries. Other countries have exhibited elements of three strategies: primary exports, ISI, and manufactured exports. Oil exporters such as Iran are an example, while Egypt and Tunisia represent countries that have continued traditional exports (cotton, olive oil, and in the 1970s petroleum), maintained an important ISI sector, and sought to promote manufactured exports with variable success.

Having described elements of simultaneity in strategy selection, we cannot deny that there may often be sequential elements at stake as well. Put simply, ISI may be adopted as *the* strategy and produce a host of unintended and undesirable consequences, at which point the country shifts to an export-led strategy. There is ample evidence of such sequential shifts in the Middle East; Turkey, Egypt, Israel, Morocco, and Tunisia have all proceeded in similar fashion. Whether sequential or simultaneous, the state continues to play a preponderant role in shaping the experiment through control of credit, foreign exchange, tax policy, and investment budgets. Stimulating the private sector or honoring the market does not mean abdicating to either. The prominent role of the state in the Korean "miracle" is instructive in this respect.

A final caveat on strategy choice is in order here, to wit, the choice is never unconstrained. It is some set of state actors that makes the choice, and the choice is bounded by a host of factors, some of which are more obvious than others. There are resource constraints: Israel cannot export oil or any other raw material on a significant scale, but it does have a highly skilled workforce. The Sudan can export cotton, but it does not have a highly skilled workforce. Saudi Arabia can export oil and import a highly skilled workforce. ISI, as noted, is ill-suited to economies with small markets, and in most instances it does not make sense to establish industries to process resources one does not have.

The choice is also constrained by the relative gains and losses that will be incurred by domestic interests, classes, and ideological factions—this indeed is the primary focus of this book. The choice will be further constrained by the country's regional and international allies, any of which may have its own image of the future and some levers with which to promote it. And the choice will be constrained by international markets and financial flows. The Sudan invested heavily in sugar refining destined for export on the eve of the collapse of world sugar markets. Countries whose external debt is denominated in U.S. dollars found themselves in the early and middle 1980s saddled with huge unanticipated servicing requirements due to the surge in U.S. interest rates and the constant revaluing of the dollar against all other currencies.

Finally, the state cannot implement all elements of a strategy. It must use agencies external to itself, perhaps the local private sector or the capitalist farming sector or the multinational corporations. Since the late 1980s few countries have not succumbed to the pressures of the international donor community to open their economies and reduce protection of domestic markets. Most countries in the region have adhered to the General Agreement on Tariffs and Trade (GATT) and to the rules and guidelines of the Uruguay Round of trade negotiations. Egypt, Israel, Jordan, Morocco, Turkey, Tunisia, and the United Arab Emirates (UAE) have joined the new World Trade Organization, the successor to GATT; Saudi Arabia has plans to join. Under the new rules of the trading game, it will be increasingly difficult to combine protected, ISI sectors with policies designed to promote exports and to open the economy to untaxed imports.

Instruments and Intermediaries

There are instruments and intermediaries that the state chooses, more or less willingly, to implement its strategy, and there are those that impose themselves, more or less, upon the state. What the state does voluntarily or is forced to do is determined to some extent by its professed ideology. But, one must hasten to add, the professed ideals of the political regime are as often as not honored in the breach.

Until the 1980s, most Middle Eastern states advocated some form of socialism, however vague the content of the label and however insincere the regime's commitment to it. Even Egypt and Tunisia, in the 1970s, as they moved toward greater reliance on the market, the private sector, and profits as incentives, still spoke of themselves as socialist states. The dominant philosophy in Israel until the advent of the Likud government under Menachem Begin in 1977 was a kind of Zionist hybrid of Fabian socialism. The Sudan, the Yemen Arab Republic (YAR), Syria, Iraq, Libya, and Algeria all have laid claim to socialism. One has the impression that their socialism, like that of Tunisia and Egypt, has consisted mainly in a large public sector and extensive welfare programs. On that score, monarchical Morocco, the Islamic Republic of Iran (as well as the Pahlavi dynasty before it), Turkey, Israel, and all the conservative princedoms of the Gulf and the Kingdom of Saudi Arabia could lay equal claim to socialism. But they do not. Morocco vaunts its political and economic liberalism, while Turkey today speaks mainly of the latter. Still we find the self-proclaimed liberals maintaining large state sectors and interfering in all aspects of market transactions. Similarly, socialist regimes tolerate and sometimes aid and abet private-sector actors in trade, small-scale manufacturing, construction, and farming. By any measure the largest and most dominant state sectors in the Middle East lie in the small oil-exporting countries, where the petroleum deposits, the producing and refining companies, and all the proceeds of oil sales are under the control of the state.

Throughout the Middle East since the 1970s Islam has come to play an increasingly important role in shaping ideology and sometimes policy. For the moment we note only that Islam reinforces nationalist suspicions of virtually all outside agencies and nations. The question for Muslims, especially Muslim thinkers, is not one of socialism versus capitalism or public versus private property but rather one of the inherent dangers in dealing with any non-Muslim power. Such dealings can never be neutral or benign but are necessarily conflictual. One may choose among lesser Satans, but the ideal is to make no choice at all.

Many scholars of developing countries have argued that their governments really have no sovereign choice of strategies—that these are determined by core capitalist countries, and the nominal differences among strategies are superficial. The international division of labor in this view is not the product of the working of the forces of supply and demand within world markets but the result of the pressure on international capital flows that are in turn determined by the dominant capitalist economies in the world system. This understanding of the dynamics of international capital flows and markets is common to the proponents of dependency and world-systems analysis, and it presumes that the major impulses toward various strategies come from advanced economies and that the range of choice is, by and large, strictly bounded. It is not difficult, for example, to explain the collapse of the socialist economies of Eastern Europe and the Soviet Union in these terms. The core capitalist countries have powerful instruments at their disposal with which to impose their models of proper economic development: multinational corporations, multinational donor and financial institutions such as the IMF and the World Bank, major private banks that hold much of the aggregate debt of the LDCs, and, in the last decade or so, control of huge flows of funds through a myriad of capital markets that have sprung up throughout the developing world.

As will become clear in several places in this book, we are not comfortable with this line of analysis, particularly with regard to its tendency to deny the possibility of a significant area of sovereign choice for developing countries. The Middle East certainly displays a wide range of experiments and strategies, and although they are constrained by external forces and institutions (one wonders how it could be otherwise under any set of international political circumstances) they are not wholly determined by them. ISI as a strategy, for example, was advocated by Latin American economists as a way of breaking or attenuating the dependency of Latin American economies upon the advanced economies of Europe and North America. It was adopted elsewhere, in Turkey for example, in that spirit. One could argue that its widespread failures show that core interests successfully sabotaged it, but one would have expected that, given the alleged power of these interests, they would have seen to it that the strategy was never adopted in the first place.

There is no question that when crises in the external accounts of LDCs become manifest in failure to service private external debt and balance-of-payments deficits the range of choice available to developing nations narrows significantly. The movement of "portfolio" money through emerging markets is increasingly influenced by levels of domestic savings and the current-account balance. When domestic savings are low, investment high, and the current-account balance in deficit, portfolio money, as Mexico discovered in the winter of 1995, heads elsewhere at literally the speed of light. Such crises, however, may be exacerbated but are seldom caused by the functioning of international markets, financial institutions, or multinational corporations. More often than not, the culprits are lagging agricultural production, inefficient industrial production systems, and costly, oversized public bureaucracies. However, once the crises become manifest, the agencies of the core gain significant leverage over policy and strategy choice in LDCs. In essence, new lines of credit and the rescheduling of existing debt and new infusions of foreign direct investment are traded against structural reforms in the economy of the developing country. Since the mid-1970s scores of developing countries have been driven toward far-reaching and painful structural adjustment programs designed in consultation with the IMF, the World Bank, and Western aid agencies, and the countries in the Middle East have been no exception (see Chapter 9).

One general observation can be made at this juncture, a much fuller treatment being saved for future chapters. ISI strategies have typically relied upon publicly owned enterprises, mainly because the initial investments have usually been very large and beyond the capacity of local entrepreneurial groups, if there are any. In contrast, as countries move toward export-led growth, there is often an attempt by public authorities to mobilize the private sector to play a significant role in these programs. The foreign donor and creditor community frequently pushes the authorities in this direction, but there may also be an independently formulated expectation that the private sector can adjust more rapidly than the public to the challenge of reducing costs, improving quality, and seeking out customers abroad for the country's products. Ideology is then left to catch up with the new reality.

Whether or not called upon to play an active part in the implementation of strategies, certain interests, strata of the population, and classes will benefit while others will be penalized, depending on the strategy or policies selected. It is the case in general that the rural sector does not benefit from ISI strategies because the state usually turns the domestic terms of trade against it. In an export-led strategy, it may be only capitalist farmers and not the peasantry as a whole that benefits from export incentives. If one looks at urban constituencies affected by ISI, one may see that organized labor in the new industries, managerial strata charged with implementing state-financed projects, and middle- and upper-income consumers may be the major beneficiaries. Large-scale industrialists in the private sector may suffer when state banking institutions and government investment programs favor public-sector enterprise. In contrast, small-scale industrialists may benefit from subcontracting on public-sector projects, especially in the construction sector.

The move toward a manufactured-export–led strategy will likely have an adverse effect on the real incomes of workers, as wages will be allowed to lag behind inflation. Moreover, if the strategy is accompanied by devaluation, a shift in the domestic terms of trade in favor of agriculture, and some reduction in consumer subsidies, all citizens in the nonfarm sector and especially those on fixed incomes will experience a sharp rise in the cost of living.

Common to both marxist and liberal schools of analysis is the assumption that forces essentially external to the state are able to control and guide it, using the state to promote or defend their interests. This is an "instrumentalist" view of the state, one that looks, in the liberal tradition, to parties, unions, and interest groups as capturing the state through elections and lobbying or, in the marxian tradition, to a dominant class controlling the basic means of production within society as being in a position to use the state to perpetuate its dominance.

We question the premises of both liberal and marxist understandings. First, the process of structural transformation and the nearly universal shift toward the preponderance of the nonagrarian, urban sector in economic and social terms produces new social actors and economic interests and undermines the old, irrespective of differing production systems, ideologies, or state formations. Second, at a less macro level, a given development strategy may set in motion a process that virtually creates new social actors. This process should be seen as an unintended by-product of the strategy choice, not as conclusive evidence that the state was acting in the interests of a class or economic pressure group that had not yet taken shape. The increasing strength of the Turkish private industrial bourgeoisie emerging out of the decades of statist, ISI-oriented politics is a case in point.

Third, in the Middle East, as in most LDCs, class alignments and interest group formation are fluid. Traditional class and economic interests have lost influence. For instance, landowning groups have been undermined by land reforms, but new and as yet unorganized commercial farming interests have begun to take shape. Nowhere have peasantries developed class cohesion. To the extent that capitalist bourgeoisies existed in the first half of this century, they were frequently made up of foreigners of one sort or another and preferred trade to manufacturing. Because industrialization has come very late to the region, the proletariat is weak. That leaves a relatively powerful state apparatus, with its legions of civil servants and managers, a relatively powerful military establishment, and a numerically important but organizationally weak stratum of craftspeople, service people, small-scale manufacturers, and myriad petty tradespeople. For the most part, these social actors are not sufficiently coherent or well defined to manipulate the state. Like any other collectivity, they may find it difficult to act collectively: The "free-rider" problem is often serious.[1] It is our contention that the Middle Eastern state, as often as not, is best seen as the instrument of the upper echelons of its own personnel and that it is in their interests to ensure that the state continues to control as much of the economic resources of the society as possible.

Departing from that premise, we go one step further. Given its relative power and relative autonomy, the state may be the creator of interests and social actors. That is, the somewhat disembodied politico-military power of the state has been used to allocate resources in the process of structural transformation in such a way that new interests are called forth and establish their own claims on resources. The policy levers at the disposal of the Middle Eastern state to act in this manner are formidable. It may own and manage the major productive assets in the economy, own and derive revenue from all mineral resources, act as the single largest employer in the economy, control if not own the major banking institutions, regulate and tax economic activities of all kinds, set basic education policy, control prices, and exercise, in Max Weber's terms, the legitimate monopoly of coercive force. Crucial struggles, then, have occurred not so much between the state and the forces in civil society that seek to control the state as within the ranks of the state elites themselves.

How the state as interest-producer works out in practice will be developed throughout this book, but a few examples of what we have in mind are in order here. Agrarian reforms in the Middle East and the implementation of new production strategies in the agricultural sector have frequently resulted in the elimination of large landowners as a major political force and the expansion of the ranks of small and middle-sized landowners, a stratum of which is allowed disproportionate access to rural credit and control over rural institutions such as cooperatives and village councils. This stratum is then in a position to take full advantage of unregulated markets for agricultural produce or to lead the way in export drives.

The groups the state favors need not be of a kind. We should expect a great deal of inconsistency in the doling out of incentives, for the state is not a monolith in its dealings with civil society. For example, in the Sudan, the state and the economy as a whole have long depended on the performance of the Gezira Scheme, in which tenants on state land grow cotton for export. The Sudanese state has traditionally sought to extract savings and foreign exchange from this scheme, and in the constant bargaining that goes on between the state and the tenant cultivators the latter have become a powerful interest group in Sudanese society. At the same time the Sudanese government has encouraged through easy credit and forfeitary land-leasing arrangements the emergence of a sizable group of private commercial farmers undertaking mechanized cultivation of sorghum destined mainly for export. Thus it simultaneously promotes policies to help it extract resources from a huge state farm and fosters a process of "primitive accumulation" among a growing stratum of capitalist tractor farmers, a stratum that thirty years ago scarcely existed.

Let us look at one final example. Turkey hopes one day to join the European Union, and to this end it has been lowering tariff walls and trade barriers in the face of more efficient European producers. The policies of Turkey in the 1980s, formulated by the then–prime minister, Turgut Özal, were to favor the country's large industrial and construction firms through tax incentives and credit policy. These policies in turn have led to the consolidation of a native capitalist industrial bourgeoisie for the first time in any Middle Eastern society.

SOCIAL ACTORS

The final vertex of our theoretical triangle consists of social actors. There is nothing neat and tidy about this category. Indeed, as we have emphasized, fluidity of class, economic, and all other interests in contemporary Middle Eastern society is a given. What needs to be stressed, however, is that, in contrast to the somewhat state-centric thrust of the discussion thus far, social actors are not inert and passive in the face of state initiatives. Societal interests and social actors penetrate the state and colonize parts of it. They form alliances with key state actors and enter into explicit or implicit coalitions with public officials, including the head of state. On occasion, they defy or resist the state through the sabotage of policies or through open resistance.

Our inclination is always, as a "first cut," to search for the material or economic incentives that shape group and individual action. Our generalizations apply best to the actions of economic interest groups (for example, the union of secondary school teachers) or of class actors (for example, private industrialists or public-sector managers). In a fundamental sense the allocation and protection of property rights by the state is the starting point for understanding interest-group and class formation. The property "regime" established by law and maintained by force at any point in time will be defended by the beneficiaries and contested by those who feel excluded.

In the last quarter of this century the array of social actors interacting with and confronting the Middle Eastern state has become far more complex than it was at the end of World War II. The middle classes—those owning "real" and intellectual (i.e., specialized educational training) capital—have grown prodigiously. Economic specialization has spawned new interests, and the creation of new wealth has slowly given those interests the ability to further their objectives. Whereas thirty years ago most social actors were "policy-takers" in the face of autonomous states that they could not significantly influence, much less hold to account, by the 1990s a process of bargaining between the state and social actors had become common. If democratic practice is to take root in the Middle East, it will be as the result of the *formalization* of this bargaining process.

That said, we recognize that not all groups are defined by economic interests alone. The new literature on Middle Eastern civil society (see Kazemi and Norton 1994; Salamé 1994) grapples with the nature of group identity. Are Islamic political movements driven primarily by religious values and fervor or by less edifying struggles for power and resources? Are ethnic groups and movements explained best by near-mystical notions of blood, ancestry, and historical injustice, or are they mainly seeking recognized claims to national resources? Are both Islamicists and ethnic movements crassly manipulated by politicians who see in religion or blood powerful implements for mobilizing a following? Undoubtedly power hunger, material betterment, group fear, and true piety all play their part. It is up to the analyst to decide what motivations predominate when. We will try our best in the coming chapters to do just that, but in each instance we will test first material explanations.

STRUCTURAL TRANSFORMATION AND INTEREST FORMATION

Europe's structural transformation over a number of centuries from an agrarian to an industrial-urban base has shaped our general understanding of the process but has not provided a model that will be faithfully replicated in developing countries. The latter may skip some stages by importing technology or telescope others. Developing countries will cope with population growth rates that Europe never confronted. So too, the process of class formation in the Middle East and elsewhere has varied considerably from that of Europe. What, schematically, are the major differences between the Middle Eastern and the European experience in the interaction of class, state, and structural transformation?

The first set of distinctions revolves around the legal institutions of private property so prominent in European history but relatively absent in Middle Eastern. In the Middle East, India, and China, Marx saw evidence for what he called "the Asiatic mode of production." The elements he saw as crucial to this mode shifted over time in his analysis (see Anderson 1980, 484–485; Islamöglu and Keyder 1977, 395), but there were some constants that we believe do define a regime peculiar to the Middle East and South Asia. The basic elements were (1) an absence, in the juridical sense, of private property in land and (2) a state that extracted tribute, through appointed intermediaries, from undifferentiated villages that combined agriculture and handicrafts and that displayed few organic linkages among themselves. Nomads and tribes competed with the state for the surplus that sedentary populations could produce. The Middle Eastern state retained the right (but not always the ability) to dispose of landed property as its rulers saw fit. What it granted were temporary rights to appropriate the produce of the land, that is, usufruct rights. In contrast to European ones, these rights were not permanent and sanctified by law but temporary privileges bestowed upon clients by the ruler—the caliph or sultan and his governors in far-flung regions of the Islamic empires.

Many historians have observed that the state's eminent domain often gave way in practice to what amounted to hereditary access to state-granted land or to the right to collect tribute in the state's name. But the arrival on the scene of a powerful sultan would, and not infrequently did, lead to the revocation of those quasi-hereditary privileges. Likewise, local notables could, in the face of a weak or financially constrained sultan, assert "stable" claims to privilege. The law was indifferent to the outcome of these power struggles; it only endorsed the right of the state to dispose of the public domain as its rulers saw fit.

Between the sultan and his government and the tribute-paying villagers and tribes lay a more or less thick stratum of tax-farmers, tribute gatherers, and rural notables. Some were military figures, such as the Ottoman *sipahis,* charged with raising tribute and troops for the sultan in exchange for fieflike estates known as timars. Others were tax-farmers pure and simple, granted the right to tax a certain population to whatever extent possible in return for turning over to the sultan a predetermined amount.

As the Middle East, from the seventeenth century on, was drawn into international trade dominated by the newly industrializing nations of Europe, and Islamic states everywhere (the Ottoman Empire, Persia, Moghul India, Morocco) dealt with military inferiority vis-à-vis the Europeans, important changes occurred in the relation of these states to their tribute-paying subjects. The need to raise revenues to pay for an enlarged and modernized military establishment pushed the sultans toward conversion of timar land into hereditary private land, while tax-farmers (*multazim*s) gained heritable and salable rights to their territories. After a time, local notables began to profit from a lucrative agricultural-export trade with Europe and were allowed to establish commercial estates (*çiftlik*s) that were tantamount to privately owned commercial farms.

The question of state revenues is crucial in grasping one of the profound differences between European and Middle Eastern patterns of economic change. For the most part, state revenues were drawn from the agrarian sector in the form of taxes in kind or in cash on land, animals, and huts. As much as 80% of state revenues may have been so derived, and as much as 15% of total agricultural production may have been absorbed in tribute (Issawi 1982, 68–69; Owen 1981, 106; Katouzian 1981). These proportions of course varied enormously in time and in place and should be taken only as orders of magnitude. The remaining 20% of state revenues came from taxes on overland trade, excise duties, state monopolies, and taxes on markets and guilds.

The paradox here is that public authorities seldom paid much attention to improving agricultural conditions so as to maximize production and, derivatively, state revenues. The one *partial* exception may have been the highly productive irrigated agrarian sector of Egypt, where the state on occasion had to concern itself with flood-control projects and the maintenance of the irrigation infrastructure. But even there, the state was mostly concerned with organizing its tribute gatherers and capturing within its net a peasantry that had nowhere to hide.

Even had the state been in all epochs more benevolent in its approach to its rural populations, there is reason to doubt that the kinds of locally inspired technological breakthroughs in agriculture that occurred in Europe would have been replicated in the Middle East. The reasons involve the ecology of the region and the existence of large nomadic populations. When we consider the vast extent of the Middle East or even its subregions, its rugged terrain characterized by mountain ranges interspersed with large desert expanses, and the prevailing aridity throughout, we can say that it would have been surprising had the Middle East duplicated European agricultural progress. Take only Saudi Arabia with its 2.2 million square kilometers, or about four-fifths of the Arabian Peninsula. This surface, the equivalent of most of Western Europe including the Iberian Peninsula and Italy, is mainly desert. Whereas European governments dealt with compact areas and generally favorable rain and soil conditions, Middle Eastern states faced staggering distances and hostile terrain that defied centralization, the habits of regular administrative practice, and the consistent maintenance of law and order.

The very ecology of the region produced a social phenomenon, the nomads, that had no counterpart in Western Europe. The nomads in the Middle East, even into the twentieth century, constituted at least 10% of the total population in most areas. Their turf was the "coastal" zones where the few well-watered areas of sedentary agriculture gave way to the desert proper. It was in these zones that they grazed their animals and pitched their tents. Their self-image was one of warriors, freemen who had only scorn for peasants enslaved to the land. Like the state, they often preyed on the very populations from which they needed tribute. Not until the twentieth century would distance be conquered, nomads subdued, and the control of the government extended on a permanent basis over all the territories of sedentary population.

What, then, of the cities and trade as a source of revenue? Urban centers have for millennia been important features in the political and economic landscape of the Middle East. We think first of the ancient cities of Jerusalem, Damascus, Antioch, and Carthage, but in the Muslim Middle Ages major cities stretched from Spain in the west to India in the east: Fez, Cordoba, Tunis, Cairo, Aleppo, Istanbul, Izmir, Tabriz, Tehran, and Baghdad were in size and diversity the rival of anything in Europe. These cities thrived on the long-distance trade linking Europe to the Far East and, to a lesser extent, to Africa. Muslim states were themselves centered in these cities and were able to tax in various ways the commerce passing through them and the crafts and services that were stimulated by overland trade. The cities were the centers as well of Muslim learning and culture.

To some extent, commerce, urban life in general, and high culture were divorced from the sedentary hinterlands of the cities (Amin 1980, 21). But whereas the state might find in the cities and caravan routes a source of income independent of the fluctuating fortunes of agriculture, its approach to urban business was hardly more benign. Writing of Moghul India, Barrington Moore observed (1967, 322): "In general, the attitude of the political authorities . . . toward the merchant seems to have been closer to that of the spider toward the fly than that of the cow herd toward his cow that was widespread in Europe at the same time. Not even Akbar, the most enlightened of the Moguls, had a Colbert."

By the eighteenth century the Ottoman and other sultanic states in the region faced a momentous fiscal crisis resulting from four factors: (1) the diversion of some overland trade to the new sea routes to the Far East; (2) overextension of the administrative capacity of the empire at the expense of settled agriculture; (3) the quest for new revenues in order to undertake military modernization that resulted in the assignation of land and tax-farming rights of a quasi-hereditary nature; and (4) the consolidation of a rural notability engaged in commercial agriculture for export. The privatization of the state's domain that we usually associate with direct colonial rule was well under way before European powers carved up the Middle East.

If we then look at the class "products" of this historical process, we find a relatively undifferentiated peasantry whose surplus was coveted by both the state and the armed nomadic tribes, urban merchants engaged in both overland and internal trade, urban artisans who produced for upper-income urban consumers as well as for peasants and tribesmen, and the legal experts of Islam, the ulema (plural of *'ālim*, "one who knows"). The ulema, along with the soldiers and the bureaucrats of the state, constituted class actors of a sort, but actors who did not necessarily own or directly control property or means of production. Rather, in the name of the state and of Islam, they exercised the authority and, frequently, the naked power to dispose of property and productive means.

DEFENSIVE MODERNIZATION AND COLONIAL TRANSFORMATION

There is no gainsaying that the mid- and late nineteenth century is a watershed in state and class formation in the Middle East. Although processes of monetization, commercialization, and privatization may be discerned prior to that period, they were greatly accelerated thereafter as the increasingly mature industrial societies of Europe contended for geopolitical and economic advantage in the Middle East.

The military threat posed by those societies, as well as by czarist Russia, had been clear for some time, and Ottoman sultans and their governors had begun to transform their military establishments along European lines. Large standing armies, modern industries for manufacturing artillery pieces and firearms, and road and railroad construction to facilitate the movement of troops and goods all required expenditures by the state on an unprecedented scale. The search for revenue led Middle Eastern states into new domestic taxation devices and into external debt to European banks.

By midcentury a so-called reform program (the Tanzimat) was under way throughout the Ottoman Empire and was echoed in Qajar Iran and in Morocco (the *nizam al-jadid*, or new order). The general tendency was to develop the legal infrastructure of private property; the European creditors of the empire argued that stable title to land and wealth would increase productive activity and hence the sultan's tax base. In Egypt the khedive, or Ottoman governor, granted private title to land to anyone who paid five years of agricultural tax in advance. In addition, the collection of taxes in cash became the norm, forcing cultivators into commercial agriculture in order to acquit their obligations. The process was not at all smooth; the Ottoman bey of Tunis in 1857 introduced a head tax in cash (the *majba*), which led to a rural revolt in 1864. The tax, which had produced 50% of the beylical state's revenues, was rescinded, and Tunis then borrowed its way into an unmanageable external debt (Anderson 1986).

The development efforts of the Middle Eastern state thus had as a direct consequence the promotion, if not the creation, of new propertied interests. The growth of a rural notability through trade and tax-farming was visible everywhere. As land became alienable, it could serve as collateral against loans. This change brought investment into agriculture and began, in parts of the Ottoman Empire, to attract foreign capital to export agriculture. Middlemen proliferated: private moneylenders, real estate banks, buyers and brokers for export crops. Frequently the middlemen were foreigners or from religious minorities that were not subject to Islamic strictures on interest: hence the prominence of Greeks, Armenians, Jews, and Coptic Christians. Increasingly, they linked the new squirearchy of commercial agriculture to foreign markets. The squirearchy itself was mainly indigenous, but we should remember that in Algeria, after the French conquest of 1830, Europeans owned the best lands and dominated the export of wine to France.

Again, in the effort to stabilize rural revenue sources, the state encouraged tribal and nomadic chieftains to settle by granting them title to what had been quasi-communal lands, while state officials, high-ranking military figures, members of the ruling family or dynasty (such as the Qajar aristocracy in Iran or the dynasty of Muhammed 'Ali in Egypt), and even "aristocratic" urban families such as those of the city of Hama in Syria established private title to what became veritable latifundia (Iraq, Iran, parts of Syria, and eastern Anatolia were particularly affected).

Similar processes were at work in the cities. The public bureaucratic function increased in importance, as did the bureaucrats themselves; the military establishment became more elaborate; and a new merchant bourgeoisie, overlapping substantially with the agents of commercial agriculture and just as frequently foreign (Figure 2.5), took root. The point we wish to stress in all this—one that informs all of our analysis—is that the state authorities can initiate broad-gauged policies in fairly unfettered fashion. Moreover, in the pursuit of specific goals, those authorities will stimulate processes of economic change whose consequences in the creation of new economic actors and class strata are as momentous as they are unanticipated.

In the late nineteenth and early twentieth centuries, Islamic states collapsed in the face of European imperialism. All of the Middle East except Turkey, Iran, and the Arabian Peninsula fell under European rule. The colonial states that were implanted were truly autonomous from the societies they governed. With modern military technology (aircraft, among other things) and administrative practices, they completed the subjugation of territories and peoples that the sultans had begun. Private property, the cash economy, and the tax collector advanced together. The colonial state added two new and vital elements: public education for a limited number of natives and the promotion of a professional civil service. The norms underlying these elements, norms that we now call Weberian, were those of achieved status, that is, position won on the basis of training and competency regardless of factors of birth, blood, or income. Even though Turkey and Iran escaped direct European control,

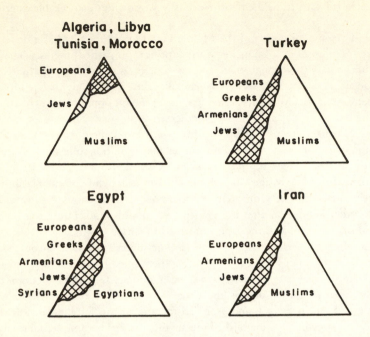

FIGURE 2.5   European and minority shares in the wealth of the Middle East: pre–World
War II. *Source:* Charles Issawi, *An Economic History of the Middle East and North Africa,*
New York, Columbia University Press, 1982, p. 9. Copyright © 1982 by Columbia
University Press. Used by permission.

their leaders attempted, more successfully in Turkey than in Iran, to apply these standards to their own bureaucracies.

The colonial state was in general expected by the metropole to be financially self-
sufficient. A modern civil service was necessary to manage roads, railroads, ports,
and power, to run the mail and telegraph services, to identify and tax the population,
to staff all echelons of local administration, and to assume all the intermediate positions between the colonial authorities and the population for which mastery of the
colonial and the native languages was essential. By the 1930s one finds a new proto-
class asserting itself. It was educated, white-collar, and salaried. Its status was dependent not on its ownership of private property—of which it might possess very little—but on its professional attainment. It was bourgeois in aspirations and lifestyle.
It was in embryo what Halpern (1963) was later to call "the new middle class."

The major achievement of the colonial state in interest formation consisted in
consolidating the position of landowners and in midwifing the birth of the new
middle class. The postcolonial state in the Middle East has gone much further than
either the Islamic or the colonial state in redrafting the class map of the region. Few

postcolonial states had, to begin with, or maintained for long strong links to wealthy classes in their societies. Syria and Iraq up to 1958, Lebanon, and Morocco were the only major exceptions. The more autonomous states, Turkey, Iran, Egypt, Algeria, and Syria and Iraq after 1958, engaged in far-reaching class engineering. The latifundists mentioned earlier were undermined by agrarian reform, and the merchant bourgeoisie was hemmed in by state regulations, price controls, public trade monopolies, and nationalizations. Foreign and minoritarian commercial groups faced systematic discrimination.

By contrast, varying combinations of agrarian reform and ISI bolstered the ranks of small landowners, left small-scale capitalist farmers at the top of the rural hierarchy, and led to rapid growth in the new middle class through mass education and bureaucratic expansion. Meanwhile, the creation and absorption into the public sector of important productive, commercial, and banking assets spawned a new managerial state bourgeoisie.

Two or three decades of state-led growth had brought to a halt or significantly slowed the process of privatization that had begun in the early nineteenth century. But the regional oil shocks of the 1970s coupled with the inefficiencies of state-led ISI opened up the possibility of a new era of privatization in the 1980s. ISI had tremendous spin-off effects in subcontracting to existing private sectors that weathered the hostile socialist or simply anticapitalist (as in Pahlavi Iran) programs of the state managers. Drawing on state business and credit from public banks and sheltered behind tariff walls put up to protect the public sector, these private sectors found themselves positioned to respond to a growing mood among public authorities that efficiency would have to take precedence over redistribution if their national economies were to survive. We are witnessing the gradual reduction of the autonomy of the state and its recapture by economic interests that the state had itself created.

Turkey serves as bellwether for the region in this process. It is one generation in advance over all its neighbors in the Middle East, having begun in economic policy and state building in the 1920s what most other countries would not attempt before the 1950s. It now contains a powerful and highly differentiated entrepreneurial bourgeoisie with a well-organized industrial segment. This bourgeoisie developed virtually ex nihilo after 1920. The war for national liberation led by Kemal Atatürk resulted in the mass repatriation to Greece of the most experienced entrepreneurs that Anatolia and Istanbul could offer. During forty years of state-led growth, the infant indigenous bourgeoisie acquired skills and capital and may now be ready, if the international economy remains hospitable, to consolidate Turkey in the ranks of the NICs and to make the Turkish state responsive to its needs.

CONCLUSION

The three variables that undergird our analysis—economic growth patterns, state structures and policies, and social actors—will be treated sequentially in the following chapters. One should not lose sight of the fact that they interact simultaneously and that the sequence in which we approach them implies neither an order of importance nor a line of causality. The next four chapters (3–6) do, however, lay out a broad contextual framework for understanding the rapid social and economic change that has characterized the region in this century. They are a necessary starting point for a full consideration of state and class. We begin with a fuller presentation of our understanding of economic growth and structural change.

NOTES

1. The free-rider problem arises when an actor cannot be excluded from the benefits of collective action. Consequently, he may shirk or fail to participate—and still reap the benefits; he gets a "free ride" on the efforts of others. See the classic treatment by Olson (1965) and the more nuanced analysis of Axelrod (1984).

3

ECONOMIC GROWTH AND STRUCTURAL CHANGE

The political economy of the Middle East is dominated by three simple facts: little rain, much oil, and increasingly many (and therefore young) people. Most of the Middle East lies in the arid zone of the Eastern Hemisphere, a zone that stretches from Morocco to Mongolia. Much of the region receives less than twenty inches of rain per year, an amount that makes unirrigated agriculture extremely risky (Map 3.1). Precipitation is also highly variable not only from year to year but also seasonally. Most of the region experiences distinct wet and dry periods. Even within the rainy season, precipitation is often quite irregular. Annual precipitation figures are often deceptive, since much rain may fall in a short space of time. For example, during 1985–1986, Tunisian rainfall was 150% above normal in March, but little rain fell during the crucial planting months of October to December. With the exception of some highland (e.g., Yemen) and coastal (e.g., the Caspian Sea region of Iran) areas, the Middle East lacks the relatively heavy and reliable rainfall of the Asian monsoons, and long, devastating droughts have occurred throughout the region's history.

Only irrigated lands could support a dense population in preindustrial times. Such areas were sharply limited: the Nile Valley of Egypt, parts of the Tigris-Euphrates Valley, and other, more localized areas. All of these irrigation systems underwent extensive changes in their long histories, expanding with stability and peace, contracting with upheaval, war, and mismanagement. Irrigation networks have faced important ecological constraints, such as increasing salinity (Hodgson 1974, 389–391), and have also created international political problems, since most of the major rivers of the region cross national boundaries. The difficult agro-ecology has contributed to the large and growing gap between consumption and domestic production of food in the region, a gap that drives much of the political economy of agriculture (Chapter 6).

MENA covers about 11–12% of the world's land area[1] (about one-third larger than the United States) and contains just under 6% of the world's population. Its

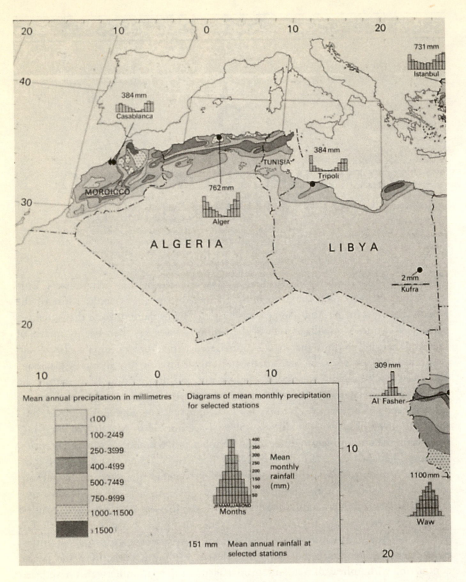

Map 3.1 The Middle East and North Africa: Precipitation. *Source:* Gerald Blake, John Dewdney, and Jonathan Mitchell, *The Cambridge Atlas of the Middle East and North Africa,* Cambridge, Cambridge University Press, 1987, p. 18. Used by permission.

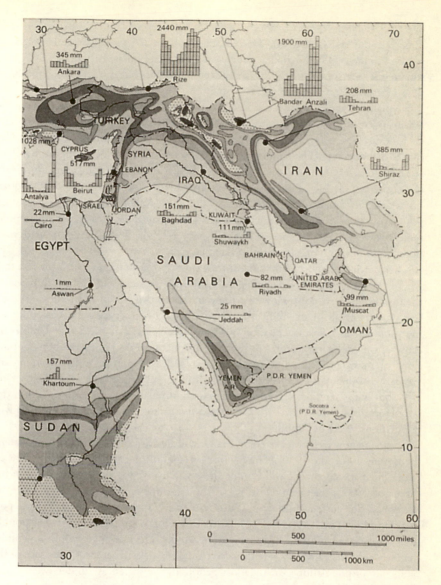

30 40 2440 mm 50 60 70

345 mm
Ankara
Rize
40
1900 mm
Bandar Anzali
208 mm
Tehran
TURKEY
1028 mm
CYPRUS
517mm
SYRIA
IRAN
385 mm
Shiraz
LEBANON
Antalya
Beirut
IRAQ
30
ISRAEL
JORDAN
151mm
KUWAIT
Baghdad
111mm
Shuwaykh
22mm
Cairo
BAHRAIN
QATAR
EGYPT
SAUDI
82 mm
UNITED ARAB
EMIRATES
1mm
ARABIA
Riyadh
99 mm
Aswan
Muscat
25 mm
Jeddah
20
OMAN
157 mm
Khartoum
YEMEN
A R
P.D.R. YEMEN
Socotra
(P.D.R. Yemen)
SUDAN
10

40 50 60
0   500   1000 miles
0   500   1000 km

30

overall population density is about 70 persons per square mile (27 per square kilometer), about the same as the United States (about 67 per square mile or 26 per square kilometer). The region is much less densely populated than India (273 per square kilometer) or China (123 per square kilometer) but more densely populated than Latin America (23 per square kilometer) (World Bank 1994g).

Such an average number is extremely misleading, however. Because of the region's aridity, only about 7% of the area is cultivated. There are over 960 Middle Easterners for every square mile (371 per square kilometer) of arable land. The most striking case is that of Egypt. The country contains 386,486 square miles (roughly 1 million square kilometers), an area about the size of France and Spain combined. But nearly the entire population of over 56 million lives in the approximately 15,000 square miles (38,850 square kilometers) of the Nile River Valley and Delta; the resulting population density of about 3,732 persons per square mile (1,441 per square kilometer) is rivaled only by that of Java and parts of India and China. The pattern of population distribution is shown in Map 3.2.

The total population of these countries is over 322 million (1993), or less than 7% of the population of developing countries (7.5% excluding Eastern Europe and the former Soviet Union). However, there are about two Middle Easterners for every five citizens of all of the industrialized market economies; Middle Easterners are more numerous than citizens of either the United States or the Soviet Union. Because of the ecological features of the region, no country supports the huge populations of monsoon Asia. The region contains three countries (Turkey, Iran, and Egypt) with populations exceeding 55 million (comparable to Italy, France, or the UK), but it also contains eleven countries with populations less than 10 million (the population of greater New York City), and two more (Iraq and Saudi Arabia) with populations less than 20 million (Table 3.1).

There are now over three times as many Middle Easterners and North Africans as there were in the late 1950s. The region's population is growing at about 2.7% per year, which means that it will double in less than twenty-seven years. Within just three generations (of twenty years each) the region's population will have increased *twelvefold*. The current number of Cairo residents is about the same as the total population of Egypt in 1919 (12–13 million). Of major world regions, only the population of sub-Saharan Africa is growing more rapidly. The rate of growth is now higher than it was in the early 1950s (although it is falling—see Chapter 4). Because of this rapid rate of population growth, most people in the region are under twenty years old (World Bank 1994g).

A large and growing percentage of these people live in cities. Although different countries use different criteria for defining a "city," which makes cross-country comparisons notoriously unreliable, about half of MENA people live in urban areas, with, again, wide variations among countries. Cities were always central to the preindustrial and precolonial social formations in the region. This importance has steadily increased; the region now contains more than thirty cities with populations greater than 0.5 million.

TABLE 3.1   1993 Population, 1992 GNP per Capita, and Average Annual GNP Growth Rate 1980–1992

		GNP per Capita	
	1993 Population (millions)	*1992 (US$)*	*1980–1992 Growth Rate*
Algeria	26.3	1,840	−0.5
Bahrain	0.5	8,030	−2.9
Egypt	54.7	660	1.8
Iran	59.6	2,200	−1.4
Iraq	19.4	–	–
Israel	5.1	13,220	1.8
Jordan	3.9	1,120	−5.4
Kuwait	1.4	–	–
Lebanon	3.8	–	–
Libya	51.9	–	–
Morocco	26.2	1,030	1.4
Oman	1.4	6,480	4.1
Qatar	0.52	15,030	−7.2
Saudi Arabia	16.8	7,510	−3.3
Sudan	26.5	–	–
Syria	1.0	–	–
Tunisia	8.4	1,720	1.3
Turkey	58.4	1,980	2.9
UAE	1.7	22,020	−4.3
Yemen	1.3	–	–
United States	225.4	23,240	1.7

Source: World Bank (1994g, 162–163).

The region also displays great diversity in per capita income (Figure 3.1). Indeed, it has more variation in per capita income than any other major region, including wealthy countries such as Israel and the UAE as well as extremely poor countries such as the Sudan and Yemen. This diversity has had important political implications.

THE NATURAL RESOURCE BASE

The region is not particularly rich in nonhydrocarbon mineral resources. A wide variety of minerals are exploited,[2] but with the exception of Algeria (mercury) and Morocco (phosphate rock) no country's output amounts to even 5% of world production. Most minerals are found in the mountainous areas of North Africa, Turkey,

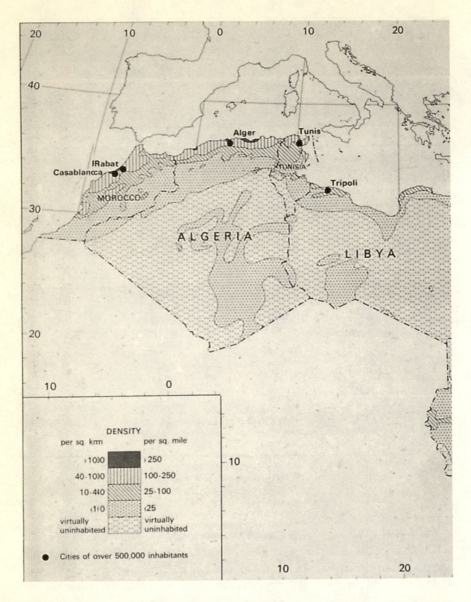

Map 3.2   The Middle East and North Africa: Population density. *Source:* Gerald Blake, John Dewdney, and Jonathan Mitchell, *The Cambridge Atlas of the Middle East and North Africa*, Cambridge, Cambridge University Press, 1987, p. 44. Used by permission.

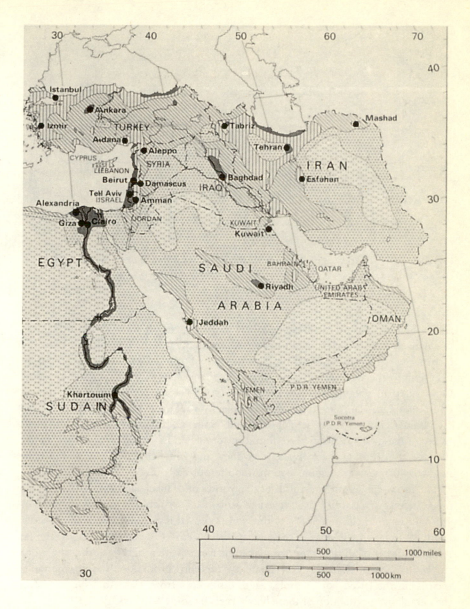

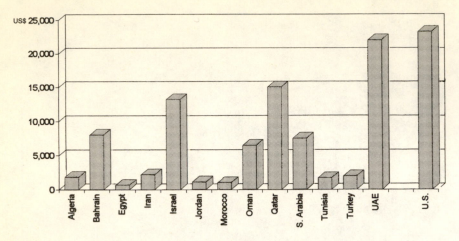

FIGURE 3.1   GNP per capita, selected MENA countries, 1992. *Source:* World Bank
(1994g, 162).

and Iran. Morocco and the Western Sahara hold over two-thirds of the world's phosphate deposits; Morocco is the third-largest producer, after the United States and the
former Soviet Union. Algeria is the region's leading iron-ore producer (ranking only
twentieth in the world), and Turkish production is about 20% less than Algerian.
Only Turkey has significant coal deposits. The 1980s saw considerable exploration
efforts and significant new finds. For example, Libya, Egypt, Saudi Arabia, and Algeria all discovered new iron-ore deposits, and Saudi Arabia discovered gold and coal.
Many of these new deposits were found in remote and isolated areas, which raised
the cost of exploiting them (Blake, Dewdney, and Mitchell 1987). All of this is in
marked contrast to the region's hydrocarbon resources.

The region has about two-thirds of the world's oil. The usual measure of available
oil is "reserves," classified as "proved," "probable," "possible," or "speculative." In
1992 the region held some 68% of the world's proved reserves (Table 3.2), of which
nearly all of it (63.8%) was in the Gulf (OPEC 1993). One country, Saudi Arabia,
has one-quarter of all the oil on the planet; its reserves are roughly ten times those of
the United States. Discovery has apparently exceeded production despite the rapid
increase in the latter. For example, Saudi discoveries from 1972 to 1992 exceeded
the cumulative production of those heady years by some 230% (OPEC 1993).

We say "apparently" because the data on "proved reserves" must be treated with
caution. The concept is defined as "reserves recoverable with present technology and
prices" (*Oil and Gas Journal*, December 28, 1988). Higher oil prices should, in theory, mean higher oil reserves, for three reasons: (1) higher prices should induce further exploration and discovery of new fields; (2) higher prices should stimulate improvements in the technology of recovery from existing fields; and (3) for existing

TABLE 3.2   Oil Reserves, 1992

	1992 Reserves (Millions of Barrels)	*% of World Reserves*
North America	32,354.00	3.1
United States	26,250.00	2.5
Latin America	140,248.00	13.5
Former USSR	57,000.00	5.5
Western Europe	22,404.60	2.2
MENA	703,323.00	68.1
Asia & Far East	47,300.30	4.6
Oceania	2,277.50	0.22
World	1,032,695.00	

Source: OPEC (1993).

wells, with existing technology, higher prices should make some additional oil recoverable. Because oil prices have such a large rent element, the last argument is not particularly apposite, particularly for MENA. In any case, additions to reserves continued after the oil price collapse of 1986. Oil reserves are not sensitive to price fluctuations. The key point remains: despite rapidly growing world production, world reserves have grown still faster, and the majority of these reserve additions have come from the Middle East.

A more serious problem with the concept of proved reserves is that some countries have been quite secretive about the numbers they release. In 1987 four OPEC countries (Venezuela, the UAE, Iran, and Iraq) released data that showed that total world proved reserves had increased by roughly 27%. The new estimate may be credible for Venezuela, where extensive surveys of the Orinoco Basin revealed very large amounts of heavy oil. The increases in Iran (90%) and Iraq (112%) are very startling, however. Could these two countries, locked in desperate military struggle, really have devoted the resources to exploration that would have led to such finds? If they had known that they had such oil before the war began (1980), why did they wait until 1987 to announce it to the world? A leading trade publication, *Oil and Gas Journal*, rather gingerly pointed out that these numbers might reflect a belief on the part of the issuing governments that oil production quotas within the Organization of Petroleum Exporting Countries (OPEC) would be allocated on the basis of "proved reserves" (December 27, 1987, 33–34). Whatever the case may be, the episode illustrates the need for caution in using data on reserves.

Nevertheless, the geographical concentration of petroleum deposits in the Middle East is indisputable. Several other geological facts matter for the political economy of oil. First, much of the world's proved reserves come from thirty-three "supergiant" fields (reserves estimated at greater than 5 billion barrels); of these, twenty-eight are in the Middle East, including nine of the ten largest fields. The largest, the Ghawar field in Saudi Arabia, contains an estimated 60 billion barrels of oil, more than twice the reserves of the *entire* United States, which come to about 25.3 billion barrels (Drysdale and Blake 1985, 314–315). Oil reserves are concentrated within the region. Four countries (Saudi Arabia, Iraq, Iran, and Kuwait) have about 75% of the region's oil reserves and about 50% of all the oil in the world.

The size of these reserves implies that events in the region will always be critical to the international oil market. It is common (although of dubious interest) to point out how long countries' reserves will last at current production rates. The data for 1992 in Figure 3.2 are significant for showing the "time horizons" of national governments, a feature that is important for understanding various regional governments' differences over pricing strategies within OPEC. Other things being equal, countries whose oil will last a long time have little interest in large price increases, since these will induce more conservation and discovery of new sources of supply.[3] The numbers are only illustrative, however. Production varies, estimates of reserves change, and patterns of resource use shift dramatically if consumers are given enough time (say, ten to twenty years) to adjust. The differences among countries are dramatic: Kuwait can go on exploiting oil for a century and a half, whereas Egypt's official reserves will last for about a generation at the average rate of production from 1972 to 1987.

More important from an economic point of view, Gulf oil is the cheapest oil in the world to produce. The estimated current cost of production of a barrel of Saudi, Kuwaiti, Iraqi, or Iranian Gulf oil is about US$1.00 per barrel.[4] By comparison, U.S. production costs range between US$4 and $6 per barrel, which is also the range

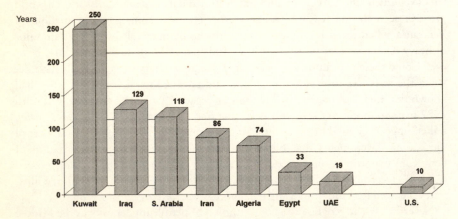

FIGURE 3.2   Approximate years of remaining oil production, 1992. *Source:* OPEC (1993).

of production costs for most other regions of the world (Atlantic Richfield 1994).[5] These low production costs are the key to the massive transferral of economic rents to the oil states, rents that fueled economic expansion and change throughout the region for over a decade.

OIL SUPPLY, DEMAND, AND ECONOMIC RENTS

Economic rents from oil production in the Middle East are huge.[6] If the opportunity cost of producing a barrel of Saudi Arabian light is approximately US$1.00 and the price of that barrel on international markets is roughly US$14.00, the economic rent is US$13.00. When the price was around US$36.50 per barrel (as it was in 1981), the economic rent was US$35.50. Even in late July 1986, when oil prices were at their post-1973 nadir of about US$8.00 per barrel, over four-fifths of the price of that barrel was still economic rent. Oil revenues of the Gulf States are almost exclusively composed of rent on a depletable natural resource.

The minimum price is given by the cost of production, but what determines the maximum price? In theory, the "price ceiling" is determined by the cost of production of the closest available substitute, often called the "backstop technology." Because crude oil has so many different uses, this price ceiling varies with the uses to which the crude will be put. Some estimates of the costs of backstop technologies made in the early 1980s are shown in Table 3.3. These price ceilings decline with time and are themselves partly a function of price. We would expect that if the price of crude oil approaches the rent ceiling and if entrepreneurs believe that this price will persist, there will be more research and development into these alternative technologies. Such activity should lower the cost of these technologies, pushing down the rent ceiling. By the mid-1990s, a common estimate of the rent ceiling was about US$25 per barrel (World Bank 1995a).

Of course, the *actual* price of crude oil is determined by supply and demand. The course of these prices is shown in Figure 3.3. Small libraries have been written on why prices rose and fell; we will sketch only the main elements of an explanation.[7]

Demand-side forces played a crucial role both in pushing prices to unprecedented heights in the 1970s and in dragging them down and keeping them low in the late 1980s and early 1990s. In the 1950s and 1960s the relative price of oil was both low and declining; the major industrialized countries increasingly switched from energy sources such as coal to oil. In 1950 oil accounted for 40% (United States), 14% (Western Europe), and 5% (Japan) of industrial nations' energy use; by 1973 those shares (of a vastly larger total) had risen to 47% (United States), 60% (Western Europe), and 76% (Japan) (Stobaugh and Yergin 1979). For both Western Europe and Japan, such a switch increased dependence on imports, especially imports from the Middle East. For the Japanese, with no indigenous oil and little coal, there was (and is) little alternative to such imports. Even today, about 70% of Japanese energy comes from oil, all of which is imported and 70% of which comes from the Middle East. Western European dependence on Middle Eastern oil also increased during the

TABLE 3.3   The Rent Ceiling in 1980: Estimated Costs of Backstop Technologies

Fuel Technologies		*Electricity Technologies*	
Production Cost (US$/barrel of oil equivalent)	*Technology*	*Generation Cost (US cents/ kilowatt hour)*	*Technology*
86 and above	Corn to ethanol Wood to high-BTU gasoline Manure to high-BTU gasoline	8.1 and above	Solar, thermal Wind Ocean thermal energy conversion Solar photovoltaic
56–85	Coal to methanol Coal gasification, high-BTU gas	6.6–8.0	Biomass (wood chips) Combined cycle, integrated coal gasification
31–55	Sugar to alcohol Wood to ethanol Coal gasification, medium-BTU gas Coal liquefaction Wood to methanol Light Arabian crude	4.1–6.5	Conventional oil-fired plant Breeder reactor Fluidized bed combustion
30 and under	Liquefied natural gas Oil sands and shales Natural gas Coal	4.0 and under	Hydroelectricity Conventional natural-gas-fired plant Geothermal, steam Light-water nuclear reactor

Includes capital costs and operations and maintenance, at 1980 prices.
Source: The Economist, December 26, 1981, 77 (citing Bechtel Corporation estimates).

1950s and 1960s as conservative governments sought greater independence from coal miners and as social democrats tried to improve environmental quality. All were drawn to the lower direct cost of oil.

The United States's dependence on oil imports increased steadily. Domestic oil producers persuaded the U.S. government to restrict imports of (much cheaper) foreign oil in 1958. Until the mid-1960s, the United States retained considerable surplus capacity, which made it (and its friends) considerably less vulnerable to threats of embargoes or to sudden price shocks. This was an unintended outcome of the system to

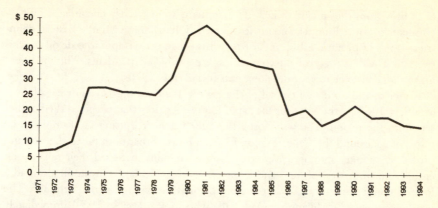

FIGURE 3.3   Saudi Arabian light crude oil prices (per barrel) in real 1994 US$. *Source:*
OPEC (1993) and (for 1994) estimate.

protect domestic producers—the so-called pro-rationing system, whereby state agencies regulated and reduced oil production. In the late 1960s and early 1970s, however, the growth of demand for energy outpaced the expansion of domestic energy supplies. Price controls inhibited the development of natural gas, and little new oil that was competitive at current prices was discovered. By 1973 the United States had no spare capacity; indeed, domestic oil production fell at a rate of 3% per year from 1970 to 1973 (Schneider 1983, 195). Oil imports, including Middle Eastern oil, supplied a steadily increasing percentage of U.S. energy needs, reaching 38% by 1974.

On the supply side, there were two interrelated dynamics, cash and control (Rustow and Mugno 1976). "Cash" refers to producing countries' attempts to get a higher percentage of the oil rents; the contest for "control" was between the nation-states and the oil companies. One might say that the history of the oil business has been that of repeated attempts to create a cartel followed by the erosion and demise of that cartel. The eight major international oil companies[8] had managed by 1953 to control 95% of non-U.S. noncommunist reserves, 90% of production, 75% of refining capacity, and 74% of product sales (Blair 1976). Interrelations among these companies were extensive, long-term (e.g., twenty-year) supply contracts and joint ventures being the most prominent mechanisms. Perhaps the high-water mark of the oil company cartel's control of world oil came in 1953, when the cartel countered Mohammed Mossadegh's nationalization of British Petroleum's (BP's) Iranian oil facilities by simply refusing to refine or market Iranian oil. When Mossadegh was overthrown and the Pahlavi shah reinstated, another joint venture was established in which nearly all of the major oil companies were represented.

Even with the low prices of the 1950s and 1960s, costs of production were so low and demand was growing so steadily that there were numerous incentives for "independent," or smaller, oil companies to enter the market and attempt to wrest a piece of it away from the "majors." Such developments were actively encouraged by governments of some European countries, especially Italy. Some Middle Eastern countries—most important, Libya under King Idris—had the wisdom to cede oil concessions to a wide variety of oil companies, especially independents. This had very important consequences for developments in the early 1970s.

In one of the ironies so typical of the region, the crushing Israeli defeat of Arab armies in 1967 set the stage for the explosion of oil prices that triggered the flood of rent into the region. The war closed the Suez Canal, requiring Gulf crude to be transported around the Cape of Good Hope, a journey that both raised the cost and provoked a tanker shortage. Western European nations increased their reliance on cheaper oil from west of Suez and from Libya in particular.[9] Libyan oil also had a lower sulphur content and was therefore favored on environmental grounds. The new government of Mu'ammar Qaddhafi (who took power in 1969) immediately demanded an increase in the "posted price" of oil.[10] Although the larger oil companies refused, the independent oil companies were more vulnerable to pressure. Libya prevailed through a classic divide-and-rule policy. Its success prompted the Gulf producers to follow suit, and nominal oil prices began to rise.[11]

Of course, the completion of the shift of both cash and control from consumers and companies on the one hand to producing governments on the other was precipitated by the October War of 1973. The decision of the Nixon administration first to resupply the Israelis (October 13) and then to give them US$2.2 billion of military assistance (October 19) prompted the Saudi embargo of the United States and the Netherlands on October 20. Oil companies cushioned the impact of this embargo on those two countries by reallocating world supply. However, the embargo created an atmosphere of panic buying on the spot (or open) market; the shah of Iran in particular took the opportunity to hold an auction in order to see what price his oil might fetch. The answer was between US$9.00 and $17.34 per barrel (Schneider 1983, 236), while the Rotterdam spot price hit $26.00 per barrel (Danielson 1982, 172).

The final price that OPEC agreed to charge customers on the "marker crude"[12] was US$11.65, a price negotiated between the "price doves," led by Saudi Arabia, and the "price hawks," led by Iran. This was to be expected, given the huge gap between the cost of production and the rent ceiling, on the one hand, and the very low short-run elasticity of demand for oil, on the other. With nearly all excess capacity inside the OPEC countries and with few short-run alternatives, consuming countries had little choice but to pay any price below the rent ceiling.

The resulting transfer of resources was massive (Table 3.4). The dramatically higher payments for oil contributed to the phenomenon of "stagflation" (recession combined with inflation) in the developed world. Inflation, in turn, slowly eroded the real gains of 1974, while recession weakened demand; real oil prices in 1978 were slightly below those of 1974. Europe and Japan responded to the change not only by passing on prices to their consumers but also by increasing tax rates on oil and by fostering the development of alternative energy supplies (e.g., North Sea oil

TABLE 3.4   Oil Export Revenues, 1974–1994 (US$ millions)

	1974	1975	1976	1977	1978	1979	1980	1981	1982	1983
Algeria	3,500	4,000	4,500	5,000	5,400	7,500	11,700	10,800	8,500	9,700
Iran	22,000	20,500	22,000	23,000	20,900	18,800	11,600	8,500	19,000	21,700
Iraq	6,000	8,000	8,500	9,500	11,600	21,200	26,500	10,400	9,500	8,400
Kuwait	8,000	7,500	8,500	8,500	9,500	16,300	18,300	14,800	10,000	9,900
Libya	6,000	6,000	7,500	9,400	9,300	15,200	23,200	15,700	14,000	11,200
Qatar	1,650	1,700	2,000	1,900	2,200	3,100	5,200	5,300	4,200	3,000
Saudi Arabia	29,000	27,000	33,500	38,000	36,700	59,200	104,200	113,300	76,000	46,000
UAE	5,500	6,000	7,000	8,000	8,700	13,000	19,200	18,700	16,000	12,800

	1985	1987	1988	1989	1990	1991	1992	1993	1994
Algeria	–	8,532	7,352	9,096	12,332	11,962	11,047	9,881	8,934
Iran	14,000	9,479	9,661	12,035	17,416	15,985	16,917	14,434	13,840
Iraq	12,000	12,179	12,234	16,109	9,492	380	1,458	752	611
Kuwait	10,000	7,418	6,749	10,300	6,202	846	6,139	9,921	10,146
Libya	10,400	2,008	1,643	2,077	3,042	2,447	2,922	2,320	2,130
Qatar	4,400	2,008	1,643	2,077	3,042	2,447	2,922	2,320	2,130
Saudi Arabia	43,700	22,885	23,879	27,663	43,559	47,180	48,711	41,370	37,077
UAE	13,000	9,362	7,893	10,462	15,551	15,818	14,634	12,868	11,910

Source: Petroleum Finance Company, Ltd., Washington, D.C., 1995.

and gas and nuclear power). However, the world's largest consumer, the United States, dithered. U.S. imports of OPEC oil continued to grow from 38% of consumption in 1974 to 47% in 1979. OPEC's market share dropped only slightly, from about 66% of noncommunist oil production in 1974 to about 62% in 1978 (Figure 3.4). The stage was set for the second oil shock of 1979.

Once again, political events opened the next act in the oil-price drama. The Iranian revolution removed about 2 million barrels a day from production; although the Saudis at first tried to make up the shortfall, they had been producing close to capacity already in an attempt to restrain further price increases, which they (reasonably) believed were not in their medium- and long-term economic interest. However, the conclusion of the Camp David Accords, with their neglect of the Palestinian issue, angered the Saudis considerably. In response, they actually *reduced* production in the immediate aftermath of Camp David, setting the stage for another round of panic buying on the spot market (Quandt 1981). The resulting record-breaking market price helped the OPEC hawks to carry the day, and the OPEC reference price leapt first to US$17.26 in 1979 and then to US$28.67 in 1980.

The resulting price hike was lower in proportional terms than that of 1973–1974 but considerably greater in absolute dollar value. The increase in revenues was prodigious (Table 3.4). Governments launched even more massive development projects

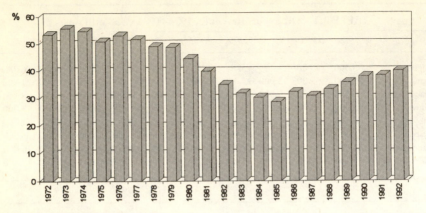

FIGURE 3.4   OPEC share of crude oil production, 1972–1992. *Source:* OPEC (1993).

than before. Never had so much been paid by so many to so few; never before in human history had such an enormous amount of wealth been transferred in such a short amount of time to governments with such (typically) small populations.[13] As we shall see, however, the wealth was shared widely, albeit indirectly, in the Middle East and North Africa through labor migration (Chapter 15).

But booms are not forever. Although it was not immediately apparent, OPEC overreached itself in 1979–1981. A comparison of the 1980 price with the figures in Table 3.3 shows that for some uses it exceeded the rent ceiling. Conserving energy became very profitable, especially once the United States decontrolled petroleum prices. OPEC soon fell afoul of both the "external" and the "internal" cartel problem. The external problem refers to the simple fact that if prices are very high, consumers and producers have incentives to change their behavior. The demand for oil is a derived demand; we want oil not for its own sake but because we want to move around, heat our homes, light our lamps, and so forth. With high oil prices, consumers had every incentive to find ways of using less oil to accomplish these ends and also (during the recession of the early 1980s) to make do with less transportation, heating, and electricity. In short, conservation was greatly stimulated. By the mid-1980s, the industrial countries were using less than 70% as much oil per unit of output as they had been in 1973 (Figure 3.5). Non-OPEC producers compounded the external cartel problem. Such producers had strong incentives, often reinforced by consuming governments, to seek, find, and exploit new sources of petroleum and alternative energy sources. Alaskan, North Sea, and Mexican oil became especially important new sources of oil, and OPEC's market share of world oil production fell from 48.8% in 1979 to 28.7% in 1985 (OPEC 1993; see also Figure 3.4).

These developments aggravated the internal cartel problem—that it is in the interests of cartel members to cheat on production quotas. Actually, OPEC lacked for-

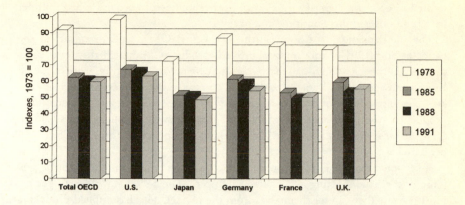

FIGURE 3.5   Oil use per unit of real GDP, 1978–1991. *Source: OECD Economic Outlook,*
no. 48 (December 1990), 35.

mal production quotas until very recently, and they are often openly ignored (e.g.,
by Iraq before 1991 and by Iran). In practice, just as OPEC was the "residual supplier" to the world market, Saudi Arabia was the "residual supplier" within OPEC.
Only the Saudis could play this role: They could vary their production from a low of
just above 2 million barrels per day (2.2 in August 1985) to a high of nearly 10 million barrels per day. (By way of comparison, their *low* figure exceeds the current production figure of any other Middle Eastern producer.) The Saudis had long demanded that other oil producers agree to production quotas and had consistently
argued that the post-1979 prices were too high. They remonstrated vainly in OPEC
councils: quota agreements, first established in March 1982, were violated almost as
soon as they were drafted. The Saudis saw their own market share steadily erode
from 21% in 1980 to 8.5% in 1985 (*Oil and Gas Journal*, December 27, 1987).
Saudi government revenues also declined, even as it had made extensive commitments to development expenditures and projects. Saudi spending began to exceed
revenues in 1983.[14]

The Saudis' patience was finally exhausted. In July and August 1986 they opened
the taps, producing about 6 million barrels per day; in late August they were producing at a rate of about 7 million barrels per day (*Oil and Gas Journal*, December 30,
1985, 65). Prices collapsed, falling to under US$10.00 in late summer of 1986. By
this action, the Saudis sent messages to fellow OPEC members ("Quit cheating; we
can take losses better than you can"), to non-OPEC producers ("Let's make a deal;
your production costs are much higher than ours"), and to investors in conservation
technology ("We can push the price down and drive you out of business").[15] Only
the last message seems to have been received. Although OPEC tried to fix production quotas, enforcement mechanisms were weak and cheating remained rife. Britain

refused to cooperate with OPEC, and prices rebounded to around US$18.00 per barrel and hovered there until the end of the 1980s.

The Iraqi invasion of Kuwait further weakened OPEC and strengthened the hands of both OECD consumers and Saudi producers. Although there was sufficient excess capacity roughly to match the increase in lost production from occupied Kuwait and embargoed Iraq, prices doubled[16] in two months as fear gripped oil markets. The rapid defeat of Iraqi forces in Operation Desert Storm and the increase in production from elsewhere (especially Saudi Arabia) swiftly brought prices back to their prewar levels. In the early 1990s prices continued to hover around US$18–14 per barrel.

A key impact of the Gulf War of 1991 has been the final demise of even the pretense of the Saudis' acting as a "swing producer." The Saudis now seek to get the most revenue they can for themselves from the market. This has implied producing close to capacity, taking advantage of the absence of Iraq from oil markets. However, the future of oil prices is highly uncertain. On the demand side, the major imponderables are policies in LDCs, whose growth—especially in East Asia—now provides most of the incremental demand for oil, but many major LDC consumers heavily subsidize oil consumption. The mix of increased demand from growth and reduced demand from the adoption of more rational policies is impossible to predict. Technological developments (such as the potential of electric cars and other photovoltaic technologies) provide additional uncertainty on the demand side. On the supply side of the market, the major uncertainty is the speed with which oil production in the former Soviet Union will rebound. All that can be said with certainty is that the demand for oil is likely to continue to rise (gradually, perhaps), while the Gulf continues to have the largest reserves and the lowest production costs in the world. Few doubt that Middle Eastern producers, and especially Saudi Arabia, will continue to play a major role in determining the future path of oil prices.

PATTERNS OF ECONOMIC GROWTH

Growth and structural change proceeded briskly in the region for thirty years after 1950 only to stagnate in the past decade and a half. In assessing the numbers in the following tables and figures, several things should be kept in mind. First, the data are often simply informed observers' best guesses; for some of the least developed and poorest countries they are of very poor quality. For all countries, data should be taken as indicating orders of magnitude rather than precise "truth." Second, many countries of the region have started the process from a very low base; in some cases (Yemen, Oman) modern economic growth began only a generation ago.

The range of wealth in the region is, as we have seen, extremely wide. Indeed, no major area of the world shows a higher variance in per capita incomes across nation-states (see Figure 3.1). The region boasts high-income countries—the UAE, Israel, and Kuwait—whose inhabitants enjoy a material standard of living like that in the developed countries. Israeli per capita GNP exceeds that of Spain, Ireland, and New

Zealand, and, unlike the high-income oil exporters, the country possesses a diversified economic and industrial structure and levels of health and literacy that rival
those in southern Europe. At the same time, the average Sudanese lives in a poverty
as extreme as any in sub-Saharan Africa, and millions of Egyptians and Moroccans
live very close to subsistence (Chapter 10). The diversity of experience with economic growth and structural change is just as wide. At one extreme, MENA contains not only industrialized and developed Israel but also Turkey, formerly the
heartland of one of history's greatest empires and a pioneer in industrialization outside of Europe and Japan. Manufacturing accounts for 23% of all output in Turkey
(Table 3.5), a higher percentage than in Italy or Hong Kong. In contrast, the region
also contains Oman, whose former sultan kept the country hermetically sealed in
medieval poverty until his son deposed him in 1970. Some less colorful distinctions
are found in the rates of growth and structural transformation, the size, efficiency,
and diversity of industrial production, agricultural-production experience, and the
composition of international trade.

Overall growth rates of GDP for 1960 to 1992 are shown in Table 3.6. Unsurprisingly, given the impact of the oil boom, the per capita output in the region grew
more rapidly than the average for LDCs. Some countries (Jordan, Saudi Arabia,
Oman, Syria, and Tunisia) grew faster than 4% per year, slightly more than doubling
per capita incomes during the past two decades. Only Israel, the Sudan, and

TABLE 3.5   **Structure of Production: Sectoral Shares of GDP, 1970 and 1992**

	Agriculture		Industry		Manufacturing		Services	
	1970	1992	1970	1992	1970	1992	1970	1992
Algeria	11	15	41	47	15	10	48	38
Egypt	29	18	28	30	–	12	42	52
Iran	–	23	–	25	–	14	–	48
Jordan	–	7	–	28	–	15	–	65
Morocco	20	15	27	33	16	19	53	52
Oman	16	4	77	52	0	4	7	44
Saudi Arabia	6	7	63	52	10	7	10	41
Sudan	43	34	15	17	8	9	42	50
Syria	20	30	25	23	–	–	55	48
Tunisia	20	18	24	31	10	17	56	51
Turkey	30	15	27	30	17	23	43	55
UAE	–	2	–	56	–	9	–	43
Yemen	–	21	–	24	–	10	–	55
United States	3	–	34	–	25	–	63	–

Source: World Bank (1994g, 166–167).

TABLE 3.6   Growth of GDP (% per year), 1960–1992

	1960–1970	1970–1980	1980–1992
Algeria	4.3	4.6	2.6
Egypt	4.3	9.5	4.4
Iran	11.3	–	2.3
Iraq	6.1	12.1	–
Israel	8.1	4.8	3.9
Kuwait	5.7	2.5	0.8
Libya	24.4	2.2	–
Morocco	4.4	5.6	4
Oman	19.5	6.2	7.7
Saudi Arabia	–	10.1	0.4
Sudan	0.7	5.6	–
Syria	4.6	9.9	1.8
Tunisia	4.7	6.8	3.8
Turkey	6	5.9	4.9
UAE	–	–	0.3

Source: World Bank (1994g, 164–165).

Morocco have grown more slowly than the average for countries of their income group, while Turkish growth has been roughly equal to the group average. Other nations, notably hapless Sudan and quixotic Libya, have stagnated.

The collapse of the oil boom and persistent policy failures (Chapters 8 and 9) have made the period 1980–1992 much grimmer. During this period output per person declined; as Figure 3.6 shows, MENA's growth performance in the immediate past has been the worst in the world. Real wages and labor productivity today are about the same as in 1970 (World Bank 1995a). Rising poverty, joblessness, and social unrest are direct results of this growth failure.

Growth was also uneven across sectors; this is the essence of structural transformation. The share of agriculture has declined in all countries (Table 3.7). Two groups of countries have seen rapid rates of growth of manufacturing: oil exporters such as Algeria, Libya, Saudi Arabia, and the UAE, all of which started in 1965 with very little industry, and countries with a longer industrial history such as Turkey, Iran, and Egypt. Tunisia, which also had little industry at independence and which exports very modest amounts of oil, also registered a high rate of growth of manufacturing output. As usual, the residual category of "services" accounts for one-third to over one-half of output; the percentage share of "industry" in national product for most countries is either the same as or slightly below what we would expect on the basis of their per capita incomes. Although Algeria and Oman have a much higher percentage of output from industry than the average for upper-middle-income countries, this is deceptive because "industry" includes the petroleum sector.

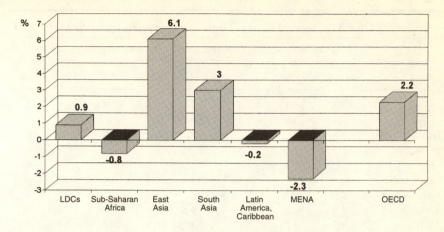

FIGURE 3.6   Per capita GNP growth, 1980–1993. *Source:* World Bank (1994g, 163).

A better picture of industrialization levels (and, as argued in Chapter 2, "sustainable" structural change) is given by the percentage of output that comes from manufacturing or by the size and growth of manufacturing value added (MVA) (Tables 3.8 and 3.9). Total MVA in the region is slightly less than that of Korea. It is instructive to compare MVA for Turkey and Iran with that of Italy, which has roughly the same number of people: Italy's MVA is ten and one-half times that of Turkey and roughly sixteen times that of Iran. Those two countries of the "northern tier" of MENA together account for over half (55%) of the region's manufacturing. Saudi Arabia accounts for another 11%. The addition of Morocco (6.9%) and Egypt (5.1%) brings the share of manufacturing for the five countries with the largest manufacturing sectors to over three-fourths of the total. Manufacturing in MENA is geographically concentrated.

Growth rates of MVA are shown in Figure 3.7. During the oil boom years they were respectable but not spectacular; the region boasted no such star performers as the Republic of Korea (16.8% per year, 1965–1985), or Brazil (11.4% per year) (World Bank 1987). Tunisia's industrial growth was approximately the same as Spain's, while growth rates in Algeria, Egypt, and Saudi Arabia exceeded those of the PRC (7.0%). The contrast with the years of the oil bust is striking: only in Morocco did the growth of MVA accelerate after 1985, and in the two major oil producers with significant industry, Algeria and Saudi Arabia, MVA declined. As we shall see (Chapters 7–9), industrial growth has been hampered by numerous political and economic problems; the search for their solution is a key to the political economy of the more industrialized countries of the area.

The pattern of distribution of MVA holds few surprises. Many countries' industries process agricultural outputs or produce textiles. Because of the labor-intensity and relatively well-established technology of such industries, most countries concentrate on them initially. The more industrialized countries have gone far beyond this

TABLE 3.7   Sectoral Rates of Growth (% per year), 1970–1992

	Agriculture		Industry		Manufacturing		Services	
	1970	1992	1970	1992	1970	1992	1970	1992
Algeria	7.5	5.3	3.8	1.1	7.6	−1.9	4.6	3.3
Egypt	–	2.4	9.4	3.9	–	–	17.5	5.8
Iran	2.8	4.5	–	4.4	–	5.8	–	0.4
Morocco	1.1	5.3	6.5	3	–	4.2	7	4.5
Oman	–	7.1	–	9.6	–	18.3	–	6
Saudi Arabia	5.3	14	10.2	−2.9	6.4	8.1	10.3	−0.3
Sudan	3.3	–	4.5	–	3.9	–	8.1	–
Syria	8.6	−0.3	9	7.6	–	–	11.1	0.3
Tunisia	4.1	3.8	8.7	3.1	10.4	6.3	6.6	4.3
Turkey	3.4	2.8	6.6	5.8	6.1	6.7	6.5	5.1
UAE	–	9.1	–	−1.8	–	3.3	–	4.1

Source: World Bank (1994g, 164–165).

TABLE 3.8   Manufacturing Value Added, Total and Regional Distribution, 1991

	Total (US$ millions)	% Regional Total
Algeria	3,334	4.6
Egypt	3,669	5.1
Iran	16,724	23.4
Jordan	505	0.007
Morocco	4,937	6.9
Oman	438	0.006
Saudi Arabia	7,962	11.1
Tunisia	1,989	2.7
Turkey	22,774	31.9
UAE	3,541	4.9
Yemen	792	1.11
MENA Total	71,340	–
Mexico	63,784	–
Italy	241,346	–
Brazil	90,062	–

Source: World Bank, (1994g, 172–173).

TABLE 3.9   Shares of Manufacturing Value Added (%), 1970 and 1991

	Food, Beverages, and Tobacco		Clothing and Textiles		Machinery		Chemicals		Other	
	1970	1991	1970	1991	1970	1991	1970	1991	1970	1991
Algeria	32	22	20	19	9	11	4	3	35	45
Egypt	17	25	35	17	9	7	12	12	27	39
Iran	30	16	20	21	18	16	7	10	26	37
Israel	15	14	14	9	33	31	7	8	41	39
Jordan	21	27	14	7	7	4	6	17	52	45
Morocco	28	32	9	23	–	10	–	17	–	19
Saudi Arabia	7	7	–	1	–	4	–	39	–	50
Sudan	39	–	34	–	–	–	5	–	19	–
Syria	37	33	40	27	3	6	2	4	20	29
Tunisia	29	20	18	17	4	6	13	8	36	49
Turkey	26	17	15	13	8	18	7	10	45	42
Yemen	20	–	50	–	–	–	1	–	28	–

Source: World Bank (1994g, 172–173).

stage, producing significant quantities of machinery, chemicals, and a host of other products. The most industrially diversified countries are Israel and Turkey; the political economy of the drive to create a competitive manufacturing sector in the latter country is examined in Chapters 7–9.

Trends in the distribution of the labor force are shown in Table 3.10. A number of features stand out. First, the percentage of the labor force in agriculture declined

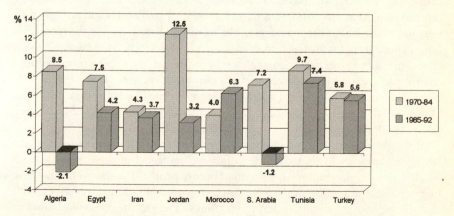

FIGURE 3.7   Growth of manufacturing value-added, 1970–1984 and 1985–1992. *Source:* World Bank (1994g, 172).

TABLE 3.10   Sectoral Distribution of the Labor Force (%), 1960–1989

	Agriculture				Industry				Services			
	1960	1970	1980	1989	1960	1970	1980	1989	1960	1970	1980	1989
Algeria	67	61	31	13.9	12	15	27	10.9	21	24	42	75.2
Egypt	58	54	46	33.9	12	19	20	12	30	27	34	54.1
Iran	54	46	36	36.4	23	28	33	32.8	23	26	31	30.8
Iraq	53	47	31	12.5	18	22	22	7.8	29	31	48	79.7
Jordan	44	34	10	10.2	26	33	26	25.6	30	33	64	64.2
Lebanon	38	20	–	14.3	23	25	–	27.4	39	55	–	58.4
Libya	53	32	18	18.1	17	22	30	28.9	30	46	52	53
Morocco	62	57	46	45.6	14	17	25	25	24	26	29	29.4
Oman	62	–	50	50	15	–	22	21.8	–	–	28	28.6
Saudi Arabia	71	66	49	48.5	10	11	14	14.4	15	23	37	37.2
Sudan	86	82	71	63.4	6	8	7	4.3	6	10	22	32.3
Syria	54	51	32	22	19	21	32	15.1	24	28	36	62.9
Tunisia	56	50	35	21.6	18	2	36	16.3	18	29	29	62.1
Turkey	78	68	58	46.8	11	12	17	14.6	6	20	25	38.6
UAE	20	–	5	4.5	33	–	38	38	–	–	57	57.3
Yemen	83	80	69	62.5	7	9	9	11	8	11	22	26.4

Source: World Bank (1994g, 210–211).

considerably in all countries (except Kuwait) over the long run, even in (stagnant and still mainly agricultural) Sudan. Whereas in 1950 between two-thirds to one-half of the workforce was in agriculture, the sector's share of total employment had fallen to a third or less by the end of the 1980s in many countries. Three notable exceptions were Morocco, Saudi Arabia, and Turkey, where farmers and farm workers were just under half of the labor force. The relatively slow decline of the farm labor force in these three countries has multiple causes; policies were more favorable to the agricultural sector than those adopted elsewhere. Second, the decline in agriculture's relative role in employment decelerated in a number of countries in the 1980s: there was little structural transformation in this sense in Iran, Jordan, Libya, Morocco, Oman, Saudi Arabia, and the UAE.[17] The explanations here vary widely but certainly include the impact of negative per capita growth.

Although industry now often employs between one-fifth and one-third of the labor force in many MENA countries, often well over half of these workers are in small establishments employing fewer than twenty people. The data also show that, in general, the proportion of the labor force employed in industry was either stable or declining in most countries during the 1980s. The growth in "service" employment is often in the so-called informal sector, inhabited by firms with very low capitalization, selling in easily entered markets, and offering low-paying, insecure jobs.

The rate and pattern of industrial growth have failed to provide enough decent jobs for all members of the rapidly growing labor force. This gap between labor-force growth and job creation is one of the central issues facing policymakers throughout the region (Chapters 4 and 5).

The problem of insufficient job creation is not the result of too little investment. In general, MENA countries have invested as high a proportion of national output as other LDCs (Chapter 8). The Algerian case is instructive here: After Algeria relentlessly invested over one-third of its output for a generation (one of the highest investment rates in history), in the mid-1980s nearly one in five workers was unemployed.

A clue to the problem may be found in Figure 3.8, which displays incremental capital-to-output ratios (ICORs) for groups of countries in the region. These show, roughly, the amount of investment required per unit of additional output. For LDCs with scarce capital and abundant labor, a lower ICOR (and therefore higher growth and employment creation) can be achieved by selecting relatively labor-intensive techniques. However, if policy creates biases toward capital-intensity, a given amount of investment will foster less growth and create fewer jobs. Algeria's ICOR during the 1970s was nearly twice as high as that in the labor-intensive, rapidly growing South Korean economy. In general, the efficiency of investment has fallen (ICORs have risen) throughout the region. Getting more output from a dollar of investment is a critical institutional and public policy task for the region.

Few of the countries of the region that do not export oil have escaped the typical LDC problem of a balance-of-trade deficit (Table 3.11). Development economists usually argue that such deficits are perfectly appropriate for a developing country *as long as exports grow commensurately.* In theory, capital *should* flow from capital-abundant developed countries to capital-scarce LDCs. However, if exports fail to grow, then the trade gap becomes a debt trap.

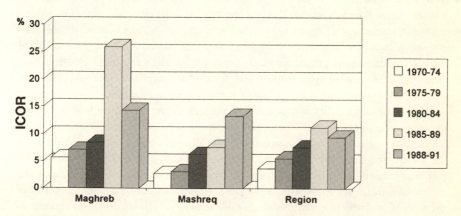

FIGURE 3.8   Incremental capital-to-output ratios, 1970–1991. *Source:* Diwan and Squire (1993).

TABLE 3.11   Growth of Exports and Imports, 1970–1992

| | Exports (US$ Thousands) | Imports (US$ Thousands) | Growth Rates (%) | | | |
| | | | Exports | | Imports | |
	1992	1992	1970–1980	1980–1992	1970–1980	1980–1992
Algeria	12,055	7,763	−0.5	4.3	12.1	−5.1
Egypt	3,050	8,293	−2.6	3.1	7.8	−1.2
Iran	18,235	26,744	−6.8	14.5	11.0	8.6
Israel	13,082	18,663	10.0	6.0	3.5	5.1
Jordan	933	3,251	19.3	6.1	15.3	−0.2
Morocco	3,977	7,356	3.9	5.5	6.6	4.4
Oman	5,555	3,674	−2.1	8.6	40.9	0.0
Saudi Arabia	41,833	32,103	5.7	−2.4	35.9	−6.2
Sudan	412	892	−3.5	0.2	−0.6	−4.8
Syria	3,262	3,365	7.0	19.4	12.4	4.6
Tunisia	4,040	6,425	7.5	6.4	12.5	3.1
Turkey	14,715	22,871	4.3	9.0	5.7	9.6

Source: World Bank (1994g, 186–187).

A number of countries in MENA now face a "debt crisis," the fruit of years of living beyond their means. Interest payments on debt as a percentage of GDP now rival those in chronically indebted sub-Saharan Africa and are similar to those that plagued Latin America in the 1980s. One critical debt ratio, the present value of debt as a percentage of exports, is shown in Figure 3.9. As a rule of thumb, any country with a ratio over 200% is said to suffer from "debt overhang": a level of indebtedness that deters private investors from risking their capital.[18] On this criterion, Algeria, Morocco, Syria, Turkey, and Yemen have important debt overhang difficulties, while the problem in the Sudan is entirely unmanageable.

Finally, the commodity composition of trade is shown in Tables 3.12 and 3.13. Of course, petroleum exports dominate the trade (and entire economies) of many countries of the region. As discussed in Chapter 2, the region has one agro-exporter, the Sudan, and three countries that export mainly manufactured goods: Turkey, Israel, and Jordan. Countries such as Egypt, Yemen, and Jordan relied heavily on the export of human beings (international labor migration) for foreign exchange until the Gulf War of 1991, which thoroughly disrupted these flows. A notable feature of the commodity composition of imports is the high percentage of food imports in countries such as Egypt, Morocco, and Algeria. Imports of fuel for countries without

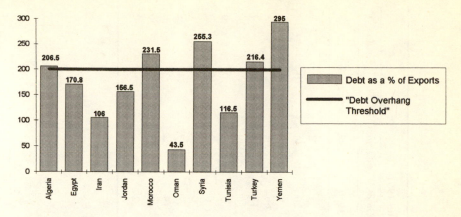

FIGURE 3.9   Value of debt as a percentage of exports, 1992. *Source:* Diwan and Squire (1993, 17).

oil and imports of capital goods (machinery) for the more industrialized countries are also evident.

CONCLUSION

It is possible to discern certain patterns in the midst of all the diversity of detail in the region. We offer a taxonomy of national economic growth and structural change patterns, dividing the countries into five groups on the basis of actual past performance and what we believe are potentially viable strategies. Needless to say, performance within any of these groups often varies considerably.

1. The coupon clippers: Libya, Kuwait, Oman, the UAE, Bahrain, and Qatar. These states have abundant oil and little of anything else, including people. They have been and will continue to be almost entirely dependent upon oil and any money earned from overseas investments. (Some—Bahrain and the UAE—have been able to play an entrepôt role, as "offshore" banks, free trade zones, and reshipment centers.) Unfortunately, in the Gulf States, the percentage of income from such sources has been cut in half during the past decade.

2. The oil industrializers: Iraq, Iran, Algeria, and Saudi Arabia. These countries enjoy substantial oil exports and revenues as well as large enough populations and/or other resources to make industrialization a real option. They should really be divided into two subgroups. The first three share the main features of large oil exports, a substantial population, other natural resources, and a chance to create industrial and agricultural sectors that will be sustainable over the long run. Tragically, all three suffer from such serious political disabilities that development has stalled in each. Its massive oil reserves place Saudi Arabia, the world's largest rentier state, in a class by itself. Although it lacks the other resources of the first three countries, its current and

TABLE 3.12 Structure of Merchandise Exports (%), 1970 and 1992

	Fuels and Minerals		Other Primary Goods		Machinery		Other Manufactures		Textiles[a]	
	1970	1992	1970	1992	1970	1992	1970	1992	1970	1992
Algeria	73	97	20	0	2	1	5	2	1	0
Egypt	5	51	68	14	1	1	26	34	19	18
Iran	90	90	6	6	0	0	4	3	3	3
Israel	4	2	26	9	5	28	66	62	12	7
Jordan	24	34	59	16	–	2	13	48	3	4
Morocco	–	15	59	30	0	6	9	49	4	25
Oman	100	94	0	1	0	4	0	1	0	0
Saudi Arabia	100	99	0	0	0	1	0	0	0	0
Sudan	1	3	99	96	0	0	0	1	0	1
Syria	62	45	29	17	3	1	7	37	4	25
Tunisia	46	16	35	11	0	9	19	64	2	40
Turkey	8	4	83	24	0	9	9	63	5	29
UAE	95	95	1	1	1	1	2	2	0	0

[a]Textiles are a subcategory of "Other Manufactures."
Source: World Bank (1987, 231; 1994g, 190–191).

73

TABLE 3.13 Structure of Merchandise Imports (%), 1970 and 1992

	Food		Fuel		Other Primary Goods		Machinery		Other Manufactures	
	1970	1992	1970	1992	1970	1992	1970	1992	1970	1992
Algeria	15	26	2	3	6	5	37	32	42	34
Egypt	23	29	9	1	12	10	27	36	29	34
Iran	7	12	0	0	8	4	41	45	44	39
Israel	14	7	5	8	8	4	30	32	42	48
Jordan	31	21	6	14	4	3	17	25	42	38
Morocco	21	14	5	15	10	10	32	25	32	32
Oman	13	19	5	2	3	3	41	42	38	36
Saudi Arabia	28	16	1	0	3	3	33	36	38	45
Sudan	21	19	8	19	3	3	27	22	41	37
Syria	21	17	8	18	5	5	28	26	38	32
Tunisia	28	9	5	8	9	9	26	30	32	47
Turkey	8	6	8	17	8	8	41	35	36	33
UAE	11	17	10	7	2	2	37	31	39	43

Source: World Bank (1987, 231; 1994g, 188–189).

future petroleum resources and access to capital are so enormous that it, too, can contemplate specializing in capital- and energy-intensive industry. Saudi Arabia has its share of economic problems, but its massive oil reserves provide it with a unique cushion.

3. The watchmakers: Israel, Jordan, Tunisia, and Syria. These four small countries have limited natural resources and must therefore concentrate on investing in human capital and on exporting skill-intensive manufactures. All have made major efforts to educate their people (Chapter 5); manufactured goods now account for 84% of Israeli, 52% of Jordanian, and 42% of Tunisian exports. Although Syria lags behind on both counts, we believe that this path is the most logical one for the country to follow over the long haul. The same would be true for any future Palestinian state.

4. The NICs: Turkey, Egypt, and Morocco. These countries either have no oil (Turkey and Morocco) or not enough to provide the basis for any long-run growth strategy (Egypt). In regional terms they have relatively large populations, relatively good agricultural land or potential, and long experience with industrial production. Turkey is clearly a full-fledged NIC, more similar to countries such as Mexico than to many countries of the region. The current regime has opted for a manufactured-export–led growth strategy. Students of the Egyptian economy have been saying that the country had no choice but to industrialize for over a generation; they are still right. The country must continue to improve its already very productive agriculture, but 360,000 square miles (932,400 square kilometers) alone cannot support 55 million people. The country has the largest skilled labor force and pool of technical talent in the Arab world. Moroccan industry, spurred by direct foreign investment and a favorable policy environment, has shown the most rapid rate of growth of any country in the region. Despite serious ecological problems (frequent droughts), its agricultural potential remains impressive. Continued industrialization, linked to agricultural development, could increase both the welfare of its people and its stature as an NIC.

5. The agro-poor: the Sudan and Yemen. These are the poorest countries of the region and ones for which the agricultural-development–led growth seems to offer the only hope. The Sudan has great agricultural potential but also enormous political, social, ecological, and infrastructural problems. Its growth performance has been the worst in the region; its immediate prospects are grim. Like the Alpine regions of Europe during that continent's industrialization, Yemen has remained agricultural while increasingly depending on emigration and remittances. The Gulf War and its aftermath have been catastrophic for Yemen, removing its main source of foreign exchange and employment. In a worst-case scenario, both countries could come to resemble "pirate states" like Afghanistan, with little public order, warlordism, endemic violence, and economic specialization in the trade in illegal drugs and arms.

This taxonomy is meant to be only suggestive; its boundaries are porous. For example, Egypt and Tunisia are partly oil industrializers. Unless important new discoveries are made soon, dwindling Algerian oil reserves will turn that country into an NIC—or a chaotic mess—in a generation. Syria and Egypt collect rents on their strategic locations, and Morocco shares some features with the agro-poor (as well as a flourishing drug trade based in the Rif). Like any taxonomy, the aim of this one is to help organize our thoughts. We should also note that this economic taxonomy does not correspond to our political taxonomy (Chapter 11).

One might object that all this is simply "closet modernization theory": the argument that all of the world will reenact the history of Europe and its overseas offspring (United States, Canada, Australia). We certainly *do* believe that the process of economic growth includes structural change; the data given above amply demonstrate the declining weight of agriculture in the economies of the region and the increase in a *kind* of industry in most cases. This process was, of course, also true of the now-developed countries. If this be modernization theory, make the most of it!

We emphatically do *not* believe, however, that the process of economic growth is smooth. It is uneven over time, over space, and over people; there are losers, and some of the winners do rather better than others. The past decade has seen retrogression and decline rather than growth and development. Furthermore, as we argued in Chapter 2, we believe that the process of economic growth and structural change is replete with unintended outcomes. And we do not believe that all (even any) of the MENA countries can or will "look like" the industrialized West or Japan, even economically. It is implicitly understood in the chapters that follow that economic growth in the region has many crucial differences from that found in the history of any now-developed country, if for no other reason than that rents have played such a critical role in regional growth. Still less do we think that Middle Eastern and North African countries will resemble the West politically or (most absurd of all) culturally. We simply argue that the course of politics cannot be understood without an understanding of the process of economic growth and structural change, a process that has a logic of its own.

Finally, we must add one more cautionary note. It is possible that "development" of the usual kind is simply not possible for the world as a whole. Ecological constraints must be taken seriously. The apparent scientific consensus on the greenhouse effect suggests that we may already have unleashed forces whose long-term effects are frightening to contemplate. Increased heat and aridity would undermine *any* development strategy in the Middle East and North Africa. If the droughts of the recent past become more frequent, the region (and the world) will face a human and ecological disaster. Understanding how such tragedies might occur and what might be done to prevent them will surely require first an understanding of the interaction of economic growth, state policies, and social actors. Even if the earth does not warm up, the continued pressure of population on scarce resources poses serious problems for the region. The political economy of population growth will be the topic of the next chapter.

NOTES

1. Excluding Antarctica.
2. The more significant are antimony, chromite, copper, iron ore, lead, lignite coal, manganese, mercury, phosphate rock, and silver.

3. Other things are usually not equal, however: Iran and Iraq have been consistent "price hawks" because the size of their populations and their development (not to mention military) needs have induced their political leaders to opt for short-run revenue gains.

4. Wellhead operating costs exclude the costs of exploration and discovery.

5. For example, the North Sea, Canada, China, and Russia. Only Mexico and other OPEC (US$3.00) and the UAE (US$2.00) have lower costs. U.S. stripper wells produce oil at a cost of about US$10.00 per barrel (Atlantic Richfield 1994).

6. Recall from Chapter 2 that "economic rent" is the difference between price and the opportunity cost of production, that is, the amount of resources required to keep a factor (or factors) of production in its current use.

7. For more details see, inter alia, Cremer and Salehi-Isfahani (1991), Heal and Chichilnisky (1991), Fried and Trezise (1993), and Yergin (1991).

8. The so-called Seven Sisters—British Petroleum (BP), Texaco, Exxon, Royal Dutch Shell, Mobil, Standard Oil of California (Chevron), and Gulf Oil—plus the state-owned Compagnie Française de Petrol (CFP).

9. Nigerian oil shipments were disrupted by the civil war that broke out in 1967.

10. The "posted price" was the price on which the companies agreed to pay royalties to the countries, as opposed to the market price, which could fluctuate.

11. *Real* oil prices were, however, roughly constant from 1970 to 1974; most of the nominal increases simply kept pace with the accelerating inflation in the industrialized countries.

12. "Marker crude" at the time was Saudi Arabian light crude oil. The price of other oils was determined by various markups or discounts from the price of Saudi Arabian light.

13. The only competitor would be the Spanish plundering of the Americas of precious metals in the sixteenth century.

14. Saudi finances have remained in deficit ever since (1983–1995).

15. Political considerations may also have influenced the Saudi decision to open the taps. The Saudis sought to deny revenue to the Iranians, who were advancing in the Fao peninsula of Iraq at that time. Some reports assert that William Casey, the director of the CIA, asked the Saudis to slash prices to deny revenue to the Soviets. When economic and political interests coincide, it is impossible to determine their relative weights.

16. To above US$40 per barrel.

17. For both Jordan (10% of labor force in agriculture) and the UAE (4–4.5% in agriculture), the lack of change in the 1980s merely says that the transformation was already largely complete.

18. Investors fear that the large size of the public debt will force the government to raise taxes either directly or indirectly via the inflation tax. In either case, a prospective investor will lose. Servicing an external debt requires an internal transfer (from private to public sectors) and an external one (from the indebted country's government to the foreign creditors). Domestic debts require an internal transfer. That these transfers must come from local sources creates fear among potential investors.

4

THE IMPACT OF RAPID POPULATION GROWTH

For good or ill, the peoples of the Middle East are multiplying rapidly. Only sub-Saharan Africa has a higher rate of population growth than the Middle East and North Africa. Although fertility rates fell during the past generation, the decline in the death rate has been swifter, accelerating population growth during the period before the 1980s. However, population growth rates have fallen quite sharply in the past ten years (from 3.2% in the mid-1980s to 2.7% in 1992). Sharp fertility declines caused this change; there are reasons to expect further drops. However, populations will continue to grow, both because fertility remains well above replacement levels and because past population growth ensures that there are many women who will soon enter their childbearing years. Even if all women had no more than two children (i.e., if fertility were to fall immediately to 2.0), more than 200 million people would be added to the population. (Population was about 317 million in 1992.) More realistic projections are for a regional population of roughly 600 million by 2025 (World Bank 1994e), some six times more people than in the 1950s.

Such numbers may be viewed as catastrophic, problematical, or even occasion for rejoicing. The old debates on the political economy of population, first incarnated as "Malthus versus Marx," have lost none of their vigor. Some neo-Malthusians believe that rapid population growth dooms any attempt at development to failure (e.g., Ehrlich 1968). Some marxists have exactly reversed this causality, maintaining that poverty and underdevelopment cause rapid population growth (e.g., Mamdani 1972). Finally, neo-Panglossians such as Simon (1982) have argued that population growth is an unalloyed blessing because, they believe, "the mind is greater than the stomach": The more talented, energetic people there are, the better off the human race will be. For them, economies of scale, accelerating human-capital formation, and rapid technological and institutional innovation put humanity on a continual upward path of progress as its numbers steadily expand.

We reject each of these extreme views, agreeing with the majority of modern demographers that population growth (1) is at least partially the result of social conditions and economic incentives (i.e., crude Malthusian "population determinism" is silly), (2) is not *solely* determined by economic conditions (and therefore family planning programs have an independent impact on fertility), and (3) exacerbates certain development problems, particularly that of providing education and jobs for the young. We believe that rapid population growth complicates the development process and generates political stresses. Policymakers must confront both of these difficulties. They can respond both directly by promoting family planning programs and indirectly by altering the incentives for couples to have children. However, both sorts of instruments are often highly charged politically.

COMPARATIVE DEMOGRAPHIC PATTERNS

Among the demographic developments in the region during the past generation (Table 4.1), several facts deserve emphasis.

Population growth accelerated in the region for roughly forty years. In 1950–1955, the rate of population growth, at 2.64% per year, was the second-highest of the major cultural-economic regions of the world. For 1970–1980 the rate had risen to 2.8 and for 1980–1992 to 3.1%; in the 1980s the region's population was growing at the most rapid rate in the world. However, in the late 1980s population growth decelerated, falling to 2.7% in 1992. Such a rate implies a doubling of population in just under twenty-seven years (Figure 4.1); the lower rate today still exceeds the rate in the early 1950s. In the simplest terms, population growth accelerated because the birthrate declined more slowly than the death rate. Since no one advocates population control by raising the death rate, population policy analysis focuses on the birthrate.

The key population issue in the region is the stubbornly slow decline in fertility. Fertility has always been high in MENA. In 1950–1955, the regional crude birthrate (CBR, defined as the quotient of the number of births and the total population) was the highest in the world, 50.5 per 1,000. The CBR fell to 45 in 1970 and then to 34 in 1992, but still only that of sub-Saharan Africa was higher (44). The region's CBR exceeds the average for LDCs (27) and for middle-income countries (24) and is only slightly below the average for the world's low-income countries, excluding China and India (28) (World Bank, 1994g).[1]

The denominator in the CBR quotient—the total population—includes men, prepubescent girls, and postmenopausal women. A more revealing statistic is the total fertility rate (TFR), which tells us roughly how many children the "average woman" will have during her fertile period.[2] By this measure, Middle Eastern women were the most fecund in the world in the early 1950s and were second only to sub-Saharan African women by the early 1980s, when Middle Eastern women were still bearing an average of six children each (National Research Council 1986). In the early 1990s the region's women were still giving birth to, on average, just

TABLE 4.1 Demographic Indicators, 1970–1992

	Population Growth		Crude Birth Rate[a]		Crude Death Rate[a]		Total Fertility Rate	
	1970–1980	1982–1992	1970–1980	1982–1992	1970–1980	1982–1992	1970–1980	1982–1992
Algeria	3.1	2.8	49	30	16	6	7.4	4.3
Egypt	2.1	2.4	40	28	17	9	5.9	3.8
Iran	3.2	3.5	45	7	16	7	6.7	5.5
Israel	2.7	2.3	26	21	7	6	3.8	2.7
Jordan	3.7	4.9	–	38	–	5	–	5.2
Morocco	2.4	2.5	47	28	16	8	7	3.8
Oman	4.1	4.3	50	43	21	5	8.4	7.2
Saudi Arabia	4.9	4.9	48	35	18	5	7.3	6.4
Sudan	2.9	2.7	47	42	22	14	6.4	6.1
Syria	3.3	3.3	47	42	13	6	7.7	6.1
Tunisia	2.2	2.3	39	30	14	7	6.4	3.8
Turkey	2.3	2.3	36	28	12	7	4.9	3.4
UAE	15.6	4.0	35	22	11	4	6.5	4.5
Yemen	2.6	3.8	53	50	23	15	7.8	7.6

[a]Per thousand.
Source: World Bank (1994g, 212).

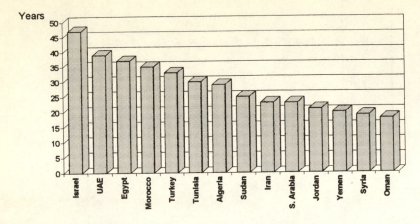

FIGURE 4.1   Doubling times of populations at 1992 growth rates. *Source:* Calculated from World Bank (1994g).

under five children apiece. Despite recent progress, there can be little doubt that MENA fertility rates are high in international comparative terms (see Box 4.1).

Fertility rates are also high in relation to incomes. It is well established that, in general, fertility falls with increases in per capita income; the relationship between fertility and income for ninety-four developing countries is shown in Figure 4.2. The relationship is not, of course, a simple one. Indeed, if everything else remains the same, higher incomes may lead to more children, since poor health at low income levels may limit the number of children that women can have. The inverse relationship may be thought of as the outcome of a highly complex social process in which new attitudes, new preferences, and new habits are generated. Or one may have recourse to the theories of economic demography, which hold, in effect, that parents start to substitute "child quality" for "child quantity" as they become richer (e.g., T. W. Schultz 1981). But for both the sociological and the economic theory of fertility, increased incomes *alone* are unlikely to reduce fertility; additional socioeconomic change is required.

The MENA evidence confirms such a perspective; fertility rates exceed what would be expected given per capita income for every country in the region except Egypt, Tunisia, and Turkey. The disparity becomes most notable for major oil-exporting countries: despite income levels roughly comparable to those of many Western European countries, fertility rates in Saudi Arabia and Libya are as high as those in the poorest African countries, whose per capita incomes are less than one-tenth those of the Gulf States. The relatively weak relationship between higher incomes and reduced fertility in the region is not confined to oil exporters: both Syria and Jordan have fertility rates much above what would be expected given their incomes. We need to explain not only why the region's fertility rates are high relative to those of other regions of the world but also why they have remained so high despite the

---

BOX 4.1
THE DIVERSITY OF FERTILITY BEHAVIOR IN MENA

Table 4.1 shows wide difference in fertility behavior across countries and regions, ranging from the extremely high rates in Oman, Saudi Arabia, and Yemen, countries that have among the highest fertility rates in the world, to the lowest rate (2.7, the same as Chile's) in Israel. Fertility also varies with place of residence and education of the mother. Recent surveys have shown that urban MENA women usually have lower TFRs than their rural cousins. In Yemen, a 1991–1992 survey found a TFR of 5.6 in cities, compared with 8.1 in rural areas. Egyptian urban women's TFR was measured at 2.9—the same as Israel's—compared with 4.9 in the countryside in 1992. And in Jordan the TFR of women in rural areas was 6.9, that in smaller cities 5.6, and that in the largest cities 4.8 (Omran and Roudi 1993). In Iran the 1986 census showed an urban TFR of 5.1, compared with 8.4 in rural areas (Bulatao and Richardson 1994). Urban TFRs in 1992 were 2.3 in Morocco and Tunisia and 3.0 in Algeria (Fargues 1994). Fargues suggests that rapid urbanization (see Chapter 10), along with other social changes, holds out the prospect of a more rapid drop in fertility than is usually predicted.

Education also has a strong effect on fertility. Women's average age at marriage rises with education: an uneducated Tunisian girl will typically marry at twenty, while one with primary education marries at twenty-two, and one with secondary education at twenty-four (World Bank 1994g). Rising educational levels are a second hopeful indicator: As we shall see in Chapter 5, in many MENA countries younger women are far more likely to be educated than their mothers. They will, however, far outnumber their mothers.

---

sustained economic growth of the decade of the oil boom and why they seem to have fallen at the same time as incomes (roughly, 1985–1995).

Modern demographers do not agree on the precise determinants of fertility. All concur that economic conditions play some role; all agree that the social position of women is highly significant; all concede that high infant mortality is correlated with high fertility rates. But different analysts accord varying weights to these and to other factors. This is not very surprising. The decision to have a child is so complex and the available data are so open to various interpretations that dogmatic positions are out of place. Accordingly, we will survey some of the plausible explanations for high fertility in the Middle East without offering a firm conclusion (inappropriate given the current state of knowledge). We do believe that the social position of women and choices by national political leaders are central to any satisfactory explanation of why MENA fertility rates are "high."

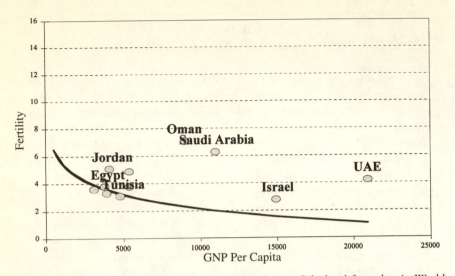

FIGURE 4.2   Per capita GNP and fertility, 1993. *Source:* Calculated from data in World Bank (1994g).

One hypothesis is that poor health conditions raise fertility rates. Most demographers agree that infant mortality is an important determinant of fertility. For a combination of economic and emotional reasons, parents are interested in *surviving* children. If many infants die, people will, on average, tend to have more children to compensate. High infant mortality rates contribute to an explanation of high fertility rates. Although infant mortality rates are high relative to those of advanced industrial countries, they have come down very sharply in the past two decades (from 139 per 1,000 on average to 58). MENA infant mortality is below the average for LDCs (65) and well below that for Africa (99) or South Asia (85). MENA fertility behavior appears to be more exceptional than the region's infant mortality performance. Conundrums appear among countries in the region. For example, Turkey has a notably higher infant mortality rate than Syria, yet fertility in the latter country is well above that of its northern neighbor (World Bank 1994g).

Economic analysis provides a useful perspective on fertility. Although, of course, any couple's decision to have a child is a complex product of social norms and personal psychology, some insights can be gained if one treats the decision like any other economic decision, as a balancing of "costs" and "benefits," recognizing from the outset that neither of these will be exclusively monetary. This view suggests that since most people like children they will tend to have *more* of them as they become richer, just as they buy more clothes, meat, radios, and entertainment. How, then, to explain the observed correlation between higher incomes and lower fertility? Economic analysts of demography argue that the key is the rising *opportunity cost of having children* as family incomes rise. In turn, this rising cost has two major components: (1) the increased amount of money that parents wish to spend on each child and (2) the higher opportunity cost of parents' time. If rising incomes do not also generate such changes, increased wealth may do little to reduce fertility.

An important component of the opportunity cost of having children is the economic activity of children: The earlier children can perform productive labor, the sooner their net contributions to the family budget will be positive. In most peasant societies, including those of the Middle East, children can and do perform numerous tasks, ranging from caring for younger children to harvesting cotton. In general, the more child labor is performed in agriculture, the lower the opportunity cost of having many children and therefore the higher the fertility rate. This aspect of the argument that low levels of development engender high fertility is certainly reasonable and is confirmed by evidence from the region. In this regard, the Middle East is little different from most of the peasant societies of the Third World.

Similarly, children perform an important function as "pension funds"—as the providers of income and care in old age. If, as in MENA, such a burden falls on the sons and if child mortality is high, an average peasant or urban poor family will rationally want to have seven births to ensure that two sons survive to provide for them in old age. Here, too, MENA countries resemble most developing countries, and therefore the "insurance" motive for children cannot explain MENA's relatively high fertility levels.

A critical component of the economic analysis of fertility is the opportunity cost of *women's* time, since women have primary responsibility for child care everywhere in the world. If women are illiterate and if they are more or less systematically excluded from alternative employment, the opportunity cost of their time will be low. When such considerations are combined with and reinforced by social pressures on women to have many children, the result is likely to be a high fertility rate.

Such an analysis suggests that the socioeconomic status of women may be *the* critical determinant of fertility rates. Here we can find a clue to our puzzle of the region's fertility rates' exceeding what we would expect given both income levels and rates of infant and child mortality. The adult literacy figures for women in the Middle East are dismally low (Table 4.2). There is much evidence that higher education is correlated with lower fertility (see Box 4.1 and Table 4.3). Educated women both want to have fewer children and are more likely to use birth control to achieve their desired family size. However, anomalies remain: fertility rates in both Jordan and Syria are considerably higher than what one would predict on the basis of income levels and female education (Jacobson 1994).

Women's employment also lowers fertility, provided that it is outside of the home. Although many Middle Eastern rural women do participate extensively in crop and livestock production, such work is typically integrated with child care and thus creates little pressure to reduce fertility. Egyptian surveys showed that women who worked for cash outside of the home had an average of 3.2 births, compared with 4.9 for women who did not (USAID 1992b). Women's participation in work that is more directly competitive with child rearing is, with a few exceptions, extremely low in the region; in 1992 women made up only 16% of the region's labor force. Female

TABLE 4.2   **Adult Literacy Rates (%), 1990**

	Female	Male	Total
Algeria	45	69	57
Egypt	34	58	46
Iran	43	65	54
Iraq	49	71	60
Jordan	70	90	80
Kuwait	67	79	73
Libya	73	87	80
Morocco	28	60	49
Oman	38	60	49
Saudi Arabia	48	76	62
Sudan	12	42	27
Syria	51	77	64
Tunisia	64	66	65
Turkey	71	91	81
Yemen	26	50	38

Source: World Bank (1994g, 216–217).

illiteracy and the absence of nonfarm, nonhousehold job opportunities for women contribute to the region's rapid population growth.

These considerations raise the question of how "culture" affects fertility and, in particular, what role Islam plays in promoting population growth. It should be obvious that the answer to the broadly stated question "Does culture affect fertility?" must be "Of course!" The social norms regulating the sexual division of labor and, indeed, all aspects of relations between the sexes powerfully shape individual actions. Specifying the precise ways in which culture influences reproductive behavior is extremely difficult, but we can offer a few general points. It is important to remember

TABLE 4.3   **Fertility and Education in Egypt, 1980s**

Educational Level	Total Fertility Rate
No schooling	5.7
Some primary schooling	5.1
Completed primary school	3.8
Completed secondary school	3.2

Source: USAID (1992b).

that most MENA countries are (or have been until very recently) largely peasant or herder societies. There are *no* peasant societies in which women are treated equally with men; everywhere the norm has been women's "social marginalization and economic centrality" (Meillassoux 1981). The importance of family life, the social and economic pressures to bear sons, and the strict control of women's sexuality are found in most peasant societies, whether Muslim or non-Muslim. Therefore, at least part of the subordination of women (and consequent high fertility rates) may be due to their position as peasants rather than as Muslims.

But this can hardly be the whole story. After all, China is still overwhelmingly a peasant society, yet its fertility rate has plummeted over the past generation. Furthermore, to an outsider Muslim societies seem especially socially restrictive for women. There are stringent practices of female seclusion and segregation of the sexes. Islamic law defines women as juridical minors; men can easily divorce women, whereas the reverse is not true; the father, not the mother, typically gets custody of the children. Some Muslim women try to have large families as a kind of "insurance policy" against divorce: a man might be more reluctant to divorce the mother of six than the mother of an only daughter.

International evidence reveals a positive correlation between Islam and fertility. Albania (a majority Muslim country) has the highest fertility rate in Europe; Muslims in Malaysia have higher fertility than other religious groups in Malaysia. In Israel, Muslim women's TFR in 1991 was 4.7, while the rate for Christians (also Arabs) was 2.3 and that for Jews 2.6 (Omran and Roudi 1993). In the mid-1980s Lebanese Christian TFRs were about 2.4, while for the Shi'ite Muslims in the Bekaa and southern Lebanon the rate was about 6 (Fargues 1994, citing Lebanese Family Planning Association, 1984). Muslims everywhere seem to have large families. However, one must avoid overly facile generalizations. Islam is a living religion; its content is in part determined by the way in which its adherents interpret their own tradition. There is *much* debate in the Muslim world over personal-status questions. Many Muslim scholars believe that many of the practices that Westerners label "Islamic" are in fact corruptions of Islam, derived from other sources such as 'urf, or customary law. They are horrified by practices such as clitoridectomy (also widely practiced in non-Muslim Africa and more rarely in West Asia) and regularly denounce them. To outsiders some of this debate may seem forced, but it is critical; only internal change that is consistent with people's beliefs has any chance of affecting such deeply personal issues as the regulation of family life. When we say that "Islam" promotes the subordinate status of women and thus high fertility, we mean "Islam as currently practiced by Muslims."

A second, complementary point is that all great cultures are flexible; they can accommodate wide-ranging changes in economic, political, and social life. For example, one might summarize the above discussion by saying that Islam places great stress on family life and considers that women's primary place is in the home. But then, of how many cultures could one say otherwise? Few would try to argue that family life is marginal in Chinese culture, yet fertility rates in China have declined more rapidly than anywhere else in the world over the past twenty years. The status of women in Chinese society was lower than in the poorest Muslim society: a married Chinese woman could own no property distinct from her husband's, divorce was even easier for men than in Muslim societies, and women were essentially the property of their husbands. Yet governments as diverse as that of the PRC, Taiwan, and Singapore have all succeeded in educating women, raising their legal status, and dramatically lowering fertility rates. "Culture" is not immutable.

The question is not whether "culture" or "belief systems" affect behavior but whether they would continue to produce high fertility *even after* substantial changes elsewhere in social and economic life. For example, it is clear that early marriage contributes to higher fertility. Few children are born outside of marriage in the Middle East; if couples are formed early in life, fertility will be higher. Indeed, recent research has shown that postponing the age of marriage was the principal mechanism for limiting fertility in preindustrial Europe and Japan (Mosk 1983; Wrigley and Schofield 1981; World Bank 1984). Early marriage is common in Islamic countries and receives social sanction and reinforcement. In the early 1980s about one young woman out of three was married before her nineteenth birthday (Lapham 1983). There is considerable variation across nations, and there have also been important recent changes. Urbanization and education increase the age at first marriage. In Kuwait the age at first marriage rose from 18.9 in 1965 to 22.4 in 1985; the percentage of women aged 15 to 19 who had married fell from 42% to 18% (Omran and Roudi 1993).

State policy affects fertility rates. A wide range of policies are available, both those that affect desired family size (sometimes called "indirect" policies), such as health and education programs, and those that affect the number of children a couple actually has (birth control). Policies in MENA have eschewed coercion and have only lightly relied on disincentives (e.g., higher taxes for larger families). The main family planning policy approach (when there has been one at all) has been to subsidize birth control technology and to disseminate information through government health networks and the media.

Some countries—Turkey and Tunisia—have followed a consistent policy of promoting family planning since 1965. The Tunisian government has pushed for universal female schooling, raised the legal marriage age, made divorce more difficult, and ensured that birth control technology is widely available. The percentage of teenage women who were married fell from 42% in 1956 to only 6% in 1975. Fertility rates have fallen from over 7 at independence to 3.8 in 1992. Turkish reforms of family law were part of Atatürk's broader developmental vision (Chapters 2 and 7). After 1965 the Turkish government promoted family planning with subsidies and propaganda, support that has continued without serious interruption.

Other countries have displayed stop-go family planning policies. Both Egypt and Iran fall into this category. Egypt launched a family planning program in 1965 that focused on the supply of birth control technology. However, the program languished under Sadat. The slogan of the time was "Development is the best contraceptive," and the focus was (in theory but not in practice) on, among other things, better health and increased female school enrollment. Gilbar (1992) argues that this shift was political—that Sadat tried to use the Muslim Brotherhood and other Islamists against the pro-Soviet left (see Chapter 14) and accordingly yielded to the Islamists' pronatalist views. Mubarak's government reversed this position, however, and, with considerable donor assistance, launched a sustained program of family planning that began to show results in the early 1990s. Iranian policy reversals have been still more dramatic (see Box 4.2).

BOX 4.2
FAMILY PLANNING IN IRAN: ON-OFF-ON AGAIN

Iranian family planning policy has undergone two sharp reversals. In 1965 the shah instituted a family planning policy that, like most such programs at the time, stressed the "supply side": the availability of contraception. This program "disintegrated" (Bulatao and Richardson 1994, 20) after the Islamist revolution. Social traditionalism and war combined to produce a pronatalist policy. The minimum age for marriage was reduced, the High Council for Coordination of Family Planning was disbanded, contraceptives became harder to get, and the government provided large families special housing and food subsidies. It is likely that these policies contributed to the reversal of fertility decline. The TFR rose from 6.5 in 1976 to 7.0 in 1986 (Bulatao and Richardson 1994; Omran and Roudi 1993). The rate of natural increase rose from 2.9% in 1966–1976 to 3.9% in 1976–1986.

The census of 1986 served as a "wake-up call" for planners, and the end of the war with Iraq in 1988 provided them with their opportunity. The government completely reversed course, establishing a Population Committee in the Ministry of Health and Medical Education. The committee set a goal of reducing total fertility to 4.0. Contraceptives were reintroduced into the primary health care system; in 1990 the government legalized female sterilization, and both male and female sterilization were offered without charge (for any man and for any woman with three or more children). Seminars and the media were extensively used to promote family planning. In May 1993 the majlis (Iranian parliament) passed a law that withdrew certain subsidies from families that had a fourth or higher-order child after May 1994.

In response to these policies and probably also to economic hardship and rising female education, the fertility rate has fallen sharply. How sharply is a matter of dispute; estimates range from 6.3 to 4.7. By any standard, this is a very significant fall in fertility, and if the lower figures are correct, "the fertility decline in the late 1980s was extraordinarily rapid, faster than the fastest recorded fertility declines in developing countries before 1990" (Bulatao and Richardson 1994, 9). Policy matters.

88 *The Impact of Rapid Population Growth*

Most countries in the region now have some kind of family planning program (Table 4.4). Yemen, which adopted a program in 1991, has, along with Turkey, Egypt, and Iran, set fertility targets for its program. Some countries, such as Israel, Kuwait, and Iraq, have explicitly pronatalist policies—always for political reasons. A number of the Gulf States have subsidy policies that provide incentives for large families. Only Iraq and Saudi Arabia openly limit access to contraceptive technology and information (Omran and Roudi 1993).

Apart from politically motivated pronatalism, neglect of family planning policy has several determinants. First and probably most important, the benefits of reduced population growth accrue in the future. We shall see repeatedly in this book that myopia characterizes most government economic policy. Second, some governments do not believe that rapid population growth is a problem; these pronatalist countries (e.g., the Sudan until 1984 and Iraq) want more people. To evaluate this position one must consider the economic consequences of population growth and the politics of ethnic differences in population growth (see below). Third, many believe that only changing economic conditions will reduce population growth. Such arguments, sometimes buttressed by appeals to Marx, are both hypocritical and false. They are hypocritical because, as we shall see in the next chapter, the region's performance in changing the basic-needs indicators such as health and women's education that are so crucial for fertility reduction has hardly been spectacular. They are false because by now there is considerable evidence that the availability of family planning exerts an independent negative pressure on fertility rates.

TABLE 4.4 Government Family Planning Policies, Early 1990s

Policy on Access to Contraceptives	Policy on Fertility Level			
	Increase Fertility	Lower Fertility	Maintain Current Fertility	No Intervention
Direct support	Israel	Egypt Iran Jordan Turkey Yemen		Bahrain Lebanon Syria
Little or no support	Kuwait		Oman Qatar	UAE
Major restrictions on access to contraceptives	Iraq		Saudi Arabia	

Source: Omran and Roudi (1993, 33).

Perhaps the critical point here is not whether governments can affect fertility (they can) but, rather, how hard they have to try—what it costs them politically. We should also ask what the role of religion is in such costs. The legal age of marriage is still only fifteen in countries such as Morocco and Turkey; raising it encounters opposition from Islamic revivalists. It is probably not accidental that Moroccan television did not begin showing family planning information until 1982, when economic crisis left little choice. Only if the government places a great deal of weight on the need to reduce population growth (as in Egypt) would a regime already hard-pressed by an Islamic opposition risk a major family planning drive.[3] The weakness of family planning policy thus becomes merely symptomatic of the wider weakness of the region's states. It is difficult not to conclude that high fertility levels are the result of political, not cultural, failure in the Middle East.

THE ECONOMIC CONSEQUENCES OF RAPID POPULATION GROWTH

Does rapid population growth matter for economic development? Although most social scientists would answer in the affirmative, there is a minority that holds that population growth is a good thing. Members of this minority can point out that in the Middle East, for example, the standard of living and life prospects of the roughly 60 million Egyptians alive today far exceed those of their 10 million grandparents in 1900. They also note that some of the development problems of the Sudan are the result of a highly dispersed population. One could accept such arguments without necessarily swallowing the more-is-better line whole, but one does need to specify just how high fertility and rapid population growth will affect national economies.

Pressure on Educational Systems

A critical feature of the demography of Middle Eastern countries is the large number of young people in proportion to the total population. A comparison of age pyramids for a few countries in the region with that of the United States is instructive (Figure 4.3). Most Middle Easterners are less than twenty years old; rapidly growing populations are young populations. It is worth noting, however, that the age pyramid for the Middle East in the nineteenth century, before rapid population growth began, would have looked quite similar. This is because declines in mortality, which drive increases in population growth, affect the survival not only of the young but also of the old; the relative percentage of young people does not shift much when the death rate falls. By contrast, a sharp drop in the fertility rate quickly reduces the proportion of young people in the population, and this proportion is further reduced by continued improvements in health that prolong old age. However, the *scale* of the problem today is entirely different; it is the absolute number of young people now rather than their proportion to the rest of the population that makes the critically important difference.

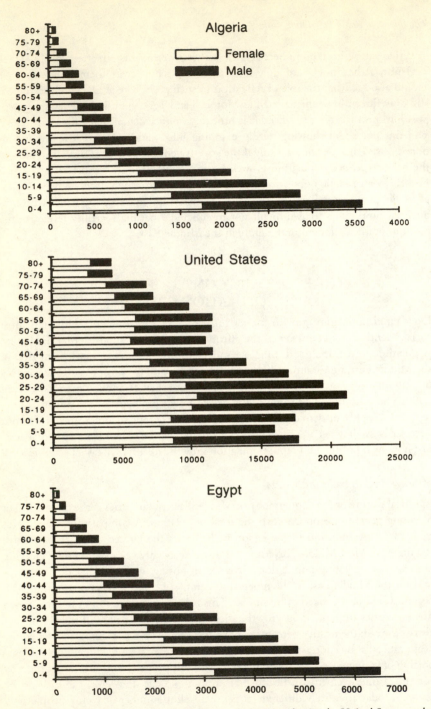

FIGURE 4.3   Distribution of population by age and sex in Algeria, the United States, and Egypt, 1980 (in thousands).

There is something approaching consensus among demographers that the amount of money spent per pupil is reduced by rapid population growth (see the discussion in National Research Council 1986). This usually takes the form of reduced teacher salaries and high pupil-teacher ratios. As we shall see in the next chapter, there is little evidence that the latter is a problem in the region; most countries try very hard to spend money on education. However, it is obviously true that a country starting to educate its children will find it more difficult to offer primary education to all of them if their numbers are growing rapidly. For example, although the total number of Algerian children enrolled in primary school nearly quadrupled from 1962 to 1978, there were still more than 1 million school-age children not in school in 1978 (Bennoune 1988). Rapid population growth swamps even the most determined attempts to diffuse basic education.

Rapid Increase in the Number of Job Seekers

The problems that a burgeoning number of young people create for society are not limited to educational difficulties. The impact on the job market is equally profound. Indeed, the rapid increase in the number of job seekers is one of the key challenges facing the region's polities and economies. Everywhere in the region, the labor force is growing much more quickly than the demand for labor. The numbers are startling. Rates of growth of national labor forces (Figure 4.4) in most cases exceed 3% per year. The regional average is 3.2% per year, the most rapid rate of growth of the labor force of any of the major regions of the developing world (Figure 4.5). This rate of growth implies that the labor force will be roughly one-eighth larger in five years and more than one-third larger in ten years. The total number of new jobs required by 2010 is roughly *67 million* (47 million for MENA as defined by World Bank plus about 20 million for Turkey)—more than the total population of the

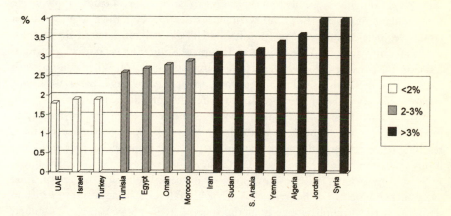

FIGURE 4.4   Growth rates of national labor forces (% per year), 1990s. *Source:* World Bank (1994g, 210).

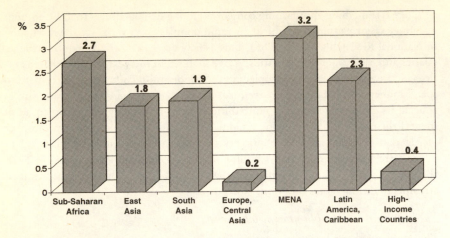

FIGURE 4.5   Labor force growth rates (%) in major world regions, 1992–2000. *Source:* World Bank (1994g, 211).

region's most populous nation, Turkey (59 million).[4] Investment requirements to employ them are large—about US$31 billion in Iran, US$30 billion in Morocco, US$25 billion in Algeria, US$14 billion in Egypt, and US$12 billion in Tunisia (Nemat Shafik, personal communication, August 17, 1995).

Two forces drive labor force growth: (decelerating) population growth and (accelerating) female labor force participation rates. Since past population growth rates have changed differentially, the future rates of growth of the labor force vary considerably across countries. In some cases, for example, Yemen, growth is accelerating; in others, for example, Tunisia, it is decelerating; in still others, for example, Morocco, it has stayed roughly the same. Iran can expect to face a surge in labor supply in the first decade of the twenty-first century. In most cases, however, the changes are small (and, given data quality problems, possibly statistically insignificant). In any case, for the 1980s, only the Nile Valley countries (Egypt, the Sudan) have rates of growth of less than 3% per year; most others are in the range of 3.0–3.5%. When coupled with the fact that these (slightly diminished) rates are applied to larger bases, we have a *demographic momentum* that ensures large future additions to the labor force.

A notable recent analysis (Fargues 1994) uses the deceleration in past fertility to predict the year when additions to the labor force will be just matched by those reaching retirement age (defined as sixty to sixty-five). The predicted year is 2015 in Tunisia, 2020 in Morocco and Algeria, 2025 in Egypt, and even farther in the future in Syria. Fargues notes that the number of new job seekers entering the labor market every year will increase to between 40% of the 1990 level in Tunisia and to 125% in Syria. Even these numbers may be optimistic, since, in many cases, the numbers used for the total fertility rate are lower than those of other sources, such as those from the World Bank, that we have used in this chapter.[5] His general conclusion, that the Maghreb is in considerably better shape than the countries farther east, seems valid,[6] but even the best performer, Tunisia, faces a demographically driven tidal wave of young job seekers for the next twenty years.

The number of job seekers will not, however, be driven by demographic forces alone. Precisely the same social force that brings down fertility rates (and thereby reduces, with a fifteen-to-twenty-year lag, demographic pressure on the labor market) also increases the number of women looking for work.[7] Rising female education both reduces fertility and raises female labor force participation. Fargues argues that, increasingly, growth in the labor force will be driven by this social (rather than purely demographic) force. He suggests that a critical determinant of women's labor force participation in the region is the *gap* between husband's and wife's education: "It is the husband, and not the children, who keeps the woman out of the labor market" (p. 169). When measured by enrollment ratios, men's education in the region is about a generation ahead of women's. Given the rapid increase in female enrollment ratios during the past decade, the next generation will have a much smaller gap than the current one. Accordingly, Fargues argues, men will be less likely to try to keep their wives out of the labor market. Rising female labor force participation will increasingly replace demography as the motor of labor force growth in MENA.

Fargues misses an important point, however. If rising women's education both reduces fertility and increases their labor-force participation, the latter effect will be felt *much sooner* than the former. The labor-market impact of reduced family size will not be felt for at least fifteen years, but the steadily rising numbers of educated young women want jobs *now*. Accordingly, the labor-market pressures are likely to be exceptionally severe in the coming decade or two.

It is perhaps not coincidental that the Islamists seem so obsessed with the position of women (see also Chapter 14). Part of their appeal is precisely the "send them back to the kitchen" rhetoric that often becomes prominent in periods of rising unemployment. There is often a (narrowing) gap in the educational level of young men and their (prospective) wives. The combination of rising unemployment among urban males, men who are not only young and relatively well educated but also unmarried (in Morocco, 80% of the unemployed in the largest cities are unmarried), with rising female labor force participation creates intense psychological pressure.

Even if the number of jobs created can match the number of jobs sought, the result will be simply some combination of stable unemployment and stagnant real wages. A rapidly expanding labor force compels the diversion of investment to providing jobs with a given amount of capital per worker. Since increasing the amount of capital per worker is typically necessary to raise worker productivity and therefore incomes, rapid population increase slows the growth of per capita incomes, ceteris paribus. Rapid population growth means that money must be spent just to create jobs rather than to improve those that already exist or to create more productive ones. It is particularly difficult to create the entry-level jobs that the (very young) labor force requires, especially when skilled older workers are so scarce. Since for nonoil (and increasingly for oil-exporting) states, funds for investment are very scarce, rapid population growth slows the pace of growth and development.[8]

Other Development Problems

Rapid population growth exacerbates other development problems in the region. Investable funds are diverted not merely from "capital deepening" but from any form of job creation to social-overhead investment (e.g., housing, sewage and water systems). Some investment may be necessary simply to repair the damage caused by population growth, as are the funds now being used to try to rehabilitate ecologically degraded areas of the Sudan. Rapid population increase contributes to the very rapid growth of cities, which are expanding at roughly twice the rate of the overall population in the region. Cairo's population of 12–13 million could double in twelve years—hardly a comforting thought for planners struggling with infrastructure that was originally planned and installed for a city of 1.5 million. Such rapid urban population growth not only diverts investment funds but also strains the administrative capacities of governments and fosters political problems. Rapid population growth contributes to a soaring demand for food in the region. Finally, by increasing the supply of labor relative to capital and by raising the ratio of unskilled to skilled labor, rapid population growth probably worsens the distribution of income.

It should be noted that population growth is neither exogenous nor a monocause of development problems. It is merely one (albeit important) variable in the ensemble of relationships in the political economy. But the rapid growth of population does exacerbate important economic development difficulties in the region, and it also poses political problems.

THE POLITICS OF YOUNG POPULATIONS

In countries with moderate or low population growth rates, political leadership is generally drawn from an age pool that contains a significant proportion, if not the majority, of the population. In North America, Western and Eastern Europe, the former Soviet Union, and Japan, not only are most citizens legal adults (about 70% of the U.S. population is twenty years old or older) but also the populations as a whole are aging. There is in these countries a much more profound sharing of experience between leaders and their major constituencies than is to be found in societies experiencing rapid population growth. Political generations are often depicted as having been shaped by national crises. For example, Churchill, Roosevelt, Truman, Stalin, and de Gaulle all spoke for a generation that shared the trauma of the world depression and World War II. In 1980 there were 57 million Americans, or 26% of the population of the United States, who were born before 1925, grew up during the depression, and were at least teenagers during World War II. That experience provided them and their elected leaders a common language and a set of symbols that were drawn from their own lives.

The situation in the Middle East, as in many developing areas, is radically different. When we note that in 1990 two-thirds of the Algerian population was under nineteen years old we can see startling political implications. First, only one third of the population are adults in the legal sense, entitled to vote and stand for election. Also, more than two-thirds of all living Algerians were born since independence in 1962. They know nothing directly of the French colonial presence or of seven years of war and devastation. By contrast, all of Algeria's presidents since 1962—Ahmad Ben Bella (1962–1965), Houari Boumedienne (1965–1978), Chadli Benjadid (1979–1991), Mohammed Boudiaf (January–June 1992), 'Ali Kafi (1992–1994), and Lamine Zeroual (1994–)—have been of the generation shaped by the revolutionary war. Their legitimacy, such as it is, stems directly from their role in the struggle against France, but for most Algerians that struggle is history, not a living memory or a shared experience.

Equally striking is the phenomenon of the Ayatollah Khomeini of Iran. Born at the turn of the century, he lived through the demise of the Qajar dynasty, the constitutional struggles of the 1920s, the consolidation of the autocratic regime of Reza Shah, the postwar confrontation between Reza Shah's son and the nationalist prime minister, Mohammed Mossadegh, and, finally, the shah's launching of the White Revolution in 1963. It was Khomeini's virulent opposition to various measures contained in that revolution that forced him into an exile that ended in 1979 with the deposition of the shah and Khomeini's triumphant return to an Islamic and republican Iran.

The majority of Iranians have been born since Khomeini went into exile. They did not live through the effervescence and occasional violence of the shah's White Revolution, which consisted of a series of measures involving land reform, female suffrage, the right of non-Muslims to stand as candidates, and the creation of a literacy corps. They did not hear or witness Khomeini's denunciations of some of these measures or his opposition to the special legal status granted U.S. personnel at that time. Even rarer are Iranians old enough to have participated in the events of 1953, when Prime Minister Mossadegh nationalized British oil interests and drove the young shah, Mohammed Reza Pahlavi, into brief exile.

One could go on with examples of the enormous disparities in age and experience of leaders and followers in the Middle East: Habib Bourguiba, born in 1903 and president of Tunisia from 1956 to 1987, and the septuagenarians that led Lebanon for years (Camille Chamoun, Suleiman Frangieh, Kemal Jumblatt, Pierre Jamayyel) are cases in point. The youngest of all Middle Eastern leaders, Mu'ammar Qaddhafi of Libya, in his early fifties, can no longer be seen as embodying the youthful élan of the bulk of the Libyan population.

There may yet be enough deference paid to age in the Middle East that the youthful majorities of the region will not reject or confront their relatively aged leaders. Khomeini's prestige among Iranians appeared undiminished at least until the cease-fire with Iraq in the summer of 1988, and hundreds of thousands of young Iranians died in the name of an anti-Iraqi crusade that he insisted on pursuing. There is evidence, however, that Islamic movements have been successful in mobilizing young people hitherto kept on the fringes of political systems that claim to represent them (see especially Chapters 12 and 14).

THE POLITICS OF DIFFERENTIAL FERTILITY

In defining the rights and obligations of citizens, the constitutions of most Middle Eastern states are blind to their ethnic or religious origins. Nonetheless, in a de facto sense, the relative weights of religious and ethnic communities are important in the political calculus of each state's leadership. There is an unstated expectation that the flows of public patronage will reflect communal weights. If the pattern of income distribution, particularly the locus of poverty, corresponds closely to ethnic or religious boundaries, then a potentially explosive situation may develop. The violent assertion of Shi'ite demands in Lebanon is a dramatic example.

The only way to know how many there are of what communities is through the national census. Censuses are carried out under the control of the national authority and can be doctored to reflect its interests. In Turkey, where since the 1920s there have been repeated assertions of Kurdish separatism in Eastern Anatolia, the national census provides no head count of the ethnic Kurds. In Iraq, where ethnicity (Kurd-Arab) cuts across religious sect (Sunni-Shi'i Muslim), the regime has typically been dominated by Sunni Arabs. Periodically there is talk of autonomy for regions in which Kurds predominate, but to delimit these regions requires a census. While negotiating over conducting a census, the regime has resettled Arabs in Kurdish areas and Kurds, who are Sunni Muslims, in Shi'ite areas. The Iraqi example illustrates the moving of people to achieve a desired census outcome. In Egypt the problem is one of adjusting census results. The Coptic Christian minority there has always protested that it has been undercounted by some 50% in Egypt's national census.

The two countries of the region in which the problem of ethnic and sectarian head counting is most acute are Lebanon and Israel. The system of political representation in Lebanon, cobbled together by the French after World War I, was founded on sectarian communities. Representatives in parliament competed for seats that were allocated in proportion to the numerical strength of each religious group in the population. The basic ratio is that for every five Muslim seats in parliament there are six Christian seats. After 1989, when fourteen years of civil war finally came to an end, the ratio was adjusted to five to five.

The original formula resulted from Lebanon's last official census in 1932. At that time the total population was 793,000. The Maronite Christians alone constituted 29% of the population, while Greek Orthodox, Armenians, Greek Catholics, and others gave the Christians a narrow but absolute majority of the population. The second-largest religious group was the Sunni Muslims, with 21% of the population. The Shi'ites were, in 1932, 18% of the population.

It was clear to everyone that the natural rate of increase of the Muslim populations was more rapid than that of the Christians. Moreover, the rate of long-term migration outside of Lebanon was higher among Christians than among Muslims. There was little doubt that a post–World War II census would show that the Christians had become a minority in Lebanon. Following the logic of the confessional system of apportionment, they would have lost the presidency and the majority of the seats in parliament. The result: no official census has been taken in Lebanon since 1932. In the past few decades there have been several informal attempts to measure the Lebanese population (Hudson 1968, 54–60). They all show that the Shi'ites have become the single largest religious group in Lebanon. Neither the Christians nor the Sunni Muslims wish to concede this fact officially.

Estimates of population distribution have varied widely (Table 4.5). The two 1983 columns reveal a discrepancy of over 1 million. Only Soffer explained the derivation of his figures, which assume 80,000 dead (more recent estimates put the death toll close to 150,000) in the civil war and the emigration of 400,000 Lebanese, half of whom were Maronite. He also put the foreign population of Lebanon at 220,000 Palestinians and 80,000 others. The Shi'ites are the poorest of all the religious sects. They are concentrated in the impoverished southern agricultural area bordering on Israel, with large pockets of relatively poor migrants in Sidon and Beirut. Their resentment over years of neglect has taken violent form. Their prominent role in the civil war in recent years is in large part motivated by their determination to win economic and political rewards commensurate with their numbers.

TABLE 4.5   **Lebanon's Estimated Population by Sect, 1932–1983**

	1932		*1983*		*1983*	
	Population	*%*	*Population*	*%*	*Population*	*%*
Total Christians	410,246	51.7	1,525,000	42.6	965,000	36.6
Maronites	226,378	28.6	900,000	25.0	580,000	21.0
Greek Orthodox	76,522	9.6	250,000	7.0	185,000	6.8
Greek Catholic	45,999	5.8	150,000	4.2	115,000	4.2
Armenians	31,156	4.0	175,000	4.9	70,000	2.6
Others[a]	30,191	3.8	50,000	1.4	40,000	1.5
Total Muslims and Druze	383,180	48.3	2,050,000	57.6	1,435,000	60.2
Sunnis	175,925	22.2	750,000	21.0	600,000	25.0
Shi'ites	154,208	19.4	1,100,000	31.0	665,000	27.5
Druze	53,047	6.7	200,000	5.6	180,000	7.7
Total	793,426	100.0	3,575,000	100.0	2,400,000	100.0

[a]Includes Jews.
Sources: First and last columns from Soffer (1986, 199); middle column from Minority Rights (1983), as cited in *Middle East,* March 1986, 41.

In Israel, questions of ethnic and religious numbers are equally sensitive, and, as in Lebanon communal boundaries correspond to differential socioeconomic status. However, in Israel censuses have been taken regularly. That very fact has produced data that alarm the Israeli establishment. The question is not so simple as how many Jews and non-Jews there are in Israel. The Jews themselves are divided between the Ashkenazim, of East European origin, and the Sephardim (or more accurately the Oriental Jews), of Middle Eastern and Spanish origin. Israel's political establishment has been dominated since independence by the Ashkenazim. As a group they are highly educated and relatively wealthy and have small families. The Oriental Jews, by contrast, occupy lower socioeconomic positions in Israeli society and are seen as more traditional. Birthrates among the Oriental Jews are higher than among the Ashkenazim, and the former and their Israeli-born offspring have become a majority of the Jewish population. They have yet to inherit the political kingdom.

Far more crucial is the question of Israeli-Arab birthrates. Over the period 1950–1993, the Israeli-Arab community grew at the extraordinary rate of 4% per annum, or from 160,000 to 785,000 out of a total population of 5 million. Non-Jews thus represented 16% of the population. Even with significant migration from abroad, the Israeli Jewish population over the same period grew by only 3.1% per annum. In the past two decades Jewish rates of natural increase and of immigration have been declining (Ben-Porath 1972, 503–539), although the influx of Soviet Jews after 1989 marginally reversed that trend.

Since the June War of 1967, Israel has occupied the West Bank, formerly under Jordanian control, and Gaza, formerly under Egyptian control, and has annexed East Jerusalem and the Golan Heights. In 1993 there were 795,000 Palestinians in Gaza and 1,150,000 in the West Bank and East Jerusalem. Israel's dilemma is twofold. First, if present trends continue, Israeli citizens of Arab origin will come to constitute as much as a quarter or a third of the population. A minority of that size, if not fully reconciled to the Israeli state, could destroy it, or at least its democratic system. Second, if Israel had decided, for security or religious reasons, to annex the West Bank and Gaza, that would have raised the proportion of non-Jews in Israel to around half. On political grounds alone, few Jewish Israelis were prepared to accept that. In a more profound sense it would have constituted the abandonment of the Zionist quest for a Jewish state. There were two alternatives: to expel the Palestinian populations from the West Bank or to concede sovereignty over the West Bank and Gaza to some sort of Palestinian entity. In 1993, after years of *intifada*, Israel and the Palestine Liberation Organization signed the Declaration of Principles that has, for the time being, cast the die in favor of the second alternative.

Although the problem has been seemingly less acute, Kuwait, the UAE, Qatar, and Saudi Arabia face politically perilous demographic situations. As does Israel, they domicile large numbers of residents without citizenship. For the most part these are migrant workers and professionals from the oil-poor countries of the region, as well as from India, Pakistan, and points farther east. In Kuwait there was also a substantial community of Palestinian refugees before 1991. In these countries not only is most of the workforce foreign but nearly half the resident population may also be foreign (see Chapter 15). Moreover, because they are worker-migrants, they are adults and preponderantly male. Illustrative sex-age charts for countries sending labor to the Gulf and those receiving labor appear in Figure 4.6. Although the economic life of these countries is dependent upon them, they have been excluded from political life. To date they have not exploited their strategic economic position to

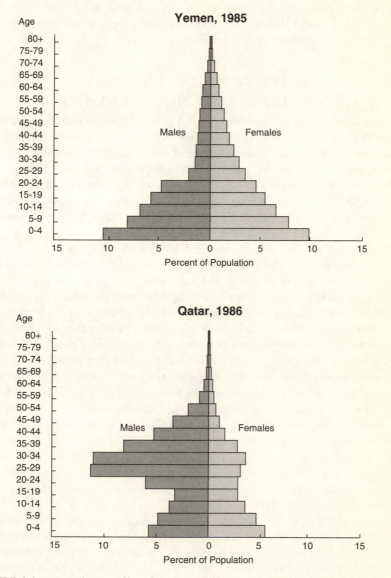

FIGURE 4.6   Age and sex profiles of Yemen and Qatar, mid-1980s. *Source:* UN (1991, 1992).

express political demands, but the fact that they might do so is sufficiently alarming that all the host states are actively pursuing policies to diminish their numbers (see Chapter 15).

Nearly every country in the Middle East is to some extent affected by the issues of counting various minorities and the different rates at which their numbers grow. In policy terms the ideal of the homogeneous nation-state in which every citizen is equal to every other is something of a myth. In that sense, the national census becomes the instrument both for determining relative weights and for granting or denying formal recognition to specific minorities.

RAPID POPULATION GROWTH AND THE WOULD-BE MIDDLE CLASS

Twenty-five years ago Halpern (1963, 62–66) wrote of the new middle class and the would-be middle class. He had in mind those educated Middle Easterners who had moved into the white-collar ranks of the civil service and the professions as well as the educated Middle Easterners who aspired to those ranks but could find no room in them. Part of the danger that Halpern foresaw was the formation of a kind of intellectual proletariat made up of upwardly mobile but frustrated young men. It must be stressed that it is only very recently that educated Middle Eastern women have entered the job market in appreciable numbers.

Over the past two decades, the structural problem that Halpern sketched has become far more acute. In the mid-1980s there were roughly 75 million Middle Easterners between the ages of fifteen and twenty-five out of a total population of around 270 million. Most of the males among them had some education—probably some 8 million had at least a secondary school diploma. Until the 1950s that much education would have qualified the recipient for a comfortable if unglamorous white-collar job, a decent standard of living, and a modicum of prestige. That is no longer the case. The young Middle Easterners recruited into the civil service and professions twenty to twenty-five years ago are not yet fifty years old. They have enjoyed rapid promotion, and some have risen to the top of their administrative hierarchies. They will not retire soon. Yet behind them are new, even larger cohorts of men and women with equal aspirations and sometimes better professional credentials. They are being offered make-work jobs or no jobs, salaries that lag behind inflation, and low social status. Their numbers are growing and will continue to grow for at least a generation. It is hard to see how and where they can be productively absorbed into the workforce. Because they are literate and politically aware, denying them material security is potentially dangerous.

It is reasonably clear that this age-group contributes significantly to various kinds of radical movements, from the street fighters of Beirut to the Islamic militants of Cairo or Tunis. One would be wrong, however, to attribute common political attitudes to an entire age-cohort. Its members are just as likely to be worker-migrants to the Gulf States or to be following conventional career paths in the bureaucracy or service sector as they are to be political activists. Yet the opportunities for them to achieve their aspirations will narrow as their numbers increase. It is not likely that they will be passive in the face of such a situation.

Middle Eastern regimes have experimented with an array of policies to contain the menace, from the creation of redundant civil service jobs to the encouragement of migration abroad. Until the rate at which jobs can be created comes into equilibrium with the rate at which this generation grows, these young people will constitute an important source of political instability in the Middle East. The region is not unique in this respect; much the same analysis could be applied to India or Mexico or a host of other developing countries. In the Middle East, however, the problem is more acute because, as a result of very high birthrates in the 1960s and 1970s, the relative number of new job seekers is also higher.

CONCLUSION

The approaches to population growth and control in developing countries have taken some peculiar twists. In the 1950s and 1960s the United States and other developed nations urged the LDCs to adopt national programs of family planning and population control. Many in the developing world saw these urgings as racist in nature—as white fear of the rising tide of blacks, browns, and yellows. Moreover, it was an era of grandiose development plans and optimism in the Third World. High rates of economic growth suggested that ever-larger numbers of people would be provided for and employed. It was assumed that larger cohorts of the young could be educated and trained so as to contribute to the growth effort rather than be a drain upon it. A striking example of this outlook is provided by President Houari Boumedienne, who in one speech (June 19, 1969) squelched a campaign for family planning that had been quietly building in Algeria. Inaugurating a huge steel works at Annaba, he said (as quoted in Waterbury 1973, 18):

> Our goal . . . over the next twenty years is to assure that our people, who will number 25 million souls, will have a standard of living which will be among the highest of the modern peoples of the world of tomorrow. I take this opportunity to say—concerning what is called "galloping demography"—that we are not partisans of false solutions such as the limitation of births. We believe that that is the same as suppressing difficulties instead of searching for adequate solutions. . . . We believe that the real solution to this problem resides in development, even if that demands greater efforts.

Few leaders in the Middle East today would be prepared to make such a statement. Indeed, despite the admonitions of Muslim leaders who tend to see the strength of Islam as lying in numbers, secular leaders have come to see the need to lower birthrates. As we have seen, even the Islamic Republic of Iran has dramatically reversed ground on its pronatalist policies and since the early 1990s has been actively pursuing policies of fertility control.

There do seem to be "carrying capacities" in various economic systems, and although they may be elastic, they are not infinitely so. To contribute to economic growth, each Middle Easterner needs good health, education, and some vocational or professional skills, but numbers have often overwhelmed the capacities of economies and administrations to provide these goods. In the next chapter we shall examine the disappointing record of the Middle East in this regard.

NOTES

1. Excluding China is necessary because that country's huge size and remarkable demographic performance makes its population dynamics atypical for LDCs. The Chinese CBR in 1992 was 19.

2. That is, "the total fertility rate represents the number of children that would be born per woman, assuming that she lives to the end of her childbearing years and bears children at each age in accord with prevailing age-specific fertility rates" (World Bank 1984, 282).

3. A comparison of the behavior of the government of Iran and Islamist opposition groups in the Arab world shows that Islamists' behavior out of power may be a poor predictor of their actions in power (Chapter 14).

4. These numbers assume that the growth rate predicted for 1993–2000 will be the same in 2000–2010. Given other demographic trends, this may be an overestimate. However, the calculation also assumes that the current (very low) levels of female labor force participation will remain unchanged. By any calculus, the magnitude of the job creation task is staggering.

5. Fargues gives a current total fertility rate of 3.0 for Tunisia, 3.5 for Morocco, and 4.6 for Algeria; by contrast, the World Bank gives figures of 3.7, 4.5, and 5.1, respectively, for these three countries (World Bank 1994g).

6. The TFR for Iraq and Syria is roughly 6, while that of Jordan is 5.2 (World Bank 1994g).

7. Fargues (1994) makes this point forcefully and at some length. His demographer's perspective (which takes a very long view) sometimes reads oddly to a political economist; to be told that the end of purely demographically driven growth in Tunisia is "not too far off" (161), in 2015, will be of small comfort to policymakers in Tunis.

8. This conclusion would be invalidated only if more rapid population growth either increased the domestic savings rate or stimulated additional capital inflows from abroad. There is no evidence to support either conjecture.

5

HUMAN CAPITAL: HEALTH, EDUCATION, AND LABOR MARKETS

Both those who lament and those who rejoice at rapid population growth can at least agree that standards of health and education must improve if poor counties are to raise their living standards. Few dispute the necessity of ameliorating health conditions and educating people as widely as possible—investing in human capital. Two strong reasons undergird this unusual consensus. First, all agree that good health and universal literacy are ends in themselves. A society that fails to educate its children and to eradicate preventable disease stands indicted of gross neglect of the general welfare. Second, analysts believe that healthier and better-educated people are more productive. There are important "virtuous circles" among education, health, fertility decline, and labor productivity. Neoclassical economists point to high rates of return on investments in human capital, while marxists stress the need for socialist regimes to liberate the productive potential of the masses. It is rare in the field of development studies to find such substantively similar conclusions emanating from such radically different perspectives.

Human-capital issues are particularly important for the countries of the Middle East and North Africa because, with the obvious exception of oil, the region is relatively poor in natural resources. Many analysts (e.g., Amuzegar 1983) therefore argue that development of human resources should lie at the center of national development plans. Unfortunately, the performance record of these countries is quite mixed. Health standards have improved during the past generation but still lag well behind what we would expect on the basis of per capita income levels alone. Although educational systems have expanded rapidly, adult illiteracy, especially among women, remains widespread. Here, as with questions of population growth, the issue of the status of women is critical; considerable evidence suggests that restrictions on women's choices block the achievment of high health standards.

Furthermore, the type of education that Middle Easterners receive too often fails to provide them with the skills and training that modern industrial and commercial life requires. Consequently, there is often a mismatch between the demand and the supply of skills; poor educational policy engenders labor-market disequilibria and exacerbates employment problems. At the same time, misconceived labor-market policies send socially inefficient signals to privately rational individuals and families; when an academic degree opens access to potential lifetime employment (even if at low wages), people will demand more higher education than society needs. Once such policies are in place, they consume scarce resources, leaving less for the more socially productive tasks of universal literacy. The past expansion of education, coupled with demography, has created a potent political force: secondary- and university-level students who often cannot find jobs consistent with their aspirations.

Despite these serious deficiencies, the current situation is nevertheless a considerable improvement over that which prevailed a generation ago. We have a glass half-empty/glass half-full situation: Current levels of health and education are unimpressive when compared with per capita incomes or with other regions, but change during the past generation has often been quite rapid. Starting from extremely low levels of health and literacy, many Middle Eastern nations have made dramatic advances during the past quarter century. They still have much unfinished business, but the achievements are undeniable. We may nevertheless fairly accuse some governments of neglecting or (even more commonly) misdirecting the "ultimate resource" of the region. In this chapter we shall examine the issues of health, education, and labor markets.

HEALTH ISSUES

Two points on health in the region stand out: Most countries have substantially improved their citizens' health conditions, but these conditions still fall well short of aspirations. "Good health" is obviously a multidimensional phenomenon; measuring it is correspondingly difficult. Two indicators are widely used as summary statements of health situations: life expectancy at birth (LEB) and infant mortality. LEB may be the single most robust indicator of national health conditions. Based on age-specific mortality rates, it tells us how long, on average, a newly born child can expect to live. It summarizes health, nutritional, and other welfare factors in a single, easily understood number. LEB figures for the region are shown in Table 5.1. Infant mortality is a second key indicator of the overall state of health of a country (Figure 5.1). Avoidable infant deaths are not only especially poignant but also symptomatic of wider health problems such as malnutrition, polluted water, and poor infant feeding practices. When just under 1 million infants die in a half-decade, as occurred in Turkey in the late 1970s, we know that much is wrong with the health conditions of the country.[1] Finally, we have seen in the last chapter that high infant mortality fosters high fertility and rapid population growth. From a demographic perspective as well as from a simple humanitarian one, understanding the causes of and remedies for high infant mortality is critical.

TABLE 5.1 Life Expectancy at Birth, 1965, 1985, and 1992

	1965	*1985*	*1992*
Algeria	50	60.5	67
Egypt	48.5	60.5	66
Iran	52	61	65
Iraq	51.5	60	–
Israel	71.5	70	76
Jordan	50	64	70
Kuwait	62.5	71.5	–
Libya	49.5	59	–
Morocco	49.5	59	63
Oman	41	63.5	70
Saudi Arabia	48	62	69
Sudan	40	48	52
Syria	56.5	63.5	67
Tunisia	50.5	62	68
Turkey	53.5	63.5	67
UAE	59	72	72
Yemen	37.5	45	53
Sweden	74	77	78
Industrial market economies	71	76	77

Health Levels and Rates of Change

Our evaluation of Middle Eastern health performance is greatly affected by whether we focus on health *levels* or on *rates of change* in those levels. From the first perspective, the region remains a relatively unhealthy place. Nearly half of the countries[2] have infant mortality rates over 50 per 1,000, which the United Nations Children's Fund (UNICEF) labels "high." Some observers believe that official data paint too rosy a picture (Kavalsky 1980). Moreover, these national numbers conceal considerable regional and social class variation. In some rural areas of the Sudan, two out of five children die before their fifth birthday; rural infant mortality rates routinely exceed urban throughout the region (el-Ghonemy 1984). In 1987 the Egyptian infant mortality rate varied from 91 in rural Upper Egypt to 44 in urban governorates (World Bank 1990b, 25). Class counts in urban areas as well: Infant mortality rates for lower and lower-middle classes in Damascus in 1976 were 83.7 and 72.8 per 1,000, compared with 55.5 and 34.4 for upper-middle and upper classes, respectively (Shorter 1985, 67). In the Middle East as elsewhere, the poor watch more of their children die than the rich.

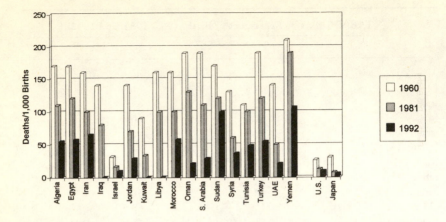

FIGURE 5.1   Infant mortality rates, 1960–1992. *Source:* UNICEF (1986).

At the same time, infant mortality is much lower than it was even twenty years ago, although performance varies widely by country (Figure 5.1), and for many countries of the region LEB has increased dramatically. A Middle Eastern child born in 1992 could expect to live eleven (for boys) or twelve (for girls) years longer than his or her parents born in 1970. Of course, LEB also varies widely by country, ranging from 52 years for a Yemeni male baby to 78 years for an Israeli or Kuwaiti girl (Table 5.1). Since the increase in LEB has been a worldwide phenomenon, we need a comparative perspective. We know that medical advances potentially affect all nations; for any given income level, LEB rises over time. However, the MENA region has done relatively well in improving health as measured by infant mortality rates and LEB in comparison with other regions of the world. Most notably, the decline in its infant mortality rates during the past generation (1970–1992) has been the sharpest of any region of the developing world (Figures 5.2 and 5.3). The MENA region has performed far better in reducing infant deaths than in lowering fertility (Chapter 4).

However, adopting a second type of comparative perspective clouds the picture. Middle Eastern health conditions are worse than would be predicted on the basis of incomes. We know that economic growth improves health. Carcinogenic industry notwithstanding, there is a clear positive correlation between LEB and per capita income; for a set of over one hundred countries, 45% of the variance in LEB (the dependent variable) may be attributed to variation in per capita income (Figure 5.4). Although no other single variable plays so important a role in explanations of cross-country differences in LEB, over half of the variance remains to be explained. Less formally, the recent experience of countries such as China and Sri Lanka shows that increased income is not a necessary condition for improving health; for both of these countries LEB is comparable to that of advanced industrial countries even though the World Bank considers them LDCs. Conversely, a highly inegalitarian pattern of

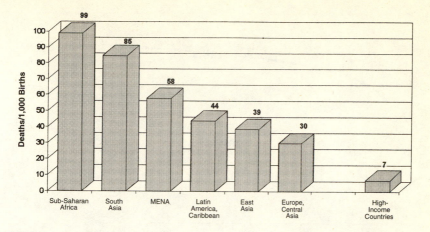

FIGURE 5.2   World infant mortality rates, 1992. *Source:* World Bank (1994g, 204–205).

economic growth may reduce infant mortality only very slowly. We need to scrutinize health performance in greater detail to understand why, despite rapid recent progress, most countries of the MENA region have poorer health conditions than their incomes would warrant.

Explanations for Mixed Health Performance

The reason so many babies and young children die unnecessarily in the Middle East does *not* seem to be lack of resources; only Latin America devotes a higher percentage of GDP to health expenditures than MENA countries (Shafik 1994b).[3] In gen-

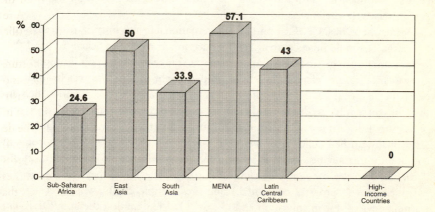

FIGURE 5.3   Percentage change in infant mortality shortfall (actual rate minus rate in high-income countries, or Sen Index), 1970–1992. *Source:* World Bank (1994g).

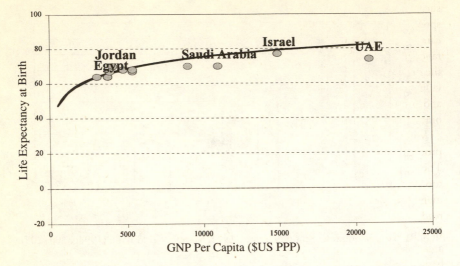

FIGURE 5.4   Per capita GNP and life expectancy, 1993. *Source:* World Bank (1994g).

eral, the problem is how the money is spent. We can approach this problem by asking what diseases kill babies (the "proximate" causes of infant death) and why they
contract these diseases or are not swiftly cured (its "underlying" causes). A great deal
is known about both of these questions. The tragedy of high infant mortality rates is
that most children in the Third World die from diseases that can be prevented, often
at very low cost. At least 40% of infant deaths are due to diarrhea.[4] Other major
child killers are diphtheria, whooping cough, tetanus, measles, poliomyelitis, tuber-
culosis, and malaria. With the partial exception of malaria, prevention of these diseases is relatively cheap with proven methods.

During the 1980s, UNICEF and other international health organizations advocated
a package of simple practices that could reduce infant mortality below 50 per 1,000:
growth monitoring, oral rehydration therapy, breast-feeding, and immunization.
Growth monitoring refers to the use of simple weight-for-age and weight-for-height
charts in infant and early child care to identify children who are malnourished and
therefore susceptible to disease. Although we can all recognize a starving person, most
of us cannot discern less advanced malnutrition without special training. Many mothers of malnourished children *do not know* that their children are suffering from this
condition until they become sick, when it may be too late to do much about it. But
if the children are brought into clinics for regular checkups, they can be weighed
and their growth progress monitored using these simple charts, which act as "early
warning-devices" for malnutrition and disease. Oral rehydration therapy (ORT) employs a simple mixture of sugar, salt, and water that when ingested enables the body to
retain the fluids whose loss is the cause of death in fatal cases of diarrhea. The cost of

such packets is less than US$0.05 apiece, and the mixing requires only a cup and a spoon. This is one of the most important and promising discoveries in infant health care in decades. Breast-feeding is essential for child welfare in the early months of infancy not only because human milk is the best "formula" for humans but also because the many antibodies in human milk provide crucial protection for the otherwise highly vulnerable infant. (After about six months a diet of human milk alone is inadequate and must be supplemented with other foods.) Finally, immunization is strongly recommended to prevent the ravages of the major infant and child killers listed above.

Middle Eastern countries have had a mixed experience with such practices. The problem with growth charts is that their use usually requires mothers to visit clinics. There are typically too few of these in most countries of the region, and the staff is too poorly paid to avoid significant delays and long waiting times. Consequently, many (especially poorer) residents use them only as a last resort, when the child is already sick and perhaps beyond simple treatment (U.S. Institute of Medicine 1979). In addition, in many countries such clinics are more abundant in urban than in rural areas, and too often the "treatment of patients by doctors is depersonalized and haughty" (U.S. Institute of Medicine 1979, 76). Although in countries such as Tunisia it was only in areas of extremely dispersed population that access to some kind of health care was a problem (H. Nelson 1979, 104), in the countries with the highest infant mortality rates, such as Yemen and the Sudan, rural outpatient clinics are rare indeed.

ORT has spread rapidly in the region. The large majority of MENA families now have access to ORT packets. (As usual, Yemen and the Sudan lag far behind.)[5] Egyptian experience is illuminating. During the 1980s, mothers' knowledge of ORT increased from 12% to 98% and the utilization of the packets by mothers rose from 27% to 68%. Only one in ten Egyptians lacks access to ORT packets. In 1980, dehydration from diarrhea killed over 100,000 Egyptian children every year; today fewer than half that number die of the same cause. Although most Middle Eastern women breast-feed their children, use of substitute infant formulas is spreading in some countries such as Yemen (Mynti 1985). One study found that Yemeni children fed with (often dirty) plastic nipples and bottles were *eight times* as likely to die as breast-fed Yemeni infants (UNICEF 1986). By contrast, breast-feeding until the age of six months appears to be nearly universal in Egypt (U.S. Institute of Medicine 1979). In contrast to the situation only a decade ago, most one-year-olds in the region have been immunized, although significant gaps in coverage exist in countries such as Turkey (72% immunized), Libya (69%), Iraq (82%), Lebanon (74%), Yemen (50%), and the Sudan (69%). In other countries, coverage is typically roughly 90% (UNDP 1994). Finally, all too often, the expansion of irrigation, an agricultural investment priority, increases the incidence of schistosomiasis and malaria.[6]

Three other measures are essential for reducing infant mortality: the so-called Three Fs, family spacing, food supplements, and female education. There is a strong correlation between infant health and the length of time between births. Too little time between births weakens the mother, thereby threatening her own health and that of her children. Short interbirth intervals are clearly the result of the failure to practice contraception, since, in contrast to practice in many sub-Saharan African societies, prolonged sexual abstinence after the birth of a child is not common in the region (Figure 5.5).

Food supplements are designed to break the synergies between malnutrition and disease. Not only does malnutrition reduce resistance but also disease can engender malnutrition by impeding the body's ability to absorb or properly utilize ingested nutrients. Compared with other Third World regions, Middle Eastern countries have done well here. The World Bank has estimated that only 10% of the people of the region receive "insufficient calories for an active working life" (i.e., less than 90% of the caloric intake recommended by the Food and Agriculture Organization/ World Health Organization [FAO/WHO]), as compared with 13% in Latin America, 14% in East Asia and the Pacific, 44% in sub-Saharan Africa, and 50% in South Asia (World Bank 1986b, 17).

There are, however, important national and international variations. For example, as many as one in five Moroccans may be malnourished, and throughout the region rural areas with scarce land appear to be worse off than urban areas, where extensive food subsidy systems prevail. Significant class biases in nutrition also exist. Typically, the lack of purchasing power, rather than failures of national (much less global) food supplies, causes hunger everywhere (Sen 1981a; World Bank 1986b). A nationwide survey conducted in 1978 in Egypt found that approximately 50% of children from low-income families suffered from mild-to-moderate protein/calorie malnutrition (U.S. Institute of Medicine 1979).[7] And, as elsewhere within disadvantaged groups, the members suffering most severely from malnutrition are children and pregnant and lactating women, hence the idea of "food supplements" to bring the supply of nutrients up to the high demands of such groups. Few Middle Eastern governments

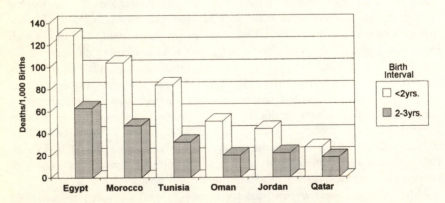

FIGURE 5.5   Birth spacing and infant mortality. *Source:* Demographic health surveys (Egypt, 1992; Jordan, 1990; Morocco, 1992; Tunisia, 1988), child health surveys (Oman, 1992; Qatar, 1991) reported in World Bank (1994e, 17).

have supplementary-feeding programs, although most have sharply reduced malnutrition through extensive, untargeted, and costly consumer food subsidy systems.

The last F, female education, may be the key to health conditions in the region. Caldwell (1986) showed that for a sample of ninety-nine countries the best predictor of both infant mortality rates and LEB was the 1960 female primary enrollment rate. He argued that nations with "exceptionally good" performances (China, Sri Lanka, the Indian state of Kerala, and Costa Rica) had relatively high degrees of "female autonomy" and that nine of the eleven worst performers were Middle Eastern, Muslim countries.[8] Since in all Third World countries women have primary responsibility for child care, it is essential that they be sufficiently well educated and accustomed to taking initiatives on their children's behalf. They must recognize early-warning signs (such as a child's failure to grow properly), understand disease origins and prevention, and be ready and able to act immediately to seek remedies. All such behavior, of course, presupposes female literacy. Caldwell argued that this kind of basic education is only a necessary, not a sufficient, condition for such autonomy. If a woman is educated but is not in the habit of venturing out of her home unaccompanied, he asserted, child health will still suffer.[9]

Most Middle Eastern mothers cannot read or write. For assessing current health, the key statistic is the enrollment ratio of the 1970s, since that is when today's (typically young) Middle Eastern mother was of school age. In 1960 most Middle

TABLE 5.2   Primary School Enrollments (%), 1991

	1970		1991	
	Total	*Female*	*Total*	*Female*
Algeria	76	58	95	88
Egypt	72	57	101	93
Iran	72	52	112	105
Israel	96	95	95	96
Jordan	–	–	97	68
Morocco	52	–	66	54
Oman	3	1	100	96
Saudi Arabia	45	29	77	72
Sudan	38	29	50	43
Syria	78	59	109	103
Tunisia	100	–	117	110
Turkey	110	94	110	110
UAE	93	71	115	114
Yemen	22	7	76	37

Figures include reenrollments and thus may exceed 100%.
Source: UNICEF (1986, 120–121); World Bank (1994g, 216–217).

Eastern girls were *not* in school. By 1970 over half were enrolled, and by 1985 three of four were in school (UNESCO 1987). Today, nearly 90% of girls in the region are enrolled, although Morocco (54% in school), the Sudan (43%), and Yemen (37%) lag behind (Table 5.2).

Here, as with questions of fertility, one must ask what, if any, is the role of Islam in generating the outcome of low female literacy and attendant high infant mortality. We argued in Chapter 4 that although people's (culturally derived) attitudes were obviously important, the impact of culture on fertility, child health, and women's education is affected by political systems. Some studies show that the percentage of Muslims in the population does not help to explain relatively low female enrollments, once incomes and other resources available for education are included (Heyneman 1993). The decline in infant mortality and the increase in female enrollment in primary school in recent history have been rapid both under regimes espousing a socialist ideology (the People's Democratic Republic of Yemen [PDRY], Iraq, Libya, and Syria) and under more conservative governments (Tunisia, Turkey, and Pahlavi Iran). With the exception of the former PDRY, none of these regimes was/is officially non-Muslim, while the Islamic Republic of Iran now has enrolled all girls in primary school. There can be little doubt that most regimes dominated by male Muslims (i.e., all regimes in MENA except Israel and, to some extent, Lebanon) have rapidly expanded the enrollment and education of women. In the first edition of this book we wrote: "It is plausible to predict that the decline in infant mortality rates in the region will accelerate as the schoolgirls of the 1980s become the mothers of the 1990s and 2000s" (112). This is exactly what has happened.

EDUCATIONAL SYSTEMS

As with health conditions, our assessment of Middle Eastern progress in education depends upon whether we look at current conditions or at the speed of change. On the one hand, present levels of literacy[10] in the Middle East are low; on the other hand, most nations have expanded educational opportunities rapidly during the past generation. Again, conditions vary considerably not only from one country to another but also between urban and rural areas and between social classes. As stressed above, the education of women has lagged but has advanced markedly in recent years from a very low starting point. Finally, the rapid *quantitative* expansion, particularly when combined with fiscal austerity (Chapter 9), has generated serious *qualitative* deficiencies in education.

Literacy Rates

In most countries, according to the World Bank, rates of literacy remain unjustifiably low (see Table 4.2). In only two countries (Israel and the UAE) can more than four of five adults read and write. More than three-quarters of adults are literate in Jordan, Lebanon, and Turkey, while Kuwait has nearly achieved 75% literacy. Literacy stands between one-half and two-thirds in Algeria, Iran, Iraq, Libya, Tunisia, Saudi

Arabia, and Syria, while less than half of adults are literate in Egypt, Morocco, Sudan, and Yemen. This is not an impressive picture. Furthermore, illiteracy is concentrated among women. In only seven countries of the region can a majority of adult women read and write; by contrast, in Southeast Asia and Latin America most women are illiterate only in Cambodia, Haiti, and Guatemala. Egyptian female literacy is about equal to that in India and lower than that in Rwanda. Again, illiteracy in the Middle East as elsewhere is concentrated in rural areas and among the poor. Although about two-thirds of urban Egyptian adults were literate in 1990, a little less than one-third of their country cousins could read and write. A 1990–1991 survey in Morocco showed a similar pattern (Table 5.3). Finally, even in countries that have devoted large resources to primary education, there are now more illiterate people than there were a generation ago. With only a few exceptions, population growth has swamped a generation of efforts to diffuse basic education.

These are unpleasant facts, and a comparative perspective affords little comfort. As before, two types of comparison seem apposite: with other regions and those with respect to per capita incomes. If adult literacy is our standard, the Middle East is relatively backward (Figure 5.6). Regional literacy barely exceeds that in sub-Saharan Africa. Only South Asia has a markedly poorer level of literacy performance than MENA. Adult literacy rates in the region are also below what we would predict on the basis of per capita incomes alone (Figure 5.7). These human-capital deficiencies place the region at a serious disadvantage in competing in international markets with countries from Eastern Europe, the former Soviet Union, Southeast Asia, and Latin America.[11]

However, a historical perspective partially mitigates this grim picture. One must remember that Middle Eastern countries launched their educational efforts from a very low base. The anciens régimes of the region did essentially nothing to educate most of their people. In some cases, education of the rural poor was actively discouraged, as on the estates of wealthy Egyptians under the Farouk monarchy (Richards 1982; Adams 1986). Arab and Berber children in North Africa were either entirely excluded from education or channeled into segregated schools under French colonial rule.[12] These countries faced severe difficulties in expanding their educational facilities after independence. There was a mass exodus of teachers, nearly all of whom

TABLE 5.3   Moroccan Literacy (%), 1990–1991

Category	Urban	Rural	National
Male	76.5	45.3	60.5
Female	51.4	12.8	31.7
Total	63.3	28.2	45.3

Source: Kingdom of Morocco (1992, 155).

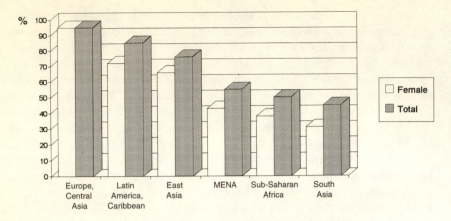

FIGURE 5.6   Adult literacy in major world regions, 1990. *Source:* World Bank (1994g, 162–163).

were Europeans: In Algeria, 27,000 of 30,000 teachers left in 1962; only one-fifth of the 20,000 new Algerian teachers were qualified (Bennoune 1988, 220). Many countries have come a long way since colonial days, when two-thirds to three-quarters of the people of the region were illiterate. By way of comparison, when South Korea shifted its development strategy to export-led growth in the early 1960s, over 70% of the population could already read and write.

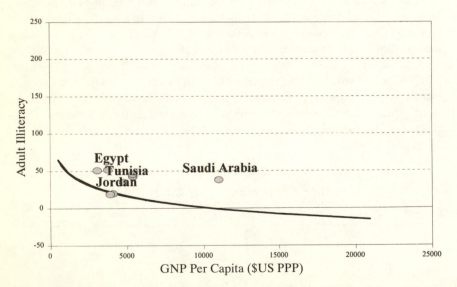

FIGURE 5.7   Per capita GNP and adult illiteracy, 1993. *Source:* Calculated from data in World Bank (1994g).

Not only do levels of literacy vary widely by country, but rates of improvement also show considerable differences. There is some dispute on how best to measure improvements in literacy. The simplest approach is to look at percentage changes in literacy rates. However, analysts such as Sen have argued that this approach biases results in favor of countries that begin with low literacy rates.[13] Sen advocated instead looking at the percentage change in literacy shortfall, that is, the percentage change in the difference between actual literacy and the goal of 100% literacy (Sen 1981b). Such a calculation is displayed in Figure 5.8. Whatever the measure, performance varies widely by country. In general, the wealthy oil-exporting states did very well during the past generation. During the past decade, the best performers (measured by the Sen Index) have been Saudi Arabia, Turkey, and Jordan, while the worst performance has been in the Nile Valley (Egypt and the Sudan).

Historical legacies alone do not explain persistently high adult illiteracy. With the exception of Iraq, Algeria, and the former PDRY, Middle Eastern countries have largely ignored the problem of illiterate adults, choosing instead to concentrate resources on educating children. Here the record is more encouraging, although some countries of the region still have much unfinished business (see Table 5.2). Overall, 98% of children are now enrolled in primary school. Enrollment is nearly universal in all countries except Saudi Arabia, Morocco, the Sudan, and Yemen. The most rapid progress has been in Oman, which went from essentially no schooling (3% enrollment) to nearly universal enrollment in one generation.[14] Enrollment of girls has also improved considerably; female primary enrollment is universal or nearly so (>95%) in eight countries. Morocco, the Sudan, and Yemen lag behind, as does Saudi Arabia to a lesser extent. When measured by the Sen Index, the most rapid progress in enrollments has been in Egypt, Iran, Oman, Syria, and the UAE, followed by Algeria and Yemen. Saudi Arabia and (especially) Morocco and the Sudan

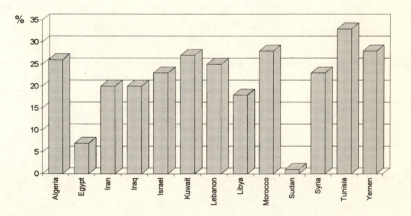

FIGURE 5.8   Percentage change in literacy shortfall (100% literacy minus actual literacy rate), 1980–1990. *Source:* Calculated from data in World Bank (1994g).

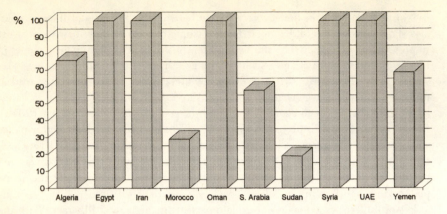

FIGURE 5.9   Percentage change in enrollment shortfall (100% enrollment minus actual enrollment rate), 1970–1991. *Source:* Calculated from data in World Bank (1994g).

have made the slowest progress (Figure 5.9). Despite the rather poor performance by populous countries such as the Sudan, primary enrollments have risen vertiginously throughout the region.

In contrast to the total number of illiterate persons, the total number of children not in school has declined in most countries since 1960. Illiteracy is increasingly a phenomenon of older people, as the numbers from Morocco show (Table 5.4). This "generation gap" may have far-reaching sociopolitical consequences (Chapter 14).

Educational-Allocation Decisions and Their Effects

Most countries of the region have made strenuous efforts to improve education. Governments allocate a relatively high percentage of expenditure to education; the

TABLE 5.4   Moroccan Literacy by Age (%), 1990–1991

Age (years)	Males	Females	Total
10–14	78.1	56.2	67.2
15–24	78.0	48.5	62.4
25–44	62.2	27.2	43.6
45–59	33.9	4.5	17.8
60+	14.1	0.7	7.1
Total	60.5	31.7	45.3

Source: Kingdom of Morocco (1992, 155, 159, 163).

share of education in government expenditure also rose from an already relatively high base during the 1980s in virtually all countries (World Bank 1994g).[15] Shares range from a low of 11.7% (Lebanon) to a high of 33.1% (Algeria), a level that the country has maintained since the mid-1970s (Bennoune 1988). Although there are exceptions (e.g., the Sudan, which allocates consistently less than 10% of funds to education), lack of spending is not the major problem with most educational systems in the region.

The real difficulty with most Middle Eastern educational systems is how the money is spent. Literacy rates remain low and children remain out of school because gender, urban, and class biases are rampant in many countries' educational-allocation decisions. Despite the improvements in female enrollment, gender biases remain. Rural enrollment rates are consistently lower than urban throughout the region, and dropout rates are higher. For example, by the late 1970s over 90% of urban Egyptian children were in school, while only 70% of rural Delta children and 60% of rural Upper Egyptian children were enrolled (Nyrop 1982). Whereas primary enrollment rates in 1977 in Algiers and Oran were over 85%, in some rural districts (e.g., Djelfa) they were less than 50% (Bennoune 1988). These gaps have narrowed but have not disappeared.

The reasons for this lie in both supply and demand. Many widely dispersed rural children are far from any school. Countries that insist on separate schools for girls and boys multiply the costs of schooling. It is especially difficult to attract women teachers to rural areas. At the same time, many rural families see no point in educating all of their children. It is quite common in the region for rural families to make sacrifices to educate at least one son; one study of Turkey found that the highest rates of return to investment in education were obtained by the sons of farmers attending primary school (Özgediz 1980), while observers of rural Egypt often note that peasant families will try to educate at least one son through high school in the hope that he will obtain a secure government job. Educating all children and especially all daughters is expensive and has low priority. Children can and do contribute to peasant family budgets at young ages by tending animals, helping with processing, harvesting cotton, weaving rugs, and so forth. And peasant attitudes toward women's status die hard; Upper Egyptian peasants asserted to one researcher in the 1980s that sending girls to school was "shameful" (Adams 1986, 142).

However, it is not simply high costs, peasant attitudes, and home economics that impede universalizing primary education in the region. Only a few countries have made investment in rural and/or female education a top priority of their educational plans; funds go elsewhere. Many countries of the region display class bias in their educational expenditures and enrollment profiles. In Morocco, for example, children from upper-income families are twice as likely to be enrolled as children from low-income families. Rural and especially rural female enrollments lag far behind those in urban areas. Throughout the region, primary and secondary education get about the same amount of money, despite the much higher primary enrollments (Shafik 1994). University education, which is far more expensive than other types, gobbles up anywhere from 33% (Jordan) to 16% (Morocco) of all educational spending (UNDP 1994).

Such allocations are extremely difficult to justify economically; much evidence suggests that, if educational spending is (properly) treated as an investment, the social rate of return[16] is highest to investment in lower grades. The most recent calculations have confirmed what has long been known: (1) both social and private rates of return are highest for lower grades, and (2) although private returns exceed social returns at all levels, the gap widens at higher levels (Table 5.5). It is politics, not economics, that dictates the bias in favor of secondary and, especially, higher education.

The politics of this all-too-common distortion in the allocation of human-capital spending is not hard to understand. First, there is, of course, some complementarity between diffusing primary education and widening more advanced educational opportunities. Someone has to teach the children, and a growing, industrializing economy needs more advanced skills as well as basic literacy and numeracy. This need is especially acute in countries that inherit little skilled labor from colonialism or the ancien régime and that are eager to defend their independence. Given the "national project" of Arab Socialist, Atatürkist, and other early developmentalist regimes in the region, it is hardly surprising that they have vigorously promoted the development of university training.

Second, the urban middle classes have had a disproportionate influence on policy. Planners themselves typically come from such backgrounds, and regimes have sought to open up more room at the top, via greater access to higher education, as a mechanism of income redistribution. And since the private rate of return to higher education remains very high, middle-class families press for space in the universities. Regimes wishing to mollify this social group have responded by rapidly expanding secondary and higher education. Vested interests, created by past state policies (by history), may be the main blockage to more socially rational and equitable allocation of educational resources (see Box 5.1).[17]

Other commonly voiced complaints about Middle Eastern education are that its quality is very low, that dropout rates are high, and that too few students master technical subjects, especially math and science. One in five Algerian primary school students leaves before completing the curriculum (Bennoune 1988). In Morocco,

TABLE 5.5 **Rates of Return on Educational Investment in MENA**

Educational Level	Social Rate of Return	Private Rate of Return	Gap
Primary	15.5	17.4	0.9
Secondary	11.2	15.9	4.7
Higher	10.6	21.7	11.1

Source: Psacharopoulos (1994, 1328).

BOX 5.1
THE MISALLOCATION OF EDUCATIONAL RESOURCES IN EGYPT

Egypt provides perhaps the most striking case of class bias in education. Forty years after Nasser's revolution, less than half of adult Egyptians can read and write, while the country boasts thirteen universities. Nearly 30% of educational spending is allocated to universities. Between 1952–1953 and 1976–1977 the number of secondary school students in Egypt rose from 181,789 to 796,411, or at a rate of 14% per annum. Primary school enrollment rose at exactly half that rate and university enrollments at more than double it, or 32% per annum. Higher-education enrollments doubled in only four years (1971–1976) and then increased another 50% by 1984 (to over 660,000). In fiscal 1984/85 higher education consumed nearly 38% of all spending on education (while nearly one-quarter of girls were not enrolled in primary school). The proportion of science students declined from 55% in 1971 to 25% in the mid-1980s, and at all levels the quality of education was very poor, dominated by rote memorization. None of this made educational or economic sense.

These trends were unintended outcomes of the worthy goal of democratizing education, a process that had started even before the military seized power in 1952. The main nationalist party, the Wafd, controlled the government and parliament in 1950 and, in what Kerr termed "a demagogic bid" (1965, 176), not only opened the secondary schools to anyone who completed primary school but also made instruction tuition-free. After the abolition of the monarchy and the establishment of the Egyptian republic, the Free Officers continued these policies. In 1957 a usually tame Egyptian parliament rose up against an attempt to restrict admission of secondary school graduates to the university and imposed a policy of tuition-free admission to universities for any Egyptian in possession of a secondary school diploma. The fatal sequence was thus established: All primary school graduates could go to secondary school, all secondary school graduates to the university, and all university graduates were entitled to a government job.

Much of the demand for secondary and higher education was a demand for the credential necessary to wait for a government job. Over half of university graduates and more than half of secondary school graduates sought jobs in the public sector (Fergany 1991). From 1976 to 1986, 90% of new jobs for Egyptians came either from the government or from emigration abroad (Handoussa 1989). The government made university education especially attractive by heavily subsidizing students and by guaranteeing government jobs to all graduates, thereby greatly increasing the private returns to university education. It is privately rational for a family to sacrifice to get a member through the university; the graduate can then join the job queue for government employment (effectively lifetime), which, although low-paying, can easily be combined with a second job and provides a kind of "income insurance." The educational system thus interacts with labor-market policies to misdirect social spending and to generate unnecessary unemployment (since graduates tend to wait for government jobs).

Even ignoring the fact that many of these graduates acquired only marginally useful skills, there is little doubt that the country's development would have been better served by shifting resources out of more advanced education toward primary schooling. Recently there have been changes in educational policies; primary enrollment is nearly universal, university enrollments actually declined in the late 1980s by about 100,000, and the government's job guarantee is in practice ignored. Vested interests are, however, sufficiently strong to keep the law on the books. This stimulates misallocations elsewhere in the economy, most prominently in the government's commitment to land reclamation, which it uses to "pay off" graduates. As we shall see in Chapter 6, this policy is creating pressure on water supplies. The ramifications of misguided educational policies can be very wide indeed (CAPMAS 1989; Richards 1992a).

---

about one-third of university students are in technical or scientific studies, 56% study the humanities and social sciences, and the remaining 12% are preparing to be teachers (*Annuaire Statistique du Maroc* 1984). These choices are individually rational; Middle Eastern students, like their counterparts in the West, select careers with an eye on the job market (Psacharopoulos 1980). Thus although agricultural studies retain their traditionally low status in the country, many students enroll in them because of expanding placement opportunities. If students are not developing the proper skills, it is because the society and, especially, the state are not sending them the correct signals.

One way to use the relatively swollen numbers of university and secondary students in countries with many illiterate adults would be to launch adult-literacy campaigns. However, only a few states of the region have ever tried to do this. In most cases, the explanation seems to be that the government fears the political impact of such campaigns; the young people who will go to the slums and villages to teach may hold more radical political views than the regime. Governments in Morocco, the Sudan, and Egypt may plausibly fear fostering contact between Islamist students and the large numbers of illiterate adults, many of whom might be sympathetic to the political messages that are usually imparted along with literacy in such campaigns. Only if a regime feels politically secure and believes that it can control and shape the content of the materials used in literacy campaigns will such efforts occur.[18]

Increasing class size has not been a key problem in Middle Eastern primary education. Pupil-teacher ratios are typically lower than the average for LDCs (34), and nearly all MENA countries have lower ratios than the Republic of Korea (34) and Costa Rica (32), both of which have invested heavily and successfully in human capital (UNDP 1994). There is little evidence that learning or later performance is linked to class size (Colclough 1982). Of course, one may well question the *quality* of the teachers whose numbers have grown so rapidly; from 1970 to 1983 the number of primary teachers nearly doubled, the number of secondary teachers more than doubled, and the number of university teachers nearly tripled (UNESCO 1975; 1980).

Probably more important than class size are pedagogical methods, teacher quality, and morale. All too often, education in the region mimics traditional madrasas (Islamic schools, where boys memorize parts of the Koran), with their emphasis on rote learning, rather than stressing problem solving, writing skills, or creativity. Few teachers, especially in poorer areas, have access to any materials but simple textbooks and paper; even these may be in short supply. Teachers in the Middle East do not enjoy markedly high social status, and rural posts are too often assigned to those with the worst academic performance. Teachers receive low pay, as do all civil servants.

Much of the money spent on education goes to teachers' and administrators' salaries. Educational quality has been crushed between constricting budgets and exploding enrollments. All available funds go to paying teachers; very little is left over to spend on books, equipment, or other educational materials. In Egypt, for example, while real educational expenditure per pupil increased over 400% from 1980 to 1989, real nonwage spending per pupil fell nearly 300%. Salaries consume over 90% of the educational budget (World Bank 1994g). These fiscal realities play a large role in the rote-memorization approach to learning from kindergarten to university throughout the region.

Given the working conditions in the poorer countries, it is hardly surprising that many teachers seek employment in the oil states. Egyptian schoolteachers can make at least *ten times* their domestic salaries in Saudi Arabia; small wonder that more than 50,000 of them are working abroad, while thousands more seek to leave. Indeed, one of the difficulties with maintaining, much less advancing, the educational systems of countries such as the Sudan and Yemen has been the departure of the small number of trained teachers to the Gulf States. Yemeni and Sudanese teachers in the Gulf, however, suffered the same fate as their fellow nationals during the Gulf crisis of 1990—expulsion (Chapter 15).

Although a more extensive discussion of the consequences of international migration is offered in Chapter 15, a few points on the impact of migration on the educational systems of both sending and receiving countries are in order. First, given the extremely low levels of adult literacy in most of the major oil-exporting countries, rapid expansion of their primary enrollments required large-scale importation of teachers. Second, such teachers had to be fluent in Arabic, and therefore Egyptians as well as Jordanians and Palestinians were prominently represented. Third, such teachers usually dramatically improved their private welfare. Fourth, there is little evidence that such emigration outflows exceeded the recruitment and training of new teachers; as noted above, pupil-teacher ratios continued to fall during the 1970s in Egypt, Jordan, and other major suppliers of teachers. Fifth, although this implies that the export of teachers had few negative consequences in countries with high enrollment ratios, the same argument is much weaker in Egypt and the Sudan. After all, the favorable pupil-teacher ratios were achieved in part by slow growth of the numerator—by sluggish improvement in the (low) percentage of Egyptian and Sudanese children in school. The Gulf crisis opened up new opportunities for Egyptian and Syrian teachers, thanks to the expulsion of Palestinians, Jordanians, and Yemenis.

Secondary Education, Social Mobility, and Politics

Prior to direct European control and the consolidation of large bureaucratic state systems, literacy in the Middle East was a skill limited to a relative few and, among Muslims, one valued more for providing access to the sacred text of the Koran than for its contribution to everyday life. As the range of government activities grew, so did the need for literate, white-collar staff: clerks, accountants, and (although not many) managers. After World War I, nationalist movements throughout the Middle East put mass education at the top of their list of demands. Their concerns were twofold. First, nationalist leaders believed that Europe's strength in large measure stemmed from its educational systems and educated citizenries. As long as Middle Eastern societies were deprived of such systems and citizens, the societies would remain backward and subjugated. Second, these same leaders decried the elitism inherent in the new school systems promoted by colonial powers in the Middle East. Secondary education was limited to a narrow stratum of the population, often the offspring of the indigenous well-to-do, whom the colonial authorities wished to keep on their side. The object of the systems was to produce the clerks necessary to staff the colonial administration itself and the banks and businesses that sustained the economic links between the colony and the metropole. Only a handful of Middle Easterners ever received a university education. With the exception of Cairo University, universities in Istanbul and Ankara set up by the independent Turkish republic, and the American University of Beirut, there were no universities in the region. The very fortunate could go to the United Kingdom (UK), France, Germany, or even the United States for advanced studies. In Algeria on the eve of the revolutionary war in 1954, out of a native population of 10 million only 7,000 were in secondary school and only 600 had gone on to university-level studies. Although the elitism of the Algerian situation was more pronounced than elsewhere, it was a difference in degree, not in kind.

Thus the colonial authorities could and did use the educational system as an instrument to bestow favors on select groups and to produce the staff that would work in the trenches of the colonial administration. The nationalist leaders who criticized the elitism and manipulativeness of these policies knew whereof they spoke. Overwhelmingly they were among the elite and not infrequently cogs in the colonial administrations' wheels.

In the interwar years a number of ideas became rooted in the popular mind, among them the belief that education and literacy are rights of all citizens rather than privileges. Once independence was achieved, nationalist leaders were held to this notion. In addition, the link between secondary education and stable, respectable white-collar employment was firmly established. All, from peasants and tradespeople to craftspeople and manual laborers, saw their children's education as the key to moving upward in society and also as a hedge against the day when they would be too old or infirm to work.

The new states of the Middle East kept their promises in various ways. On the one hand, there was the temptation to yield to popular (i.e., middle-class) pressure and open the gates of secondary and university education nearly as wide as those of primary education. In most cases the financial costs of such a policy appeared prohibitive. Typically, per student outlays in secondary school are two to three times higher than in primary school, and university outlays may be ten times higher. The demands for and costs of teacher training for secondary education are also commensurately higher. Alongside these concerns was the realization that the economy needed skilled craftspeople, technicians, and low-level supervisory personnel as much as or more than it needed civil servants. Secondary education has nevertheless become much more widespread in the past twenty years (Table 5.6). MENA secondary enrollment rates are now the highest of any region in the developing world (though, again, not for girls). The increasing flood of secondary school students into the labor market constitutes a critical challenge facing economic policymakers and political strategists (see below and Chapter 14).

Those with the lowest secondary enrollment ratios in general are also the poorest, the Sudan and Yemen. The richest economies tend to have higher ratios, but Jordan and, especially, Egypt appear to be exceptional performers in comparison with their per capita incomes. Despite this apparently excellent performance, only Jordan and, to a lesser extent, Israel have ratios that approach those of upper-income countries. In 1992 the ratio in the United States was 90%, in Japan 97%, in France 100%, and in South Korea 88%. The same bleak and politically ominous scenario as that sketched above for Egypt (Box 5.1) can be run for a number of other states, especially those that followed programs of state-centered socialism (Syria, Iraq, Tunisia, and Algeria, in particular). Moreover, as in the case of rapid population growth itself, the "problem" is one posed for the society and economy as a whole. For any individual the private returns to any education are very high; to be frustrated in one's career aspirations is better than to be denied those aspirations in the first place.

With that in mind, we may turn briefly to Morocco, a former French protectorate, a monarchy with no socialist pretensions, and a country where there is a severe weeding out of students between primary and secondary school. Yet here again we see an accelerated expansion of secondary and university enrollments while primary school enrollments increase slowly. In 1992 Morocco spent over 18% of its GDP on education. It is important to remember that as secondary and university

TABLE 5.6   Enrollments in Secondary and Higher Education (%), 1970–1991

	Secondary				University	
	Total		Female		Total	
	1970	*1991*	*1970*	*1991*	*1970*	*1991*
Algeria	11	60	6	53	–	–
Egypt	35	80	23	73	18	19
Iran	27	57	18	49	4	12
Israel	57	85	60	89	29	34
Jordan	–	91	–	62	27	25
Morocco	13	57	7	29	6	10
Oman	–	46	–	53	0	6
Saudi Arabia	12	22	5	41	7	13
Sudan	7	20	4	20	2	3
Syria	38	50	21	43	18	19
Tunisia	23	46	13	42	5	9
Turkey	27	51	15	40	6	15
UAE	22	69	9	73	2	11
Yemen	03	31	–	–	–	–
Thailand	62	83	65	86	18	22
Philippines	46	74	–	75	28	28
Indonesia	16	45	11	41	4	10
China	24	51	–	45	1	2
MENA	24	56	15	51	10	15
Latin America	28	57	26	54	15	18
East Asia	24	50	–	47	4	5

Source: World Bank (1994g).

enrollments grow more rapidly than primary enrollments, their share of total outlays grows even more rapidly.

In sum, the costly effort throughout the region to expand secondary and university education has to some extent backfired because it has proved impossible to maintain exacting standards of instruction at the same time. Schools, whether urban or rural, are primitive; drafty and cold in the winter, ovenlike in the spring. They are run-down because of inadequate budgets for maintenance; there may be no or very little artificial lighting, broken windows, missing blackboards, primitive and insalubrious plumbing, and classrooms crowded with benches and desks looking like relics from a war zone. The din has to be heard to be believed. The students who suffer through this are often ill-clothed and ill-fed and must return to homes where there is no place to study and perhaps little understanding among the older generation of what modern education is all about.

It is moot under these circumstances whose morale is lower, that of the students or that of the teachers. For the latter, pay is low, student-teacher ratios high, and support equipment nonexistent. That teachers resort to rote learning punctuated by long periods of chanting and calisthenics in what passes for the schoolyard is hardly surprising. Nor is their absenteeism. Young male teachers, thrust as bachelors into village schools, face long periods of sexual and social frustration. The teaching profession, like the diplomas it produces, has lost its prestige. Normal schools attract the least capable university students. It is a miracle that the system functions at all.

In this situation, privileged classes have reproduced themselves in part through their ability to put their children through an educational process that gives them career advantages and excludes most of their compatriots of a similar age. Thus, despite the professed ideal of the region's governments to make the educational system without cost and open to all, a number of practices have developed that have maintained its class bias.

One avenue is offered through private schools, although it is safe to say that nowhere in the Middle East is there a truly elite system of private secondary schools such as one finds in the United States, the UK, or even India. At one time Victoria College in Alexandria or Robert College in Istanbul played such a role, but that is no longer the case. Christian missionary schools in the past were occasionally sought out because of high-quality education and foreign-language training, but their day, in societies that are preponderantly Muslim, has passed. The Christian minority of Lebanon has always maintained good private educational institutions, and perhaps even the civil war has failed to disrupt them. We are currently witnessing a resurgence of private Muslim education, especially at the primary level. Its aim is, however, to safeguard Muslim values and practices rather than to promote the interests of a privileged class.

A second prop for the protection of privilege comes through the acquisition of foreign languages, especially English. Whether one points toward a career in industry, foreign trade, or banking and finance, mastering English, German, or French may be requisite to rising to the top. This brings us to the consequences—perhaps unintended, perhaps not—of Arabization, or Persianization, or Turkishization. Having all one's young citizens learn the national language is a logical and laudable policy, a blow for democratization and cultural revitalization. But those who learn only Arabic, Turkish, or Persian will be able to rise only so far in the civil service, in professions such as medicine or engineering, or in modern industry and finance. Some critics have seen in the efforts to Arabize a plot on the part of the privileged to keep control of the commanding heights, for their children can afford secondary schools with quality instruction in foreign languages and are likely to do their university studies abroad or in disciplines that require foreign-language competency.

This question is most relevant for formerly French North Africa. There indigenous civil service and professional elites were educated almost exclusively in French. Even after independence, French continued to be the official language of the government and the military. Such a situation was seen as absurd, as the local populations were very largely Arabic-speaking and thus unable to share the discourse of those who governed them. The governments of Tunisia, Algeria, and Morocco began to Arabize school and then university curricula while slowly promoting Arabic as the main language of government. In theory, a North African today, monolingual in Arabic, has an equal chance with one who knows more than one language to achieve any position in society. In practice, it is probably still the case that entry into the technocratic and intellectual elites requires a mastery of French or English. The offspring of incumbent elites are the most likely to have that competency.

In many Middle Eastern societies the public school system may be the only one available to the well-off. Facilities and teaching quality are supposed to be uniform throughout the system. Everywhere it is the central government that finances school budgets, so the local tax base is not relevant to school quality. Still, schools in urban areas are better-equipped and better-staffed than in the rural world, and schools in wealthier districts tend to have lower student-teacher ratios and an atmosphere more conducive to learning. These kinds of variations in what are supposed to be systems of uniform quality are common throughout the world. One may add to them the fact that although the public system is free to all eligible children, the well-off can afford books, pens, and pencils, decent clothing, and decent food and housing for their offspring, giving them a range of material advantages over the poor.

Going well beyond these types of class bias is the phenomenon of tutorials. Most of our evidence is drawn from Egypt, but the logic of the phenomenon is so compelling that we feel that it must manifest itself elsewhere as well. In Egypt at the end of the secondary cycle students sit for a general exam. The scores obtained on the exam determine the university faculties to which they will gain admission. Engineering and medicine require the highest scores and are, indeed, the most sought-after faculties. In short, high scores on the secondary school exam determine access to the faculties that will produce the next generation of elites.

Enter the underpaid teacher and the anxious middle-class parent. The teacher wants to supplement his or her meager income, and the parent wants to give his or her child a leg up. The result is fee-based tutorials to prepare for the exams. Depending on the subject matter and the number of students in the tutorial, the fees can be very high, sometimes more than a low-income Egyptian may earn in a year. In this manner a parallel educational system grows up, based on fees, a system that favors the rich and penalizes the poor. The parallel system helps ensure that the children of the well-to-do accede in disproportionate numbers to those professional disciplines that will be most highly regarded in terms of income and prestige.

Having stressed educational strategies that reflect class bias, we must even more strongly emphasize that the mass educational systems set up in most Middle Eastern countries have been catalysts for real social mobility. The evidence for this assertion is fragmentary; systematic studies of the socioeconomic background of secondary- and university-level students have not been carried out. We do not know how profound has been the democratization process in higher education. All indications, however, point in the same direction, to wit, that the children of lower-middle-income strata, the petty bourgeoisie of crafts- and service people, the clerks, the teachers, and the agrarian smallholders, have seized the educational opportunities offered to them and moved well beyond their parents in status and wealth. The phenomenon was first observed in the 1930s, when in various countries admission to institutes of higher education but, most important, to officer's candidate schools was determined by competitive examination. Hardworking, ambitious, intelligent offspring of the lower-middle class outperformed all others and entered educational and professional domains that had been reserved to the upper classes. Gamal 'Abd al-Nasser, the son of a rural functionary, and a number of others who overthrew the Egyptian monarchy in 1952 entered the military academy between 1936 and 1938 and attained the rank of colonel in the postwar years. A similar process got under way in Syria a few years later and yielded Hafiz al-Assad and other officers of rural, lower-middle-class background.

With independence, the process accelerated. One of the most striking examples is that of Damascus University, where in 1968 half the student body was of rural origin and only 65% of the students had fathers with university education (Hinnebusch 1979, 28–29). Rapidly expanding public bureaucracies, educational systems, state enterprises, and military establishments provided a growing job market for these young people. They also became functionaries in some of the more coherently organized political parties, such as the Republican People's party in Turkey, the Ba'ath party of Syria and Iraq, and the Neo-Destour (New Constitution) party of Tunisia (now known as the Constitutional Democratic Rally [RCD]).

By contrast, it would appear that the offspring of peasants, salaried workers, and common laborers—that is, the majority of the low-income strata—have not gained access to secondary and university education in numbers that come near to being proportional to their weight in society. This simply reflects their lower representation in the primary school system (see above). Cutting across income levels is the continued bias against females throughout the educational system. Thus the democratization of education in the Middle East has been incomplete and promises to remain so.

In recent years in many parts of the Middle East, there have been reassessments of mass-educational policies and sometimes timid, camouflaged attempts to slow the rate of increase in secondary school enrollments and to restrict admission to the universities. Such attempts are usually accompanied by efforts to orient primary school students and those who fail general secondary school exams toward vocational-training institutes. As in the United States, such institutes have been regarded as dead ends, and students and parents alike have gone to great lengths to avoid them.

All governments of the region have for years stressed the need for vocational and technical training for their youth. Egypt's goal in 1985 was to provide primary and preparatory education to all children and then orient 60% of secondary students toward vocational and technical training. The remaining 40% would follow the traditional secondary school curriculum, with admission to university as the final target. Egypt is a long way from achieving this distribution, as are all other states in the area. Again, if we take Egypt as representative, we find that most of the vocational students are being trained in commerce, probably simple accountancy, and relatively few in industry and skilled trades. As in many developing countries, there is still a marked preference for white-collar, desk-bound employment. The old respect for craftsmen does not appear to have survived into the twentieth century. Even when herded into vocational education, Middle Eastern students opt for potentially white-collar skills in accountancy rather than certifying themselves as electricians, mechanics, or plumbers.

These attitudes may be changing, however. The great construction boom of the 1970s in the Gulf States created a heavy demand for masons, carpenters, electricians, and the like. Wages for these trades rose rapidly not only in the oil-rich countries importing labor but in the sending countries as well. Within a few years, plumbers or mechanics in Egypt could earn far more than a university-educated civil servant. Moreover, in addition to the oil boom, a technological transformation of the region was taking place. In the cities, high-rise buildings entail elevators, which in turn require maintenance. Air-conditioning in places of work and private homes also requires maintenance, and so do tractors and diesel pumps in the countryside. In short, there is a booming market for skilled repair persons, whose relative wages do not seem to have changed with the oil bust. Substantial incomes can be earned in these fields, but that realization is slow in dawning on a populace obsessed with the respectability of university education and white-collar jobs.

It is not at all clear that a bigger public effort to promote vocational training would remove these bottlenecks. Too often, it appears, vocational training is mired in routine. There is little interaction with the markets for which the students are presumably being trained. The same skills are taught in the same way year after year without regard to changing needs and changing technologies. The result is students who may have to be retrained by their employers. In fact, it may make good sense for public authorities to help likely employers to design their own on-the-job training. For many trades this takes place anyway through the traditional system of master and apprentice. If one looks in any auto mechanic's workshop or notices who is carrying the plumber's tool bag, one is likely to see a boy learning the trade. Whether he also goes to school is irrelevant. He may be paid little more than subsistence, but working side by side with the master he will become familiar with a range of real-life situations—such as dismantling five different kinds of automobile engines—that the vocational trainee will not face. Such private, on-the-job training is almost everywhere superior to public or "official" training. Given the structure of labor markets (see below), it is unsurprising that publicly funded vocational training has largely failed.

The secondary and vocational school environment provides a special political chemistry. The main actors, students and teachers, have particular characteristics.

The teachers are themselves young and most often male. They are of course educated but may well have aspired to a loftier or more remunerative career than teaching. As mentioned earlier, they may have too few resources and too many students to carry out their job effectively. Often they are politically aware, if not active, and today they—and their students—constitute fertile recruiting ground for Islamist movements. In the Arab countries they may be monolingual in Arabic and resent the fact that this precludes their ascent to elite status. In sum, secondary school teachers are seldom content with their lot or with the system for which they work.

The same can be said for many secondary school students. Although they may have survived the screening process after primary school, access to university-level studies will be available to, at most, a quarter of them. And for those in vocational schools that possibility does not exist at all. We have, then, physically mature adolescents, often from low-income backgrounds, a cut above the mass of primary school students and with ambitions to match. They too are politically aware and at a point in their lives when high-risk political action may appeal to their sense of adventure or at least relieve their frustration. In their teachers they may find mentors not much older than themselves who can focus their actions.

Finally there is the school itself, a physical locale that brings the actors together on a day-to-day basis. As is the case for the mosque or the church, it is very difficult for the authorities to control political activities among people who congregate in a perfectly legal manner. When there are disturbances in schools, they are highly visible and noisy and spill out to disrupt life in entire city neighborhoods or small rural towns. The issues that trigger protests, the violence that may ensue, the reprisals, arrests, and police beatings immediately resonate through a much broader stratum of the population—parents, siblings, and other relatives, who all have a stake in the secondary student's education. A student protest over poor food in the canteen or increased fees may rapidly activate many people with a more extensive list of grievances (see Chapters 10 and 14).

These patterns are neither very new nor unique to the Middle East. Some of the region's better-known political leaders came out of the teaching corps or received their political baptism as secondary school students. Probably the single most important Muslim political leader of the first half of the twentieth century was the Egyptian Hassan al-Banna, monolingual in Arabic and a primary school teacher, who founded the Muslim Brotherhood in 1929. Of a very different political persuasion were Michel Aflaq and Salah Bitar, the Syrian secondary school teachers who founded the Ba'ath party that now rules in Syria and Iraq. Several of the nationalist movements in the Middle East, such as the RCD party of Tunisia, the Istiqlal of Morocco, the National Liberation Front (FLN) of Algeria, the Wafd of Egypt, and the Ba'ath, relied to some extent on schoolteachers and students to develop the local infrastructure of their organizations. Whether we consider the adolescent Gamal 'Abd al-Nasser experimenting with the Young Egypt party (Misr al-Fatat) in the 1930s or the lycée student Ait Ahmad Hocine, who was a militant in the Algerian People's party (PPA) and later one of the six historic chiefs of the Algerian revolution, we see a pattern of the political awakening and active political involvement of secondary school students from the 1930s on.

Leaders of the independent countries of the region are acutely aware of the strategic importance of both students and teachers at this level. Habib Bourguiba of Tunisia was able to harness them to his Neo-Destour party but lost some of them to his more militant rival in that party, Salah Ben Yussef. The shah of Iran, after 1963, tried to mobilize students and teachers in literacy campaigns in the countryside, while Houari Boumedienne, president of socialist Algeria, put them to work in 1972 on a survey of landholdings prior to an agrarian reform (Leca 1975). Kemal Atatürk and his successor, Ismet Inönü, saw secondary school teachers as the vehicles for promoting the secular values of the Turkish republic. Village institutes were created to train rural youth to be teachers and to carry the message of republicanism, secularism, and statism to the traditional rural populations. People's houses, functioning as local cultural centers, were set up to propagate the new credo to people outside the school system. In Egypt, during its most pronounced socialist phase in the mid-1960s, the single party, the Arab Socialist Union, relied on local schoolteachers, veterinarians, co-op officials, and other white-collar functionaries to break the influence of local landowning groups (Harik 1974, 81–100).

These efforts at co-optation often ring hollow among the targeted groups. Part of the reason stems from the yawning gap in age between the political elites relative to the students they are trying to control (see Chapter 4). The co-opters lack credibility. In addition, as we argue throughout this book, the period of austerity since the mid-1980s has made access to real jobs something of a lottery in which the bulk of the student population draws losing tickets.

Islamic movements have exploited this situation to their advantage. They have always viewed the school system as a crucial battleground control of which may yield control of the hearts and minds of the students. In some ways political Islamic groups seek political power not for its own sake but rather because it would provide them control—so they believe—over the cultural and educational institutions and the mass media. To the young, therefore, they offer leadership that is closer to them in age and spirit than the aging leadership of the status quo and values that stress probity, the separation of the sexes, and religious faith. They move along three tracks: (1) the assault, direct or indirect, on the bastions of political power, (2) the infiltration of the public education system, and (3) the establishment of private schools under their direct control. In Algeria since 1991, the struggle has been violent and waged extralegally by the Islamic Salvation Front (FIS). In Turkey the Welfare party has waged its struggle at the ballot box. The goals of the two movements vis-à-vis youth and the educational system are roughly the same.

The Universities

Prior to the twentieth century, the Middle East had no modern public universities. There were a few higher institutes of Islamic studies such as the Qarawiyin in Fez, Morocco, and Egypt's prestigious al-Azhar. The first university on the Western model in the region was the American University of Beirut, which was private and established as part of the Protestant Mission in Lebanon. By 1925 Cairo University had been chartered as a fully public institution, and national universities were started in Turkey and Iran. The Hebrew University was founded in Jerusalem, in Mandate Palestine, in 1925. These aside, there were no universities in the region until the 1950s and 1960s.

With full independence throughout the region, there was an explosion in the establishment of universities and in the number of students attending them (see Box 5.1). Algeria, which had no universities in 1962, now has eleven. Yemen's San'a University, founded in 1970 with 64 students and 9 teachers, now has 12 faculties and over 36,000 students. Tehran University was founded in Iran in 1934, and by the middle 1970s another eight universities had been established, with total enrollments around 60,000; ten years later, enrollments had more than doubled (to over 145,000). By the end of the 1980s Turkey had an equivalent number enrolled. In the region as a whole, the proportion of the age-group eighteen to twenty-three years old attending institutes of higher learning grew from 4% in 1960 to 10% in 1980 to 15% in 1993. In addition, tens of thousands of Middle Easterners pursued university educations abroad.

The institutional expansion within the region necessarily sacrificed educational standards. For many years the growing economies and governments of the Middle East could absorb all the graduates the universities produced almost regardless of the quality of their preparation. By the 1970s, however, administrations were clogged with fairly young civil servants, expansion of public-sector enterprises had slowed, and, except in the Gulf, the construction booms of the 1960s and 1970s were over. The formation of a "dangerous" class of the educated unemployed had begun.

Universities and institutes of higher learning exhibit a greater degree of class bias than secondary schools. There has undoubtedly been a certain measure of democratization, as we saw with respect to the University of Damascus, with members of the lower-middle class in particular bettering their position through access to a more open educational system. Still, findings from a survey of university applicants carried out in Turkey in the mid-1970s may be applicable throughout the region (Özgediz 1980, 507). Only 30% of all applicants were from rural areas, while 47% were from the three major cities, Istanbul, Ankara, and Izmir. The success rate in passing entrance exams was three times higher for applicants from upper-income strata than for those from lower-income groups.

The first universities were all located in major cities. Cairo alone has three universities and well over 200,000 students. No regime likes to see that kind of concentration of potentially volatile young, educated people in one place. In recent years there has been a general move throughout the Middle East to establish provincial campuses. This policy serves several purposes. It demonstrates to more remote regions the government's concern to make higher education directly available to their populations. It helps satisfy the relentless demand from all sectors of the population for university education. And it eases the concentration of students in economic and political capitals, where their agitation is highly visible and disruptive. The strategy does not always work. For over fifteen years the University of Assiut in Upper Egypt has been a hotbed of clashes among Islamic student groups, other students, university authorities, and the local police. Many of the provincial universities dispense a thoroughly mediocre education. Even more than the older universities, provincial universities are understaffed, underfinanced, underequipped, and overpopulated. In most instances they are monuments to political expediency.

Middle Eastern universities are preeminently and self-consciously political. Various elements within them claim to speak for the nation's intelligentsia as well as for the generation that will furnish the nation's leaders. By its very organization the university, in its research and instruction, touches upon all the issues that are of great moment to the nation as a whole. All the political currents of the nation will be manifested within the university. There is a constant battle within its walls for control over the institution, and, particularly in the authoritarian systems that typify the region, the conduct of that battle is seen as a bellwether for the entire polity.

Student elections of one kind or another may be more hotly contested and less easily controlled than other elections in a given society. In the absence of other indicators of shifts in public opinion or in the relative weights of political forces, such elections are closely scrutinized. Every regime will have its tame student association or union to enter the fray. In single-party regimes, such as those of the Ba'ath in Syria and Iraq, the RCD in Tunisia, or the FLN in Algeria, the student union will be directly affiliated to the party. So too will associations of professors and administrators. In this way the university is supposed to remain a place of learning subordinate to the regime, but it seldom works out that way in practice. Although student or faculty activists may be a minority of the university population, they are ubiquitous, visible, and highly motivated.

The Middle Eastern university is enveloped in contradictory symbols and practices. Its origins are Western, and most countries of the region at least honor the fiction of the physical and intellectual inviolability of the university. However, the sanctity of academic freedom as well as the campus itself is frequently violated. In many countries the university is called upon to "serve the revolution" or contribute to the development of the nation, slogans that mean in fact that it should remain subservient to regime goals, if not politically inert.[19] When university organizations or movements criticize the government precisely for betraying the revolution (e.g., Algeria in 1966 after Boumedienne seized power from Ben Bella), thwarting the development of the country (Iran throughout the 1970s and Turkey in 1978–1979), or capitulating to its enemies (Egypt in 1971–1972 and in all the years since the 1979 Camp David Accords), then the spokespersons for those organizations are denounced as agents of foreign powers. The Moroccan monarchy on occasion has simply drafted troublemakers into the armed forces.

The freedom of teaching and research is highly circumscribed. There may be subjects that cannot be researched and questions that cannot be asked. Classes will typically have their share of police informers. Some regimes have resorted to strong-arm tactics, with party-affiliated toughs enforcing the proper line, breaking up unauthorized meetings, and intimidating student leaders. Israeli authorities have since 1967 engaged in a running battle with Palestinian students and faculty at Bir Zeit and al-Najah Universities on the West Bank. Still, the spirit of the university as an institution with a peculiar responsibility to the fate of the nation is kept alive, and university students are often prepared to take great risks in making their views known. The best among them will in all likelihood be the nation's future leaders. In fact student militancy has often been the stepping-stone to high official position, as incumbent leaders identify their challengers and set about co-opting them. It is for all these reasons that in national power struggles contenders may see capturing the university to be as strategically important as capturing the armed forces.

LABOR MARKETS

The "human-capital" metaphor suggests that better health and education make people more productive. But these potential benefits can materialize only if labor markets can match these healthier, better-trained individuals with jobs that utilize their skills. If no jobs or, more likely, the wrong kinds of jobs are created, some combination of unemployment (quantity adjustment) or lower real wages (price adjustment) will ensue. Educational systems and choices and labor markets are closely linked; if markets send distorted signals, privately rational choices will spawn socially inefficient outcomes.

Labor-market structures and dynamics in MENA are problematic. Too few jobs are created, and for decades many government policies have stimulated the acquisition of credentials rather than of marketable skills. We saw in Chapter 4 that the region's labor force is growing at the most rapid rate in the world. Unfortunately, the demand for labor has not been keeping up, and the structure of labor markets—primarily, the preponderance of government employment in national labor markets and intrusive regulation of (larger) private employers—further impedes job creation.

The employment problem may be the most politically volatile economic issue facing the region for the coming several decades. Despite data deficiencies, several generalizations may be made: Current levels of unemployment are high, and the problem will probably get worse in the near to medium run. Unemployment primarily affects young, semieducated, urban people, whose anger fuels political unrest. Unemployed youth provide fertile ground for Islamist radicalism throughout the region (Chapter 14).

Unemployment

The quality of the data on unemployment (Figure 5.10) varies widely; cross-country comparisons are especially problematic. Surveys are episodic and use different methods. The most common method of measuring unemployment is to count the number of workers who have registered for government jobs. So long as workers have not found such jobs, they are listed as unemployed; if they take jobs in the private sector,

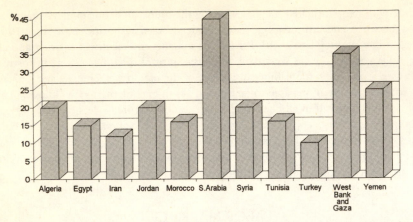

FIGURE 5.10   Unemployment rates, selected countries, early 1990s. *Sources:* Al-Qudsi, Assaad, and Shaban (1993); Wilson and Graham (1994); World Bank (1993b; 1993c; 1994a; 1994b; 1995).

they are stricken from the list. Such a system creates incentives for people to wait for the secure, "respectable" job if they can or surreptitiously take a job in the informal sector if they must. All data must be treated with considerable caution.

Nevertheless, the outlines of the situation are visible. Four generalizations can be hazarded. First, unemployment is greater in cities than in the countryside; second, unemployment is mainly an affliction of the young; third, educated workers are more likely to be unemployed than uneducated ones (although this depends, to some extent, on the definition of "educated"), and fourth, unemployment rates for women exceed those for men.

Unemployment is largely an urban phenomenon. For example, in Morocco, measured, open unemployment rates are nearly four times higher in cities than in rural areas, 20.6% compared with 5.6% (Kingdom of Morocco 1991). Over 70% of the Iranian unemployed in 1990/91 lived in cities (Amuzegar 1993, 66). This suggests that rural labor markets are far more flexible than urban markets and that rural-urban migration sharply reduces the rate of growth of the rural labor force. Agriculture and informal rural labor market outcomes are best explained with supply-and-demand models such as wage flexibility. The best-documented case is Egypt. A recent study (Richards 1994) found that an essentially neoclassical model best explained the large changes in Egyptian farm labor markets during and after the oil boom. Both supply and demand were inelastic with respect to the wage, and real wages were (and remain) very flexible, rising and then falling sharply with international oil prices. Supply shifts explain these real wage changes. These in turn are primarily the outcome of international labor migration. All of this is entirely compatible with a flexible wage model.[20]

Measured, open unemployment in agriculture is very low. Of course, there exists significant seasonal unemployment, which is a factor in rural poverty. Agricultural workers often also work in services, construction, handicrafts, and/or small-scale manufacturing (see, e.g., Radwan and Lee 1986 on Egypt), in part as a means of off-setting the inherent seasonality of agricultural work. It is fair to say that "unemployment" by the usual definition is much more of an urban than a rural problem. This is perhaps partly because rural-urban migration reduces the rate of growth of the rural labor supply. The rural population is growing much less rapidly than the urban population, despite the (generally) higher fertility rates in the countryside (Chapter 10). Further, it is precisely the young and the (semi) educated who have always had the greatest desire to leave rural areas. In an important sense, unemployment is "exported to the cities," where it has significantly different political consequences from what would be expected if it were concentrated in rural areas. For example, most sociological studies (e.g., Ibrahim 1994; Roy 1994) find that the most likely members of Islamist groups are recent immigrants from the countryside who have some education.

Most of the unemployed are young. To some extent, this is hardly surprising: youth unemployment is *always* higher than unemployment for older workers. In OECD countries, for example, youth unemployment is roughly two to three times higher than prime-age unemployment. In the United States in 1990 the total unemployment rate was 5.5%, whereas the unemployment of sixteen-to-nineteen-year-olds was 16.2%, that of twenty-to-twenty-four-year-olds 9.6%, and that of workers older than twenty-five, 4.4%. Consider the similar (but much higher) rates of measured unemployment in Algeria in the same year (Table 5.7).

In Morocco, nearly half (45.5%) of the unemployed are between the ages of fifteen and twenty-four. Young people are roughly twice as likely to be unemployed as older workers; the unemployment rate for (urban) fifteen-to-nineteen-year-olds in Morocco was nearly 40% in 1990/91, compared with a total rate of 20% (Kingdom of Morocco 1992).

Explanations for youth unemployment in OECD countries stress the lower "commitment" of the young to the job market. Unencumbered by families to support, youths can more easily spend some time looking for jobs, switch jobs, and so on. In short, they are better-equipped for the job search than older workers. They can

TABLE 5.7   Algerian Unemployment by Age (%), 1990

Age-Group	Unemployment Rate
15–19	64
20–24	46
25–29	17
All workers	18.4

Source: World Bank (1994a).

afford to wait. We do not know what percentage of total youth unemployment in the region may be accounted for by such job-seeking behavior, but some of the high measured youth unemployment is, in fact, *voluntary*, fractional unemployment.

If young people with the means and desire to search for "better jobs" become an increasing percentage of the total labor force, then the total unemployment rate will necessarily rise. A substantial (but as yet unquantified) fraction of the high unemployment rates in MENA is "demographic unemployment." In Egypt, for example, between two census years the percentage of the labor force between fifteen and twenty-four years of age rose from 22% (1976) to 31% (1986); similar trends are visible elsewhere in the region. This demographic perspective on the unemployment problem in the region suggests that the longevity of this part of the problem is inversely related to the duration and strength of past family planning programs. Governments that started long ago trying to reduce the total fertility rate are more likely to reap the rewards today of decelerating labor force growth. In most countries, unfortunately, such a happy development is at least fifteen to twenty years away (Fargues 1994).

Not all youth unemployment is voluntary, and not all of it can be ascribed to past demographic surges. The educational failures described above also have played a role by failing to equip young people with marketable skills. Government employment and rigid labor markets play a major role in generating youth unemployment. It is notable that youth unemployment is a serious problem in Southern European countries, reaching 38% in Spain, 31% in Italy, and 25% in Greece in 1993 (as cited in Shlaes 1994). The usual explanation for youth unemployment on the northern shore of the Mediterranean stresses rigid labor markets, not demography. The demographic explanation for youth unemployment will take us only so far.

Most analysts agree that unemployment is concentrated among the (relatively educated) youth in MENA. There are, however, some skeptics. For example, a World Bank study of Jordanian returnees from the Gulf States found no relationship between unemployment and level of education. Al-Qudsi, Assaad, and Shaban (1993) conclude that university graduates are not the group most affected by unemployment, but other evidence supports the notion that unemployment is concentrated among the *relatively* educated. For Jordan, for example (Figure 5.11), unemployment is a monotonically increasing function of education: the higher the education, the more likely is unemployment. These numbers, however, may be biased by the year of the survey: 1991, when the Jordanian labor market was flooded by workers expelled from the Gulf. For other countries, unemployment is highest for the semi-educated, those with intermediate educational attainments. Morrison (1991, 46) has aptly articulated this perspective: "Urban unemployment [in Morocco] is . . . in the nature of a waiting list from which those who have virtually no hope of a job by reason of personal handicap (no primary education or professional training) have struck themselves off." Moroccan official statistics (Kingdom of Morocco 1992) show the same inverted-U relationship between unemployment and education (Table 5.8).

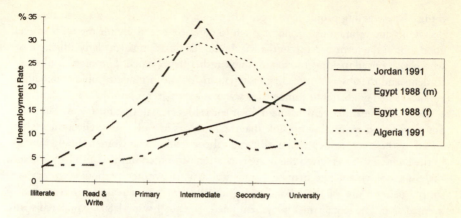

FIGURE 5.11   Unemployment rates by education level, selected countries, early 1990s.
Source: Al-Qudsi, Assaad, and Shaban (1993).

Some unofficial estimates place the rate of unemployment of holders of the *bac-calauréat* at over one-third (Morrison 1991).

Several implications follow from this relationship between education and unemployment. First, the evidence is consistent with the general notion that the unemployed wait for jobs. Educated people are likely to conduct longer job searches for jobs than illiterate workers because they can (reasonably) hope to find a good job, whereas the illiterate know that they have almost no such chance and must take the first job available. Second, a basic determinant of unemployment is the relative rates of growth of the number of "qualified" (school-leavers), on the one hand, and the number of jobs created in the modern sector, on the other. Third, the very high rates of unemployment among secondary school-leavers suggest that "a little knowledge is a dangerous

TABLE 5.8   Moroccan Urban Unemployment (%)
by Educational Level and Sex, 1990–1991

| Educational Level | Unemployment | | |
	Male	Female	Total
None	7.4	17.4	10.9
Primary	22.1	37.2	25.3
Secondary	20.6	45.8	27.0
Higher	20.8	29.8	20.6

Source: Kingdom of Morocco (1992).

thing." These young people have received enough education to have altered their expectations and aspirations but not enough to compete effectively for the (very scarce) good jobs in the formal sector. In the Maghreb, this situation particularly afflicts those who have received their instruction in Arabic rather than French. The large numbers of students and the absence of reading materials in Arabic on modern subjects ill equips Arabic-trained graduates to compete for scarce modern-sector jobs.

Generally, measured female unemployment is higher than that for males. The Gulf States are an exception. It is possible that the numbers in Gulf States reflect the higher wealth of these countries plus the strong social convention that women should remain in the home. However, given the rising education of women in the Gulf, the lower female unemployment rate may be a statistical artifact; women without jobs may be simply defined out of the labor force. Morocco provides a reasonably well-documented case. The female unemployment rate in 1990/91 was 31.8%, compared with 16.7% for men; roughly 40% of the urban unemployed were women (Kingdom of Morocco 1992). A student of Moroccan labor markets has noted that not only do women experience higher overall rates of unemployment but women's unemployment rises more rapidly in economic downturns than men's (Morrison 1991).

In MENA countries, as elsewhere, women may have a lower commitment to the labor market, entering and leaving to accommodate family needs (both of income and child rearing). Female unemployment, even more than that for men, may also plausibly be attributed to rising education. "In the four years 1978–82 the number of working women who had benefited from higher education increased by 110% (48% for women with secondary schooling)" (Morrison 1991, 50). Morrison found that educated women, even more than men, "refused to leave the working population and to enter the informal sector."

Much anecdotal evidence suggests that women are differentially and adversely affected by changes in public-sector job availability. Young women and their families need reassurance that they will be safe in the workplace and that others will perceive their employment as "respectable." For many women, this means either working directly with male family members (e.g., in a small family-owned shop) or working in a large, modern office. Public-sector jobs offer respectability and regular, relatively short hours—working conditions that are particularly attractive to women.

Finally, women in the region can afford to be unemployed: they can wait. Families will support daughters, sisters, and wives rather than have them take inappropriate jobs. Women's unemployment, like most unemployment in the region, is consistent with Gunnar Myrdal's hypothesis that "unemployment is a bourgeois luxury"—something that only those with some means can afford. Economic austerity, with its cuts in government budgets (Chapter 9), is likely to impose a particularly high price on educated women.

Labor-Market Structures

We may divide urban labor markets into three major sectors: public, private formal, and private informal. The public sector is in turn divisible into bureaucracies and state-owned enterprises. Public employment is very secure: it is almost impossible in many cases to lose one's job. However, this greater security is often purchased at the price of lower wages. Until recently, the public sector has often provided the first jobs for the growing masses of educated and semieducated young men. Public-sector employment dominates most MENA labor markets (Figure 5.12).

The private formal sector varies greatly in size but is often the smallest of the three sectors. There are several definitions, but usually a minimum of ten to fifty workers is required to classify an enterprise as belonging to this sector. Additionally, workers in it are assumed to have some job security, although less than in the public sector. Private formal-sector workers often receive higher wages than their counterparts in the public sector. In some countries (e.g., Turkey, Tunisia) many may belong to trade union organizations. Some analysts (e.g., Harberger 1971) treat this and the public sector as "protected" sectors, offering wages above market-clearing levels, a situation that naturally creates queues of workers seeking these jobs.

Finally, there is the private informal sector. The definitions of this sector vary considerably in the literature. Sometimes the term is used as a euphemism for "slum dwellers" or "poor people." Some analysts (e.g., Charmes 1986) treat it as a residual category, embracing all jobs and activities that do not fall into either the public or the private formal sector. Some define it as consisting of all self-employed persons plus those employed in firms with fewer than ten workers and the unskilled, casual laborers employed by larger firms. One careful study for Egypt argued that the informal sector there consisted of (1) small-scale manufacturing and handicraft work, (2) itinerant and jobbing artisanry (masons, carpenters, tailors), (3) personal services (servants, porters, watchmen), and (4) petty services and retailing activities (car washers, street hawkers and vendors, garbage collectors) (Abdel-Fadil 1983). A critical feature everywhere is that informal "firms" are unregistered and untaxed.

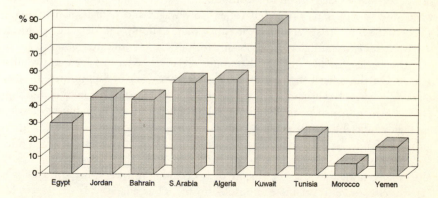

FIGURE 5.12   Percentage of labor force employed in the public sector, selected countries, early 1990s. *Source:* Al-Qudsi, Assaad, and Shaban (1993).

Despite the diversity of definitions, all agree on certain characteristics. There are few or no barriers to entry in the informal sector. Capital per worker is very low, and incomes fluctuate considerably both seasonally and annually. The sector usually employs a higher proportion of women, children, and young adults than other sectors. Some analysts argue that both the output markets and the labor markets are highly competitive (Kuran 1980). Others see competition as restrained by the limited area of search of both employers and employees: Information on this labor market is thought to be highly imperfect (Hansen 1985). We do not yet have enough detailed, rigorous studies to be able to assess these arguments.

How large is the informal sector? Given the diversity of definitions, it is not surprising that we find considerable difference of opinion. In Egypt, for example, one analyst (Abdel-Fadil 1983) has argued that about 16% of the urban labor force was employed there, whereas two others believe that it is closer to 41–43% (Hansen 1985; Charmes 1986). Numbers also vary across countries: YAR, 70%; Turkey, 36%; Iran, 35% (World Bank 1979; Kuran 1980). Most recently, the World Bank has estimated the sector at 30% of nonfarm employment in Algeria, 40% in Egypt, 63% in Morocco, and 35% in Tunisia (World Bank 1995c). Given the differences in definitions and the often rather poor data quality (many of the members of the urban informal sector escape enumeration by labor force surveys or censuses), we may conclude that the informal urban sector employs at least one-third to one-half of the labor force. This is roughly comparable to what has been found in studies in other parts of the Third World (Sethuramen 1981, 214). There is also anecdotal evidence that the share of this sector in employment is growing under the impact of economic reform.

From an employment perspective, the key structural feature is the rigidity in both public and private formal sectors that government regulations have created. Most MENA countries experience a kind of "labor-market dualism," with two radically different labor-market mechanisms. On the one hand, we find an essentially neoclassical labor-market mechanism in the informal sector (and agriculture), with flexible wages and low unemployment but (often) low wages and high levels of poverty. These markets are relatively "efficient": they match supply and demand. Unfortunately, these "efficient markets" are mainly for poorer, less educated workers. Needless to say, these are not the jobs that young, relatively educated men and women want.[21] On the other hand, government employees work in "administered" labor markets, where job slots and wages are determined by bureaucratic criteria, not supply and demand. Such labor allocation mechanisms dominate the public sectors and are highly inflexible. Large public sectors raise unemployment not only by reducing growth (Chapter 9) but also by creating an inflexible labor-market structure.

A plausible story, based on the Egyptian case, goes like this: Young people seek to obtain jobs in the public sector, despite their declining real wage, because such jobs (1) are very secure (it is almost impossible to fire a bureaucrat), (2) are respectable (which is important for "marriage-market" considerations for both men and women), and (3) permit considerable moonlighting. At middle levels, such jobs may also have some value because they make it possible to collect rents (bribes, in plain English) and/or to become a member of a vertically organized network of patronage. The jobs also provide pensions. In order to obtain government jobs, graduates must place themselves on a government list. However, people's names are removed (in theory) from the list if they obtain other jobs. They must, therefore, either be unemployed or work surreptitiously. Their families bear the costs of their waiting because of the benefits just listed.

Similar stories can be found elsewhere in the region. For example, it is worth noting that, in the late 1980s, the Algerian government hired most school-leavers, in a manner similar to the Egyptian experience of a decade earlier. An implication is that even more trouble lies ahead for Algeria. Jordanian labor markets combine high unemployment of the educated with immigration for unskilled work; there is strong evidence that young Jordanians will not take low-paying unskilled (or, in some cases, semiskilled) manual jobs. Jordanian analysts often stress the role of a job as a status indicator—especially relevant for marriage concerns and other social factors. The result is high unemployment, combined with large numbers of (often Egyptian) immigrant workers.

An interesting contrast may be found in Morocco. As in Egypt, the informal sector seems to be mainly competitive but fragmented into many "micromarkets"—for example, in Fez, where construction industry artisans and unskilled workers of Saharan origin dominate employment. Agriculture is also competitive, with marked seasonal fluctuations and much unpaid family labor. Interestingly, although, as elsewhere, in the modern sector unemployment is a rising function of education, there is some dispute on the importance of "waiting for a government job." Morrison (1991) seems to think the phenomenon does exist, while Pissarides (1993) is more skeptical. The available data suggest that at least it has less impact in Morocco than elsewhere on the economy as a whole.

The public-sector wage mechanisms are similar in all cases. The differences (such as they are) across countries seem to be mainly explained by differences in the share of the public sector in total employment. In Jordan, Algeria, and Egypt, the public sector dominates urban employment. In Yemen, nearly 40% of urban workers are employed by the government. In Kuwait and elsewhere in the Gulf, the government is the overwhelming employer of nationals. By contrast, the public sector in Morocco employs less than 10% of the labor force. The roots of youth unemployment, with its potentially explosive political consequences, may be traced to statist economic policies.

There is also often an antiemployment bias in laws regulating private employment. In some countries it is very difficult for private employers to fire workers, particularly after they have been employed for more than six months to a year. The result is that firms either substitute capital for labor or evade regulations by avoiding expansion beyond a small size. Such government policies impede some of the more productive segments of the informal sector from becoming an "engine of growth" as small business can often be. Dismantling such regulations is necessary to foster job creation.

None of this is intended to suggest that labor-market structures and institutions alone are responsible for deficient job creation. Clearly, given the growth of the labor force documented in Chapter 4, rapid economic growth is essential. The impediments to such growth, however, are often similar to the blockages to job creation discussed here: excessive statism (Chapters 8 and 9).

CONCLUSION

Nearly all Middle Eastern governments have promised their citizens health, education, and jobs. Until this century, jobs were not much of a problem for an overwhelmingly agricultural population, which was also ignorant and often sick. Progress in both domains has been rapid and real, but starting from such low bases has meant that many Middle Easterners—infants who die young or adults who remain illiterate—still suffer from the twin scourges. The progress registered is not commensurate, by international standards, with the average levels of income and per capita GDPs of these countries. Moreover, the rapid increase in population in the region will make the effort to catch up extremely costly. Past population growth means that during the next quarter-century the number of people below the age of fifteen will double (Shafik 1994b). At the same time, government budgets are increasingly constrained (Chapter 9).

The existing educational system has helped the current generation of school-leavers to fall between two stools: On the one hand, their aspirations have been raised, making them reluctant to take manual, low-status jobs. On the other hand, the overcrowded, underfunded, rote-memorization educational system provides them with few of the skills that a modern-sector employer would want. Few students develop the "ability to respond to disequilibria" that Theodore Schultz felt was the essence of human capital. The quality problem must be addressed even as the quantitative demands remain very heavy.

The only solution is to continue reallocating limited resources toward more socially efficient uses. In some countries (e.g., Jordan) spending on primary and secondary education has increased, while university education is increasingly financed privately through tuition and donations (Shafik 1994b). Much more of this will be necessary, because public funds are simply too scarce to waste; any subsidy must be paid for, and subsidizing higher education is a poor social investment. The region must improve both the quantity and the quality of education if it is to stimulate the necessary economic growth. The World Bank estimates that MENA children must have about nine years of education by 2010 for the region to achieve international competitiveness (World Bank 1995a). Given demographic trends, primary enrollments will have to increase by 50% and secondary enrollments by 200%. If quality is to be enhanced at the same time, the amount of money spent will have to more than double. Enhanced efficiency and a greater role for the private sector will be necessary if the region is to cope with the challenges of rising demand for education in the next generation. At the same time, reform of labor markets—specifically, reducing the role of government employment and ending regulations that deter private employers from hiring workers—is essential. As usual, vested interests and faltering leadership are the main obstacles to success.

NOTES

1. According to UNICEF, between 1975 and 1980 the average yearly number of infant deaths was 167,000 in Egypt, 195,000 in Turkey, 181,000 in Iran, 104,000 in Algeria, and 103,000 in the Sudan. The number of such deaths, when summed over these countries over an eight-year period, is some six times larger than the death toll of even the most brutal military conflict in recent regional history, the Iran-Iraq War. Informed observers estimate the total number of casualties on both sides of that eight-year conflict at approximately 1 million.

2. Including the "political entity" of the West Bank and Gaza as a country.

3. As usual, there are substantial variations across countries. In 1990 Morocco spent about 2.6% of GDP on health (of which public spending was 0.9%), while neighboring Algeria spent 7.0% (5.4% public) (World Bank 1993b, 211).

4. Diarrhea kills by dehydrating and "starving" its victims, whose bodies cannot absorb the nutrients in their food. The disease caused some 45% of the deaths of children between birth and five years of age in Rabbet in 1981 and 49% of these in Tunis in 1982. Such diseases are the leading cause of child death in Egypt and in other countries (UNICEF 1986).

5. While the unweighted average access for all other MENA countries exceeds 90%, only 16% of Yemenis and 22% of Sudanese had access to ORT in 1992 (UNDP 1994).

6. The emergence of a chloroquine-resistant strain of malaria in Africa, a strain that is now spreading in the Sudan, is alarming. Unlike other diseases in the region, malaria is neither simple nor cheap to control or cure.

7. By the end of the 1980s, despite falling per capita incomes and rising unemployment, "no sharp deceleration of positive trends in health and nutrition was apparent" (Alderman 1993, 125). The rapid spread of ORT helps reduce child malnutrition, which has important synergies with diarrheal disease.

8. A comparable result can be obtained through multiple regression analysis of UNICEF data. Having a higher percentage of the population adhering to Islam *reduces* LEB, controlling for income per capita. However, the adverse impact of Islam is entirely explained by female illiteracy; when a variable for female illiteracy is introduced, the percentage of the population that is Muslim ceases to have any explanatory power (that is, its coefficient becomes statistically insignificant) (Richards 1987).

9. Cross-country regression analysis fails to support this (plausible) contention: As noted above, when controlling for female illiteracy the percentage of the population that is Muslim has no effect on LEB or on infant mortality. Presumably it would if "female autonomy" (which, under any reasonable definition, must be judged low in many Muslim countries) had an impact on health independently of female literacy.

10. Unless otherwise stated, "literacy" means "adult literacy" in this chapter.

11. The Moroccan case is instructive: Moroccan primary enrollment rates were 38% below the average for lower-middle-income countries in 1990 (44% below for girls); secondary enrollment rates were 38% below (47% for girls); adult literacy rates were 40% below (53% for women) (World Bank 1993b).

12. Segregation in Algerian schools formally ended in 1948, but the system remained strongly biased in favor of *colon* children until independence.

13. Since, in that case, the percentage change will be greater, the lower the original literacy number: for example, an increase of literacy from 10% to 20% (100% change) seems more impressive than a change from 80% to 100% (a 25% change). For a full discussion, see Sen (1981b).

14. Omani enrollment is not yet quite universal. The 100% figure includes some repeaters, since not all girls are enrolled.

15. Algeria, Egypt, Iran, Israel, Jordan, Oman, Morocco, Saudi Arabia, Syria, Tunisia, Turkey, and Yemen.

16. The social rate of return on an investment is the internal rate of return, calculated using international (as opposed to distorted domestic) prices and taking into account externalities.

17. It is estimated that closing the gender gap in MENA education would require spending less than 0.5% of GDP. It is interests and deficient political will at the top, not lack of money, that slows educational advance in the region (Shafik 1994b).

18. The actual performance record of the campaigns in Algeria, the PDRY, and Iraq is itself quite mixed. In Iraq, although US$700 million was spent, approximately $350 per person reached by the campaign (Sousa 1982), adult literacy was still only 60% in 1990.

19. In September 1961 Syria broke its political union with Egypt and brought about the demise of the United Arab Republic. Students at Cairo University and elsewhere demonstrated in favor of the union and against Syria. Egypt's President Nasser closed down the universities for having demonstrated at all.

20. There is also some (modest) evidence that labor markets do not clear even in peak season in Egypt (Richards and Martin 1983). This information comes from a small-sample survey and seems compatible with some kind of "efficiency-wage" argument. But most evidence (such as it is) suggests wage flexibility in farm labor markets.

21. There is some evidence (Richards and Martin 1982; Assaad 1994) that these markets are not perfectly competitive because of asymmetric information problems. Such issues also arise in OECD labor markets, but we have much less information on these problems in MENA. They are not, however, very likely to be major explanators of unemployment.

6

WATER AND FOOD SECURITY

The Middle East cannot produce enough food to feed its population. Rapidly escalating demand and sluggish supply response have made it the least food-self-sufficient region in the world. The emergence of this "food gap" does not mean (as some
have implied) that agricultural supply has stagnated. Although this has happened in
some cases, the more common experience has been that both public and private responses to the food deficit have failed to restore food self-sufficiency. This, however,
is not necessarily a bad thing. Indeed, food self-sufficiency is physically impossible
and economically undesirable for the region.

The water constraint dooms dreams of self-sufficiency. The water situation in the region grows more serious daily. Renewable water resources per capita fell from 3,500
cubic meters in 1960 to 1,500 cubic meters in 1990. Population growth ensures that
these numbers will fall further in coming decades; the World Bank projects that there
will be only 667 cubic meters per person by 2025, compared with a worldwide average
of 4,780 cubic meters per person in that year (World Bank 1994f) (Figure 6.1). Ten
countries' (plus Gaza's) water use already exceeds 100% of renewable water supplies;[1]
water quality problems plague another ten (Table 6.1).[2]

The demand for water has been driven up by population growth, rapid urbanization, and expanding irrigation. If income growth resumes, this will also increase
water demand.[3] Water used by households and industry has a much higher economic value than water used in agriculture. Consequently, as the water becomes
scarcer, agriculture will have to get by with less. Most authorities agree that Israel
and Jordan, for example, will have little choice but to save water by cutting back on
irrigated agriculture, increasingly using recycled waste water for farming, and also
making investments in expensive technologies such as desalination. Although there
is scope for greater efficiency in irrigation, there is simply not enough water in the
region to permit food self-sufficiency.

Food self-sufficiency is, however, a very different concept from food security, which
is an insurance concept. Ensuring food security means guaranteeing that consumers
are reasonably certain of being able to eat properly. Policymakers all too often conflate
food security with food self-sufficiency, and the resulting policies are transforming

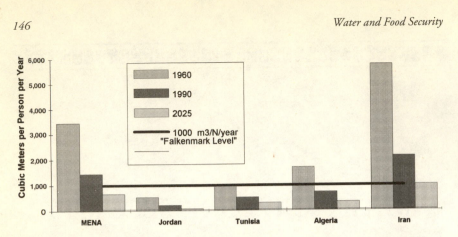

FIGURE 6.1   Renewable fresh water available per person, selected countries, 1960–2025.
Source: World Bank (1994f).

TABLE 6.1   Severity of Water Quantity and Quality Problems, Early 1990s

	Water Quantity *Problems*[a]	
Water Quality *Problems*	*Low*	*High*
High	Algeria, Egypt, Iran, Iraq, Lebanon, Morocco, Syria, Tunisia	Gaza, Jordan
Low		Bahrain, Israel, Kuwait, Libya, Oman, Qatar, Saudi Arabia, UAE, Yemen

[a]*Low:* water use <100% of renewable supplies; *high:* water use >100% of renewable supplies
Source: World Bank (1995b).

agricultural production and relations between both rural and urban citizens and their
states throughout the region.

THE FOOD GAP

A sketch of the stylized facts of food security must distinguish between two quite different decades, the oil boom of 1970s and the austere 1980s.

The Exploding Food Gap of the 1970s

During the 1970s, rapidly increasing populations and oil rent fueled per capita income growth, quickly raising the demand for food. The increase in incomes was not limited to oil exporters but also enjoyed by the poorer countries because of large-scale migration for work in the oil-exporting countries. Demand growth has three determinants: population increase, per capita income advance, and the income elasticity of demand.[4] We have seen that MENA population growth rates are among the highest in the world. Such population growth rates in themselves pose a challenge to food producers, but the very rapid growth of incomes during the 1970s compounded the task. For five countries, per capita GDP grew more than 5% per year, with incomes doubling in fifteen years. With the major exception of the Sudan, per capita incomes advanced swiftly in the region during the oil-boom years.

The impact of this income growth upon food demand depended, of course, on the specific foodstuff. Demand for cereals for direct food consumption (as opposed to use as livestock feed) grew at approximately 3.7% per year from 1966 to 1980; although this was mainly due to burgeoning population, increasing incomes accounted for roughly 25% of this growth. Demand for cereals for livestock feed grew more rapidly (4.8% per year); about one-fourth of all cereals consumed in the region is eaten by animals (Paulino 1986, 26). Income growth particularly stimulated the growth of consumption of meat, fruits, and vegetables. In the Middle East as everywhere, when people get richer they eat more of everything, especially animal and horticultural products.

Domestic supply response was sluggish in the 1970s because of the Dutch Disease—policies that excessively taxed and limited investment in the agricultural sector. Cereal production was especially weak, caught between rising labor costs, marginal rainfall, and government-imposed price disincentives. By contrast, the production of higher-value crops such as fruits, vegetables, and livestock did much better. Almost everywhere, the food gap could be plugged with imports: abundant foreign exchange and improving terms of trade[5] permitted a dramatic increase in food (and especially cereal) imports.

The levels of dependency on food imports of the 1970s prompted widespread alarm. The risk of a politically motivated food embargo became something of an obsession with many government planners. The effectiveness of the "food weapon" was probably overrated; only a multilateral embargo could be effective, and even Iraq after the Gulf War has been allowed to import food. Bilateral embargoes (e.g., by the United States) would simply open lucrative markets for European Union (EU) or Australian wheat, a fact not lost on the U.S. farm lobby. Heavy reliance on food imports does, however, entail political risks. Three countries of the region purchase at least 20% of their total food supply from the United States: Egypt (25%), Israel (34%), and Morocco (20%). Furthermore, the percentage is higher in some cases for highly strategic wheat supplies: Egypt gets nearly 50% of its wheat and wheat flour, *the* staple food in the country, from the United States. Such dependence, even on friendly countries, makes policymakers nervous. And of course, no country in the world relies exclusively on comparative advantage and market forces in its food system.

Unsurprisingly, therefore, state reactions to the imbalance between domestic supply and domestic demand for food have not been limited to increasing imports.

From the economic point of view, states could either focus on diversifying their exports (thereby increasing the stability of their foreign-exchange earnings) or launch programs to increase the proportion of domestic supplies to total consumption. Increasingly, the water constraint will force most countries of the region to adopt the former approach. In the 1970s, however, few were prepared to undertake the kind of economic policy reforms that such an export-oriented food security strategy would have required. Many still are not (see Chapter 9). In contrast, nearly all have implemented at least some import-substituting agricultural policies.

Partially Redressing the Balance in the 1980s

During the 1980s, income growth collapsed in the region as a whole and turned negative for many countries. Consequently, population growth became the sole source of additional demand for food. The deceleration in demand provided a temporary respite for harried agricultural planners, who had succeeded in formulating and implementing significant policy shifts.

The rise in the percentage of consumers' food that came from abroad during the 1970s was disquieting to policymakers, who considered reliance on foreign supplies risky economically or politically. In the early 1980s subsidies of inputs usually either continued or increased (although this had begun to change by the end of the decade) while taxation of output through price policies typically eased. Governments often began to allocate a larger share of investment to agriculture, and many urban entrepreneurs entered the production of horticultural crops, poultry, and livestock. By now, the latter constitute a significant "farm lobby" in most countries, a fact of considerable relevance for water policy (see below).

In part because of these policy shifts, most countries' agricultural sectors managed at least to keep up with population growth during the 1980s. Different sources present conflicting information on trends in food self-sufficiency in the Arab world. Data from the Arab Organization for Agricultural Development suggest modest improvement in some food self-sufficiency ratios (Figure 6.2). By contrast, an analysis of FAO data suggests that population grew, cereal production stagnated, and cereal self-sufficiency remained unchanged (Richards 1996). This implies that per capita consumption of cereals declined for the region as a whole. Perhaps the safest conclusion to draw from these disparate studies is that food self-sufficiency at least did not deteriorate during the 1980s. This is a markedly different experience from that of the oil-boom years.

The increases in output were largely the result of additional inputs. The arable area continued to increase in those countries that experienced the strongest agricultural growth, and irrigated land expanded nearly everywhere. Fertilizer use increased but at a diminishing rate. Mechanization, especially tractorization, continued unabated throughout the region. The farm labor force either continued to grow or resumed growing after an oil-boom-induced decline in most countries. The boom of the 1970s drew labor out of agriculture: in Algeria, Iraq, Jordan, Syria, Yemen, Libya, and Egypt, the adult male farm labor force actually declined during the

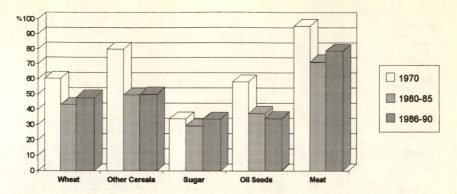

FIGURE 6.2   Arab self-sufficiency ratios for selected commodity groups, 1970–1990.
Source: Sadik and Barghouti (1994).

1970s. However, the 1980s largely reversed this Dutch Disease phenomenon in all but Iraq, Jordan, and Libya. In short, MENA agricultures used more land, more water, more fertilizer, more machines, and more labor—all just to keep up with population growth (see Figures 6.3–6.7, Table 6.2, and Box 6.1).

The Fading Mirage of Food Self-Sufficiency

If income growth resumes, the challenge of growing demand for food will become still more acute. Given the increasing scarcity of water, food self-sufficiency will be increasingly out of reach. But is food self-sufficiency really necessary to achieve food security? Most economists think not.

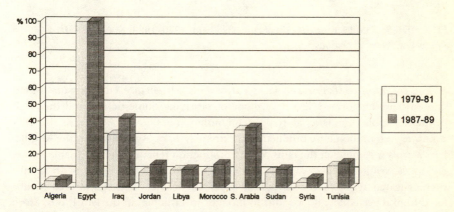

FIGURE 6.3   Percentage of cultivated land under irrigation, 1971–1989.
Source: Calculated from *FAO Production Yearbook* (various years).

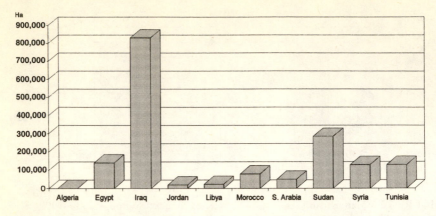

FIGURE 6.4   Increase in irrigated land area, 1980s. *Source: FAO Production Yearbook* (various years).

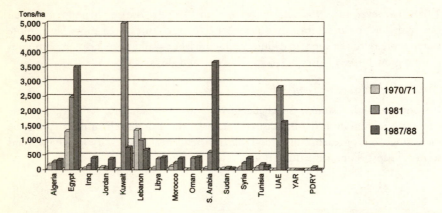

FIGURE 6.5   Fertilizer use per unit of cultivated land, 1970–1988. *Source: FAO Production Yearbook* (various years).

The common conflation of food security with self-reliance tacitly assumes that domestic production is a less risky mode of satisfying domestic demand than dependence upon international trade. Common sense suggests otherwise. In arid zones, relying on domestic production is extremely risky. Agriculture in the Middle East is truly a gamble on the rains. Cereal production remains highly variable in the region, as weather shocks plague staple food production. Only Egypt, with its entirely irrigated agriculture, escapes from repeated weather shocks, and even it suffered from repeated low floods (due to drought in Ethiopia) in the late 1980s. Elsewhere in the region the situation is far worse. In Syria, for example, food production would fall below the average by more than 5% *every third year*, and planners in the

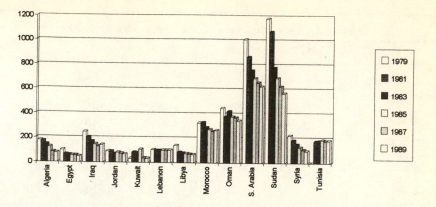

FIGURE 6.6   Tractors per hectare of cultivated land, 1979–1989. *Source:* Derived from *FAO Production Yearbook* (various years).

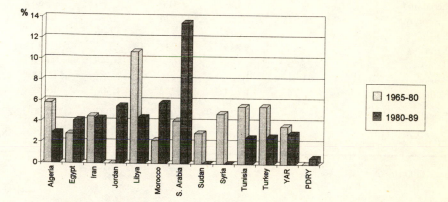

FIGURE 6.7   Growth rates of agricultural output, 1965–1989. *Source:* Calculated from *FAO Production Yearbook* (various years).

Maghreb must find supplementary foreign exchange to buy such "unusual" amounts of food four years out of ten.

The devastating (climatologically unrelated) droughts in the Maghreb and the Sudan underscore the climatic threat. In Morocco, production of wheat fell by nearly 40% from 1976 to 1977, while in the Sudan, millet and sorghum output fell by 38% and 58%, respectively, in 1982 and 1983 and continued to fall the next year (*FAO Production Yearbook,* various years). The social, economic, and political impacts were severe: Some 4 to 5 million northern Sudanese were forced from their homes, moving either into the Nile Valley or farther south to less severely affected areas. In addition, multitudes of drought refugees fled to North African cities.

TABLE 6.2   Agricultural Labor Force (thousands), 1960–2000

	1960	1970	1980	1985	1990	2000
Main oil-exporting countries						
Algeria	1,990	1,394	1,262	1,301	1,342	1,387
Iran	3,220	3,547	4,026	4,082	4,199	4,331
Iraq	972	1,125	1,081	1,043	1,049	1,073
Oman	97	102	140	140	163	165
Saudi Arabia	871	1,019	1,333	1,490	1,599	1,729
Subtotal	7,296	7,337	7,979	8,210	8,210	8,803
Main non-oil-exporting countries						
Egypt	4,364	4,765	5,158	5,526	5,902	6,786
Jordan	199	162	66	63	59	51
Lebanon	199	130	106	90	86	69
Morocco	2,195	2,333	2,594	2,746	2,860	2,950
Sudan	3,376	3,601	4,331	4,606	4,866	5,348
Syria	685	785	707	713	747	848
Tunisia	663	559	668	648	630	549
Turkey	10,991	11,361	11,146	11,385	11,418	11,335
Yemen	1,174	1,232	1,212	1,306	1,432	1,769
Subtotal	23,846	24,928	25,988	27,083	28,000	29,705
Total	31,142	32,265	33,967	35,293	36,479	38,508

Source: FAO (1986).

Serious drought returned to North Africa in the early 1990s. All agricultural sectors in the region outside of Egypt must contend with meager, variable rainfall. There is little evidence of either marked improvement or deterioration in variability over time for the region as a whole. Relying on domestic production is a very risky strategy for ensuring food security in MENA.

Fundamentally, arid zones like MENA cannot escape geography: water is and will become increasingly scarce in the region. So long as water is needed for photosynthesis, there will be serious barriers to the achievement of self-sufficiency in food or agriculture anywhere outside of Turkey or (potentially) the Sudan. Everywhere but in the Gulf, agriculture uses about 85% of the region's water. Water problems are especially acute in the Mashreq and the Arabian peninsula, where unsustainable rates of usage are increasingly common. Increasing pollution of water is also a growing problem. In many countries, the demand for water will likely exceed renewable freshwater supplies by the end of the decade; by 2025, per capita water availability

BOX 6.1
THE VARIETY OF AGRICULTURAL PERFORMANCE

The aggregate data on agricultural performance conceal significant differences among countries and among crops. Agricultural performance was only weakly linked to overall economic growth during the 1970s; countries with high over-all GDP growth rates have included agricultural success stories, such as Syria in the 1970s, and relative failures, such as Morocco. The two extremes may be Turkey, intermittently the sole cereal exporter of the region, and the Sudan, which has experienced famine in 1983/84, in 1987/89, and in the early 1990s. In the 1980s the best performers were Jordan and Morocco, while Syrian agriculture stagnated. Saudi agriculture was in a class by itself, but its extraordinary growth was fueled by massive subsidies (depending on the year, domestic wheat prices were 600 to 1,000% above world prices) and unsustainable exploitation of fossil water.

The rate of growth of production of various crops has also varied widely. In general, in the Middle East as in Latin America, output of "luxury" foods such as fruits, vegetables, poultry, and livestock products has increased more rapidly than that of cereals. Much of this increase is simply the result of the higher income elasticity of demand for horticultural and livestock products. Until very recently price and credit policies also contributed to these trends. Such developments do little to reduce the food gap. They may actually increase it; for example, increasing poultry production stimulates feed imports.

---

for all purposes could be as low as 700 cubic meters. Food self-sufficiency is an expensive, wasteful, and ultimately doomed food security strategy.

Fortunately, food security can be obtained through trade. Middle Eastern political economies will have to emulate other economically successful but agricultural-resource-poor nations to achieve food security in the years ahead. But how can national leaders be persuaded of this when, for example, irresponsible opposition politicians claim that self-sufficiency is possible and fault the government for "selling out to foreigners" and "failing to protect the nation"?[6] Implementing credible economic reforms faces formidable political obstacles (Chapter 9), but because of policy and, still more, physical constraints on increased food production, countries of the region will increasingly have to export in order to eat.

POLICY IMPEDIMENTS TO OUTPUT GROWTH

We may (loosely) divide the policy constraints on food production into two parts: (1) skewed access to land and other "property-rights" problems and (2) limited incentives for farmers. Farm output growth is also constrained by investment problems; these will be taken up as part of the discussion of the key physical constraint, limited water supplies.

Land Tenure

Despite the usual diversity across countries of the region, we shall hazard five generalizations concerning land tenure and property rights. (1) Prereform land tenure
more nearly resembled the bimodal pattern of Latin America than the small peasant
systems of East Asia. (2) The state was, and remains, exceptionally active in shaping
patterns of land tenure. (3) Land reforms implemented roughly between 1953 and
1975 reduced but did not eliminate the inequalities inherited from the past. (4) The
state has had mixed success in substituting itself for the expropriated landlords as
marketing agent, crop selector, and so forth. (5) States have recently retreated from
land reforms and especially from public-sector agriculture, a retreat that is part of a
wider trend toward increased reliance on the private sector. States have created social
actors through land reforms and other policies with regard to property; the actors so
created now often constitute an important force shaping policy—a farm lobby.

During the nineteenth and early twentieth centuries, large landholdings emerged
in many MENA countries. Relations between the state and local social groups and
expanding markets for crops provided opportunities for private aggrandizement.
States typically resisted this process: rulers tried to remove intermediaries between
themselves and the tax-paying peasantry. The success or failure of such policies depended on local, regional, and international political forces.

The intrusion of European colonialism always fostered bimodalism.[7] The pattern
was most striking in the Maghreb, where agrarian changes resembled those of Latin
America: foreign conquerors seized the best agricultural land for themselves, relegat-
ing the indigenous inhabitants to marginal areas for subsistence farming, to wage
labor on the European modern farms, or, commonly, to both (see Box 6.2). "Indirect" colonial rule generated a similar result in Iraq and Egypt. Charles Issawi has
aptly summarized the prereform land-tenure systems: "large estates, accounting for a
quarter to four-fifths of privately owned land and in the main tilled by sharecroppers; a huge number of very small peasant proprietors, often with highly fragmented
holdings; short and precarious leases; high rents . . . large debts, rising land values;
and a growing landless proletariat earning very low wages" (Issawi 1982, 138).

Land reform swept through the region in the quarter-century after World War II.
Echoing David Ricardo, critics charged that wealthy landlords were economic
drones, failing to invest their profits and rents domestically. Although modern historians reject this portrait (Davis 1983; Tignor 1984), there is little doubt that the
land-tenure systems fostered huge social inequities and impeded human-capital formation. The real impetus behind land reform was political. Reformers expropriated
enemies: Nasserists dispossessed the family and friends of King Farouk; Syrian
Ba'athists (often 'Alawi or Druze) took away the lands of urban (typically Sunni)
merchant absentee landlords; the Algerian FLN seized the farms of fleeing *pied noir*
colonists; Iraqi nationalists and communists dispossessed the sheykhs who had often
supported the deposed Hashemite monarchy. Even the shah of Iran, shortly after he
was reinstalled by the United States in 1953, agreed to launch a land reform, mainly

BOX 6.2
COLONIALISM AND LAND TENURE

In Algeria between 1830 and 1880 *colons* and/or the French state seized nearly 900,000 hectares of land in Algeria; by 1962, 30% of the cultivated area was owned by *colons*, of which some 80% was held in large farms of over 100 hectares (Smith 1975). By 1914 nearly 20% of the arable land in Tunisia was in European hands, and over half of it belonged to only sixteen extremely wealthy absentee owners; by 1953 Europeans held nearly 1 million hectares in Morocco, concentrated in the fertile, well-watered plains of the west and north; the Italian Fascists seized some 500,000 hectares of land in Cyrenaica (Libya). The dispossessed indigenous population was forced onto more marginal lands, while the European farms enjoyed privileged access to government loans and other favors (Abun-Nasr 1971; Nouschi 1970). Population growth shortened fallows, extended cultivation into ever more marginal land, and reduced the amount of land available to each peasant family even as large estates continued to expand (van der Kloet 1975).

The British in Iraq shored up the sheykhs and aghas as counterweights to (nationalist) urban groups and to the king (Batatu 1978, 78–100; Dann 1969, 4). By confirming the registration of formerly tribal land in the names of sheykhs, the British and later the independent Iraqi government placed vast amounts of cultivated land in a few hands. By 1953, 1.7% of landowners held 63% of the land, while nearly two-thirds of the population held less than 5% of the land; over three-fourths of the rural population was landless (al-Khafaji 1983, chap. 7).

In Egypt, Muhammad 'Ali had initially attempted to eliminate all intermediaries between the state and the peasants. When internal economic difficulties and British pressure forced him to decentralize, he granted land to court favorites, military officers, and the like. These actions created a class of large, typically absentee landlords known as "pashas." By 1900 large (over 50 *feddan*) farms (1 *feddan* = 0.42 hectares = 1.03 acres) covered 40% of the cultivated area of the country (Baer 1962; Owen 1986; Richards 1982).

because he believed that this would weaken his opponents, such as friends of Mossadegh (himself a landowner) or the Shi'i ulema (Hooglund 1982; Katouzian 1981). Large landlords have ceased to exist as a political force in any country that has had a significant agrarian reform.[8]

The contributions of land reform to equity and economic growth were mixed. The Egyptian agrarian reform, which became the model for other Arab regimes, affected only 12% of the land area. Landless workers were excluded, since only tenants were believed to have the necessary agricultural experience. This pattern was repeated in Algeria, where the permanent workers seized the estates of the departed *colons*. When the land seizures were institutionalized under *autogestion* (self-management), temporary and seasonal laborers received nothing (Zghal 1977). Subsequent reforms of the 1970s affected some 30% of the rural population (Tuma 1978).

The administration of land reforms often created serious production problems. Governments sometimes removed large landowners, who often had also supplied credit and seed to tenants, without replacing them with anyone else. This was a function of continual political upheaval, as in both Iraq and Syria during the 1960s, and of the lack of sufficient cadres, a problem that was more serious in Iraq than in Syria and that had become less acute by the late 1970s (Springborg 1981).

Most land-reform beneficiaries were obliged to join government-sponsored service cooperatives. Peasants farmed their own lands as private property, but input supply, marketing, and often crop choices were regulated by the cooperatives. The cooperative system, pioneered in Egypt, also appeared in Tunisia, Algeria, Syria, Iraq, and the former PDRY. Such cooperatives became the principal instrument for channeling resources out of agriculture toward industrial projects. Land reform was the handmaiden of state-led industrialization strategies. Some scholars (e.g., Hansen 1992) have argued that the disappearance of the large owners in Egypt removed a powerful lobby on behalf of all farmers, leaving the farm sector exposed to the significant taxation increases that such growth strategies entailed (Hansen 1991). However, few countries succeeded in mobilizing the agricultural surplus for industrial investment via land reforms and cooperatives. Land reforms also failed to create a wide domestic market.

Land reforms' limited coverage, the states' use of cooperatives to distribute and subsidize inputs, and history's legacy often combined to generate a "new class" of rural rich, the more prosperous sections of the peasantry. Large landlords had been eliminated, while official cadres relied on the wealthy peasants for information and for social activities. Such farmers dominated their areas and ensured that government policies and cooperatives favored or at least did not threaten their own interests (Adams 1986). Nevertheless, reforms throughout the region greatly reduced the gross inequities in land tenure that were inherited from the pre–World War II era.

For the past decade, the trend has been toward much greater reliance on private farming and on market incentives in agriculture. Throughout the region, the extensive experience with large-scale state farms has been disappointing. Whether in Tunisia in the 1960s, in Iraq and Syria in the 1970s, or in newly reclaimed lands in Egypt, wholly public-sector farms have been abandoned. In Algeria, 2,000 "self-managed" farms have been subdivided into 6,000 smaller and more specialized units, while "other land is being leased to state farm workers or coop members who want to farm privately" (USDA 1987, 23). Privately owned large farms have fared little better; in Pahlavi Iran the large "farm corporations" set up by the shah not only disrupted rural society but also failed to outproduce medium-sized peasant holdings by any of several measures (Moghadem 1982). Small may not be beautiful, but big is surely sluggish: economies of scale are very limited in agriculture. As the food security problem loomed ever larger, governments from Algeria to Iraq turned to the private sector to solve their domestic agricultural supply problems. For such a strategy to succeed, however, incentives had to be provided.

Price Signals

Heavy taxation has been a serious impediment to the growth of agricultural production in MENA. The mechanisms chosen to transfer resources out of the farming sector have distorted farmers' incentives and misallocated scarce resources. Two types of so-called price policies were particularly destructive: (1) direct or sectoral taxation, in which government marketing agencies enjoying monopsony power offered farmers prices well below those prevailing on world markets, and (2) the indirect or macroeconomic taxation implicit in an overvalued real foreign-exchange rate. Both types of taxation originated in import-substituting industrialization programs; the choice of such a development strategy thus implies bias against agriculture (Little, Scitovsky, and Scott 1970; Johnston and Kilby 1975; Timmer, Falcon, and Pearson 1983). Both of these forms of taxation were used extensively; both had the predictable effect of slowing production growth. Consequently, as food security fears increased, such taxation mechanisms were in some countries gradually reformed.

The first mode of taxation typically relied heavily on government marketing monopolies. These were extensively used by national governments throughout the heyday of ISI economic development strategies and were closely linked to the land reform/"cooperative" systems described above. Indeed, such "cooperatives" are best understood as taxation devices rather than cooperatives in the American or European sense. In the Sudanese Gezira Scheme, for example, the Sudanese government's cotton-marketing monopoly permits the government to pay farmers below the international price and pocket the difference.[9] Until the early 1990s Egypt followed a similar system for cotton, sugar, and rice, as well as imposing extensive quantity and area controls for other crops. Algeria, Morocco, and Tunisia did the same; the Algerian government's interventions were the most extensive, but even supposedly "liberal" Tunisia fixed the producers' prices for eight of the major farm outputs.[10]

Sectoral price policies engendered inefficiencies and may have retarded output growth. It is widely agreed that farmers are highly responsive to price signals *among* crops. Because some crops are more heavily taxed than others, farmers reallocate land, labor, and purchased inputs toward less taxed, more profitable crops. The resulting distortions can be extensive. For example, Egyptian farmers fled from cotton and rice into horticultural crops and from wheat into clover (see Box 6.3), whereas Sudanese farmers in the Gezira switched their land and labor away from heavily taxed cotton toward sorghum, peanuts, and wheat. In Algeria, value added in (taxed) cereals stagnated between 1974 and 1986; during this same period value added in vegetables grew at 7.4% per year and that of fresh fruit at 4.3% (World Bank 1987; *FAO Production Yearbook*, various years).

Such static resource misallocations mattered. In Egypt the value of the allocative distortions amounted to some 7% of total GDP and fully 30% of agricultural GDP

BOX 6.3
EGYPTIAN PRICE POLICIES

The Egyptian government used its monopolies over domestic marketing (implemented through the cooperative system) and over international trade to pay farmers prices below international levels. In the 1970s, regulations and controls affected cotton, wheat, rice, sugarcane, beans, and winter onions. All of these crops were taxed. Livestock products, in contrast, were protected because of consumers' preferences by explicit tariffs and the complex bureaucratic hurdles placed before importers until 1987. Horticultural crops (fruits and vegetables) were entirely unregulated.

As a result of these policies, and despite area controls, cotton yields stagnated, and the area planted in wheat declined in favor of birsim or Egyptian clover. Farmers had ample incentives to divert variable inputs (labor, fertilizer) away from (heavily taxed) crops like cotton and wheat. Finally, foreign-exchange scarcity in the mid-1980s led to restriction of nonwheat agricultural imports, which increased the degree of protection of crops that competed with cotton (Dethier 1991). Egyptian price policies not only robbed the country of the foreign exchange that it could have obtained through exporting cotton (in which the country has a strong comparative advantage) but also exacerbated the food gap by retarding wheat production.

Egypt began dismantling these policies in the late 1980s and accelerated the process after the Gulf War (see Chapter 9). In 1995 only cotton and sugarcane retained controls. The decontrol of wheat prices, combined with a technological innovation, had quite dramatic results in the late 1980s. Adapting higher-yielding varieties of wheat to Egyptian conditions proved a challenging task. When, however, the release of the new variety coincided with decontrol of the wheat market and large price increases, output rose by over 40% in four years. It is now recognized that the country has a strong comparative advantage in wheat (World Bank 1993a) and that the long struggle to develop a locally adapted high-yielding variety and to free domestic prices has paid off handsomely.

(Dethier 1989; Hansen 1991). In the Sudan the incentive bias against cotton reduced the average yield of that crop by roughly 50% between 1974 and 1980/81 (World Bank 1985) (see Box 6.4). Since cotton is that country's largest export, farmers' responses to such policies exacerbated the country's severe balance-of-payments problem. In the early 1980s some 15% of the value of Moroccan agricultural GDP was transferred out of the sector (Tuluy and Sallinger 1991). There is little doubt that the resource reallocations brought about by distorted price signals had important efficiency consequences.

BOX 6.4
INEFFICIENT PARASTATALS AND AGRICULTURAL
STAGNATION: THE SUDAN

The Sudanese government regulates all aspects of cotton crop production. Administrative and exchange-rate problems have often prevented the timely delivery of inputs; for example, in 1989 some 15% of the cotton crop was lost because of the late delivery of sacks. The situation with spare parts is still worse. These problems interact; officials of the parastatal Agricultural Corporation are obliged to spend much time in Khartoum trying to secure allocations of foreign exchange for inputs, and this diverts their energies from on-the-ground management activities. Unclear lines of responsibility between the Agricultural Corporation and the Ministry of Irrigation impede management of public irrigation systems. Because of the accumulation of weeds and silt in canals, the crop intensity in the irrigated subsector fell from 75% to 57% (a decline of some 300,000 *feddans*). Another parastatal, the Earth Moving Corporation, has a silt removal capacity of 10.2 million cubic meters per year, while silt deposits are estimated at 16.7 million cubic meters per year. Significantly, the government of Sudan prohibited private entry into this activity despite its own incapacity to deliver the needed service. Ginning losses in Sudan are some 300–400% above international norms. The parastatal Sudan Cotton Company has a monopoly over ginning and exports. Cotton growers (the tenants of the Gezira and Rahad Schemes) and the input suppliers (the Agricultural Corporation) are insulated from the success or failure of the Sudan Cotton Company, so they do not press for reform (World Bank 1990c).

Overvalued exchange rates also blunt farmers' incentives. Such overvaluation creates excess demand for foreign exchange, which is then usually rationed by (often complex) government regulations. These policies lower the value of exports and raise the value of imports, while also increasing the prices of nontraded domestic goods relative to products that are traded internationally. The first effect hurts producers of export crops (e.g., cotton, rice, vegetables) and of the major import-competing crop, cereals. Furthermore, government rationing of scarce foreign exchange usually favors industrial and military users; farmers are often last in line, finding that they must pay higher prices for inputs or consumer goods if, indeed, they can get them at all. The increase in the relative price of nontradables to tradables also hurts farmers, because a large portion of the sector's costs is nontradable inputs such as land and labor, while its outputs are, of course, tradables. All of these effects reduce farmers' incomes.

In Egypt, for example, exchange rate overvaluation increased the taxation of agriculture by 50–200%, depending on the year, between 1970 and 1985 (Dethier

1991). The overvalued Turkish lira more than compensated for the sectoral subsidies that politically active Turkish farmers were able to obtain during those fifteen years.[11] A similar phenomenon occurred in the Islamic Republic of Iran, which also combined sectoral subsidies (input credits, price supports) with a seriously overvalued real exchange rate.

As usual, the variation in countries' experience with both direct and indirect agricultural taxation is wide. Although foreign-exchange largesse is supposed to be detrimental to agriculture in models of the Dutch Disease, countries with surplus capital often found ways to offset such problems. Their hefty oil rents eliminated the need to transfer resources from agriculture to other sectors, their demand for food was growing the most rapidly of all the countries in the region, and their food security fears were acute. In response, major oil-exporting governments lavishly subsidized their farmers. The most extreme case of this is the experience of Saudi Arabia (see Box 6.5).

As food security fears mounted, more and more countries began to reform their price policies. Already in the 1970s, four countries (Jordan, Morocco, Libya, and Saudi Arabia) actually subsidized their wheat producers even when taking exchange-rate overvaluation into account. Moroccan cereal farmers came to enjoy increasing protection (i.e., subsidies) during the 1980s; the ratio of Moroccan to international prices (calculated at market exchange rates) rose from 140% in 1984 to 180% by the end of the decade (Tyner 1993). The Syrian government paid wheat farmers about

---

BOX 6.5
SOWING OIL RENTS IN SAUDI ARABIA

Saudi Arabia paid farmers from five to six times the international price of wheat during the early 1980s while simultaneously subsidizing inputs; the effective rate of protection (the combined impact of protected output prices and subsidized inputs) may have reached 1,500% in the late 1980s (Wilson and Graham 1994). Saudi government loans to farmers rose from under US$5 million in 1971 to over US$1 billion in 1983; from 1980 to 1985 the Saudi government spent some US$20 billion on agriculture, mostly in the form of subsidies (*Economist*, April 6, 1985, 80–83). The results have been spectacular for the key food security crop: wheat output rose from less than 3,300 tons in 1978 to over 3.9 million tons in 1992—at an estimated cost of $2.12 billion in subsidies. The kingdom is the world's sixth-largest wheat exporter. Libya, Kuwait, and the UAE also offer generous farm incentives. These policies are, to put it mildly, dubious both economically and ecologically, but food security concerns and the vested interests of subsidy recipients (often well-placed ruling-family members) have swept these concerns aside.

30% more than the international price in the early and middle 1980s; maize farmers received over twice the international price, while sugar beet, sugarcane, and cotton farmers also received prices above international levels (World Bank 1986a). Some countries' farmers may enjoy prices above international levels because of "natural protection" due to transportation barriers: thus farmers in the YAR in 1982 received, on average, cereal prices that were 360% above those prevailing on international markets (World Bank 1986a, annex 1).

The impact of price distortions on aggregate farm output (and on sectoral growth) is less clear than their impact on the cropping pattern. As Binswanger (1989) has pointed out, the basic argument for inelasticity of aggregate farm output was made over forty years ago (by Johnson 1950): aggregate sectoral output can increase only if more resources (land, labor, and capital) are utilized or if there is technological change. Binswanger reviews a series of econometric studies of aggregate supply response from around the world; although there are the usual methodological debates and conundrums, the conclusion is clear: aggregate supply elasticities are very low in the short run, usually below 0.2 and often below 0.1. Several studies of Egyptian agriculture indicate that the responsiveness of the entire sector to shifts in its terms of trade is rather low (e.g., Alderman and von Braun 1984).

As usual, however, the longer the time period, the greater the response: price distortions may inhibit technological change and/or bias its direction in socially undesirable ways (Valdes 1989). Even if *elasticities* are low, a large *output response* could occur: for example, if prices rise 100%, then output could rise by 10–20%—a result that regional policymakers would certainly welcome (Braverman 1989). The most sensible conclusion is probably that price reform is a necessary but not sufficient condition for agricultural growth. In some cases, complementary price policy shifts and technological innovations have led to dramatic output gains, as the Egyptian example in Box 6.3 shows. The available evidence strongly suggests, however, that technological and physical constraints are likely to be at least as important as price policies over the medium and long run.

WATER AND THE IMPERATIVE OF A
NEW FOOD SECURITY STRATEGY

Five key water problems face most nations of the region in the coming decades. (1) Water is becoming increasingly scarce, whether measured by some simple indicator such as supplies per capita or by more sophisticated projections of water demand. (2) Water quantity problems are exacerbated by water quality problems, which become increasingly serious as nations seek to solve water quantity problems through reuse of water. Technologies exist to do this safely, but they require considerable funds and careful management. Neither of the latter is abundant. (3) From an economic perspective, the burden of adjustment to increasingly scarce water must fall on the agricultural sector, because the economic value of water is much lower in farming than for domestic or industrial use. Politically, however, such a shift is very difficult; past government programs to reclaim or redistribute land and increase domestic agricultural production have created powerful interest groups that will oppose reallocation of scarce supplies away from their farms. (4) Government water management systems suffer from lack of funds and are geared to a situation of relatively abundant water. (5) Most water resources in the region are rivers and aquifers that cross international frontiers. There is a sharp clash between economic/engineering logic, which would favor managing a river basin as a unit, and political considerations, marked by fear and distrust of one's neighbors.

Water Quantity

Since water supplies throughout the region are essentially fixed (with a few exceptions), as population grows the total amount of water per capita must decline (see Figure 6.1). But such information is not sufficient to answer the question whether there will be enough water, since, of course, much depends on how the water is used. Of the various empirical measures of water scarcity one of the most popular is that developed by Malin Falkenmark, who estimated that a country was "water-stressed" if it had less than 1,000 cubic meters per person per year of available water supplies (Falkenmark 1989). The calculation includes an allocation for agriculture as well as estimates for domestic and industrial use. An alternative measure has been created by Hillel Shuval, who takes the current estimate for municipal and industrial use in Israel (about 100 cubic meters per person per year) and adds an additional 25 cubic meters for gardening and miscellaneous to arrive at what he calls the "minimum water right" of 125 cubic meters per person per year (Shuval, personal communication). A comparison of these rough indicators with the estimates of available resources in 2025 illustrates the dimensions of the emerging challenge.

Discussions of water quantities often refer to "water needs." Since water is necessary for life, of course, there is some amount of water that is a basic need or a human right, but that amount is very small in relation to most uses of water. In the United States, for example, drinking and cooking account for only 1.5% of residential use (Gibbons 1986). And, as Figure 6.8 shows, most of the water in the region, as in most countries, is used not by households directly but by farmers.

In consequence, water economists typically split the demand for water into two parts: a small amount treated as a "merit good," a basic need to which everyone is entitled, and the rest of water use, better viewed not as a "need" but as a "demand." Water for large domestic use (e.g., watering lawns) or for industry and agriculture is to be treated as a commodity like any other: as a good the demand for which depends on its price, people's incomes, and the prices of substitutes and complements. The key concept then becomes the economic value of water (see Box 6.6).

Thinking of water *demands* instead of water *needs* complicates the simple picture of population growth pressing against fixed supplies. First the bad news: water is like food—people demand more of it as their incomes rise. From this perspective, the water situation is, if anything, even more serious than the picture presented in Figure 6.1.

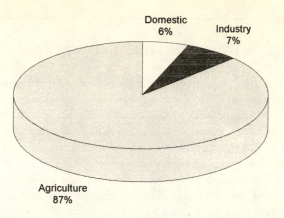

FIGURE 6.8   Sectoral water use in MENA, 1992. *Source:* World Bank (1994f).

Fortunately, the demand approach also offers good news: the demand for water, although price-inelastic, is by no means completely unresponsive to price. A World Bank review estimated that the price elasticity of domestic water demand averaged −0.45 (cited in World Bank 1994d); a recent modeling exercise for Egyptian agriculture estimated the price elasticity of demand for irrigation water at −0.37 (Hazell et al. 1994). Everywhere in the region, water use is heavily subsidized. In many countries, not even the costs of operations and maintenance of water systems are recovered. In none are the capital costs (some US$12.5 billion per year) recovered from users. The price of water for most users in the region is zero.[12] Mechanisms to raise the private cost of water to users may well be critical to the management of increasing scarcity. As we shall see, however, the creation of such mechanisms faces formidable institutional, managerial, technological, and political challenges.

Water Quality

One approach to dwindling per capita water supplies is to try to recycle water. Water analysts distinguish between water *use* and water *consumption*. For example, water used by a household is all the water that it takes from taps and pipes, but water consumed by the household is only that fraction (typically about 50%) that does not then flow back out into the system as waste water. In crop production, use is the water applied to the fields; consumption is the water lost to the system through evapotranspiration. The rest may return to the river or seep into aquifers, where it can often be tapped as groundwater. An indication of the ratios of use to consumption for different uses in Egypt is shown in Figure 6.9.

To the extent that water can be reused, water supplies can be augmented so that more users can be accommodated. However, using water reduces its quality, even if consumption is low. This is most obvious in industry, where the ratio of consumption to use is often very low (e.g., 1:6) but the quality of the water coming out of a factory is very different from the quality of the water that flows in.

BOX 6.6
THE ECONOMIC VALUE OF WATER

Like any commodity, water must be scarce to have an economic value. If water is scarce, the "shadow price" of water is the amount by which one additional unit of water (say, 1 cubic meter) will increase our utility. Put differently, we should be willing to pay a price for water that is just equal to its contribution to our goals. For domestic uses, water economists treat the household as the final consumer. Under some reasonable assumption (e.g., that expenditures on water are a small percentage of total expenditures), price, willingness to pay, and marginal utility are all the same. For drinking water, surveys in the Cairo slum of Embaba have shown that consumers are willing to pay up to £E4.00 per cubic meter (more than US$1.17 per cubic meter at mid-1995 exchange rates), which is more than the cost of producing water by desalination.

Willingness to pay for water on the part of industrial and agricultural users is determined by the marginal value product of water. Water is an input into industrial and agricultural production processes. Farmers are willing to pay a price for water that is just equal to the marginal physical product of water (e.g., the amount of additional cotton made possible by one more cubic meter of water) times the price of that output. Industrial values are lower than domestic users' willingness to pay but higher than that for farmers. For example, the marginal value product of water in Egyptian sugarcane production may be as low as £E0.1 or about US$0.04 (World Bank 1993a). This means that (1) agriculture is the "residual user" of water, and, within agriculture, the residual users are those producing crops with low marginal value products (a cubic meter of water used for tomatoes in Egypt produces about £E0.8—eight times more value than water used for sugarcane) and (2) economic reforms that increase crop prices also necessarily raise the demand for water. Economic reform without reform of the water system will exacerbate water shortages.

Repeatedly used irrigation water increases in salinity. Some crops (e.g., rice) are more salt-tolerant than others, but there are always limits on recycling. Increased concentrations of heavy metals and toxic organic substances pose still more serious challenges. These problems are exacerbated by outmoded treatment plants, poor managerial practices, and inadequate and/or underenforced pollution control regulations. For example, Algerian waste water from households and industries is usually dumped untreated into rivers and the Mediterranean because of nonfunctioning treatment plants. Industrial waste water from lead-paste machinery used in battery manufacture is dumped into the Zarqa River in Jordan, causing problems for downstream farmers in the Jordan Valley. Excessive (often subsidized) fertilizer use in

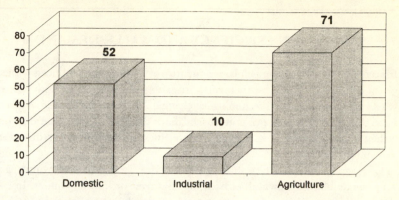

FIGURE 6.9   Percentage of water used that is consumed, by sector, in Egypt, early 1990s.
Source: Egyptian Ministry of Public Works and Water Resources.

Tunisia has led to the eutrophication of some reservoirs. Many countries have serious water quality problems (see Table 6.1).

It may be possible to increase the reuse of water safely in most MENA countries but only if treatment technologies and, especially, institutions and management systems improve dramatically. Recyling of water and its concomitant, greater water-use efficiency, can certainly reduce pressure on supplies, but doing so will require significant changes in behavior and incentives at all levels of the water system.

The Implications of Agriculture's Being the Residual User

As water demand increases, some users will not be able to obtain all the water they want—or formerly obtained. A simple thought-experiment illustrates the situation. Suppose that, at a zero price, all consumers can have all the water they want (as has been the case in countries such as Egypt until very recently). Now suppose that, as rising population and incomes push up demand, demand exceeds supply at a zero price. Assume further that water is priced. As the price rises, uses whose economic value is less than price will be terminated. For example, if the only source is desalinated water, at an average cost of approximately US$1.00 per cubic meter,[13] only domestic users will buy water. At such a price there will be no agriculture at all: even for high-value crops in a productive farm system like Egypt's, the marginal value product of water is less than US$0.30. This situation, in which increasing water scarcity forces irrigated farming to do with less and less water, is becoming increasingly apparent in very water-scarce countries such as Israel, Jordan, and the West Bank and Gaza (see Box 6.7). Forecasts in Israel, for example, suggest that agriculture will have to rely almost exclusively on recycled waste water in the not too distant future. Economic logic strongly suggests that agriculture, as the marginal user, will bear the brunt of increasingly limited water supplies. The implications for food security strategies are obvious: food security cannot be achieved through domestic production.

BOX 6.7
IRRIGATION EFFICIENCY AND WATER DEMAND

It may be objected that a much larger quantity of food can be produced with a given volume of water by increasing irrigation efficiency. Certainly there would be gains from such technological change. The best experience is that of Israel, where crop yields per unit of land have doubled at the same time as water use has fallen by 50%. Certainly more efficient irrigation can reduce the demand for water.

One must, however, be cautious here. Excess irrigation water must go somewhere; often it flows either back into the river or into an aquifer. In either case, there is often scope for reuse of the water. In such a "closed system," enhanced irrigation efficiency creates additional water supplies only by improving the quality of water. How large such an effect is seems not to be well-understood. Perhaps the safest conclusion in the present state of knowledge is that improved irrigation efficiency, though desirable, is no panacea for increasing water scarcity. The percentage of water used in agriculture (and, therefore, the total amount of water) will necessarily decline as municipal and industrial demands grow. The main role of irrigation efficiency may be to ensure that food production does not decline with reduced water use. Technologies such as drip irrigation are thus not an answer to regional food security problems.

As so often happens, however, the political calculus yields a very different answer. The region's states have sponsored irrigation expansion for decades, in some cases (Egypt) for over 150 years. The interests that have been created, including national bureaucracies and prosperous farmers, are formidable indeed. Farmers can invoke nationalism as a defense for subsidized water: in Israel, irrigated farming is closely connected to the Zionist dream of "making the desert bloom"; in Jordan, the Jordan Valley Authority aims to strengthen Jordanian farmers along the border with the West Bank and Gaza; in Egypt, plans to funnel Nile water to the Sinai through the El Salaam canal seem motivated by political desires to populate the Sinai with Egyptians (lest, it is said in private, Israel reassert claims to the area).

States have invested in irrigation hoping to reduce national food dependency. The problem of food security is visible today; the problems of increasing water shortages are only now becoming acute. Once again, the lethal politics of the region have encouraged a short time horizon for planners that favors the short run over the future, but in this arid region, nature's revenge is often cruelly swift.

Irrigation has also provided the state with an opportunity to extend its authority in the countryside and to pursue its "vision" of development. The Egyptian government insists on pursuing land reclamation and concomitant irrigation expansion to the fringes of the Nile Valley, although most studies show that the returns to water in such uses are very low. The Moroccan government has used irrigation development partly as a kind of substitute for land reform and partly as a mechanism for bestowing benefits on the rural notables who constitute such an important source of political support (Leveau 1985; Swearingen 1987). Morocco continues to be firmly committed to irrigation expansion (see Box 6.8).

The result of past irrigation expansion is that powerful vested interests block adoption of better management strategies for coping with scarcity. Farmers oppose the imposition of operations and maintenance charges, often claiming (with some justice) that the quality of service is so poor that they should not have to pay for it. As with the broader case of economic reform, however, it is important not to overestimate the strength of the farm lobby: Israel has significantly cut water subsidies to agriculture during the past decade despite the protests of its strong farm lobby, and recovery of operation and maintenance charges is being debated (for the first time) throughout the region.

Farmers will strongly oppose water charges. This is understandable: water has had a zero price, but as it has become scarce its value has been capitalized into the value of land. Farmers reasonably view the imposition of water fees as an expropriation; they feel that they have already paid for the water. The pricing of water also raises religious (and therefore political) objections in Muslim countries. For these reasons, some analysts recommend granting farmers tradable water rights. Such a system would give the rents of water to farmers rather than to the government and simultaneously create incentives for water conservation (Rosegrant and Binswanger 1994). The concept is intriguing; so far, no country in the region has tried this approach.

Financial and Managerial Constraints

Most countries in the region heavily subsidize water use, particularly in agriculture. In particular, water charges rarely cover even operations and maintenance costs, much less the opportunity cost of water in alternative uses. Consequently, about US$12.5 billion of yearly investment in water resources go unrecovered. Some 45 million people lack access to safe water, and 85 million do not have adequate sanitation. Merely solving these last two problems will require some US$55 billion in new investment over the next ten years (World Bank 1995b). These are not small sums, but they do not include additional dams and canals or rehabilitation of obsolete treatment plants. To make matters still worse, many smaller dams in the region are increasingly threatened by siltation of reservoirs.

Morocco illustrates the dimensions of the problem. Investment in dams has stabilized in the past fifteen years at 7% of total government investment. The planned expansion of irrigation of 250,000 hectares by the end of the decade is projected to cost US$25 billion. Public spending on irrigation infrastructure is planned to double from 0.4% of GDP in 1988–1994 to around 0.7% of GDP in 1995–2000. Total investment in the mobilization and distribution of water resources is projected to reach 2% of GDP by the year 2000. There are serious questions concerning the

BOX 6.8
MOROCCAN IRRIGATION

The commitment of the Moroccan government to irrigation has deep roots. Older Moroccans can remember the implications of complete dependence on rain-fed farming in a climate so prone to drought. A drought that began in 1935 and lasted for over two years in southern Morocco deprived several hundred thousand Moroccans of food. The rural exodus was so massive that roadblocks were established and the population was diverted to camps. Half a million people became entirely dependent on government food distribution. The experience led to the creation of the first major irrigation perimeter in which land was allocated to Moroccans rather than to French *colons*. There was worse to come: in 1945 Morocco was hit by the most severe drought of the twentieth century. For eight months there was no rain whatsoever. Half of Morocco's livestock perished; a massive relief operation was undertaken to distribute grain brought in from the United States, Canada, and Argentina. Distribution weaknesses meant that relief stations could distribute only 6–9 kilograms per person per month; since an average person needed about 15 kilograms per month, widespread starvation ensued.

With such a historical background, it is hardly surprising that the government of Morocco is so committed to the development and extension of irrigated agriculture. Irrigation development has another attractive feature: it allows the government to reward its friends and to strengthen its support among leaders in rural communities. Ever since 1961 its rural development programs have sought, successfully for the most part, to strengthen rural elites who have long been among the key supporters of the monarchy (Leveau 1985). Perhaps 9,500 to 9,000 large landowners own some 2.2 million hectares, or nearly 30% of the country's farmland (Swearingen 1987, 187). They constitute a critical constituency for the palace, as do the much larger number of smaller farmers who know perfectly well that their relative wealth is in large measure the result of public investment.

Public investment in large dams and infrastructure has been the key. According to Swearingen (1987), from 1912 to 1956 (the French Protectorate period) fourteen dams were constructed. In the first ten years of independence (1957–1967) three dams were built. In 1968 the government proclaimed a "politique des barrages" designed with the assistance of the World Bank, and by 1991 fourteen more dams had been completed. The goal, originally proclaimed by the French Protectorate, has been to bring the total area under irrigation to 1 million hectares. Current plans call for the completion of twelve new dams by the end of the decade. The largest, the Al Wahda dam on the Ouerga River in the Sebou Basin, will be the second-largest dam in Africa, smaller only than the Aswan High Dam in Egypt. Fifty-one additional dams are planned for the coming thirty years.

impact of these plans on continued fiscal stability, the linchpin of the government's economic reform program (World Bank, 1994d; see also Chapter 9).

The managerial constraints are no less severe than the financial. The current system of centralized public-sector management of water systems breaks the link between suppliers' incentives and users' needs. Privatization of municipal water systems (i.e., turning them into public utilities) could greatly improve not only access to capital but also managerial efficiency and responsiveness to users' needs. Water bureaucracies in the region suffer from the many ills of public-sector management (Chapter 8). Poor pay and performance and haphazard ministerial coordination (in most countries, a number of ministries have responsibility for different aspects of water systems) are among the most serious.

As water becomes increasingly scarce, governments will have little choice but to devise mechanisms for choosing which consumers do *not* get all the water they want. Whether this is done by administrative diktat, by differential taxing of land planted in water-using crops, by volumetric pricing of water, or by tradable water rights, *some* mechanism for rationing scarce water will have to be found. The course of these changes will be central to the region's political economy in the decades ahead.

International Hydropolitics

However serious the domestic political impediments to the management of scarcity, they pale beside the international political complications. Many countries in MENA depend for much of their water supply on sources that are either outside of their boundaries (rivers) or shared with other countries (aquifers). The major international rivers in the region are the Nile, the Jordan, and the Tigris-Euphrates. Internationally shared aquifers include the Eastern Erg (Algeria and Tunisia), Nubian Sandstone (Egypt, Sudan, and Libya), the Saq Formation/Disi aquifer (Jordan and Saudi Arabia), the Ras al-'Ain aquifer (Turkey and Syria), and the Yarkon-Tanimim and coastal aquifers (Israel and the West Bank and Gaza).

Sharing water with one's neighbors creates very severe problems. We have seen how water is used and reused. Water can be diverted or polluted by upstream states, leaving downstreamers with either less water or poorer-quality water or both. International law is generally unhelpful, and, in any case, only two of the rivers are governed by even limited agreements (the Nile Agreement of 1959, signed by Egypt and the Sudan, and the Israeli-Jordanian Peace Agreement of 1994, which contains a water protocol). Beyond accords to share flow data, there are no agreements governing the other international water resources.

Needless to say, in the volatile political environment of MENA, such sharing of water resources creates serious difficulties. From an engineering and economic perspective, water basins and aquifers are best managed as units. However, if leaders are reluctant to rely on international trade for food, they are still more reluctant to entrust their water supplies to foreigners. It does not help that upstream and downstream states often have serious political differences over other issues (e.g., Turkey,

Syria, and Iraq; Israel and Jordan before 1994; Israel and Syria; Jordan and Syria; Israel and the West Bank and Gaza). Even Egypt and the Sudan, which have normally enjoyed reasonably cordial relations, recently confronted the specter of conflict over water: As accusations and counteraccusations flew between Cairo and Khartoum in the wake of the assassination attempt on President Hosni Mubarak, Sudan threatened to "cut off Egypt's water." The fact that the Sudanese lack the engineering capacity to do such a thing did little to dampen hysteria in the Cairo press. Water conflicts are potentially serious throughout the region.

Two important points need to be emphasized: First, the increasing pressure on existing supplies of surface water and aquifers among the sovereign nations of the region has introduced into foreign policies and interstate bargaining a range of issues that have traditionally been seen as domestic and none of the business of one's neighbors. For example, the on-field efficiency of water use in a given agricultural sector may be scrutinized by neighbors who contest the status quo or the "real" needs for water of a state with which they share a river or aquifer. Even the selection of crops with different crop-water duties may appear on the international bargaining agenda.

Second, the reluctance of sovereign states to put their claims to water at risk by integrating storage and delivery infrastructure across international boundaries may stymie any future attempts to create regional water markets. The only way in which quantities of water could be transferred among riparians in an international basin is through dams, reservoirs, pumping stations, irrigation grids, and pipelines running across boundaries. Narrow concerns for national and food security may prevent such integration even at the cost of suboptimal solutions such as overexploitation of limited national water resources or investment in costly desalination technologies (see Box 6.9).

CONCLUSION

The future of the region is nonagricultural. There is simply not enough water available for countries to become self-sufficient in food, even if they were willing to bear

---

BOX 6.9
WAS THE ASWAN HIGH DAM WORTH IT?

Egypt's agriculture had been dependent on the Nile flood for millennia, but the country's irrigation system underwent a fundamental transformation in the nineteenth century with the transition to year-round irrigation, a transformation that concluded only in the 1960s with the completion of the Aswan High Dam. There are certain inescapable facts about Egyptian irrigation development: (1) Summer irrigation made possible the production of cotton on a substantial scale and was thus an important part of that country's integration into the international economy during the nineteenth century. (2) Year-round, dependable irrigation makes it possible for Egyptian yields to be among the highest in the world; for example, the High Dam allowed maize (until very recently the main rural foodstuff) yields to increase by over 70%. (3) The expansion of irrigation not only redistributed land, especially in the nineteenth century, but also increased the role of the state in the countryside. (4) Political forces have determined the pattern and timing of irrigation investment, with the result that the technological externalities that often accompany irrigation development were ignored and neglected (Waterbury 1979; Richards 1982).

The debate on the merits of the High Dam at Aswan has raged for at least thirty years. Although its problems were and are serious, the achievements of the dam are too often overlooked. First, there is no doubt that some form of "over-year storage" for Nile water was absolutely necessary to provide increased irrigation water to keep up with the country's expanding demand for food. Egypt's food security problem would have been *much* worse much earlier without the dam. When the annual Nile flood was unusually low in 1972, the country's agriculture suffered relatively little—thanks to the dam. The devastating droughts that ravaged Ethiopia and Sudan in the early 1980s would have severely affected Egypt also had it not been for the dam. Even with the dam, disaster has been narrowly averted; the level of Lake Nasser was only 147 meters in August 1988 (at 145 meters, the turbines of the dam would have had to be shut down). Second, there was really no alternative to the dam; all other technically feasible approaches faced insuperable political obstacles. It is hardly surprising, given the need and given the alternatives, that the High Dam at Aswan was constructed.

The technological externalities were severe, however. Some of these were unique to the High Dam: problems of shoreline erosion (because all silt was trapped behind the dam), decline in fish catches in lakes and in the Mediterranean, scouring of the Nile banks, and high evaporation losses of the water stored in Lake Nasser. However, the most serious problems were really not qualitatively different from problems that had repeatedly plagued the extension of year-round (i.e., summer) irrigation in Egypt for more than half a century: inadequate drainage and disease. The incidence of schistosomiasis and ancylostomiasis in Egypt is very ancient but was certainly exacerbated by earlier (khedivial and British) irrigation works just as it was by the High Dam. From the point of view of agricultural production, however, the main problem with irrigation expansion both was and is the neglect of drainage. The ecological consequences of such neglect are straightforward: all water contains soluble salts and minerals, and even if farmers use water with maximum efficiency, inadequate drainage will permit these salts to accumulate, dramatically lowering soil fertility. By the late 1970s, this problem afflicted some two-thirds of Egypt's cropland. Massive investments funded by the World Bank have since largely overcome it.

the (considerable) costs of such an economically inefficient strategy. They will increasingly have to export in order to eat, to reform and revamp their water allocation mechanisms, and to find new, often unpalatable ways of cooperating with their neighbors. Such shifts, in turn, will require a rather dramatic change in the role of the state in the economy. We devote the next three chapters to this central issue.

NOTES

1. Bahrain, Israel, Jordan, Kuwait, Libya, Oman, Qatar, Saudi Arabia, the UAE, and Yemen.

2. Algeria, Egypt, Gaza, Iran, Iraq, Jordan, Lebanon, Morocco, Syria, and Tunisia.

3. According to the World Bank, for LDCs as a whole, the average income elasticity of water demand is approximately 0.30.

4. The formula is $D = n + ye$, where D = the rate of growth of demand, n = population growth, y = the rate of growth of per capita incomes, and e = the income elasticity of demand, or the percentage change in quantity demanded for every 1% change in income.

5. In 1970 a barrel of oil would buy roughly one bushel of wheat; by 1980 the same barrel would purchase six bushels, and even in May 1986 a barrel (of US$14.00) oil would still buy over three bushels.

6. As argued by a Muslim Brotherhood delegate in Jordan's parliament in February 1994.

7. Bimodalism refers to a land-tenure system that combines a small number of owners holding very large estates with a large number of owners holding very small farms.

8. The shah's land reform provoked Ruhollah Khomeini to attack the policies so vociferously that he was forced into exile in Iraq, thus beginning the long saga that culminated in the revolution of 1978–1979.

9. The list of disincentives to Sudanese cotton production in the late 1970s was formidable: an overvalued exchange rate, explicit taxes on cotton, allocating the input costs of *all* crops in the Gezira Scheme to cotton, and long (sometimes up to two-year) delays in payments. Many of these problems were ameliorated in the early 1980s.

10. In the early 1980s price controls applied to cereals, olives, wine grapes, sugar beets, milk, dates, beef, and poultry; prices for pulses, lamb, forage crops, fish, and most vegetables and fruits were uncontrolled (Cleaver 1982, 36).

11. Sectoral policies (e.g., price supports) transferred *into* agriculture a nominal sum equal to 1.3% of GDP, but when the impact of exchange-rate overvaluation is included 3.8% of GDP was transferred *out of* agriculture between 1961 and 1985 (Hansen 1991).

12. This is not true for all users. Urbanites who buy drinking water from water vendors typically pay the full cost of water provision, while farmers who pump groundwater pay both the capital and the operation and maintenance costs of such services. The current situation, in which some users pay the full costs while others pay nearly nothing, is both inefficient and highly inequitable.

13. The cost of desalinating brackish water using reverse osmosis is now about US$0.65 per cubic meter, while that for sea water exceeds US$1.00 per cubic meter (World Bank 1994f).

7

THE EMERGENCE OF THE PUBLIC SECTOR

Our concern in this chapter is to document and analyze the prodigious growth in the economic functions of the Middle Eastern state. Despite more than a decade of economic crisis and adjustment, the relative shares in the economy of the Middle East's public sectors have not diminished. There is little that is unusual about the region in this respect. What is striking, however, is the relative lack of variation in the degree and scope of state intervention across countries that otherwise differ greatly.

Middle Eastern states are big; they employ large numbers of people as civil servants, laborers, and managers—sometimes, as in the case of Egypt, as much as half of the nonagricultural workforce. These states monopolize resources; they control large investment budgets, strategic parts of the banking system, virtually all subsoil minerals, and the nation's basic infrastructure in roads, railroads, power, and ports. Whether size and resources translate into strength is a question to be examined on a case-by-case basis. Certainly the potential for strong states is there, especially when resources are coupled with control over, or control by, the military. There is, unsurprisingly, abundant contrary evidence that size spawns red tape and administrative paralysis, that resources are diverted into corruption and patronage, and that authoritarian leaders cannot push administrative agencies at a speed and in the directions that they would like.

Though attenuated after years of economic stagnation and crisis, the legitimacy of an interventionist state has long been widely accepted in the Middle East. This does not mean that most Middle Easterners accept the legitimacy of the particular state under which they live—that frequently is not the case. Rather, it has been conceded in the abstract that the state and its leaders have a right and an obligation to set a course for society and to use public resources to pursue that course. Two principles flowing out of the Western liberal tradition are given short shrift. One is that state authorities, to the extent possible, should confine themselves to the maintenance of law and order, regulation (but not too much) of economic life, provision of basic social-welfare benefits (health and education), and defense of the borders. The Middle Eastern state has taken on functions vastly more complex than these, and its citizenry has endorsed the effort. The other is that the emphasis is on the ends of state intervention, and checks and balances are seen not as preventing abuse of power but as impeding the state's progress toward its goals. Therefore, to some extent, there has been an acceptance of a high concentration of power—economic, administrative, and military. It can be argued that in Muslim society political authority is legitimate only insofar as it promotes the interests of the community of believers, the *umma*. This yields an organic image of society, a living community whose "health" the state must maintain.

Religious and cultural antecedents notwithstanding, it is our conviction that it is more the politics of decolonization and development than history and culture that account for the interventionist, organic state in the Middle East. The caretaker states of the colonial era, concerned with law, order, and taxation, have logically evoked their opposites, states that impinge upon all aspects of their citizens' lives. Moreover, the postcolonial state has seen as its duty the reparation of all the economic damage resulting from colonial policies. It has had to mobilize human and material resources on an unprecedented scale. The goal has been to overcome "backwardness" and build a prosperous, educated citizenry, a diversified economy, and national power. These tasks and goals are culture-blind. Hence we find basic similarities in the goal orientation and interventionism of states in societies as widely varied in cultural origins as Indonesia, India, Burma, Ghana, and Tanzania.

THE STATE AS ARCHITECT OF STRUCTURAL TRANSFORMATION

It is not only outside observers but also the leaders of Middle Eastern states themselves who see their tasks in terms of "engineering," architecture, blueprints, and the like. They are designing new societies, and the state is that collection of agencies that will enable them to build what they have designed. Ideologies vary but not the perceived need for state intervention. And no state in the region has been able to forgo the exercise of elaborating a national plan.

The point of departure for the state is backwardness—a condition, it is alleged, imposed on the region by imperial powers. Its three major components are (1) an economy mired in the production of cheap agricultural commodities requiring an unskilled workforce, (2) the perpetuation of this system of production by denying education and the acquisition of modern skills to all but a privileged few, and (3) the forcible integration of this backward agrarian economy into an international division of labor. To remedy backwardness requires a supreme effort, a kind of military campaign on three fronts. Only the state can coordinate the campaign and mobilize the inherently scarce resources needed to carry it out. So, along with the engineers and architects there are the inevitable Bonapartes, and, as Tunisia's Habib Bourguiba has demonstrated, they need not all wear a marshal's uniform.

The area has an inadequately educated, poor population and an agricultural system characterized by small pockets of high productivity in a landscape of low yields and by the inefficient use of scarce capital. However ironic it may seem in retrospect, the leaders of the state saw the need for intervention in order to avoid wasting scarce resources. The comprehensive and rational planning effort anticipated would require an inventory of available resources, a strategy for their development and utilization over time and in light of the profound structural changes that would take place in the economy and society as the plan unfolded, and the construction of the economic levers needed to implement the plan.

Throughout the region it was assumed that the private sector could not be relied upon to undertake this kind of resource mobilization and planning. The least critical saw the private sector as too weak financially, too close to a commercial and trading rather than an industrial past, and too concerned with short-term profit to be the agent of structural transformation. More severe critics emphasized the greed and exploitativeness of the private sector, its links to interests in the metropole, and its tendency to export capital rather than reinvest profit. Private sectors might be tolerated, but nowhere, save in Lebanon, did they enjoy legitimacy. Reliance on private entrepreneurs and on the law of supply and demand to allocate scarce resources would be wasteful, it was believed, and would not extricate the economy from its trap.

As important as efficiency for the state leaders was equity. Gross inequalities in the distribution of assets in Middle Eastern societies, not to mention absolute poverty for large segments of the population, were associated with the colonial system of exploitation. A more equitable distribution of assets within society became a universal goal throughout the area, again regardless of ideology. Some states pursued redistribution with greater conviction than others, but all espoused it as an ideal. The Great Depression, leading to absolute declines in the standard of living of rural populations, and the privations caused by World War II sensitized Middle Eastern elites to these equity issues. It was again assumed that the private sector could do little to alleviate them, and, if left to its own devices, would probably aggravate them.

The Middle Eastern state took upon itself the challenge of moving the economy onto an industrial footing, shifting population to the urban areas, educating and training its youth wherever they lived, raising agricultural productivity to feed the nonagricultural population, redistributing wealth, building a credible military force, and doing battle with international trade and financial regimes that held it in thrall. These were goals widely held if poorly understood by the citizens at large. There were no impediments, then, to the expansion and affirmation of the interventionist state.

ATATÜRK AND THE TURKISH PARADIGM

The Republic of Turkey has been an example if not a model for many of the other states in the Middle East. Because it achieved real independence in 1923 after successful military action against European forces (Italian, French, and Greek) that were bent on dismembering all that remained of the Ottoman Empire, Turkey showed what could be done to thwart imperialism. It possessed an inspiring leader, Mustapha Kemal Atatürk, "father of the Turks," who built a secular, republican, nationalist system in Anatolia. His sweeping reforms, from the abolition of the caliphate to the introduction of the Latin alphabet, have been too well studied to require treatment here (see, inter alia, Lewis 1961). For our purposes it is important that by the late 1930s Turkey was endowed with a credible military structure, the beginnings of a diversified industrial sector, and a rapidly expanding educational system.

Atatürk's contemporaries, including Reza Khan of Iran, who was to found the Pahlavi dynasty, looked on with varying degrees of admiration.[1] So too did Arab nationalist politicians such as Habib Bourguiba of Tunisia, who would lead their countries to independence. There were also students and young army officers in the turbulent 1930s who learned from the Turkish experience lessons that they would come to apply in the 1940s, 1950s, and 1960s. An Iraqi officer who later participated in the Golden Square conspiracy to oust the British from Iraq attended Atatürk's funeral and wrote (Salah al-Din Sabbagh, quoted in Hemphill 1979, 104): "I saw signs of progress which amazed me . . . a social revolution in education and economics, and in cultural and spiritual affairs. I saw the pride of the Turks in their fatherland, pride in their nationalism, their self-reliance and their independence."

In April 1931 Atatürk issued a manifesto containing six principles that were to be embodied in the 1937 Constitution of the Republic. He declared that the society and the Republican People's party (RPP) that he headed would be republican, nationalist, populist, secular, etatist, and revolutionary. The principles of etatism (a term meaning "statism" taken from the French and retaining a strong Bonapartist flavor), populism, and revolution will be our main concern here. The first provided legitimation for a strongly interventionist state. Populism meant that the masses were the object of political and economic policy and that distributive issues were at the top of the policy agenda. The revolution lay in Turkey's rejection of empire along with the sultanate and caliphate, its militant republicanism, and its confrontation with the imperial powers of Europe. Within a few years of the enunciation of these principles, Turkey embarked upon an economic experiment that was to be emulated in several countries following World War II (Hershlag 1968, 74): "Turkey became first among the backward countries to conduct an experiment in planned development with its first five year plan in 1934." It also built a large public-enterprise sector and pursued a policy of import-substituting industrialization under the auspices of the state.

Turkey's trajectory toward this experiment was erratic, and there is no question that the world depression forced it to revise profoundly the strategy that had prevailed in the 1920s. It is important to review these antecedents. First, Turkey was in a shambles after World War I. The empire itself had been destroyed, and the Arab portions had fallen under French or British control. The basically agricultural economy had been badly damaged, especially in the fighting against the Italians, French, and Greeks. Then, after the signing of the Treaty of Lausanne in 1923 between

Turkey and the major war victors, an enormous exchange of population took place. By 1926 perhaps 1.3 million Greeks had left Anatolia, taking with them vital skills in commerce and trades. In their place came 400,000 Turks, mainly peasants from Thrace, whom the rural world could absorb only with difficulty.

Turkey inherited the Ottoman debts, which were finally settled at the end of the decade. It was fortunate that no reparations were imposed upon it as a successor to the empire that had fought on the side of Germany in that war. The fact that Turkey had signed a treaty of friendship with the USSR in 1921 may have militated against vindictive policies on the part of the allies. The Lausanne Treaty did impose restrictions on Turkey's ability to place tariffs on imports from Europe and hence to protect its own nascent industries. Nonetheless, Atatürk was determined from the outset to promote Turkey's industrialization and to liberate its economy from dependence on the West.

In contrast to what was to transpire after 1931, the republic's strategy was to rely on private-sector initiative and to avoid taxing the peasantry in order to finance industrial growth. The Organic Statute of 1924 declared private property and free enterprise to be the basic principles of the state. Its credo, not always honored, was that "the task of the state begins where the activity of private initiative ends." With the founding of the Iş (Business) Bank in 1924 to finance private enterprise, the state showed its willingness to foster the growth of an indigenous capitalist class (F. Ahmad 1981; Boratav 1981).

Again in contrast to what came later, the new republic implemented policies that were relatively favorable to the rural world. In 1924 the 'ushr tax, or tithe, was abolished. This tax had generated as much as 29% of government revenue. Its abolition was of particular benefit to smallholders and poor peasants. In its place the government introduced a land and unutilized-property tax that fell most heavily on wealthy landlords. Throughout the 1920s agricultural prices were allowed to rise. Although agricultural production was at an abnormally low ebb following the war, it grew by an impressive 58% between 1923 and 1932, while cereals alone increased by 100%. At the same time urban consumers had to pay high prices for commodities controlled by government monopolies: tobacco, salt, sugar, matches, alcohol, gasoline. In many ways this was the inverse of the urban bias that was to develop in the 1930s and 1940s, when factory smokestacks were referred to derisively as "Atatürk's Minarets."

After 1929, with the onset of the world depression, agricultural prices collapsed. No nonagricultural private sector had yet emerged that could pick up the slack in the economy, even supposing that world economic conditions would have allowed such a development. As soon as the tariff restrictions of the Lausanne Treaty had expired in 1929 and before the onset of the depression, Turkey introduced higher tariff barriers to protect local industry. As the world crisis affected the Turkish economy, there was not time enough to see if the private sector would respond to the protective measures.

When, on April 20, 1931, Atatürk launched the etatist experiment, he said (Hershlag 1968, 69), "We desire to have the Government take an active interest, especially in the economic field, and to operate as far as possible in matters that lend themselves to the safeguarding of vital and general interests, or, in short, that the Government ensure the welfare of the nation and the prosperity of the state."

In May 1932 Turkey negotiated a historic interest-free twenty-year loan from the Soviet Union for the equivalent of US$8 million. This may have been the first loan of its kind to a developing country, and no other such loan was made by the USSR for the next twenty-five years. It was to be used to buy Soviet equipment for two sugar refineries and a textile mill at Kayseri. Repayment was to be made in Turkish exports to the USSR. The Soviets set up a special trade agency, Turkstroj, to implement the loan agreement, and in 1935 it negotiated with the Sümer Bank created by Turkey especially to manage the project financing of its First Five-Year Plan. A pattern of economic assistance was thus established that was repeated in Egypt, Algeria, Syria, Iraq, Iran, and Morocco in the 1950s, 1960s, and 1970s.

In the year following the loan Turkey drew up the five-year plan, and its implementation began in 1934. Atatürk, like nearly every head of state we shall consider in these pages, headed a coalition of interests and ideological perspectives within his government and party. Left-of-center figures who had been offstage during the 1920s were given much more prominence during the etatist era. There was much more talk now of the "Kemalist Revolution," and the private-sector strategy of the earlier years was abandoned. Rather than the state's being the handmaiden of a growing private sector, it was now to seize the "commanding heights" of the economy and bend the private sector to its will. In this new atmosphere the state technocracy and party ideologues could denigrate the private sector and talk of the necessity of state intervention. The left-of-center voices found a forum in the journal *Kadro* (cadre, or party organizer). The secretary general of the RPP, Recep Peker, was known to be an advocate of forced-pace change "to tear away from a social structure the backward, the bad, the unjust and harmful, and replace them with the progressive, the good, the just, and the useful elements" (cited in Karpat 1959, 72). Finally, the prime minister, Ismet Inönü, a man who saw etatism primarily in terms of the political and administrative obligations of the state, was to some extent eclipsed by Celal Bayar, who saw the need for much more aggressive economic intervention on the part of the state. Bayar came out of the Iş Bank and became minister of economy in 1932 and then prime minister, replacing Inönü, in 1937.[2]

The five-year plan was a blueprint for ISI, emphasizing local processing of Turkey's primary commodities and minerals. A major part of the program lay in developing the textile industry, utilizing Turkish cotton, and selling to a large domestic market. This kind of thrust is often associated with the so-called easy phase of ISI. Other industries of a similar nature are food processing, sugar refining, and simple assembly. But Turkey went somewhat farther, launching projects in basic chemicals—superphosphates, chlorine, caustic soda—as well as in cement, iron, paper and cellulose, artificial silk, and hemp.

Even prior to the First Five-Year Plan, the Turkish state owned several enterprises; there were processing plants associated with the tobacco monopoly, beet sugar refineries, a shoe factory, wool mills, and a cotton-weaving plant. It had taken over power generation and the railroads from foreign interests. The plan added some twenty new enterprises to the public patrimony. A State Office for Industry was set up in 1932 and by 1936 was empowered to inspect the accounts of private-sector industries and to enforce price and wage controls. The Central Bank had been established in 1930 as the bank of issue. In 1933 the Sümer Bank was created and absorbed the Bank for Industry and Mines. Sümer Bank provided financial management and supervision to state-owned enterprises, planned new projects, and invested in others coming under the plan. By 1939 Sümer Bank's holdings accounted for 100% of production in artificial silk, paper, cardboard, iron, and superphosphates, 90% of shoes, 80% of steel and lubricants, 70% of coke, 62% of leather, 60% of wool, and 55% of cement (Hershlag 1968, 92). The Iş Bank went well beyond private-sector financing to invest in a number of joint ventures. The Eti Bank to finance mineral exploration, extraction, and marketing was set up in 1935. In this way the state in the 1930s had the financial leverage to orient all economic actors in accordance with plan priorities.

Work on drafting the Second Five-Year Plan was started in 1936, and the plan itself was formally adopted by the Grand National Assembly in September 1938, just before Atatürk's death. Over a hundred new enterprises were planned. The first efforts at "industrial deepening" were projected. The Zonguldak-Karabük region was slated to become a heavy-industrial-growth pole, built around coal, steel, and cement and serviced by its own Black Sea port. A major effort was to be made in power generation, basic chemicals, engineering, and marine transport. Part of the plan was to disperse industry in order to benefit backward areas, especially Eastern Anatolia, as well as for strategic reasons.

Some of the seemingly inevitable side effects of this sort of big-push strategy began to make themselves felt during the 1930s. The government ran a growing deficit due in large part to an outsized bureaucracy. The civil service, not including the military or part-time personnel, reached 127,000 in 1938 and 184,000 in 1945 (Karpat 1959, 129). About 35% of the budget went into their salaries. The size of the civil service was due not so much to the overproduction of university graduates that characterized most of the Middle East by the 1960s as to the absorption of the personnel of the Ottoman bureaucracy set up to administer an empire. The deficit of the government stood at TL13.8 million in 1930/31 and TL125 million in 1939/40. Over the same decade Turkey was obliged to borrow abroad, from the Soviet Union, Germany, and the UK. Still, in contrast to other countries in the region in the 1960s and 1970s, Turkey was able to finance most of its investment out of its own resources. The level of investment was modest by postwar standards; the government was investing annually about 5% of national income, with another 5% coming from the private sector.

World War II interrupted the Second Five-Year Plan, and a period of severe privation ensued. Import substitution continued of necessity as Mediterranean shipping was disrupted during the hostilities. A major shift in the political domain after the war, leading to a two-party system and the victory of the Democrat party, which had come to oppose etatism, ushered in a liberal economic phase during the 1950s. Only after a military takeover in 1960 did Turkey return to etatism. By that time it had been joined by another half-dozen states in the region.

REPLICATING THE PARADIGM

It would be an exaggeration to say that other states in the Middle East slavishly imitated the Turkish experience. In fact, state-led ISI spread throughout the developing world in the years after 1945 and, as a strategy, had a logic independent of any single country's efforts. We shall see that among Middle Eastern states, the tremendous growth in publicly owned assets and the development strategies associated with them had varying sources of inspiration, some external and some internal.

We are distinguishing here between public-sector enterprise and other governmental agencies that employ the bulk of the civil servants. Generally, public-sector enterprises have their own statutes, personnel policies, and salary and wage scales. They are companies in the legal sense that make and sell products or deliver services for a fee. They enter the national marketplace directly and usually with great impact.

If we look at the developing world as a whole around 1980, we find impressive statistics on the weight of public sectors in their economies. On average the output of public-sector enterprise, exclusive of financial institutions (banks, social security and pension funds, insurance companies), accounted for 8.6% of GDP; these enterprises on average employed 47% of the manufacturing workforce in the organized sector, utilized 27% of all manufacturing investment, and, on average, ran deficits equivalent to 5.5% of GDP (World Bank estimates). State-owned manufacturing enterprises frequently accounted for 25–50% of value added in manufacturing. Some Middle Eastern states, especially Egypt, Algeria, and Syria, were well above these averages: Egyptian state-owned enterprises accounted for around 60% of value added in manufacturing and Syrian ones for 55%. The output of Algeria's and Egypt's state-owned enterprises reached 13% of GDP, while Syria's was close to 11%. Turkey's state-owned enterprises were, in 1980, producing about 8% of GDP and accounted for 25% of value added in manufacturing.[3]

The question of publicly owned assets is important to this study in two ways. First, the assets are always the instruments of a given state's development strategy. In that sense, they shape production, absorb and allocate scarce resources, and orient patterns of consumption. This may help or hinder the development of private-sector activity. They are always instruments of political preemption and control. Second, when we speak of publicly owned assets we are obviously dealing with a fundamental aspect of property relations and hence of class. What the state owns private individuals or firms do not. In theory, public ownership is ownership by the "people." The state acts as custodian, manager, and fiduciary on behalf of citizen-owners. The latter monitor the state through their representatives in parliament or the party or on the boards of directors of public enterprises. But this is almost everywhere a fiction. The state builds public enterprise to pursue ends that it alone defines.

The last statement, however, begs some crucial questions. The state cannot be taken as a homogeneous bloc. It always contains diverse interests and factions that prevail at different times and in different combinations. Furthermore, crude indicators of ownership and economic weight such as those presented in the preceding paragraph tell us little of intent or direction. The states in the Middle East with the weightiest public sectors are to be found among the frequently conservative oil exporters. Moreover, in Turkey in the 1950s, despite the professed liberalism of the Democrat regime, the public sector actually grew. More important, public enterprises may implicitly or explicitly be put, in part, at the service of the private sector (Turkey in the 1920s) or be designed to marginalize the private sector over time (Egypt after 1961). The weight of the public sector in the two cases may not differ much, but direction and intent are quite different.

The final begged question is whether the managers of public assets, those "atop the commanding heights" or "in control of the major means of production," come to constitute a dominant class that seeks to reproduce itself and to exclude others from the assets it controls. We shall try to advance some tentative answers to all these questions in the remainder of this chapter.

Arab Socialism and State Enterprise

One set of Arab states adopted the Turkish paradigm and went well beyond it. These states' strategies were explicitly socialist and populist, hostile to the indigenous private sector and to foreign capital, and aimed at far-reaching redistribution of wealth within their societies. The strategy has not always been sustained and on occasion has been officially abandoned (e.g., Egypt after 1974, Tunisia after 1969, the Sudan after 1972). The principal experiences we have in mind are those of Egypt (1957 to 1974), Algeria (1962 to 1989), Syria (1963 to the present), Iraq (1963 to the present), Tunisia (1962 to 1969), the Sudan (1969 to 1972), and Libya (1969 to the present). What all these have in common is a blueprint for the radical transformation of their societies and economies. In these states the campaign for growth, equity, and national economic sovereignty was no mere metaphor. Indeed, Habib Bourguiba of Tunisia likened his country's quest for development to a jihad and said that Tunisians should be dispensed of the obligation to fast during the month of Ramadan just as if they were warriors.

A number of basic assumptions underlay these experiments. The first of these was that profit and loss should not be the primary criteria for assessing public-sector performance. Rather, the creation of jobs, the provision of cheap goods of first necessity, the introduction of new economic activity to remote or poor regions, and the achievement of self-sufficiency in goods of a strategic or military nature would be more appropriate tests of success. Second, it was assumed that the operation of supply and demand was inferior to planning and the application of administered prices. In market situations, goods of first necessity (food and clothing) are often the objects of speculation, and because demand for them is relatively inelastic, prices may rise precipitously. The state had to set prices so that such goods were always within reach of the poorer strata. Similarly, the price of inputs and credits supplied to priority industries should not reflect their scarcity value.

The large-scale private sector was seen as untrustworthy. Most of the regimes under consideration nationalized it or sharply curtailed its activities. The private enterprise that remained was subjected to state licensing and price and wage controls and had to compete with the public sector for scarce credit and foreign exchange.

Foreign investment was viewed with suspicion. Entire sectors of the economy, such as basic metals, chemicals, and minerals, were reserved exclusively for public-sector enterprise; neither foreign nor domestic private capital was to be allowed in them. The favored form of collaboration with foreign capital was through turnkey projects and management contracts in which foreign investors acquired no equity in the host country. Socialist Algeria, in the 1970s, was able to do billions of dollars' worth of business with the United States, France, Japan, and other countries through such formulas.

The setting up of closed sectors for public-sector enterprise underscores another assumption: that there is nothing inherently inefficient about monopolies. In many instances state-owned enterprises enjoyed monopolies in entire lines of production or were the sole purchasers (monopsonists) of certain inputs (raw cotton or sugar beets). Egypt, after 1961, took matters further, putting the entire banking, insurance, and foreign-trade sectors under public ownership. The supply of investable funds and the importation of vital production inputs thus became a state monopoly. For all this to work—to promote overall growth, industrialization, and a more equal distribution of income—required that the planners anticipate the interaction of all the economic variables that, today, computer models chew over, that the managers pursue efficiency even while protected by tariffs and monopoly status, and that the civil servants put in an honest day's work. By and large none of those requirements were met.

Egypt.   Egypt was the first Middle Eastern country in the postwar era to adopt a strategy of radical transformation. In many ways it was far more integrated into the world economy than Turkey. It had been one of the leading exporters of raw cotton for nearly a century. The British occupation after 1881, the economic dependency on Britain that ensued, and the role of the Suez Canal in world trade made Egypt's a classic colonial economy. As in Turkey, the world depression and World War II set Egypt on the path toward ISI. It was the Egyptian private sector, partly indigenous and partly foreign, that led this effort.

In 1952 the Egyptian monarchy was overthrown by a military coup led by Col. Gamal 'Abd al-Nasser and a group of his colleagues known as the Free Officers. From 1952 to 1956 Egypt promoted public-sector growth but, as did Turkey in the 1920s, did so either to help the private sector or to undertake projects that the private sector could not finance or manage. The old Aswan Dam was electrified to augment Egypt's power supply, and it was decided to promote a new, giant dam at Aswan to increase hydropower generation severalfold and to ensure a predictable supply of irrigation water to the agricultural sector. Work was begun on an iron-and-steel complex at Helwan and on a large fertilizer plant at Aswan.

It was not until the Suez War of November 1956 that the public sector grew at the expense of the private. Because of the participation of Britain and France, along with Israel, in a direct attack on Egypt, all assets owned by the former two in Egypt were taken over by the Egyptian government. The attack itself had been provoked by Egypt's nationalization in July 1956 of the Suez Canal Company. With the wartime sequestrations of banks, trading companies, insurance companies, utilities, and some manufacturing enterprises, the Egyptian state found itself in possession of a very substantial patrimony. It was only then that the term "socialism" was adumbrated and that left-of-center voices in Nasser's coalition gained greater prominence. In 1957 Egypt contracted its first loan for economic assistance from the Soviet Union, followed in 1958 by a Soviet loan to help build the Aswan Dam. In 1957 Egypt began its first five-year industrial plan, with strong emphasis on state enterprise. By 1960 it considered itself ready for a five-year plan for the entire economy.

After 1956 there was some evidence of private-sector disinvestment and profit-taking and of growing suspicion between the private sector and the regime. The privately held Misr Group and Bank Misr had been essentially taken over by the state by 1960. The new Ministry of Industry was empowered to license and regulate all private industrial activity. The elaboration of the First Five-Year Plan was carried out without consulting the private sector, although the latter was called upon to mobilize about 55% of all investment over the five-year period.

The failure of the private sector to do so allegedly provoked a wave of nationalizations through the Socialist Decrees of July 1961. In one fell swoop, the Egyptian state took over most large-scale industry, all banking, insurance, and foreign trade, all utilities, marine transport, and airlines, and many hotels and department stores. The bulk of agricultural property remained in private hands, but new desert reclamation projects were owned by the state.

The First Five-Year Plan embodied a straightforward ISI strategy, combining aspects of the easy (textiles, sugar, automobile assembly, pharmaceuticals) and hard (heavy engineering, steel, chemicals, and fertilizers) phases. It generated 1 million new jobs and growth rates of 6% per annum. Yet in 1965 it ended in crisis.

The Achilles' heel of ISI, whether under public or private auspices, is the economy's ability to earn foreign exchange. For the major oil exporters that at one time or another pursued an ISI strategy (Iran, Algeria, Iraq) this was not a major problem, but for Turkey, Egypt, and Syria it certainly was. As Turkey learned in the 1930s, ISI often reduces imports of one kind—for example, finished textiles or refined sugar—only to increase imports of another kind—for example, raw materials such coking coal for new steel plants or capital goods such as turbines and power looms. Egypt's new industries were designed to market their products in Egypt. They did not have the economies of scale and basic operating efficiency that would have allowed them to export to other markets. Thus, although they needed imports to function, they could not generate the foreign exchange to pay for them.

To finance its Second Five-Year Plan, Egypt had little choice but to try to borrow more heavily abroad. It was not very successful, and even the Soviet Union was reluctant to extend new lines of credit. At the same time, the state's large outlays on construction and social services drove up domestic demand without commensurate increases in the supply of goods, so that inflation reared its head. Finally, the fact that few state-owned enterprises were profitable and many were being padded with redundant personnel in an effort to create jobs meant that the government had to resort to deficit financing to cover their losses. In short, although rates of growth in production and the delivery of services were quite respectable, the Egyptian state nonetheless faced an external and a domestic fiscal crisis.

The Second Five-Year Plan, which, like Turkey's, would have led to industrial "deepening," had to be abandoned for want of adequate financing. Then came Egypt's disastrous defeat in the June War of 1967 and Israel's occupation of the Sinai Peninsula. Egypt lost its oil fields there, the Suez Canal was closed to traffic, and tourism was badly disrupted. Egypt went into severe recession. Its strategy for radical structural transformation through public-sector enterprise had to be revised.

President Nasser died in September 1970, and his successor, Anwar al Sadat, cautiously pursued a policy of economic liberalization aimed at reforming and streamlining the public sector, stimulating the private sector, attracting foreign investment, and promoting exports. Public-sector enterprise was subjected to sharp criticism for its chronic inefficiency and huge operating deficits. Although Egypt continued to produce five-year plans, they had clearly lost their mystique, and the notion of socialist transformation was downplayed. Egypt's initial blueprint, the crises that developed in its implementation, and the revision of the blueprint constitute a sequence that has been repeated elsewhere in the region.

Even though heavily criticized, Egypt's public sector continued to grow throughout the 1970s. Entering the 1980s it included 391 companies employing about 1.2 million workers. The market value of its assets was about £E38 billion. In 1983/84 its wage bill stood at £E5.7 billion (over 20% of GDP) and over the period 1975 to 1982 had grown at 19% per annum. It accounted for 22% of total value added in the economy. The return on its total investment was only 1.5% per annum. Counting public authorities that ran everything from the Suez Canal to the Aswan High Dam, along with the civil service, the public and governmental sector in the early 1980s, before the structural adjustment effort began, had 3.2 million employees— more than a third of the total workforce and over half of the nonagricultural workforce—and over £E90 billion in assets. Total public expenditures in 1980 represented 60% of GDP, total government revenues 40% of GDP, and the public deficit 20% of GDP. As one observer put it, "There are few, if any, developing countries in the world with such high proportions" (Ahmad 1984, ix).

Algeria.   Algeria is one of the few LDCs to rival Egypt in terms of the weight and extent of its public sector. To a greater degree than in Egypt, the overall size of the Algerian public sector was the result of ideology and long-term policy.

Independent Algeria emerged in 1962 out of seven years of revolutionary warfare against the French. Many of the leaders of the National Liberation Front (FLN) were committed socialists and occasionally marxists. The nature and intensity of their struggle made it inevitable that Algeria would confront France and the imperialist world in general. International business interests and the Algerian private sector itself were seen as likely enemies of Algeria's revolution (Leca 1975, 124). At no time did the state see its role as helpmate to the private sector as did Turkey during the 1920s or Egypt up to 1957. The National Charter of 1976 reiterated a position that had been constant since 1962 (Benissad 1982, 29):

> In Algeria, private property cannot be a source of social power. It cannot be the basis for exploitative relations between the owner and the workers. It can only function to the extent that it does not prejudice the interests of the laboring masses, nor constitute a brake or obstacle to the inexorable evolution of our society toward socialism. . . . In the industrial domain, the intervention of the national private sector is restricted to small-scale enterprise involved in the last stage of industrial transformation, downstream of the production or the imports of the public and socialist sectors.

From 1966 to 1989 the commanding heights of the economy were reserved to the state. Collaboration with foreign firms was extensive but was carried out on a contract basis involving turnkey projects, technical assistance, and purchase of technology. Direct investment was carefully avoided. Like all states in the region, Algeria was the exclusive owner of all subsoil minerals. French companies that had developed the country's petroleum and natural gas deposits were nationalized between 1969 and 1971, giving the state exclusive control over their production, refining, and marketing. The hydrocarbon sector, after the surge in world petroleum prices in 1973, came to represent over 30% of GDP.

In many ways Algeria could not have avoided heavy state intervention even if its official ideology had not been socialist. On the eve of independence, nearly all of the French settler community in the country, nearly 1 million strong, packed up and left. This was an exodus even more devastating than that of the Greeks from Turkey in 1922–1923. The French settlers had dominated modern farming, skilled trades, the small industrial sector, and government services. The new state inherited agricultural, industrial, and residential property, and the first two were given over to "worker self-management" units. In the agricultural sector, over 2 million hectares were cultivated by about 130,000 permanent workers on 2,000 farms. The state owned the farms, but, in theory, the workers had full control over their operations. The same formula was applied to industrial units. These consisted of about 400 small-scale enterprises, only 5% of which employed more than 100 persons, with a total workforce of 15,000.

In the early years, when Ahmad Ben Bella was president, the experiment in self-management was seen as putting power in the hands of the working people and constituting a barrier to the emergence of a dominating and domineering bureaucracy and technocracy. The period 1962–1965 was one of near-romantic populism and socialism, but already one could see government agencies arrogating basic decision-making power in all spheres of production. The FLN, which had seen many of its militants absorbed into the civil service, could do little to defend the populist experiment, and the workers themselves soon reverted to apathetic clock punching.

The romantic period came to an end in June 1965 when the minister of defense, Houari Boumedienne, overthrew Ben Bella and ushered in an era of "rational" top-down planned development that, implicitly, saw the masses as a source more of disruption than of revolutionary support. Worker self-management was paid lip service but deprived of any effective autonomy.

Boumedienne met one significant challenge from Ben Bella's old coalition. In December 1967, Tahar Zbiri, the army chief of staff, and Abdelaziz Zerdani, the minister of labor, who was close to the General Confederation of Algerian Workers (UGTA), tried to engineer a coup against Boumedienne. Zerdani saw the Algerian development strategy moving toward authoritarian state capitalism in which the workers would be made to pay a heavy price while their unions would be muzzled. He appealed to his old friend Zbiri, like himself a Berber from the Aurès Mountains and a former guerrilla fighter. The coup attempt failed, the conspirators fled, and Boumedienne, in close concert with his minister of industry, Abdesslam Belaid, pushed Algeria down the very path that Zbiri and Zerdani had tried to bar.

With the First Four-Year Plan, 1969–1973, Algeria launched a program built on heavy industry. Oil and natural gas were to serve two ends: First, they would be the feedstock for a modern petrochemical sector producing fertilizers and plastics; second, the earnings from their export would pay for the importation of plant and capital goods for steel manufacture and vehicle assembly. It was expected that the agricultural sector, especially the self-managed units, would be an expanding market for the new products (fertilizers, irrigation pipes, tractors). The local private sector was regarded as irrelevant to the effort, and foreign firms were seen mainly as providers of technology. The slogan was "Sow oil to reap industry."[4]

By the time Algeria initiated its Second Four-Year Plan, world petroleum prices had quadrupled. In contrast to Egypt, Algeria faced no financing problems in the mid-1970s. In that sense, its experience emphasizes some of the inherent weaknesses of state-led ISI, for by the late 1970s important elements of the strategy had been called into question. Rather than the agricultural sector's generating demand for new industrial products, there was a general decline in agricultural production, especially in the self-managed sector. Algeria became a major importer of food. Insufficient domestic demand coupled with tariff protection and monopoly position meant that public-sector industries operated below capacity and at high cost. They had little hope of exporting except to some of their East European creditors. Finally, some of the imported technologies, for example, in natural gas liquefaction, were so sophisticated that costly units were frequently shut down for technical reasons.

Near the end of his life, President Boumedienne acknowledged the shortcomings of his approach. In his "state of the nation" address of March 1977, he warned (as cited in Nellis 1980, 410): "Management is henceforth a battle to win, just as we have won that of investment. In truth, the problem of the management of the economy, and more particularly the production and service units will constitute our major concern for the coming years."

Boumedienne died on December 27, 1978. His successor, Chadli Benjadid, a former liberation army commander and a man who had supported Boumedienne in 1965, was elected president in 1979. During his tenure, which ended in 1991, Algeria's public sector was extensively overhauled (see Chapter 9). However, it still dominates the Algerian economy. In the late 1980s there were some fifty public-sector companies and twenty authorities with assets valued at over US$100 billion, employing 80% of the industrial workforce and accounting for 77% of industrial production. Add to this 260,000 civil servants and 140,000 teachers and other employees of the educational system and one has 45% of the nonagricultural workforce on the public payroll. Finally, the Algerian state in the late 1970s was able to invest the equivalent of 25–30% of GDP annually. This could not be achieved, however, without stimulating inflation and increasing the external debt, which stood at US$23.3 billion in 1987 (World Bank data). The collapse of international petroleum prices in 1984/85 forced Algeria to question the very premises of the strategies it had followed since the mid-1960s.

Syria and Iraq. Since 1953 Syria and Iraq have fallen under the domination of the same pan-Arab party, the Ba'ath, or Arab Renaissance party. Since its founding in Syria after World War II, this party has called for Arab unity and socialism and has tried to propagate its message throughout the Arab world. The major obstacle to its spread was perceived by its leaders to be Nasser's Egypt, especially when that country entered its socialist phase after 1961. Many of the policies of state intervention implemented by the Ba'ath in Syria and Iraq sprang in part from its socialist ideology, but just as important were the fears of Ba'athi leaders that Egypt's socialist transformation would dazzle the radical youth of the Arab countries.

Both Syria and Iraq, in contrast to Algeria, had substantial indigenous trading and landowning bourgeoisies and no foreign settler communities (see, inter alia, Batatu 1978 and Khoury 1983b). Prior to the Ba'ath's coming to power, both countries pursued policies whereby the state helped the private sector through the development of infrastructure and banking credit. Neither country had made significant advances in industrial production, although Iraq enjoyed the revenues from a sizable oil sector.

In the 1950s, under the Iraqi monarchy, oil revenues gave the state tremendous leverage in the economy. The public Development Board annually absorbed 70% of those revenues and invested them mainly in infrastructural development. It was this policy that required deferred consumption and contributed to a situation in which elements of the Iraqi armed forces overthrew the monarchy in July 1958.

Almost immediately the new regime, led by 'Abd al-Karim Qassim, disbanded the Development Board and replaced it with a Planning Board and a Ministry of Planning. There was a major shift in investment away from infrastructure and agriculture and into industry. The Ministry of Industry was empowered to promote public-sector projects and to supervise and license private-sector activities (Penrose and Penrose 1978, 253).

The new regime, however, was not Ba'athist. Qassim was merely a nationalist army officer with leftist leanings. He tried, unsuccessfully, to balance Nasserist, communist, and Ba'athist forces within his coalition, contend with Kurdish dissidence, and implement far-reaching agrarian reform. All the contenders battled for the hearts and minds of the officers' corps, and in February 1963 a group of Ba'athi officers overthrew and killed Qassim and set up a government presided over by Colonel 'Abd al-Salam 'Arif. This new regime moved in early 1964 to nationalize all banks, along with thirty-two large industrial and commercial firms. With these moves the state's share in large manufacturing concerns rose to 62% of gross output, 46% of employment, and 55% of wages. Once more the state had captured the commanding heights, and most observers concede that Iraq acted in order to steal Egypt's thunder (Batatu 1978, 1,031; al-Khafaji 1983). It was not, however, until 1972–1975 that full nationalization of the petroleum sector took place.

The nationalization coincided with the first big increase in world petroleum prices. With the oil sector under state ownership, the state's share in GDP rose to 75% in 1978, although if the petroleum sector is excluded the state's share was a more modest 23%. By 1977 there were some 400 public-sector enterprises, employing 80,000 workers. They absorbed over 60% of all industrial and commercial investment (Stork 1982, 36; al-Khafaji 1983, 36). Total government employment in 1977 reached 410,000, or nearly half of Iraq's organized workforce. Adding to this 250,000 members of the armed forces (a figure that rose to over a million in the 1980s), 175,000 in the Ba'ath militias, 260,000 in the police, 120,000 pensioners, and thousands of schoolteachers, we find that by 1980 one in four Iraqis was on the state payroll (Batatu 1978, 123). Saddam Hussein's public sector had a far more sinister aspect. Not only was it heavy with police and intelligence personnel but, it is estimated, it came to employ about a quarter of the workforce as part-time paid informants (al-Khalil 1989, 38).

Between 1958 and 1961, Syria had been a member, along with Egypt and North Yemen, of the United Arab Republic (UAR). In those three years, under Egyptian pressure, land-reform measures were undertaken as well as some steps toward expanding public-sector enterprise. Egypt's Socialist Decrees of July 1961 alarmed the Syrian private sector, which feared they would be applied in Syria. In league with sympathetic army officers, these elements brought off a coup d'état that took Syria out of the UAR and installed a somewhat conservative, pro–private-sector military regime in Damascus.

In March 1963, a month after the Ba'ath had come to power in Iraq, yet another military coup brought the Ba'ath to power in Syria. A year later, in May 1964, the regime took over the country's banks, and in the wake of private-sector protests in Hama seven enterprises of "reactionary capitalists" were nationalized. Then in January 1965 the regime undertook far-reaching nationalizations. Assets worth US$50 million were taken over, and the public-sector share in industrial production rose from 25% to 75%. Again, part of the motive was to demonstrate to organized labor that Syria's socialist experiment was as radical and devoted to workers' welfare as Egypt's (in general, see Hannoyer and Seurat 1979; Chatelus 1982; Longuenesse 1985). In fact, Syria structured its public sector exactly on the Egyptian model, using general organizations to supervise production in specific sectors such as textiles, chemicals, and metals.

A more radical wing of the Ba'ath seized power in 1966, but its militancy was manifested mainly in confronting Israel and sponsoring Palestinian guerrilla attacks. This faction's image was battered in the June War of 1967, and, in 1970, after an internal trial of strength, Hafiz al-Assad, the minister of defense and commander of the air force, took power. The shift to some extent resembled that from Ben Bella to Boumedienne. Assad is an organization man, mistrustful of the masses and of revolutionary adventures. He has relied on the large power structures of the country—the armed forces, the bureaucracy, the Ba'ath party, and the public sector, perhaps in that order—to control, preempt, and police, rather than mobilize.

Between 1970 and 1982 employment in public-sector enterprises rose from 57,000 to 119,000, or half the industrial workforce. In just two years the public-sector wage bill doubled, from 3.5% to 6% of GDP. In 1979 Syria's total workforce was about 2.1 million, of which about a third were engaged in agriculture. Combined public-sector and civil-service employment probably totaled 350,000. There may have been 230,000 Syrians in uniform and, although there is some overlap with the preceding categories, perhaps 200,000 members of the Ba'ath party (Drysdale 1982, 5–7). Some 220,000 workers, in both the public and the private sector, were unionized and under Ba'athi supervision. Again, as we have found in all the preceding experiments, the state not only owned the major means of production but controlled through the payroll, the party, and the armed forces the most strategically situated elements of the workforce.

This dominance in Syria and elsewhere was achieved at the expense of economic efficiency. The strategic sectors became used to their privileges and to low levels of performance. The state hesitated to alienate them by asking more of them or paying them less. This held true especially for the military; in 1981 Syrian defense outlays were 13% of GNP, placing it among ten nations worldwide to spend more than 10% of GNP on defense. Inflation and a growing external debt (according to the World Bank, it increased tenfold between 1970 and 1983 to $2.3 billion) plagued the economy, especially after the Syrian intervention in Lebanon in 1976.

Tunisia. Since its independence in 1956 and up to 1987, when Gen. Zine Ben 'Ali deposed Habib Bourguiba on the grounds that he was medically unfit to govern, Tunisia maintained uninterrupted civilian rule. Nonetheless, during those same years it built an interventionist-state system that resembled those of Egypt, Turkey, and Algeria. Bourguiba founded the Neo-Destour party in the 1930s, rallied the small-scale trading and commercial groups, the professionals and intelligentsia, and the trade unions, and led the coalition to power (Moore 1965).

Although the French settler community in Tunisia was smaller than that of Algeria, it nonetheless dominated the modern private sector. There was no such mass exodus of settlers as had occurred in Algeria, but the fact remained that there was no indigenous industrial bourgeoisie upon which the new state could rely to promote the country's structural transformation.

From the outset, then, much as in Turkey in the 1920s, Bourguiba built a powerful state apparatus, to some extent gutting the Neo-Destour of its best cadres, subordinating the trade unions, and using the state to mobilize capital and raw materials to stimulate private activity. In 1962 Tunisia launched its first three-year plan, followed by a series of four-year plans. The state's role in resource mobilization was, until the 1970s, overwhelming (Table 7.1).

Tunisia in the 1960s was quite literally boxed in between the Arab world's two most ostentatious socialist experiments, Algeria's to the west and Egypt's to the east. By 1964 Bourguiba had decided that it was necessary to give a more radical cast to the Tunisian strategy. In October 1964 the Neo-Destour party became the Socialist Destour party and called for the "coexistence" of the public, private, and cooperative sectors. The First Four-Year Plan, 1965–1968, was to embody a socialist transformation of the economy: cultivators were to be grouped into agricultural cooperatives, and state enterprise would spearhead the industrialization drive. A young intellectual, Ahmed Ben Salah, active in the Neo-Destour and the unions prior to independence, was made secretary of state for planning and national economy and was the driving force behind the experiment.

Both the extent and the pace of state intervention had been dictated by Bourguiba's failing health. The Combatant Suprême, as he liked to be known, feared that the socialist experiment would be jeopardized if he were to die before it had been implemented. But Bourguiba's health was restored, and Ben Salah, by forcing the

TABLE 7.1   Evolution of Total and Industrial Gross Fixed Capital Formation in Tunisia (%), 1962–1981

Gross Fixed Capital Formation	Three-Year Plan 1962–1964	Four-Year Plan 1965–1968	Four-Year Plan 1969–1972	Four-Year Plan 1973–1976	Four-Year Plan 1977–1981[a]
Total					
Public sector	74.7	70.9	59.1	53.2	64.7
Private sector	25.3	29.1	40.9	46.8	35.3
Industrial					
Public sector	84.7	86.7	60.5	43.7	63.6
Private sector	15.3	13.3	39.5	56.3	36.4

[a] Average for first three years of the plan.
Source: Signoles and Ben Romdane (1983, table 4, 119).

pace of cooperative formation, alienated much of the regime's petty capitalist and small landowning constituency. In 1969, Bourguiba turned on Ben Salah and put him on trial for treason. The statist experiment was overhauled, and Tunisia adopted a strategy of stimulating its private sector and promoting exports to the EEC. The shift in emphasis is shown clearly in Table 7.1 (see also Chapter 9). Still, the Tunisian state remained, until the late 1980s, a dominant force in the economy and, through its modest oil exports, had substantial revenues at its disposal. Those rents explain the rising share of the state in gross fixed capital formation after a decline in the early 1970s. In 1982 the public-enterprise sector alone employed 180,000 persons, or over 11% of the workforce.

The Sudan. The Sudanese economy is, among the major countries of the region, the most heavily dependent on its agrarian sector. About 70% of the population is rural, and half the workforce is employed in farming, animal husbandry, or fishing. Prior to independence in 1956, Sudanese industry was based on agricultural processing: cotton ginning, seed crushing for edible oil and feed cake, and soap manufacture. After a military coup d'état in 1958, the Sudanese state began an ISI strategy built around public enterprise. Once again the Egyptian example proved contagious, and, as in Algeria, Egypt, Syria, and Iraq, the Soviet Union stepped in with technical assistance, planning advisers, and soft loans. The strategy was maintained during a turbulent return to civilian control between 1964 and 1969 and then was accelerated when Major Ga'afar al-Nimeiri seized power in May 1969. His coalition initially had a strong marxist and communist faction that engineered several nationalizations of foreign banks and indigenous private firms.

In the summer of 1970 Nimeiri purged his government of its communist and marxist members and within a year began to denationalize the assets he had just taken over. In the early 1970s the regime acted to support private-sector growth within the general ISI framework, but state enterprise remained the dominant economic force in the economy. Public companies dominated the sugar, textile, cement, food processing, and canning sectors and had a significant share of leather, edible oils, soap, and detergents. The million-hectare Gezira Scheme was owned by the state; cotton and groundnuts were grown on the scheme by 100,000 tenant farm families. One of the largest state-owned farms in the world, it has for years been the backbone of Sudan's rural economy. The state also owned all mineral deposits, including some oil deposits in the south-center of the country, the Sudanese railroads, and all hydro- and thermal-power systems.

As has been the case for the other countries under consideration, the state in the Sudan was the country's principal employer. With over 400,000 people on the public payroll in 1977, exclusive of the armed forces, the state employed 8% of the entire workforce and 21% of the nonagricultural workforce (Table 7.2).

Libya. The Jamahiria, or "mass state," of Libya represents the unacknowledged combination of romantic revolutionary and Islamic programs with a kind of cynical

TABLE 7.2   Growth in Public Employment in the Sudan, 1955/56–1976/77

	1955/56	1976/77
Central government	31,283	119,115
Local government	80,000	157,457
Public corporations	65,125	132,144
Total	176,408	408,716

Source: Sudanow, December 1977, 11.

authoritarianism. As in all the major oil-exporting nations, the state dominates the economy by the simple fact of owning the petroleum and controlling the proceeds of its sale. That was the case under the Idrissid monarchy, and it has been the case since 1969, when the monarchy was overthrown by the then-lieutenant, now colonel, Mu'ammar Qaddhafi. He eventually elaborated a new theory of the state of the masses, the Jamahiria, in which all productive units and all workplaces were to be directly governed by popular congresses. Bureaucratic hierarchies, top-heavy party structures, and elaborate command channels were all depicted as antithetical to true popular democratic control. Libya's experiment, on paper, was one of worker self-management with a vengeance (see Fathaly and Palmer 1980).

Beginning in 1979 Qaddhafi led an assault on private-sector interests unrivaled anywhere in the Middle East. He expropriated all private industry. In 1981 all bank deposits were seized without warning, and a program to abolish retail trade by replacing it with state-owned supermarkets was begun. By this time three-quarters of the workforce was on the public payroll (Anderson 1986). The Libyan state and regime never really relinquished effective control of production and administration to popular committees. The oil and banking sectors were kept under tight state control, as were and are the 60,000–70,000 men and women in the armed forces. Libya had multiyear development plans like other countries we have considered, and the leadership did not allow the "people" to question, much less change, any of the plans' major parameters.

Liberal Monarchies

It may be that socialism entails a significant public sector, but the converse is not true. The monarchies of pre-1979 Iran, Jordan, and Morocco all professed liberal economic credos in which the private sector was to be the leading force. The role of the state was, once again, that of handmaiden to the private sector. Yet if we look at statistical indicators of state activity, we see that these three countries possessed public sectors of a size and weight equal to those of the socialist countries. The experience of these monarchies highlights the general point that one should not confuse state ownership with socialism. Some "radical" regimes have waved the flag of public ownership to demonstrate their socialist bona fides, while "liberal" regimes have passed over in silence the substantial assets they control through state ownership.

Iran. Next door to Turkey in Iran a would-be Atatürk appeared on the scene following World War I. Colonel Reza Khan of the Persian Cossacks had de facto taken over the Iranian state by 1924, and it was his intention to proclaim a republic, have himself made president, and build a state system as Atatürk was doing in Turkey. The Shi'ite clergy of Iran, however, vehemently resisted the plan for a republic and persuaded Reza Khan to proclaim himself shah (emperor) in 1925 and found the Pahlavi "dynasty."

Aside from this nontrivial distinction, Reza Shah set about building a nation in the ethnically and geographically fragmented society he inherited from the Qajars. The state apparatus and the armed forces grew side by side, and, as in Turkey, the depression pushed the Iranian state into ISI. The private sector benefited from credit provided through the state Industrial Bank as well as from high tariff walls against imports. But the state did not wait to see how the private sector would respond to these incentives, and by 1941 there were public enterprises in textiles, sugar, cement, and iron and steel. Through consumption taxes and trade monopolies, the Iranian state, over the period 1926–1940, was able to invest some US$400 million in industry and infrastructure, a very substantial sum for that era. Another US$120 million was invested by the private sector. All this was done with very little foreign borrowing. The modest revenues from the sale of oil in those years were turned over to the military (Issawi 1978). Iran was neither populist nor revolutionary, but it was just as etatist as Turkey.

Reza Shah was sent into exile in 1941 by the Allies, who feared his collaboration with the Axis. His young son, Mohammed Reza Pahlavi, became the new shah. He did not consolidate his grip on power until his showdown in 1953 with the prime minister, Mohammed Mossadegh, a nationalist leader who brought under state ownership the British-controlled Anglo-Iranian Oil Company. After that time, Iran's economic strategy marched on three legs: petroleum exports, continued ISI, and a division of labor between the public and private sectors. State enterprise undertook the deepening process in iron and steel, copper, machine tools, aluminum, and petrochemicals, while a dynamic private sector, sometimes in joint ventures with foreign capital, moved into finished metals and special steels, synthetic fibers, paper, automobile assembly, and sugar. Iran in 1944 established a Plan and Budget Organization and launched its first national plan. In this respect it was well ahead of all countries in the region except Turkey.

This kind of division of labor was what one would have expected—it reconciled the regime's professed economic liberalism with a strong state presence in the economy. But in the 1970s a very significant shift in the division of labor occurred, one that contains lessons about the logic of public enterprise in the Middle East. With the first great surge in petroleum prices in 1973/74, the shah's state had at its disposal a tremendous volume of rents. Neither the shah nor his advisers nor the state technocracy proposed investing these rents in private-sector growth. Rather, the new funds allowed the state to expand and consolidate in an atmosphere in which public authorities either disregarded or were actively hostile to the private sector (Razavi and Vakil 1984, 66; also Katouzian 1981, 237).

The dream of the Great Civilization had established a subjective development goal in the shah's mind. It was then necessary to refine the strategy of development. This was to be a big-push type of industrialization financed by oil revenues. Given that oil reserves were seen to have a twenty-year horizon and that the shah probably knew himself to be fatally ill, the speed with which the big push was to be implemented was to be of paramount importance in the shaping of expenditure patterns.[5]

Those expenditure patterns revealed a dramatic reorientation in the 1970s (Table 7.3). In 1973 the shah prophesied that by 1980 there would be no more than 2 million people, or 300,000 farmers, left in Iran's agricultural sector (Katouzian 1981, 304). In essence, he had resurrected his father's blueprint: a powerful state and a powerful military establishment. By the end of the 1970s, government investment and consumption represented 43% of GNP. Military expenditures, which neared US$10 billion in 1978, were the equivalent of 10% of GNP. One-quarter of the nonagricultural workforce, 1.5 milllion people, were on the public payroll.

A few general propositions can be extracted from this example. First, regardless of the ideology of the regime, one of the major factors making for the expansion of the state's economic role is the *control* it offers the nation's leaders over resources and people. It denies those resources and people to other contenders for power. In this sense it is doubtful that the shah ever wanted a powerful and autonomous private sector to develop in Iran. A prosperous, subordinate, parasitic private sector, yes; a true national bourgeoisie, no. When given his monopoly over Iran's external rents in the 1970s, the shah showed the real content of his liberalism.

Has the Islamic Republic of Iran reversed this pattern since 1979? The question is of more than passing interest, for Iran's Muslim state could be something of a harbinger for the rest of the region. The constitution of the Islamic republic is explicit on the role of the public sector, which is to include "all major industries, foreign

TABLE 7.3   Public and Private Shares in Gross Fixed Capital Formation in Iran (billions of rials), 1963–1977

Gross Fixed Capital Formation	Third Development Plan 1963–1967	Fourth Development Plan 1968–1972	Fifth Development Plan 1973–1977
Public	74	146	734
Private	77	141	319

Source: Razavi and Vakil (1984, 76).

trade, major mines, banking, insurance, power, dams, major irrigation systems, air, sea, land and rail road transport." Shortly after Khomeini's return to Iran, a wave of nationalizations took place in June and July 1979 involving 27 banks, insurance companies, and heavy industries, such as the Iran National Auto Works, with 12,000 workers, and the Behshahr Industrial Group, with 13,500. By the end of 1982 the National Industrial Organization controlled about 600 enterprises, with 150,000 employees. In addition, the Foundation for the Disinherited (Bonyad-e Mostaz'afin) was created to take over the assets of the Pahlavi family, the Pahlavi Foundation, and the expropriated property of the shah's entourage, including farms and apartment buildings (Bakhash 1984, 178–184).

There was, then, no rollback of the state under the Islamic republic, yet it is clear that the new regime was deeply divided on the issue of state ownership and intervention in the economy. The Guardianship Council, whose duty it is to monitor the constitutionality of legislation, in 1982 declared unconstitutional land-reform measures passed by the parliament as well as the law giving the state a monopoly in foreign trade. At the same time, an important faction of radicals in the parliament sought to use the state to engineer a far-reaching redistribution of wealth in Iranian society. In early 1988 Khomeini's pronouncements showed that he was leaning in the direction of the more radical, statist elements. Since his death, and despite the emergence of the more pragmatic Hashemi Rafsanjani, the same tension continues unresolved (see Chapter 9).

The Kingdom of Jordan.   The Jordanian economy is small and, since the Israeli occupation of the West Bank in 1967, severely truncated. It is dynamic and growing but highly dependent on external assistance. In 1976/77, for example, when GNP stood at US$1.7 billion, external assistance exclusive of military aid stood at US$500 million.

The Jordanian state has controlled the economy in three ways. First, as the direct recipient of the external assistance, it has been able to channel investment in the ways it sees fit. This channeling has taken the form of large-scale joint ventures with state, foreign, and local private capital in fertilizers, cement, petroleum refining, and so forth. State pension and social security funds as well as the Housing Bank and the Industrial Development Bank have been the conduits for substantial public finance. In 1980 the state had a significant equity stake in private firms in mining (42%), manufacturing (23%), tourism (27%), and transport (20%) and owned 90% of the shares of the Jordan Phosphate Mines Company, 100% of the Jordan Automatic Banking Company, and 99% of the Agricultural Products Manufacturing Company (Rivier 1980, 111, 206). The second lever in the hands of the state has been the phosphate sector, the country's single largest export and foreign-exchange earner. The third lever has been the defense budget, which stood at US$246 million in 1978, or 15% of GNP.

The Jordanian private sector, a large proportion of which is of Palestinian origin, has been given the lead in promoting exports of fruits, vegetables, and manufactured goods to Arab and regional markets. If it were not so internally divided between Palestinians and non-Palestinians, Jordan would have been a good candidate for an export-led growth pattern à la Hong Kong or Singapore. Its relatively well-educated and hardworking population and its no-nonsense political leadership might have been sufficient to attract foreign investment and technology. There is no way, however, given its small population and narrow resource base, that Jordan could have pursued an ISI strategy.

The Kingdom of Morocco.   Morocco and Iran up to 1979 followed similar development strategies. Morocco, like Iran, had a substantial trading bourgeoisie that was never totally eclipsed by French economic interests during the protectorate, 1912–1956. The country's economic ideology has always been liberal and pro-private-sector. Yet, like the shah, King Hassan II may be reluctant to see a national bourgeoisie with its own resource base gain an undisputed foothold in the economy. Finally, although Morocco is not an oil exporter, it has been the world's leading exporter of phosphates, and through the giant public holding company, the Cherifian Phosphates Office (OCP), it controls the most important sector of the economy.

The state's control of the economy has taken the form of direct ownership of assets (mines, railroads, dams, sugar refineries) and equity positions through public holding companies. The OCP and the Cherifian Foreign Trade Office (OCE) own assets themselves and have a controlling interest in a host of affiliated enterprises. The OCE, for example, between 1965 and 1975 helped launch twenty-five branch operations involved in citrus exports and wound up controlling about US$5 billion in assets. In addition, the state controls a number of special investment agencies such as the Caisse de Dépôt et de Gestion, which handles social security and pension funds, and the National Bank for Economic Development, which has been a favored channel for World Bank credits.

The post-1973 surge in world petroleum prices was followed closely by a large jump in world phosphate prices. The Moroccan state found itself in control of windfall rents and, just as had occurred in Iran, used them not to invest directly in the private sector but to expand the public sector. The 1973–1977 plan was revised in midcourse, with public investment targets rising from 11 billion to 29 billion dirhams (ca. US$6 billion), destined mainly for the steel, sugar, cement, and chemical sectors. The number of public-sector firms increased from 137 in 1970 to 238 in 1976 and state equity in them from 700 million to 2.2 billion dirhams (el-Midaoui 1981, 234–238; el-Malki 1982, 175). The share of the government and the public sector in total gross fixed capital formation reached 19% in 1977 (Table 7.4). The Moroccan state employed well over 400,000 persons in the civil-service and public sector. There were at least another 150,000 in the armed forces and police. At least one-quarter of the nonagricultural workforce was on the public payroll.

Since the big push in public-sector expansion in the mid-1970s, phosphate prices have tumbled, and Morocco's military involvement in the Saharan war cost the country on average US$300 million per year for a decade. The government by 1983

TABLE 7.4   Sources of Gross Fixed Capital Formation in Morocco (millions of current dirhams and % GDP), 1968–1977

Gross Fixed Capital Formation	1968	1970	1972	1975	1977
In millions of current dirhams					
Government[a]	500	580	710	2,150	4,650
Public enterprises	950	1,050	950	3,400	4,530
Of which: transfers	(390)	(500)	(400)	(1,190)	(1,940)
Other sectors	740	1,360	1,520	3,310	6,170
Of which: housing	(250)	(440)	(580)	(1,130)	(2,180)
Total	2,190	2,990	3,180	8,860	15,350
In percentage of GDP					
Government[a]	3.1	3.0	3.1	5.6	9.6
Public enterprises	5.8	5.4	4.2	8.9	9.4
Of which: budget transfers	(4.2)	(2.6)	(1.7)	(3.1)	(4.0)
Other sectors	4.5	7.0	6.6	8.7	12.8
Of which: housing	(1.5)	(2.3)	(2.5)	(3.0)	(4.5)
Total	13.4	15.4	13.9	23.2	31.8

[a] Includes civilian investments only.
Source: World Bank (1981, 25).

had been driven into large public deficits and a cumulative external debt of around US$10 billion. It was obliged to restrict its current expenditures and investment and to revert to its pre-1974 policy of stimulating the private sector and luring in foreign investment. Although the number of enterprises in which it had a majority stake increased, the share of the state in total equity of these companies declined.

Princes and Kings of Oil

The most conservative regimes in the Middle East, the princedoms of the Gulf and the Kingdom of Saudi Arabia, are also those with the largest state sectors. They are conservative in the sense that they share nonrepublican forms of government, a concern for the protection of Islamic values, a fierce anticommunism, and dominant classes with roots in older maritime and transdesert trading communities.

Their economies have been swamped by oil revenues. They combine small populations (Saudi Arabia is by far the biggest, with about 11 to 12 million inhabitants), little or no agriculture (with the exception of Saudi Arabia; see Chapter 6), no tradition of manufacturing, and a common resource, oil, that has generated tremendous rents. The share of the oil sector in the gross national products of these countries reached the following levels in 1980: Saudi Arabia, 66%; Kuwait, 51%; the UAE, 65%; Oman, 69%

(World Bank data). Kuwait's lower figure merely signals that its rents had diversified and that the country had begun to draw significant revenues from its foreign investments.

With this kind of financial clout at the disposal of the state, it was inevitable that all new investment programs would fall within the state sphere. For most of the princedoms, industrialization will never be a realistic option except in the petrochemical field, where public enterprises have formed joint ventures with foreign multinational corporations (Kubursi 1984). Private-sector activity is booming and occasionally crashing, as in the Kuwaiti stock market (known as Suq al-Manakh) scandal of August 1982 (Beblawi 1984, 232–234). But such activity is confined to trading and speculative investment, while the public sector dominates the productive sectors and, of course, the civil service.

The civil administration has grown prodigiously in all these countries. Kuwait's expanded from 22,000 in 1963 to 146,000, of whom 90,000 were foreigners, in 1980. Saudi Arabia's grew from 37,000 in 1962 to 232,000 in 1981, to which we should add another 81,000 part-time or nonclassified employees (Ayubi 1985; see also Islami and Kavoussi 1984; Chatelus 1982, 23). The entire native Saudi workforce in 1980 totaled 1.5 million, and there were 800,000 foreign workers in the country. Ayubi saw this expansion as a function of increased educational output unaccompanied by significant industrialization. Public employment serves the purpose of political control of the educated. It also serves as window dressing: "a respectable and modern looking tool for distributing part of the oil 'loot' and for 'disbursing' largesse camouflaged in the language of 'meritocracy and national objectives'" (Ayubi 1985).

Saudi Arabia has gone farther and established a giant public-enterprise sector, with over forty corporations in housing, storage, agriculture, and basic industries. In the plan period 1976–1980 alone, Saudi Arabia disbursed US$290 billion, which went into infrastructure, port development, and new industrial cities at Jubail and Yanbu. The 1980–1985 development plan, although less spectacularly funded, was designed to put Saudi Arabia on an industrial footing. The then–oil minister, Ahmad Zaki Yamani, prophesied that Saudi Arabia would soon rank alongside Argentina, Brazil, and South Korea as a semi-industrialized country (*Middle East Journal*, March 1984, 25–27). Whereas the goal may be to shift some of the burden of industrialization onto the private sector, it is likely that even if significant industrialization takes place, it will involve mainly public-sector joint ventures with foreign capital.

Israel and Post-Atatürk Turkey

Israel, for obvious political, social, and religious reasons, is a case apart, but in the structure of its economy, the weight of the state, and some of its ideological predispositions it has shared many features with the socialist states of the Arab world and with Turkey. This sharing is all the more striking in that before there was any Israeli state at all, the Zionist community in Palestine had well-organized party and union structures and cohesive farmer-soldier communities in the kibbutzim. That a powerful and somewhat autonomous state grew out of such a highly structured civil society says much about the logic and attractiveness of the interventionist state.

It was David Ben Gurion, the first Israeli prime minister, who developed the doctrine of etatism (in Hebrew, *mamlachtiut*) and subordinated to the state his own socialist labor party, the MAPAI, and its powerful trade union affiliate, the Histadrut. The Histadrut included in its membership about 70% of Jewish wage earners in Palestine. In addition, the new Israeli state asserted its control over the Zionist defense force, the Haganah, which had fought successfully to achieve and then defend Israeli independence.

What Ben Gurion did in absorbing the labor movement into the state sector, robbing the kibbutzim of their most dynamic leaders, and putting the MAPAI and the Israeli Defense Forces under state control is not unlike the process undertaken by another charismatic civilian, Habib Bourguiba, in Tunisia after 1956. As Ben-Dor pointed out (1983, 109), "there was an overwhelming paradox in a man trying to use his party as a base of power from which to destroy the party-state linkage."

There were, however, a number of factors that made Israel's experiment in state building unique. First, there was the "acquisition" by the state of all the property previously owned by Arab Palestinians who had left their homes during the hostilities of 1948 (cf. Turkey in 1923 and Algeria in 1962). Second, the Jewish immigrant population of Israel doubled between 1948 and 1952, most of the newcomers were "Oriental," and the state had to undertake their economic, cultural, and social integration into what had been a predominantly Ashkenazi society. Third, Israel, like Jordan, has always been dependent on external assistance and financial flows, and it is the state that controls their disbursement. Between 1950 and 1974, for example, such assistance totaled US$19.5 billion. Finally, the state runs Israel's military-industrial complex. Defense outlays were the equivalent of 17% of GNP in 1972 and 30% in 1979, probably the highest proportion in the world at that time (in general, see Rosenfeld and Carmi 1976; Arian 1985; and Kimmerling 1983).

What had emerged in Israel by the late 1960s was a large, paternalistic welfare state with vaguely socialistic objectives and extensive public ownership. In this system, "the citizen would be perceived as an object available for the activities of the state and its bureaucracy, this latter serving as [a] paternalistic body deciding what was good for the citizens and for the collectivity as a whole. By definition, the reasoning of the authorities was better than and took precedence over the individuals and groups" (Kimmerling 1983, 99).

The Israeli variant of statism was given practical effect by state-owned or state-controlled enterprise. Histadrut in the 1970s had 1.5 million members, or 80% of the employed workforce. It in turn had controlling interests in several corporations: Solel Boneh in construction, the Koor holding company, with 250 industrial, financial, and commercial firms under its control (Koor was one of the Fortune 500), Bank Hapoalim, and others. There were 200 corporations in Israel in which the government had at least 50% equity. In addition there were some 450,000 persons on the public payroll, including the professional military, teachers, and municipal employees. Arian

**TABLE 7.5   Public and Private Shares in Investment in Turkey (%),
by Plan Periods, 1963–1987**

Investment	1963–1967	1968–1972	1973–1977	1979–1983	1984–1987
Public	48.0	44.0	46.4	46.1	56.2
Private	52.0	56.0	53.6	53.9	43.8

Sources: Celasun (1983, p. 103); TÜSIAD (1988, p. 9).

(1985, 36) estimated that in the late 1970s about 52% of the Israeli workforce was employed by the state and Histadrut, with the remaining 48% in the private sector.

The Israeli economy paid a heavy and familiar price for *mamlachtiut*. Huge government deficits resulting from indexing wages to the cost of living, heavy defense expenditures, and various forms of subsidies produced triple-digit inflation in the mid-1980s. Despite flows of concessional aid and grants, Israel's external debt had risen to US$12.5 billion in 1980, or 62% of GNP, the highest ratio in the Middle East. After the Labor Alliance lost power to the Likud in 1976, there were important modifications in the Ben Gurion formula, and some efforts at containing government expenditures and promoting exports through devaluation were undertaken. In 1986 Israel implemented a determined inflation-reduction program, cutting government expenditures, temporarily freezing prices and wages, and increasing tax receipts.

Since Atatürk's death in 1938, Turkish development strategy has oscillated in intent, but the weight of the public sector has remained predominant. In the decade of the 1950s—the first ten years of two-party democracy—the Democrat party, led by Adnan Menderes and Celal Bayar, rejected etatism in favor of a liberal economic policy to benefit commercial farmers and the industrial bourgeoisie. Nonetheless during the 1950s eleven new state-owned enterprises were started, the initial objective of selling off some public enterprises was abandoned, and the share of public in total investment rose from 38% in 1952 to 62% in 1959 (Roos and Roos 1971, 43).

The brief military takeover in 1960 ushered in another period of national planning and state-led ISI. This thrust was modified in the Second Five-Year Plan, 1968–1972, to put a greater burden of investment on private industry. Subsequently, the RPP government under Bülent Ecevit, with the Third Five-Year Plan, 1973–1977, resurrected the statist strategy, giving new authority to the State Planning Organization and stressing intermediate and capital goods industries (Walstedt 1980, 85–87; Hale 1981, 198–200).

At the end of the 1970s, the state sector remained the economy's center of gravity. The public share in total investment had stayed fairly constant for twenty years (Table 7.5), while public investment in the manufacturing sector had risen from

34% in 1965 to 65% in 1980 (World Bank 1982, 218). Employment in state-owned enterprises had grown from 362,000 in 1970 to 646,000 in 1980, or the equivalent of 16% of the nonagricultural workforce. In the manufacturing sector alone, state-owned enterprises accounted for 32% of value added, 36% of employment, and 43% of investment.

STATE CAPITALISM, THE STATE BOURGEOISIE, AND THE PROCESS OF ACCUMULATION

There is remarkable consensus among observers of widely differing political viewpoints that the interventionist state in the Middle East (and elsewhere) gave rise to a state bourgeoisie that controls but does not own the major means of production and to a process of accumulation that is called state capitalism.[6]

As Fitzgerald has pointed out (1977, 70, 87) for Latin America, there are two fundamental types of state intervention and capitalist accumulation. Both aim at structural transformation of the economy. They are not mutually exclusive and, as the Turkish case has shown, may oscillate over time. The first is a process whereby the state helps nurture or strengthen a private sector. It does so, as noted in the preceding pages, in several ways. It provides roads, railroads, ports, and electrical power to stimulate economic activity in general. Through its basic industries and mines it provides raw materials (coal, oil) and semimanufactured goods (iron, aluminum, chemicals, synthetic fibers) that feed directly into private production. It provides cheap credit and protective legislation. It may take over failing private enterprises. In this process of accumulation, the state transfers surpluses on its own operations, profits if any, and external rents to the private sector and tries to absorb all major risks for that sector.

This has been the predominant process of accumulation in the Middle East, although it is important to remember that it is frequently interrupted and that within the state sector itself there are always powerful lobbies that decry the handmaiden role. It is worth repeating that the state, when it gains access to an increased volume of external rents, uses those rents to expand its own activities with little regard to the private sector: thus Iran and Morocco after 1973/74 and Tunisia after 1977, when its own oil revenues shot up. Structural crises may also provoke episodes in which the state sector mobilizes resources by and for itself, as did Egypt and Syria in the 1960s. By and large, however, we see the handmaiden process at work in Turkey since 1950, in Egypt since 1974, in Tunisia since 1969, in Morocco since 1956, in Iran since 1963, and in the Sudan since 1972. Israel also fits somewhat awkwardly into this schema. Leftist critics of the Baʿathi experiments in Syria and Iraq are wont to attribute the same role to state intervention in their economies (e.g., al-Khafaji 1983; Longuenesse 1979), but our view is that in both countries there are dominant coalitions committed to state power and, to some extent, to a socialist vision of society such that the private sector is encouraged only insofar as it remains subordinate to the state, the party, and the plan.

The second process of accumulation is one in which the state undertakes all the resource mobilization and infrastructure development functions mentioned above but captures the surplus of its own activities, of a substantial portion of private-sector profits, and of external rents in order to finance its own expansion. Its goal is to dominate all aspects of resource allocation and to seize, once and for all, the commanding heights of the economy. When this process is under way, the slogans of "socialist transformation" or the "noncapitalist path" have generally been used to describe it.

Turkey in the 1930s flirted with this strategy. Egypt explicitly adopted it with the Socialist Decrees of 1961 and then gradually dropped it after 1974. Algeria has described itself in those terms since 1962, although after Boumedienne's death in 1978 the regime became more attentive to private-sector interests. Tunisia between 1964 and 1969 adopted and then abandoned the strategy. Whatever the critics may say, Iraq and Syria have both adhered to it since 1963. Finally, it may be that Libya, since 1975, has gone further than any country in the region outside the marxist regime in the former PDRY in strangling the private sector.

The term "state *capitalism*" calls attention to a basic dynamic in both processes: State enterprise, whether in the service of the private sector or of itself, may not involve any major revision of the relations of workers and managers to the means of production. The simple fact of public ownership does not mean that the profit motive disappears or that the workers gain control of the surplus value of their own labor. "Exploitation," the counterpart of the drive for financial profit, does not disappear. Again, critics on the left are especially inclined to see the state technocracy substituting itself for the private sector without any fundamental change in the relations of production. It is true that no regime has rejected financial efficiency and the generation of a surplus as legitimate criteria, among others, for measuring public-sector performance. There may be "exploitation" in the process in the form of surplus transfers from agricultural populations to the service and industrial sectors. The fact, however, that public-sector enterprises generally operate at a loss, reveal low levels of managerial performance, and carry more workers than they need must give us pause in labelling them "state capitalism."

We approach the concept of a state bourgeoisie with the same caution. There is a compelling logic to the *assumption* of a dominant state class. After all, much of this chapter has inventoried the size and strategic importance of the assets owned by the state. They do constitute the major means of production, except in the agrarian sector, where the state nonetheless has the means to orient production. It stands to reason that the professional managers of public assets could develop the attributes of a class, standing as they do in a similar position in relation to the means of production and sharing a common set of interests and goals, that is, class consciousness. The existence of such a class is all the more plausible in that conventional class actors are weak or in decline. The old landowning classes have been destroyed by land reform, while an industrial bourgeoisie has yet to emerge. The managers of public assets might be expected to fill this class vacuum, but the fact is that there is little evidence that they have ever done so.

This judgment is based upon an observable paradox in the identity of the state bourgeoisie. It cannot really ensure its own incumbency or its reproduction as a state class. A dominant capitalist bourgeoisie will, in the marxist view, perpetuate its control of the means of production and pass that control on to its offspring through the juridical device of private property until the final showdown with the proletariat. But members of the state bourgeoisie have no legal title to their offices; they cannot transfer them, and the higher they are in the state hierarchy the less likely it is that they will hold their own positions for very long. The fate of economic "czars" in the region is illustrative: Aziz Sidqi, the driving force behind Egypt's industrialization in the 1960s, disappeared from the scene in the 1970s; Algeria's minister of industry, Abdesslam Belaid, met the same fate after 1980, although he reappeared briefly after 1991. Toward the end of his regime, the shah of Iran put under house arrest some of his longtime advisers such as Prime Minister Amir Abbas Hoveida. Bourguiba tried his own acolyte, Ahmed Ben Salah, for treason.

The survival of the members of this class is dependent upon three factors: (1) their ability to move from position to position within the state hierarchy, (2) their technical competency, making them marketable in *any* milieu, and (3) their ability to build nest eggs (farms, businesses, investments, foreign bank accounts) outside the state sector. Seen in this light, the state bourgeoisie is a strange class indeed. Property is not the source of its power; it has no juridical claim to the positions that are the source of its power; and it cannot and may not even want to reproduce itself as a state class (Waterbury 1991).

At any point we can see it as a class merely by identifying those who are in formal positions of power and the resources they control. Thus Walstedt saw that in Turkey (1980, 187) "a self-perpetuating power group was born, linking bureaucrats, labor unions, and local politicians, that was far more powerful than any private capitalist power blocks operating in Turkey." Waterbury (1983, 260) saw 200,000–300,000 members of the state bourgeoisie in Egypt. But where are it and its offspring going? Perhaps into a private sector that it has helped to foster? to other sectors within the state? out of the country altogether? Or, finally, perhaps back and forth across a public-private divide that for years has had little operational and, in states such as Kuwait or Saudi Arabia, very little juridical meaning?

When social scientists do not know what is happening, they invoke "transitional phases." We can do no less. Powerful interventionist states with large public sectors and the groups that dominate them grew out of, on the one hand, the need to promote the structural transformation of their "backward" economies and, on the other, a kind of class vacuum in which a temporarily dominant class emerged on the strength of its education and competency rather than its property. The process of state intervention has contributed directly to the demise of some classes (large landowners, traditional trading bourgeoisies, craftspeople) and promoted others (capitalist farmers, bureaucratic middle classes, a small-scale manufacturing bourgeoisie). The process of intervention has also resulted in deep-seated crisis in the state sector itself and in the economy in general, calling into question the feasibility of continued intervention on the same scale as in the past. We are witnessing in several Middle Eastern societies a cautious retreat of the state and hence a gradual weakening of the state bourgeoisie. In some instances this is best seen as an effort to rationalize state intervention and to make it more efficient. Algeria is a case in point. In others, such as Turkey, an assertive private entrepreneurial sector is ready to take over from the state the role of leading the development process. Falling in between are countries like Egypt and Tunisia, where economic liberalization measures have been introduced in the absence of strong, self-assured private sectors (see Chapter 9). In the mid-1990s, after ten to fifteen years of reform and adjustment in several economies, it is still hard to know if we are at the dawning of a new era in which the state will confine itself to regulating market economies or merely in a period of stocktaking and statist regrouping.

Whatever the answer, what has changed—and changed dramatically—over the past thirty years is the confidence that leaders and led once placed in the efficacy of state intervention. That confidence is largely gone, and the positive legitimacy granted state intervention has been replaced by a kind of resignation born of habit and the lack of alternative agents of change.

NOTES

1. It is important to remember that for many Muslims Atatürk is probably the most despised leader of the twentieth century precisely because he abolished the caliphate and tried to subjugate the Islamic establishment in Turkey.

2. Atatürk died in November 1938. İnönü became president, and Bayar resigned as prime minister. The latter returned to prominence after 1950 when Turkey's first open elections brought the Democrat party, of which Bayar was a founder, to power.

3. A number of advanced industrial nations, especially Austria, Italy, France, and the UK, reveal similar proportions.

4. The strategy owed a great deal to the French economist G. Destanne de Bernis (1971).

5. The fear that time was running out, as noted earlier, impelled Bourguiba to delegate broad powers to Ahmed Ben Salah in Tunisia's version of the big push.

6. On the state bourgeoisie, see, for example, Amin (1980, 8), Batatu (1979, 110), DERSA (1981, 263–283), Hannoyer and Seurat (1979, 127–133), Hussein (1971, 137–186), al-Khafaji (1983, 39–44), Longuenesse (1979, 9), el-Malki (1982, 163), Nellis (1980, 417), Raffinot and Jacquemot (1977, 99), Trimberger (1978, 119), Walstedt (1980, 187), Waterbury (1983, 232–262; 1991).

8

CONTRADICTIONS OF
STATE-LED GROWTH

It is now widely acknowledged that both state intervention in the economy and the public-enterprise sectors have, by and large, malfunctioned financially and economically. Other than in petroleum and banking, public enterprises have failed to generate profits and constituted a net drain on state resources; to remain afloat they have required subsidized credit and inputs, foreign exchange at preferential rates, and constant flows of working capital and new investment. At the same time, public enterprises have not solved many of the social and economic problems they were designed to address.

In many respects state-led growth achieved a great deal. Both absolute and per capita national output grew at respectable rates in most countries of the region even before the massive infusion of oil rents during the 1970s and early 1980s. Structural transformation, whether measured by the share of industry in output or by employment, also proceeded at rates that were not unfavorable in international comparative perspective (see Chapter 3). This performance was no mean achievement considering the rapidity of population growth, the heavy burden of defense expenditures, the limited natural resource base apart from oil, the initially low levels of literacy, and the perennial political instability of the region.

However, industry was seldom internationally competitive; because of both price and technical inefficiencies, many "infant industries" never grew up. Overvalued exchange rates and domestic-price distortions led to serious misallocations, some of which we have documented earlier for both agriculture and industry. Too often, the wrong price signals led state managers and private economic actors to produce the wrong things with the wrong combination of inputs. Heavy industry grew rapidly, while agriculture and light industry were relatively neglected. International comparative advantage was often ignored. For example, in two of the leading industrial nations, Egypt and Turkey, much investment took place in industries in which profitability was actually negative if international prices were used for the calculation.

Furthermore, the multiple goals of state-owned enterprises (supplying cheap inputs to other industries, providing jobs for the rapidly expanding labor force) often gave the managers of these industries little incentive to minimize costs, even with a given technology. Capacity utilization was often poor (for example, the Algerian steel plant at El Hadjar operated at only 40% of capacity in the early 1980s [Nelson 1985, 208]), leading to higher unit costs, which had to be either subsidized from the state budget or passed on in the form of higher costs to other industries. Usually the former approach was adopted.

Allocative efficiency and "X-efficiency"[1] were not the only problems with the state-led-growth strategy. The stress on heavy industry and import substitution failed to create sufficient jobs for the rapidly expanding workforce, and, as we have seen in Chapter 6, the relative neglect of agriculture until the late 1970s contributed to the widening food gap. Finally, many countries continued to rely on external sources of investment capital and to accumulate large external debts. The goals of both social justice and national economic independence proved elusive.

Many countries of the region tried to invest more resources than were saved domestically. The "resource gap" (gross domestic investment [GDI] minus gross domestic savings [GDS]) was large and in percentage terms considerably larger than that for other LDCs (Table 8.1). There was, and is, great variability in this indicator across countries and over time. Unsurprisingly, during the oil boom the oil-exporting countries typically saved more than they invested. Indeed, this phenomenon led to the creation by the World Bank of a new category of developing country, "capital-surplus oil exporters," composed, prior to the collapse of oil prices in the mid-1980s, of Saudi Arabia, Libya, Kuwait, and the UAE. Other oil exporters, principally Iran, Iraq, and Algeria, had adequate national savings to meet investment.[2] Another group of countries (Sudan, Morocco, Tunisia, Egypt, Syria, Turkey, Israel) had resource gaps in 1985 ranging from 2 to 11% of GDP. Two other countries (the former YAR and Jordan) had massive gaps, 36% and 44% of GDP respectively. Mainly because of heavy debt repayments, domestic savings exceeded domestic investment in all middle-income countries from 1980 to 1985.[3] In comparison with this reference group, MENA countries had very large resource gaps, filled for the most part with continued foreign borrowing and with aid from the United States, the EEC, and the capital-surplus oil exporters of the Gulf.

There were several reasons for this resource gap, but the inefficiencies of the state-owned enterprises certainly made an important contribution. For example, the "budgetary burden," or net deficit, created by these enterprises was 4% of GDP in 1978–1981 in Tunisia and 3.5% in Turkey in 1978–1980 (Floyd 1984). These deficits contributed to high rates of inflation, which, in their turn, led to overvalued real exchange rates and therefore to uncompetitive exports and domestic-price distortions. The failure to develop internationally competitive industrial (and agricultural) exports, combined with rapidly expanding domestic incomes and demand, exacerbated the deficit of the balance of trade. The public sector, originally created in part to generate foreign exchange, too often simply absorbed it.

TABLE 8.1   MENA Resource Gaps, 1965, 1985, 1993

	GDI/GDP			GDS/GDP			Resource Gap		
	1965	1985	1993	1965	1985	1993	1965	1985	1993
Algeria	22	36	29	19	38	28	−3	2	−1
Egypt	18	25	17	14	16	6	−4	−9	−11
Iran	17	–	29	24	–	30	7	–	1
Iraq	16	–	–	31	–	–	15	–	–
Israel	29	16	22	15	9	14	−14	−7	−8
Jordan	–	31	30	–	−13	−13	–	−44	−43
Kuwait	16	21	23	60	30	30	44	9	7
Morocco	10	22	23	12	12	17	2	−10	−6
Oman	–	30	17	–	43	27	–	13	10
Saudi Arabia	14	31	24	48	21	27	34	−10	3
Sudan	10	7	–	9	−3	–	−1	−10	–
Syria	10	24	16	10	14	7	–	−10	−9
Tunisia	28	27	29	14	20	20	−14	−7	−9
Turkey	15	20	27	13	16	22	−2	−4	−5
UAE	–	31	25	–	59	33	–	28	8
Yemen	–	21	20	–	−15	3	–	−36	−17
LDC average									
Middle-income	22	21	23	21	23	22	−1	2	−1
Lower-middle income	18	20	23	15	19	22	−3	−1	−1
Upper-middle income	24	22	23	24	26	21	0	4	−2

Source: World Bank (1987; 1995g).

The failure of state-led growth to close the twin gaps between domestic savings and investment and between exports and imports contributed to the accumulation of large foreign debts (Table 8.2). In most cases, there was a marked increase in external indebtedness and a rise of the debt-service ratio (debt repayment as a percentage of export revenue). Although these debts were not nearly so large in absolute terms as those of Latin American debtors like Brazil (about US$125 billion) or Mexico (about US$100 billion), they were large enough to narrow the options for policymakers and to increase the influence of international lending agencies in the policy process.

Finally, just as the goals of efficiency, growth, and national independence were only partially achieved, the ideal of increasing equity also proved elusive. The employment problem clearly was not solved, and the gap between rich and poor often

TABLE 8.2 Total External Debt, 1993	
	External Debt (US$ millions)
Algeria	25,757
Egypt	40,626
Iran	20,550
Iraq	86,000
Israel	25,770
Jordan	6,972
Morocco	21,430
Oman	2,661
Sudan	16,561
Syria	19,975
Tunisia	8,701
Turkey	67,862
Yemen	5,923

Source: World Bank (1995d; 1995e).

either widened or remained roughly constant. It appeared to many observers that those equity gains that were achieved had a high efficiency cost, as in expensive consumer-subsidy programs or in the swelling ranks of redundant public-sector employees. And, as we have seen, the education and health systems seldom promoted a real equalization of human capital in the region.

Despite high levels of redundant labor in state-owned enterprises, disguised and open unemployment remains a serious problem in most Middle Eastern societies. Some redistribution of wealth has taken place through public-sector-employment drives and the location of state-owned enterprises in backward areas, but the distribution of income in most Middle Eastern countries remains highly skewed (Chapter 10). The state-owned enterprises have not—again, except for the petroleum sector—contributed to exports, while their import needs and hence claims on foreign exchange have remained high. Finally, although the prominence of agriculture in economic activity has diminished, it has been the service sector more than industry that has picked up the slack. It is not at all clear that centralized planning and state enterprise have accelerated the process of structural transformation.

Despite this generally acknowledged situation and the need for reform, little has been done in the past fifteen years. There have been efforts to stimulate the private sector, and there has been talk of "privatization," that is, selling equity in state-owned enterprises to private investors. By and large, however, the economic weight of public enterprise in the Middle East has been little diminished.

THE CONTINUED DOMINANCE OF
PUBLIC-SECTOR ENTERPRISE

State enterprise has arisen within two broad developmental frameworks. The first is an explicitly socialist and redistributive one in which equity issues take precedence over profit-and-loss criteria in assessing state activities. When reform is first called for in such systems, it is in terms of making the public sector more efficient, reducing the deficits of specific enterprises, increasing monetary incentives for workers, allowing price increases, linking budgetary support and banking credit to performance, and perhaps even reducing the personnel list. The shift here is toward state capitalism. That shift began in Egypt in 1965, when Nasser first denounced the inefficient performance of the public sector, and in Algeria sometime between 1967 and 1969. Discipline, productivity, and profitability become the watchwords of the new era, but frequently they remain slogans more than effective guides to improved performance.

The second framework is represented by the state-capitalist experiments, in which socialism is never at issue and profitability, at least in theory, always takes precedence over redistribution. Even by these criteria, however, the performance of state-owned enterprises in nonsocialist countries such as Turkey, Iran, Morocco, and Saudi Arabia has been lackluster. When the issue of reform is raised in these countries, the main elements of the proposal are to use more public resources to stimulate private-sector activity directly and to privatize public-sector assets.

In neither framework have many steps been taken toward reform and privatization. After thirty or more years of strong state intervention in the economy, powerful bureaucratic, managerial, and political interests stand in the way of any diminution of state economic activities.

It is not always possible to discern which groups, organizations, or class interests carry the most weight in promoting or defending the state's role in the economy. Organized labor is generally a staunch supporter because of relatively high wage levels and benefit packages and, above all, because of job stability and relatively light workloads. In many ways unions in the public sector constitute a labor aristocracy (for example, the unemployed in many Middle Eastern countries outnumber those in the public-sector labor force by two to one [see Chapter 5]) and defend their privileges in the name of socialism and the toiling masses. When regimes begin to promote state capitalism, the unions find themselves in a difficult position. They sense that the public sector is under fire and seek to defend it against its critics. Yet they do not want to pay the price of greater efficiency, which entails higher productivity: more output per hour of work for the same pay. They may resist the introduction of incentive systems that reward individual or group performance and insist that pay and promotion be based on nondiscriminatory and "nonexploitative" seniority systems. In other words, they may try to sap the very logic of the state-capitalist thrust. Union leaders generally know that this is a dangerous game; if public-sector performance does not improve, its critics will inevitably call for disinvestment and privatization, an even worse outcome for the unions than state capitalism.

The managers of public assets are likely to resist efforts at reform. Frequently they have formed alliances of convenience with labor that have led to low productivity and high enterprise deficits. Managers may well prefer periodic bailouts from the state to the harder option of exacting higher levels of performance from the workers and from themselves. They have generally been drawn to the public sector by its salaries and "perks," which are better than those found in the civil service and even in parts of the private sector. Although in the 1970s, when rates of inflation were high throughout the area, these salary advantages eroded, it is still the case that the work is less demanding and jobs and promotion are more secure than in the private sector. Individual managers may have good prospects for shifts into the private sector, but most public-sector managers will prefer the quasi-sinecures they have. The opportunities for side payments and moonlighting compensate for deteriorating salary levels.

Some segments of the civil service will also have a strong interest in the perpetuation of large public sectors. Whereas the autonomy of individual enterprises varies from country to country, in all instances government ministries directly oversee their activities. They draw up and supervise sectoral and enterprise budgets, review contracts, help design projects, and control personnel procedures. Thus, in the Ministries of Industry, Agriculture, and Defense, where the bulk of state enterprise is concentrated, extensive bureaucracies have developed to monitor them. The Ministry of Planning may plan public-sector activity, while the Ministry of Finance controls enterprise budgets, credit flows, and rates of corporate taxation (see, inter alia, Roos and Roos 1971, 64). Auditing agencies check the books of hundreds of public-sector firms. Any reduction in the size of the public sector could lead to a reduction in the ranks of supervisory personnel. Civil servants may therefore resist recommendations for greater operational autonomy of state enterprises in the context of state capitalism and recommendations to sell off parts of the public sector.

For some twenty years up to the early 1980s, the external donor community showed some predilection for public enterprise and direct state intervention in the economy. The degree of that predilection was not at all uniform. For example, the U.S. Agency for International Development (USAID) has never been a strong supporter of public enterprise, although there was a time when the U.S. government saw the Tennessee Valley Authority as a model for regional uplift that could be exported to the developing world. The attractiveness of public-sector enterprise to other donors lay in the possibility, so it seemed, of bypassing cumbersome entrenched bureaucratic agencies in order to promote specific projects (e.g., fertilizer industries) or programs (e.g., diffusion of new varieties of wheat). For bilateral donors there was also the attraction that large public-sector enterprises could become important purchasers of equipment and technology from the donor's home economy. The point is that although the donors, since the advent of Margaret Thatcher in the UK and Ronald Reagan in the United States, have become the major proponents of public-sector reform and privatization, not so long ago they supported public-sector expansion.

Parts of the private sector frequently find it in their interest to have a large public sector alongside them. Large public enterprises in basic metals, plastics and petrochemicals, and other semimanufactures such as cotton yarn may support private-sector manufacturers with a regular and cheap supply of inputs—Turkey, Algeria, and Iraq are all notable in this respect. Likewise, the public sector may prove a reliable and not very cost-conscious purchaser of private-sector goods, from automobile components to army uniforms. Several observers have concluded that the stirrings and growth of the private sector in several Middle Eastern countries, notably Turkey and Egypt, are an assertion of class interests and that they are the principal force behind the gradual abandonment of state regulation of the economy. Private interests, sustained over decades by state contracts and protection, are alleged to be sufficiently powerful to force the state into retreat or at least to put it more directly at the service of the private sector. Doubtless, some private interests will benefit from the process of liberalization that we summarize under the rubric "economic reform." We do not believe, however, that private class interests *caused* such policies. Moreover, it is not clear that most private interests would have a stake in the reform of the public sector. They can have the best of both worlds through an inefficient public sector that continues to feed business to the private sector and by comparison makes private enterprise performance look good (see Chapter 9).

The public sector and the civil service together have been an important source of state revenues and savings that will not easily be abandoned or allowed to run down. State employees represent a captive source of income tax and social security payments. Taxes and payments are simply deducted from salary and wage payments; evasion is virtually impossible. Income tax and even social security payments outside the public sector are very difficult to collect and generally represent a tiny proportion of total government revenues. For example, in 1980, 60% of Egypt's total wage bill was paid out to civil servants and public-sector employees. Social security payments represented 10% of all government revenues, income tax on salaries of government personnel another 5%, and profits tax on public-sector enterprise, returns on public assets, and public sector self-financing another 40%. Indirect taxes (sales tax, stamp duties) and tariffs and customs, a substantial proportion of them levied on goods produced in or imported by the public sector and the government, accounted for another quarter of total revenues. External assistance represented 13% of total revenues. The remaining 7% came from corporate and income tax revenues from the nongovernmental sector and the proceeds on bond sales (Waterbury 1983, 202). The state sector in Egypt, taken in its broadest sense, was the source of most state revenues and by the mid-1990s the locus of a captive workforce of over 4 million.

It may well be that public sectors and big government tend to conserve their predominance in Middle Eastern economies, seemingly regardless of the ideologies of individual regimes, because of the extraordinary power they offer political leadership to preempt resources from actors outside the state system, to finance state activities, and to control strategic sectors of the workforce. It does not surprise us to see leaders of self-proclaimed socialist regimes defending their public sectors, but at first blush it seems surprising to see large public sectors in nominally liberal or liberalizing economic systems such as those of Egypt, Jordan, or Tunisia. The economic risks of inefficient public enterprise may not outweigh the political risks of giving up the leverage over resources and people that public enterprise provides.

It is the political calculus of these two kinds of costs that determines the manner in which political elites respond to the poor performance and fiscal burdens characteristic of public-sector enterprise. To some extent equity (in the form of redundant labor, relatively high remuneration, and low productivity) and inefficiency have been combined and paid for through deficit financing and borrowing abroad. When foreign creditors refuse to advance new lines of credit until the fiscal mess is cleared up, a painful day of reckoning can no longer be postponed.

The timing, pace, and content of reform efforts in the MENA region have varied widely across countries (see Chapter 9). Common elements with major political consequences are the efforts to restrain public expenditures, to hold in check if not reduce the size of the public-enterprise sector, to stimulate private enterprise and investment, and to remove subsidies on consumer goods, agricultural and industrial inputs, and credit. In addition, there have been efforts to liberalize foreign trade, to reduce the tariff protection of domestic producers, and to stimulate the export sectors of the economy. Each of these moves produces winners and losers. Combining them in the reform effort will send shock waves through well-established coalitions of economic interests and beneficiaries of the status quo.

THE POLITICAL ECONOMY OF
STRUCTURAL ADJUSTMENT

The failures arising from mismanaged ISI and public enterprise have been general across all the countries in the region. They were doubtless exacerbated in countries with no or very limited petroleum reserves by the increase in world petroleum prices in the 1970s. Growing import bills coupled with stagnant exports led to burgeoning trade deficits that had to be financed by foreign borrowing, both commercial and multilateral. The reaction of most Middle Eastern countries to inflation in their import bill for petroleum and nonpetroleum products was to promote the expansion of their economies, perhaps with the long-range hope that such expansion would lead to increased exports.

Turkey, for example, found itself in one of the region's gravest economic crises in the late 1970s. It was governed at the time by fragile and changing political coalitions, dominated by the Republican People's party (led by Bülent Ecevit) and the Justice party (led by Süleyman Demirel). Neither of these protagonists could afford to promote economic austerity for fear of alienating a significant part of the electorate. The result, in the words of Celasun (1983, 11), was that despite the oil crisis and related external shocks, Turkey attempted to preserve its growth momentum under the Third Plan (1973–1977) through rapid reserve decumulation and massive external borrowing. Instead of relying upon internal adjustment to promote balance of payments improvement, the various coalition governments pursued expansionary policies, while allowing a decline in marginal savings ratios, and negative import substitution in the energy and manufacturing sectors.

Other countries replicated this scenario to some extent, although Turkey was unique in the nature of its party-competitive political system. What we see, then, is some degree of imported inflation, combined with high domestic-investment levels. The latter, unaccompanied by significant increases in domestic production, led to high domestic inflation. Governments responded to the inflation by resorting to ill-considered deficit financing in order to maintain salary levels and to cover the operating losses of public-sector enterprises. Foreign resources were used to pay for current consumption rather than to increase production. Eventually, as foreign debt snowballed, current borrowing was used to some extent to cover payments on past debt.

Without some fundamental restructuring of the basic parameters of the economy, the vicious circle described above would lead to debt default and economic collapse. It was to address the issues of restructuring the economy that the World Bank, in cooperation with the IMF and other multilateral lenders, developed strategies and multiyear loan programs for structural adjustment. These were no longer conjunctural, designed to deal with a particular balance-of-payments crisis or short-term disturbance in economic performance, but rather aimed at the basic assumptions of development strategy. Ideally, structural adjustment could and should take place without sacrificing growth, but even then, the process necessarily entrains deflation and austerity for important segments of the population. Whether structural adjustment programs are leveraged by the World Bank and other donors or begun spontaneously out of domestic considerations (India has been notable in this latter respect), they go to the very heart of structural transformation: the balance between agricultural and nonagricultural sectors and the adjustment of policy and investment in favor of the former; the balance among public, private, and foreign enterprise; the amount of resources devoted to the public sector writ large; and the balance between the ISI sector and sectors capable of promoting exports.

The first steps toward austerity and restructuring were frequently taken in the wake of balance-of-payments crises. Typically, the affected country turned to the IMF in order to borrow in excess of its quota in the Fund. The IMF in turn disbursed these funds in "slices" (tranches) as the country took a sequence of steps to prevent a recurrence of the balance-of-payments shortfall. These first measures became part of a short-term stabilization program or standby agreement. Often the reform measures included reductions in government spending and increases in interest rates to dampen the rate of inflation and stimulate savings. Between 1956 and 1984 Egypt, Iran, Israel, Morocco, Syria, Tunisia, and Turkey entered into a total of fourteen such agreements.

Short-term remedies often proved inadequate to address structural problems, and issues of structural adjustment to be carried out over several years became part of the agenda. In the early and mid-1980s, Turkey, Egypt, the Sudan, Tunisia, and Morocco were all wrestling with structural adjustment programs. Even countries that had experienced no severe balance-of-payments problems, such as Algeria and Iraq, had, because of problems of food security, unemployment, and poorly integrated domestic markets, spontaneously moved in the direction of structural adjustment. Although countries that undertake structural adjustment programs at the behest of their major creditors frequently complain that economic reform is being rammed down their throats heedless of potential political upheaval, the converse may also be true. The oil boom of the 1970s allowed the shah of Iran to finance large capital-intensive projects in the public sector, continue to neglect agriculture, and generate high rates of inflation in an overheated economy. His failure to use Iran's petroleum rents for structural adjustment set the economic stage for his own downfall. As Bienen and Gersovitz (1985) have argued, stabilization and structural adjustment programs are at least as likely to contribute to political stability as to undermine it.

The simple fact is that the imbalances caused by years of unsuccessful state-led ISI exact a high political price one way or another unless the country is able to borrow abroad indefinitely the resources that it cannot generate at home. Otherwise some sort of "biting the bullet" is unavoidable. Let us briefly review some of the typical measures that will have to be undertaken.

Generally, government deficits will have to be reduced to some target level—say, 4% of GDP. To do this governments may have to implement salary and hiring freezes and slash investment budgets. Such measures go to the heart of the state's role as employer of last resort and may deny public-sector enterprise the flows of investment to which it has become accustomed. Second, devaluation of the national currency may be called for. The object here is to promote exports, and it may be the agricultural sector that can most quickly meet the foreign demand induced by the new exchange rate. However, all imports will become more expensive. Industries reliant on imported raw materials and capital equipment will see their operating costs soar; urban consumers used to cheap food imports will likewise be hit; the military will find that its penchant for fancy imported armaments is costing much more. The short-term effects of devaluation can be devastating before its long-term benefits begin to be felt.

Structural adjustment programs will generally seek to stimulate national savings by raising interest rates. This in turn will tend to dampen consumption and inflation while making borrowing more expensive. The end of cheap or subsidized credit in the long run will encourage more careful project selection and a more efficient utilization of capital, but the short-term effect may be to put many firms out of business and many people out of work.

There will be measures to reduce administrative interference in pricing mechanisms and to allow supply and demand to determine price levels. Subsidies of consumer prices and inputs in the manufacturing sector may be reduced or phased out, increasing the cost of inputs and the final price of manufactured goods. Subsidies on fuel, fertilizers, and agricultural-credit rates may be ended, raising the costs of agricultural production. Thus, despite a range of anti-inflation measures (reduced government spending and credit squeezes), the cost of living, especially for urban populations, may rise dramatically.

Structural adjustment generally entails a revision in the terms of trade prevailing between the agricultural and nonagricultural sectors. Policies that have held down the producer prices of agricultural commodities that feed into local industries (sugarcane, cotton, sugar beets) or of basic food crops (wheat, rice, oil seeds) may be raised to stimulate production. Presumably if production does increase, the prices of such commodities will eventually fall, but the near-term effect may also be to raise the cost of living for urban populations and the cost of production for the manufacturing sector.

Finally, there will be an effort to streamline the public sector and to stimulate the private. Public-sector enterprises will be called upon to increase productivity, reduce costs and idle capacity, generate a financial return on their investments, and, ideally, meet their investment needs out of their own earnings rather than relying on government financing of their deficits. The effort to make the public sector more efficient will mean that redundant labor will gradually be let go, no new hiring will take place, and management will be called upon to concern itself with issues of inventory controls, waste reduction, market research, and quality control. At the same time, new sources of commercial credit to the private sector may be opened, and the public sector may find itself competing with local private or even foreign joint-venture enterprise in areas where it had previously enjoyed a monopoly position. It will be the private rather than the public sector that is targeted to lead an export drive to reduce the country's balance-of-payments problems.

To summarize: Successful structural adjustment will require at a minimum reduced government spending; a shift of investment resources from the urban to the rural sector and from the public to the private sector; a move away from a planned economy to one in which the market plays a major role in allocating resources; and, in the most general sense, a move to an economy in which equity concerns may be "temporarily" sacrificed to those of efficiency. The process is inevitably painful. Standards of living for people on fixed incomes and/or low- and middle-income urbanites may decline; privileged labor unions may find their wages and benefits eroding; educated and skilled youth may face an economy generating very little employment. Short-term economic contraction, it may be argued, is the price that must be paid to assure future sustained growth, but getting from the short to the longer term often proves politically perilous, if not fatal.

Two kinds of pitfalls must be avoided. The structural adjustment "medicine" must not be so powerful as to lock the economy into a downward spiral of contraction, business liquidation, unemployment, and slack demand. Judicious resort to government pump priming and foreign borrowing to keep the economy expanding will be called for. But the second pitfall is related directly to seeking that delicate balance between

austerity and growth. The application of stabilization and structural adjustment programs may be so diluted that they achieve the worst of both worlds—a deterioration in
standards of living for important segments of the population without the structural reforms that would set the stage for further growth.

There are basically three kinds of response to such pressures that national leaders
may adopt. The first is outright rejection of structural reform, generally citing the
deleterious consequences for equity and the likelihood of economic stagnation. In
Turkey's turbulent party-competitive system in the 1970s, none of the major political leaders could afford to advocate belt tightening. A second gambit is to adopt a
posture of rejection of some or all of the recommended reforms but quietly to pursue
their implementation. Both Sadat and Mubarak of Egypt from 1976 on followed
that tactic to some extent. The risk, of course, is charges of hypocrisy and subterfuge
when and if the game is revealed (Bienen and Gersovitz 1985, 749; J. Nelson 1984,
986–991). Finally, leaders may accept the reforms but claim that they are being implemented purely out of domestic concerns and because they make sense. One
might view the reforms introduced in Turkey after the military takeover in September 1980 in this light.

The major risk, however, at least as it is perceived by political leadership, is that
austerity will provoke violence, especially among urban populations. Cost-of-living
rioting in Middle Eastern cities has severely tested the regimes of Morocco in 1965,
1982, and 1984, Tunisia in 1978 and 1984, Egypt in 1977, Algeria in 1988, Jordan
in 1989, and the Sudan, where it may have been the catalyst to the overthrow of
Nimeiri in March 1985. We have already noted the crisis into which Turkey's expansionary policies had driven the economy in the 1970s. Even before the military
seized power in the midst of escalating civil violence, the civilian government, in January 1980, introduced sweeping policy changes that included sharp increases in the
prices of public-sector goods, elimination of a wide range of price controls, a major
currency devaluation, export incentives, favorable legislation for foreign investors,
and curbs on government spending. It is moot whether this program could have
been implemented with the same force had the military not intervened to put an
end to civil violence as well as to open democratic life. The trade unions and universities were muzzled, and the return to civilian government in November 1983 was
under the strictures imposed by Turkey's senior officers. The figures in Table 8.3 give
some indication of the impact of the austerity measures.

In Egypt, the challenge of structural adjustment was first posed unequivocally in
1976. The country had fallen in arrears on payments on its commercial debt; the
government deficit and domestic inflation were growing in lockstep, the public sector was riddled with idle capacity and large aggregate losses, and price disincentives
prevented agriculture from taking up the slack. Egypt entered into a standby agreement with the IMF in the spring of 1976. Part of the reform package was to reduce
the level of subsidies of several consumer goods in order to lower the deficit. In November 1976 President Sadat faced Egypt's first openly contested parliamentary elections since 1952. He put off action on subsidy reductions until January 1977. When

TABLE 8.3   Unemployment and Wages in Turkey, 1979–1983

| Year | Unemployed | Wages (TL/day) | |
		Gross	Net[a]
1979	189,467	75	41
1980	263,354	56	29
1981	341,336	52	33
1982	468,654	50	31
1983	549,081	51	32

[a] Net of insurance payments, income tax, stamp tax, and "financial balance tax."
Source: Central Bank, Republic of Turkey (1984, 110).

the price increases were announced, three days of severe rioting ensued in Alexandria, Cairo, and several other Egyptian cities. Sadat immediately revoked the price increases, and the stabilization program was shelved.

That Egypt's economy did not then founder was the result of great luck and some skillful political maneuvering. In the fall of 1977 Sadat made his historic trip to Jerusalem in search of a peace that might, among other things, enhance Egypt's image as a home for foreign investment and lighten the burden of military expenditures on the economy. In fact, the Camp David Accords of March 1979, which established formal peace between Egypt and Israel, led to Egypt's ostracism from the Arab world and a drying up of Arab aid and private investment in the Egyptian economy.

In the late 1970s, however, other processes, unplanned and unanticipated, were in train. The booming oil economies of the region needed manpower at all skill levels to implement their gargantuan development plans. By 1980 hundreds of thousands of Egyptian migrant workers were remitting to the home economy upwards of US$3 billion per year. The recovery of oil fields in the Sinai Peninsula after years of Israeli occupation coincided with a second surge in international petroleum prices. By 1980 Egyptian oil exports were earning the country US$4.5 billion per annum. The surge in oil prices also was reflected in increased transit fees in the Suez Canal. According to the IMF, these fees earned the economy nearly US$1 billion in 1981/82. Finally, the peace between Israel and Egypt did stimulate tourism, which in 1980 generated US$700 million in revenues.

Egypt was awash in unanticipated foreign exchange, and it became increasingly dependent on foreign rents (Figure 8.1). These external resources could have been used to cushion the impact of the structural adjustment process initiated in 1976 and aborted in 1977. Instead they were used to pay for increased consumption, mainly in the form of imports and increased consumer subsidies. They allowed

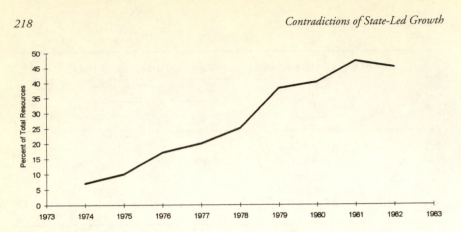

FIGURE 8.1   Share of exogenous resources in total resources in Egypt, 1974–1982.
Source: IBRD (1983, 5).

Egypt to avoid structural adjustment rather than to make the process less painful. By the middle 1980s, a global oil glut was manifest, and the bottom dropped out of international oil prices. Egypt's oil earnings plummeted, the demand for Egyptian labor in Arab oil-exporting economies slackened and the flow of remittances began to diminish, tanker traffic through the Suez Canal tapered off, and numerous terrorist incidents in 1985 and 1986 scared away tourists. Ten years after first nibbling at the bullet, Egypt was once again faced with the entire structural adjustment package. In the early 1980s, the World Bank and other donors became increasingly alarmed at Egypt's economic prospects in light of softening petroleum prices and the lack of domestic economic reform. A 1983 World Bank report put the matter succinctly and starkly:

> Egypt's public finances are extraordinary in several respects compared to those of other countries at similar income levels. The public sector's dominance in its economy requires the mobilization and expenditure of a vast amount of resources. Total public expenditures are 60% of GDP, total revenues are 40% of GDP and the public-sector deficit is 20% of GDP. There are very few, if any, developing countries in the world with such high proportions. These heighten the normal fiscal issues of the efficiency, equity and development impact of public-sector economic operations.

The reforms envisaged by the bank and others involved the following:

- Reduction of consumer subsidies, which were running at about £E4 billion per annum in the early 1980s or circa 7% of GDP.
- Energy pricing and conservation: Petroleum products in Egypt were priced at about 16% of the world prices prevailing in the early 1980s; this indirect subsidy to the rest of the Egyptian economy was worth US$2.5 billion per annum.

- Exchange-rate management and trade policy (i.e., devaluation and export promotion).
- Tax reform to introduce a unified, global income tax-rate structure.
- Agricultural production policies to improve the terms of trade between the agricultural and nonagricultural sectors and to promote agricultural exports.
- Public-sector reform, giving state-owned enterprises greater financial and managerial autonomy and requiring them to sell their products/services at their real market value and to pay market wages to attract skilled labor but also to shed redundant unskilled labor. (The bank did not at this time recommend privatization or divestiture.)

These reforms were advocated at a time when bank forecasters sketched out oil-price scenarios that they thought were fairly pessimistic. They saw a decline in world prices to about US$25 per barrel but thought that price would hold, at least in nominal terms, throughout the 1980s. In fact, by 1986 the price had dropped to around US$15 per barrel. Egypt's day of reckoning seemingly could no longer be postponed.

In the mid-1980s Egypt had become one of the world's major debtor nations, with over US$38 billion in foreign obligations (not including Soviet military debt) and annual debt service charges in excess of US$4 billion (i.e., as much as or more than earnings from the export of oil). Since the late 1970s, Egypt's military debt to the United States had grown to US$4.5 billion, and interest on that debt ran at 13% per annum. "Peace," as anyone would have predicted, did nothing to lessen the economic burden of Egypt's military preparedness. In 1986 Egypt had fallen US$1 billion in arrears in some of its foreign payments.

The Egyptian government's internal debt in the middle 1980s had reached nearly £E30 billion or about US$20 billion at the market exchange rate prevailing at that time. The budgetary deficit of the government, already at 16% of GDP in 1981/82, increased to over 20% in the mid-1980s. An acceptable level from the point of view of the World Bank and the IMF is around 4%. The annual financing requirements of state-owned enterprises alone at that time were well in excess of £E1 billion and were met largely by overdrafts on public-sector banks and the printing of money.

President Hosni Mubarak came to power in 1981 after the assassination of President Sadat by Muslim extremists. The new president was only too aware of the depth of alienation of large segments of Egypt's youth, faced with a soaring cost of living and a shrinking domestic job market. To take on structural adjustment reforms at the very moment that external markets for Egyptian labor were beginning to contract must have seemed as politically suicidal as it was economically inevitable.

Several other Middle Eastern states have to varying degrees shared in Egypt's distress. The *Economist* (July 20, 1985) surveyed one of these states and noted the following symptoms: an inflation rate of 180–200% per annum, the highest per capita foreign debt in the world (US$6,200 per person), unemployment running at 10% of the workforce, an absolute decline in the standard of living, and an annual growth rate of GNP of about 1%. The causes of the disease were seen as lying in a defense establishment that annually absorbed 20% of GNP, a massive welfare state, subsidies of basic consumer goods, the indexing of wage increases to the cost of living, a "huge socialist bureaucracy—encompassing not only trade unions but also banking, transport, farming, insurance, education," the dampening of private initiative through public quasi-monopolies, and "irresponsibly disbursed American aid." Public-sector expenditures were at a level equivalent to 30% of GNP and the deficit in 1984 at about 16% of GNP. The trade deficit had reached US$2.5 billion. The country surveyed by the *Economist* was Israel.

Prime Minister Shimon Peres promoted austerity measures that went much farther than any attempted in Egypt. He slashed the government budget from US$12 to US$10 billion, including outlays for housing, education, welfare, and civil service salaries. Some US$800 million in subsidy reductions were being planned. Simultaneously, the government set its sights on promoting high-tech exports as well as military hardware, the latter of which earned the country over US$1 billion in 1984.

We are at the end of a major developmental phase in Middle Eastern societies and in LDCs as a whole. State-led growth has brought about a certain amount of structural transformation, but rapid population growth has overwhelmed the income-raising effects that such transformation was presumed to yield. The state has overextended its capacities to manage and guide increasingly diversified economies. It was able to give a big push to industrialization but unable to deal with the complexities of industrial deepening, the efficient use of labor and capital, and the need to export in highly competitive world markets. Part of the complexity and diversity that state intervention brought about lay in the creation of new social actors and interests that benefited from state policies (land-reform beneficiaries or the recipients of subsidized credit) or from state business (the whole range of subcontracting). Over time, these groups became entrenched in their economic niches, absorbing resources and saving and investing in such a manner that they developed some economic autonomy and the means to lobby effectively vis-à-vis the state. Indeed, many state functionaries joined their ranks.

These beneficiaries of the decades of ISI have not yet lost all their leverage in the political system, but their claims to public resources and favorable public policies are under challenge. The international donor community and international capital markets have exerted pressure for change that is difficult to resist. The discrediting of centrally planned economies in Eastern Europe and the former Soviet Union has deprived the upholders of the status quo of a viable economic model. Structural transformation under conditions of austerity will be far more difficult politically than it was when large public outlays and ISI went hand in hand.

NOTES

1. "X-efficiency" arises when an enterprise's total costs are not minimized because the actual output from given inputs is less than the maximum technologically possible level.

2. Iran and Iraq joined their poorer brethren in facing a resource gap once they embarked on their mutual slaughter, but there are no international data on this issue for these two countries after 1980. Unofficial estimates placed Iraq's debt at as much as US$90 billion, while Iran had entirely depleted its accumulated reserves at the end of the war (*Middle East*, July 1988).

3. The difference between domestic savings and domestic investment was +2% for all middle-income countries, −1% for lower-middle-income countries, and +4% for upper-middle-income countries.

9

THE CHECKERED COURSE OF ECONOMIC REFORM

"Economic reform" is a generic term for the shift in state economic policy toward greater reliance on market forces, increased emphasis on the private sector, improved public-sector decisionmaking, and wider opening to international markets. Although the specifics vary, many of the region's states have moved in this direction. These changes are best understood as the product of the difficulties and contradictions of state-led growth and influence from abroad. The changes face difficult political hurdles. Economic and political logics conflict. Structural adjustment programs are "packages": they have an internal, logical coherence. But political logic enjoins precisely the opposite: it is the height of political folly to offend everyone at once—which is what the economic logic often implies. Further, the benefits of reform are always uncertain, and losers may be better placed to act collectively than winners. Reforming an economy is a serious political challenge.

Reform opponents hardly hold all the cards, however. Reform advocates have certain opportunities; macroeconomic reforms cause considerable pain in the short run, but stabilization can also provide benefits to most people in the country. This is the more likely to be the case the more parlous the state of the economy before reform. By bundling together reforms (such as trade reforms) that redistribute benefits from small but well-organized interest groups to the diffuse, disorganized public with the macro changes that most people recognize are necessary and inevitable, opposition to the former can be blunted (Rodrik 1994). Reforms often come in a crisis period, when the opposition is disorganized and/or discredited. This situation may provide reformers with a temporary opportunity that they would be wise to seize vigorously. In contrast to reformers in the newly democratic countries of South America or Eastern Europe, however, long-term authoritarian incumbents in MENA enjoy no "honeymoon period" in which to implement such a strategy.

The ability of losers to block reform can easily be exaggerated. Middle Eastern presidents and kings have many mechanisms at their disposal for rewarding friends and restraining enemies. Losers from reform can be persuaded, bought off, or co-erced into compliance, while winners can be encouraged to organize and demand continued change. However, overcoming the opposition of losers requires skilled and determined leadership. As we shall see, this quality has too often been lacking in the region's would-be reformers.

The current conventional wisdom in the Middle East is that its economic reform programs are the result of leaders' survival strategies. Despite the caveats just offered, it is highly unlikely that executives in MENA are so strong that they can ignore *all* interest groups. Accordingly, the structure and speed of reform are given by the lead-ers' need to do just enough to solve critical balance-of-payments problems while si-multaneously placating key domestic interest groups.

The view of reform as a regime survival strategy cannot explain why such a strat-egy is *credible*. Why should private investors believe the (still unaccountable) kings and presidents of MENA when they verbally embrace economic reform? Why shouldn't private actors assume that the government is simply trying to extricate it-self from the current foreign-exchange crisis, after which it will revert to arbitrary, statist, expropriating behavior? If private investors lack confidence in government re-form pronouncements, they will not invest, and without greatly increased private in-vestment economic reform cannot succeed. Credibility is key (see Box 9.1).

Reformers have at least three (not exclusive) strategies available for enhancing their credibility: building a reputation for reform consistency, blocking retreats, and getting help. Building a reputation takes time; the longer a government persists, the better. One encouraging sign is that so far few reforms that have actually been imple-mented have been reversed (although budgetary indiscipline returned in Turkey in the early 1990s). At the same time, few bridges have been burned. Difficult-to-reverse (and therefore credibility-enhancing) reforms such as privatization have moved at the slowest pace of all reforms in the region. Many countries have, how-ever, emulated Ulysses and the Sirens and have used other actors to tie them to the mast. International agreements with the IMF, the World Bank, the Paris Club, and so forth persuade skeptics because these institutions themselves have credibility. Structural adjustment loans from the World Bank and Letters of Intent with the IMF are international treaties, not to be abrogated with impunity (although back-sliding and partial fulfillment are the norm). The imprimatur of the IMF boosts re-form credibility with private investors. Agreements with the European Union have a similar effect.

Reform credibility is also shaped by *domestic political alignments*. In particular, the reform's credibility partly depends on perceptions of the relative strengths of winners and losers. Economic agents may rationally perceive a reform measure that imposes costs on a well-organized group as likely to be opposed and reversed. Such a reform will, ceteris paribus, be perceived as less credible than reforms whose costs are largely borne by weaker, unorganized groups. The capacity of winners and losers to act col-lectively is an important component of reform credibility. For example, the relative success of Moroccan reforms may be partly explained by the fact that the beneficiaries

---

BOX 9.1
PRIVATE-SECTOR INCREDULITY

The meager inflows of foreign direct investment (FDI) and the continued large sums of money held offshore by MENA nationals suggest that credibility is a serious problem. The region captured only 3% of the roughly US$62 billion of FDI inflows into the developing world in 1993. In sharp contrast to the situation in Asia and Latin America, these inflows have been static since the mid-1980s. The offshore funds held by MENA nationals are estimated by the IMF at around US$600 billion. The estimated offshore holdings of hard currency by Egyptians exceeds US$80 billion, nearly twice the size of Egypt's current international debt. The estimated US$6.2 billion of Jordanian external savings is over 160% of Jordan's GNP, and Syria's US$26.1 billion is over 160% of its GNP. Unsurprisingly, the region's capital market is tiny by international standards: in thirty-eight "emerging markets" with a total capitalization of $1 trillion ($1 \times 10^{12}$) in 1994, Arab bond and equity market capitalization amounted to approximately US$91 billion ($91 \times 10^9$), or only 9% (Azzam 1994; Diwan and Squire 1993). The key to successful reform is attracting these funds back to MENA countries, where they can be invested in job- and foreign-exchange-creating enterprise. With only a few exceptions, however, most MENA countries have not, apparently, persuaded domestic or private investors that their reforms to date are serious enough to warrant committing funds to them.

---

of reforms—wealthy industrialists, rural notables in rain-fed agriculture, and the beneficiaries of the irrigation projects—were already staunch supporters of King Hassan. The king's opposition had long been found among organized labor and petty functionaries, particularly schoolteachers. Economic reform, made necessary by the external balance-of-payments crisis, afforded the king an opportunity to reward his friends and punish his opponents. His reform pronouncements were perceived as credible, and substantial private foreign direct investment flowed into Morocco. Their credibility was at least in part a function of the executive's political strategy and the configuration of winners and losers from reform.

A SURVEY OF COUNTRY EXPERIENCES

There is a wide range of country experience in supplying the necessary leadership to overcome interest-group blockages, surmount credibility problems, and stimulate private investment. Although none of the countries of the region has firmly established its credibility, some have done much better than others. Moroccan, Tunisian, and (perhaps) Jordanian reforms are often perceived as credible, while Egyptian, Syrian, Iranian, and Algerian reform pronouncements are greeted with skepticism. Turkish reforms achieved a high level of credibility in the mid-1980s only to deteriorate more thereafter.

Different regimes have different configurations of interest groups, institutions, bases for regime legitimacy, and leadership patterns. Accordingly, this discussion of reform will be organized by regime type: socialist republics (e.g., Algeria, Egypt, Syria, Tunisia, Yemen), Arab monarchies (e.g., Jordan and Morocco), Islamic republics (Iran and Sudan), and secular democracies (Israel and Turkey). Reform is also strongly influenced by the presence or absence of significant external rents. No leader takes on the hazards of economic reform unless there is little alternative. The cases examined below range from relatively successful ones such as Morocco and Tunisia to much less successful ones such as Iran and Algeria. Egypt falls somewhere in between, with Turkey illustrating a reform process that began well but later faltered.

Egypt

Egypt's prereform situation, though extreme, is illustrative of the reform challenges faced throughout the region. On the eve of the Gulf War, the Egyptian economy was a shambles. Growth turned negative in the late 1980s; by 1990 the country had amassed international debts of nearly US$50 billion; its debt/GNP ratio of roughly 150% was arguably the highest in the world. Real wages of unskilled workers had plummeted by 40% in four years, while civil servants earned only about half of their 1973 salaries (Richards 1992b). The level of open unemployment had roughly doubled during the decade. The quality of government health, transportation, and educational services had declined precipitously from already dismal levels. The situation was increasingly exploited by Islamist extremists.

At the core of Egypt's macroeconomic crisis were three macroimbalances: gaps between domestic savings and investment, imports and exports, and government revenues and spending. The collapse of oil revenues and the mounting losses of public-sector companies undermined public savings, while private savings were deterred by negative real interest rates on Egyptian pound deposits and by great uncertainty on the part of private wealth holders as to the direction and credibility of economic policy. Investment flowed into infrastructure rather than into tradable goods production; investment was increasingly inefficient and capital-intensive, creating few jobs.

By 1989 the current account deficit was 7.2% of GDP, and by 1991 it was 10.2% (World Bank 1991). Since roughly two-thirds of Egyptian imports are intermediate and capital goods, there was relatively little room for import compression. Export developments during the 1980s were dominated by the decline in the value of petroleum sales, which fell from US$2.9 billion in 1983 to US$1.36 billion in 1987. Other tradables failed to fill the gap created by the decline of oil. Cotton export volume in 1990 fell to one-third that of the early 1980s, when it had already declined by 50% in comparison with 1974. In 1987 the deficit of agricultural trade was some US$2.8 billion, about one-third of the total trade deficit. Industrial exports performed only slightly better. Invisible earnings fared better. Tourism grossed over US$2 billion per year on the eve of the Gulf crisis in 1991 and provided the only really bright spot of the economy in the late 1980s. Workers' remittances outperformed most predictions until the Gulf crisis, averaging roughly US$3.4 billion from 1982 to 1989.

Egypt, like so many middle-income countries, plugged the twin gaps by borrowing from abroad, largely from foreign governments. Although there are conflicting estimates of debt because of underreporting and multiple exchange rates during the past two decades, a rough estimate would be that Egypt's foreign debt climbed from about US$2 billion in 1970 to some US$21 billion in 1980 to just under US$50 billion in early 1990 (see Amin 1995); in 1990 debt-service payments consumed over 25% of exports. The situation in mid-1990 may fairly be characterized as one of crisis, in which foreign exchange for wheat imports was hard to locate and only last-minute help from the Gulf States narrowly averted an American aid freeze for failure to service military debt.

The twin gaps were exacerbated by the government deficit. Although its size fell somewhat at the end of the decade, the average deficit for FY 1982/90 was 21.2% of GDP; the deficit in 1991 was some 21.9% of GDP. Revenue fell with oil receipts, while spending was inelastic downward for the usual political reasons: blockage by vested interest groups that would lose sinecures and economic rents and fear of popular wrath over subsidy cuts. Some 80% of government spending consisted of subsidies, public-sector salaries, interest on the public debt, and the military. The last two were sacrosanct, forcing all adjustment on the spending side onto the first two.

As new foreign lending dried up in the latter half of the 1980s, the deficit was increasingly financed by the banking system. Inflation accordingly rose to roughly 25%, with the usual baleful results: further distortion of price signals, sharply negative real interest rates that exacerbated the savings-investment gap, and (thanks to fixed nominal rates) a steadily increasing overvaluation of the exchange rate. Such underpricing of increasingly scarce foreign exchange discouraged the production of traded goods and favored imports over exports; in short, it greatly exacerbated the trade gap.

Microeconomic distortions reinforced macroimbalances. Egyptian price distortions of the 1970s and 1980s were internationally notorious. The divergences between private and social rates of return in industry were little short of astonishing (World Bank 1983).[1] In the second half of the 1980s, price reforms began to be implemented in agriculture, but cotton remains underpriced even today. Prices in Egypt have borne little relation to opportunity costs.

Price distortions interacted synergistically with the regulatory environment to create a producer's nightmare. One example is the increase in capital-intensity. On the one hand, the price of labor relative to capital rose as labor emigration pushed up wages, while accelerating inflation and financial regulations created strongly negative real interest rates. Supervisory personnel, so crucial to successful labor-intensive production, was particularly scarce during the migration boom. At the same time, laws that made it almost impossible to fire workers converted labor into overhead.

Regulations were—and remain—voluminous, ubiquitous, opaque, and arbitrarily enforced.

The Gulf War created an entirely new situation. In a fine example of the use of others to create credibility, the government adopted a reasonably conventional stabilization and structural adjustment package, endorsed by the IMF, in exchange for massive debt relief. Such a bargain was attractive both economically and politically. Economically, the reduction of up to US$20 billion of debt cut yearly interest payments by US$2 billion for the next ten years. Politically, the deal was easier to sell domestically, since the government could plausibly argue that its creditors were shouldering part of the burden of past mistakes. By front-loading the reforms, international donors hoped to change the payoffs facing the government; if they failed to reform, they would not enjoy subsequent tranches of debt relief.

By some measures, macroeconomic stabilization has done very well. Debt relief and banking reform are the keys here. The United States forgave the roughly US$7 billion of military debt. Some 15% of the debt was forgiven in May 1991 following the IMF's approval of an eighteen-month standby arrangement (later extended another six months). A further 15% was forgiven in September 1993, when the IMF concluded that the first set of reforms had been successfully implemented, and agreement was reached on an extended fund facility. The final 20% of debt was to be forgiven in July 1994, contingent on satisfactory compliance with the terms of the extended fund facility, which emphasizes continued fiscal reform, trade liberalization, and reform and privatization of both financial and real goods sectors. This last step has not materialized, and the reasons are revealing.

Thanks to the banking reform package, Egyptians have been turning dollar holdings into Egyptian pounds, generating current account surpluses. International reserves have soared, rising from US$2.68 billion in 1990 to US$10.8 billion in 1992 and an estimated US$16–18 billion in 1994. The savings and investment gaps are now being filled with private-capital inflows. Price reforms in the agricultural sector have also proceeded according to plan, and the government has increased its real revenue by replacing indirect taxation with sales taxes.

Fiscal reform has also been very successful: government deficits have been slashed, plunging from over 20% of GDP before the war to 4.7% in FY 1992/93. By 1993/94 the overall budgetary deficit was 2% of GDP. Fiscal discipline has combined with tight monetary policy to cut inflation from over 25% in 1990 to 8% in 1994.[2] The contrast between the situation today and that prevailing before the Gulf War is striking.

The bad news is that real-goods-sector reforms have lagged behind financial and macro changes. Indeed, the very success of the banking reform has reduced pressure on the exchange rate, which has led to real overvaluation estimated by the IMF at 25–40%. The balance of trade has remained heavily in deficit (it is now slightly above US$5 billion) because of the lackluster performance of exports. Nonoil exports actually *fell* by 20% from 1991 to 1994.[3] The Egyptian government refuses to devalue, while the IMF insists that this is necessary. This is one of the two causes of the current impasse, the other being the sluggish pace of privatization and deregulation. Even today, the Egyptian government has privatized only 20 of 314 state-owned enterprises, and, perhaps most important, the regulatory swamps remain entirely undrained.

The growth of nontraditional exports has slowed as local costs have risen and the exchange rate has appreciated. The banking system is awash in cash, but the public's holdings are mainly in very short-term (one-to-three-month) instruments. Any shock to confidence could lead to rapid conversion of Egyptian pounds to dollars, precipitating a sharp, sudden devaluation. It is notable that despite Islamist violence this has not happened; wealthy Egyptians are betting on the government and accord some credibility to the reform process. An additional problem is that the high capital inflows lead to an overvaluation of the real effective exchange rate, which in turn reduces incentives to produce the traded goods that are necessary to create jobs. Yet devaluation, as urged by the IMF, could easily lead to heavy, destabilizing capital outflows.

Private investors' vote of confidence is highly tentative: short-term liquid savings have yet to be translated into investment in the real economy. Only such investment can generate sustainable employment growth. There has been little progress on privatization. It is true that the Egyptian government has agreed to Basle standards for asset valuation and has formed public holding companies to increase the autonomy of public-enterprise managers. Two large bottling companies have been sold, but otherwise privatization is mainly confined to tourism (hotels). High interest rates and, especially, the general lack of public confidence in the stability of a level playing field for private and public enterprise have so far stymied private investment in tradable-goods production. In other words, three years and 2 million new job seekers after adopting the reform package, little has been done to correct the fundamental weakness of the Egyptian economy, *the weakness of private investment in labor-intensive tradable-goods production*. Structural adjustment, as opposed to stabilization, has barely begun. On the one hand, the government clings to the industrial dinosaurs of the Nasserist era. On the other hand, it has failed dismally to provide an adequate social safety net. Implementation of the Social Fund was greatly delayed as diverse ministries and public personalities fought for access to its very considerable resources. While the government dithers, the Islamists move in and win support by providing their own assistance.

Egyptian reform began only in 1991 and has moved cautiously even since then. Three factors best explain this pattern: the structure of interest groups, the personality and priorities of the leadership, particularly President Mubarak, and the availability of substantial international rents.

The principal losers from economic reform were precisely those upon whom the regime had traditionally relied for support and whose ability to act collectively was institutionalized under Nasser: organized labor and managers in state-owned enterprises, government bureaucrats, and holders of import licenses and other rent seekers. Egyptian reformers faced a powerful phalanx of vested interests that blocked the adoption (and still more, the implementation) of policy change. The strength of such groups can, however, be overstated. These potential losers from reform face free-rider problems in opposing reform and, given Egypt's highly centralized political system, would probably fall to a determined effort by the president. The president, however, chooses to move as slowly as possible.

Leadership is always important for reform, but, arguably, in Egypt it is especially so. The Egyptian political system is extremely centralized, with most key decisions being made by the president and his closest advisers. The men close to Mubarak are very much men of the old order; there has been very little turnover in the cabinet and hardly any in key portfolios. Mubarak, a military man, has surrounded himself with bureaucrats—not a set of backgrounds that is conducive to wholehearted embrace of market-friendly reform. Mubarak is no "technopol," or economist-turned-politician, like Carlos Salinas or Turgut Özal. His experience of the Sadat assassination is said to have reinforced his caution, and he has surrounded himself with mediocrities. Now that the regime has ample foreign-exchange cover, the danger is that he will see no reason to persevere with reform, particularly in the regulatory area.

Economic rent provides the third prong of the dilatory reform strategy. Until the mid-1980s, oil rents, whether directly in the form of oil export revenues or indirectly as workers' remittances from the Gulf and Iraq, permitted the Egyptian government to pursue business as usual. The collapse of oil rents in the early to mid-1980s greatly increased the pressure for reform. Although there were some reforms (particularly of the government budget), a consistent reform program was not even formulated until mid-1986, not implemented until May 1987, and abandoned in November 1987. Throughout the 1980s the government procrastinated as problems mounted, long after oil rents had dwindled.

Strategic rents permitted reform dalliance. Egyptian leaders were able to exploit their unique position as the largest Arab nation and the only one to have signed a peace treaty with Israel to extract concessions from the United States, the EEC, and, through these, international agencies such as the IMF and the World Bank. Official development assistance averaged 4% of GDP throughout the 1980s and rose to 9% between 1990 and 1993. The Mubarak government skillfully utilized strategic rents to delay reforms for half a decade after the oil-price collapse of mid-1986, seized the opportunity for debt relief afforded by the Gulf War, and, despite foreign pressures, reformed at its own glacial pace. This pace does little to provide jobs to the rapidly rising number of young job seekers. The combination of interest-group structures, strategic rents, and the personality of the president has yielded relatively low reform credibility.

Algeria

Despite oil rents and rapid growth, Algeria could not escape the contradictions of its statist, inward-oriented development strategy (see Chapter 8). The key weaknesses of the Boumedienne strategy were excess capacity, overcentralization, unemployment, massive rural-urban migration, and serious neglect of agriculture. These problems elicited halfhearted reform measures that helped delegitimize the government as they imposed hardships but failed to deliver a restructured economy.

The situation in the early 1980s was increasingly difficult. Labor productivity had actually declined in both the hydrocarbon and the nonoil public-industrial sector. The rate of worker absenteeism ranged between 10 and 20%, about one-fifth of workers left their jobs each year, and "factory discipline became extremely unsatisfactory" (Bennoune 1988, 141). The iron-and-steel complex at El Hadjar was operating at only 40% of capacity in the early 1980s, thereby forfeiting economies of scale and raising costs to all final users of its output. Two-thirds of Algerian basic food was imported, and unemployment rose to 16% in the cities. Housing was extremely scarce. The regime slowly, inexorably sowed the dragon's teeth by providing young men with incentives to move to the cities, where they found no jobs, no housing, and, therefore, no wives.

These problems can be traced to the strategy of concentration on heavy industry and to management problems of state-owned enterprises. The economic argument for developing heavy industry was based on linkage effects: These industries were to provide the basic materials for others that would supply the population with its needs. It is true that basic metals and energy industries have high forward linkages, but they are also very capital-intensive and create relatively few jobs. Worse, in Algeria they were run as monopolies, giving enterprise managers little reason to be efficient. Furthermore, the location of these industries in and around the major cities of Algiers, Constantine, and Oran further stimulated rural-to-urban migration, already massive because of rapid population growth and the neglect of agriculture. This exacerbated the severe problems of the cities.

Beginning in 1982, the regime of Chadli Benjadid began to tinker with this system. Initially, some 66 huge state-owned enterprises were broken up into 474 smaller companies by 1985, with more following. Successive decrees were issued that were intended to decentralize decisionmaking in state enterprises. Other changes included the reallocation of public investment away from heavy industry, incentives to attract foreign investors, and measures to revive the agricultural sector. The autonomy of management was strengthened, and capacity utilization rose from an average of 30–40% in the late 1970s to 75% in 1984. Industrial workers received bonuses linked to productivity.

The regime tried to encourage both domestic and foreign private investment. The private sector accounted for about one-fourth of manufacturing output in 1985; its activities continued to be concentrated in light-industrial products. As elsewhere in the region, private entrepreneurs existed in a symbiotic relationship with the public sector, obtaining inputs from the public sector and/or selling their output to the giant monopolies. The 1982 investment code reduced the tax rate on profits and expanded credit for industries likely to generate foreign exchange (e.g., tourism). The amount of foreign currency that such firms could legally import was doubled, and the establishment of some 660 new private firms was approved. Private foreign direct investment rose from virtually zero to US$280 million in 1984. Whereas previously nearly all contracts with foreign companies had been turnkey arrangements, for the first time foreign firms were allowed to operate facilities (in joint ventures) in the country. The two most visible were in telecommunications (Sweden's Ericsson Company) and automobiles (Italy's Fiat Corporation).

A critical force driving all of these policy changes was the country's mounting indebtedness. In 1985 the World Bank reported Algerian debt at US$15 billion, while for the same year the OECD's figure was about US$24 billion. Despite austerity programs of reducing investment spending, pruning government recurrent expenditures, and slashing imports by over 10% in one year, the government was forced to return to international capital markets in 1987.

The restructuring of the economy under Benjadid failed to alleviate debt and failed to cope with unemployment; in 1986 about 116,000 new jobs were created, while about 173,000 new job-seekers entered the labor market. As labor force growth accelerated, growth of output declined to 3% during the 1980s. Urbanization accelerated; the urban population growth rate rose from 4.1% in the 1970s to 4.8% in the 1980s (Bennoune 1988). International debt continued to mount, reaching US$26.5 billion in 1991, by which time a vicious civil war was well under way. Algerian perestroika had failed.

Algerian reform in the 1980s was fundamentally an attempt by reform-minded technocrats grouped around Chadli Benjadid to square the circle: to overcome the Boumedienne legacy of excess capacity, low productivity, overcentralization, excessive capital-intensity, galloping urbanization, and one of the most seriously neglected agricultural sectors in the region while still maintaining state control of the economy. It was a classic case of reform as survival strategy.

Much of the impetus for Algerian reform was the mounting pressure of servicing the country's international debt. Benjadid's team argued in 1982–1983 that reform was necessary in order to avoid rescheduling the debt, but, in marked contrast to its Maghreb neighbors, Algeria deliberately avoided entering into an agreement with the IMF. Its reform was "structural adjustment with a nationalist face," designed in part to avoid the perceived humiliation of "losing sovereignty" to the IMF.

This reform, decidedly "heterodox," was fundamentally flawed. The key problem was conceptual: the government eschewed implementing the centerpiece of all structural adjustment programs, devaluation of the real exchange rate. A real devaluation is also an increase in the price of tradables relative to that of nontradables and, among tradables, an increase in the price of exportables relative to that of import-competing goods. It is difficult to promote agriculture, create jobs, and foster the private sector without such a change in relative prices. However, out of the same kind of nationalist pride that so infuriated Keynes in the interwar period, the Algerian government refused to devalue the dinar. It was unwilling to cut the link between state-owned enterprises and budgetary subsidies; the "soft budget constraint" remained flaccid. Consequently, it had difficulty restraining public spending and, therefore, inflation. By maintaining fixed nominal interest rates, it produced negative real interest rates, underpricing capital. The heterodox, nationalist reform in Algeria was, until the agreement with the IMF in 1989, a "*Hamlet* without the Prince." Unsurprisingly, it was not credible.

Poor conceptualization was accompanied by poor implementation. Large sections of the ruling FLN never accepted the need for reform. Middle- and lower-level functionaries impeded the shift to the market at every opportunity. Suspicion of market activities remained high in these quarters, and even as legal changes dictated from the top removed obstacles to private-sector activity, bureaucratic resistance blocked their realization. Although reform intensified after the riots of 1988, with agreement with the IMF in 1989 and continued reform until 1993, economic reformers increasingly had to vie with hard-liners arguing that the reforms were responsible for the rise of the FIS and the Islamist insurgency. After the assassination of Mohammed Boudiaf in June 1992, the government of Abdesslam Belaid, who had been minister of industry under Boumedienne, abandoned reform in favor of a more traditional, FLN-style policy of favoring state enterprises. The government persisted in this approach until, in the spring of 1993, the Bank of Algeria could no longer service the country's international debt, forcing the government to begin serious negotiations with the IMF. By then, of course, internal violence had increased considerably.

The political dynamics of economic reform doomed the process from the start. The reformers were, initially, a group around Benjadid. He found few supporters for his reformist intentions in the dominant FLN or in the armed forces. Some have argued that he used the Islamists (the FIS) as a counterweight to the FLN and some army elements in an attempt to "open a space" for his reforms (Leveau 1993). One is reminded of Sadat's (ultimately personally fatal) use of Islamists as a counterweight to pro-Soviet Nasserists in the 1970s. This political strategy had serious weaknesses. The government's legitimacy eroded significantly both before and during the reform decade of the 1980s. As one analyst puts it, the FLN "had become valued by most Algerians by what it could deliver, not for what it stood for politically or ideologically" (Vandewalle 1992, 190). As the regime's ability to deliver faltered, its legitimacy evaporated. Further, implementing highly visible reforms that changed little reduced the constituency for reform and aroused public skepticism.

Public disillusionment in Algeria was particularly strong because the regime (1) was widely perceived as thoroughly corrupt and out of touch with the needs of ordinary Algerians, (2) never intended to make a real "break for the market," and (3) pursued flawed reform policies from 1982 until 1988. Even when sensible macroeconomic policies were finally put in place after the 1988 riots, it was too little and too late: urban young people were far too alienated, and even at this late date the dinosaurs of the FLN and the bureaucracy continued to block the market-oriented reforms that alone had a chance of creating jobs. Finally, the politics of encouraging the Islamists as a counterweight to antireform elements assumed that the government would retain control of the political game, but the FIS soon became at least as strong as and then stronger than the reforming technocrats around the president. Events since 1992 have simplified the triangle of political forces of presidential reformers–FLN/army–

Islamists by removing the first group as significant players. Such polarization forms the backdrop to today's current bloody drama.

We cannot know yet whether the Zeroual government will be able, against the odds, to implement economic reform while negotiating a political settlement with the Islamists. There are some positive signs: it replaced the entire upper echelon of the army, signed an agreement with the IMF, and tried to open a kind of dialogue with more moderate Islamist elements while waging a determined military struggle against the terrorists. Usually, however, moderate moves by one segment of the ruling elite (the so-called *conciliateurs,* grouped around Zeroual) are matched by harshly repressive countermoves by the *eradicateurs*, generally thought to be led by the chief of staff, General Lamari. The breakdown of talks between government and opposition in October 1994 and the continuous spiral of violence are hardly encouraging.

The deepest problem remains the credibility of the current commitment to reform. Quite apart from the climate of physical insecurity and violence, why should private investors believe that the old guard of the FLN, which retains significant power, will not continue to sabotage the implementation of reform? Although this process is under way, it has yet to happen in the upper reaches of the leadership. One is certainly entitled to ask whether this leopard can change his spots, particularly in the middle of a fight against a very nasty pack of hyenas. The structure of interest groups, the presence of large hydrocarbon rents, and the absence—until it was too late—of reformist leadership seem the key explanators of reform's failure.

Tunisia

Tunisia offers a striking exception to the generally weak economic reform performance of socialist republics. Although it has had difficulty privatizing—for the same reasons as similar regimes—its history of pragmatism in development since 1969 has paid off. In a manner reminiscent of Mexico's economic (though not political) reform under Salinas, Tunisian reform has built credibility in three ways. First, the effort started at least a decade ago, and the government has very carefully lived up to all of its commitments. Second, it has worked very closely with the IMF and the World Bank in constructing and implementing reform programs; Tunisian reform has been highly orthodox. Third, the president has visibly backed the decisions of the Western-trained and -oriented technocrats whom he has placed in charge of economic policymaking. The generally high level of competence of the Tunisian civil service has helped ensure adequate implementation of reform measures.

Like other countries of the region, Tunisia followed the usual inward-oriented, statist approach to economic development immediately after independence. In the early 1970s it pioneered the "opening up" (*infitah*) approach better-known from Sadat's Egypt. Despite early attempts to attract foreign direct investment, the private sector remained relatively small. In 1981 state-owned enterprises still accounted for about 60% of the value of manufacturing output. The budgetary burden of state-owned enterprises increased to 4% by 1978–1981. Private investment was largely limited to consumer goods production and tourism. Even for consumer goods, the government continued to manage large firms, often trying to attract joint-venture partners.

As elsewhere, the approach before 1986 was mainly one of streamlining the existing economic strategy of state-led growth, in which the government dominated the commanding heights of the economy, supplying the intermediate goods that private industry needed. The complex of controls over prices, investments, trade, credit, and foreign exchange remained in place, as did its corollary, misallocation of resources.

Events in the 1980s made this policy unsustainable. The government tried to "grow through" external shocks such as the international recession of the early 1980s, drought, rising European protectionism, and falling oil prices. Tunisian debt continued to mount, rising from 38% of GDP in 1980 to 63% in 1986. Because of strong internal demand, an overvalued currency and deteriorating terms of trade, the current-account deficit widened from 5% of GDP in 1980 to 11% in 1985–1986. The government's budgetary deficit reached 5.2% of GDP in the five years before 1986, while the resource gap averaged 9% from 1981 to 1985.

The Muhammed Mzali government instituted some halfhearted reforms, including the change of consumer-subsidy programs that provoked the riots of January 1984. The government then retreated, but the problems became even more severe; by the summer of 1986 the country had only a few days of import cover left. At this point, the government had little choice but to turn to the IMF and accept the standby agreement that it had proudly avoided for so long. In August 1986 it embarked on a new round of economic reform.

Devaluation of the currency, export promotion, reduction in import protection, liberalization of banking and prices, budgetary austerity, and privatization were, as usual, the key elements of the structural adjustment program in Tunisia. Most targets were met, and the economy's performance improved significantly. Economic growth for 1987–1992 was 4.3%, compared with 2.8% for the previous five years. Exports have grown strongly and have been diversified; exports of manufactures grew at 15% per year, and workers' remittances rose until the Gulf War. Private savings rose, as did foreign direct investment, which increased from US$75 million in 1989–1990 to US$215 million in 1992 and US$316 million in 1993. Inflation fell to 8%, and the balance of payments improved despite the adverse shock of the Gulf War. Debt accumulation decelerated markedly in the second half of the decade, and the ratio of present value of debt to export of goods and services improved, falling from 170% in 1986 to 125% in 1991. Tunisia does not suffer from a significant debt overhang problem. In 1991–1992 it achieved a positive food trade balance for the first time in twenty years. The efficiency of investment improved: ICOR fell from 7.7 in 1980–1984 to 3.8 in 1988–1991. These are significant achievements.

The program has some weaknesses. Government savings have performed relatively poorly. Financial reform has fallen behind schedule; the Central Bank is often accused of excessive regulatory intervention, with the result that a truly modern, competitive banking sector has yet to emerge. There are persistent reports of collusive behavior among bankers, especially through the Association Professionnelle des

Banques. Although most agricultural commodities have been deregulated, price controls are maintained on cereal grains, milk, sugar, and oil.

The weakest component of reform has been privatization. Between 1987 and September 1991, less than 1% of the book value of the over two hundred state-owned enterprises in existence in 1987 had been privatized. As is typical of privatization programs worldwide, the first phase of privatization was the divestiture of small and medium-sized enterprises in services such as tourism and construction. The next phase, in which larger industrial enterprises must be privatized, will be more politically difficult.

From a labor-market perspective, the changes have been essentially a matter of running faster just to stay in place: despite faster growth, the number of the unemployed (but not the unemployment rate) continues to rise. It would, of course, have risen faster without the reforms, but young men's politics is rarely determined by ceteris paribus arguments. Nevertheless, compared with other countries in the region, Tunisia has a reasonably good record of job creation.

Despite the problems, Tunisia is justifiably praised by the World Bank and the IMF as one of the most successful reformers in the Arab world. The government is clearly committed to further reforms. During 1993–1994 it strengthened its credibility by making the dinar convertible, creating a foreign currency market, adopting a unified investment code, and taking some limited steps to institute a stock market. Over 85% of imports are tariff-free. Tunisia's associate status with the European Union further strengthens the credibility of its reforms.

Private investors evidently find the reforms credible. The presence of a high level of human capital by regional standards is attractive to private investors. Tunisia has the highest literacy rate (65%) in the region, and over 90% of the labor force under thirty-five years old is literate. Foreign executives comment that Tunisia is the only Arab country in which they can find adequate skilled labor and, especially, middle managers. Tunisia received some 18% of total foreign direct investment (FDI) flows into the region in 1992. Its economy, compared only with those receiving some FDI,[4] was only 4% of the total. Disproportionately, foreign investors are betting on Tunisia.

Without minimizing Tunisian achievements in economic reform so far, it is fair to say that the next phase will be more difficult. Most of the needed changes will pose significant political challenges. Powerful domestic political interest groups oppose further privatization and liberalization of the labor market. Reduced budgetary deficits will be difficult because public investment needs to increase to provide the kind of improved infrastructure that private investors seek. Local and foreign investors are not particularly keen to see domestic tariff walls further reduced. For years the bureaucracy has been closely linked to the political party patronage system. Without personal connections, coping with the regulatory issues remains difficult.

Perhaps the key problem is continuing to convince investors, both domestic and foreign, that the current government will really provide a level playing field for the private sector, abandon its myriad levers of control, and streamline the bureaucracy and make it accountable. The problem is made still more difficult by a paradox: political stability is essential to greater private investment, but deregulation of the economy deprives the government of important control mechanisms. The Ben 'Ali government seems determined to make haste slowly in its attempt to foster a market economy in Tunisia, but no one should doubt that there is urgency; 800,000 new jobs need to be created by the end of the decade. Nevertheless, the achievements of Tunisia show that sound policies can go very far toward ameliorating the socioeconomic problems that underlie crises such as those in Algeria and Egypt.

Morocco

Morocco initially faced similar imperatives and blockages to economic reform as other countries in the region. In Morocco as elsewhere, the roots of structural adjustment can be traced to the legacy of state-led import-substituting industrialization, the commodities price boom of the 1970s, and the accumulation of international indebtedness (Chapters 7 and 8). The resource boom of the 1970s also had the usual Dutch Disease effects: the real exchange rate became increasingly overvalued, shifting incentives away from tradable-goods production. Moroccan experience paralleled that of neighboring oil countries.

Even at the height of the boom, part of state expansion was financed by foreign borrowing. Expansion continued into 1976 even as phosphate prices collapsed (falling by 47%), swelling the budget deficit to 20% of GDP (Morrison 1991). Expenditures rose with the beginning of the Saharan War, the increased cost of consumer subsidies (rising from 1% of GDP in 1973 to 6.9% in 1974) (Horton 1990), unwillingness to cancel investment projects, and the political fear of canceling public-sector salary increases. Although some initial steps toward stabilization were taken in 1977, the Moroccan government, along with many others, hoped that the adverse price shock was temporary and tried to "grow through the recession." Accordingly, its foreign debt rose from 20% of GDP in 1975 to nearly 60% (at US$10 billion) in 1980, when service payments consumed 32.7% of exports. As the burden of debt became increasingly unmanageable, the government was forced to undertake stabilization measures. As usual, the initial impetus for stabilization came from outside: foreign creditors refused to continue to finance budgetary deficits, forcing the country to turn to the IMF for assistance. In Morocco, as in other countries of the region, the first key agent of change was external.

Because of the high political costs of austerity, most countries of the region have found adjustment policies difficult to sustain. Here, too, the experience of Morocco initially seems similar. Beginning in 1978 it reduced public spending on investment, increased taxes, restricted civil servants' salary increases, and slowed the growth of credit to private companies. However, in 1979 it retreated, granting a 10% rise of average civil servants' salaries and a 30–40% increase in the minimum wage. It also expanded food subsidies even as the prices of imported farm products rose. A second attempt at implementing a stabilization program was aborted when an extremely sharp rise in consumer prices (50%) and the government's decision to reduce subsidies on food products led, in spring 1981, to major rioting in Casablanca. In the two years (1981–1983) following the Casablanca "bread riots," Morocco pursued an expansionist policy by borrowing more and more from abroad. Foreign public debt continued to rise, reaching US$11.8 billion (84% of GDP) in 1983 (Morrison 1992). Drought added to the difficult situation, accelerating rural-urban migration and increasing the need for food imports. The number of state-owned enterprises rose to 700 in 1984. By 1981–1982 the current-account deficit had risen to 12.6% of GDP (from 8% in 1980) (Morrison 1992). By the middle of 1983 currency reserves were almost exhausted, forcing the government to institute emergency measures to restrict imports. As elsewhere in the region, exogenous shocks and political blockages seriously delayed the implementation of stabilization and structural adjustment.

By 1993, however, Morocco was (with some justification) being held up as a textbook case of successful economic reform. The World Bank's regional director for the Middle East and North Africa summarized the achievement: "Morocco is perhaps the only country in the world which has, at the same time, created a realistic hope for a durable solution to its foreign debt problem, put in place a basic program of structural adjustment, re-established a sound balance of payments situation, instituted monetary stability and stifled inflation while carrying through economic growth at about 4% a year" (*Economist Intelligence Unit*, 1992, First Quarter). The ingredients of the new policy package were the familiar ones of nominal exchange rate devaluation, budgetary discipline, tariff reduction, real interest-rate increases, and privatization.

Moroccan economic reform may be divided into two phases. During the first period (roughly, 1983–1986), the government focused on macroeconomic stabilization through contractionary fiscal and monetary policy, along with other measures to achieve a devaluation of the real effective exchange rate, principally the 1985 floating of the dirham. During this phase most adjustment took place on the spending rather than the revenue side of the public ledger, with investment spending being especially hard hit.

During the second phase of adjustment the government continued to pursue active demand management but increasingly concentrated on stimulating supply. On the demand-management side, the government has recently announced convertibility of the dirham (except for capital transfers). Inflation was held steady at an average rate of 7.2% during the 1980s. Consequently, the real exchange rate fell by roughly 40% during the decade (22% during the first phase of adjustment), greatly increasing the competitiveness of Moroccan manufactured and agricultural exports and the incentives for Moroccan workers abroad to repatriate their savings. Remittances reached US$1.3 billion by 1989, covering 24% of imports. On the supply side, the government liberalized trade by abolishing many price controls, reformed the capital market, and shifted agricultural incentives. Fiscal reform measures were also instituted: a value-added tax (VAT) was introduced in 1986, followed by a corporate profits tax in 1987 and a global income tax in 1989. Government revenues recovered somewhat, and this permitted some modest increases in spending, especially capital expenditure.

The results have been encouraging: GDP expanded at an average annual rate of 4.0% during the 1980s, with manufacturing growing slightly faster (4.1%). The export response was strong, while import growth decelerated. Exports rose from 18% of GDP in 1965 to 25% in 1990. The composition of exports also shifted markedly, with large increases in farm and factory goods. Both the balance of trade and the balance of payments improved.

These gains were the result of an increasingly efficient economy as the structure of Moroccan production conformed more closely to its comparative advantage. Policy shifts assisted this process. Trade reforms reduced the maximum tariff from 400% in 1983 to 44% in 1988, and the government announced a goal of a uniform 25% tariff rate.[5] Morocco has joined the WTO and has entered into negotiations with the European Union for a NAFTA-style free-trade agreement, the "Mediterranean Initiative." The country has maintained a high rate of domestic savings and of investment, but the resource gap has become increasingly easy to fill because of accelerating inflows of foreign direct investment, which rose from US$1 million in 1986 to US$85 million in 1988 to US$165 million in 1990 to US$320 million in 1991. Morocco gets roughly 20% of all FDI in the region (World Bank 1995a).

Experience throughout the world strongly suggests that privatization is the most difficult step in economic reform. Although Morocco has only recently begun to take steps in this area, its past achievements and its progress to date with the early preparatory stages of privatization strongly suggest that it will persist here. The government has announced its intent to privatize a wide range of companies; the Ministry of Economic Affairs and Privatization has slated 112 state entities for privatization by the end of 1995, including 75 companies and 37 hotels (Saloman Brothers 1992). Tender documents have been issued and bids received for a number of companies, and initial awards have been made for several hotels. Foreign investors are decidedly bullish on Moroccan privatization.

Morocco's performance in economic reform has been all the more remarkable because it has been accompanied by growth: GDP expanded at an annual average rate of 4.0% during the 1980s. Manufacturing expanded at 3.8% per year. This is relatively unusual. Economic restructuring is necessarily deflationary in the short run.[6] For example, in Latin America, where they speak of the 1980s as the "lost decade," manufacturing grew at 1.7%; in Mexico, to which Morocco is often now compared, manufacturing expanded at 1.4% during the 1980s (World Bank 1994). Thanks to the expansion of Moroccan industry, the demand for urban manufacturing labor grew at 5.5% from 1979 to 1983 and accelerated to 8.8% from 1985 to 1990, but despite this rapid expansion the numbers of the urban unemployed rose from 322,000 in 1982 to 519,000 in 1984 to 803,000 in 1990/91. The national unemployment rate rose from 12% to 16% during the period; the rate for the more politically volatile urban areas was over 20% in 1990/91, compared with about 12% a decade earlier (Morocco 1992). One can only imagine the consequences of adjustment in Morocco without economic growth!

The poorest urban Moroccans benefited: minimum wages in manufacturing rose after 1987, and hundreds of thousands of new, unskilled jobs were created. Growth was possible because of good weather (raising agricultural output, incomes, and purchases from cities) and the large increase in exports. Expenditure switching was relatively more important than expenditure reduction in restoring macroeconomic and external payments balance.

Moroccan reform has been highly credible for four reasons: (1) The government has used others to this end, crafting its reforms in close consultation with international agencies. (2) The king has provided crucial leadership and visibly supported the key technocrats, who, moreover, enjoyed considerable longevity in their posts. (3) The beneficiaries of reform were already key supporters of the king. (4) The regime has avoided any backtracking on reform.

The country has also enjoyed good luck. In general, Morocco can expect to face recurrent drought, but during the late 1980s it experienced successive years of good weather, leading to a series of exceptionally large harvests. Farm bounty reduced rural-urban migration by raising rural incomes, and agricultural job creation just kept pace with new entrants to the rural labor force. It is possible that having good weather when it was so badly needed also reinforced popular perceptions of the king's possession of baraka or a special blessing from God.

Domestic political alignments were also very helpful. King Hassan has used his great political skill to build and strengthen a proreform coalition composed of two critical groups of winners in the economic reform process: large private-sector Moroccan capitalists and rural notables. Moroccan capitalists have benefited from the opening of the economy, the growth of output, and the influx of foreign capital for joint-venture investment. The king himself is the country's largest capitalist, owning roughly 15% of the nation's largest diversified holding company, Omnium Nord-Africain. Unlike Ben 'Ali and the RCD, King Hassan can privatize without necessarily losing political patronage. He has been able to adopt a Louis XIV strategy: *L'état, c'est moi!*

Other, older and more traditional linkages between the king and the business elite have also been strengthened by his strong support of probusiness reforms. Some "new men" have been created by the expansion of export-oriented industry; although they have benefited from the economic adjustment policies, they are less well connected politically. They constitute a potential additional source of support for the king's policies.

Rural notables, long a pillar of the regime, have benefited from the fact that structural adjustment has favored agriculture in general and the rain-fed subsector in particular as agricultural investment has been reoriented toward them. Sound exchange-rate management has also helped this sector by providing incentives for Moroccan workers in Europe to send back remittances that have been critical in reducing rural poverty. But the main source of benefits in this subsector may have been sheer luck.

The large rural population subsisting in this subsector benefited from a series of high-rainfall years in the late 1980s. Long-standing political control mechanisms, which rely heavily on patron-client relations, further reinforced political stability in rural areas.

For both economic and political reasons, the king has also been able to overcome opposition from losers. The losers in the reform process were largely urban. Economic growth, job creation, and increases in unskilled wages have helped to mitigate the challenge to the regime from the urban poor. Politically, the king has pursued a two-pronged strategy. On the one hand, he has continued to use a wide variety of divide-and-rule mechanisms. On the other, he has embarked on a political liberalization process including the release of political prisoners and the holding of elections. In November 1993 he even offered the opposition cabinet positions. Although these processes are hardly above criticism, they do suggest a shift in political strategy toward greater reliance on a certain degree of accountability in order to strengthen the government's legitimacy with the urban population. The king has also used to his advantage both his traditional religious role as Commander of the Faithful and the patriotism engendered by the Green March and the Saharan War. He has been able to draw on a relatively rich associational life, and these associations have long been prevented from forming effective system-challenging coalitions.

Yet the same features that have contributed to Morocco's relative successes also help to explain its shortcomings. There are five threats to continued Moroccan success: First, despite skillful debt management, the ratio of the present value of debt to exports—some 230% in 1991—remains high. Large public debts weaken financial systems. Historically, countries with ratios above 150% have had difficulty attracting long-term capital investment because investors fear that older investments will be honored rather than their own (Diwan and Squire 1993). Servicing the debt requires internal (public to government) and external (Morocco to rest-of-world) transfers. Potential investors reasonably fear that such a debt overhang will increase the probability of tax increases; domestic investors may fear being crowded out. The number of claimants on the public purse raises uncertainty for new investors, deterring investment. Debt overhang threatens the success of Moroccan reform.

Second, Moroccan educational achievements lag behind those of other developing countries with comparable per capita incomes (Chapter 5). The educational situation is especially shocking for women; most women are illiterate, rural women's literacy levels are at Fourth World levels, one-third of rural girls and one-tenth of urban girls are not in school, and even in the top quintile of the income distribution only a bare majority (52.4%) of women can read and write (Kingdom of Morocco 1992). Moroccan economic growth will not be sustainable so long as the talents of half the population are so grossly underutilized. Morocco now competes internationally almost entirely on the basis of low labor costs, but such a strategy is not sustainable over the long run. Foreign private businesses often cite the paucity of a cadre of "sergeants of industry"—the skilled workers, foremen, and middle managers who are essential to the success of modern private enterprise—as a barrier to investment. Educational failures may yet doom Moroccan reform.

Third, nepotism and favoritism are rife. The presence of perhaps US$3 billion of cannabis exports from the Rif is worrisome. The area has also become a transshipment point for hard drugs, such as cocaine from Colombia. The FBI's Operation Dinero revealed that the Cali cartel was using Morocco as a staging area for European operations (Fox 1995). So far it appears that the government has avoided the state-within-a-state phenomenon of, say Colombia. However, Rifis have long had relatively hostile relations with the palace; it is difficult to imagine that massive drug trafficking does not have the connivance of the Ministry of the Interior. Corrupt governance may yet undermine Moroccan growth.

Fourth, many Moroccans worry about the longevity of the king. Moroccan kings have traditionally been challenged during their early years. Few believe that Crown Prince Sidi Mohammad will fare differently. Most observers also doubt that the son's political skills are equal to his father's. Political reformers in the palace are aiming to the right of Spain—trying to forge a constitutional monarchy in which the king has more power and the parliament less than in Morocco's neighbor to the north—but die-hards fear and resist such a transition. The lack of strong political institutions to consolidate the power of modern elements in the political economy is cause for concern.

Finally, of course, there is fear of spillover from Algeria. One need not assume a domino effect; Moroccan nationalism is strong (many Moroccans believe that western Algeria rightly belongs to them). However, unless growth remains strong enough not only to provide jobs for new entrants to the labor force but also to raise wages, Islamists will find Morocco fertile ground.

Iran

The Iranian economy has declined precipitously since the revolution. Income per capita in 1992 was estimated to be about 38% below what it was in 1979. (Of course, much of this—as throughout the region—is simply the result of the fall in oil prices.) Population growth *accelerated* during the revolution while output stagnated. The rate of natural increase rose from 2.9% between 1966–1967 and 1976–1977 to 3.9% between 1976–1977 and 1986–1987; the total fertility rate in 1994 was 6.2 (Bulatao and Richardson 1994). The regime has recently reversed itself on family planning, which is now vigorously encouraged (see Box 4.2), but because of the fertility bulge of the recent past the labor force is projected to grow at over 4% per year for the coming decade. All of these figures are among the highest in the region. Unsurprisingly, employment creation has not kept up with additions to the labor force, which is nearly 50% larger now than at the time of the revolution. Measured unemployment rose from 10% to 14%, and more than two-thirds of new jobs created since the revolution have been in the public sector. More than 80% of college graduates work for the state. Iran displays all the usual regional symptoms of high and rising unemployment of semieducated young people.

These failures need to be weighed against the increase in consumption per capita of various foodstuffs in urban areas, the apparent narrowing of rural-urban income gaps, increases in enrollment ratios, and declines in infant and child mortality. The only way to explain the combination of falling incomes per capita and increasing consumption of food is to posit an increase in the equality of income distribution, in which a higher share went to people with a higher marginal propensity to consume food. It seems that the simplest description of Iran under the mullahs is "shared poverty." As Jahangir Amuzegar points out, however, other evidence contradicts the picture of rising equality (Amuzegar 1993). For example, data from expenditure surveys shows rough stability in the Gini coefficient in both rural and urban areas (Karshenas and Pesaran 1994). Perhaps the consumption figures have been doctored for political purposes, or perhaps national income accounts are faulty because a very large percentage of Iranian national income is in the underground economy. These are not mutually exclusive hypotheses. In any case, the shared-poverty perspective seems the best available explanation.

The Iran-Iraq War greatly stimulated the centralization of economic decisionmaking and led to the creation of statist, command-economy-style allocation mechanisms. The war also imposed serious costs on the economy, in particular the destruction of infrastructure. The government implemented price controls, rationing of consumer goods, a deliberately overvalued exchange rate, strict quantitative regulation of imports, and tight controls over banking. It also constructed the familiar regulatory maze for private investors, who needed to obtain numerous permits.

Industrial performance has been unimpressive. In the wake of the revolution, some 580 companies, all of them medium- to large-scale enterprises, were nationalized. Like most developing countries, Iran displays marked industrial dualism, a large number of very small firms coexisting with a much smaller number of medium- and large-scale enterprises. This division also nearly coincides with a private-public split; all large-scale industries and the large majority of medium-scale enterprises are run by the public institutions. In 1990/91 public enterprises accounted for 73% of industrial value added, 72% of employment, and 65% of investment (Amuzegar 1993). The revolution greatly increased direct state management of Iranian industry. Accordingly, manufacturing output stagnated during the 1980s (actually declining at a rate of 0.1% per year, according to the World Bank [Amuzegar 1993]). Some industries fared far worse than this: automobile production in 1992 was only 15% of the pre-1979 level. Growth revived during the 1989–1992 period, when the manufacturing sector grew at double-digit rates. However, much of this growth was capital-intensive and absorbed less than 10% of the new entrants to the labor force during this period.

This poor performance has two sources: the revolution itself and the usual problems of statist, inward-oriented policies. The revolution and ensuing war may be blamed for political interference in management, labor strikes, exodus of managerial skills, and electrical power shortages. Inward-oriented policies such as tariffs and a grossly overvalued exchange rate insulated firms from competition, permitting inefficiency to flourish and creating a vested interest in the continuation of these policies. It is easy to understand why Rafsanjani's reform pronouncements at least pay lip service to privatization. However, progress here has been halting and inconsistent, and reform has stalled.

Agriculture has performed far better than industry. This is consistent with the critiques of the Pahlavi regime voiced during the revolution. Agricultural output increased by 54% from 1980 to 1990. Nearly all of this growth took place before 1986, and most of it was the result of increases in acreage, not increases in yields. Roughly compatible with this observation is the fact that, although fertilizer consumption increased by one-third, the number of tractors roughly tripled. Agricultural growth was due partly to the Pahlavi inheritance, especially the investment in large multipurpose dams and primary irrigation channels, and partly to the government's own policies. It offered very generous subsidies to cereal producers; wheat producers received subsidies equal to 80% of the cost of production, and the government purchased 85% of the crop. These policies had two goals: to pump oil money into rural areas and to achieve food self-sufficiency. The first seems to have been achieved. Although larger farmers received the lion's share of the benefits (as in the United States), smaller farmers also benefited. Demand, however, outstripped domestic supply, and imports continued to supply about 25% of consumption.

There have been the usual negative consequences of the distortions in relative prices that self-sufficiency drives always entail. The creation of a government monopoly in grain trading reduced efficiency. Very heavily subsidized cereal prices encouraged the plowing up of marginal land that had been used for livestock grazing. This not only reduced livestock productivity but also contributed to soil erosion, which, in turn, accelerated the silting up of reservoirs and undermined some traditional farming systems for managing rangelands. The policy mix also encouraged overpumping of ground water, damaging aquifers. Pahlavi agricultural neglect was replaced by unsustainable subsidization and relative price distortion under the mullahs. Meanwhile, the decline in public agricultural investment to one-third of its earlier level created substantial backlogs for rehabilitation and maintenance of existing structures.

In their gross mismanagement of the exchange rate, the mullahs very much resemble the Algerians in the 1980s. As the price of tradable relative to nontradable goods, the exchange rate is linked to all goods and services. Until 1989/90 the exchange regime was tightly controlled and very complex, with some twelve different exchange rates. Although reform in 1991 simplified the system (to three rates) and reduced controls, in 1993 the free-market price of foreign exchange was *twenty times higher* than the official rate (in 1982 it had been twice as high). Attempts at reform have been feeble and then typically reversed.

In general, the Islamists in Iran have increased the centralization of the economy, redistributed income toward the poor and the rural areas, instituted unsustainable agricultural policies, and mismanaged the macroeconomy. They have failed to meet the challenge of jobs, have a very mixed record on food, and have little to their credit in the area of water management. Perhaps most fundamental, however, they have not succeeded in enticing private investment into job-creating production of labor-intensive goods and services. Private economic agents continue to view the regime's commitment to a market economy with skepticism.

The Islamic Republic of Iran has always rested on a coalition of groups with disparate economic interests. The coalition has included populist, unemployed or underemployed youth and students, urban lumpens, conservative *bazaaris* (merchants), mullahs, and segments of the professional middle class. At the time of the revolution, the opposition to the shah seems to have been as widespread as Polish opposition to communist rule. Like Solidarity, the initial coalition led by Khomeini was a very large tent indeed. Over time it seems to have narrowed, but the regime still rests on an uneasy alliance of two very different sets of interests: populist lower and lower middle classes and prosperous mullahs and those with whom they do business.

More specifically, Amuzegar discerns two main groups of political actors: "radicals," a grouping of "economically dependent radical *mullahs* (of mainly poor, provincial origin) and . . . left-wing elements infiltrating the high ranks of the bureaucracy," on the one hand, and "conservatives," with "strong financial and blood ties to the *bazaar* [who] have tended to represent the interests of landlords and the urban bourgeoisie," on the other (Amuzegar 1993, 32). Members of a third group, formed since Khomeini's death, the "pragmatists," have "close affiliations with the wealthy, but . . . have mainly *managed* and handled national wealth rather than *owned* it" (32). This last group is the core of Rafsanjani's support for economic reform. The private oligopolists and rent seekers of the Pahlavi regime were expropriated only to be replaced by the "economic mullahcracy" of the *bonyads* or foundations. They are often joined by wealthy *bazaaris,* who enjoy monopoly power as holders of quotas and licenses—classic rent seekers, who obstruct change. These organizations are now deeply entrenched and offer substantial opposition to Rafsanjani's reformism.

Such a configuration of interests suggests that economic policy will oscillate, and this is indeed what has happened. At the beginning, the populists seemed to have the upper hand, and a number of their views were incorporated into the constitution. They remain very active today. But much of their activism was blunted; the vacillation on land reform is a good example, as is the current intense conflict over exchange-rate management. Yet even in early 1995, students in Teheran took to the streets to protest against price increases. It is important, however, that these are government-mandated price increases, *not* price decontrol in the sense of permitting prices to be set by market forces. Reforms have been haphazard, inconsistent, and stop-and-go. The strength of populist, statist elements within the ruling coalition has helped to ensure that traditional, highly liquid investments dominate private Iranians' portfolios. Iranian reform has not been credible.

Turkey

Turkey was a regional pioneer in adopting economic reform. Its structural adjustment program has stimulated exports, particularly nontraditional ones. The country has shifted its development strategy from import-substituting industrialization to export-led growth. However, successive governments have found it extremely difficult to implement austerity measures. The government continues to run large deficits and then compensate for the ensuing inflation by frequent small nominal devaluations. In recent years, however, the gains of the mid-1980s have been endangered by budgetary indiscipline and accelerating inflation. Turkish experience highlights the difficulties of consolidating economic reform in a politically fragmented parliamentary democracy.

Turkey's economic crisis in the late 1970s was grave. It was governed by fragile and changing political coalitions dominated by the Republican People's party (led by Bülent Ecevit) and the Justice party (led by Süleyman Demirel). Neither of these protagonists could risk promoting economic austerity for fear of alienating a significant part of the electorate. The result was that

> despite the oil crisis and related external shocks, Turkey attempted to preserve its growth momentum under the Third Plan (1973–1977) through rapid reserve decumulation and massive external borrowing. Instead of relying upon internal adjustment to promote balance of payments improvement, the various coalition governments pursued expansionary policies, while allowing a decline in marginal savings ratios, and negative import substitution in the energy and manufacturing sectors. (Celasun 1983, 11)

At the beginning of the reform process, the government announced a sweeping structural adjustment policy with devaluation of the currency, fiscal austerity moves, and trade and parastatal reform. A crawling peg was adopted for the currency, tariffs were cut, and many quantitative export restrictions were lifted. Parastatals were reformed; management obtained the authority to set prices and was required to phase out subsidies. From 1981 to 1985 exporters received tax rebates and subsidized credit while nonexporting firms faced sharper increases in the real cost of borrowing. Average tariff rates fell precipitously; the average tariff rate was 11% (the same for all goods) on manufactures and only 17% on manufactured consumer goods, the most protected sector (Öniş and Webb 1994).

Turkish manufactured exports responded very strongly to this new policy environment. Manufactures jumped from one-third of exports in 1980 to three-quarters in 1985, with continued strong performance thereafter (manufactures were 66% of total exports in 1989 and 72% in 1992). There was considerable diversification of manufacturing, and the sector's efficiency rose. Turkish consumer durables became competitive in the discriminating markets of the European Union and the Gulf.

Agricultural performance was mixed. The rate of growth has been roughly equal to or slightly below the rate of population growth. The growth of agriculture accelerated, from 2.16% in 1972–1979 to 3.7% in 1980–1988 (World Bank 1995d). More recent performance has been weaker. Cereal imports in 1989 were roughly three times greater than in 1970. This had no implications for national food security because of the strong industrial export performance. Sectoral price policies (i.e., price supports) transferred *into* agriculture a nominal sum equal to 1.3% of GDP between 1961 and 1985, but when the impact of overvaluation is included some 3.8% of GDP was transferred *out of* agriculture. When the impact of industrial protection and therefore the internal terms-of-trade effects are included, the total volume of resources transferred out of agriculture through price changes was 2.9% of GDP. There were also price distortions between crops, which engendered efficiency losses. When nonprice policies (i.e., investment and other public spending) are included, the picture changes somewhat, but the basic point remains: without including the exchange-rate effect, from 1961 to 1980 about 0.7% of GDP was *transferred into* agriculture. What sectoral policy gave, however, exchange-rate policy took away: when exchange-rate changes are included, the positive effect of sectoral policy was overturned, and about 1.1% of GDP was *transferred out of* agriculture. Structural adjustment removed some of the exchange-rate biases against agriculture without, as we shall see, eliminating subsidies. Structural adjustment reversed the increasing biases against tradable goods of the 1970s.

Because of the weaknesses of privatization, price liberalization in some cases included the freeing of prices by monopolistic parastatals. This had adverse impacts on their customers, who were numerous in rural Turkey. Turkish farmers saw huge increases in fertilizer prices (some 1,000% from 1979 to 1982—over 600% in one year, 1980) and in other inputs. Although specialists dispute the issue, despite the reforms of the exchange rate and relaxation of import restrictions the terms of trade seem to have turned against agriculture during the 1980s. There were clearly significant short- to medium-run adjustment costs, including the loss of some 100,000 agricultural jobs. There have been efficiency gains, and the sector has been modernizing rapidly: despite the large increase in fertilizer prices, fertilizer use per hectare in the late 1980s was 63.7 kilograms per hectare, compared with 15.7 in 1970–1971. Turkish farmers, long a mainstay of center-right parties (e.g., Menderes's Democrat party and its two successors, the Justice and the True Path), were hurt by the way in which reform was implemented. This proved a serious weakness when democracy resumed.

National indebtedness and balance-of-payments difficulties remain a problem. Turkish debt soared from US$42 billion in 1992 to over US$60 billion in 1994 (World Bank 1994d). Such borrowing had the usual causes. The two key weaknesses of the reform effort (in addition to its electoral impact on farmers) were the failure of privatization and the lack of budgetary discipline. Even in 1994, some fifteen years after the first reform program, the government was negotiating with the IMF over privatization, which the international agency believes could help to retire some US$5 billion in debt and would send a very strong signal to private investors. Successive governments have been loath to privatize, fundamentally because state-owned enterprises provide any government with potential patronage. Özal, for all his strengths, did little in this area.

Even more serious, the government has proved incapable of controlling the budget. The public-sector borrowing requirement (budget deficit plus parastatal borrowing) fell during the 1980s, from 9% in 1981 to 6.5% in 1988 (World Bank 1994d).

Inflation was reduced but remained high by regional standards, averaging some 40% during the decade. Unfortunately, however, deficits ballooned in 1988 and since then have risen steadily. Inflation rose to over 150% in 1994; it fell back to double digits in 1995.

The persistent budgetary deficit is fueled by parastatal borrowing, which remained at 2.6% in 1994. Just as important were export subsidies, large public spending by municipalities, and the spending of the special off-budget Ministerial funds, a type of spending that often expands greatly in the period preceding elections. Neither the military regime nor successive democratic governments have been able to eliminate the large subsidies inherited from past policies. Rather, the subsidies have been restructured and reoriented to favor exporters, especially in manufacturing, and to win popular support for otherwise unpopular programs (Waterbury 1992). Turkish structural adjustment has always lacked one of the three "IMF pillars," fiscal austerity,[7] and this has inevitably undermined the credibility of reform. The crawling peg has prevented this inflationary pressure from overvaluing the real exchange rate, but as inflation accelerates this mechanism becomes increasingly difficult to manage.

The Turkish government is clearly committed to a more market-oriented development strategy, but despite the best intentions it has failed to implement a consistent structural adjustment package of the IMF type. It has been argued recently that the inability to restrain government spending may be the political price that must be paid to implement the other measures. Specifically, Turkey is now governed by a center-right coalition in which economically strong but electorally weak (because few) business interests must seek allies among those who have sustained losses from structural adjustment (Waterbury 1992). Consequently, the governing center-right political parties must spend large sums of public money not only to foster export drives but also to compensate losers. In a democratic environment such as Turkey's, it has proved very difficult to implement the classic structural adjustment package.

Numerous forces contributed to the credibility of Turkish reform in the 1980s, particularly in the period 1983–1988. The acute crisis that immediately preceded the reform disorganized losers (who, in the case of militant trade unions, were also violently suppressed once the military seized direct control of the government). It also permitted the government to offer large benefits to the population very quickly; the shortage of foreign exchange led to severe shortages of common consumption items such as coffee and also disorganized production by depriving enterprises of imported inputs. The government bundled trade reforms together with the generally beneficial macroeconomic changes that unblocked foreign exchange, and this strategy reduced opposition to the former. The reform was also strongly supported by the IMF, the World Bank, the United States, and other NATO/OECD nations that dispensed loans and eased the foreign-exchange constraint immediately following the onset of reforms. In this sense the reform process was financially front-loaded.

The leadership of Turgut Özal was critical. As a Western-trained technocrat, he was committed to reform, and he proved a very skillful politician in assembling a team of like-minded technocrats and insulating them from political pressures. He also made good use of a "honeymoon" period created by the circumstances of his rise to power. Since he had resigned as head of the economic team under the generals in the wake of the "bankers' crisis" in 1982, he was able to stand for election against the military's preferred candidate as the symbol of change, opposing not only the old order of the 1970s but also military rule. Özal forged a center-right coalition to support his reform, incorporating key business leaders and also, as junior partners, various Islamist political elements. He institutionalized this coalition in his Motherland party. Unfortunately for the durability of reform, this coalition soon splintered. The institutional structure of Turkish politics supported Özal's key role. The state bureaucracy had long been far more powerful than any set of interest groups, which tended to take direction from the state rather than vigorously press their own demands. Thus the reform effort benefited from determined, skillful leadership operating within institutions that magnified its power.

Unfortunately, key weaknesses became increasingly salient after 1988. Patronage politics and the decision to seek a military solution to the Kurdish problem fueled government spending and spawned large budgetary deficits. These, in turn, stimulated inflation. Patronage politics may, in turn, be partly the result of weakly institutionalized political parties, which simply try to buy voters' support (Öniş and Webb 1994). Ministerial off-budget funds proved, as Öniş and Webb put it, a "sorcerer's apprentice" devised by the reformers to insulate technocrats only to have the institution swamp any attempt to control spending and restrain inflation. Kurdish policy now costs Turkey some US$500 million per year; the total cost is estimated at US$8 billion. The budgetary drain (not to mention the political cost) is heavy.

Other developments have also weakened reform. The center-right coalition's vote is now divided between the Motherland party and the True Path party. The alienation of the farmers proved particularly costly electorally. The death of Özal left a leadership vacuum that Tansu Çiller of the True Path party has been unable to fill. The resurgence of inflation, continued heavy rural-urban migration, public bickering within the political elite, and the weakness of social services has opened a wedge for the Islamic Welfare party to win mayoralties in Istanbul, Ankara, and elsewhere. Cultural politics, as well as ethnic politics, is becoming increasingly salient and distracts from the task of economic reform.

The current situation in Turkey is difficult. Although inflation has recently receded from its 1994 peak, it remains entirely unconquered. Ethnic violence (Kurd vs. Turk and also Alevi vs. Sunni) is rising along with unemployment and falling wages. The political pressures for redistributive measures are strong. Unless these are very carefully implemented, however, they will prove unsustainable. There is little reason to believe that a weak government embroiled in a civil war will be able to provide such carefully crafted, well-targeted measures. Turkey could easily fall into the reform cycle so familiar to students of Latin America, where unsustainable populist policies alternate with harshly repressive austerity.

CONCLUSION

There are strong commonalities as well as important differences among MENA countries' attempts at economic reform. The origins of reform are very similar in all cases: for reasons examined in Chapters 7 and 8, nearly all pursued variants of state-led ISI, and nearly all suffered from the by-now well-known contradictions of that strategy. No country has been able to afford the luxury of simply ignoring these imperatives.

In some ways, the responses to these problems have been very different across regime types. Reforms have been strongest in Turkey (until 1988), the Arab monarchies, and Tunisia, weakest in the Islamic republics and the socialist republics adopting homegrown reforms. In most socialist republics (Algeria and Egypt—and one could add Syria and Yemen), the regimes' primary political constituency (mainly state-owned-enterprise employees, government bureaucrats, and political party hacks) stand to lose the most from economic reform. These regimes have spent decades grounding their claims to legitimacy in an ideological commitment to equity based on state enterprise. Their tendency to attempt to craft their reforms without outside assistance (Algeria, Syria) further reduces reform credibility. However, the successful reform in Tunisia suggests that the critical variable may be vigorous reformist leadership.

Such leadership is certainly present in monarchies such as Morocco and Jordan. The Arab monarchies also rest on very different political constituencies and have very different claims to legitimacy, claims that give Islam a much larger role (see also Chapter 11). The configuration of both interests and ideology makes reform somewhat easier. The kings have made good use of a pro-Western orientation, letting the IMF and the World Bank boost their credibility. But such regimes, too, face considerable difficulties with entrenched interests, excessive past promises of state largesse, and defective governance.

The Islamic republics display policy oscillation that destroys reform credibility. These regimes rest on a disparate coalition of economically conservative urban merchants and redistributionist students and street youth. The diverse elements of this coalition struggle against each other to achieve their economically incompatible goals. A leadership that stresses religio-cultural issues above other problems tacks now toward the market, now toward state controls. In Iran, different interests have taken over different institutions that compete with each other. Their antagonism to the West prevents them from creating credibility by using the IMF. The result is economic paralysis.

Turkey's experience illustrates the classic problems of reform in a democracy. Vigorous leadership took advantage of crisis to promote exports and forge a center-right coalition with important popular support. Reform credibility was enhanced by perceptions of Özal's strength, by the political insulation of the change team, and by close cooperation with international agencies. However, the government could not restrain public spending or inflation when political competition resumed. Progress on privatization was also slow. Reform bogged down toward the end of Özal's life, and his departure from the scene was a serious blow to continued progress. Turkey offers a disheartening example of the fragility of reform even under relatively favorable circumstances.

Despite these differences, all MENA countries have one feature in common: their reforms have, after at least a decade in many cases, done little to change the weight of the public sector in their economies. Lip service is paid to expanding the role of the private sector, but there is usually far less here than meets the ear. The contrast with Latin America, Eastern Europe, and Russia is striking. In the space of eighteen months Russia privatized some 15,779 medium-sized and large enterprises; by July 1994, less than three years after the demise of the USSR, over 86% of Russian industrial workers were employed by the private sector (*Economist*, April 8, 1995). No MENA country comes at all close to the speed and depth of this shift in the world's original socialist economy. The leaden hand of the state remains all too firm in regulatory behavior as well. As we have seen (Box 9.1), the result has been that investors shun MENA economies. Most countries of the region are very far indeed from having created a regulatory and legal environment that is conducive to private investment in job-creating activities. As MENA countries procrastinate on reform, the stresses of lagging incomes, slow job creation, and tenuous food security mount.

NOTES

1. The social rate of return on investment is calculated using opportunity costs, which are international prices for tradable goods, while the private rate uses actual domestic prices, reflecting taxes and subsidies.

2. Some of this may be deceptive, however: the losses of state-owned enterprises have been transferred to the banks, removing their subsidies from the budget but changing little else.

3. From US$1,983 million in 1991/92 to US$1,566 million in 1993/94 (U.S. Embassy, Cairo, 1995).

4. These countries were Egypt, Israel, Jordan, Morocco, Oman, Saudi Arabia, Tunisia, and the UAE. Libya received 7% of FDI inflows in 1992; since it does not report GDP figures to the World Bank, we have excluded it from the comparison. Its inclusion would not alter the conclusion (World Bank 1995a).

5. Moroccan tariffs remain high, however; the average tariff rate is now 37% overall but considerably higher for export commodities. This may be compared with the average LDC rate in 1987 of 34% and that for Europe and the Middle East of 26% (data from World Bank). Protection of export industries was also Korean practice under Park (1961–1973).

6. The key, of course, is getting growth to resume quickly after the initial stabilization. Tunisia was able to do this, as was Turkey from 1983 to 1992 except during the Gulf War.

7. The other two being, of course, nominal devaluation and trade reform.

10

URBAN POLITICAL ECONOMY

The Middle East has long been dominated by its cities. Even in 1800, after several centuries of decline, perhaps 25% of the population of Greater Syria and 10% of Egyptians lived in cities of over 10,000 (Issawi 1969, 102–103). Cities dominated their rural hinterlands and were focal points of the extensive international trade system linking Europe to Asia. Landlords and rulers alike lived in the cities, not in the countryside as did their European feudal counterparts. The medina was the center of gravity of economics, politics, religion, and intellectual life.

This historical legacy continues today. The cities of the region hold most of the industry, a large and growing percentage of the labor force, and the bulk of government officials. They contain most of the modern health facilities and universities; they are the centers of drama, film, television, publishing, and intellectual life generally. Their residents enjoy higher incomes and better standards of health and education than their rural cousins. Cities also display severe economic and political problems, many of which are caused by rapid urbanization: acute housing shortages, insecure and unremunerative employment, water, power, and sewage failures, and political riots.

The overall picture of urbanization is shown in Table 10.1 and Figures 10.1–10.3.[1] The region is more urbanized than East Asia, South Asia, or sub-Saharan Africa, less so than Latin America (where over 70% of the population lives in cities). In the larger countries of the region (Morocco, Algeria, Egypt, Turkey, Iran), from two-fifths to over half of the population live in cities. In many cases, the urban population is concentrated in one or two very large cities. Over 40% of urban Moroccans live in Casablanca and neighboring Rabat; Baghdad contains more than half of all urban Iraqis and nearly 20% of the total population. In 1970 Beirut was home to over 60% of the urban population of Lebanon. The region's (and Africa's) largest city, Cairo, holds over 12 million inhabitants, making it roughly as large as New York City. From 1985 to 1990, the most rapid growth, however, was in secondary cities[2]—6%, compared with a growth rate of 3.8% for the nineteen largest cities with populations over 1 million in 1990 (World Bank 1995a).

TABLE 10.1	Urbanization Indicators, 1970–1992			
	% Urban		*Urban Growth Rates*	
	1970	*1992*	*1970–1980*	*1980–1992*
Algeria	40	54	4.1	4.9
Egypt	42	44	2.5	2.5
Iran	42	58	5.0	5.0
Israel	84	92	3.2	2.1
Jordan	51	69	5.5	6.0
Morocco	35	47	4.1	3.8
Oman	5	12	8.3	8.2
Saudi Arabia	49	78	8.3	6.5
Sudan	16	23	5.0	4.1
Syria	44	51	4.1	4.1
Tunisia	44	57	3.7	3.4
Turkey	38	64	3.7	5.6
UAE	57	82	20.4	5.0
Yemen	13	31	7.0	7.3

Source: World Bank (1994g).

As have cities throughout the Third World, MENA cities have grown swiftly. Although urban population growth is very important, rural-urban migration is probably the critical component of the process—but, as usual, the data are uncertain and there is much variation across countries.

THE PROCESS OF URBANIZATION

The diverse weight of cities in populations within the region, ranging from a low of just under 25% in the Sudan to over 90% in Kuwait and Israel, is broadly consistent with a simple expectation: the higher the per capita income, the higher the percentage of the population that is urban. Of course, this is not a causal statement; indeed, it is much more plausible that increased urbanization and rising per capita incomes are both the result of economic growth and, especially, of industrialization.

One of the most important aspects of urbanization in the region is its speed. The number of urban Middle Easterners has risen from 35 million (about a third of the population) in 1960 to 135 million (slightly over half) in 1990 (World Bank 1994e). This rapid growth has had three sources: reclassification,[3] natural growth of the urban population, and rural-urban migration. Although it is impossible to give precise estimates of the relative weight of each of these factors, evidence suggests that rural-urban migration usually accounts for at least half of the growth of cities.

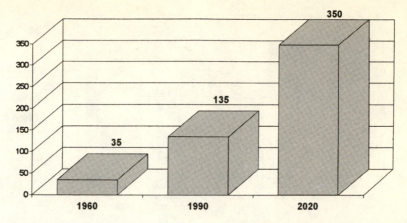

FIGURE 10.1   Urban population of MENA (in millions). *Source:* World Bank (1994e).

A very crude calculation would begin by assuming that rates of natural increase (fertility minus mortality rates) are the same in urban and rural areas and then approximate the rate of rural-urban migration (plus reclassification) as the difference between the rate of growth of cities and the overall rate of population growth (Table 10.2).[4] Keeping in mind the crudeness of the data and the assumptions, several generalizations may be made. Rural-urban migration accounts for about one-third to roughly half of the growth of cities in Iran, Jordan, Morocco, Oman, the Sudan, Tunisia, and Yemen. This is roughly the same ratio common elsewhere in the developing world (Todaro 1984; Sethuramen 1981). In several other countries, the role of migration in urbanization was rather larger. In the period 1965–1980, more than half of urbanization in six countries (Jordan, Lebanon, Libya, Oman, Tunisia, and the

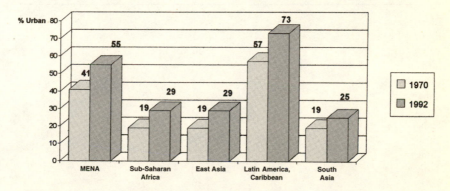

FIGURE 10.2   Urban dwellers as percentage of total population for major world regions, 1970–1992. *Source:* World Bank (1994g, 221–222).

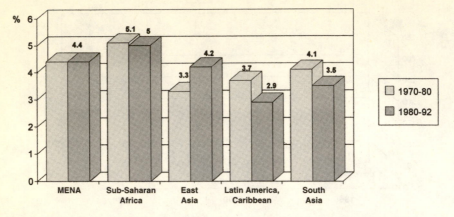

FIGURE 10.3   Urban growth rates, 1970–1980 and 1980–1992. *Source:* World Bank
(1994g, 221–222).

former YAR) can be explained by rural-urban migration; by this measure, the role of
migration declined in the 1980–1992 period in Jordan, Oman, and Tunisia, while it
rose in Algeria and Turkey. By contrast, Egypt shows a low rate of rural-urban migration so measured.[5]

   This methodology seriously underestimates the importance of rural-urban migration in urban growth. First of all, the assumption that the rate of population growth

**Table 10.2   Estimated Contribution of Rural-Urban Migration to
Total Urban Population Growth (%), 1980–1992**

	% Growth
Algeria	43
Egypt	4
Iran	30
Jordan	38
Morocco	34
Oman	48
Saudi Arabia	25
Sudan	34
Syria	20
Tunisia	35
Turkey	59
UAE	20
Yemen	48

Source: World Bank (1994g 223).

is the same in rural and urban areas is dubious. A priori, we would certainly expect both fertility and mortality rates to be lower in urban areas. As we have seen, much of the variance in fertility rates can be explained by income differences, and average urban incomes are typically higher than rural ones. Female literacy is higher in the cities, and infant mortality is usually lower; both suggest that urban fertility should be lower than rural. However, since mortality is also very probably lower in urban areas, it is uncertain whether overall rates of natural increase are lower in the cities than in the villages. The fact that health improvements have been more dramatic than fertility changes suggests that rural population growth rates probably exceed urban rates.

For some countries we have direct evidence that urban rates of fertility and mortality have been considerably lower than rates in rural areas. For example, the Turkish rural population grew roughly 40% faster than the urban population in the 1970s (Kuran 1980). When differential population growth is included in the analysis, about 60% of urbanization in Turkey before 1980 is attributable to migration (Todaro 1984). Similarly, Egyptian rural fertility exceeded urban; in 1975–1976 the total fertility rate was 3.9 in Cairo and Alexandria, 5.0 in urban Lower Egypt, 6.0 in rural Lower Egypt, and 6.8 in rural Upper Egypt (National Academy of Sciences 1982, 3). However, mortality rates were also higher in rural areas, so the rates of population growth in urban and rural areas may not have been significantly different.

What is more, the high rates of natural increase in the cities are not independent of rural-urban migration. There is much evidence that this form of migration is often undertaken by whole families and is especially prevalent among the young. The transfer of population of childbearing age to the cities obviously raises the rate of urban natural increase (Todaro 1984). A substantial portion of children born in the cities have parents who have recently arrived from the countryside. When this factor is taken into consideration, it seems clear that, for most countries of the region, rural-urban migration is the single most important explanation for the rapid growth of urban areas.

In any case, the absolute numbers of rural migrants to cities have been very large during the past generation. For example, in the mid-1970s in Turkey, up to 650,000 rural residents arrived in the cities every year; by the 1980s, 800,000 arrived every year (Danielson and Keleş 1980). From 1968 to 1977 just under 1 million rural Iraqis moved to the cities, especially to Baghdad and Basra (Sluglett and Sluglett 1987). Between 1967 and 1979, 1.3 million Algerians moved from the countryside to the cities (Bennoune 1988). Rural-urban migration is a crucial process in the political economy of the region.

It is no secret why rural people move to the city. Throughout the world, economic motives predominate in the decision to migrate. The most widely accepted model of the process (Todaro 1969) posits that the decision to migrate is based upon the difference between the incomes that rural migrants expect to earn in the city and those that they can earn in the countryside. This framework combines the rural "push" with urban "pull" factors. Some more recent arguments have held that migration may be part of a family strategy of income maintenance; one brother goes to town to seek work, while others remain behind (Stark 1984). However, the evidence in the region suggests that most rural-urban migration is of entire families; this seems to be the case for Iraq (Sluglett and Sluglett 1987), Iran (Kazemi 1980a), Turkey (Danielson and Keleş 1980), Egypt (Hopkins 1983), and Morocco (World Bank 1981). Still more complicated models have been formulated, trying to link together all of the different markets that might influence the migration decision (so-called computable general equilibrium models [Kelley and Williamson 1984]). Such models stress the role of terms of trade between agriculture and manufacturing and faster productivity growth in (usually urban-based) manufacturing.

Although differences in rural versus urban wages and incomes in MENA are not excessive by developing-country standards, they are substantial, usually on the order of 1.5 to 3.0.[6] Of course, a potential migrant has to consider the risk of failing to find a job in the cities—a risk usually measured by urban unemployment rates. Measuring unemployment in developing countries is difficult. Official, measured unemployment rates are often high in the region, but they are often quite low for unskilled workers (Chapter 5). Even if we take the higher numbers at face value, however, and even if we assume that rural workers have no difficulty finding jobs in the countryside, migrating to the city is still a good investment.[7]

In fact, the incentives to migrate to cities are even stronger than the simplest version of the Todaro model implies. First, we have seen in Chapter 5 that many of those listed as unemployed are actually working in low-paying, irregular jobs in the informal sector. In some countries (e.g., Turkey, Iran), rural migrants are often first employed in this sector. Second, there is direct evidence that migrants obtain urban jobs fairly quickly; a World Bank study in Morocco found that more than 70% of migrants found work in less than three months and that the urban unemployment rate in 1976 for urban residents born in the countryside was less than half that for those born in the city (World Bank 1981, 247).

It may be objected that the cost of living in rural areas is lower than in the cities. Two points should be considered here. First, such cost differentials are rarely as large as the differences in nominal wages. Although housing may be more expensive in the cities, extensive food-subsidy systems, usually confined to the cities, reduce food costs for urban dwellers to the same levels as those in rural areas or even lower. Since food usually constitutes over half of the total expenditure of poor persons in MENA countries,[8] food subsidies significantly reduce rural/urban cost-of-living differences.[9] Second, other benefits of urban life such as better educational and health facilities further widen the gap between real incomes in urban and rural areas.

Finally, in some cases people have left rural areas because they could not survive there. Much of the recent growth of North African and Sudanese cities is due to the influx of drought refugees, people whose crops or rural employment prospects were wiped out by bad weather. Government neglect of rural areas (Algeria) or misguided policies (Iraq, Iran) have also played a major role in creating incentives for rural people to move to town.

Two other tributaries of rural-urban migration flows are spreading rural education and (during the oil boom) the Dutch Disease. Young men who receive some education pour out of the countryside in large numbers, often taking their families with them. One study of rural migrants to Tehran found that over two-thirds were literate, compared with overall rural literacy rates of about 20%. Over two-fifths of farmers with a primary education wanted to move to the cities (Kazemi 1980a). This is, of course, a universal phenomenon; educated people everywhere leave the farm for the cities. One of the ironies of development is that successful educational programs in rural areas swell urban populations.

The Dutch Disease likewise fostered rural-urban migration. The shifting of the terms of trade against agriculture, the disproportionate concentration of spending in the cities, and, especially, the construction boom of the 1970s widened the gap between rural and urban incomes, increased the probability of finding jobs in the cities, and thereby stimulated migration. In some countries this process interacted with the phenomenon of international labor migration. In Egypt, for example, nearly half of the urban construction labor force left the country to work in the Gulf States. Since the demand for domestic construction labor shot up at the same time, the incentives for unskilled rural residents to move to the city became overwhelming.

HOUSING AND INFRASTRUCTURE

Probably the most visible and pressing problem facing both the increasing numbers of urban residents and their governments is the provision of adequate housing. The rapid growth of urban populations has ensured that demand for housing would outstrip supply, spawning shortages, overcrowding, and/or soaring rents. Governments often allocated substantial sums to housing even while implementing regulations that hindered private housing construction. But since government housing expenditures have been perceived as diversions from growth-enhancing industrial investment, they have often been severely constrained. Public utilities have been inefficiently managed and underfunded, with their outputs heavily subsidized. The result has been poor, intermittent service and inadequate coverage. Urban infrastructural deficiencies, like other economic problems, will not be ameliorated unless the role of the private sector increases.

A few examples may illustrate the magnitude of the problem. Moroccan cities have been growing by 1,000 people *every day*. Although the supply of housing units roughly doubled between 1973 and 1977, the shortfall increased from 390,000 units in 1973 to 800,000 units in 1977 (World Bank 1981). In Algeria, where public enterprises dominate the construction business, public construction of housing fell from 90,000 units in 1986 to 30,000 in 1991; during this period the annual incremental demand for housing was 200,000 units. The shortage is estimated at over 2 million units; the average occupancy rate is 8.5 persons per unit, one of the highest ratios for any middle-income country (World Bank 1994a). The situation in Egypt is equally grim: a huge housing deficit (of over 2 million units) was accumulated between 1960 and 1979. Much of the existing housing stock is decidedly substandard: in 1982 23% of urban households had no electricity, over one-sixth had no access to potable water, and nearly two-thirds lacked sewage hookups (Mohie el-Din 1982).

Much of modern Cairo, where vast districts (Masr al-Qadima, Sayyida Zeinab, Darb al-Ahmar, Gamalia, Bulaq) are almost uniformly run-down and substandard,[10] deserves the term "slum." More than a half million Cairenes live on rooftops, and well over a million live in and around the tombs of the City of the Dead. New construction has lagged slightly behind new households, and therefore the gap remains vast (World Bank 1990b). Further, much of the new housing is extremely expensive and certainly well beyond the reach of most young men seeking to start a family. At the same time, rent control makes some luxury flats overlooking the Nile rent for the price of an off-season watermelon.

As usual, there are sharp differences in access to housing by social class. At the upper end of the social scale, every city in the region has neighborhoods of well-maintained, comfortable, often elegant housing inhabited by the well-to-do. In the Maghreb, upper- and middle-class Moroccans, Tunisians, and Algerians often occupied the dwellings of the (often hastily) departed French. Moroccan cities boast new residential developments, with comfortably low densities; even densely populated Cairo has its favored districts (such as Zamalek, Doqqi, and Maadi). The problem of urban housing in the MENA countries is, as everywhere, primarily a problem of the relatively poor.

The class bias of the housing problem partly reflects two facts: (1) In all countries, most housing construction is in the private sector, which, of course, responds to ability to pay, and (2) public-sector housing and, indeed, subsidy schemes for low-income housing in general have been inadequately funded or misconceived or both. In some cases, class bias has been an official element of policy; in the Moroccan plan of 1973–1977, the first goal of housing policy and spending was to meet the needs of those with the ability to pay (World Bank 1981). In Tunisia, although the large majority of units built under the 1977–1981 plan was designed to satisfy the needs of the poor, the average cost of new units was out of reach for the poorer half of the population (H. Nelson 1979, 101).

Some policies intended to benefit the poor have been misguided. Two of these seem especially prominent: rent control and attempts to clean up shantytowns. Official rent control in Cairo has had the usual effects: (1) it depressed private investment in housing, (2) it led to the substitution of "key money" for rent and other ways of circumventing the rules, and (3) it discouraged people from moving, presumably either reducing the flexibility of the labor market, increasing the demand for (grossly inadequate) urban transportation, or both. In short, it engendered inefficiencies with little compensatory increase in equity (Mohie el-Din 1982).

Most of the cities of the region are surrounded by squatter settlements: neighborhoods of relatively poor urbanites, with nonexistent or insecure title to the land they occupy, living in dwellings made of very crude materials. The various national names illustrate their nature: *bidonvilles* (tin-can cities: Morocco, Algeria), *gourbivilles* (peasant-style mud-hut towns: Tunisia), or *gecekondu* (housing built overnight: Turkey). In 1981 about one-quarter of urban Moroccans and Turks lived in such settlements; in some cities the proportion was much higher. Nearly two-thirds of the population of Ankara live in *gecekondu*, with over two persons per room. Southern Tehran, northern Cairo, Omdurman, and Casablanca have similar conditions. Most of these people are recent rural migrants. One study for Turkey estimated that 85% of the inhabitants of *gecekondu* came from the countryside (Danielson and Keleş 1980).

Until fairly recently, states were hostile to these urban formations, which not only were unsightly but often forced urban administrations to extend already over-stretched electric, water, and sewage facilities. Governments tried to prohibit such construction and even attempted to tear down existing structures. Residents resisted these actions (in Iran and Turkey), however, and economic reforms implied greater fiscal austerity and increased reliance on the private sector; both suggested that the government should leave shantytowns alone. Many governments have now revised their policies, embracing at least some of the arguments of John Turner, who observed over twenty years ago that shantytown residents, like anyone else, would try hard to improve their own housing if they felt secure (Turner 1969). Self-help reha-bilitation of the *bidonvilles* is now government policy in Morocco; the Turkish government tries to offer low-cost loans to cooperative housing projects in the *gecekondu*. The available evidence vindicates Turner and the new policy approach. Turkey's *gecekondu* are considerably more substantial than equivalent shantytowns in Latin America, more solidly built and usually connected to electricity (*Economist*, June 18, 1988). The *gourbiville* residents of Tunisia replace the original mud walls first with brick, then with cement block.

Other components of urban infrastructure also show serious problems. Although national statistics indicate that the large majority of urbanites have access to drinking water and sanitation, in fact there are numerous shortages due to poor maintenance. Solid-waste collection is adequate in the larger cities, but disposal is a serious prob-lem. In Tetouan, Morocco, wastes were simply piled up until they caused landslides. Waste collection is woefully inadequate in the smaller and medium-sized cities, which, as we have seen, are the most rapidly growing urban agglomerations. Air pol-lution is very serious in many cities: the levels of lead in the air in Cairo may cause brain damage and mental retardation in small children. Solutions to these problems will cost money: the World Bank estimates that solving the problem of municipal solid-waste collection for the region as a whole will require US$4–6 billion of invest-ment over a ten-year period (World Bank 1995b), while solutions to water-distribu-tion and air-quality problems will be still more expensive. Governments are unlikely to be able to afford to provide services at below cost to urbanites if coverage is to be extended and health hazards are to be reduced. Although privatization of municipal utilities (as in Argentina) can contribute to a solution, we have seen in Chapter 9 that few MENA countries have proceeded very far with anything along these lines.

For all the urban problems of the region, one remains relatively minor in compar-ative terms: street crime. In sharp contrast to many Latin American, sub-Saharan African, or North American cities, major Middle Eastern cities have very few areas that are unsafe for men to walk in at any hour. People complain, as everywhere, about crime, but there is nothing even remotely resembling the anomie and random violence of Lagos, Bogotá, or Los Angeles in Cairo, Istanbul, or Casablanca. It is a tribute to the social cohesiveness of Muslim societies that this nearly universal plague of the modern world has been relatively mild in the region.

INCOME DISTRIBUTION AND POVERTY

All governments in the region have proclaimed that reducing poverty and achieving a more equitable distribution of income are central goals. The determination of whether they have achieved these goals is plagued by practical and conceptual problems. First, the data for most countries are of uneven quality and employ different concepts, rendering hazardous evaluation of changes over time and, even more, cross-country comparisons. No country in the region except Israel has the thorough and effective income tax collection system that generates the data sets with which scholars of the OECD countries work. Instead, most information about income distribution comes from sample surveys. Respondents may not tell the truth about their incomes, fearing that the tax collector is peering over the shoulder of the survey researcher, and data from such surveys may therefore undercount both the very poor and the very rich. It is not unusual for the national income implied by such surveys to fall well short (e.g., by 20%) of national income measured by macroeconomic data. All data on poverty and wealth distribution must be used with caution. There is, in fact, very little information on poverty or distribution *of incomes.* Nearly all data refer instead to *expenditures.* Although these are quite useful for measuring absolute poverty, their exclusion of savings makes them a much less reliable indicator of equity. Unless otherwise stated, all data referred to in this section are expenditure rather than income data.

Arnold Harberger (1984) has argued for the primacy of poverty alleviation over income distribution concerns. He contends that whereas there is no consensus over questions of equity, there is substantial agreement on what constitutes destitution (absolute poverty) and consensus that destitution is unacceptable. There is, however, no consensus on how best to eliminate destitution. Although we sympathize with this argument, it is impossible to separate poverty issues from distributional questions. Since the days of Adam Smith or even before, political economists have recognized that poverty is a relative social concept. Constructing poverty lines typically uses distributional criteria. The most common method proceeds in two steps. First, one defines a minimum food basket without which a person would be malnourished. This is itself a social, relational idea. Nowhere in the world do people spend *all* of their income on food; even starving people will not go naked, everyone needs *some* shelter, and so forth. Therefore, the second step in constructing a poverty line is usually to increase the amount needed for food by some percentage. This percentage is usually the average percentage that households in the third decile from the bottom of the income distribution spend on nonfood items. This procedure automatically introduces distributional elements into poverty measurement.[11]

It is easy to see that such a procedure leaves much room for debate. Analysts will disagree about the minimum diet (because the amount of calories someone needs depends upon that person's size, occupation, geographical location, etc.), the cost of that diet (what prices do the poor really pay?), and the amount of nonfood consumption that is necessary to avoid destitution. In short, because poverty is a relative, social concept, it is unsurprising that even within the same society we can find quite different estimates.

Most of the poverty measures listed below are of the head-count variety: having defined a poverty line, the researchers then count the number of households or persons below that line. In some cases, they also have tried to measure the "poverty gap"—the amount by which the spending of the poor falls short of the line, usually expressed as a percentage of aggregate consumption. When available, this information is also given.

There are several broad-brush estimates of poverty in MENA. The World Bank defined an absolute poverty line as spending of less than US$370 (in purchasing-power-parity) per person per year. Since this line was constructed by looking at consumption patterns in low-income countries and most MENA nations are middle-income countries, these numbers may be regarded as lower-bound estimates of absolute poverty (Table 10.3).[12]

A second overview comes from the International Fund for Agricultural Development (IFAD), which tried to estimate rural poverty only. In contrast to the World Bank, IFAD uses nationally defined poverty lines (Table 10.4). These data suggest that although poverty remains the fate of a substantial number of Middle Easterners, the problem is less severe in MENA than in most other regions. Using the World Bank's very conservative criterion, only East Asia has a smaller percentage of poor people to total population. The IFAD numbers suggest that rural poverty is less severe in MENA than in any other region of the developing world. The World Bank data also suggest that the poverty gap is relatively small. Taken together, these data describe a poverty problem that, however painful, is less dire than that for most other parts of the developing world. This is plausibly explained as the consequence of past redistribution of assets and of the large role of the state in guaranteeing a minimum level of consumption in urban areas. Neither of these has occurred on anything like the same scale in, for example, Latin America.

TABLE 10.3 Absolute Poverty in 1985: MENA in Comparative Perspective

Region	Number (millions)	Percentage of Population	Poverty Gap
Sub-Saharan Africa	180	47	11
East Asia	280	20	1
South Asia	520	51	10
Middle East and North Africa	60	31	2
Latin America and Caribbean	70	19	1

Source: World Bank (1990d, 29).

TABLE 10.4   **Rural Poverty in 1988: MENA in Comparative Perspective**

Region	Percentage of Rural Population That Is Poor
Asia	31
Sub-Saharan Africa	60
Middle East and North Africa	26
Latin America and Caribbean	61
Total of 114 countries	36
LDCs	69

Source: Jazairy, Alamgir, and Panuccio (1992, 2).

Three caveats are necessary, however. First, even if other regions do worse, having a minimum of 60 million poor, between one-fourth to one-third of the population, is sobering. Second, as noted earlier, for several reasons the World Bank numbers must be treated as lower bounds. For example, this poverty line (US$370 per person) is far below average purchasing-power-parity (PPP) per capita incomes for most countries.[13] Third, both data sets fail to reflect the impact of the regional downturn after the collapse of oil prices in the mid-1980s and subsequent austerity. Fourth, there is considerable variation among countries.

IFAD's data set gives some insight into the variation among countries for rural poverty. The situation varies widely, from 15% poor in Tunisia to 85% poor in the Sudan (Table 10.5).

TABLE 10.5   **Rural Poverty, Selected Countries, 1988**

Country	Percentage of Rural Population That Is Poor
Algeria	25
Egypt	25
Iraq	39
Jordan	17
Lebanon	15
Morocco	45
Sudan	85
Syria	54
Tunisia	15
Yemen (former PDRY and YAR)	30

Source: Jazairy, Alamgir, and Panuccio (1992, 386–387).

For a still smaller subset of countries (Morocco, Tunisia, Egypt, and Jordan) we have a series of estimates of poverty that, despite their flaws, allow at least some very tentative generalizations about poverty changes over time:

Morocco. The poverty problem is very serious in Morocco by any standard. Roughly comparable data exist from surveys conducted in 1984–1985 and 1990–1991. The poverty line used for 1990–1991 is higher than the World Bank's line.[14] Regardless of the choice of poverty line, two statements may be made: (1) rural poverty is higher than urban and (2) poverty declined in the late 1980s (Table 10.6).

Tunisia. The Tunisian government has set its poverty line low by international standards. Setting a poverty line below the World Bank's line in a middle-income country like Tunisia suggests a serious undercounting of poverty. The government's estimate of rural poverty in 1985, for example, is less than half that of IFAD (15%) and only 23% that of the ILO (31%) (Radwan, Jamal, and Ghose 1991). Nevertheless, the numbers do show a consistent, uniform reduction in poverty overtime (Table 10.7).

Jordan. Jordan has seen a sharp increase in poverty between 1986 and 1992. Depending on the poverty line, between 2 and 20% of the population were poor in 1992, compared with negligible poverty in the mid-1980s. The government of Jordan commonly uses a number near 20% to describe its current situation. Rural poverty (30%) exceeded urban poverty (15%) in 1992. Although 68% of the population was urban in that year, the number of poor people was divided roughly equally between cities and countryside. The poverty gap also increased from 1986 to 1992. The key explanators of these trends are the collapse of growth following the end of the oil boom and the impact of the Gulf War and crisis of 1990–1991 (World Bank 1994b).

Egypt. Regardless of the poverty line chosen, Egyptian poverty fell between 1974–1975 and 1981–1982 but rose again by the early 1990s. Agricultural wages (a good proxy for unskilled wages and therefore incomes of the poor under flexible labor-market conditions [Chapter 5] rose by 350% from 1970 to 1985 but then fell

TABLE 10.6   Moroccan Poverty Trends (%), 1984/85–1990/91

	1984/85	*1990/91*
Urban	17.3	7.6
Rural	32.6	18.0
National	21–26	13.1

Source: World Bank (1993b, 4).

TABLE 10.7 Tunisian Poverty Trends (%), 1967–1990

	1967	1975	1980	1985	1990
Urban	n.a.	26.5 (34)	11.8	8.4 (16)	7.3
Rural	n.a.	18.0 (43)	14.1	7.0 (31)	5.7
National	33	22.2	12.9	7.7	6.7

Sources: World Bank (1993c, 50–51), reporting Tunisian government data; for numbers in parentheses, Radwan, Jamal, and Ghose (1991, 53).

by over 40% by the end of the decade. A tentative picture of poverty trends may be obtained by combining various estimates—a risky procedure, since the definitions and coverage of sources diverge. Nevertheless, the picture that emerges is consistent with the broad outlines of recent Egyptian economic history: stagnation in the late 1960s/early 1970s, oil boom in the mid- to late 1970s, and stagnation again in the late 1980s (Table 10.8).

What policy differences can explain this heterogeneous performance? In general, poverty will fall if economic opportunities (particularly jobs) are created for poor people and if the poor can seize those opportunities. If governments adopt policies that are inimical to growth and to job creation and if they fail to provide adequate education to the poor, poverty will rise. Many governments have singularly failed to reform their economies and, therefore, to stimulate the growth that alone can alleviate poverty (Chapter 9). Without growth, there will be little job creation, and the labor force is growing rapidly. Increasing poverty will inevitably result. Furthermore, too many MENA countries have failed to provide the poor with the basic skills of literacy and numeracy that would make it possible for them to seize new economic opportunities. Only a sustained period of credible economic reform, resumed growth, and investment in human capital can reduce poverty in MENA on a sustainable basis. Poverty has fallen the most dramatically in Tunisia, which has come the closest to implementing the twin policies described above. Both Tunisia and Morocco illustrate the importance of economic reform and growth in reducing

TABLE 10.8 Egyptian Poverty Trends (%), 1958/59–1990/91

	1958/59	1974/75	1981/82	1990/91
Rural	35	44.0	24–30	54.5
Urban	30	34.5	22–30	35.9

Sources: 1958/59 and 1974/75: Radwan (1977); 1981/82: lower estimate, World Bank (1991); higher estimate, Korayem (1987); 1990/91: Korayem (1994, 28).

TABLE 10.9	Distribution of Expenditure (%), Selected Countries					
	Bottom 20%	*Second* 20%	*Third* 20%	*Fourth* 20%	*Top* 20%	*Top* 10%
Algeria (1988)	6.9	11.0	14.9	20.7	46.5	31.7
Egypt (1990–1991)						
Rural	7.6	12.5	16.8	22.1	41.1	26.5
Urban	6.8	11.1	15.2	20.2	46.8	32.6
Jordan (1991)	6.5	10.3	14.6	20.9	47.7	32.6
Morocco (1990–1991)	6.6	10.5	15.0	21.7	46.3	30.5
Tunisia (1990)	5.9	10.4	15.3	22.1	46.3	30.7

Sources: Egypt: Korayem (1994, 32); all others: World Bank (1994g).

poverty, while Egypt illustrates the poverty implications of dilatory reform and poor human-capital performance. Admittedly, the data upon which these generalizations are based are very weak; we have much to learn about the impact of policy on poverty in MENA.

If the poverty data are opaque, the data on distribution are murkier still. The World Bank reports expenditure distribution data for only four MENA countries (Table 10.9). In general, although the distribution of expenditure is not so unequal as in Latin America, expenditures are less equally distributed in MENA than in countries such as Korea or Indonesia.

It is even more difficult to make reasonable statements on trends in distribution over time. For Egypt, Korayem has produced estimates for 1981–1982 and 1990–1991 that show an increase in inequality: the Gini coefficient rose from 0.32 to 0.38 for urban areas and from 0.29 to 0.32 for rural areas. This would be consistent with the dilatory reform pattern sketched in Chapter 9: halfhearted reforms before the Gulf War allowed some privileged sectors to benefit but failed to stimulate employment growth.

URBAN POLITICS AND POLITICAL VIOLENCE

The region's working class, for all its geographical diversity, has a few commonalities. It is growing, and it is a composite of the urban-born and recent arrivals from the countryside, responding to the gap between urban and rural incomes. In many countries (e.g., Algeria, Tunisia, Egypt, the Sudan, Turkey, Syria, and Iraq) it is segmented by sector of employment (government/private, formal/informal) and degree of job security. Many of these people are self-employed, and a large fraction of wage earners work in small establishments, in which industrial relations are personalized, often even a family affair. The working class is also united by relatively low incomes, the constant problem of finding jobs (if not for fathers, then for sons), and overcrowded living conditions. Most members receive at least some consumption subsidy from the state, which both makes it possible to survive and politicizes consumption. These people have many grievances and often express their frustrations politically.

Large and medium-sized cities in the Middle East, as in other LDCs, may be a stage for disruption and violence. The theatrical potential of cities evokes a level of concern on the part of governing elites that the countryside, no matter how important economically, can seldom match. Relatively small groups of determined people—from spontaneous rioters to urban guerrillas—can disrupt and paralyze urban centers that sit astride national communications grids (railroads, ports, telephone systems, the international airport) and contain heavy concentrations of industry, the chief bureaucratic installations of the government, the foreign diplomatic and press corps, and the major universities.

In the 1940s and 1950s the expectation was widespread that the shantytowns of the developing world would provide an endless stream of young, poor, unskilled, uprooted males ready to answer any appeal to violence. The image that developed was one of individuals stripped of their village, family, and kin associations, thrust into a money economy in which jobs were scarce and exploitation of the unskilled common and in which anomie predisposed the uprooted to seek a new identity in radical movements through targeted and random violence. The picture, although not wholly inaccurate, has major flaws. Shantytown populations have by and large turned out to be fairly responsible urban dwellers (J. Nelson 1979). Often they have reconstituted kin, ethnic, and religious associations in their new abodes. We have seen that generally they have been able to find work. When city authorities have legalized access to the land on which they had been squatters, they have invested their labor and earnings in home improvement. They are upwardly mobile, and however grim the shanty slums may appear to the outsider, their inhabitants vastly prefer life there to life back in the village. For the most part, shantytowns have not been hotbeds of political agitation and violence.

At the same time, a third or more of a given city's population may live in the inner city, with its old, decaying, substandard housing, much of which may be condemned and is certainly unsafe to inhabit. These residents may be second- or third-generation migrants or trading and craftspeople of long standing in the city. Second-generation migrants may have forgotten why their parents left the village and see only the poor services offered them by the municipality—the broken sewers, crowded schools, collapsing buildings, and mounds of refuse that often make these quarters more forbidding than the shantytowns (see Wikan 1980). The solidly urban service and craftspeople may recall a bygone era when they enjoyed higher status and a higher level of income, before modern industrial production, department stores, and the like invaded their world. In short, residents of these quarters may be more violence-prone than those of the shantytowns.

Another source of potential actors is to be found in the ranks of organized labor. Trade unions present a command structure for and sometimes a tradition of confrontation and militancy. They can respond rapidly, coherently, and on a sustained basis to unfair labor practices (plant- or industry-specific), cost-of-living issues, or ideological and political causes. Strikes among dockers or bus and train drivers can shut down cities and ports, and worker demonstrations of whatever nature may act as a catalyst to the involvement of other, less organized groups. But because organized labor is usually a small fraction of the entire workforce, governments are willing to make large financial settlements to buy the goodwill of union leaders. Conversely, in most Middle Eastern countries strikes are illegal, and the threat of arrest and imprisonment is not idle (as the secretary general of Tunisia's UGTT, Habib Achour, learned in 1978). Corporatist arrangements through which the state co-opts union leadership have been the preferred strategy for dealing with labor (see Chapter 12).

High school and university students are viewed by municipal and national authorities with particular alarm. They have relatively little to lose—few are married or hold jobs—and are therefore willing to take big risks. Terminating their education is a real threat, often acted upon, but committed university militants may discount that threat, and many high school students may feel that their education is of little worth anyway. It is, moreover, part of student culture everywhere to take political stands, to be the nation's or the movement's conscience, to confront, be bloodied, go to jail (on Egypt, see 'Abdalla 1985). No Middle Eastern society has been spared student agitation and violence, and in some (Morocco in 1965 and 1984, the Sudan in 1964 and 1985, Turkey throughout the 1970s, Egypt in 1968 and 1977, Iran in 1978–1979) regimes have been shaken or fallen. When students go into the streets, they draw not only other students but perhaps organized labor and the slum dwellers as well.

Although they tend not to be the initiators, segments of the urban trading and merchant strata may be important actors in urban-based challenges to the authorities. The concerted clanging down of iron shop shutters in congested urban commercial districts is a time-honored and dramatic signal that even the better-off have had enough. Shopkeepers have closed down to support the war against the French in Algiers in 1958 and to oppose Israeli occupation of the West Bank, sporadically since 1967 and on a regular basis since 1987, the awarding of a monopoly in tobacco trade to foreigners in Tehran in 1896, the abandonment of Islam as the state religion in Syria in 1966, and the regime of the shah in his final months in Iran in 1978.

Finally, we should pay attention to what marxists would call lumpen elements. All cities are full of people who in fact are rootless or, if organized, are so in ways that enjoy no respect or legitimacy: beggars, prostitutes, drug dealers, scavengers, drifters, and derelicts. Time and again, political protest draws in the lumpen elements, and organized confrontation may degenerate into random looting. Few observers in the past decade or so have failed to note the striking presence of the very young in all forms of urban violence. These are preadolescent or early-adolescent street urchins, kids playing hooky, runaways, orphans, and beggars. They take physical risks that even older students avoid, and they suffer casualties that the authorities generally try to cover up.

By looking at specific instances of urban violence we may better appreciate how these various elements combine (see Denoeux 1993). One of the most frequent forms of violence has been the cost-of-living riot or demonstration. The issue has become acute as various countries try to reduce their deficits through cuts in consumer subsidies, but there were instances of this form even in the 1960s. A sharp rise in the price of sugar in Morocco in 1965 triggered massive rioting in Casablanca, with scores of dead, and led to the suspension of parliament and a state of emergency that lasted for the rest of the decade. In June 1981 there was a repeat of this scenario in Casablanca, with sixty-six "officially" killed (six hundred by other accounts).

In August 1983, the Moroccan authorities reduced consumer subsidies on average by 20% and raised public-sector salaries by an equal amount. No violence occurred immediately, but in January 1984 riots broke out all over northern Morocco, as well as at Oujda and Marrakech. This time Casablanca was not a major locus of the violence. Poor political management had allowed several grievances to come together simultaneously. Secondary school students were already on strike because of an increase in the fees required to sit for the *baccalauréat* exams. In northern Morocco, where contraband trade with the two Spanish enclaves of Ceuta and Melilla helps prop up economic life, very high exit fees were imposed on Moroccan traders. Rumors, probably well founded, were rife that new subsidy cuts were in the offing. Finally, in preparation for an Islamic summit at Casablanca, a number of Moroccan cities had been stripped of their police to protect the conferees. Student strikes and demonstrations turned into cost-of-living riots, and the local forces of order in several cities were unable to contain them. Twenty-nine persons "officially" lost their lives, but some estimate the real number at around four hundred (Clément 1986).

Similar cost-of-living riots occurred in Tunis and other Tunisian cities in 1978 and 1984 (in the latter, eighty-nine were officially killed), in Egypt in 1977 (about ninety dead), and in Khartoum in 1982 and 1985 (number of dead unknown). Surely the most quixotic of these outbreaks was the one in Beirut in the summer of 1987, when Lebanese interrupted their civil war to demonstrate against the precipitous drop in the international value of the Lebanese pound. Algeria, which for nearly twenty-five years had experienced little urban violence, was rocked by cost-of-living riots in the fall of 1988, and the Kingdom of Jordan followed suit in the spring of 1989.

National leaders are loath to admit that these riots reflect real grievances, for that would be to admit that the government cannot feed its own people. Generally, the head of state blames the riots on outside agitators—Zionism, Khomeini, marxists, or Qaddhafi have always been ready at hand. Nevertheless, the same heads of state typically give away the game by rescinding the measures that gave rise to the protest: Sadat, Bourguiba, and King Hassan all responded in that manner. Needless to say, with such precedents it becomes all the more difficult to reintroduce the measures, just as these precedents make it more likely that people will resort to violence in the future.

We should be cautious, however, in accepting counter-claims of pure spontaneity for cost-of-living riots. Organized political groups, from Muslim militants to marxist radicals, are generally forewarned of impending shifts in government pricing policies and ready to incite allied groups to go into the streets. It is unlikely that their actions are decisive, but there may be more orchestration to some riots than meets the eye. In the winter of 1986, thousands of Egypt's security police, made up of young, rural, extremely underpaid but armed conscripts, rioted against an alleged plan of the government to extend their tour of duty by one year. A number of those arrested were found to have amounts of money on them equivalent to several months pay. The conclusion, never proven, was that Muslim groups had paid many of them to protest.

There have been outbreaks of violence or demonstrations driven by political issues. Perhaps the most important is the one that occurred in Cairo on January 26, 1952. In a day of rioting and arson, downtown, "European" Cairo was set ablaze as denizens of the Old City (low-income, substandard housing) and of the tombs in the City of the Dead went on a rampage. These Black Saturday riots had been triggered by an assault on an Egyptian police post in the Suez Canal Zone by British troops who suspected the police of harboring terrorists. The riots introduced such a sense of interregnum and *fin de régime* that Nasser and his coconspirators accelerated their plans to seize power and did so the following July.

Hanna Batatu recounted that in March 1959 the Iraqi Communist party (ICP) tried to pressure Gen. 'Abd al-Karim Qassim, the Iraqi head of state, into giving the party four seats in the cabinet. At that time the party probably had no more than 2,000 members, but it was able to put *half a million* people in the streets of Baghdad. Surely very few of them were committed marxists. Many of them may have come out of the "somber wretchedness" (Batatu 1978, 49) of the largely Shi'ite slums, and there were surely students and members of the white-collar intelligentsia.

Perhaps those half-million Iraqis responding to the marching orders of the ICP were in composition similar to the millions of Iranians who demonstrated against the shah exactly twenty years later. In Iran a broad coalition of urban interests sustained direct confrontations with the Iranian police and military for most of a year. Although Ayatollah Khomeini's recorded instructions and urgings, sent from his exile in Paris, may have been the real force behind the movements, other groups, including students, bazaar merchants, organized labor, and radical political organizations, all contributed to what became an urban-based revolution.

Ashraf and Banuazizi (1985) noted the absence of participation of slum dwellers in the violence and, like Kazemi (1980b), stressed the involvement of second-generation migrants and the urban unemployed. They estimated the scope of the violence during the twelve months of 1978, a period of cyclical urban riots and mass demonstrations, as follows (1985, 22):

Number of demonstrations	2,483
Number of participants	1,600,000
Number of strikes	1,207
Number killed	3,008
Number wounded	12,184

In the last two months of 1978, demonstrators were joined by an estimated 5 million workers and employees involved in strikes, and in the first two months of 1979 virtually the entire adult population demonstrated in one fashion or another against the shah.

The final two examples we shall look at are (so far) atypical for the region as a whole. One is Turkey's urban violence during the 1970s, the patterns of which were more akin to those in Argentina, Italy, and West Germany of the same period than to anything in the Middle East. The Turkish political arena underwent a kind of centrifugal process by which radical leftist, fascist, and occasionally Muslim militant groups took up arms and fought among themselves. There appears to be little doubt that fascist groups such as the Grey Wolves were the primary instigators of the troubles. They fought for control of university campuses, assassinated both one another and "marked" political leaders, and used the shantytowns as hideouts. By 1980 twenty to thirty Turks were being killed every day, and the total number of political deaths had reached five thousand.

The beginning and the end of the decade were marked by military takeover, in each instance partially justified by the need to restore law and order. It was organized labor that provided the occasion for the first intervention (Bianchi 1984, 202):

> In June 1970 industrial workers in the Istanbul-Izmit area joined in a massive march to protest a new law regulating union organization and collective bargaining. The march soon erupted into a workers' riot involving over one hundred thousand demonstrators in the largest and most violent worker protest in Turkish history. Tanks and paratroopers were mobilized to quell the rioting, which had caused large-scale damage at over one hundred work sites. The organizers of the demonstration were accused both by the government and rival labor leaders of fomenting class warfare and staging a rehearsal for a proletarian revolution. Nine months later, after the government's economic austerity policies had led to an unprecedented wave of political protest that included virtually every organized sector of Turkish society and urban guerrillas had launched a Tupamaro-type campaign of bank robberies and kidnappings, the General Staff deposed the beleaguered Justice Party government in what many feared was a rehearsal for a Turkish "Eighteenth Brumaire."

During the 1970s, labor continued to disrupt the economy, if not urban life per se. The figures in Table 10.10 show the growth in strike activity. In 1977 the 80,000 members of the Metalworkers' Union went on strike for eight months. The combination of political organizations settling accounts with arms and growing labor agitation as the two-party system polarized between the secular and increasingly left-leaning Republican People's party of Bülent Ecevit and the center-right, probusiness Justice party of Süleyman Demirel finds no equivalent anywhere in the Middle East.

Lebanon and Beirut offer the other special case. When civil war broke out in 1975, many assumed that it would go on only so long as it did not disrupt commerce and banking. That point was reached and passed within a few years. Anyone who stayed in Beirut, Tripoli, Sidon, or their immediate hinterlands had to be either armed or in a position to hire protection. As the fighting increased, many business-

Year	Strikes	Strikers	Days Lost
TABLE 10.10	Strike Activity in Turkey, 1963–1980		
1963	8	1,514	19,739
1970	72	21,150	220,189
1977	59	15,628	1,397,124
1980	220	84,832	7,708,750

Source: Margulies and Yildizoğlu (1984, 18).

people and much of the intelligentsia left the country. The streets were given over to armed militias, some affiliated with older political parties, such as the Christian Phalanges (Kata'ib), with the Palestinian resistance, or with the various Shi'ite factions. It is clear that in Lebanon the young men of the slums, the squatter settlements, and the refugee camps took over the cities and staked out highly fortified enclaves. The small-scale merchants, traders, craftspeople, and service people who stayed on had to pay off the local powers, but as money came in from outside to finance the war and found its way into the pockets of the militias and their dependents, business was good.

The carnage lasted fourteen years and caused the death of an estimated 150,000 Lebanese and Palestinians. It is hard to discern any longer what causes and issues drove the violence. Religion and confessional balances, greater economic equality among religious confessions, the survival or liquidation of the Palestinian refugees, and the never-ending need to avenge an avalanche of deaths were all at stake. Power hunger and habit transformed Beirut into a city where no central authority held sway and where violence was the norm and its absence a curiosity.

The cities of Iran and Lebanon may point toward the future. Every outbreak of urban violence in the Middle East since the Iranian revolution has had an Islamic component, and in some instances that was the only component. In late 1979 the Great Mosque at Mecca was seized by a heterogeneous group of Saudi fundamentalists and allied pilgrims from all over the Muslim world. It took weeks for Saudi security forces to flush them out. In the summer of 1987 Iranian pilgrims, under instructions from Ayatollah Khomeini, staged demonstrations at Mecca that Saudi security forces confronted with force. Over two hundred demonstrators and policemen were killed.

After President Sadat's assassination by Muslim extremists in October 1981, hundreds of those associated with the plot made their stand in large provincial cities, especially Mansura in the Delta and Assiut in Upper Egypt. In the latter, pitched battles were fought and several hundred were killed. The violence there pales in comparison to the confrontation between Syria's Muslim Brotherhood and its archenemy, the Alawite regime of Hafiz al-Assad. The Brotherhood, accused of an assassination campaign against Alawite army officers, holed up in the old Sunni city of Hama. Assad ringed the city with artillery and leveled parts of it. The death toll may have been in the tens of thousands.

In January 1980, armed bands, apparently having infiltrated from Libya, briefly seized the Tunisian mining town of Gafsa and proclaimed a set of Islamic revolutionary goals. Since then the Tunisian regime has periodically met militant Islamic groups with force. Neighboring Algeria has dealt ruthlessly with similar challenges, and its cities have been relatively free of Islamic agitation. The riots of the fall of 1988, however, were to some extent led by prominent Muslim spokesmen. In the fall of 1990, as the United States mobilized an international coalition to oust Iraqi military forces from Kuwait, both Morocco and Tunisia were rocked by urban demonstrations and riots on a very large scale. As in Algeria in 1988 and in Jordan in 1989, there was undoubtedly an element of socioeconomic protest against the harsh economic reforms the governments of all three countries were pursuing, but that protest was deeply suffused with cultural and religious protest as well.

We seem to be seeing developments that neither the older vision of violence going hand in hand with massive migration and unemployment nor the more recent vision of the docile shantytowns and perhaps violence-prone second-generation migrants would have predicted. Urban violence now is taking a predominantly religious form. Its organizers and to some extent its shock troops are drawn from a particular stratum of the urban population. They tend to be young men, and some women, from provincial cities who had come to the metropolis to pursue higher education. They tend to come from solid families rather than broken homes, and they have been raised within an Islamic value system. In confronting the big city, they are shocked by the luxury, debauchery, cosmopolitanism, and materialism that these conurbations typically display. The university campuses themselves appear to be venues of uncontrolled mixing of the sexes and centers for the propagation of debased Western mores. These young people are thus a segment of the rural lower-middle class with professional aspirations and high religious ideals. They are willing and able to organize small, disciplined groups that infiltrate state agencies, the junior officers' corps, and the security forces. Alternatively, if they feel that the corrupt state monster cannot be taken from within, they withdraw into small cellular communities and, like the Prophet at Medina, prepare to take society from without (see Ibrahim 1980; Sivan 1985; al-Ansari 1986; Ayubi 1991a).

Such leaders and groups do draw on other sectors of urban society, and, indeed, in Lebanon the slum dwellers appear to have been the shock troops for all the contending factions, be they religious, partisan, or mercenary. These groups will also often enlist the support of militant members of the ulema, who lend the lay militants some doctrinal legitimacy, and they may count on support from a broad spectrum of actors from well-to-do officers in the armed forces to schoolteachers, clerks, and petty traders.

By the turn of the century the Middle East will be overwhelmingly urban, and it is likely that in most countries there will be a number of cities with several million inhabitants. These growing urban markets may well drive up the prices of rural produce and thus stimulate agricultural production. That is the good news. The urban populations will, however, bear the brunt of the austerity measures introduced as part of structural adjustment programs. Except for the very rich, all urban dwellers will suffer, but the ones who will feel the pain most acutely will be those on fixed incomes and those with the educational qualifications for middle-class status but for whom appropriate employment will be in increasingly short supply. Managing the national economy and managing the cities will become coterminous.

NOTES

1. Because these numbers are based on different national definitions of "urban," they are only suggestive of rough orders of magnitude.

2. A secondary city is defined as having a population between 100,000 and 1 million.

3. "Reclassification" means a change of a given village from the "rural" to the "urban" category simply because of the increase in its population.

4. That this procedure seriously underestimates the role of rural-urban migration in the urbanization process (see below) more than compensates for the overestimation that results from including reclassification with migration, especially if, as is likely, rural population growth rates exceed urban ones.

5. More detailed estimates suggest that migration accounted for some 65% of Cairo's growth between 1935 and 1965 but only 10% from 1966 to 1976 (Omran and Roudi 1993). Rural-urban migration has resumed and probably accelerated since the mid-1980s.

6. Some examples are Syria, 1.7 (el-Ghonemy 1984, 26); the YAR, 2–4 (World Bank 1979; Commander and Burgess 1988); Egypt, 1.7 (el-Ghonemy 1984); Iran, 3.2 (Nattagh 1986); Turkey, 1.5–3.0 (Danielson and Keleş 1980); Tunisia, 2.1 (el-Ghonemy 1984); Morocco, 2.2 (el-Ghonemy 1984); Jordan, 2.5 (el-Ghonemy 1984); and the Sudan, 2.8 (el-Ghonemy 1984). It is common for the ratio between low-income urban and low-income rural to be at least 2.5 (e.g., Turkey, 2.7 [Dervis and Robinson 1980, 112]).

7. The expected value of moving to the city is given by the formula $E(v) = P(U)(YURBAN) - P(R)(YRURAL)$, where PU is the probability of finding an urban job, $YURBAN$ is urban income, PR is the probability of finding a rural job, and $YRURAL$ is rural income. As long as $E(v)$ is positive, it pays to migrate. Assuming that $P(R) = 1.0$, we may rewrite the formula as $E(v) = P(U)(YURBAN/YRURAL) - 1$. Using one of the highest measured employment rates cited (25%), the probability of finding a job is 75% ($1 -$ unemployment rate). This implies that as long as urban incomes are even one-third higher than rural incomes, migration will pay.

8. One study estimated that the poorer 44% of Moroccan households spend over 80% of their income on food (USAID 1986, 18); poor Egyptians spend about 60% of their incomes on food (Radwan and Lee 1986, 96).

9. Because food subsidies there are also effective in rural areas, this is less true for Egypt than for other countries of the region (see below and also Alderman and von Braun [1984, 37–51]). However, during the 1970s the rural price index increased more rapidly than did the urban (Mohie el-Din 1982, 24), a further indication that differences in cost of living did little to offset incentives for cityward migration.

10. For an extensive discussion, see Waterbury (1978).

11. For a thorough and rigorous discussion, see Sen (1981a, chap. 2).

12. The 95% confidence interval around the point estimates in Table 10.3 for MENA are 13 and 51; any estimate of the percentage of the population that is poor between 13% and 51% cannot be ruled out (World Bank 1990b). The World Bank has since revised downward its estimates of regional poverty (World Bank 1995a).

13. More technically, the ratio of per capita GNP to the poverty line, both in PPP dollars, is unreasonably high when compared with a similar calculation for the United States. In the United States, GNP per capita is about 6.5 times greater than the poverty line (US$14,335 for a family of four in 1992), whereas corresponding MENA figures are Egypt, 9.9; Jordan, 11.4; Morocco, 8.8; and Tunisia, 13.8 (Danziger and Weinberg 1994 for the U.S. figure; remainder of figures calculated from data in Table 2.2).

14. US$624 PPP for urban and US$552 PPP for rural in Morocco, compared with US$370 PPP by the World Bank.

11

POLITICAL REGIMES: AS THEY ARE AND AS THEY VIEW THEMSELVES

We are on treacherous ground but in good company when we try to label the political regimes of the Middle East (see, inter alia, Binder 1957; Hudson 1977). "Regime" refers not only to a type of government but also to ideology, the rules of the game, and the structuring of the polity in a given nation. "Regime change" is no mere changing of the guard or cleaning out of City Hall; it is, rather, profound structural change in all forms of political activity. Regime change may be revolutionary, as in the violent shift from a monarchical to a republican regime in France in 1789 or from Pahlavi dynastic rule to the Islamic republic (some would say "theocracy") in Iran in 1979. Regime change may, however, be relatively peaceful and incremental. Turkey moved between 1946 and 1950 from a single-party, authoritarian regime to a two-party system with openly contested elections. Egypt has been creeping hesitantly since 1971 from Nasser's single-party, authoritarian socialist regime toward a more liberal multiparty system in which private economic interests have come to play a legitimate role. Hinnebusch (1985) has characterized the Nasserist regime as "authoritarian-populist" and Sadat's as "post-populist authoritarian-conservative."

There is no dearth of cumbersome labels for Middle Eastern regimes, and both their number and terminological complexity testify to the difficulties observers encounter in making coherent generalizations about the nature of these regimes. There are a number of pitfalls into which one easily stumbles. The first one is that in the Middle East, not without reason, we tend to personalize regimes, equating or confusing them with their founders. We talk of the Nasserist, Kemalist (Atatürk), or Bourguibist systems, and doubtless for these giant figures there is a good deal of truth in equating their systems with their personae. Waterbury (1983) argued that the death of Nasser in 1970 in itself signaled the end of a regime and necessarily set the stage for a new one. But it is an abuse of the term "regime" and of empirical reality to succumb to the temptation to see all leadership changes as constituting regime changes. Constant and violent power struggles within the Baʻath hierarchy in Syria and Iraq since the mid-1960s have not constituted regime changes. The triumph of the more managerial Hafiz al-Assad over the more populist Salah Jadid in Syria in 1970 or the eclipse of Ahmad Hassan al-Bakr in the face of Saddam Hussein in Iraq were only in-house power shifts and did not significantly alter the nature of the Baʻathi-military regimes of those two countries.

A second pitfall is taxonomic; we tend to classify regimes merely by describing what they appear to be doing at a given point in time. Rather than capturing the essence of the process of regime formation, consolidation, and decay—that is, classifying by understanding the *dynamics* of regimes—we say that regime X is "authoritarian-socialist," "radical Islamic," or "patriarchal-conservative." Now that public-sector enterprises are everywhere being compared unfavorably with those of the private sector and there is considerable talk of putting the former on the auction block, at least one scholar is using the term "authoritarian-privatizing regimes." In this way there is a tendency for each regime to become its own type, and when the regime changes a new type must be invented to describe it. All one needs to do is summarize what the new regime does in a new hyphenated label.

One must be on the lookout for a third pitfall. One way to avoid superficial and descriptive labeling is to focus on the dynamics of social and economic change within societies and how they are or are not reflected in the nature of the regime. This may enable us to see the extent to which regime change is the product of social and economic change. For instance, in 1962 there was an abrupt regime change in North Yemen. The quasi-medieval theocracy known as the imamate was overthrown through a military coup d'état and a socialist republic proclaimed. Legally, a profound change had occurred, but Yemeni society had scarcely changed at all. By contrast, one could argue that the downfall of the shah of Iran in 1979 and the proclamation of the Islamic republic came as the result of rapid and profound social change in Iran in the 1960s and 1970s. The large cohorts of literate, urban, upwardly mobile Iranians that the shah's own educational system had spewed forth could no longer be contained within the paternalistic, authoritarian, and repressive regime he had inherited from his father. Although an Islamic republic was surely not the only possible regime alternative to the shah and the shah's downfall itself was not inevitable, Iranian society was clearly ready for some profound restructuring of the polity.

We have here classified regimes in part according to how they manage publicly owned assets (Chapters 7 and 8). The three major categories are (1) regimes that use these assets to generate surplus for further state expansion at the expense of the private sector, (2) those that use assets to act as a handmaiden to private entrepreneurs, and (3) those that seek to transfer public assets to private hands. We have tried to delimit the major factors leading given regimes into one or another of these modes as well as the likely consequences of their adoption. In what follows we extend the analysis to the major policy domains of the region's regimes in order to move beyond descriptive understandings of their dynamics.

SOCIALIST REPUBLICS

Of all the regime types that have characterized the Middle East since World War II, the most prevalent has been the socialist republic. As was the case for economic growth strategies and state intervention in the economy, the Turkish republic of the 1920s and 1930s, although never espousing socialism, was the forerunner and the model for several regional neighbors. Egypt, Syria, Iraq, North Yemen, the Sudan, Tunisia, and Algeria all replicated to some extent the Turkish model. One should also include Qaddhafi's "mass state" in Libya and the former PDRY of South Yemen. Not only are these regimes numerically dominant, but they have also demonstrated considerable longevity: Egypt, 1952–present, with a significant regime transformation beginning in 1971; Syria, 1963–present; Iraq, 1963–present; Algeria, 1962–present, with a major constitutional change in 1989; Sudan, 1958–1964 and 1969–1985; North Yemen, 1962–1991; Tunisia, 1956–present, with a major shift in political philosophy after 1987; Libya, 1969–present; and South Yemen, 1968–1991.

Atatürk's Turkey

The interwar experience of Atatürk's Turkey set the main themes and gave them real meaning in the construction of the Turkish polity. The quest for independence and national sovereignty—the ability to stand up to the great powers—was seen as rooted in a strong industrial economy and a cohesive citizenry. Former Ottoman *subjects* had to become proud Turkish *citizens*—educated, enlightened, free of the fetters of religious obscurantism, hardworking, and patriotic. Atatürk was a practitioner of nation building—a term that was to come into vogue in the Western modernization literature long after his death.

Nationalism, etatism, republicanism, revolutionism, populism, and secularism were the watchwords of the Turkish experiment. The six-hundred-year-old Ottoman Empire and the Islamic caliphate were ended in 1923. Atatürk and his lieutenants, inspired by the writings of Ziya Gökalp, himself inspired by Emile Durkheim's *The Human Division of Labor*, sought a society in which all class conflict and parochial loyalties were subordinated to citizens' functional or occupational roles. "Solidarism," the building of an integrated, conflict-free society, characterized an outlook that spread throughout the Middle East. Religion was to be the affair of individuals, not of the state, which would remain resolutely secular and rationalist, especially in the education it dispensed through the public school system. The political guarantor of the nation's integration was to be a single party, to mobilize the citizenry rather than to compete for power against other parties, which, in any case, were only sporadically tolerated. The Republican People's party, while the creation of the regime, became an important organization in its own right.

As we have already pointed out, the Turkish experiment put the state center-stage. This was to be an activist, interventionist state rather than a set of agencies and bureaucracies over which political factions fought for control. Together with the military, the Turkish state rose above society and sought to reshape it in the image that Atatürk and his lieutenants thought desirable (see Trimberger 1978). This was a state with a purpose and with goals—to build a modern nation and modern Turkish citizens. The hurly-burly of electoral politics, the unfettered expression of political differences, or, worse yet, the outbreak of class conflict could, it was believed, only deflect the state from its lofty purpose.

This understanding of the proper role of the state and of the uses of public power spread throughout the Middle East in the post–World War II era and was at the heart of the socialist republican experiments. The late Malcolm Kerr, in a powerful essay on Arab radical notions of democracy (1963, 10–11), wrote that this radicalism was

> characterized by a moral preference—not just a tactical preference—for maintaining the maximum degree of unity of purpose and action at all political and social levels, by an emphasis upon the virtues of group solidarity and the evils of individual self-absorption and self-seeking, by a mistrust of competition, bargaining and the promotion of special interests, and by a vision of strong government as a liberator rather than a danger to liberty.

Kerr noted that the Islamic reformers of the early twentieth century (principally Egypt's Muhammed 'Abduh) had arisen from the first attempts to organize the Muslim community as a "morally purposeful society" under one leader (the caliph), with a common interest in service to God under a single law (the shari'a) that assured the moral and political solidarity of all members. In this conceptualization "power is good or bad according to the righteousness of its possessor" (Kerr 1963, 10).

Atatürk tried to redefine its purpose and to strip it of its religious underpinnings, but the morally purposeful state was still the linchpin of his nation building. Many other Middle Easterners, while seeing much to admire in republican Turkey, were disturbed, indeed often shocked, by Atatürk's vehement secularism. Tunisia's Habib Bourguiba, among the Arabs, came closest to emulating Atatürk's ideas and practices, but few other Arab leaders dared try to separate national from religious identity or "church" from state.

We may note now, in anticipation of discussion to come, that the strengthening of Islamic challenges to many of the existing Middle Eastern states can be seen in large measure as stemming from the conviction that these states have failed in their mission. Some Muslim activists believe that the republican socialist mission was misconceived if not blasphemous. Atatürk, for many pious Muslims, is the villain who ended the caliphate and separated the Turkish state from serving the community of Muslim believers (the *umma*). What Islamic radicals seek to do is to put the state, once again, to its God-given purposes of promoting the unity and strength of the *umma*. There is, thus, conflict over state purposes but no conflict over the belief that power used for the right purposes should be unchecked and unbalanced.

Nasser's Egypt and Bourguiba's Tunisia

In July 1952 a group of Egyptian officers of the rank of colonel or below seized power and ended the monarchical rule of the descendants of the old Ottoman governor in Egypt, Muhammed 'Ali (1804–1841). A republic was soon proclaimed, and a respected senior officer, Gen. Muhammed Naguib, was made its president. All existing political parties were abolished in 1953, and in 1954 the Muslim Brotherhood (al-Ikhwan al-Muslimun), although not legally a party, was abolished after one of its members attempted to assassinate Col. Gamal 'Abd al-Nasser. Having swept the political arena clean, the new regime sought to build its own monopoly political organization from the top down. It was called the Liberation Rally, and its founders' programmatic priorities were largely embodied in its slogan, "Unity, Discipline, and Work." With the parties and politicians who had lived on factionalism and debilitating partisan conflict out of the way, the new leaders hoped that the populace would close ranks, put its shoulder to the wheel, and—led by the armed forces, the embodiment of the nation's will to survive—stand up to the imperialist powers.

In these early years the talk was much more of revolution than of socialism. It was only after 1956 and the acquisition of extensive economic assets taken over from the British and the French (see Chapter 7) that a socialist ideology gradually took shape. But whatever Nasser's understanding of socialism, he was always clear about the need for unity and solidarity. Egypt's second monopoly party, founded in 1957, was called the National Union. As he was to say frequently thereafter, it was not a party, because parties meant partisanship, and partisanship meant dividing the body politic, and that would not be tolerated. The National Union was, rather, an assembly of the whole nation—the organizational manifestation of its unity of purpose.

After the abrupt nationalizations of 1961, the regime committed itself to socialism and the building of yet another monopoly party, the Arab Socialist Union (ASU). Nasser's goal was to use this party to extend Egyptian influence throughout the Arab world. Within Egypt it tried to organize the citizenry along functional lines. There were five broad categories—the peasants, the workers, the intellectuals and professionals, the national capitalists, and the troops—bound up in what was called the Alliance of Working Forces. One of the objectives of the socialist revolution and the Arab Socialist Union was to achieve "the melting away of class differences." As in Atatürk's Turkey, the rhetorical emphasis was on unity, cohesion, devotion to the national cause as defined by the state, and the peaceful resolution of class differences by the redistribution of national wealth through state policies. A unified Egypt would carry the socialist revolution to the rest of the Arab world, and greater Arab and socialist solidarity would protect the region from the forces of neoimperialism and from Zionism. Reality and rhetoric did not mesh very often, but we are concerned here with trying to capture the spirit of the experiment.

The origins of the Bourguibist and Destourian regime in Tunisia were far different from those of Nasserist Egypt. Habib Bourguiba, a young lawyer from Monastir in Tunisia, captured the nationalist movement of that country from an older generation of leaders and in 1934 founded a mass-based party, the Neo-Destour (New

Constitution) party. The party came to mobilize organized labor, white-collar professionals, the intelligentsia, and provincial merchants and commercial farmers into a powerful coalition. The Neo-Destour helped win independence from the French in 1956, and Bourguiba served as president for thirty-one years until he was deposed in the fall of 1987.

Bourguiba had all of Atatürk's instincts; his project for Tunisia was republican (he ended the old quasi-monarchical institution of the dey), secular, populist, and, more than Atatürk's, imbued with a kind of French rationalist vision of the state that was Napoleonic in spirit. Socialism was not initially part of the project, but redistributive policies certainly were. In 1964, however, Tunisia entered a short-lived socialist era. The Neo-Destour party became the Socialist Destour, and the new minister of planning, Ahmed Ben Salah, formulated a state-led plan for the formation of agricultural cooperatives and public-sector industrialization. Egypt to the east and Algeria on Tunisia's western border were ostentatiously promoting similar socialist experiments, and Bourguiba may have felt compelled to climb on the bandwagon.

The experiment, having been implemented too rapidly, raised considerable opposition within Bourguiba's old coalition, especially among provincial merchants and capitalist farmers. In 1970 Ben Salah was dismissed and eventually jailed. The socialist experiment was ended, but all other aspects of the Bourguibist state remained. It must be stressed that Bourguibism, while similar to Atatürkism, differed in one major respect—it was resolutely nonmilitarist. Bourguiba always argued that Tunisia could never be a credible military power and that the building of a large military establishment would only consume scarce investment and perhaps thrust Tunisia into the cycles of military intervention in politics that had plagued the rest of the Middle East. Tunisia would have to use diplomatic skill rather than military power to defend its independence.

Twenty years after independence most observers saw Tunisia as one of the best-organized polities in the Arab world. Hudson (1977) compared Arab regimes in terms of three levels of political legitimacy. The first, personal legitimacy, refers to popular support and respect for leaders that does not necessarily extend to the programs and institutions they seek to develop. The second type of legitimacy is ideological, whereby citizens respect a regime's professed ideology and principles but not necessarily its leaders, who may fail to honor those principles. Finally, there is structural legitimacy, whereby citizens respect and accept the rules of the political game, the programs of the government, and the way in which goods are distributed in society. In Hudson's view, Bourguiba and the Tunisian regime enjoyed legitimacy on all three dimensions and in that sense were probably unique in the Arab world: "Tunisia may be considered as perhaps the most politically modern of the revolutionary Arab states, in terms of secularism, rationality, and institutionalized participation. Certainly it has been one of the most stable" (1977, 378).

Yet even as Hudson wrote, he noted that in 1975 the National Assembly proclaimed Bourguiba president for life. The proclamation foreshadowed a breakdown in the rationality of the regime—the reinforcement of the cult of the indispensable leader, a violation of the ideal of meritocracy and political accountability. Like Atatürk before him, the leader (the *za'im*, as such power figures are known in the Arab world) apparently did not trust the citizens created by the new rationalized political system to choose or change their leaders. For all their emphasis on national unity and purpose, the leaders of the socialist republics never leave office voluntarily. Atatürk and Nasser died in harness, and Bourguiba, in his eighties and senile, was ushered into retirement by General Zine al-Abdine Ben 'Ali, the man he had appointed minister of defense. None of these leaders could accept the full political logic of the systems they sought to build.

With age and physical decline, Bourguiba became more and more manipulable by figures in his entourage. There were, in the 1980s, occasional flashes of his old political skills, but the modernizing presidency became increasingly the focal point of intrigue and personal vendettas—as if Tunisia had tired of the French model of the state and had resurrected the Ottoman seraglio. In June 1986, at the congress of the Socialist Destour, Bourguiba simply appointed a new central committee, a body supposedly elected by party members, and dismissed the careful and unflamboyant Prime Minister Muhammed Mzali, a man who had been seen as his successor.

President Ben 'Ali has changed little in the Bourguibist system except to rename the party the Democratic Constitutional Rally (RCD by its French acronym). The new order was no less corporatist than the old, only faintly more liberal, and, given the man at its head, far more wedded to the military and security than had ever been Bourguiba's.

North Yemen and the Sudan

North Yemen and the Sudan experienced regimes in the past twenty-five years that were to some extent Nasserist in their structures and programs, but the societies onto which these regimes were imposed were and are very much different from that of Egypt or Tunisia, let alone Turkey. North Yemen is still a tribal society, with backward agriculture and very little industry. It is, moreover, divided between the mainly Shi'ite tribesmen, from whom the former imams were drawn, and urban Sunni Muslims, from whom the merchant class is drawn. Sunni officers seized power from the imam in 1962, proclaimed a republic, and reached out to Nasser's Egypt for support. Some Shi'ite tribes rejected the new regime and looked to Saudi Arabia to help restore the imamate. Five years of civil war ensued in which a large Egyptian expeditionary force found itself incapable of subduing the tribes in their mountainous home territories. The Egyptian expeditionary force was withdrawn at the time of the June War of 1967, and the contending Yemeni factions reached a fragile modus vivendi that preserved the republic but restored royalist leaders to positions of power. Factional struggles within the Yemeni military, backed by tribal allies, finally yielded a military regime in 1978, headed by 'Ali 'Abdullah Salih, a Zaydi Shi'ite, who has been head of state ever since.

North Yemen's immediate neighbor to the south was the former British Protectorate of Aden, which in 1968 became the People's Democratic Republic of Yemen, an avowedly marxist regime. Over the years it proved unable to impose marxist secular rationality on its tribal base. The dominant marxist elite was itself divided along tribal lines, and those divisions erupted into a bloody civil war in 1986. The victor was 'Ali Salim al-Baidh, but no sooner had he consolidated his grip on power than the PDRY's long-standing patron, the Soviet Union, drifted toward collapse and abandonment of its international commitments. Without economic or military support from the USSR, al-Baidh was obliged to save his regime by seeking unity with North Yemen. With an economy even weaker than that of the North and only 20% of the combined population of 12 million, he was in a weak bargaining position. He was nonetheless able to bargain for rough parity in an elected parliament and in government ministries. Moreover, the military establishments of the two entities were not integrated. Unity was proclaimed in May 1990.

In late April 1993, elections to the new parliament were held in the presence of international observers. Observers hailed the birth of a new democracy in this unlikely corner of the Arab world. But, as in Algeria's aborted elections of 1991, the democratic process proved destabilizing and self-destructive. South Yemen's Yemeni Socialist party came in third behind two northern parties, Salih's General Congress party and the Reform party representing Islamists in alliance with the Hashid tribal confederation, both of which fiercely opposed unity with the "atheist-marxist" forces of the South. Al-Baidh read the results in strictly regional terms; the South that he controlled could never make political inroads into the North and would inevitably be subordinated to Northern interests. With Saudi support the South in effect seceded from the union. Salih refused to accept the dissolution of the union and went to war to prevent it in the summer of 1994. A unified Yemen was restored, the old forces of the socialist South crushed, and the experiment with democracy, for the time being, shelved. Salih, in power for sixteen years, became the head of both Yemens, unified by military force and unfettered by any democratic constraints.

The Sudan, the largest country in Africa in surface area (Algeria is second), is also one of the continent's poorest. Like North Yemen, it is still overwhelmingly rural and agricultural, with its 28 million inhabitants (in 1994) scattered over a territory the size of the United States east of the Mississippi. One-third of the population, living in the southern region, consists of black Nilotic and Bantu tribes who for the most part are neither Muslim nor Arabic-speaking, while the rest are of mixed Arab and black African stock, Sunni Muslims, and speak Arabic.

In 1958, only two years after independence, a military regime was established under the leadership of Gen. Muhammed 'Abboud. Bearing some resemblance to the Nasserist regime in neighboring Egypt, it put an end to a multiparty system that had ineffectively governed the country between 1956 and 1958. It emphasized themes of national unity and solidarity and tried to deal militarily with dissidence among the southern populations. It drew up a national economic plan and promoted state industries.

The growing war in the south was the principal cause of the downfall of the 'Abboud regime in 1964. For five years civilian parties and politicians, organized around the country's two major Muslim brotherhoods (the Ansar and the Khatmiya), sought to construct a liberal political system and to bring an end to the fighting in the south. Failing on the second count, they crippled their liberal experiment.

In May 1969 Col. Ga'afar al-Nimeiri seized power and established a regime that was explicitly Nasserist. A few months later Mu'ammar Qaddhafi established a similar regime in Libya. Both Nimeiri and Qaddhafi looked to Nasser as a revered leader, as a source of inspiration for their own experiments, and, ultimately, as a protector who could come to their rescue if need be. Nasser died only a year after the two young officers had come to power.

Nimeiri, in his first two years, dealt with the religious power centers in the Sudan, taking on the Ansar militarily, dispersing its adherents, driving its leaders into exile, and seizing its rural properties. He then turned on marxist supporters in his government and, in a bloody sequence of coup and countercoup in July 1970, physically eliminated several prominent marxists and communists. As had Nasser in 1953, Nimeiri had cleared the political arena, and into it he cast the Sudanese Socialist Union, yet another "alliance of working forces" derived directly from Egypt's Arab Socialist Union. Central planning was resurrected, and there was a great surge in the funding of public-sector industries. Most important, Nimeiri negotiated an end to the fighting in the south and granted local autonomy to the three southern provinces.

But Sudanese society was neither ready for republican socialism nor prepared to tolerate the authoritarian politics of young army officers. As in Yemen, traditional tribal and regional loyalties to brotherhoods and religious leaders were very much alive, and Nimeiri eventually became absorbed in elaborate games of patronage, payoffs, and the balancing of rivals that sapped the regime of much of its socialist energy. These games were interspersed with a half-dozen attempted coups, the frequency of which may have driven Nimeiri deeper into drink (the only habit he shared with Atatürk) and corruption. Although only half Bourguiba's age, Nimeiri lost the logic of his political project and succumbed to the intrigue of his own seraglio. He probably never enjoyed much legitimacy of any sort; he was personally uncharismatic, his ideology was muddled and unconvincing, a blind imitation of Egypt's, and his political and economic structures never took root. His one achievement, ending the civil war in the south, was undone by his penchant for the strategy of divide-and-rule, which eventually alienated his own supporters among the southern populations.

In the early 1980s Nimeiri became a kind of "born-again" Muslim. He threatened to apply shari'a throughout the country, including the non-Muslim south. By 1983 the south, led by John Garang, was again in full revolt. In the north, Nimeiri combined a ferocious Muslim piety with a vast spoils system by which his civilian and military cronies pilfered the public purse. The Sudanese intelligentsia and uncorrupted elements of the armed forces overthrew him in March 1985. A fragile civilian regime was reestablished under the leadership of Sadiq al-Mahdi and the Ansar. He was reluctant to rescind Nimeiri's promulgation of shari'a in the south, and therefore the civil war raged on.

Nimieri ruled sixteen years, exactly as long as Nasser, but at the end of the period he had left virtually nothing of his experiment behind. The Sudan's third brush with democracy, 1986–1989, once again produced policy paralysis and an unresolved civil war. In 1989 yet another military coup, led by Lt. Gen. Omar al-Bashir, brought a self-proclaimed Islamic republican regime to power. Bashir's spiritual and political guide was Hassan al-Turabi, founder of the Sudan's Muslim Brotherhood. Oxford- and Sorbonne-educated, articulate, and sophisticated, Turabi has cast himself as the dominant voice of political Islam in the Muslim world, filling the void created by the death of Khomeini.

The Islamic regime has prosecuted the war in the south with a calculating zeal unrivaled in the Sudan's recent history. What human rights organizations have identified as its deliberate use of famine as a weapon in the civil war has elicited plausible charges of genocide. Within the regions that it more or less controls, the new regime has established its own dominant party, the National Islamic Front (NIF). It has sought with some success to marginalize the older politico-religious parties, the Democratic Unionist party (allied with the Khatmiya) and the Umma party (allied with the Ansar). As in Iran, religious corporatism is combined with ferocious repression of tribes, non-Muslims, and intellectual dissidents.

The economy is marginally less state-dominated than under Nimeiri, but that is an inevitable result of the enfeeblement of the state by two decades of economic crisis and the enormous outlays on the military campaign in the south. Moreover, since the time of Nimeiri the Sudan has lost access to IMF and World Bank funds, and the Bashir goverment, in coming to power by overthrowing a democratically elected government, rendered any rapprochement with these and other Western sources of funds highly unlikely. By the mid-1990s only Iran and possibly Iraq could offer any assistance to the Sudan.

The result is that the Sudanese state and economy have fragmented. Public finances cannot maintain a coherent regional administration and pay schoolteachers and postmen, much less invest in infrastructure and regional development. The NIF may be able to project its Islamic message more effectively in neighboring Arab countries such as Egypt or Tunisia than in the hinterlands of the Sudan itself.

The Radicals

Socialism in the Middle East has not been inspired by doctrinaire marxism or sustained by coherent socialist political parties. Rather, the appending of the term "socialism" to various loosely structured political fronts has symbolized commitment to equity and distributive issues, public ownership of some means of production, the acceptance of private property, and the drive for development—the mission of the purposeful state. It has not meant indoctrination, the moral and spiritual reshaping of human beings, or the assumption that social action must be organized along class lines. It certainly has not meant the dictatorship of the proletariat or even the direct control of publicly owned enterprises by the workers themselves.

By and large, all the Middle Eastern socialist regimes except the PDRY have adopted similar outlooks. What has made some more radical than others has generally been their conduct of foreign policy rather than their domestic politics. Thus in their domestic policies the regimes of Algeria, Syria, and Iraq in the 1970s and 1980s had come, de facto, to resemble those of Egypt or Tunisia, but all three were aggressively anti-imperialist, too friendly with the USSR to suit the United States, and, significantly, bogged down in foreign adventures—Algeria in the Saharan War with Morocco, Iraq in large-scale hostilities with Iran, and Syria in the Lebanese cockpit.

Algeria. That Algeria is not more revolutionary and radical is something of a surprise. Algerian socialism and its organizational underpinning, the National Liberation Front (FLN), were shaped in eight years of brutal warfare with France between 1954 and 1962. The FLN at the time of independence was not a top-down party like the Arab Socialist or the Sudanese Socialist Union. Like the Neo-Destour, it had come out of the crucible of nationalist struggle, but in Algeria that struggle had been violent and prolonged. Some believed that once independence had been won the FLN would lead Algeria down a Marxist-Leninist path similar to Cuba's.

Organizationally and in terms of its leadership, the FLN was a heterodox coalition of all the major participants in the war for liberation. Its secular, socialist, and even marxist image was owed to the young intellectuals who had constituted its "external team" and who had made the Algerian cause known throughout the world. Their radical views were embodied in the two fundamental documents of the revolution, the Tripoli Program of 1962 and the Charter of Algiers of 1964. Algeria's first president, Ahmad Ben Bella, was not unsympathetic to their views. In the early years of independence the radicals were able to promote worker self-management (with Yugoslav advice) on agricultural land taken over from departing Europeans and in abandoned or nationalized factories. Algeria also became a major voice in the nonaligned movement and identified strongly with Palestinians, the African National Congress of South Africa, and liberation fronts in Vietnam, Angola, and Mozambique.

But alongside the articulate and cosmopolitan radical intelligentsia were other major forces far less committed to the radical transformation of Algerian society. The guerrilla fighters were mainly mountain and steppe Berbers, fervent nationalists and pious Muslims eager for their share of the spoils of victory but by no means doctrinaire socialists. Indeed, they had always been suspicious of and hostile toward the citified and seemingly atheist intellectuals.

The guerrillas (mujahedin) did not have a monopoly of arms in independent Algeria. The major armed forces were large professional armies that had been trained and billeted in Tunisia and Morocco but had seen little action in the final years of the war. Their principal spokesman was Houari Boumedienne, the first minister of defense and the man who would seize power from Ahmad Ben Bella in June 1965. Boumedienne was a graduate of Egypt's major center of Islamic learning, al-Azhar. He had little sympathy for Ben Bella's secular socialist allies or for the ragtag bands of guerrillas that had borne the brunt of the fighting.

Boumedienne's seizure of power ushered in an era that was in many ways Nasserist. The new president, like Atatürk, Nasser, and Bourguiba, was obsessed with rational and orderly national development. He liked good organization and good management, and, as we have seen in Chapter 7, he launched Algeria onto the path of state-led heavy industrialization. The era of romantic socialism and strident internationalism ended; the era of the planner and the technocrat began.

The FLN, while enjoying a legal monopoly within the political arena, was increasingly marginalized under Boumedienne (Leca 1975; Roberts 1984). Rather than an instrument of mass mobilization it was to be, like the ASU in Egypt, an instrument to control Algerians while the state marshaled the nation's resources for the development effort. Real power passed to the armed forces and the bureaucracy. In the absence of a national parliament and a permanent constitution, the supreme authority in the country was the National Council of the Algerian Revolution (CNRA). Typical of the secretiveness of Boumedienne, the full membership of the CNRA was not made public. Several of the members came from the so-called Oujda Group, military associates who had been with Boumedienne in Oujda, Morocco, during the revolution and when the first units of the Army of National Liberation were being trained. Few, if any, Middle Eastern regimes had ever so divorced themselves from their mass base or so discouraged popular participation as Algeria's. Boumedienne himself was a private, dour man who never sought popular acclaim. Yet, ironically, toward the last years of his regime it could be said that Boumedienne, his statist, technocratic socialism, and his efforts to remake the Algerian economy all enjoyed considerable legitimacy.

That legitimacy was not unmitigated. In 1976 the regime organized debates in all sectors of society to formulate a new national charter. Sharp criticism of corrupt officials and heavy bureaucratic procedures poured forth. After this letting off of steam, the national charter was approved. Notably, it talked of Algerian socialism's consisting in a transclass alliance. The idea of internal class struggle was played down, while that of Algeria as a "proletarian" state struggling against the forces of imperialism was emphasized (Nellis 1983, 372). With that the regime went back to business as usual until the death of Boumedienne in 1978.

He was succeeded by another member of the Oujda Group, Chadli Benjadid, who presided over a profound political and economic transformation of his country. He ruled from 1978 until January 1992, when he was deposed. Economic crisis dictated a thorough overhaul of state expenditures and macroeconomic policy that in turn opened the way to political transformation. Algeria, as a major exporter of petroleum and natural gas, was particularly hard hit by declining international prices of both commodities in the mid-1980s. As a major exporter of labor, it was simultaneously squeezed by the closing-off of European labor markets that had for two decades or more been open to Algerian migrants. Algeria had no choice but to undertake stringent austerity measures in order to bring its external accounts into some balance and to begin structural adjustment (see Chapter 9).

As in other countries in the region, the austerity measures were the proximate cause of cost-of-living riots in October 1988. These were, in Algeria, particularly bloody, resulting in thousands of deaths. The regime was shaken. As we have argued elsewhere, deep economic and political crisis, while inherently fraught with danger, offers political leaders opportunities for initiating far-reaching change. Chadli Benjadid saw that opportunity in October 1988 and seized it.

The grievances that provoked the riots went far beyond short-term material problems, signaling the delegitimization of the regime and particularly of the FLN. Benjadid took the opportunity to dissociate himself partially from the single party and, as president, to rise above it. A year before the riots he had approved a law allowing the free formation of associations in Algeria without any prior approval by public authorities. Immediately after the riots he submitted to referendum a new constitution that was given overwhelming approval. It omitted any mention of socialism and any reference to the state as guarantor of the citizens' well-being.

With the new association law and constitution in place, Benjadid moved Algeria rapidly toward its first democratic elections, first for local assemblies, then for the parliament. An Islamic opposition, the Islamic Salvation Front (FIS by its French acronym), was legalized and allowed to contest the elections. Its two principal leaders, Abbasi Madani and 'Ali Belhadj, put together a mass movement in the space of a year and in June 1990 swept the local elections, winning nearly two-thirds of the votes cast. About one third of the electorate abstained. Algeria's political establishment was shocked, but Benjadid plunged ahead with the preparations for the elections to the national assembly or parliament.

Formerly one of the most closed and least participative military authoritarian regimes in the Middle East, Algeria was on the verge of an astounding democratic transition in which an Islamic party was permitted to contest for power at the national level. The stakes were high. It was widely feared that if the FIS won the parliamentary as it had the local elections it would have sufficient votes to amend the constitution or do away with it altogether—in other words, that Algeria's entry into democracy might simultaneously be its exit. The Algerian senior officers' corps was particularly alarmed at the prospect of an Islamic electoral victory. It feared that the FIS would end its monopoly on political power, set the country back technologically, and turn the schools into centers of religious indoctrination. Algeria's politically active women feared being forced out of public life and employment and back into the home. Secularists feared that an FIS victory would see the imposition of shari'a throughout the land. The firebrand denunciations of democracy by Belhadj in particular did nothing to allay these fears.

In December 1991 the elections were held. The balloting system followed was the French, with an initial vote for all candidates followed by a runoff between the two leading candidates in any district in which no candidate won a clear majority in the first round. The authorities believed that enough contests would be decided in the second round that, through alliances, the FLN could prevent the FIS from winning an outright majority. The calculus proved disastrously wrong, and the FIS, while winning a million fewer votes than it had in 1990, stood poised after the first round of voting to win an absolute majority in the parliament. The second round was never held, and in January 1992 the senior military moved to depose Benjadid, arrest Belhadj and Madani, and dissolve the FIS.

The military reverted to the closed, secretive style of the Boumedienne years, putting the country under the control of the High Council of State. It brought back to the presidency Mohammed Boudiaf, one of the historic leaders of the revolution (1954–1962), who had been in exile in Morocco for many years. Boudiaf proved far too independent, and when he began to crack down on corruption in the government and military he was assassinated, on June 29, 1992. The FIS was blamed for his death, but many Algerians, including his widow, remain convinced that the military eliminated him.

Since then Algeria has sunk into civil war. With its leadership in jail, parts of the FIS took up arms, allegedly with the help of mujahedin returning from years of combat in Afghanistan, where they had fought the Soviet occupying forces. Eventually a renegade armed wing known as the Armed Islamic Group broke from the FIS and fought the Algerian security forces and civilian adversaries in the cities and in the countryside with horrific savagery. Intellectuals, unveiled women, foreigners, and members of the political and military establishment were ritually slaughtered and sometimes mutilated. There is no question that the security forces resorted to the same methods and attributed the victims to the "fanatical" actions of the Armed Islamic Group and the FIS.

Returning to its closed military authoritarianism, Algeria began to lose its administrative and security grip on parts of its territory. In early 1994 the High Council of State was formally disbanded and the minister of defense, Lamine Zeroual, made president. He pursued the initiation of a dialogue with the FIS, especially its jailed leaders, and other forces in the opposition. No observers were convinced that he had the backing of the military, and no one could imagine the compromise that might allow the violence to end. Could new elections conceivably be held with FIS participation, and, if so, according to what rules? By aborting the last round of elections did the regime doom for the foreseeable future any possibility that the FIS could try the democratic path once again? Finally, would the Armed Islamic Group, which had little use for either the "moderates" in the FIS or for democracy, play any role but that of spoiler?

Anticipating a more detailed discussion in Chapter 14, we can suggest what kind of regime would be established if the FIS or some political movement like it were to come to power. As Lahouari Addi has argued (1995), the FIS has adopted all the populist themes of the FLN but with an Islamic twist. The Muslim people of Algeria are to be the beneficiaries of the revolution; the Muslim state must stamp out corruption and redistribute wealth; the economy must be harnessed for the protection and spread of the Islamic revolution, and therefore the state must maintain control of key economic sectors and strengthen the armed forces. An Islamic Algeria would be expected to join other Islamic polities in resisting the economic and cultural incursions of the West and in confronting Israel militarily.

Economically, an Islamic regime's choices would be limited. There are no wealthy Islamic benefactors to offer it significant financial support; Saudi Arabia, the only candidate for such a role, has no reason to encourage such regimes. The international financial institutions dominated by the advanced Western nations and Japan would insist on adherence to orthodox structural adjustment programs. An Islamic Algeria would have difficulty attracting foreign private capital unless it followed similar guidelines. If it could not afford populism, redistribution, and high military outlays, it would come to resemble the regime it replaced (or the Turabi-Bashir government in the Sudan), one surviving on the strength of a narrow coalition, strangling political participation, following orthodox, contractionary economic policies, and ruling by force and intimidation.[1]

Iraq and Syria. Since 1963 Iraq and Syria have been ruled by national branches of the same party, the Ba'ath or Arab Renaissance party. Founded after World War II by two French-educated schoolteachers from Syria, Michel Aflaq (Greek Orthodox) and Salah Bitar (Sunni Muslim), it took as its mission capturing power somewhere in the Arab world and then working for Arab and socialist unity. The irony is that in the 1960s the Ba'ath contested Nasser's Arab Socialist Union for preeminence among the region's youth, and Nasserists and Ba'athists divided the Arab world between them. The enmity between Nasserists and Ba'athists took a violent turn in Iraq in 1959, but it was eclipsed by the rivalry that developed between Ba'athist Syria and Iraq after 1968. It is hard for the outsider to discern any profound doctrinal differences between the two regimes, and one suspects that older geopolitical rivalries between two states sharing the Euphrates Basin may have as much to do with the enmity as anything else.

The structures of the two regimes are rather similar. Although in both countries civilians built the party (Aflaq and Bitar in Syria and the Shi'ite civil servant Fu'ad Rikabi in Iraq), they were tempted to recruit supporters among the officers' corps and seek power by means of coup d'état rather than the ballot. Unlike the Neo-Destour, which fought openly for Tunisian independence, the Ba'ath won power through stealth. Its popular base of support in both Syria and Iraq has always been narrow. In Iraq around 1980 the Ba'ath had only 25,000 full members, although there were 1.5 million "supporters" (Helms 1984, 87). Hinnebusch (1979, 21) put party membership in Syria at 100,000 in the mid-1970s. The Ba'ath has always had a Leninist predilection for a vanguard rather than a mass-based party.

The military allies of the Ba'ath have tended to take it over and marginalize it much as Boumedienne did the FLN in Algeria after 1965. In Iraq there is the Revolutionary Command Council (RCC), which groups the major military figures of the regime and, like Algeria's CNRA, is the real locus of decisionmaking. Alongside it is the Ba'ath Regional Command (the Iraqi branch of the Ba'ath), whose membership is quite similar to that of the RCC. Finally there is the National Command, supposedly the heart of the pan-Arab organization, of which Michel Aflaq (d. 1989), at odds with his native Syria, was the titular head. The National Command has no power at all.

The structures of the Syrian Ba'ath do not greatly differ from those of Iraq prior to 1980 and the outbreak of war with Iran. The military retains effective power but uses the Ba'ath party to legitimize its preeminence. In February 1971 Hafiz al-Assad, a senior air force officer and a member of the Ba'ath since his youth, was reappointed to the presidency by a body called the People's Council. The council had itself been appointed by the Ba'ath Regional Command and included 173 Ba'athis, 40 Nasserists, and 8 Communists. Assad clearly wanted to portray himself as president of *all* Syrians.

Nonetheless, the Syrian Ba'ath party has remained well organized and pervasive; it is not a paper organization like the Sudanese Socialist Union. Sadowski probably had it right in this assessment (1985, 3): "Twenty-two years in power have changed the Ba'ath from a revolutionary movement into a virtual appendage of the state. But this transformation did not destroy the party's influence. Along with the army and the bureaucracy, it remains one of the foundations of the Assad regime."

Both Iraqi and Syrian politico-military elites tend to be drawn from regional and sectarian minorities. In Syria, Assad, many of his closest associates, and a number of those upon whom he trampled before and since seizing power in 1970 have been drawn from the Alawite religious sect, an offshoot of Shi'ism, and from the poor hinterland of the Latakia region. As Hinnebusch noted (1979, 17), "The Ba'ath recruited from all those who were outside the system of connections, patronage or kin on which the old regime was built: the educated sons of peasants, the minorities, the rural lower middle class, the 'black sheep' from lesser branches of great families." The wearing of the Ba'athi label and the espousal of Ba'athi socialism has not been enough to persuade many (mostly Sunni) Syrians that Assad's regime is other than a clan of power-hungry Shi'ites masquerading as socialists.

Still, Assad has reached out to Sunnis, especially in the urban business class. Since the Syrian armed forces entered the Lebanese civil war in 1976, Syrian involvement in Lebanese affairs has generated a lucrative flow of legal and illegal cross-border trade in which the supporters of the regime, Sunni and Shi'ite alike, have claimed a share. Syria's participation in Operation Desert Storm against Iraq in 1991 won it financial support from Saudi Arabia once the Iraqi occupation of Kuwait was ended. The Syrian economy has, as a result, grown significantly, allowing Assad to erect a fairly big tent under which to gather a broad coalition of public and private, civilian and military, and Sunni and Alawite economic interests.

The end of the cold war and the withering of Soviet/Russian support for its Ba'athi clients in Syria and Iraq produced different responses in the two regimes. Assad exploited Syria's crucial role in the peace process between Israel and its Arab neighbors, knowing that its loss of a great-power patron did not deprive it of all leverage vis-à-vis the United States. Allying itself with the UN-sponsored force to drive Iraq from Kuwait was a calculated risk (not one very popular among Syrians or most other Arabs) but one that paid off handsomely. In the subsequent peace negotiations Syria has been a stubborn but responsible negotiator. Assad has demonstrated to the Syrians and to the region as a whole that he is still a player, courted and visited by foreign ministers and heads of state. As a consequence he has been able to proceed with cautious economic liberalization (Heydemann 1992) while blocking any meaningful political liberalization.

The Ba'ath came briefly to power in Iraq in the winter of 1963, on the shoulders of the military, and was moved out by a "palace" coup led by 'Abd al-Salam 'Arif, a Nasserist of sorts, who sought close relations with Egypt. An agreement with Egypt of May 1964 provided for a loose form of union between the two countries and for the setting up in Iraq of the Arab Socialist Union–Iraqi Region. Egypt had temporarily won Iraq from the Ba'ath. In terms of domestic policy, however, there was little to choose between Nasserists and Ba'athists. 'Arif's nationalization of over thirty industrial firms in May 1964 would have fit easily into a Ba'athi program, as would all other aspects of his state-led growth (see Gotheil 1981; Penrose and Penrose 1978; Springborg 1981).

The June War of 1967, in which the Iraqi armed forces played no significant role, may have undermined whatever legitimacy the 'Arif regime still enjoyed. In July 1968 the Ba'ath came to power once again through a military coup. Iraq's new president was Gen. Ahmad Hassan al-Bakr, but the real power of the regime lay with the prime minister, Saddam Hussein, a Ba'athi militant since his student days and a hardened veteran of the nation's internal police. Few Middle Eastern leaders have ever had as much experience with "dirty tricks" as Saddam Hussein.

Both Saddam and al-Bakr, along with several other stalwarts of the new regime, were from central Iraq, especially the provincial town of Takrit. Iraq's new masters were bound by shared blood, their home region, and the fact that they were Arab Sunni Muslims. The Takriti clan in Iraq has become the functional equivalent of the Alawite clan in Syria. There has been bloodletting among Takritis but not rivaling the violence wreaked on Shi'ite fundamentalists, Kurdish dissidents, and any others foolish enough to challenge Saddam. When al-Bakr died in 1982, Saddam, in the midst of the war he had launched against Iran, became president. He has nurtured a cult of his own personality that is unparalleled in the Middle East.

His state, like Assad's, rests on the pillars of the armed forces, the police, the bureaucracy, the party, and his clan. Iraq's ideology has no more teeth in it than Tunisia's. Batatu has dismissed the 1968 Ba'ath party constitution as formulating "a mild form of middle-class socialism." It tries to combine acknowledgment of Islam and pan-Arabism with the ideals of social justice, the end of exploitation, the right to use private property subject to state regulation, and "a guided national economy based on the cooperation of the public and private sectors" (1978, 1084). Like Syria's, the Iraqi regime has redistributed income, promoted growth, spread literacy, and for a time improved the economic lot of its citizens.

Saddam Hussein gradually transformed Iraq into a police state of unparalleled proportions in the Arab world. After eliminating all real enemies inside Iraq, he had to rule by terror and the systematic seeding of suspicion and fear among all Iraqis. As

noted in Chapter 7, as much as a quarter of the Iraqi workforce may have been associated with spying and intelligence gathering for the regime. Neighbors informed on
neighbors, children on parents, classmates on classmates, so that civil society was at-
omized and rendered mute (al-Khalil 1989).

The eight years of war with Iran (1980–1988) only deepened the culture of repression and fear. They also witnessed the subordination of all economic activity to
the war effort. Despite its petroleum exports, Iraq contracted something like US$80
billion in foreign debt during the 1980s, most of it owed the Kuwaitis and Saudis,
whom Saddam Hussein had no intention of repaying. When hostilities with Iran
came to a close, he proclaimed that Iraq was liberalizing its economy, privatizing
some of its public enterprises (sold, of course, to his friends), and opening the economy to foreign investment.

Saddam had expected in particular that Kuwait and Saudi Arabia would provide
much of that investment, all the while forgiving Iraqi debts. The investment did not
materialize, and the issue of the debt was not resolved. It was, in part, for these reasons that he invaded Kuwait in the summer of 1990, perhaps with the intention of
proceeding on to Saudi Arabia. Also, the invasion was Saddam's response to the end
of the cold war. His reaction to the loss of his Soviet backers was to proclaim his intention of leading an Arab crusade against Israel while he and the rest of the Arabs
had the arms and technology to do so. Time, he argued, was not on the side of the
Arabs in a unipolar world. No other Arab state openly shared his analysis, and Kuwait
and Saudi Arabia seemed more concerned about recovering some of the money they
had "lent" to Iraq. Saddam meanwhile was trying to demobilize some of the million
men under arms in Iraq and absorb them into a depressed civilian economy crying
out for new investment. Seizing Kuwait would, at a minimum, bring its large oil reserves, its access to the Persian Gulf, and its infrastructure under his control.

It is not our intention here to revisit Operation Desert Storm and the crisis surrounding it. Let us note simply that Iraq's infrastructure was shattered, its military
capabilities greatly reduced, the Kurds placed under a kind of UN trusteeship, and
the southern part of the country beaten into submission by Saddam's Republican
Guard after an aborted Shi'ite insurrection. What we want to stress is that more than
a decade of war has transformed the Iraqi state and economy into something for
which we have no ready labels. We simply do not know how the economy functions
in a country the northern, Kurdish fifth of which escapes the control of the central
authorities entirely and the southern, Shi'ite third of which is treated as enemy territory. As in the Sudan and, to a lesser extent, Algeria, there is no longer a unified national economy or an administration present and functioning in all parts of the
country. Because of international sanctions imposed as a result of its occupation of
Kuwait, Iraq cannot market its oil. The regime presumably lives off of contraband
and billions of dollars stashed away before the invasion in foreign bank accounts.
Again like the isolated regimes of the Sudan and Algeria, Saddam's regime hunkers
down in the central, Sunni third of the country, playing upon Sunni Arab fears of
Kurdish or Shi'ite domination were Saddam to be overthrown. If those fears are insufficient to exact obedience, repression and terror are ready at hand.

South Yemen. The marxist experiment in South Yemen to which we have already alluded found its unlikely home in the British Protectorate of Aden. South Yemen, socially and ecologically an extension of the North Yemeni highlands, receives less rainfall and thus has only limited agricultural potential. Traditionally it survived on maritime trade. Its remote, arid valleys were populated by highly stratified tribal lineages dominated by a religious notability, the sayyids, putatively descended from the Prophet (Bujra 1971). The sayyids dominated trade and helped carry Islam to the Far East (e.g., Malaysia, Indonesia). In this peculiar society the British established one of the world's major ports, Aden, servicing the British fleet and shipping in transit to India and beyond. With the opening of the Suez Canal in the last third of the nineteenth century, the port of Aden became a vital link in Red Sea maritime traffic. It was made a crown colony, and its hinterland was put under a British protectorate.

In the port a modern workforce developed consisting of dockers, maintenance personnel, clerks, customs officials, suppliers, traders, bureaucrats, schoolteachers, and the like. Many were drawn from the tribal interior and, like many other Middle Eastern peoples, as individuals struck an indeterminate balance between their status in the modern world and their deeply rooted identity in blood-tribal and religious networks. Throughout the 1960s, while the rest of the Arab world consolidated its independence and while the civil war wore on in neighboring North Yemen, nationalist agitation in the port of Aden grew in strength. Abdullah al-Asnag, a labor leader, founded the People's Socialist party, which in turn was part of the National Liberation Front (NLF), to spearhead the movement. The NLF in 1968 took over the government of South Yemen from the departing British. With independence, the NLF adjusted its internal alliances. The organized labor wing and especially Asnag, its moderate leader, lost out to a group of intellectuals and a rural constituency of poor tribal peasants who had long chafed under the dominance of the sayyid class. Something of a Maoist scenario was enacted: revolutionary intellectuals allied with oppressed peasants surrounded and captured the city.

The NLF was an explicitly mobilizational party seeking to activate the working class, which included women, students, and soldiers. It was also the supreme authority in the land, eclipsing the government and the Supreme People's Council as the locus of decisionmaking. The NLF can be conceived of as a vanguard party, penetrating all sectors of society through mass organizations set up along familiar functional lines: peasants, workers, soldiers, students, women. On paper there would be little to distinguish the NLF from the Ba'ath, but it would seem that its effective role in running the state and the level of indoctrination of its cadres clearly set it apart from all other Arab revolutionary parties.

From the mid-1970s on, predictable cleavages between moderate and radical wings of the NLF were exacerbated by the country's economic crisis. In the early years of the decade, the regime had backed a liberation front in Dhofar province, part of the Sultanate of Oman, in the hope of spreading and consolidating the revolution. The front was eventually subdued, however, through a combination of Jordanian, Iranian, and Pakistani military support to the Omani sultan and the largesse of a Saudi Arabia awash in foreign exchange after the surge in international oil prices in 1973.

The PDRY was in desperate economic shape in the mid-1970s. It had lost business through the closing of the Suez Canal after the June War and also had to pay much higher prices for its petroleum imports. Saudi Arabia was willing to bail the PDRY out of its difficulties in exchange for the abandonment of the Dhofar Liberation Front and some move away from the regime's espousal of Marxism-Leninism. The chairman of the Presidential Council, Salim Robaya 'Ali, was sympathetic to the Saudi overtures, while 'Abd al-Fattah Ismail, secretary general of the NLF (renamed the Yemen Socialist party [YSP] in 1978), was opposed.

Robaya 'Ali prevailed for a time; the regime became regionally well-mannered, although it hosted a large Soviet military presence and maintained close relations with the revolutionary regime in Ethiopia and the most radical factions of the PLO. But the conflict between socialist radicals and moderates had not been definitively resolved. Moreover, when once again it burst forth, it was clear that older forms of tribal loyalty contributed to what appeared to be purely ideological or strategic disputes.

For a time, when 'Abd al-Fattah Ismail replaced Robaya 'Ali as president, the radicals appeared dominant, but in 1980 he in turn was replaced by the moderate 'Ali Nasr Muhammed, who became both president and secretary general of the YSP. Ismail went into exile in Moscow, but his supporters put increasing pressure upon the regime for his return. Curiously, the Soviet Union was not eager to have Ismail back in the PDRY, devoted marxist though he was. The USSR cautioned 'Ali Nasr against allowing him to return, but in February 1985, yielding to internal pressure, 'Ali Nasr did so anyway. Over the next year Ismail mobilized his supporters to take over key positions in the party's politburo. It was simply a question of time before that politburo would calmly depose and dispose of 'Ali Nasr. Against this creeping coup d'état, 'Ali Nasr launched a preemptive coup in January 1986. He seemed to lack the heart to fight his opponents to the end, and as armed conflict engulfed the city of Aden he fled to his tribal homeland at Abyan and then into exile. Ismail and the hard-liners were back in power.

The end of the cold war spelled the end of any viable marxist regime in South Yemen. As we have seen it also spelled economic crisis such that unity with the North appeared to be the only way for the South to survive economically, no matter what ideological and political concessions its leaders would be forced to make. Despite the relatively good deal al-Baidh ultimately obtained in terms of the division of ministerial and governmental positions, the 1993 elections indicated that the YSP itself would remain a weak and beleaguered party in the union. Al-Baidh in essence withdrew from the union, and in the ensuing civil war the YSP and the South as a whole were crushed by the armies of 'Ali 'Abdullah Salih.

Libya. In 1969, then-Captain Mu'ammar Qaddhafi overthrew the Libyan monarchy and proclaimed an Arab republic faithfully modeled on that of Nasserist Egypt. Within a year Nasser had died and Qaddhafi was left to deal with an Egypt under Sadat that was rapidly opening its economy to foreign investment and seeking rapprochement with the West. After a few quixotic attempts at full union with Egypt, Qaddhafi went his own peculiar way. In 1977 he introduced what he called the Jamahiria, or "mass state," the intent of which was to abolish all intermediaries between the people, or masses, and their leaders. There were to be no political parties or mass organizations, which would only produce new oligarchs. All agencies, enterprises, and places of work were to be run by the employees themselves, through revolutionary people's councils, and formal administrative hierarchies were to be dismantled or at least closely supervised by these councils. Simultaneously, the mass state sought to terminate wage payment for work, nationalize retail trade, and end all rents—all this in the name of the eradication of exploitation.

The blueprint was breathtaking, but its implementation has not been visible. Key bureaucracies built around the oil and banking sectors seem little affected by massism, and there is no evidence that the armed forces have been taken over by the revolutionary committees. In June 1986, after the U.S. air strike against Libya, Qaddhafi in typical fashion unilaterally (that is, without consulting the revolutionary committee movement in whose name he spoke) resurrected the Revolutionary Command Council, including four officers who had participated in the 1969 coup d'état against King Idris.

The idea of the mass state seems vacuous when it is recalled that, like Saudi Arabia's and Kuwait's, 40% of Libya's workforce is foreign, as is 50% of its managerial and professional personnel. Foreigners cannot be members of revolutionary committees, and it is inconceivable that they are not paid wages. Libya in the final analysis is simply another rentier state with an idiosyncratic and autocratic leader who confuses theatrics with institution building. His staging is for the benefit of the Libyans, but without oil rents and worker migrants the show would end. We suspect that the Libyan "model" will have little appeal elsewhere.

The PLO. A brief discussion of a possible and future Palestinian state finds its logical place here in that since 1967 the Palestine Liberation Organization and its major constituent al-Fatah have followed an ideological trajectory similar to that of the radical socialist republics. In the wake of the June War of 1967 and the Israeli occupation of Gaza, the West Bank, the Golan Heights, and East Jerusalem, the PLO, led by Yasser 'Arafat, emerged as an armed movement to resist the occupation. At that time its ideology was leftist and secular and called for the "liberation" of all of Palestine, including Israel in its pre-1967 borders, and the establishment of a democratic, secular, socialist Palestine in which peoples of all faiths could reside.

Over time this vision and the organization itself were buffeted by the same forces as other regimes and movements in the region. Internally, throughout the 1970s and 1980s, the voice of political Islam grew stronger and was embodied in HAMAS (the Arabic acronym for the Islamic Resistance Movement), an organization that was initially encouraged by the Israelis as a counterweight to the PLO but soon developed a life of its own. HAMAS had no use for socialism or secular cohabitation in Palestine and resisted any compromise with the Israelis.

At the same time the Soviet Union became a less reliable and, because of its occupation of Afghanistan, less desirable friend of the PLO. Thus, the PLO and al-Fatah drifted ideologically toward more nationalist and proto-Islamic positions and tactically toward a more accommodationist position vis-à-vis the increasingly dominant United States and its client, Israel. In 1989, 'Arafat and the PLO accepted the existence of Israel and declared their readiness to live in peace with Israel on the basis of UN Resolution 242, calling for Israeli withdrawal from the occupied territories. It was thus an extremely misguided reversion to older rhetorical and political stances when in 1990 'Arafat and the PLO blessed Saddam Hussein's occupation of Kuwait and his blustery threats against Israel. Having sided with the loser and alienated Saudi Arabia, the PLO and 'Arafat had to pay dearly.

When the formal peace talks among Israel, Jordan, Syria, and the Palestinians, launched in Madrid under the joint auspices of the United States and Russia, failed to produce significant results, Israelis and Palestinians met secretly in Oslo, Norway, to iron out the details of what became the Declaration of Principles (DOP) and the historic handshake of Prime Minister Yitzhak Rabin and Chairman 'Arafat at the White House in September 1993. The DOP called for a transition period and direct negotiations toward a final settlement. During the transition Israel would initially withdraw from the town of Jericho in the West Bank and from the Gaza Strip. Further withdrawals would take place so that elections could be held in both Gaza and the West Bank.

The scheduling of those elections is hostage to the sputtering peace talks, but when and if they are held they will constitute the first step toward the establishment of a sovereign Palestinian entity lodged between Jordan and Israel. There is much that can go wrong: determining the status of Israeli settlers and that of Jerusalem could present insurmountable obstacles. But if they are overcome, the Palestinian state that will emerge will be a far cry from its origins in 1967. It is likely, on the basis of polls in the mid-1990s, that al-Fatah would win about half of Palestinian votes in any elections, while HAMAS could count on no more than 13%. A Fatah-dominated government would have to make compromises with other, mainly Islamic, partners. It would have to substitute for older goals of liberation and romantic violence the practical necessities of facilitating trade, manufacturing, tourism—in short, private and foreign investment. Many Palestinians will feel that history has robbed them of their rights, but that sense of injustice will only be contained if the new state can help make their lives more prosperous and the prospects for their children acceptable.

The important point here is that the Palestinians may be ready for a move toward democratic practice far more genuine than anything seen among their Arab neighbors. The long years of the *intifada* prior to 1991 and its reinforcing of Palestinian civil society, the distance of its leaders-in-exile, and the high levels of literacy and political awareness among its population have given the Palestinians of the occupied territories the sense of self and the practical experience to move beyond the tired paternalistic authoritarianism of other Arab regimes—a paternalism, be it noted, shared all too much by Yasser 'Arafat. It is more than a straw in the wind that the figures cited above on relative party strength were drawn from polls conducted regularly by the Centre for Palestine Research and Studies. Few if any Arab countries dare ask their citizens these kinds of questions.

LIBERAL MONARCHIES

The kings, princes, and sheykhs of the Middle East have fostered very different polities from those of the socialist republics. The purposeful state, bent on development and military might, its citizenry tightly organized, mobilized, and, above all, unified, has not characterized the monarchical systems of the region. Of course, it has not even characterized the socialist republics themselves, which, more often than not, have failed to achieve unity or development.

The distinction we wish to make is subtle and not always apparent from the written record. The shahs of Iran, father and son, were modernizers and little tolerant of ethnic and sectarian cleavages in their society. As did Atatürk, they dealt with these cleavages by force. King Muhammed V and Crown Prince Hassan of Morocco likewise dealt ruthlessly with Berber dissidence in 1959. Monarchs seem as concerned with integration as republican presidents. They have also espoused the cause of economic development and have marshaled state resources and large technocracies to pursue them. All have paid lip service to an even distribution of national wealth. Most, in function of their own national resources, have sought military credibility; the last shah was obsessed by that goal.

What, then, makes the monarchs different? In our view there are two main factors. First, all claim some degree of divine right to rule. Even King Hussein of Jordan, a descendant of the Prophet, can invoke his blood as a qualification to rule. The shah claimed that he spoke to God and that the Pahlavi dynasty had a divine mission to rule Iran. The king of Morocco uses the Koranic title Commander of the Faithful. King Fu'ad, father of Egypt's last monarch, Farouk, had tried in the 1930s to lay claim to the caliphate, which had fallen victim to Atatürk's militant secularism. The point is that the monarchs do not rest their legitimacy on the expression of popular will or sovereignty. They are responsible not to the people but to God. The distinction may be somewhat artificial in that few Middle Eastern leaders, republican or monarchical, have ever enjoyed much legitimacy, but the rival sets of symbols evoke powerful emotions.

The second factor has to do with the handling of diversity and pluralism. Here the monarchical game is subtle and close to hypocritical. Monarchs speak in terms of the nation and decry the fractious elements in society that impede national unity, but they do not deny these elements legitimacy so long as they behave according to the rules of the game as the monarchy defines them. What the monarchs want is a plethora of interests, tribal, ethnic, professional, class-based, and partisan, whose competition for public patronage they can arbitrate. None of these elements can be allowed to become too powerful or wealthy, and the monarch will police and repress or entice and divide factions that are becoming too entrenched. The monarch's rule is to divide, chastise, and regulate but not to humiliate or alienate important factions. The shah in the 1970s, fat with oil revenues, thought that he could violate this rule.

The rhetoric of this game is paternalistic; kings talk of themselves as fathers to their societies or, as King Hassan has described himself, as a shepherd to a flock of occasionally errant sheep. They suggest that if all behaved selflessly and for the national good, all would be better off, but, alas, children will be children, and kings must settle their petty squabbles. They are thus *above* all factions and party to none, especially in that they answer to God alone.

But they must have the factions and the squabbles. It is their role of arbiter and supervisor of the distribution of patronage and state resources that makes kings relevant to the political game. They must propagate the belief that were they ever to disappear, the system would disintegrate into a chaotic war among all the petty contenders for spoils. Their populations have not always believed in their indispensability, and monarchies have been overthrown with some regularity: King Farouk of Egypt in 1952, King Faisal of Iraq in 1958, the imam of Yemen in 1962, King Idris of Libya in 1969, and the shah of Iran in 1979. The first four fell to military coups that may or may not have expressed popular sentiment; only the shah was the victim of direct popular action.

The monarchy of independent Morocco emerged out of the French protectorate (1912–1956). The nationalist Independence party had used King Muhammed V as the symbol of the nationalist struggle, but with independence the king took his distance from the party, abetted its scission, from which the National Union of Popular Forces emerged, in 1959, and encouraged the formation of rival parties. In other words, he deliberately increased the number of factions and political clans in the system, the better to assert his role as arbiter. Shortly after independence, Berber dissident movements in the Middle Atlas and Rif Mountains elicited a sharp military response, but at the same time Mohammed V encouraged the formation of a Berber party, the Popular Movement. (His wife, the mother of King Hassan, is a Middle Atlas Berber.)

Mohammed V died in 1961 and was succeeded by his son, Hassan II, whom he had put in direct control of the royal armed forces. Hassan never relinquished his control over the military, although he was nearly overthrown by it twice, in 1971 and in 1972. He assiduously followed the divide-and-rule tactics of his father, weakening parties, trade unions, and regional interests but never destroying them or pushing them out of the political arena. Even the Moroccan Communist party, dissolved a few years after independence, was allowed to reestablish itself legally in the mid-1970s. King Hassan puts himself forward as the final protector of all interests—the parties against military intervention; the military against civilian bungling, the Berbers against the Arabs, and the Jews against the Muslims.

Monarchs position themselves above the contending forces in the political arena in a way that makes it easier for them than for the leaders of the socialist republics to allow contested elections and some modicum of democratic practice. The monarch can portray himself as a disinterested but authoritative arbiter of the contending interests whose sole concern is the well-being of his people. Hassan II is no exception, and since the mid-1970s multiparty elections, neither free nor fair, have taken place on a fairly regular basis. Given an improving economy and twenty-five years of political tranquility, Hassan II, while not loved by all, has convinced most Moroccans that the monarchy is vital to the country's stability.

Reza Khan, the founder of the Pahlavi dynasty, was, it will be recalled, inclined to follow Atatürk's path and model his state after Turkey's republic. Although he was persuaded to adopt a monarchical form of rule, much of his reign was characterized by the crushing of all regional, tribal, and ethnic dissidence and the building of a centralized state and a powerful military. Although Reza Khan built a powerful state, he left a place in its political arena for the weakened tribal leaders, for regional interests, and for the clergy. As in Morocco, as long as these groups played by the rules laid down by the shah, they could represent their interests legitimately.

The shah's son, Mohammed Reza Pahlavi, even after surviving his confrontation with the nationalist prime minister, Mohammed Mossadegh, in 1953, never managed the political game with the same forcefulness and assurance as his father. His efforts to fabricate political parties (see Chapter 12) and to exclude other parties of the Mossadegh era or before, such as the Tudeh and the National Front, merely produced a kind of vacuum that could be filled only by clandestine political groupings, either radical Islamic or radical secularist, and the notorious internal police, the Iranian Security and Intelligence Organization (SAVAK). Rather than dealing with formally constituted parties and interest groups as the king did in Morocco, the shah tried to manipulate large categories of the population—the secular intelligentsia, the clergy, the bazaar or traditional retailing bourgeoisie, a new state-dependent private entrepreneurial bourgeoisie, organized labor, and civil servants. Heady with the massive oil earnings accruing to the state treasury in the 1970s, the shah neglected many of these constituencies; he found himself in the late 1970s with only two sources of support, the armed forces and the United States, and a large source of indifference, the peasantry. All other constituencies had turned against him. He had lost his role as the accepted, indeed indispensable, arbiter of the political game.

Other monarchs also profit from cleavage and enhance their relevance to the functioning of state power by perpetuating it. King Hussein bestrides the cleavage between a majoritarian, highly educated Palestinian population and a largely Bedouin minority that dominates the Jordanian armed forces and key government positions. The Bedouin look to King Hussein to protect their privileged position and to "contain" the Palestinian intelligentsia and entrepreneurial bourgeoisie. Jordan is eloquent testimony to the fact that the cleavages that allow monarchs to survive are precisely those that can and do bring them down.

It should not be surprising, then, that it was King Hussein who took the risk of holding parliamentary elections in 1989 and 1993, the latter following the Declaration of Principles establishing peace between the Palestinians and Israelis. Both elections were free, although the electoral system used in 1993 favored individual candidates at the expense of parties, especially the Muslim Brotherhood. The Islamic vote was strong but not dominant in both elections, and many Palestinian voters abstained. Nonetheless, the elections allowed King Hussein to portray himself as above all parties and the safeguard of national integrity. His being a descendant of the Prophet helped.

Similarly, the Sabah ruling family of Kuwait finds itself astride major cleavages. There is a Shi'ite minority that is sometimes seen as a fifth column for Iraqi or Iranian interests, but basically the fault line is unidimensional. Over 40% of the population is non-Kuwaiti, as is a majority of the workforce (see Chapter 15). The economy and the administration are thus dependent upon these more or less long-term worker-migrants. The Sabah family cannot claim to speak for or represent the foreign workers, but it can and does manage relations between them and the native Kuwaiti population. A large component of the nonnative workforce was once Palestinian, but because the PLO backed Iraq's occupation of Kuwait and because some Palestinians were accused of collaborating with the Iraqi forces of occupation, several hundred thousand Palestinians were expelled from Kuwait and sent primarily to Jordan.

Kuwait first introduced a parliament, in which the country's wealthy merchants were represented, in the 1930s (see Crystal 1990). However, once the Kuwaiti state and the Sabah family had control of the country's increasing petroleum rents after World War II, the need for merchant support dwindled. The parliament, as in Jordan, led a precarious existence and was frequently dismissed by the sovereign. The rescue of Kuwait from Iraqi annexation and occupation by Operation Desert Storm came at a price; both domestic constituents and external backers pressured the Sabahs to take steps to reestablish democracy. In October 1992 elections for the National Assembly were held in which only about 70,000 male Kuwaitis of proven Kuwaiti ancestry, out of some 625,000 native Kuwaitis, could vote (Gause 1994:6, 188–189). Nonetheless, Kuwait had rejoined the ranks of the liberal monarchies.

The Kingdom of Saudi Arabia cannot claim similar status. It has been run since the 1920s by and largely for the sprawling royal family, descendants all of the founding patriarch, King 'Abd al'Aziz Al Saud, who now number in the thousands. The incorporation of commoners into the political establishment comes through cooptation, often on the basis of technical merit and competence but not as the result of electoral victories.

The Saudi monarchy does resemble the others in that it straddles social and regional cleavages within the country. These include the Shi'ite minority in the east of the country and, more important, the Najd, from which the royal family comes, and the Hijaz, which contains the holy cities of Mecca and Medina and is the home of Saudi Arabia's traditional trading and merchant families. Finally, Saudi Arabia, as the paradigmatic oil rentier state, has for decades relied upon the a large pool of migrant labor, both skilled and unskilled. The bulk of the latter had traditionally come from Yemen, but because North Yemen leaned toward Iraq when it occupied Kuwait the Saudis expelled some 700,000 Yemenis from the country. Since Operation Desert Storm there has been some return flow of Yemeni workers to Saudi Arabia, but there has also been an influx of Pakistanis, Indians, Filipinos, Egyptians, and others (see Gause 1994; Krimly 1993; Chaudhry n.d.).

Despite Saudi Arabia's crucial geopolitical significance and place in U.S. strategic thinking, the monarchy came under some pressure after Desert Storm to put on a more liberal face. It eventually did so, on August 20, 1993, when King Fahd appointed a sixty-member Consultative Council. This body was made up of non-elected representatives of prominent families, businesses, religious leaders, and the government. It was to consult and advise the sovereign but not to legislate. In this respect it conformed to the Quranic injunction that the leader of the *umma* should consult in the conduct of the affairs of state with those of experience, wealth, and wisdom. Even this modest nod toward liberalization must be placed against the monarchy's resort to conservative Islamic clergy to fend off the growing political Islamic challenge from within.

ESTABLISHED AND WOULD-BE DEMOCRACIES

There are only three countries in the Middle East that have indulged in liberal electoral politics for sustained periods of time: Israel, Lebanon, and Turkey. The Sudan had three chances, in 1956–1958, 1964–1969, and 1986–1989, while Egypt has pursued a highly controlled liberal experiment since 1976. Turkey has oscillated between freewheeling electoral politics in the 1950s and 1970s and military rule in the 1960s and early 1980s. Since 1983 another and so far successful attempt has been made to revive civilian electoral politics. Only Israel since its creation in 1948 has maintained a democratic regime, but that distinction must be qualified by its strict policing of the Arab populations it inherited in 1948. The Israelis have only recently allowed autonomous Arab parties to function in their political arena.

Turkey failed to achieve a stable party system, and in the 1970s it suffered from a series of coalition governments with interests so diverse that no coherent economic policy could be implemented. Sound economic management fell victim to the political expediency of the Justice party, the lineal descendant of the Democrat party of the 1950s and of the Republican People's party—now "radicalized" and more overtly socialist under the leadership of Bülent Ecevit than at any time under Atatürk. The military, as already noted, put an end to this situation, tried to put Turkey's economic affairs in order, and then, under carefully controlled circumstances including the banning of most parties functioning before the 1980 coup, allowed new elections to be held in 1983. Turgut Özal's Motherland party won a narrow majority, and he became prime minister.

Turkey is subject to a kind of democratizing pressure, however, that no other country in the region faces. There is a national consensus of sorts that Turkey should join the European Common Market. To do so will require not only a far-reaching restructuring of the Turkish economy but also adherence to European legal standards of liberal democracy. Rule by generals, repression of labor, and suppression of Kurdish organizations cannot be made compatible with entry into the EU.

In November 1991 the Motherland party was voted out of power and replaced by a coalition of the True Path party, the successor to the Justice party, and the Social Democratic Populist party, one of the descendants of the Republican People's party. Turkey demonstrated its ability to change party governance through the ballot box. Moreover, the True Path party went on to select Tansu Çiller as its leader and the first female prime minister of the republic. In 1994, in municipal elections, the Welfare party, a thinly disguised Islamic party (the constitution prohibits the formation of openly religious or ethnic parties), swept several cities, including Istanbul and Ankara. In future national elections it could poll a quarter to a third of the vote.

There are three points to be made with respect to Turkish democracy. First, it appears to be here to stay and may have some demonstration effect for its regional neighbors. Second, it allows for change through the ballot box; most, but not all, Turks can find a way to be represented or identify a candidate reflecting their preferences. Third, it may show how political Islam can be accommodated within a democratic system.

Lebanese democracy after independence in 1946 fascinated Western political scientists. Here was a society that the French protectorate authorities had organized along sectarian or confessional lines. Seats in parliament were distributed in a ratio of six to five between Christians and Muslims and subdivided among the several sects in both religious communities. The 1943 National Pact, elaborated by the principal leaders of the Maronite and Sunni sects, consecrated the French arrangement. Henceforth a Maronite Christian was to be president, a Sunni prime minister, and a Shi'ite president of the Chamber of Deputies. Positions in the civil service and the armed forces were likewise distributed along confessional lines.

In a manner most theorists of modernization would find reprehensible, Lebanon had quite literally enshrined religion in politics. People ran for office or voted, won jobs or lost them, and occasionally came to blows as members of specific sects. Despite the lack of separation of "church" and state, somehow the system seemed to work. The press was free, debate open and vigorous, and elections held on a regular basis (although not without tampering), and Lebanon served as a small island of political refuge and free enterprise for the rest of the region.

Yet the fragility of the confessional balance was apparent to some early on (see especially Hudson 1968). Most obvious was the fact that confessions became more rather than less rigid as offices and spoils were distributed along confessional lines. Except at the elite level there were few crosscutting alliances, although candidates did have to seek votes outside their own confessional constituencies. The point is that the meaningful units in electoral alliances were always confessional.

Second, although population growth and migration gradually transformed the Christians into a minority (see Chapter 4), they continued to control the presidency and a majority of the deputies. Camille Chamoun, who was president up to 1958, altered the constitution so that he could succeed himself, thereby triggering a brief civil war that presaged what was to happen in 1975. Chamoun was forced from the presidency and replaced by Gen. Fu'ad Chehab (a Maronite), who restored law and order and talked about deconfessionalizing Lebanon. He was unable to make much headway, as his talk of position through merit seemed to non-Christians to favor Christians, who enjoyed generally higher levels of education and training.

The fruits of Lebanon's booming merchant economy were not equally shared. The oligarchs of the economy came from all sects but were dominated by the Maronite banking elite. Yet the sharing of economic interests among the very wealthy cut across confessional lines, and, some have suggested, the oligarchs saw it as to their advantage to promote confessional conflict so that class-based politics might be avoided.

Finally, after the June War of 1967 and the conflict between King Hussein and the PLO in 1970, nearly 200,000 Palestinians, many of them armed, sought refuge in Lebanon. They were not citizens and could not vote, but because they were mainly Muslim, Lebanese Christians feared that their gradual absorption into the local arena, were that to happen, would mean the loss of any semblance of balance among confessions. It was the Maronite Christian Phalange party that precipitated the civil war in 1975 in an attempt to disarm or expel the Palestinians. In the ensuing years the Lebanese state collapsed and at least four statelets (Maronite, Druze, Shi'ite, and Palestinian) emerged, the Lebanese armed forces became only one of several militias, and confessionalism became a question not merely of voter identification but of life and death.

After fourteen years of war, the Lebanese may have lost as many as 150,000 people out of their tiny population. With Saudi Arabia and Syria as intermediaries the fighting was finally brought to a halt through a negotiated agreement known as the Ta'if Accords. These were finalized in the Saudi city of that name in 1989, and, among other things, they reaffirmed the confessional nature of politics but adjusted the Christian-Muslim ratio to fifty-fifty. The Syrian military presence in Lebanon was given an open-ended lease on life: in essence the Syrians would not leave before they wanted to and certainly not before Israel closed down its security zone and Lebanese client army in the south. All militias were to be disarmed, but in practice Hizbullah, the dominant Shi'ite militia in the south, enjoying Iranian backing, remained fully armed. It will not be disarmed until Syria no longer regards it as a useful bargaining chip in peace negotiations with Israel.

After the Ta'if Accords, in 1992, Lebanon held elections to its parliament, which many Maronites boycotted in protest of Syria's continued presence but in which candidates loyal to Hizbullah participated and did well. Unlike the situation in Turkey, it is far too soon to say that Lebanese democracy has been reestablished. It will be a generation at least before the wounds of the civil war heal, and true normalcy will come about only when both Syria and Israel terminate their military presence in the country. But even if that condition were met, the porosity of Lebanon's confessional system will always invite outside meddling. Lebanon is probably fated to exhibit entrepreneurial exuberance and political fragility.

Israel's democratic system is old and vigorous but should not be taken for granted. As in Turkey, old political coalitions such as the center-left Israel Labor party

(MAPAI), which dominated Israeli politics in the first two decades, have broken down and reassembled. Now the major cleavage in Israeli Jewish society is between secularists with some commitment to socialism and a strong welfare state and a conservative coalition increasingly characterized by an aggressive religious nationalism. Menachem Begin's Likud alliance, which dominated Israeli politics from the mid-1970s to the mid-1980s, has been home for Israelis favorable to private-sector growth, religious claims to the occupied territories, and repressive policies toward Israel's Arab minority. The bulk of Likud's following has come from Oriental and Sephardic Jews, who tend to be somewhat less educated than the dominant Ashkenazi elites and somewhat lower in the hierarchy of incomes. They have been joined in recent years by a half-million immigrants from the former Soviet Union who have had no experience with democracy, but their votes have gone more to the Labor party than to Likud. Although there are those in Likud and on the right in general who are passionately committed to the Zionist dream and Jewish retention of the occupied territories and may be prepared to sacrifice democracy for their goals, there are also new business interests that see peace and regional stability as vital to their economic future.

Ultimately, the question is, as in Lebanon, whether the system can absorb a large, possibly majority, non-Jewish population and still preserve the logic of one citizen, one vote. There are 800,000 Arab citizens of Israel, dating from 1948, and 1.3 million Palestinians in the West Bank and East Jerusalem and another 880,000 in Gaza. The 1993 general elections, which brought the Labor party, led by Yitzhak Rabin, back to power, signaled the electorate's determination to end the *intifada* and push forward the peace talks begun in Madrid. Thus, part of the answer put forth by a narrow majority of Israelis is to relinquish the West Bank and Gaza, the protests of the 150,000 Jewish settlers there notwithstanding. As for the 800,000 Arab Israeli citizens (who will soon become a million), they constitute the great gamble of the future. After nearly fifty years within the Israeli economy and polity, there is some evidence that they have become a distinct political entity, proud to be Palestinian but not ready to join a Palestinian state; willing also, if given the benefit of the doubt by Jewish Israelis, to behave as responsible citizens within an Israel at peace with the Palestinians and with its other Arab neighbors.

THE ISLAMIC REPUBLICS

There are two Islamic republics in the Middle East: the Iranian and the Sudanese. We will have more to say about both in Chapter 14, and we have already touched on the Sudanese experience above. We shall focus here on Iran since 1979 and a revolution that sent tremors throughout the region. The establishment of the Islamic republic under the guidance of the Ayatollah Khomeini merits the term "revolution" because it effected the complete dismantling of the shah's political regime, the remaking of Iran's foreign policy and alignments, and a cultural transformation. In the final analysis, however, it did not bring about a full social or economic revolution.

Years of war had fattened a class of profiteers and speculators in scarce goods, a phenomenon common to nearly all war situations, while the regime allowed many of its own to live off sinecures in the public sector and the foundations. In some cities in the mid-1990s, when the regime tried to bulldoze shantytowns, the reaction was the same as it had been under the shah—riots and violent confrontation. In addition, the public-enterprise sector, with its center of gravity in petroleum extraction, refining, and petrochemicals, remained large. There has been little talk of privatization. Much of the property and assets taken over from the Pahlavi family and those accused of collaboration with the old regime remain grouped in state-owned foundations that spin off handsome revenues for the cronies of the new power elite.

Like the socialist republics, the Islamic republic has consistently stressed unity, combining the overriding element of being Muslim with the secondary element of being Iranian. In the months following the departure of the shah, various ethnic and linguistic groups forcefully put forward claims for greater recognition in the new polity than had ever been accorded them under the shah. As Ayatollah Khomeini and the clergy consolidated their grip on the new state, mainly through the elimination of leftists and liberal moderates such as Bani Sadr and the venerable Mehdi Bazargan, these claims were denied. Revolutionary Guards were dispatched to crush Kurdish, Turkomen, and other groups agitating for a new place in the republic. When war broke out with Iraq in September 1980, this kind of subnational agitation became at once blasphemy and high treason.

Although pluralism is officially condemned, the new regime does share one characteristic with the monarchies we have examined, and that is the denial of the principle of popular sovereignty. Sovereignty is God's alone, and although in the Islamic republic the people elect their representatives, those who rule are ultimately responsible to God rather than to the people. Rulership cannot be inherited; rather, it is the duty of the council of the foremost clerics to judge and select the best-qualified leaders to the ends of protecting the believers, applying God's law, and preserving the republic. Moreover, a Constitutional Council reviews all parliamentary legislation to ensure that it conforms to the shari'a and the Iranian constitution. The principle in operation here is the "trusteeship of the jurisprudents" (*vilayet al-faqih*), whereby the elite of the clergy, on the strength of their learning, ensure that the people, in practicing Islamic democracy, do not stray from "the straight path."

The new regime has been concerned with equity issues made all the more acute by eight years of war with Iraq. It has not rolled back the shah's land reform measures, and it has invested significantly in rural infrastructure and power generation. But the majority of Iranians are urban salary or wage earners. The inflation generated by the war has lowered their standards of living dramatically. Unemployment among educated male youths is very high, and perhaps 20% of the workforce is unemployed. The combination of unemployment and inflation means that many Iranians must survive in the informal sector, often engaging in contraband trade, drugs, and smuggling. It is no small irony that pious Islamic Iran and secular socialist Algeria have in many ways become mirror images of each other.

The Ayatollah Khomeini died in June 1989 having grudgingly blessed an end to hostilities with Iraq. The heroic, romantic phase of the Islamic revolution had come to an end, and the mundane task of reconstruction and economic reform had begun. It fell to the new and uncharismatic president, 'Ali Akbar Rafsanjani, to take up this task. The incumbency of this cleric indicated the continuation of what Shaul Bakhash (1984) has dubbed Iran's "mullacracy." The man who took on the role of the revolution's spiritual guide, 'Ali Khamanei, was and is like a second head of state. The mullahs control the major institutions of the state, the parliament, the Foundation for the Disinherited, and the Revolutionary Guard. Although there is some evidence that younger Iranians have begun to lose faith or interest in the Islamic regime, it is doubtful that we shall soon see a retreat of the clergy from politics.

For someone who is male, Muslim, and loyal to the notion of an Islamic polity and reveres the memory of Ayatollah Khomeini, Iran is a vibrant, contentious, and—dare we say it?—democratic place. Iranian political cleavages are predictable and unmysterious. There are so-called radicals, both clerical and lay, who want to confront the impious West, especially the United States, spread the revolution through Lebanon and the Sudan, and one day confront Israel. If there is to be an Iranian nuclear device, it will be because of them. They partially overlap with social and economic radicals who want to tax the rich, punish the speculators, and redistribute wealth to the poor. They oppose the economic reforms so far unsuccessfully advocated by Rafsanjani.

Arrayed against them are so-called pragmatists. Some seek a more conciliatory policy toward the West in order to attract investment and promote trade. They may or may not condone the support extended by the radicals to their Shi'ite allies in Lebanon and their Sunni friends in the Sudan. They are apt to respect private property and want to encourage the private sector to invest. They are prepared to work with Western creditors, including the World Bank, to control government expenditures, reduce inflation, and deregulate the economy. Finally, there are voices, even among the clergy, who suggest that they have had their day in power, made a hash of it, and should if possible gracefully retreat to their madrasas, where they enjoy some comparative advantage.

In 1995 none of these tensions within the political establishment had been resolved, but the issues are being debated in a remarkably open way. The country has not fallen under the control of a religious police state. It is not ruled by the military. There are possibilities for a peaceful transition to a postmullacracy.

FUTURE REGIMES: SOME SPECULATIONS

The past fifteen years have put the state and political formations of the Middle East under enormous stress. The boom and bust of the regional petroleum economy, the tacit abandonment of any viable military option against Israel, the related rise of militant Islamic challengers to the incumbents, the rigors of economic stabilization and adjustment, and the exit of the Soviet Union as a major patron for several regimes in the system have challenged the credibility and viability of nearly every state. Yet the center has held. Regime change took place in Iran in 1979 and less obviously in the Sudan in 1989. Otherwise stasis has been the hallmark of the recent past.

Still, one senses a precariousness in the status quo. Incumbents and regimes are aging. King Hussein (the longest-ruling head of state alive), has been in power since 1952, King Hassan since 1961, Yasser 'Arafat since 1967 or before, Hafiz al-Assad since 1970, Mu'ammar Qaddhafi since 1969, 'Ali Abdullah Salih and Saddam Hussein since 1978, and Hosni Mubarak since 1981. Even when heads of state have changed, as in Algeria or Tunisia, the political system has not, and it is tired. Many of the incumbents have lost any sense of national purpose, any "project" (*mashru'*) with which to capture the imagination of their peoples. They offer halfhearted economic reform, which still hurts large segments of their citizenries, without offering real political opening through which grievances might be expressed. Yet civil society—the full panoply of social actors mentioned in Chapter 2—has grown in size, complexity, and voice. The Islamists have captured a significant part of it, but whether they merely reflect a high level of frustration among the citizenry as opposed to a genuine quest for an Islamic state is moot. Incumbent leaders do not want to find out which it may be.

The advent of the Islamic Republic of Iran in 1979 represented the most profound regime change of the past quarter-century, but it produced no domino effect whatsoever. Thus, it is unlikely that if, say, Algeria were to fall under the control of an Islamic, populist regime, its neighbors, as distant as Egypt, would follow suit. This is not to say that Egypt or any neighboring state would be indifferent to such a change, but its contagion effect might be limited. Most incumbent regimes have dealt with their Islamic challengers by police repression of the militants, all the while cloaking their own actions in Islamic rhetoric. They have, in this manner, sought to co-opt or neutralize what might be called the moderate Islamic center. The question is whether rhetoric and some patronage will suffice to disarm all the centrist critics. King Hussein decided in 1989 that the lesser risk was to open the political system, let the center voice its grievances, and keep it within the bounds of law by offering it participation in the electoral process. Chadli Benjadid in Algeria, in 1990 and 1991, took a similar gamble but, through poor design of the voting system, lost badly. Will either of these experiments inspire other leaders in the region?

It is, perhaps, to Turkey that we should turn. Turkey's political evolution has often presaged what has transpired in the Arab world. Turkey has, in all but name, allowed an Islamist party to participate in a democratic system that has functioned impressively since 1983. The Welfare party runs several cities and has representatives in the Grand National Assembly. It is not inconceivable that in the next national elections it could win a plurality and thus the prime ministership. Were that to happen (it is not the most likely scenario), the odds are that the elections would stand and the party would abide by the constitution and the electoral rules in place.

It would be astounding were Welfare to win more than 25% of the vote, and an outright victory could occur only because the rest of the electorate was divided among three or four other major parties. We suspect that in most countries in the region the Islamist vote would at most be 30% of *registered* voters. Where elections have been held—the Sudan in 1986, Jordan in 1989 and 1993, Algeria in 1991, Yemen in 1993, northern Iraq in 1992, Lebanon in 1992, Pakistan in 1993, and Morocco in 1994—Islamist parties did not come close to winning outright majorities.

This discussion has implied that if change is on the horizon, it may be toward greater democracy. Equally likely, however, are further turns in the authoritarian cycle. Ben 'Ali in Tunisia, Bashir and Turabi in the Sudan, a succession of leaders in Algeria, and a number of failed plots against Saddam Hussein in Iraq indicate that the old politics of coup and countercoup have not passed from the scene. Leaders who come to power by this route will preserve the discredited methods of rule of their predecessors but proclaim a new mission or the relaunching of the old. They will denounce the corruption of their predecessors and their selling out to nefarious foreign forces and, if the offenders are still alive, put them on trial for treason. Then they can turn to the economic mess they will have inherited.

NOTES

1. The Algerian saga is of immense importance to the region and the world. It deserves far more analysis than we have granted it. Those who wish to delve more deeply into its crisis may consult Leveau (1993), Kapil (1990), and Vergès (1993).

12

SOLIDARISM AND ITS ENEMIES

The integrated, cohesive citizenry about which Middle Eastern leaders have spilled oceans of ink and over which waves of rhetoric have crashed remains an impossible goal. The erosion of optimism and elite will that accompanied the long and dangerous wielding of power has been matched by the disillusionment and cynicism of citizens. Sensing that alienation, leaders have been driven to divide and rule rather than to unite, to contain rather than to mobilize, to repress rather than to inspire. The rhetoric of solidarism still prevails, but political practice has deviated sharply from the older goals. Some of the obstacles to the new society have lain in older forms of social and political insurance: clans, ethnic groups, tribes, and religious sects, units that, among other things, protect their members from the vagaries of powerful states and markets (see Migdal 1987). To see these forms as atavistic is to lose sight of their redefined roles in the new state systems of the contemporary Middle East.

Underlying but separated from them is the bedrock of Islam, which provides a set of standards by which political leadership is judged. When leaders who profess adherence to Islam fail in their statist enterprises, they are seen as exposing the *umma* to mortal danger. If they are unaware of their error, they must be removed and replaced by rightly guided leaders. But if they err knowingly, it is possible that they are the agents of satanic power. For many Muslims, Atatürk, Nasser, and Mohammed Reza Shah were all such agents.

There are, by contrast, obstacles to solidarism of quite a different order. Leaders nearly obsessed with control have emasculated the very political organizations they created to mobilize and integrate the masses. At the same time, in organizing strategic sectors of the working population they have created real occupational associations that have gained organizational and political skills and substantial bargaining power. Concomitantly, the disbursement of large state-investment budgets and the very real economic growth that has occurred in some Middle Eastern societies have transferred resources to white-collar workers, skilled trade unionists, capitalist farmers, and a few entrepreneurial groups that are now in a position to contest, cautiously, certain state policies. Endowed with resources and accumulated experience, they can now bargain directly with the state and its agents, and, as we pointed out in Chapter 2, such bargaining may be the prelude to more formal democratic processes.

Finally, had Middle Eastern leaders been able to nurture some sort of broad ideological and programmatic consensus, it might have been possible to keep all these old and new actors within the political game. But ideologies fabricated by house ideologues or, worse yet, by bureaucrats in Ministries of Culture, Information, and National Guidance have failed to penetrate strategically placed elites, let alone the people as a whole. There is, we argue, a kind of organizational and ideological vacuum in the Middle East that several sorts of actors are trying to fill. Incumbent elites with the economic and coercive might of the state at their disposal still have the upper hand, but they may lack the conviction or confidence to use it. Secular liberals are a tiny minority, but they may have some historical momentum on their side. Islamists have enthusiasm and popular symbols but (see Chapter 14) few answers to questions of governance and economic management.

SMALL GROUPS AND CLIENTELIST POLITICS

One trap we must avoid is seeing older forms of political organization and action as direct reenactments of their forebears. Tribe and tribal loyalty in the twentieth-century Middle East are qualitatively different from their seventeenth- or eighteenth-century antecedents. So too are sects, ethnic groups, families, and coteries. What has changed momentously is the degree of state and market penetration into all sectors of Middle Eastern society. Just as economic subsistence is a thing of the past, so too is political isolation. Central authorities are now able to make effective claims on ever-growing proportions of societies' wealth, but they tend to do so in arbitrary and sometimes punitive ways. Markets, having captured large producing populations, do not behave predictably. And for those who play the national political game the stakes are high, with death, torture, imprisonment, exile or, at best, forced retirement as probable outcomes. Parties and formal associations have not yet provided effective means to protect members from the new order. People retreat into or invent "security groups" as much to protect themselves as to promote their interests. One may find in a small band of friends or members of one's tribe, ethnic group, home region, or religious sect a framework for mutual support, accountability, shared obligations, or plain psychological reassurance that no formal organization can offer. Putnam (1993) has termed these small-group resources "social capital."

The more people adhere to these unrecognized, loosely organized forms of political and social action, the more the formal associations and political parties lose their cohesion and viability. Leaders have so far reacted in one or both of two ways: beating the political fragments into submission and, abandoning solidarism, trying to manipulate them through state patronage. A third way, democratic pluralism, as we have seen in the previous chapter, has been tried by very few.

What Bill and Springborg (1994, 84–135) have called the genes of Middle East politics are congeries of small and nonexclusive units that have varying degrees of cohesion and durability. Throughout the area we find political and economic actors associating with small clusters of cronies of similar status. The members of these groups help each other along in their careers, for it is likely that at any particular time some will be doing better than others and can promote the interests of the less fortunate. People who are from the same village or region or perhaps from the same university class or who are of common descent or related through marriage may come together in such groups. Whether it is a question of Iran's *dawreh*s (circles) or Egypt's *shilla*s, cronyism is an important form of political and economic insurance.

One often hears of clans in Middle Eastern politics. Sometimes we find fairly persistent coteries at the elite level, such as the Oujda Group in Algeria, but these groupings are fragile, and power struggles within them can be brutal. Despite the fact that a member of the Oujda Group, Chadli Benjadid, succeeded Boumedienne to the presidency, most of its other stalwarts have disappeared from the scene. Again, several members of Egypt's Revolutionary Command Council (RCC), which seized power in 1952, were classmates in the staff college in the late 1930s and served together in various postings and in the 1948 war with Israel. Over the years after 1952, members dropped away in disgrace, exile, or early retirement.

We hear also of the Takriti clan in Iraq and the Alawi clan in Syria. Unlike the two examples mentioned above, these clans combine cronyism with common regional and sectarian loyalties. Moreover, both Hafiz al-Assad and Saddam Hussein have to some extent surrounded themselves with confidants from their own lineages. One should not doubt for a minute that, were there to be a violent change in governing elites in Iraq or Syria, the new incumbents would ferret out all real or suspected members of the Takriti and Alawi clans; that realization makes elite clans cling to power all the more tenaciously, frequently at the expense of their rationalist and egalitarian ideals.

Yet another manifestation of small-group genes lies in pervasive patron-client networks. Unlike clusters of cronies, clientelistic groupings bring together people of very different status and power. The patron is the power wielder, and his clients need his protection. In turn they render him a number of services that enhance his power and hence his ability to act as their protector. The classic example in the Middle East and elsewhere is the large landowner. He monopolizes in a given locale the most precious fixed asset, land. He controls access to it, and his clients are his tenants, laborers, and sharecroppers. He protects them physically, supplies them agricultural inputs and monetary credit, assists them if they fall ill, and helps them pay for extraordinary events such as marriages and funerals. The clients in turn produce for him, supply him free labor for a host of menial tasks, vote for him if elections are an issue, and fight for him if he is attacked by outsiders. In this classic example the patron controls what are called "first-order resources"—land and money. As long as he maintains his local monopoly, his clients will have little choice but to seek his protection. Migration may be an option, but in some countries, such as Iraq in the interwar years, peasants with outstanding debts could not legally migrate. Peasants are chronically in debt. Agrarian reform has everywhere eroded the power of the classic rural patron.

Today, with the growth of large bureaucratic states that invade and regulate all aspects of one's life, the patron is more likely to be a broker. Although he may continue to control first-order resources, his real services to his clients will come through his ability to deliver public goods or to protect his clients against various forms of state action. In this sense he brokers access to state resources. He may help procure a birth certificate, a work permit, a commercial license, a passport, or any of the other vital pieces of paper that the modern state routinely requires but does not routinely deliver. He may help place a son in secondary school or the university, find a migrant a job in a public agency or factory, get the courts to drop charges for a misdemeanor, or swing a loan through the agricultural credit bank. What the patron receives in return is somewhat amorphous. In the few systems in which votes count he will surely receive votes, but his relative weight in the political system may well hinge on his ability to demonstrate the size and cohesion of his group of clients. If he is perceived as being able to "deliver" his clients, even in elections where official candidates receive 99.9% of the votes, or to keep them out of street demonstrations, strikes, or land seizures, the higher authorities will make sure that public resources sufficient to maintain his clientele are put at his disposal.

As the socialist and solidarist élan of several of the radical republics began to wane, the large, all-encompassing parties that they set up became simple conduits for the distribution of state patronage. Party cadres, rather than educating, indoctrinating, and mobilizing the populations with which they dealt, fell into the role of broker, establishing their reputations on their ability to deliver state resources to their clients. Intended to be members of the vanguard, they became ward heelers. The party thus became an instrument in the slow drift of the leadership into divide-and-rule politics; the cadres were there not to encourage the masses to do something but to reward them for doing nothing. Putting as kind a light on this as possible, some observers have referred to this arrangement as a "social pact or contract."

THE FAILURE OF PARTIES

There has been an abundance of political parties, but, with the exceptions noted in the previous chapter, they have never contested elections. Seldom have they sought to represent constituents or, as organizations, challenged their own regimes. Those enjoying legal monopolies on "representing" citizens, such as Egypt's ASU or Algeria's FLN, rejected the label "party"—having no rivals, they needed no partisans. Through some mysterious chemistry from which freedom of speech, open debate, and freedom of choice were notably absent, the front or union would distill the essence of the popular will and transmit it, for policy action, to the regime's leaders. It did not take long for the citizens to recognize this hokum for what it was.

More liberal experiments fell into their own kinds of sham. Iran, Morocco, and Jordan, monarchical regimes with carefully policed multiparty systems, and Sadat's Egypt all boasted party-competitive systems. But like several of their socialist counterparts (and, in Egypt's case, like its predecessor) the parties that were to compete for power were created from above, and the outcome of elections was more or less known in advance (al-Ansari 1986, 203). The shah of Iran habitually dabbled in the fabrication of parties. In the 1950s he established a loyal opposition party, Mardom, and a loyalist party, the Melliyun; eventually they came to be known as the "Yes" party and the "Yes Sir!" party. After 1963 the shah replaced his two creations with the Modern Iran party, run by the young technocrats who engineered the White Revolution. Then in 1975 he founded the Renaissance party and made Iran a one-party state.

We should not overlook the ground-up parties, organized in nationalist struggle or in defense of specific interests and classes. We have already discussed the Neo-Destour of Tunisia, but the Wafd party of Egypt, standard-bearer of Egyptian nationalism, is back in action again thirty years after Nasser dissolved it. Morocco's nationalist Independence party hangs on in the king's carefully controlled political arena. In some countries communist and socialist parties, often born in illegality and the objects of constant repression, have developed strong organizations and toughened cadres that compensate for their small membership. As Islamist groups increasingly capture the allegiance of the region's youth, leftist parties will find it hard to replace their aging leadership.

Against the few examples of successful party organization, a pervasive gloom envelops partisan activity in the Middle East. There are four main reasons for this. The first, outlined above, is that parties have been created from the top down and seldom strike roots in the population in whose name they claim to speak. With a stroke of a pen Sadat dissolved Egypt's ASU in 1975, and there was not the slightest murmur from the "masses" or the party's cadres. The same fate befell the Sudan's SSU in 1985, and there the "masses" were positively jubilant.

The second reason is the hesitancy of leaders to use the parties they have created to mobilize the people, to cause them to participate in national politics and share responsibility. Time and again, parties have been used to control and *de*mobilize the populace. Infiltrated by police informers, parties have become associated with the repressive apparatus of the state—in Iraq, Saddam Hussein, a "policeman," runs both the party and the government. Cadres are all too often bureaucrats who have been seconded to the party from the civil service and whose careers will ultimately be determined in their ministries.

Third, the economic strategies of many Middle Eastern states have brought forth a technocratic elite of planners, financial experts, managers, and engineers whose quest for orderly and disciplined change reinforces the party's mission as an instrument of control, especially in the workplace. Boumedienne's Algeria best represents this concept of party organization and technocratic supremacy.

Finally, where parties were alive and well prior to independence, there was a marked tendency afterward to drain them of their best cadres to staff government agencies in an ever-expanding state apparatus. Party militants became government bureaucrats, and the parties were left with no mission and very few experienced organizers. The Neo-Destour, the Ba'ath in Syria and Iraq, and Algeria's FLN have all fallen victim to this phenomenon.

THE TENETS OF SOLIDARISM

The word "corporatism," to the best of our knowledge, does not exist in any of the languages spoken in the Middle East, and despite a vast body of literature (e.g., Schmitter 1974) only Bianchi (1984) has examined a Middle Eastern political system in corporatist terms. Although the term may be foreign to the Middle East, its logic certainly is not. To oversimplify, corporatist ideologies conceive of societies as organic entities much like the human body. Societies have functioning parts that perform specific kinds of tasks. The brain (the government) and the nervous system (the party) control these parts and make sure that they work harmoniously together to achieve a desired end (once again, the teleological mission of the state and society). They *must* work harmoniously together; just as one's arms and legs cannot be at odds with one another if one is to walk, so too the functioning parts of the society must be coordinated for the body to live healthily. Occasionally diseases set in; foreign bodies (the Jews in Nazi Germany) must be purged; conflict may produce paralysis; a specific functioning part may atrophy.

The corporatist imagery comes out of European fascism. It condemns two kinds of conflict models of politics: the marxist and the liberal. In an organic society there is no place for class conflict or any organization along class lines. Likewise, open competition among a myriad of opposed interests and parties cannot be accepted. In the corporatist model, conflict is pathological.

Thus corporatist systems structure organization and representation around the major functional groups in society—agricultural producers, industrial producers, entrepreneurs, white-collar workers, the armed forces. We have already seen how this sort of categorization has manifested itself in Egypt, Algeria, and elsewhere in the Middle East. Such functional categories cut vertically through horizontal strata of wealth and poverty; agricultural producers may range from a landless tenant to a capitalist farmer, entrepreneurs from a street vendor to a factory owner, and so forth. Corporatism prescribes representation by function and wedges people of disparate power and resources into the same functional box.

Whatever historical and cultural predispositions there may be for the twentieth-century manifestations of corporatism, we argue that those manifestations must be seen as new and culturally neutral. They emerge as a function of state-building and market penetration in an age when governments can ill-afford to condone wide disparities in the distribution of wealth. Resource scarcity, which is inherent in the development process and no more so than when LDCs are struggling with structural adjustment, provokes conflict. Corporatism becomes an arm of the struggle to regiment large segments of the population that are officially entitled to a fair share of the national pie but in fact are denied that share as resources are channeled away from consumption toward investment and speculation. It is rare that the relatively disenfranchised masses—peasants, workers, low-income white-collar workers—feel that they are adequately represented through corporatist structures, and they are quite literally bought off by consumer subsidies, guaranteed employment schemes, and a blind eye to moonlighting, peculation, and low productivity.

A predisposition to corporatism may emerge from the nature of military organization. No modern organization more resembles the corporatist ideal than the military. Here is a relatively large, complex organization divided into functionally specific services, in turn subdivided into functionally specific corps (e.g., engineers, logistics, supply, communications) and task-defined field units (artillery, infantry, armor). The activity of all functioning parts is minutely planned and supervised by the chiefs of staff and chiefs of operations. Although the lines of hierarchy—of subordination and command, of officers and recruits—are sharply drawn, the military ethos calls for harmony among all units and all levels of command. Insubordination entails court-martial, dishonorable discharge, and, in time of hostilities, death. The military is a quintessentially purposeful organization, and all of its functioning parts must be subordinated and directed to the pursuit of specific goals. Although it is hard to advance concrete evidence, we can plausibly speculate that the prevalence of government by the military in the Middle East over the past thirty years may have brought to power men who, by their training and the evolution of their military careers, were disposed to organize civil society along corporatist lines (see Box 12.1).

Corporatist organization and ideology have done battle with four major sociopolitical issues: the role of political parties, class antagonism, labor organization, and ethnic and sectarian conflict.

BOX 12.1
ATATÜRK'S CORPORATISM

The great innovator Atatürk in May 1935 set forth his conception of society in terms that were to be echoed throughout the Middle East after 1950 (quoted in Özbudun 1981, 88):

> The source of will and sovereignty is the nation. The Party considers it an important principle that this will and sovereignty be used to regulate the proper fulfillment of the mutual duties of the citizen to the state and of the state to the citizen. We consider the individuals who accept an absolute equality before the law, and who recognise no privileges for any individual, family, class, or community to be . . . populist. It is one of our main principles to consider the people of the Turkish Republic, not as composed of different classes, but as a community divided into various professions according to the requirements of the division of labour for the individual and social life of the Turkish people. The farmers, handicraftsmen, labourers and workmen, people exercising free professions, industrialists, merchants, and public servants are the main groups of work constituting the Turkish community. The aims of our Party . . . are to secure social order and solidarity instead of class conflict, and to establish harmony of interests. The benefits are to be proportionate to the aptitude, to the amount of work.

Corporatism and Parties

Many Middle Eastern leaders have seen partisan competition as divisive, destructive, and a potential conduit for direct foreign intervention in domestic affairs. The common pattern has been the dissolution and legal abolition of all political parties and the establishment of monopoly fronts to represent "all the people." Egypt from 1953 on, Algeria since independence in 1962, and the Sudan between 1969 and 1985 established corporatist monopolies in the ASU, the FLN, and the SSU. The Ba'ath regimes of Iraq and Syria and the Socialist Destour of Tunisia have allowed for coalitions of the dominant party with small marginal groupings such as communists, Nasserists, and liberals, but there has never been any question of these groupings' being allowed to organize freely or to play anything but a subordinate role.

Corporatism and Class

Corporatist regimes sometimes deny the existence of class antagonisms, as in Atatürk's 1935 speech, or acknowledge their existence but refuse to allow any organization along class lines. This notion was at the heart of Nasser's socialism, which sought the "melting away of class differences" through a peaceful and harmonious redistribution of national wealth. There is no question that everywhere corporatism has been aimed at containing marxists and any attempt to incite class conflict, but while European corporatism was aimed directly at containing the radicalization of the industrial proletariat, that class has yet to acquire much weight in the Middle East.

Corporatism need not be a mechanism for the defense of the interests of the upper bourgeoisie; in fact it is more likely to appeal to middle- and lower-income groups. But almost never does it seek to give proportionate and effective weight to the poor majority of the adult populations of the Middle East. Nasser's distribution of 50% or more of elected seats in the ASU and the National Assembly to peasants and workers was window dressing.

Corporatism and Labor

Corporatist regimes pursue dual strategies vis-à-vis labor. One is to encourage organization and unionization. Strategically placed labor, mainly in public-sector enterprises and the transportation sector, may receive favorable wage and social-benefit packages. Such workers are co-opted by the corporatist state; their leaders are given significant roles in the "party" organization, in legislative assemblies, and sometimes in the government itself. In exchange for favorable unionwide wage-and-benefit packages, union leadership is expected to keep the rank and file in line. The second strategy is to segment the labor force, relying on the organized-labor elite to keep the economic wheels turning while looking over its shoulder at the majority of unorganized labor in the urban informal sector, in the private sector, and in the countryside—workers who would clearly love the jobs of the labor elite.

In Algeria Boumedienne purged the unions (the peak organization, the General Confederation of Algerian Workers [UGTA]) of militant leadership in 1967 and subordinated them to his statist industrialization drive. The 1971 Charter of Social-ist Management of Enterprise installed an ineffective system of worker participation in management. Every major workplace would have an elected assembly of workers, but the latter included management as well as labor. The clear goal of socialist man-agement was to increase production, not promote proletarian democracy (DERSA 1981, 132; Nellis 1977, 549).

Labor leaders co-opted into the corporatist power structure must walk a fine line between serving the state leaders and maintaining some semblance of credibility among the rank and file. Sometimes the balancing act is impossible to maintain. In 1966 the dominant Türk-Iş labor confederation in Turkey condemned a strike in a glass works. This led to the hiving-off of a faction of Türk-Iş and the founding of the radical Confederation of Progressive Trade Unions (DISK). By 1970 DISK had 40,000 members and Türk-Iş 700,000, but DISK became an active element in the agitation of the 1970s. When the military took over in 1980, DISK was disbanded and many of its leaders were arrested.

A similar process unfolded in Tunisia. The General Confederation of Tunisian Workers (UGTT) had been a pillar of the Destourian coalition before and after inde-pendence. Whenever labor leaders appeared ready to use its organizational strength in any way that conflicted with regime goals, Bourguiba had them removed. Throughout the 1970s and the readjustment of the Tunisian economy after the Ben Salah statist experiment, the UGTT was led by Habib Achour. In 1978 cost-of-living riots broke out in several Tunisian cities. The UGTT rank and file was hit hard, yet the regime wanted Achour to condemn the violence. In order not to lose support among his following, Achour had to distance himself from the regime. As a conse-quence, he was jailed, but the relative autonomy of the UGTT had been asserted.

Cost-of-living riots occurred once again in January 1984, when the regime sought to reduce consumer subsidies. It could no longer rely on the relatively pampered members of the UGTT to remain aloof from the agitation. During the Sixth Five-Year Plan, 1982–1986, the regime called for a "social dialogue" and announced that the consultative Economic and Social Council would be transformed into the Na-tional Council for Social Dialogue and that in each ministry social peace commis-sions would be created (Baduel 1983). But corporatist discipline appeared to have broken down. After Achour was once again jailed, the UGTT called in May 1984 for a boycott of local elections and even threatened to run its own list of candidates in the 1986 legislative elections.

Corporatist discipline is always hard to maintain. Sometimes the regime will toler-ate strikes and labor agitation in the private sector but forbid them in the public, as public enterprise is the motor of national development and, in any case, is owned by "the people." Such double standards have seldom precluded public-enterprise strikes. In 1977, only a year after the adoption of a new national charter, there were 129 strikes, involving 31,000 workers, in the Algerian public sector (DERSA 1981). Egypt experienced major strikes twice in 1968, as workers demanded that military officers responsible for the debacle of the June War of 1967 be given severe sentences by the military tribunals. In 1977 dockers in Alexandria sparked three days of cost-of-living riots that spread through most Egyptian cities. The prospect of privatization in 1995 triggered strikes in public-sector textile firms, especially in Kafr al-Dawar.

One of the unexpected results of corporatist experiments is to inculcate organizational skills and eventually some sort of autonomy from the state in the very functional groups the experiment was designed to control. The evolution of the Confederation of Egyptian Labor is instructive. Its autonomy was limited in the Nasserist-socialist era, when rhetoric in favor of the working man was at a high pitch. During the Sadatist era of economic liberalization, the confederation's leadership was co-opted into prominent official positions, and its leader, Sa'ad Muhammed Ahmad, was made minister of human resources, a post he held for nearly a decade. By the time of Sadat's death in 1981 "the Confederation had become the largest, wealthiest and most representative association in Egyptian society" (Bianchi 1986, 438). Under Mubarak it became an effective veto group, notably in preventing any further joint ventures between public-sector companies and foreign investors. Corporatism had thus "provided union leaders with new means for defending workers' interests and, ironically, for limiting the decisional autonomy of the authoritarian regime in critical issues" (Bianchi 1986, 434).

Increased autonomy need not entail greater radicalism. The trend in Turkey and Egypt and perhaps elsewhere is toward the development of unions and professional associations into important economic enterprises in their own right. With dues, special funds, and pension funds at their disposal, unions and associations have invested in businesses, run cooperative-housing schemes and hospitals, launched banks to mobilize their members' savings, and even participated in joint ventures with foreign capital. In this way the organizations develop a stake in the overall smooth functioning of the economic system; their members' interests are better served through the general ability of the economy to generate profits, an ability not enhanced by strikes and agitation.

The gradual distancing from close corporatist control that several Middle Eastern labor organizations have undergone has been replicated to some extent in business and professional associations (especially those of lawyers, journalists, and engineers). Corporatist organizations, like public-sector enterprise, have tended to fall into the hands of bureaucrats, clock punchers with little motivation. Just as production and profits have suffered in the parastatals, ideological commitment and indeed unity itself have suffered in corporatist fronts. The decay of corporatist structures has paralleled the erosion of the elite's confidence in its ability to change society. Rather than displacing patronage, corporatist structures have simply absorbed it. Social harmony then becomes a function of patronage carrots and the formidable stick of highly trained police.

Corporatism, Sectarianism, and Ethnicity

Ethnic and sectarian identity and conflict have vexed Middle Eastern leaders as much as they have fascinated outside observers (see Khoury and Kostiner 1990;

Esman and Rabinovich 1988). We shall deal all too cursorily with the topic here. Communalism and sectarianism have been viewed in the modernization literature as anachronisms that will slowly erode in the face of economic development, literacy, and nation building (inter alia, see Lerner 1959). As any observer of the persistence of racial discrimination in the United States knows, however, issues of blood, skin color, and creed are not readily susceptible to treatment through public policy. It may in fact be easier to redistribute wealth through public policy than to wash away these parochial loyalties, prejudices, and conflicts.

The major corporatist experiments in the Middle East have to some extent foundered on the rocks of ethnic and sectarian loyalties. As early as 1926 Atatürk confronted a Kurdish rebellion with Islamic overtones in Eastern Anatolia, representing the first major challenge to the new secular, republican regime. Nasser was challenged by the Muslim Brotherhood in 1954 and 1965. Coptic Christian and Muslim confrontations became commonplace in Egypt during the Sadat era, and eventually Muslim extremists assassinated him. Bourguiba early on had to back away from his own secularizing proclivities, and today Tunisia has one of the strongest Islamist movements in the Arab world. Finally, Lebanon was nearly destroyed as a nation by sectarian strife—not just Muslims versus Christians but Shi'is versus Sunnis versus Druze versus Maronites, and so on.

The issues become murky when sect or ethnic groups overlap with relative wealth or deprivation. Lebanese Shi'is have for long been the underclass in Lebanon's economy, whereas the Maronites have formed the core of the business elite (Nasr 1985). Oriental Jews in Israel have been in a situation similar to that of the Shi'is in Lebanon. In North Yemen in the early 1960s, Shi'i tribesmen fought Sunni townsmen, and in 1986 Southern Yemeni marxists fought among themselves along clan lines.

In certain instances a multidimensional overlap of ethnic origin, distinctive language, shared sect, geographic location, and a common economic way of life makes the ethno-sectarian issue particularly intractable. The outstanding examples in the Middle East are the Kurds and the southern Sudanese. The Kurds, perhaps 20 million strong, inhabit a mountainous homeland sprawling across the borders of Turkey, Iran, and Iraq. All three countries have suppressed attempts at Kurdish self-determination. The shah and later Ayatollah Khomeini dealt successfully but not definitively with sporadic Kurdish insurrections. In Iraq, however, Kurdish dissidence has been chronic and has seriously hindered Arab-dominated elites in Baghdad from consolidating their rule. Since the end of the Gulf War in 1991, the northern Kurdish zone of Iraq has lived under an internationally enforced no-fly zone, affording the Kurdish populations there a precarious autonomy. The black, mainly Nilotic[1] populations of the southern Sudan make up roughly a third of the country's population and occupy a third of its land area. These people are non-Arab, speak tribal languages other than Arabic, are for the most part non-Muslim, and live as cattle raisers, fisher folk, or subsistence farmers in the vast swamps and savannas of the south. Since 1955 there has been a chronic state of civil war in the southern Sudan, interrupted for about a decade, 1974–1983, during the Nimeiri regime. The fighting has periodically led to the toppling of regimes (1964 and 1985) and crippled the economy. Since 1989, the Islamic government of Bashir and Turabi has prosecuted the war in the south in the name of Islam and the application of shari'a.

More often the issues are less clear-cut. Ethnic and sectarian groups may not be geographically fixed, may have considerable degrees of inequality among members, and may share important characteristics with majority populations, such as language (e.g., Shi'ite Arabs in Iraq) or religion (e.g., Muslim Berbers in North Africa). The result is a multidimensional set of actors. It is hard to know at any point what factor is driving the actors—ethnicity, region, religion, or class status. What we should bear in mind is that ethnicity and sectarianism should be seen as resources that can be drawn upon when they best suit the needs of an individual or a group. They need not be a badge that is worn constantly and with unalterable intensity (see Kasfir 1979). When communal tensions run high, when clans are settling scores, or when sectarian or ethnic witch-hunts are under way, individuals cannot shed the ethnic or sectarian labels with which they were born. In calmer circumstances, however, individuals may as easily act in terms of their occupations or their material interests.

The Kurds and the black populations of the southern Sudan are peoples seeking at a minimum regional autonomy and, in the case of the Kurds, national independence. These populations have at various times sought to opt out of existing systems. That desire was not shared by all Kurds or by all southern Sudanese. Today the leaders of the rebellion in the southern Sudan claim they seek a socialist transformation *within* the nation. Still, these two movements have seen little to be gained from the regimes with which they have done battle. In contrast, most ethnic dissidence has had as its aim to opt *into* existing political systems—to use violence or its threat to extract more resources (roads, schools, clinics, industrial projects, and so forth) from the central authorities. Even though the Turkish authorities give no recognition to their Kurdish minority, they have nonetheless invested heavily in dams, hydropower projects, and agricultural schemes in the Kurdish heartland. The Kurds of the Islamic Republic of Iran have also tried to fight for a more favored position in the newly established republic. Similarly, the Berbers of Algeria and Morocco have confronted the central authorities to enhance their position in the political establishment and to draw more resources to their home regions. Their status is highly complex. Their regions of origin are generally mountains or steppes and generally poor. For this very reason out-migration has been heavy. Several North African cities are majority Berber in population, and hundreds of thousands of Berbers have worked in France and other European countries. Berbers are a crucial part of the North African urban proletariat. Finally, in both Algeria and Morocco many Berbers enjoy elite status, with prominent roles in the state technocracy, party leadership, and the officers' corps. The interests of North African Berbers are not homogeneous, and for that very reason there has never been a unified Berber front, much less a movement, to opt out of existing political systems (see Gellner and Micaud 1972; Roberts 1982; 1983).

When religious identity is invoked, it tends to take two forms. First, religious minorities generally adopt a defensive posture, trying to guarantee some degree of legitimacy and freedom of practice within the majority society. Some minorities have not fared well, and none worse than the Baha'is in Iran. Historically in the Middle East, the most violent repression of a religious minority was that of the Armenians in Turkey at the beginning of this century, and since 1948, when the state of Israel was founded, Jewish minorities in the Arab countries have experienced varying degrees of repression even though the right to practice their religion has never been questioned. The second form is that taken by religious movements within the dominant Islamic majority. Here the objective is to transform existing political systems, to force them from without or to change them from within to adhere to the shari'a and to Islamic principles. There is no question of opting out here, only of exerting the force of the putative majority in whose name Muslim militants claim to speak (see Chapter 14).

In summary, no sectarian or ethnic group can be analyzed or understood within its own terms of reference. In every instance there will be at stake elements of the distribution of scarce resources, of making concessions that might jeopardize national unity, of reacting to minority demands in such a way as to call the regime's legitimacy into question. Just as sectarian or ethnic groups are the enemies of corporatist solidarity, so too are they often the enemies of class formation and consciousness. Sectarianism and ethnicity more often than not cut across class lines. No corporatist or class-based organization has succeeded in fully co-opting or defanging ethnic and sectarian groups. Until national political systems can provide institutions and rules of political conduct that are reliable and respected, such groups will continue to act as buffers against the arbitrary use of state power.

Let us note finally that minorities have the pesky habit of living on strategic real estate: Iraq's Kurds live in the oil-bearing region of their country, and their dissidence is a loaded gun pointed at the head of the Iraqi regime. So too, the southern Sudanese sit on that country's recently discovered oil reserves but, more important, control the headwaters of the White Nile. Central authorities almost always suspect strategically located minorities of colluding with hostile foreign powers to destroy the nation, and sometimes those authorities are right.

THE FAILURE OF IDEOLOGY

For over three decades the official ideologies spawned in the Middle East shared several common themes, all similar to if not derived from Atatürk's and the Turkish republic's six principles. National strength, meaning freedom from imperial control coupled with a strong economy and strong armed forces, was both a goal and a promise. Building a new citizen and a new sense of citizenship was a second ideological tenet, something that would be achieved once foreign control had been ended and domestic oppressor classes such as large landowners and compradors eliminated. Mass literacy, public health, and a booming planned economy would take care of the physical and work needs of the population, giving each adult a new sense of dignity and self-worth. The psychic needs of the populace would be satisfied through the mass party, which would educate new generations in nationalist and civic duties. Every regime espoused the equitable distribution of the benefits of economic growth. Some called this concern "socialism" and some did not.

Curiously, all of these themes can be found in the Western modernization literature of the 1950s and 1960s. The literature of nation building could, in spirit, have
been written by Atatürk or Nasser. The shah of Iran, King Hassan of Morocco, King
Hussein of Jordan, and, indeed, the Saudi monarchy have been as concerned with
modernization and national strength as the more obvious socialist republican leaders. If one examines the rhetoric of the White Revolution launched by the shah in
1963, one finds familiar themes of destroying the feudal landowners through agrarian reform, redistributing national wealth through the sale of shares to workers in
private and public industry, bringing literacy to all the people, and liberating
women. Ten years later the shah added the national-military dimension, proclaiming
that within a decade or so Iran would become a world military power.

Had the planned, state-dominated economies worked up to expectations, had the
expansion and increasing quality of education and social services kept pace with
unchecked population growth, and had Middle Eastern nations built measurably
powerful military establishments (only Turkey, the Middle East's sole member of
NATO, and Israel can be said to have done so), then perhaps the accompanying ideologies might have had some impact upon broad strata of Middle Eastern society.
But the many performance failures, from unprofitable public enterprise to repeated
military setbacks for some Arab armed forces, rendered the rhetoric hollow and ultimately a target for derision and anger. Khoury (1983a) has rightly written of regime
"exhaustion," the collective playing out of a set of policy and ideological options by
an entire generation of Middle Eastern leadership. The statist, socialist, and implicitly secularizing experiments of the past three or four decades have resolved few of
the problems they promised to tackle. Other than in Iran and perhaps Saudi Arabia,
the one option that has not been tried is Islamic government, and, by default, its
hour may yet come. Still, one must underscore the fact that some fifteen years after
Khoury wrote his article, the same "exhausted" regimes still cling to power.

THE ISLAMIC CHALLENGE

Many Muslim theologians and lay people believed that the dominant statist experiments after World War II were totally misguided in their attempts to define a separate and diminished religious sphere, to separate Islam from politics, to reduce the
ulema to mere bureaucrats, to bury the shari'a in an avalanche of Western-inspired
civil law. Nearly all political leaders could feel the repressed heat of Muslim militants; Nasser, Atatürk, and the shah, among others, broke up their organizations and
put the leaders in jail. Significantly, however, nearly all republican constitutions in
the Middle East state that the president must be a Muslim, and several declare that
Islam is the religion of state and that all law must conform to the shari'a. Leaders
from Nasser to Saddam Hussein have frequently invoked Muslim themes in an
attempt to legitimize their rule, and few have failed to make the pilgrimage, ostentatiously, to Mecca. And we should not forget that several "secularizing" leaders, including Nasser and Boumedienne, were in fact pious Muslims who performed their
religious duties regularly.

If the Islamic Republic of Iran and the republic of the Sudan are harbingers of the nature of Islamic governance and discourse, then it is reasonably clear that they have invented neither an entirely new political language nor innovative political and economic policies. In fact, as noted in the previous chapter, what they attack is *secular* solidarism, under which men, not God, make laws for men. Iranian and Sudanese leaders are just as apt as their sworn enemies to invoke an organic image of society coupled with a purposive, mission-guided state. For these leaders solidarity is inherent in the *umma*, the community of Muslim believers, who will march as one if their leaders are truly pious, devoted to God, and learned in the laws of Islam (see Box 12.2).

The current rise of Islamic militancy is partially a function of the hesitancy of incumbent elites to continue to repress and harass militant groups. It is not that these

---

BOX 12.2
KHOMEINI'S SOLIDARISM

Ayatollah Khomeini, in lectures given to students of religion in Najaf, Iraq, in early 1970, envisioned the *fuqaha* (sing. *faqih*), those well instructed in Islamic law, as the future corps of governors of the *umma* (quoted in Algar (1985, 137–138):

> As for the supervision and supreme administration of the country, the dispensing of justice, and the establishment of equitable relations among the people— these are precisely the subjects that the *faqih* has to offer. For it is the *faqih* who refuses to submit to others or fall under the influence of foreigners, and who defends the rights of the nation and the freedom, independence, and territorial integrity of the Islamic homeland, even at the cost of his life. It is the *faqih* who does not deviate either to the left or to the right. . . .
>
> The entire system of government and administration, together with the necessary laws, lies ready for you. If the administration of the country calls for taxes, Islam has made the necessary provision; and if laws are needed, Islam has established them all. There is no need for you, after establishing a government, to sit down and draw up laws, or, like rulers who worship foreigners and are infatuated with the West, run after others to borrow their laws. Everything is ready and waiting. . . .
>
> Fortunately the Muslim peoples are ready to follow you and are your allies. What we are lacking are the necessary resolve and armed power, and these, too, we shall acquire, God willing. We need the staff of Moses and the resolve of Moses; we need people who are able to wield the staff of Moses and the sword of the Commander of the Faithful (peace be upon him). . . .
>
> Today we have 700 million Muslims in the world, 170 million or more of whom are Shi'is. They are all ready to follow us, but we are so lacking in resolve that we are unable to lead them. We must establish a government that will enjoy the trust of the people, one in which the people have confidence and to which they will be able to entrust their destiny.

groups are so powerful but rather that the population as a whole alternates between indifference and hostility toward the elites. Although relatively few might welcome Islamic government, a far broader swath of the population shares the militants' moral indignation. Aware of this popular state of mind, elites hesitate to confront the militants for fear of isolating themselves further.

A more common and powerful explanation has to do with the current socioeconomic context. As social scientists, we have a tendency to explain a given phenomenon in terms of others. In this instance we see the strengthening of militant, and sometimes violent, Islamic groups in terms of unemployment among the educated and semieducated, bleak career prospects, resentment of those who have done well for themselves, often through illegal means, and a quest for justice. This understanding is surely "true" to some degree, but it assumes that if economic and employment conditions could be improved, then militant Islam would lose its constituency. It diminishes the place in Islamic identity of piety and faith. One of Morocco's best-known Islamic leaders, Abdesslam Yassin, chided a French social scientist, François Burgat, precisely for falling into this analytic error (Burgat 1993, 75): "I find this explanation a little too easy and that it does not take into account the subjective factor. People do not come to Islam as an alternative for their social misfortunes. People come to Islam in response to a call, a call which goes very far and deep in the human soul."

There is one last sociological phenomenon that should be mentioned. Both individually and collectively, there is frequently an espousal of militancy for militancy's sake, virtually without regard for its ideological content. Individual leaders have often oscillated between political extremes—marxists or leftist radicals in their youth and Islamic fundamentalists in their autumn years (Akram Hawrani of Syria and Ahmad Ben Bella of Algeria are examples). What may best explain these gyrations is the simple desire on the part of many politically aware Middle Easterners to do something to move their societies and to challenge the corruption and complacency of incumbent elites. In May 1959, according to Batatu (1979, 900), the Iraqi Communist party pressured the government of 'Abd al-Karim Qassim for greater representation in the cabinet. Although the party had no more than 20,000 members, it was able to put 300,000 demonstrators into the streets of Baghdad. What did these people understand by their demonstration? How much marxism could they possibly have mastered? Can we see as their counterparts twenty years later the hundreds of thousands of Iranians who repeatedly filled the streets of Iranian cities in support of Ayatollah Khomeini? Did the latter know anything more about the doctrine of trusteeship of the jurisprudents than the former had known about the class dialectic? Probably not. What we may presume the masses saw in both movements was a tool with a cutting edge and leaders prepared to help them shape their own destinies.

DEMOCRACY WITHOUT DEMOCRATS?

Solidarism, whether of the secular authoritarian or Islamist variety, has had difficulty dealing with electoral democracy. Both solidarisms speak constantly in the name of the people while at the same time depicting conflict as unnatural. Electoral democracy entails rule-bound competition, appeals to specific interests, and attacks on one's adversaries. It also entails a good measure of unpredictability—something that the Algerian regime learned in December 1991. Solidarism and corporatism assume harmony of interests and predictable, if not planned, outcomes in political and economic life. Solidarists want to speak in the name of the people but not to talk to them. Consequently, Middle Eastern regimes have paid lip service to popular democracy but have tried to control results through the single party, resort to referendums and plebescites, and the restrictive licensing of all political groups. Outside Israel and Turkey (and Lebanon from 1946 to 1975) there have been no sustained experiments in electoral democracy in the region.[2]

That situation may be changing. Three interrelated factors are of major importance. First, the international context has changed dramatically in the past decade. The collapse of the regional oil economy (see Chapter 3) forced many Middle Eastern countries to cut back public expenditures and to turn to domestic private sectors to pick up the slack in investment budgets. Simultaneously, with the collapse of the Soviet Union and the end of the cold war the flow of strategic rents to several Middle Eastern countries dropped off sharply. Thus, and second, the military establishments and regimes of the region could no longer make the same outsized claims on national wealth that had facilitated their grip on power in earlier decades (see Chapter 13). Finally, the economic crises have forced governments in the region to increase the tax burden on their own populations. The easiest targets are urban lower- and middle-class consumers and wage earners, who are assessed through value-added taxes on goods and services and income taxes at the source of income.

There is, then, a political sea change under way. The large, urbanized middle classes of the region are being called upon to yield tax revenue to beleaguered governments. Private sectors, once attacked and derided by "socialist" regimes, are being asked to invest. Foreign creditors, especially the World Bank, condition assistance on thoroughgoing deregulation of economic life and privatization of state-owned assets. In the face of these factors, it will be very hard for the praetorian regimes[3] of the Middle East to maintain the right to regiment political life and to deny real political participation to the groups and strata that they seek to tax or from which they are removing entitlements such as subsidies and employment guarantees. We may, therefore, be witnessing the development of a bargaining relationship between state agents and various constituencies in society. It is not yet a question of the formal representation of these interests in the political system but rather one of the implicit recognition by the state that these interests will have to be guaranteed certain rights before they will voluntarily part with their money.

This would be a novel development both in historical and contemporary terms. The state-dominant systems of the Middle East have, by and large, made policy behind closed doors through which only safe and sure allies were ever granted entry. Civil society was a policy taker. Most often, groups adversely affected by new policies would react, after the fact, by bribing officials for dispensations or by engaging in various forms of noncompliance and sabotage. In the extreme, victims of new policies could revolt or exit the system altogether, but they had few formal channels for expressing grievances, much less influencing policy.

The new environment encourages lobbying, that is, the *pre*-policy exercise of influence. If the state wants investment, it may have to draft legislation that promotes specific private interests. Consultation with those interests before policy is made thereby becomes more and more common. It will be recognized that private interests are concerned with macroeconomic policy as well and will voice their views on exchange rates, interest rates, tariffs, inflation, government spending, taxation, and so forth.

In the broadest terms, then, the trend is away from the crafting of personal agreements after policy has been made toward collective action on the part of increasingly well-defined interests that begin lobbying before policy is made. In Turkey, beginning in 1979, the Turkish Businessmen's and Manufacturers' Association (TÜSIAD) has followed this trajectory, and since the mid-1980s a similar trend can be seen in the evolution of the Egyptian Businessmen's Association. As various countries seek to encourage exports, we can expect to see exporters' associations becoming more involved in the policymaking process. The ultimate weapons of private-sector interests are investment strikes and capital flight. The US$600 or so billion held by Middle Easterners outside the region shows how much is at stake. Once openly acknowledged and legitimized, such bargaining relations can be seen as a public good, that is, one to which others cannot be easily denied access. In other words, there may be spillover effects; other interests, including trade unions and professional organizations, may seek the right to bargain with state agents before policy is made. It will be hard for regimes to grant or deny such rights selectively.

It needs to be stressed at this point that we have not identified any philosophical democrats in this process. Bargaining is not formal democracy, although, as it is institutionalized, it may lead in that direction. Nor are the bargainers democrats; rather, they may be pursuing the protection and promotion of their interests with little regard to the broader implications of the process. With that in mind, let us consider another path to democracy.

Political struggle in the contemporary Middle East has often been of the winner-take-all variety. Faction A wins out over Faction B and then sets about destroying the remnants of Faction B, either literally or by seizing its assets. No constitution could sanction such outcomes, so the struggles are generally nasty, violent, and extralegal. Because the stakes are so high, the struggles tend to drag on; one need only note the civil wars in Lebanon (1975–1989), the Sudan (1955–), northern Iraq (1975–), and Algeria (1991–). These struggles often end in stalemate, and prolonged stalemate may then promote a negotiated pact that involves power sharing. Power sharing requires rules, guarantees, and formulae for representation. Once again, the protagonists may bring their hatreds and contempt for their adversaries to the table. Tolerance and respect for others may not be operative. All that is in play is a recognition that it is better to win something than possibly to lose everything. The Ta'if Accords of 1989 that brought the fighting in Lebanon to a close and reestablished an elected government were not signed in a burst of fellow feeling. For that reason they are fragile, but if the protagonists live by them for some period of time they may become incorporated into the mores of both leaders and followers. If a winner-take-all outcome is to be avoided in Algeria, one must hope that the military regime and the FIS (or, more accurately, the Armed Islamic Group) will fight to a weary stalemate, at which point third parties may suggest formulae for power sharing.

There is no magic to elections. There are several ways in which they can poorly serve the institutionalization of democratic procedures. For example, throughout the colonial era Britain and France repeatedly held rigged elections to ineffective legislative bodies. For an entire generation of Middle Easterners democracy was tantamount to a colonial charade in which only a pampered native elite took any real interest. Mohammed Reza Shah's conduct of the democratic game in Iran between 1953 and 1978 produced much the same popular disdain for the process.

There are elections or electoral situations that prove profoundly destabilizing. A basic tenet of democratic theory is that the process will be sustained only as long as major contenders feel that they have a chance to win, no matter how far in the future (Przeworski 1991, 30–31). When the Turkish constitution forbids sectarian or ethnic parties, then any such interests are told that they have no hope of winning within the system. Their alternative is to go outside it and attack it. Similarly, when the Algerian military suspended the second round of voting in the 1991 legislative elections, the message for the FIS was that it could have no future in a democratic Algeria. Conversely, Algerians were told that the country had no democratic future so long as the FIS tried to participate. In the same vein, election results may send a message to some contenders that further participation is futile. The Yemen Socialist party took the results of the 1993 legislative elections as a definitive and negative commentary on the ability of the party to win votes in the North, where the majority of voters reside. It therefore opted to try to secede from the union with the North rather than continue to play the democratic game. The 1986 elections in the Sudan told the NIF that its voter base was too narrow to win a majority or even a plurality, and it opted for an alliance with the military and accession to power through a coup d'état.

For international actors, especially the United States, that profess a commitment to the spread of democratic institutions throughout the region, there is sufficient uncertainty about the size of the "Islamic vote" to give them pause. The Algerian experience of 1991 reinforces the apprehension that democracy might yield Islamist majorities in several countries, primarily Egypt, Tunisia, Algeria, and perhaps Palestine. If these countries joined forces with Iran and the Sudan, the peace process between Israel and its Arab adversaries would likely end. The new regimes would not only seek confrontation with Israel and the West more generally but could claim a credible popular mandate to do so. We indicated in the previous chapter that we are doubtful that Islamist parties could win majorities anywhere in the region. Whether or not we are right, not much international leverage is being used to promote democracy in the Middle East.

CONCLUSION

The radical authoritarian regimes of the Middle East are ideologically exhausted but still powerful enough to repress and to cling to power. The liberal monarchies have made greater concessions to pluralism and electoral democracy but not yet enough to permit one to say that a true democratic transition is under way. Islamists in Iran and the Sudan and their imitators elsewhere use a political rhetoric similar to that of the radical republics they so despise, adding God to the familiar themes of social solidarity and political harmony.

Economic change, driven by shifts in the international economy and the end of the cold war, may be creating situations in which resource-starved governments of whatever ideological persuasion must turn to their citizens for taxes and in so doing enter into a contractual arrangement with them. Governments may be held to account, and citizens may be empowered. It is far too early to predict this outcome with any assurance, but the logic of the current situation points in that direction. It may not be necessary for a generation of convinced democrats to take charge of the transition. Leaders mired in stalemated conflicts and willing to bargain with constituents whose resources they need could be enough to launch, if not sustain, a transition from solidarism to democratic pluralism.

NOTES

1. The populations of Equatoria province are, however, largely Bantu.

2. For fuller treatments of democratic experiments and prospects in the Middle East, see Garnham and Tessler (1995), Deegan (1994), Hudson (1994), Salamé (1994), Vatin et al. (1992).

3. Samuel P. Huntington (1968, 195–198) develops the notion of praetorianism and defines it simply as the intervention of the military in politics.

13

THE MILITARY AND THE STATE

Throughout recorded history the Middle East has been the arena for sweeping military encounters. Enduring geopolitical struggles between the two great river systems—the Nile and the Tigris-Euphrates—date back to the pharaonic and Babylonian dynasties. As perhaps the world's most important crossroads, the area has been fought over by Greeks, Romans, Assyrians, Persians, Turks, Mongols, Crusaders, and, latterly, the imperial powers of nineteenth-century Europe. As Islam spread across this area, it was carried, so to speak, in the saddlebags of Muslim generals. Kemal Atatürk, the Gazi, or warrior, is but the most recent in a long line of military heroes of epic proportions.

THE MILITARY IN MIDDLE EAST POLITICS

History aside, this century has been marked throughout by a high level of conflict and warfare. Since World War II, armed conflict has been carried out on a scale and with an intensity that has been rivaled only in theaters such as the Indo-Pakistani or the Indo-Chinese since the 1930s. The area has witnessed one major war for national liberation and independence in Algeria (1954–1962). Among independent states, the most salient example is the Arab-Israeli conflict, which has resulted in four major wars and several thousand deaths. Accompanying this intractable confrontation have been extraordinarily bloody civil wars in Lebanon (1976–1989), the Sudan (1959–1971 and 1983–), North Yemen (1962–1968 and 1994), and Oman (early 1970s), while the Iraqi government has sporadically fought its Kurdish minority. King Hussein of Jordan engaged armed elements of the PLO in savage battle in September 1970, and Algeria and Morocco have fought each other since 1976 in the ex-Spanish Sahara, which Morocco has claimed as its own territory but which the Polisario Liberation Front, with Algerian backing, has tried to win for itself.

The most spectacular and grisly of these conflicts has been the Iran-Iraq War, which raged from 1981 until a cease-fire in the summer of 1988. In most ways it was a conventional war, with large regular and irregular armed forces confronting each other with very high levels of firepower and means of destruction, including poison gas. Perhaps as many as a million died in what became a conflict to rival those of Korea in the 1950s and Vietnam in the 1960s. Not long after the end of formal hostilities, Iraq invaded and occupied Kuwait in the summer of 1990, and a UN force led by the United States drove Iraq from Kuwait, in Operation Desert Storm, in the winter of 1991 (see Box 13.1).

Alongside these major military confrontations, there has been a constant stream of smaller incidents: brief border skirmishes (Egypt-Libya, Morocco-Algeria), shows of force (Jordan-Syria, Syria-Iraq, Israel versus all its neighbors), and invasions of longer or shorter duration (Turkey in Cyprus, Libya in Chad, Israel and Syria in Lebanon, Iraq in Iran, and then Iran in Iraq). Since 1991 Turkey has on three occasions moved thousands of its troops into northern Iraq in an effort to eliminate the bases of Kurds from Turkey organized in the guerrilla movement known as the Kurdish Workers' party (PKK).

This simple listing of military conflicts says nothing about causes and motives; they are complex and specific to each particular theater or conflict. All that it tells us is that the Middle East has had more than its share of military violence and, predictably, has devoted more of its human and material resources to defense and warfare than many other regions of the developing world.

It is also undeniable that Middle Eastern societies have experienced prolonged periods of rule by the military. Military or quasi-military government has been the rule rather than the exception. Even when, de jure, regimes are headed by civilians, the power wielders may be military officers who have left their uniforms in the closet. Atatürk himself was the first general to follow this path and to insist that those of his officer colleagues who wished to pursue political careers do likewise. Ismet Inönü, his vice president and successor, led the way in resigning from the armed forces. Still,

BOX 13.1
THE COSTS OF WAR

At the conclusion of Operation Desert Storm, Iraq's war with Iran and its invasion and occupation of Kuwait had incurred costs and external obligations totaling US$600 billion, nearly three times Iraq's total earnings for oil sales over the period 1931–1990 (al-Nasrawi 1995):

US$232 billion	cost of repairing war damage
US$67 billion	value of assets destroyed
US$97 billion	reparation payments owed Iran
US$100 billion	payments to UN compensation fund for victims of the occupation of Kuwait
US$100 billion	war-related Iraqi external debt

it is hard to see Atatürk's regime as other than quasi-military. Next door to Turkey, Reza Shah, commander of the Iranian cossacks, founded a monarchy, but throughout his rule his regime was reliant upon the military. His son Mohammed Reza Pahlavi continued to depend on his military establishment and in fact owed his throne in 1953 to the initiative of Gen. Fazlollah Zahedi, who, in coordination with the U.S. Central Intelligence Agency (CIA), arrested the civilian prime minister and opponent of the shah, Mohammed Mossadegh.

As the Arab countries gained their independence, several fell under nearly uninterrupted military rule. Since 1949 Syria has known only brief periods of civilian rule. Today Hafiz al-Assad may wear a suit to work, but he and his fellow Alawite officers constitute the power elite of the government and of the Ba'ath party. Iraq since the toppling of the monarchy in July 1958 has had constant military rule, although, as we have seen, Saddam Hussein comes out of the police rather than the military. Several of his closest associates from his home area of Takrit are strategically placed in the military and in the Iraqi Ba'ath party. Similarly, the YAR, the PDRY, the Sudan between 1969 and 1985 and again after 1989, Algeria since 1965, and Libya since 1969 have been ruled by the military.

One should not, however, underestimate the possible significance of the "civilianization" of military regimes. Over time, moves that initially may be largely symbolic, such as dropping military titles and substituting mufti for uniforms, may lead to a real transfer of power and control to civilian hands. That transfer took place in dramatic fashion in Turkey in 1950, although the military has intervened in politics in 1960, 1971, and 1980. In Egypt and Algeria in the past decade nonmilitary technocrats have played increasingly prominent roles in economic and social policymaking, though the two presidents, Hosni Mubarak and Chadli Benjadid, were once professional military officers and maintain close links to their senior officers' corps. Key positions in internal security and administration, national defense, and foreign affairs are still reserved for senior officers. The confrontation between the military and the FIS in Algeria has in many respects led to the remilitarization of the regime, making it the most praetorian of any in the Middle East.

In all the major monarchies—Jordan, Morocco, Iran from 1923 until 1979, and Saudi Arabia—the king is intimately linked to the military. Members of the royal family, if not the king himself, direct the Ministry of Defense, command key units in the armed forces, and review all promotions in the officers' corps. Before becoming king, Hassan of Morocco was put in command of the royal armed forces, and King Hussein, whose throne is dependent upon the support of the largely Bedouin Jordan Legion, has always been a king in uniform.

A handful of regimes have had a reputation for civilian predominance. Tunisia enjoyed uninterrupted civilian government from 1956 to 1988. The size of the military was contained, few military men played any role in the civilian administration, and there were no serious attempts at military intervention. Bourguiba single-mindedly built his coalitions among civilian forces and insulated his regime from military influence. In recent years, however, the size and cost of Tunisia's military have been growing substantially. Moreover, it was the minister of defense, Gen. Zine al-Abdine Ben 'Ali, who deposed Bourguiba in 1988.

We have already discussed Turkey's peculiar oscillation between civilian and military rule since 1950 (Chapters 11 and 12). It has been more than fifteen years since the Turkish military last deposed a civilian government, but the continued use of the military in an effort to eradicate the PKK has given the armed forces continued leverage in Turkish politics. If ever Turkey is to join the European Union, it will have to convince its European partners that its civilian institutions are firmly and irrevocably anchored.

There was a time when Lebanon appeared to be a solid civilian republic, but appearances were deceiving. Civil war broke out in Lebanon in the summer of 1958, at the time of the overthrow of the Iraqi monarchy. The violence provoked U.S. military intervention. President Camille Chamoun, a civilian, was judged to have mishandled the situation and was replaced by Gen. Fu'ad Chehab, like Chamoun a Christian. For six years under Chehab, Lebanon was under lightly veiled military rule. Between 1964 and 1976, Lebanese presidents were civilian, but their presence did not head off the civil war that after 1975 devoured civilian institutions, the Lebanese armed forces, and the country itself.

Israel has apparently escaped military rule, but soon after independence Prime Minister David Ben Gurion feared a coup d'état engineered by the leaders of the outlawed Jewish terrorist organizations (principally, the Irgun, led by Menachem Begin). It is an irony of sorts that Begin went on to become prime minister himself some thirty years later through the ballot box. More important, however, is the thorough intermingling of the civilian and military spheres in Israeli politics and in the economy. Israel is a nation in arms. It has fought four major wars. It has faced terrorist threats of various kinds. It maintains a large defense industrial base, and many public activities are regulated by concerns of national security. The military does not have to seize power in Israel, because on most issues it is already positioned to get what it wants. Moreover, many of Israel's most visible politicians have come out of the military: Moshe Dayan, Yitzhak Rabin, Haim Bar-Lev, Ezer Weizmann, Rafael Aytan, and Ariel Sharon, to name but the most illustrious (for a contrasting view, see Gutmann and Landau 1985, 191).

In Iran, the shah's enormous repressive apparatus, built on the armed forces and the secret police (SAVAK), was neutralized by persistent street demonstrations and strikes orchestrated by both the Iranian Muslim organizations and the radical leftist groups. It would be hard to describe the Islamic Republic of Iran as civilian but equally hard to describe it as a military dictatorship. The regular military has been contained by a dominant coalition of the clergy (the mullahs) and the irregular Revolutionary Guards (Pasdaran). It is this coalition that, with Khomeini's fervent blessing, prosecuted the war with Iraq. The Islamic republic is thus a strange, if not unique, mutant of Huntington's praetorian state, led by "priests" and armed religious militants.

GOOD GUYS OR BAD GUYS?

In the 1950s and 1960s, in the literature generated under the rubric of "political development," there was a tendency to look upon military regimes in LDCs with some favor. Military officers were seen as modernizers, men with a nationalist vision, a strong sense of discipline and organization, and a commitment to the values of a meritocracy. For many observers, the military could build a nation out of the heterogeneous religious, ethnic, or linguistic particles of its society—transforming the economy, developing the infrastructure, expanding the educational system, and seeing to it that hard work and competence were rewarded with official recognition and advancement. "The army in politics cannot become an institution above the battle. It intervenes as a partisan, representing a new class with whom the majority in the country does not yet share a common consciousness" (Halpern 1963, 274). In short, the military's vision was national whereas that of its compatriots was parochial; it was organized and disciplined while the civilian population was still mired in the supposed fatalism and petty jealousies of traditional societies; it believed in performance though its countrymen trusted in fate or luck. If freewheeling democracy had to be sacrificed, temporarily, to the exigencies of building a nation and transforming an economy, that appeared an acceptable price to pay.

By the late 1960s neither the military nor its presumptive class allies were viewed with the same enthusiasm. Huntington, in his influential book, *Political Order in Changing Societies* (1968), wrote with faint distaste about praetorian regimes as perhaps necessary evils to restrain popular demands for social and economic benefits that hard-pressed governments could not meet. The praetorians provided the order that would allow economic development to proceed without unmanageable unrest. Although in the past twenty-five years the Republic of Korea has best exemplified the kinds of praetorian functions Huntington attributed to Third World militaries, the counterparts in the Middle East that come closest to his model are Iran under both shahs, Turkey under Atatürk,[1] and Algeria under Boumedienne. The experiments of Nasser in Egypt and the Ba'athi military in Syria and Iraq do not fit well because they have neither really suppressed popular demands for economic benefits nor driven forward the development process to the degree that they had hoped.

In an analysis of Latin American politics in the 1960s and 1970s, O'Donnell advanced a variant on the praetorian model that he called "bureaucratic authoritarianism" (1978). He argued that LDCs that pursue strategies of import-substituting industrialization eventually come to a point when the "easy" phase ends and a process of "deepening" must be initiated. This entails moving from the manufacture of consumer goods to the manufacture of intermediate and capital goods—sophisticated machinery, heavy engineering goods, and the full range of basic metals. It may entail cutting costs so that industries that have grown fat on captive domestic markets can compete in international markets. O'Donnell predicted that as deepening got under way it might require a military authoritarian regime to discipline the workforce and hold down wages. The military would ally itself with elements of the civilian technocracy responsible for designing and planning the deepening strategy and with foreign multinational corporations that would provide the technology and expertise.

This model, developed largely with Brazil and Argentina in mind, has been judged deficient even for Latin America (Collier 1979), and in the Middle East the only regime that has approximated it has been Turkey. In the early 1960s the Turkish military did pursue industrial deepening, behind high tariff walls and in the absence of much foreign investment. It was, however, the military intervention of 1980 that best approximated O'Donnell's model. That intervention was provoked by years of growing political violence and a profound economic crisis that called into question Turkey's long-standing ISI strategy. The generals, allied with civilian technocrats, muzzled the labor unions and the universities, cut social outlays, and pushed through an export-led growth strategy that required Turkish industry to become competitive in international markets. What was at stake was not deepening but rather export promotion.

It is difficult in the 1980s to unearth anyone who finds merit in military or quasi-military rule. The downfall of the shah, Ferdinand Marcos, Nimeiri, and the military regimes in Argentina, Brazil, Chile, and elsewhere was greeted, at least initially, as a blessing. Similarly, the collapse of the party-police states of Eastern Europe and the former USSR was seen as testimony to the failure of such regimes to provide materially or psychically for their own citizens. Whatever degree of order and discipline the military has been able to provide, it has been outweighed by the choking off of the free flow of information and ideas and the blocking of the assumption of responsibility on the part of ordinary citizens for their economic and political affairs.

Although the military clings stubbornly to power in the Middle East, its role as a transforming and dynamic institution has been discredited nearly everywhere. There is among the middle classes of the region a general sense that the military must be pushed out of politics and out of economic management. Among countries that have experienced military rule, only Turkey appears to have achieved lasting civilianization. In other countries there has been backsliding. The Sudan has reverted to military rule, Tunisia fell under it for the first time in 1988, Algeria since 1991 has deepened its praetorian character, and the Yemens are now forcibly united under the rule of a general.

THE ECONOMIC WEIGHT OF THE MILITARY

Conventional wisdom has long posited that heavy outlays on defense and warfare divert scarce resources away from directly productive investment and human-capital formation. For once, conventional wisdom may be right. A counterargument with respect to the LDCs is that large defense expenditures may act as an economic stimulus. They finance heavy industry (armaments), the acquisition of advanced technologies, the formation of skilled personnel, from truck drivers to radar operators, and the provision of employment. Defense expenditures or a large military establishment may attract foreign aid and investment and thus enhance the country's foreign-exchange position. The argument has provoked a great deal of debate (summarized in Deger 1992), and many studies have found that defense outlays bear a high opportunity cost, shifting resources from "high-growth development projects" that entail a reduction not only in public outlays but in dependent private outlays as well. Only countries flush with foreign exchange (e.g., Saudi Arabia before 1986) show any positive correlation between defense outlays and economic growth; otherwise, the two compete with each other.

What can the Middle East tell us about this argument? Unfortunately, nothing very conclusive (on Egypt and Israel, see Barnett 1992). When defense expenditures in all regional groupings in the developing world are compared, those in the Middle East certainly come out the highest. When oil prices were at their peak, Middle Eastern countries were spending US$40 billion a year on defense, with Iran and Saudi Arabia leading the way. Petroleum revenues of course allowed some countries to indulge in this luxury, but Egyptian outlays were about US$3 billion and Syria and Morocco about US$2 billion. Of the fourteen countries worldwide that in the late 1970s spent more than 10% of their GNP on defense each year, eight were in the Middle East. Chatelus (1984, 19) calculated that Syria in the early 1980s was spending ninety-three times as much on defense as on health.

One might suppose that such defense burdens would cripple most economies, at least those without significant petroleum earnings. But there is no correlation in the Middle East between defense expenditure as a proportion of GDP and rates of growth (Table 13.1). Moreover, large outlays and relatively high rates come together in a few instances. One cannot conclude from this that defense expenditures contribute more than direct public or private investment to economic growth, nor can we assume a causal relation between high defense outlays and growth. We may estimate, counterfactually, the returns on alternative uses of the moneys devoted to defense, but practically nowhere in the world is there any assurance that reduced defense budgets would result in increased outlays on, say, social welfare or infrastructure. Defense outlays are laden with the symbols and sentiments of national pride and survival. People seem prepared to accept disproportionate public investment in defense. They and their leaders may find less justification in using equivalent resources to reduce adult illiteracy or line irrigation ditches.[2]

Similarly, big defense establishments attract foreign-resource flows because they represent important markets for arms exporters and because they are located in geopolitically strategic regions. Through the supply of arms and military expertise great and lesser powers can buy political and strategic leverage that no other sphere of economic activity can offer. In the same vein, there is often a large concessional component in the pricing and the financing of the arms deliveries; indeed, in the Middle East, billions of dollars' worth of arms have been given away annually. As is the case with domestic military expenditures, it is unlikely these grants would have ever materialized, at least not on the same scale, for nonmilitary development purposes.

TABLE 13.1   Economic Weight of Middle Eastern
Military Establishments, 1979–1993

		Military Expenditures	
	Average Growth GNP (%)	% GNP	% Central Government Expenditure
Bahrain	−2.9	5.93	15.01
Egypt	2.8	9.33	16.75
Iran	2.6	6.77	28.60
Iraq	−11.5	35.68	59.31
Israel	2.0	17.65	26.17
Jordan	1.2	15.90	35.77
Kuwait	−4.3	19.95	30.97
Oman	3.4	22.35	42.65
Saudi Arabia	−3.6	19.44	40.30
Syria	2.4	15.05	42.25
Turkey	2.4	4.23	18.95
UAE	−4.4	6.62	50.56
PDRY	−1.5	16.30	23.19
YAR	3.8	9.87	28.29

Figures represent averages over the 1979–1993 period. Figures for PDRY and YAR are for 1983–1989, and figures for Iraq and Syria are for 1983–1993.
Source: U.S. Arms Control and Disarmament Agency (1995); World Bank (1995d).

The collapse of oil prices and its ripple effect on the region's economies had a substantial impact on the military establishments of the Middle East. From an average of 17% of GDP in 1983, military expenditures for the countries of the region fell to 9% in 1993. Nonetheless, relative to the other major regions of the world, the Middle East remained the most generous in military spending (see Figures 13.1 and 13.2 and Sadowski 1993). Moreover, as can be seen in Table 13.1, reductions in military expenditures were not uniform; they have crept up over time in Tunisia and surged in the Sudan as the government in Khartoum has stepped up the military campaign against the southern insurrectionary forces.

The beginning of peace negotiations in 1991 between Israel and its Arab adversaries raised hopes that the region might one day benefit from a large "peace dividend" (see el-Naggar and el-Erian 1993). Such hopes are ill-founded, because there are several theaters of ongoing military tension in the region that are not directly related to the Arab-Israeli conflict, for example, Iran-Iraq, Saudi Arabia–Yemen, Turkey-Greece, Iraq–Saudi Arabia, Iraq-Kuwait, Iraq-Syria, Israel-Iran, Syria-Turkey, Egypt–the Sudan, and Algeria-Morocco. These unresolved conflicts will be used by the parties to

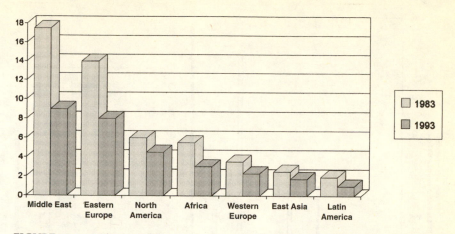

FIGURE 13.1   Military spending as a percentage of GDP, 1983–1993. *Source: The Economist,* July 15, 1995, 60.

them to justify continued high levels of expenditure and arms acquisition. They do not include ongoing or unresolved civil wars, such as those in Iraq, the Sudan, Turkey, and Lebanon. Turkey's prime minister in 1994, Tansu Çiller, claimed that her country was spending 5% of GDP annually in its war against the PKK.

The data on arms sales to Middle Eastern countries since the end of Operation Desert Storm are indicative. Over the period 1991–1993, some US$20 billion in arms were transferred to Saudi Arabia and Kuwait alone. Iran has been spending about US$2 billion a year in arms purchases. Both Iran and Syria have acquired missiles from North Korea and the PRC. As soon as Salih had ended the secession of South Yemen from the Yemeni union in 1994, he contracted with Moldava to purchase thirty MIG-29 fighters for US$300 million. The simple fact is that major arms suppliers such as the United States will not forgo the opportunity to resolve balance-of-payments problems by selling arms to countries already replete with them and located in war zones (see Figure 13.3). In addition, the countries of Eastern Europe and the former Soviet Union may have little else to export than surplus Soviet equipment. Some will try to export weapons-grade uranium, for which Iran appears to be an eager buyer.

The weight of the military can be measured in other ways. In several of the large Middle Eastern states there has emerged what President Dwight Eisenhower once termed a "military-industrial complex." Israel, Egypt, Turkey, and Iran, most notably, have developed extensive armaments industries that occupy a particularly important niche in their economies. For one thing, the military-industrial sector includes some of these economies' most advanced technological undertakings—research into and direct use or manufacture of strategic technologies, including supercomputers, nuclear fission, lasers, advanced telecommunications and remote

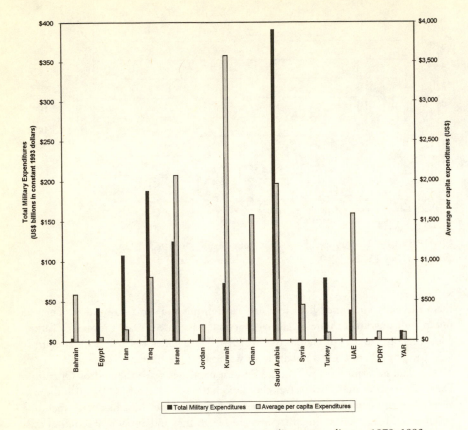

FIGURE 13.2   Cumulative and average per capita military expenditures, 1979–1993.
Source: U.S. Arms Control and Disarmament Agency (1995).

sensing, telemetry, and missiles. Further, these undertakings are almost exclusively within the public sector. Although in Israel and Turkey some component manufacture is contracted out, the transfer and adaptation of high technology with obvious civilian applications is monopolized by the military establishment, and anyone who has the expertise and desire to work with such technologies becomes a servant of that monopoly. The military-industrial complex tends to invade the civilian sector of the economy, competing directly with private producers and providers of services. Finally, these growing economic domains have become important sources of foreign exchange through sales of arms. Arms exports have been crucial to Israel's balance of payments for many years, but Egypt too, partially as a result of Iraq's needs for arms, saw the value of its military exports rise from some US$1 billion in 1986 (see Springborg 1987) to an estimated US$4 billion in 1988/89, according to the U.S. Arms Control and Disarmament Agency.

Turkey's military industries employ over 40,000 people, and in 1985 Turkey exported some US$400 million in arms. These factories and facilities are involved in

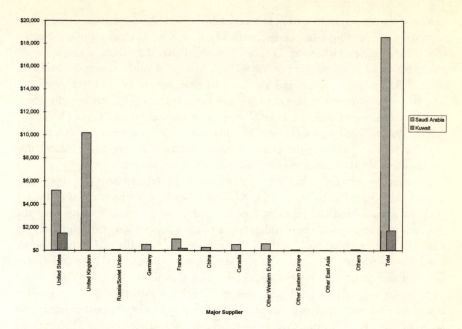

FIGURE 13.3   Arms transfers (US$ millions), 1991–1993. *Source:* U.S. Arms Control and Disarmament Agency (1995).

overhauling M-48 tanks, manufacturing optical equipment, and manufacturing and assembling Huey helicopters and F-1 jet fighters, submarines, patrol boats, tank guns, and missiles. Significantly, some of Turkey's large private industrial conglomerates are licensed to manufacture ground-to-air missiles, Black Hawk helicopters, heavy trucks, and armored vehicles (see Karaspan 1987; *Middle East Economic Digest,* September 7, 1985).

Egypt's defense industry is several decades old. Under Nasser it expanded from manufacture of munitions and light arms into aeronautics and even took an ill-fated leap into ballistic missiles. But real expansion occurred under Sadat, especially after 1975, when Saudi Arabia and some other Gulf States agreed to finance the Arab Military Industrialization Organization (AMIO) to produce a range of advanced weapons for the Arab countries. Egypt became the home for the AMIO, and when, as a result of the Camp David Accords, the Arab financiers pulled out of the project, it became an entirely Egyptian undertaking. Between the AMIO and the original defense industries, in 1986 the complex included some twenty-four factories, with a workforce of 70,000 to 100,000 and production worth about US$350 million per year (Stork 1987). It manufactured components for MIGs and assembled French Alpha jets, helicopters, and, at Benha Electronics, radar systems.

During the 1970s the shah of Iran sought to make the Iranian military the dominant force in the Gulf and a rival to India in the Indian Ocean. The purchase of arms and military technology ran at more than US$4 billion per annum and led to contracts and licensing arrangements with a host of multinational suppliers: Northrop, Lockheed, Bell Helicopter, Leyland, Daimler-Benz, and others. The Islamic republic inherited this complex but had to look to other sources of supply: the PRC, the USSR, Sweden, Turkey, and the international arms market. Likewise, Saudi Arabia, on the strength of its petroleum revenues in the 1970s, has bought entire military technologies and industries. For instance, Saudi Arabia's Peace Shield air-defense system is bringing in billions of dollars in radar equipment and computers. In the two years following the end of Operation Desert Storm, Saudi Arabia imported about US$19 billion in arms and defense-related matériel.

It is Israel, however, that has gone the farthest in the development and sophistication of its military industries. Israel's technical expertise is without equal in the region. Its research-and-development facilities put it on an equal footing with the most advanced nations of the world. It is one of the world's major arms suppliers. Its scientists have provided Israel with all the requisites to assemble and deliver nuclear bombs and warheads. The country had the necessary expertise to design and manufacture a jet fighter, the Lavi, possessing all the capabilities of the U.S. F-16C. Israel wants to be self-sufficient militarily and in all technological domains, but its own armed forces could never generate sufficient demand to sustain, economically, the range of military industries that national security would require. In 1990 its two largest armaments industries had a combined turnover of US$2.3 billion. For such industries to be viable, Israel must seek markets abroad.

Perhaps the most important aspect of the Middle East's military-industrial complexes is that they have tended to become powerful economic enclaves and, because of their strategic nature, not fully accountable to parliaments or auditors. They are in a position to harness important private-sector clients and, indeed, to invade civilian markets. They own property, productive assets, and financial institutions, and they can negotiate foreign and domestic loans and put out contracts. Frequently it is alleged that these assets and points of leverage are used by the officers' corps to line their own pockets and those of their clients.

Turkey may have pioneered in the building of a military-economic enclave. After the military coup of 1961, the Armed Forces Mutual Assistance Fund (ÖYAK) was set up. Its financial resources come from a 10% levy on the salaries of all commissioned and noncommissioned officers, and the purpose of the fund is to pay these officers pensions upon their retirement. By the middle 1970s some 80,000 officers were paying into this fund. Its assets were estimated at US$300 million by 1973, and a decade later Bianchi (1984, 70) described it as "the country's largest and most diversified industrial conglomerate." At the time it had controlling interests in the Turkish Automotive Corporation, the MAT Corporation (truck and tractor manufacture), the ÖYAK Insurance Company, TÜKAS Food Canning, and a cement plant and owned 20% of Petkim (petrochemicals), 8% of Turkish Petroleum, 42% of ÖYAK-Renault (automobile assembly and manufacture), and 7% of a Goodyear subsidiary (Ayres 1983).

ÖYAK has bridged a gap between the military establishment and the private economic sector. Since Ottoman times and even under Atatürk, the military has seen itself as an independent entity, a guardian of the nation's interests and, to some extent, a watchdog against private greed. It has always depended upon state budgetary appropriations for its needs. Now ÖYAK and other special funds are dependent on direct investments in the national economy and in joint ventures with foreign and domestic corporations. The economic interests of the officers' corps have become firmly wedded to the performance of the Turkish economy and to that of its private sector.

Egypt, especially since the advent of Field Marshal Abu Ghazala in 1981, has followed a similar path. Military industries had already claimed a portion of civilian markets for products including truck motors, telephone equipment, optical lenses, fans, and air conditioners. Annual production for civilian consumption reached about US$300 million in the early 1980s. In 1978 the National Service Projects Organization was established, and once Abu Ghazala got hold of it its range of activities was greatly expanded. The army corps of engineers assisted civilian contractors in bridge and road construction. Armed forces communications experts implemented the refurbishing and expansion of the telephone systems of Cairo and Alexandria. Most spectacular was the armed forces' direct entry into food production, allegedly so that in time of hostilities they could ensure their own supply of food. What transpired was a capital-intensive plunge into desert reclamation, hothouse cultivation of vegetables, and commercial production of eggs and poultry. Springborg estimated the value of food produced by the military at £E488 million (roughly US$200 million) in 1986. Private producers have cautiously complained, particularly after military production drove down the price of eggs, that by using conscripts as free labor the military had an unfair advantage over the private sector. These protests may be outweighed by the ability of the military to let lucrative contracts to private firms, ensure supply or produce to designated wholesalers, and, through a network of retired officers relocated in private and joint-venture firms, maintain a far-flung system of clients and cronies.

The Syrian military has followed the same path. It was drawn into the Lebanese civil war in 1976 and wound up in effective control of eastern and northeastern Lebanon as well as of access to Beirut. Mildly austere, socialist Syria thus met anarchic Lebanon, where freewheeling entrepreneurs still managed to thrive in the midst of the fighting. Lebanon imported a range of consumer goods that Syrians craved, and the armed forces found themselves in a position to control the movement of such goods. The result was predictable: a sprawling black market in everything from tape decks to automobiles, operated by Syrian officers, with astronomic profits distributed through several subnetworks. Even without this profiteering spawned in the Lebanese cockpit, the Syrian military controls an important economic enclave. It has been involved in public works, construction, basic industry, farm production, and the manufacture of batteries, bottled mineral water, and furniture. The largest military corporation is the Military Housing Organization (Longuenesse 1985, 18).

THE MILITARY AND NATION BUILDING

Recent studies of state formation in Western Europe have emphasized the crucial role of military rivalry and war (for example, Tilly 1975). It is argued that the perceived need to build powerful military forces obliged central authorities to extend their administrative grip on their societies, reduce the autonomy of the feudal estate, and extract through taxes the resources needed to pay for the military effort. Over time this process gave rise to strong, centralized states and, because war was inherent in the scheme, to protonationalism.

We may legitimately ask whether in the Middle East a singular process is under way. The answer is an equivocal no or, perhaps, not yet. Certainly war or its threat has been a constant in regional affairs since World War II, but with a few exceptions this has not notably promoted national integration and a common national identity. Perhaps our time horizon is simply too short. Moreover, because arms and what we have called strategic rents have been so readily available, and on soft terms, to Middle Eastern belligerents, the region's states have not had to develop an extractive capacity commensurate with their military burdens.

Nonetheless, there are very important exceptions to these generalizations. There is little doubt that war has been a determinant in shaping Israel's national identity. There, the nation in arms is an everyday reality. The Israeli defense forces have, moreover, been used since 1948 as a primary instrument for integrating the culturally diverse Jews of the Diaspora, teaching them Hebrew, socializing them to the values of the state, and erasing differences among them through a common uniform and shared drudgery. (The only non-Jews who participate in this experience are the Druze.)

Like Israel, the Turkish republic was born and consolidated as the result of military victory, a commodity that hardly any other Middle Eastern society has enjoyed in recent centuries. It may be stating the obvious to say that, whereas defeat or perceived inferiority provokes a divisive search for culprits and traitors, military success can be claimed by all elements of a nation and serve as a symbol of national accomplishment. Thus in 1931 Atatürk could credibly claim a grandiose role for the Turkish armed forces (Tachau and Heper 1983, 20): "the Turkish nation has . . . always looked to the military . . . as the leader of movements to achieve lofty national ideals. . . . when speaking of the army, I am speaking of the intelligentsia of the Turkish nation who are the true owners of this country. . . . The Turkish nation . . . considers its army the guardian of its ideals."

We can hardly address this issue without considering Iran and Iraq. In 1988, after these two countries had been at war for over eight years, they reached a tenuous cease-fire. They are both societies with profound religious, linguistic, and ethnic cleavages. They contain colossal obstacles to national integration. Yet one of the astonishing elements of the combat was that each nation more or less maintained unity in the ranks. The Shi'ites and Kurds of Iraq did not defect from Iraq's war effort despite having ethnic or sectarian brethren on the other side; likewise, Iran's Kurds and Arabs did not break ranks. However, after Iraq's armed forces were crushed in Operation Desert Storm, both Iraqi Kurds and Iraqi Shi'ites rose in a failed revolt against Saddam Hussein. Clearly war had not yet forged an Iraqi identity that could displace those of sect or blood.

THE REGULAR MILITARY AND CIVILIANS IN ARMS

The several self-proclaimed revolutionary regimes of the Middle East have all had to confront in one way or another the issue of arming the people. In Algeria, Iran, Israel, and the PDRY, where the people were to some extent already armed when new regimes were founded, the issue was particularly sensitive. In other countries, such as Morocco and the Sudan, irregular guerrilla forces had to be absorbed into the regular military.

We can state as a general rule that the regular military views with alarm the arming of civilian militias and party paramilitary groups, not to mention the poking about in military affairs of political commissars. Regimes have come unstuck over this issue. In 1965 Ahmad Ben Bella, the president of Algeria, contemplated arming civilian groups under the auspices of the National Liberation Front. His minister of defense, Houari Boumedienne, saw this as an implicit statement that the Army of National Liberation was incapable of defending the revolution and that Ben Bella wanted a paramilitary force loyal to him to hold Boumedienne's power in check. In June 1965 Boumedienne toppled Ben Bella, and there was no further talk of party militias.

A similar drama unfolded in Syria in the late 1960s. Salah Jadid, a senior Alawite officer and leader of the military command in the Ba'ath, sought to organize a Ba'athi militia to engage Israel in guerrilla warfare. This was clearly a major issue in driving him apart from his erstwhile ally, Hafiz al-Assad, who was minister of defense. In September 1970, in the wake of King Hussein's crushing of the PLO in Jordan, Assad had Jadid arrested and took over the presidency of the republic.

In Morocco, Algeria, and the Sudan, the regular military had to disarm and absorb into its ranks the remnants of guerrilla forces. In Morocco these came from liberation armies operating, in the two years prior to independence, in the northern mountains, the southern deserts, and some big cities, while in Algeria they came from the guerrilla armies in the interior *wilaya*s, or military zones, of the FLN. In the Sudan, after the granting of autonomy to the southern provinces in 1971, the Sudanese army absorbed large numbers of freedom fighters into its ranks. One of them, Col. John Garang, deserted in 1983 and has led a major insurrectionary movement (the Southern People's Liberation Army [SPLA]) in the south ever since.

If and when Israel and the Palestinians reach a definitive settlement, the PLO will face the task of sorting out the armed components of the organization, creating what will surely be no more than a well-trained police and disarming, demobilizing, and integrating into the civilian economy the rest. Perhaps the greatest challenge will be to close down the armed wing of HAMAS, which is not part of the PLO.

Iran offers an example of irregular forces cohabiting uneasily with the regular military. The key actors are the Revolutionary Guards or Pasdaran, who became nationwide militia at the service of the Islamic Republican party (until that party was disbanded in late 1987). Many of the leaders came out of the radical secular leftist

Mujahidin al Khalq before 1979. They were introduced to radical Shi'ite Islam through the teachings of Ali Shariati and were drawn to Ayatollah Khomeini because of his fiercely anti-imperialist and antidespotic stance. After Khomeini came to power, these militants turned on their erstwhile leftist allies, hounding them out of the country or physically eliminating them. They organized the revolutionary tribunals that meted out arbitrary justice to a host of presumed enemies of the republic. They waged war against the Kurds and were instrumental in the seizure of the U.S. Embassy in Tehran. With time they took on the role of a security-force-cum-vigilante group in the countryside.

The regular armed forces were relatively powerless to oppose the ascendancy of the Pasdaran because the senior officers' corps had been so badly compromised in its loyalty to the shah. The armed forces were given an opportunity to refurbish their image in the war with Iraq and to some extent did so. But the Pasdaran, along with the ill-trained volunteers, or *basij,* enhanced their image in Iran through human-wave assaults on Iraqi positions and other suicidal exploits.

The Pasdaran have become a very powerful force in Iranian politics. Perhaps numbering 200,000, they are armed, control substantial financial resources through institutions such as the Foundation for the Disinherited, and espouse a common militant brand of Shi'ism. They have had powerful allies among the mullahs, such as the former prime minister Mir Hosayn Mousavi, and numerous allies in the majlis.

It is in Israel that one finds the most "comfortable" equilibrium between the professional military and armed civilians. The Israeli defense forces were born in the kibbutz movement and the irregular Haganah before independence in 1948. Although the Haganah was rapidly professionalized after 1948, it has never forgotten its civilian origins. More important, Israel's ability to mobilize its adult population quickly and its system of reserve training for all males until an advanced age have blurred most boundaries between soldiers and civilians. Israelis board buses and sit on park benches with their weapons with the same nonchalance as a businesswoman with her attaché case. Because the military is so closely integrated into Israeli society, the nation's leaders do not fear an armed citizenry.

CONCLUSION

On the whole, the prominent and long-lasting role played by the military in Middle East politics has been harmful. By and large, military regimes did not achieve the kind of structural transformation of their economies or the industrial deepening that they invariably announced as their goals. However, the heavy outlays on the military and on war preparedness that their incumbency has entailed appear to have done little to impede fairly rapid economic growth. The real question is whether this growth could have been more rapid still in the absence of such heavy spending. It has certainly been the case that direct rule by the military has not enhanced the military performance of the region's armed forces.

The military has been the catalyst, or at least the conduit, for the introduction of advanced technologies into the region. Military industries and research-and-development facilities are often the most advanced of their nations and have a wide range of civilian applications. It is less clear, however, to what extent these technologies are merely imported as opposed to being absorbed into the scientific community. At a more mundane level, and with the major exception of Israel, the armed forces of the Middle East have not been extensively used to impart literacy and vocational training to their recruits. Because most countries maintain some form of universal conscription and most recruits may come from rural backgrounds, there is a real opportunity to build the nation's human resources during the years in which its youth is in the ranks, but that opportunity has not been widely seized.

The military has done more to build state apparatuses than to create strong economies. We noted in Chapter 12 that the very nature of military training and the functional division of the armed forces may have predisposed officers to a corporatist vision of society as a whole. Thus, together with the strengthening of the state apparatus and of the public sector, we find military rulers structuring the political arena along corporatist lines. Order has taken precedence over mobilization, organic unity over pluralism, discipline over spontaneity.

War and military rule have been the two most salient characteristics setting the Middle East apart from other regions of the world. That combination has also been the major obstacle to the emergence of more liberal political practices if not to democracy itself. Despite a slowly diminishing grip on national wealth, the military everywhere is deeply entrenched. The many unresolved regional conflicts will enable it to exert claims to substantial resources. The civilianization of Middle Eastern political systems will come very slowly and, in some instances, as in the Sudan, may be halted altogether by alliances of Islamist movements with military sympathizers.

NOTES

1. For two positive views of Turkey's "modernization," see Lerner (1959) and McClelland (1963).

2. Of course, if people prefer private consumption to defense outlays, even if investment and growth do not increase, social welfare will rise if defense spending falls (and, by hypothesis, private consumption rises).

14

IS ISLAM THE SOLUTION?

"Islam is the solution!"—the rallying cry of Islamist political parties—appears on walls in virtually every popular quarter in the Middle East and North Africa. In this chapter we ask whether this slogan is true in a particular, limited sense: Is Islam the solution to the development problems described in this book? We do *not* ask whether Islam is the solution to *other* problems, such as that of personal salvation, a just moral order, or gender relations. Islamists will, of course, object that one cannot separate the solution to development problems from such wider questions. We disagree, and we also think that the answer to our limited question is no. We concede that Islamic precepts can contribute to improved governance, but we deny that Islamists offer solutions to the region's pressing development problems.

We must make absolutely clear from the outset what we mean—and do not mean—by "Islamist." Although it is an obvious point, it cannot be repeated often enough that *not all or even most Muslims are Islamists*. For example, the largest Muslim country in the world, Indonesia, does not depend on Islam for its solutions to problems of development. Classed by the World Bank as belonging to that superstar group of developing countries, the "high-performing Asian economies," Indonesia has perhaps the world's best record of macroeconomic management of the Dutch Disease (the difficulties that attend a sudden, large influx of foreign exchange). Its economic managers swiftly dealt with the problem in the late 1970s by adopting and implementing highly orthodox macroeconomic policies. In marked contrast to most Middle Eastern countries, Indonesia responded with similar agility to the fall in oil prices during the 1980s. Moreover, the gains from sound management have been widely shared; whereas in 1972 roughly 68 million Indonesians were "poor," by 1982 only 30 million were poor, and the percentage of the population that was poor had fallen from 58% to 17% (World Bank 1990d). The number of poor Malaysians was roughly halved during the same period of time. There is no question that Muslims can govern their economies with great skill in Southeast Asia, as did the Turks under Özal and as do the Moroccans under King Hassan and the Jordanians under King Hussein.

We are also presumably not talking about "fundamentalist Muslims." If this is a meaningful category (which is dubious), then it surely includes the Wahhabis of the House of Saud. Although the Saudi economy has had its share of shocks, dislocations, recessions, and the like, the economic management of the country has been reasonably good. The management practices of the Saudi Arabian Monetary Authority have been quite conservative; its relations with equally conservative colleagues in Western and Japanese banking circles are excellent. Saudi Arabia has accumulated rather disquieting levels of internal and external debt, but in this it resembles a host of other LDCs. These problems have everything to do with interests and institutions and essentially nothing to do with ideology and religious beliefs.

We use the term "Islamist" to describe that subset of Muslim theorists and political activists who believe that a return to the shari'a is the single most important issue facing the Muslim world today and that the imposition of Islamic law and the dictates of the Islamic tradition offer clear, coherent, and straightforward solutions to the problems facing Muslim societies. Islamists oppose existing non-Islamist regimes; in particular, they oppose the Saudi regime, denying it the Islamic legitimacy that the House of Saud so assiduously cultivates.

In considering the political economy of Islamism, we begin by sketching our understanding of the origins of the movement, its sources of support, and its nature as a political coalition. Then we inquire into the likely performance of Islamists in power by examining both their economic theories and (where possible) their economic practice.

ISLAMISTS IN OPPOSITION

Islamist movements are loose coalitions of three elements: a counterelite composed of businessmen and professionals, a second stratum of frustrated intellectuals and unemployed or underemployed university or secondary school graduates, and a mass base of the young, semieducated unemployed. In some cases, the Islamists are able to recruit from the ranks of the urban lumpenproletariat, where militants compete with criminal gangs of smugglers and drug dealers. There is also some evidence that the movements' militants are getting younger and less well educated (Ibrahim 1994). The core of the Islamist movement, however, remains the young, semieducated, newly urbanized unemployed.

These young people harbor deep grievances. They are personally and collectively frustrated. As we have seen (Chapters 4, 5, and 10), education and exposure to the wider world have broadened their horizons, but the grim realities of the job and housing markets have dashed their hopes. Their key problems are their inability to find jobs, especially jobs that match their expectations, and the lack of suitable housing. These two combine with more prolonged education to induce them to postpone marriage, often for a very long time. In a culture that teaches that sex is proper and good but only within marriage, this situation is deeply frustrating. Because young people everywhere are trying to establish their identity, they care about their relationships with others. This is one reason jobs and marriages matter so much. The "politics of identity" so often noted by cultural specialist students of Islamism is fueled by the youth of the membership of these movements. For demographic reasons, the percentage of young people in the populations of these countries has been growing.

Islamism is also usefully conceived as the new nationalism in Arab countries. The young of today are as attracted to nationalism as were their fathers and grandfathers. They perceive the wider community of Muslims as attacked and abused, and they identify with those who resist these attacks. They are all, at least in their dreams, "Afghans"—the name given the young Arabs and Turks who fought for the mujahedin against the Soviets in Afghanistan.

The Islamist movements arose out of the failure of the old order. Specifically, their grievances need to be placed in the context of the grandiose promises and squalid performances of national development strategies in the region since independence. We will review three phases: the ISI phase, the oil-boom era, and our current era of austerity and economic reform. We have seen how ISI policies increased industrial production and opened educational systems, particularly for secondary and university education. They also fostered excessive capital-intensity, which retarded job creation, generated severe balance-of-payments constraints, which slowed growth, and discriminated against agriculture, which fostered rural-urban migration.

The oil boom of the 1970s further blunted incentives for production of tradables via the Dutch Disease and stimulated rural-urban migration. It also fostered large-scale labor emigration from poor countries to the Gulf States, including Iraq (see Chapter 15), the rise of new, often Islamist financial intermediaries channeling the flow of remittances back home, and the acceleration of state largesse. States trying to pursue the partial, halting liberalization known as *infitah* encouraged Islamist militants as counterweights to the socialist left. The counterelite of Islamist businessmen and professionals was also greatly strengthened in this period.

The oil bust of the 1980s and 1990s witnessed declining resources, governmental retrenchment, and tentative, often noncredible economic reform efforts. The economic downturn and government budgetary austerity coincide with the acceleration of new entrants to the labor force, coming on top of a legacy of economic failure. Government spending cutbacks and administrative deficiencies further rend an already tattered social safety net, and this creates opportunities for Islamist movements, who have moved to provide their own services.

In short, government policies during the past three decades have fostered a counterelite of Islamist business and frustrated educated youth, accumulated potential recruits for the movement through economic failure, provided them with numerous grievances, and evacuated critical spaces in the political economy. Islamist movements cannot be understood without a grasp of the uneven and sometimes stalled developmental processes that we have chronicled throughout this book. However, as we have argued in Chapter 12, the phenomenon of Islamism cannot be *reduced* to these developmental problems. Blocked careers, unemployment, rampant corruption, unavailable housing all set the context for Islamism, but they are poor predictors of exactly who will participate in such movements. Young, unemployed, frustrated young men throughout the region can turn to Islamism, to drugs and crime, to psychoanalysis, or to indifference, muddling through, dogged hard work, or any number of other, personal coping strategies. The decision to join a revolutionary movement is a deeply personal, idiosyncratic one. Socioeconomic contexts are important for understanding these movements, but they by no means fully explain them.

From a political perspective, it is not enough that a counterelite exists or that its followers have grievances or that individuals idiosyncratically choose to try Islamism as a solution to their problems. For a movement to matter politically, the aggrieved must be able to act collectively, which means that they must be able to overcome the free-rider problem. Two classic ways of overcoming this problem are through small group size and the provision of "contingent incentives," desirable private goods that are obtainable only by joining the group (Olson 1965). Both of these mechanisms are prevalent among Islamists.

Islamist groups are usually informally organized, relatively small groups composed of close friends and relatives. The prototype for this aspect of Islamist politics (as for so much else) is the Muslim Brotherhood. From the outset, "the entire movement was built around small, semi-independent cells geared to the particular needs and aspirations of their members." The fundamental organizational building block of the movement was a group of five to ten persons called (significantly, for a politics of identity) *al-usra* (the family) (Denoeux 1993, 94). The tradition has been replicated among Lebanese militias, networks of Iranian mullahs, Egyptian *jama'at al-islamia*, and the Algerian FIS. Members of such small networks can more easily monitor, detect, and deter free-riding.

Islamist groups also typically provide contingent incentives. For example, Islamist student *jama'at* in Egypt provide their members with low-cost lecture notes and textbooks, minibus transportation for (veiled) women, and access to the study groups and tutoring services necessary to pass examinations. Islamic organizations provide day-care centers, private medical clinics and even hospitals, and schools. During the 1970s the radical Takfir wal-Hijra group in Egypt provided its male members with wives, housing, and access to work in Saudi Arabia (Ayubi 1991a; Kepel 1986). The Lebanese Hizbullah provided stipends, pensions, and an array of social services, such as schools, vocational training institutes, clinics, hospitals, and orphanages (Denoeux 1993).

The Islamists' ability to supply private goods is partly a function of government action.[1] First, as noted earlier, many states permitted or even encouraged Islamist organizations in the 1970s. Since there are typically dynamic economies of scale in institutional formation, this provided a critical advantage to Islamists. Second, state cutbacks in the supply of goods and services, whether because of political collapse (Iran in 1978) or budgetary austerity (Egypt, Algeria, and others), increases the opportunities for competitive supply of these goods and services by Islamists. Third, private resources are necessary to supply such goods; these Islamists have, either from wealthy

Islamist businessmen or, in some cases, from governments—especially, depending on the case, Saudi Arabia before 1991 and Iran. On all three counts, Islamists are increasingly able to supply the contingent incentives that help to overcome free-riding.

Islamists also have some potential for managing free-riders because they are not reluctant to use coercion, because they continually interact with each other, and, in some cases, because of genuine piety and deep conviction. The logic of collective action suggests that Islamists have high collective-action potential. Of course, this by no means ensures that they will be able to seize power; it merely suggests that they are likely to remain a force to be reckoned with for some time to come.

ISLAMISTS IN POWER

Islamist Economic Theory

Modern economists will look in vain for a coherent, specifically Islamist theory of economic behavior or economic policy. Islamists have numerous disagreements and often offer diametrically opposed interpretations.[2] Reasons for this diversity include different approaches to the sources and, as in any religion, the existence of scriptural statements with diametrically opposed economic policy implications.

Islamists take different approaches to the Islamic sources. These differences are often quite ancient and certainly long precede the rise of modern Islamism. However, the Islamists continue the tradition of debate over interpretations of the sources. Although not all Muslims would agree, we may identify five sources: (1) the Quran, (2) the Sunna, (3) *ijma'* (consensus), (4) for Sunnis *qiyas* (analogical reasoning), for Shi'ites *'aqil* (reason), and, for Shi'ites, (5) *ijtihad* (reinterpretation).

The Quran, of course, is the fundamental text for all Muslims, who believe that God dictated its words to Muhammad. This unique, inimitable, and (as Muslims believe) miraculous text contains verses revealed in Mecca, which deal largely with theological issues, and others revealed in Medina, which deal with the organization of an Islamic society and state. Verses may also be divided into the obvious and the veiled, the latter being allegorical. Muslims do not, and have not for centuries, agreed on precisely how to interpret this text.

The Sunna, the "way" or "practice" of the Prophet, stands second only to the Quran as a source of Islamic thought of all types. Formally, it consists of stories (hadith) about the acts, injunctions, and statements of the Prophet that were told by his companions and ultimately written down. There are numerous differences among the orthodox Sunni legal schools (and still more between Sunni and Shi'a ones) concerning the accuracy of these stories. For example, although Ahmad ibn-Hanbal, founder of the Hanbali school, accepted over 40,000 hadith, Abu-Hanifa, founder of the Hanafi school, reportedly accepted only 17 (Nomani and Rahmena 1994).

Muhammad reportedly said, "My community will never agree on an error." But who, exactly, is "the community"? The Hanafi school maintains that the answer is "the community of jurists"; this is also the orthodox Shi'ite position. The Maliki school maintains that *ijma'* is legitimate only if it is reached by the residents of the city of Medina, while Shafi'is believe that the community is that of all Muslims.

Some Islamic schools of thought give considerable weight to reasoning by analogy (*qiyas*). Shi'ites stress reason itself (*'aqil*) and *ijtihad* or reinterpretation and innovation. It is perhaps the latter that has permitted the acceptance (to a degree) of Khomeini's entirely new concept of "government by jurists" (*velayet-i-faqih*), a concept for which there is no record in any of the other sources.

Even when scholars agree on which source to use, they disagree on what they mean. Nothing in the Islamic sources allows Islamists to answer with any precision one of the key questions of political economy: how do we assess the claims of equity and social justice, on the one hand, versus the claims of the legitimacy of private property, on the other? Muslims, like the rest of us, endlessly debate this issue. For Muslims the debate goes back at least as far as the Third Caliph, Uthman, who banished a man named Abu Zarr (a companion of the Prophet) for condemning hoarding by the rich and for demanding the redistribution of wealth (Nomani and Rahmena 1994, 60). One can easily support either position with Quranic quotations. The Quran repeatedly legitimizes "trade based on goodwill" and the sanctity of private property. Indeed, it sanctions the cutting off of a hand for violating private property rights (theft). Yet the same Quran uses the word "justice" more than a thousand times. Similarly, most Islamic jurists agree that the purpose of the shari'a is to promote life, religion, reason, progeny, and property. Proponents of a basic-needs or redistributionist policy will appeal to the need to promote life, while their conservative, laissez-faire opponents will defend the principle of property (Nomani and Rahnema 1994).

Although by now there exists a considerable corpus of Islamist economic writing, economic matters are not central to the Islamist political agenda in the way that they have been for, say, marxists.[3] It is useful to distinguish economic politics, political-system politics, and cultural politics, and Islamist politics is, of course, preeminently a politics of culture. Islamist politicians are concerned with language, symbols, dress codes, sexual mores and the family, and enforced social conformity to standards of piety. They are much less concerned with questions of economics; as the Imam Khomeini is alleged to have remarked, "The revolution is about Islam, not about the price of melons."

Several important consequences follow from the subordinate role of economics in Islamist politics. Islamists are likely to take a highly pragmatic approach to economic management. This, of course, is all to the good if the alternative is a dogmatism of left or right, but one person's pragmatism is another's expediency or even incoherence. If the modern economic history of developing countries teaches any lesson it is that consistency in economic policy is essential. The very marginality of economics within Islamist politics suggests that consistency may easily yield to expediency. It does make it easier for them to hold together a coalition of disparate economic interests, but satisfying these diverse groups economically is likely to be quite difficult (Box 14.1).

BOX 14.1
ISLAMIST ECONOMIC POLICY IN OPPOSITION

In opposition, Islamist movements have displayed a high degree of opportunism in their economic policy pronouncements. Consider the case of Syria's
Muslim Brotherhood. The Ikhwan's declared economic policy prescriptions
were driven by the desire to differentiate the Ikhwan's views from those of the
hated Ba'ath. A recent analysis[1] distinguishes three periods: from 1968 to the
early 1970s, the fall of 1980, and post-Hama massacre in 1982. In the first period, Islamists adopted an apparently liberal view. The Ikhwan stressed that
some economic functions must remain in state hands "because they are essential." However, individuals had natural rights, which included the right to
own property. Consequently, laws were needed to buttress these rights. This
position was designed to differentiate the Ikhwan's position from the centralizing, orthodox socialist Ba'ath party line of the time. In the fall of 1980 the
Syrian ulema began discussions with and tried to bring together different Islamist movements into the Islamic Front (al-Jabha al-Islamiyya). The Syrian
government had embarked on a halting perestroika at that time. Although the
Front's manifesto stressed the right to private property and demanded the
breakup of state farms, it also called for state subsidies to small firms. Government spending was to be allocated in accordance with the needs of regions,
not on ethnic criteria. Public-sector workers were to receive shares in public-
sector firms, and working conditions were to be improved for all workers in
both public and private sectors. After the Hama massacre, the badly damaged
Front tried to make an alliance with opposition elements of a Nasserist or dissident Ba'athist hue. Consistent with a fundamental indifference to economic
policy issues, it took a much vaguer, sketchier position on economic questions
so as to conform more closely with the statist preferences of its would-be coalition partners.

NOTES

1. The following is based on an oral presentation by Fred Lawson of Mills
College at the seminar "The Moral Economy of Islamism," Institute of International Studies, University of California, Berkeley, March 8, 1995.

Economic development is not easy; as the East Asian experience shows, successful
development requires a single-minded focus on growth. Needless to say, this is most
unlikely to be true of Islamists. More specifically, much evidence suggests that the
insulation of technocrats from political pressures is essential for sound macroeconomic
management and successful implementation of economic reform. It is difficult to
imagine an Islamist regime affording such insulation to its economists; instead, it is
likely that their every move will be scrutinized for religious rectitude, variously interpreted by whichever political group seems to have the ear of key decisionmakers.

This, at least, is certainly the experience in Iran to date. Islamist governments will adopt unsound economic policies because their priorities are elsewhere, as in the recent Sudanese government decision to create additional states, at a total estimated cost of £S5 billion, at a time when the budgetary deficit already exceeds £S25 billion. With the politics of culture in command, sound economic management is likely to be undermined.

The cultural-politics aspect of Islamism has one final economic implication. Because Islamists are explicitly anti-Western, they tend to prefer national, regional, or (at a minimum) Islamic world partners for trade and investment. In practice, of course, they will deal with anyone they must to survive. However, the xenophobia of many Islamists does pose problems. For example, the hostility to Western investment of some is, of course, a barrier to the acquisition of technology. Iranian opponents of economic reform charge that such policies amount to a sellout to foreigners. Finally, the obsession with national food self-sufficiency prominent in the two existing Islamist states is a deeply flawed agricultural development strategy (see Chapter 6).

Utopian assumptions about human behavior may be the core theoretical problem with Islamist approaches to economic issues. This judgment is hardly original; many scholars of these movements concur with it (see, e.g., Ayubi 1991a; Nomani and Rahmena 1994; Kuran 1992a; 1992b; Roy 1994). Essentially, Islamist thinkers abolish by assumption the core problem of political economy: the problem of scarcity in a world of self-interested actors. Islamists assume, instead, that the former problem is best solved by the diffusion of selfless behavior. *Homo Islamicus* is contrasted to *Homo Economicus*. But what if most people, for better or (more likely) for worse, are better described as self-interested than as altruistic? Institutions designed for *Homo Islamicus* will work poorly in such a world.

The Islamists' key concept is a particular interpretation of the Islamic notion of *tawhid* (unity). Whereas for non-Islamist Muslims the concept applies to God, who is "unique, transcendent and without associates" (Roy 1994, 40), for Islamists it applies to the ideal (Islamic) society, which is to have no conflicts of interest and no factions, parties, or disputes. They argue that since the Quran states that God has created everything in the right amounts to meet human needs, scarcity is the result of human avarice and greed. Islamists do not deny that people have unlimited wants (and, therefore, that scarcity exists); rather, they argue that the goal of public policy should be to change this—to make people into sober, altruistic *mutaqqin* or ideal Muslims.

Perhaps this conception originated in the small, close-knit society of the Companions of the Prophet—a group of perhaps seventy persons who accompanied Muhammad in the flight to Medina (*hijra*). The strength of altruistic notions within such a small group would be consistent with the modern notion of altruism as declining in strength as the size of the group increases. (As any infantry officer will tell you, men risk death not so much for "the cause" as for their "buddies.") Utopian conceptions also have a strong appeal for the young people who are disproportionately represented among Islamists.

The Islamist position is that harmony and social order will be achieved by the promotion of individual virtue—by individuals' altering their behavior to conform with Divine Revelation. However laudable such a goal may be for individuals, it is a poor basis for public policy formation. Unrealistic behavioral assumptions lead to unworkable institutional designs whose inevitable failure provokes sharp disappointment, repression, and hypocrisy. At least since the seventeenth century, Western political thinkers have abandoned the notion that religious exhortation could be relied upon to restrain destructive human behavior. The alternative advocated by St. Augustine and Calvin—repression—merely displaces the problem to the level of the sovereign. Beginning with Machiavelli and Vico and culminating in the Scottish Enlightenment and Adam Smith, we try—whenever possible—to "make private vices into public virtues." Most notably in economics, we seek to control the social consequences of greed by pitting greed against greed. Every businessperson would love to be a monopolist, but we simply create rules that make this very difficult. We take human viciousness as given; we try to design institutions, to create "rules of the game," that assume that many of us most of the time and all of us some of the time will behave selfishly, perhaps even callously. Our debates then turn on when such behavior can produce socially desirable outcomes.

It must be said, however, that even most Westerners have never been entirely happy with this rather stark view of political order. Many contemporary Western thinkers stress the importance of community, solidarity, "law abiding as a public good," and so on. Clearly Islam has a great role to play in providing standards of public and private conduct that can strengthen both economic performance and political order and liberty. Such moral codes (perhaps "social capital"), however, are probably better thought of as supplements to the defensive institutional designs just described than as their basis. If a large number of people behave altruistically, then institutions designed for a world of selfish actors will still work well; the reverse, alas, is not true. By making unrealistic assumptions about human behavior, Islamists are likely to craft repressive and arbitrary institutional structures. This may have considerable importance for economic management.

Much of Islamist economic thought is concerned with applying specific injunctions found in the texts to modern contexts. The most important of these is *riba,* the injunction against usury, which forbids the payment of interest. The fundamental idea seems to be that such behavior is a form of gambling, which is presumptuous in the face of Divine Will. Although this injunction has some disadvantages, actual practice suggests that there is often less here than meets the eye.

Prohibiting interest has its problems. The interest rate is a price: the price of time, or waiting. Setting the price of waiting or price of capital at zero is an extreme form of subsidizing capital. When a good is scarce, it must be rationed. If it is not rationed by price, it will be rationed by quantity—by queues. This leads (typically) to inefficiency, rent seeking, and corruption. Other disadvantages include subsidizing capital-intensive production, potentially depressing savings (or, at least, savings channeled through the banking system),[4] harming risk-averse lenders (e.g., retirees), and, arguably, intensifying the informational asymmetries that are common in capital markets (when all capital is converted to equity, the need for knowledge about the borrower increases).

These may, however, be merely theoretical issues. In practice, evasion and compromise seem the norm. "Fees" for "management expenses" and other euphemisms are often used to charge interest without using the word. In some cases, banks assert that they are paying "shares" (since dividing profits is permissible) to depositors, usually simply as a ruse to pay interest. One Iranian financial instrument that claims to be doing this has tracked the U.S. Treasury Bill rate with remarkable accuracy and apparent impunity.

Alternatively, paying zero interest to depositors may be very lucrative. The prohibition of interest seems to affect Islamic banks' liability positions far more than their asset portfolios. If depositors (lenders) believe that interest is immoral and are willing to lend to a bank at a zero price and if that same bank can make loans internationally (where, of course, positive real rates of interest prevail), the practice of the (partial) prohibition of interest will be very profitable indeed.

The hadith stating that "water, grass, and fire" are communal property is widely interpreted to mean that actually pricing water or pasture land at its opportunity cost is *haram* (forbidden). It is acceptable, of course, to charge operation and maintenance fees. Instituting such charges would, in most countries of the region, be an important step forward in the struggle to economize on increasingly scarce water (see Chapter 6), but in the years ahead it is unlikely to be sufficient. Nevertheless, it seems likely that a little ingenuity could surmount the problem of pricing water (e.g., through tradable water rights, which seem to be acceptable) just as it has the problem of pricing time (i.e., charging interest).

The hadith in question does not necessarily create an Islamic "tragedy of the commons." After all, for many centuries Muslim nomads have vigorously defended long-established tribal rights to particular areas of rangeland. Current problems with managing common-property resources in Muslim countries have far more to do with population pressure and the interventions of centralizing national governments (including inappropriate subsidies and taxes) than to shari'a.

Zakat, or Islamic taxation, is a final specific injunction typically recommended by Islamists. There is disagreement over its interpretation. Local governments in the former YAR used the notion of *zakat* in taxing migrant remittances, spending the proceeds locally on badly needed physical infrastructure. If calling such a tax *zakat* increased taxation's legitimacy and hence taxpayer compliance, any economist would approve. Some of the more literal interpretations of *zakat*, however, raise economic difficulties. In the most rigid interpretation, *zakat* is to be levied on gold, silver, and various specific commodities. Gold has an exemption of 3 ounces, silver one of 21 ounces. At recent prices, this would be an exemption of over US$1,000 for gold but about US$100 for silver. An attempt by the government of Zia ul-Haq in Pakistan to levy a 2.5% *zakat* tax on personal savings led to Shi'ite protests and discouraged bank deposits and savings. Such an interpretation of *zakat* would further reduce tax transparency. Since no country has a transparent tax code, this problem is nothing extraordinary.

In conclusion, Islamists do not offer any internally coherent and consistent theory of economics founded on reasonable assumptions about human behavior. The vagueness of their economic writings, the marginality of economic issues to their political project, their utopian assumptions about human conduct, and their diversity in these, as in other, matters vitiate attempts to construct an Islamist economic model.

Intellectually fashionable literary theories notwithstanding, neither the laws of economics nor the laws of addition are culturally relative. An unbalanced budget is an unbalanced budget, and inflationary finance will always undermine attempts at exchange-rate management. Self-interested behavior is here to stay; large groups of people who follow its dictates will generate outcomes that are reasonably predictable. Demand curves still slope down, diminishing returns still exist, and opportunity cost is present, wherever there are people. Every modern government that has claimed to be able to manage the economy in terms of contradictory principles has come to grief. Muslim economists, trained largely at Berkeley and Harvard, have done an excellent job managing the Indonesian economy. Iranian mullahs have done much worse, as have the lawyers of the Sudanese National Islamic Front.

One often feels that, given the richness of the Islamic tradition, it is possible to justify nearly any economic proposal. It seems very likely that the configuration of the specific *interests* that undergirds any Islamist government, combined with specific *institutional structures* and the *political exigencies* of the moment, will be far more important than ideology in determining that government's economic policy. As a counterpoint, however, it is conceivable that the compatibility of Islamism and modern economics might be similar to that of Islam and the ancient Persian theory of kingship. The Persian notion of the absolute monarch was hardly compatible with early Islamic notions of the caliph as one selected for leadership by the consensus of the Islamic community, and yet, some hundred years after the death of the Prophet Muhammad, the caliphate mimicked all the trappings of Sasanian (Persian) kingship. The gap between core Islamic beliefs and the practice of rule of virtually the entire period of Muslim government is huge.[5] This analogy suggests that however wide the gap between Islamist conceptions and modern economic theory, in practice Islamists might manage an economy no worse than those currently in charge (which is not saying very much: see Chapter 9).

Islamist Economic Management

It is well to remember that policymaking practice *never* conforms to rigorous theory. In some cases, the discrepancy can be quite striking, as recently in Argentina, when Carlos Menem was elected as a populist/Peronist and implemented an orthodox structural adjustment program. To paraphrase Dr. Johnson, there is nothing like the prospect of no money to focus the mind. Even in cases less extreme than Menem's Argentina, policies always have to be adjusted to political realities. Economics demands consistency, and politics abhors it (Chapter 9). The requirements of coalition formation and/or maintenance will usually take precedence over economic logic in economic policy implementation. It will perhaps be especially likely to do so when the economic policies in question cause significant hardship to many people—which is the normal case with economic reform. Even determined, tough, and skillful economists-turned-politicians such as Turgut Özal have to retreat in order to advance—back away from some reforms in order to stay in power. The key determinants of actual economic policymaking under Islamism are the same as anywhere else: the balance of interests, the structure of institutions, and the timing of events.

Interests. Existing Islamist regimes rest on a disparate coalition of economically conservative urban merchants and professionals and redistributionist students and street youths. The diverse elements of the Islamist coalition struggle against each other to achieve their economically incompatible goals. Such a coalition is possible *precisely because economic politics is secondary to cultural politics.* As always, the relative weight of different elements of the coalition will vary, as will the Islamists' ability to forge coalitions with other groups. In Turkey in the 1980s, for example, non-Islamist politicians brought Islamists into a center-right coalition as an attempt to broaden the popular electoral appeal of an economic program that, in the short run at least, would benefit a relatively small, already well-off social segment. In the Sudan, the National Islamic Front, whose main support comes from secondary and university students, especially in Khartoum and the western provinces, and smaller traders, merchants, and other entrepreneurs who were excluded from the main rent-seeking networks of previous regimes, has tried to form a coalition with Baggara militias (Jamal 1991; Keen 1994; see Box 14.2). The long-run economic interests of marginalized Baggara raiders and a rising new elite of merchants close to Turabi are no more compatible than those of Algerian industrialists and the young shantytown dwellers who support the FIS.

The main consequence of such a disparate coalition for economic management is that promarket reform programs lack credibility (see Chapter 9). A leadership that places culture in command tacks now toward the market, now toward state control. There is nothing very unusual about this—policy inconsistency is the norm—but whereas in some countries economic technocrats are insulated from such pressures, this is not likely to happen under Islamist regimes. We should expect their economic policies to be contradictory and, therefore, relatively ineffective. If anything, as the case of Iran (Chapter 9) suggests, Islamist regimes are likely to do worse than the average LDC in forging credible economic reform commitments.

Institutions. Throughout the region, institutions of government are generally rather weak. The rule of law, in particular, is noticeably absent; governmental corruption is typically pervasive, and political parties are commonly feeble. Governments often make up for these institutional weaknesses with ham-fisted repression and flagrant buying of support through patronage. Neither is conducive to the forging of a successful market economy. Strong states in the region are typically also obsessed with control and, therefore, postpone market-oriented reform (Chapter 9).

BOX 14.2
POLITICAL COALITIONS IN THE SUDAN

The Islamist NIF seeks to undermine the support for the Ansar Brotherhood (affiliated with Sadiq al-Mahdi) in the western Sudan (Kordofan and Darfur) as well as the Khatmiya Brotherhood, which has long had a strong presence among Khartoum merchants and both merchant and military elites from the riverine areas north of the city. Mahdi had created a reformed Ansar political organization that stretched down to the village level in the western Sudan after his reconciliation with Nimeiri in 1977. Drought, population growth, the influx of weapons from Chad, generational change, and the spread of mechanized farming combined to reduce grazing opportunities for Baggara tribesmen in the west and to provide them with the means to attack the Dinka to the south. They organized *muraheleen* (militias) that began raiding and committing a wide range of atrocities and human rights abuses (including the revival of the slave trade) among the Dinka. The NIF and Bashir tried to co-opt these traditional Ansar supporters by officially recognizing them in the People's Defense Act of October 1989. The Baggara militias are, however, highly independent, in some cases reaching their own accommodations with the Dinka-dominated SPLA. The current government seems to seek their support by encouraging them to attack the south, thus fostering famine. Not only is promotion of famine useful as a weapon against the SPLA but it is also part of the NIF's ongoing struggle to supplant the Ansar in the west (Kean 1994; Africa Watch 1990).

Weak states remain in power exclusively through governmental largesse and therefore have difficulty controlling fiscal balances. Strong states will not and weak states cannot make credible commitments to a market economy.

Islamist states are likely to be very similar to other Middle Eastern countries here. Obviously, the governmental capacity of Iran far exceeds that of the Sudan, but in Iran the government has been unable to contain patronage politics, and this has led to large fiscal deficits and, consequently, an overvalued real exchange rate. Sudanese implementation incapacity was legendary before the Islamists took over; there are few signs of change under the Bashir-Turabi regime. We have already seen that Islamist governments are highly unlikely to insulate their technocrats; an independent central bank is almost unthinkable in an Islamist state.

Islamists may add a further source of governmental incapacity: dual power. They inherit a governmental apparatus that they regard as permeated by the mores of the old order. As do all revolutionaries, they face the dilemma of balancing their desire to purge the bureaucracy of their opponents, on the one hand, with the need to maintain functioning institutions, on the other. They purge, but they also add bureaucratic layers in the form of some supervisory agency or agents to ensure the Islamic rectitude of the bureaucracy. These agencies have considerable power, provide employment for the revolution's shock troops of the street, and rarely know anything at all about modern organizations. The organizations may also have been instrumental in the conquest of power and so enjoy a particularly strong position within the government. Ensconcing religious ideologues in implementing agencies is unlikely to improve the quality of economic management, and additional layers of bureaucracy hardly enhance policy implementation.

Exigencies. The circumstances of taking power are also very important. It makes a difference whether a regime takes power through violence or by electoral means and, if by violence, whether through a little-opposed coup, as in the Sudan, or through mass revolutionary upheaval, as in Iran. The Sudanese coup, of course, must also be situated in the context of that country's vicious civil war. Obviously, civil wars and violence are breeders of extremism and statism. War Islamism will be highly statist, as will any war economy. All Turkish governments to date have been either short-lived military caretakers or elected coalition governments. If Islamists ever have major input into Turkish economic policy it will most likely be via the latter path. This will be extremely important for their policy choices.

Where Islamists take power also matters greatly. The inherited institutions, the internal fissures in the country, and (perhaps especially) the *target of nationalism* vary considerably across countries. Any consideration of the role of the Islamist Jamaʻat-i-Islami in coalition governments in Pakistan must include the existence of the High Court and an independent judiciary and the experience of "on-and-off" elections. To the extent that Islamism represents nationalism, one must consider the target of this nationalism. In the Arab world, this is likely to be the United States and Israel. Elsewhere, as in Central Asia or the Caucasus, it is far more likely to be Russia. In Algeria, it may be mainly France.

Depending on when, how, and where Islamists take power, they may find themselves embroiled in wars, whether of their own choosing or imposed upon them by external forces. It is difficult to manage an economy and still more difficult to meet economic development challenges while fighting a war. War everywhere, always diverts resources from development, generates very strong inflationary pressures, and greatly expands the role of the state in the allocation of resources (Chapter 13). To the extent that Islamists are revolutionaries, we might expect them to become embroiled in wars, with their inevitable economic consequences. Perhaps, if there were a peaceful transition to Islamism, the outcome would be different. But there seems to be little reason to expect that transitions will be peaceful (although Turkey is a potential exception).

We should be cautious about generalizing from the experience of existing Islamist regimes that took power during the cold war and during the oil boom, both of which provided anti-American regimes with leverage that is not available today.

Large subsidies from oil states are unlikely to be available in the future (the Saudi regime subsidized many Sunni Islamist movements such as the Muslim Brotherhood until the Gulf War), and the cushion of workers' remittances that was crucial is unavailable today.

The Middle East today has two Islamist states, Iran and the Sudan, and, in Turkey under Özal, a government that might be called Islamist-supported. The three cases range from the highly statist to the pragmatic, compromising, mixed-record neoliberal. This is consistent with the general argument that coalitions and circumstances, not texts and theories, are the main determinants of Islamist economic policies. We have examined the Iranian case in Chapter 9; here we turn to the other, the Democratic Republic of Sudan.

Actually Existing Islamism: The Sudan

Since the Islamists have only been in power in the Sudan for roughly five years, it is even more difficult to offer an evaluation of their performance than it is for Iran. Sudanese data are often nonexistent and nearly always of very dubious quality. The Sudan is a vast country with extremely weak infrastructure in the best of times, racked by civil war and now excluded from the main organizations that compile internationally comparable economic data, the IMF and the World Bank. We see economic performance in the Sudan through a very dark glass indeed.

The Islamist regime has taken some positive steps. It has ended export and import licensing, devalued the exchange rate, announced cuts in some subsidies, and scheduled privatizations. Given the configuration of interests that underlies the regime, it is reasonable to expect that some privatizations will occur. These are positive steps, though, of course, much will depend on precisely how the reforms are implemented. It is fair to say that the Bashir-Turabi regime has gone at least as far with economic reform as previous Sudanese governments.

There are also some less encouraging signs. The macroeconomic picture is grim. The regime seems to be entirely incapable of controlling inflation, which rages at over 150% per year. Some of this may be due to one-shot reforms such as the cuts in consumer subsidies and the devaluation of the Sudanese pound. However, the core inflationary problem is the very large governmental budgetary deficit. The government is spending large sums on war, and its fiscal capacity is weak. Until the deficit is brought under control, the Sudanese economy will continue to flounder. The regime has simply stopped servicing its debt, and this will deprive it of future capital inflows. Debt overhang is substantial and is exacerbated by the failure to service the debt. Trade is collapsing.

Some optimists point to the recent upsurge of food production as the result of the government's crop-switching policy. Here several cautions are in order. First, it is impossible to reject the hypothesis that the recent upsurge is simply cyclical, driven by the climatological cycle. There may be a mild upward trend, but it is less than population growth. Second, of course, food self-sufficiency is neither necessary nor sufficient for food security. The latter has continued to deteriorate under the Bashir regime at both the national and the household level. At the national level, since exports have collapsed, the country cannot buy food; given its own policies, it will receive little food aid. This leaves its food supply entirely at the mercy of the African monsoon—a high-risk policy. At the household level, the picture is worse, of course. Shortages of gasoline and other inputs have led to food shortages in various areas (e.g., northern Kordofan), while even in the capital, plummeting real wages jeopardize many citizens' entitlements to food. And the regime and the SPLA deliberately foster famine as an instrument of war in the south (Africa Watch 1990).

In short, the record to date of the Islamist regime in the Sudan is fairly bleak—but not worse than that of the Sudanese government under Mahdi or Nimeiri. Good intentions do not make a functioning market economy. The regime is internationally isolated and embroiled in war. These features push policies toward autarky and statism. Other tendencies may emerge later, but new vested interests are likely to be created in the interim. If the Iranian regime seems to offer its citizens shared poverty, perhaps the Sudanese will offer shared famine. After all, there are precious few economic policy success stories of any kind in sub-Saharan Africa. It is most unlikely that the Islamists of the Sudan will do much better than the grim, run-of-the-mill decay of the rest of the continent. Although it may not be doing much worse than most MENA regimes in reforming the economy, it offers little evidence that "Islam is the solution."

Neoliberalism in Islamic Guise?

Many believe that there is no contradiction between Islamist government and neoliberal (i.e., promarket) economic reform. Roy (1994) for example, argues that this is the case for groups that he characterizes as "neo-fundamentalist" (in which he includes the FIS in Algeria).[6] It is often argued that Islamists are staunch supporters of private property rights and that they oppose that bane of Middle Eastern economic life, a vast, overblown state sector. We are often told that they will privatize, deregulate, and generally manage their economies as the World Bank and the IMF would want them to do.

There is some evidence to support this view. Certainly the Sudanese "Program of Economic Salvation" often reads like a World Bank document. It is also true that the Egyptian Muslim Brotherhood strongly opposed Nasser's nationalizations. Many of the supporters of the NIF in the Sudan and the Muslim Brotherhood in Egypt (and elsewhere) are prosperous businessmen who might be expected to favor fairly orthodox economic programs and policies.

History clearly shows, however, that Islamic governance itself is entirely compatible with arbitrary, even confiscatory behavior toward private individuals. Islamists often differentiate their views on private property from Western perspectives by saying that private property in Islam is subject to "social obligations." For example, the Iranian constitution "requires property to meet three conditions: that ownership must not 'go beyond the bounds of Islamic law,' that the property itself should 'contribute to the economic growth and progress of the country,' and that the property must not 'harm society'" (Amuzegar 1993, 28). These are worthy goals, but who decides when they are fulfilled? In Iran, it seems that the majlis decides, and "there is evidently no constitutional protection against arbitrary confiscation of property by a *Majles* law" (Amuzegar 1993, 28). All of the problems sketched above—the role of multiple possible interpretations, the tension between the claims of society and the claims of the individual, and, above all, the absence of a methodology for designing institutions that takes a realistic view of human behavior—should make us cautious about thinking that an Islamist regime will *necessarily* be neoliberal.

This argument also works, however, in reverse: nothing in the "theory" of the Islamists *necessarily prevents* their adopting a neoliberal model. Precisely because cultural politics, not economics, is at the center of their agenda, it is not difficult to imagine situations in which Islamists might support neoliberal economic policies. We should seek the explanation for Islamist neoliberalism in the same place as the explanation for Islamist statism: in the configuration of interests, the institutional structure, and the specific conjuncture of Islamists acquiring/sharing power. This general point may be illustrated by an example of the use of Islamism in neoliberal programs: Özal's Turkey (see also Box 14.3).

Turkish Islamists did not make economic policy. The Özal government's economic policies were managed by a highly Westernized elite of technocrats recruited from American institutions such as the Wharton School and insulated from political pressures by the prime minister. Many of these technocrats—the so-called princes (e.g., Rüşdü Saracoğlu)—had nothing but contempt for Islamists. Economic policy under Özal may have deviated from neoclassical orthodoxy (e.g., persistent budgetary deficits, export subsidies), but Islamism had little to do with these divergences from the IMF model.

However, the Motherland party was undeniably a coalition of proreform business interests *and* Islamists. Özal himself had run for office (and lost) in 1977 as a candidate of the National Salvation party, and his older brother was a prominent religious leader. As John Waterbury has noted, the neoliberals in Turkey (and elsewhere) have a serious problem when competing with a populist opposition: their program offers few benefits to most people in the short run. Of course, reformers believe (with considerable justification) that reform is essential for reviving economic growth and increasing the demand for labor. These, of course, are necessary conditions for raising real incomes and reducing poverty. But in the short run reformers offer austerity and other wrenching changes that make them unpopular. When economic politics alone is concerned, the center-right coalition is necessarily a narrow one. The appeal of a party espousing neoliberal economics can, however, be broadened considerably by including cultural conservatives—in this case, Islamists—in the coalition.[7]

Not only do such elements bring significant electoral benefits but these benefits can be obtained a relatively modest cost. This was an important consideration, since budgetary resources were scarce because of the attempts at austerity. Özal maintained his coalition in the usual manner of conservative Turkish governments, through the use of patronage. Accordingly, the public sector did not shrink during the reform period of the 1980s. Özal also insulated his technocrats and centralized

BOX 14.3
PAKISTAN UNDER ZIA UL-HAQ

Pakistan under Mohammed Zia ul-Haq is an example of Islamist-supported neoliberalism outside of MENA. The Islamist regime of Zia ul-Haq in Pakistan was, initially, simply a coalition of the military and the Jama'at-i Islami (JI) party—or, perhaps more accurately, simply a military dictatorship whose leadership happened to embrace the ideological prescriptions of that party. Such commitment may have been sincere, but it also provided a convenient means of relegitimizing the armed forces, whose reputation had been badly damaged by the debacle of East Pakistani secession and military defeat by India in 1971. The generals reached out for support from urban commercial traders and other small-scale urban entrepreneurs. Because Zia supplanted the populist, nationalizing, pro-Sindhi (and, implicitly, therefore, pro-Shi'a) Bhutto government, the Islamist government of Pakistan was able to appeal to larger industrialists and elements of the Punjabi and Muhajir elite. Enjoying support from Saudi Arabia and the United States (after the Soviet invasion of Afghanistan) and buoyed by the workers'-remittances boom of the late 1970s and early 1980s, Zia embraced economic reform, signing a structural adjustment loan with the World Bank. The demise of the program and the limited privatization (disappointing to larger industrialists) occurred for the usual reason: the government was reluctant to abandon a source of patronage (Noman 1988).

Zia invited the JI to join the cabinet in August 1978. It received important economic portfolios, such as Petroleum, Mining, and Water Power, and Production and Industry. Pro-JI intellectuals played important roles in the core of Zia's unofficial advisers. Finally, a prominent JI member, Kurshid Ahmad, became minister of planning. He soon resigned, however, denouncing the budget as "un-Islamic." Some observers believe that the resignation was purely political: the JI wanted to run as oppositionist in the forthcoming elections, since it hoped that, in alliance with the Pakistan National party, it could control the civilian government that would result from these elections. Zia, however, outmaneuvered the JI, partly by divide-and-rule tactics in which he fostered other, rival Islamist parties. The JI soon became disillusioned with Zia (Nasr 1994).

Zia hoped that the JI would provide him both with a vital organizational resource to help to smash Bhutto's supporters (the People's party) and with useful ideas. The JI was helpful in (temporarily) accomplishing the first goal; it failed entirely to achieve the second. As the leading scholar of the movement (Nasr 1994, 194) puts it:

> Aside from abstract notions about the shape and working of the ideal Islamic state, the party had little to offer in the way of suggestions for managing its machinery. Its notions about the working of Islamic dicta in economic and political operations provided Zia with no coherent plan of action. Just as the Jama'at became disappointed with the politics of Zia's regime, so the general became disillusioned with the practical relevance of the Jama'at's ideas.

government decisionmaking, relying on government decrees rather than legislation. As Önis and Webb (1994, 137) note, this heightened investors' uncertainty and reduced the credibility of the reforms.

An important mechanism for such centralization was the extrabudgetary funds. These predated Özal's tenure (there were thirty-three in 1980), but his government greatly expanded their number and role, adding seventy-three by 1990. The revenue from the funds rose from 1.3% of GNP in 1981 to over 11% in 1990, exceeding half of public-sector revenues (Önis and Webb 1994, 151–152). These funds permitted a ministry to evade legislative oversight and fiscal discipline. Interestingly, such funds were also often officially "Islamically managed," that is, interest-free, "profit-sharing" funds. Such an approach may also have been a mechanism to appeal to the culturalist wing of the Motherland party.

Islamists were induced to support a neoliberal program, even to the point of joining a coalition with secular neoliberals in the Motherland party. Perhaps unsurprisingly, however, their cooperation was short-lived. Many of the Islamists defected from the Motherland party to the Prosperity party, while some rural conservatives joined the True Path party of Süleyman Demirel. All of this is explicable within the general framework of garden-variety interest-group politics, and understanding outcomes also requires knowledge of the institutional setting (e.g., the tradition of executive independence/insulation dating to Ottoman times and the long experience with the horse-trading of parliamentary democracy). The keys to understanding the role of Islamists in the Turkish neoliberal experiment are the ones enumerated earlier: the configuration of interests, the institutional matrix, and the specific constraints and opportunities offered by the timing of reforms.

CONCLUSION

That Islamist economic management is likely to be unexceptional may not matter much politically. As we have seen, economic mismanagement is widespread in MENA; only a very severe crisis threatens any regime. In fact, for repressive regimes (as Islamist—and most other—MENA regimes are likely to be) the crisis can be very deep indeed before it threatens regime stability. Redistributive policies can buy support or at least acquiescence for quite some time. Further, distributing benefits to its supporters is more important to regime survival than overall efficiency or economic growth. The extreme case of this may be the Sudan, where fomenting *muraheleen* raids and depredations against the non-Muslim south increases support for the NIF among elements of the Baggara even as it enslaves and starves southerners. Islamist regimes have considerable powers of repression, and they do not hesitate to deploy them. As the history of the Soviet Union clearly shows, poor economic managers can survive in power for decades.

The final question must be whether Islamist mismanagement is likely to be so bad as to provoke a regime-challenging crisis. Neither we nor anyone else knows. It seems likely that the mounting challenges of jobs, food, water, and the environment will get steadily worse, simply because of population growth. These pressures are likely to be an essential part of the deep background of any crisis in Islamist (and other) regimes in the region, but regime crises are conjunctural events in which leadership, timing, and chance all play major roles.

It may be that Islamist economic mismanagement will simply reinforce the "Africanization" of the Middle East—its progressive transformation into an economic backwater. The presence of oil and weapons of mass destruction suggests that the outcome may be somewhat less sleepy than that, however. The consequences of Islamist economic errors may create strong temptations for governments to deflect popular discontent into aggressive foreign adventures. Whatever the case, we believe that the answer to the question posed at the beginning of this chapter is no.

NOTES

1. This is a good example of Bates's (1990) argument that collective-action potential is everywhere and always partly a function of state actions and policies.

2. A cynic might ask how different they are from Western economists in this; at least for microeconomics, however, there is wide agreement among the latter on the method of reasoning and on many of the policy implications of that reasoning.

3. For example, an expert on Algeria states bluntly, "Algerian Islamism had virtually nothing to say about economic policy" (Roberts 1994, 124).

4. In theory, the injunction against interest requires all loans to take the form of equity participation. Since this is a more risky form of lending, if lenders are (as is widely assumed) risk-averse, ceteris paribus, Islamic banking laws will reduce the supply of loans.

5. The great historian of Islam of the past generation, Marshall Hodgson, put it this way: "the caliph was to be a major figure, successor to the Great King of the Iranian empire. . . . he even ought to have a certain religious aura, foreign to the spirit of the *Shari'ah* . . . but close to that of the old Sasanians. When the caliph was addressed—as he was—as 'the shadow of God on earth,' the *'ulama'* scholars could only be profoundly shocked" (Hodgson 1974, 280).

6. Roberts (1994) shares this view.

7. One may usefully compare this strategy with that of Christian Democratic parties in Western Europe or the Republican party in the United States.

15

REGIONALISM, LABOR MIGRATION, AND THE FUTURE OF THE OIL ECONOMIES

Middle Eastern intellectuals have long dreamed of unity. Before the rise of secular nationalism, Muslims cherished a vision of one polity under one ruler: the Dar ul-Islam, ruled by the caliph, the Prophet's successor. Such dreams live on among Islamists, sometimes mixed with Arab nationalist hopes for secular unity. There have been several attempts to realize these visions politically. The best-known was the formation of the United Arab Republic under Nasser, when Egypt and Syria merged for three years (1958–1961). However, Nasser's reforming military regime coexisted uneasily with a Syrian polity still dominated by wealthy merchants and landlords, and the system collapsed when Syria withdrew in September 1961. More quixotic gambits emerged from Tripoli, as Qaddhafi's Libya attempted to merge with Egypt, Sudan, Tunisia, Syria, and Morocco. These ventures have puzzled political pundits and yielded very little in the way of concrete political unification. Operation Desert Storm dramatically exposed the emptiness of claims of Arab political unity.

Limited regional economic intercourse contributed to these failures. Like most LDCs, MENA countries primarily sold their goods, purchased their imports, and admitted capital from the developed countries of the West, not from each other. Trade is now increasingly with other LDCs but not with the rest of the region. During the past twenty years, economic integration of the region has accelerated dramatically in some ways while remaining limited in others (Kerr and el-Yassin 1982).[1]

A simple measure of integration would be the movement of goods and factors of production across national boundaries in the region. MENA integration into world goods markets has actually *declined* from already low levels during the past decade. In contrast to all other regions of the developing world, MENA saw trade as a percentage of output fall (World Bank 1995a). Trade with other Maghreb and Mashreq countries[2] changed little during the 1980s: in 1990 only 6% of total trade was intraregional. Even if oil is excluded from trade, intraregional trade still amounts to only 10% of the total (Shafik 1994a and Figure 15.1). The inward-oriented policies explored in Chapters 7–9 leave little room for integration into goods markets: national markets remain highly protected. Until economic reform has succeeded in a number of countries, the prospects for trade integration remain slight.

Integration of factor markets has gone much farther. Governments have dominated the investment process in most countries, whatever the official ideology. The major oil-exporting countries spent most of their increased incomes between 1974 and 1984 on their own internal-investment projects. Most of the surplus was held in short-term liquid assets in the OECD countries, but some money was channeled toward their poorer neighbors as economic aid—both direct, bilateral assistance and contributions to "development funds" and other multilateral agencies. Generally speaking, increasing domestic spending programs and (by the mid-1980s) plummeting real oil prices slashed such aid as a percentage of donor's GNP (Figure 15.2). The Gulf War and the ensuing massive deficits in Saudi Arabia further reduced such assistance, but even in 1993 the Saudi government was giving away proportionally 80% more of its national income than the most generous OECD donor, Norway.[3] Such aid made up a large proportion of total investment in recipient countries between 1973 and 1987.[4]

The various private, public, and mixed banks in the region engaged in lending to LDCs gave preference to other MENA countries and countries in the wider Islamic world. Lending policies have typically been conservative, concentrating on areas where managers already have some expertise, such as petroleum refining, tourism, and real estate.

Perhaps the most notable attempts to use capital as an instrument of economic integration have been the region's various development funds. The earliest of these (the

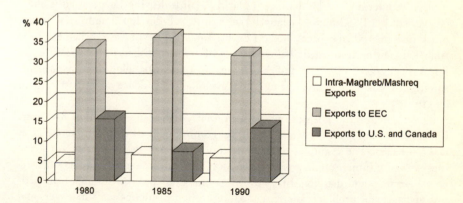

FIGURE 15.1   Geographical destination of exports, early 1990s. *Source:* Shafik (1994a).

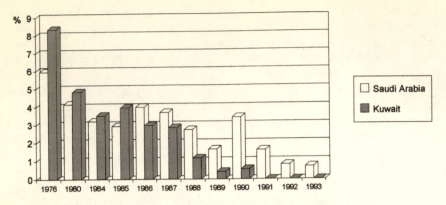

FIGURE 15.2   Foreign assistance as a percentage of GNP, Saudi Arabia and Kuwait, 1976–1993. *Source:* World Bank (1994g).

Kuwait Fund for Arab Economic Development) was founded in 1961, to be followed by the Arab Fund for Economic and Social Development, established by the Arab League in 1968, and the Abu Dhabi Fund for Arab Economic Development, founded in 1971. These funds are run along World Bank lines, extending loans for development projects ranging from railroads and fertilizer plants to sewage and water supply systems to livestock and crop production schemes.

The Arab Fund has had the most self-conscious political agenda. In addition to making development loans to specific countries, it has sought to promote the regional economy in at least three ways. First, it has invested in the Pan-Arab Communications Network, including the development of an Arab communications satellite. Second, it has promoted the development of the Arab Military Industrialization Organization to manufacture weapons for Arab armies. The international aspects of this project were terminated by the Camp David Accords, leaving Egypt to go it alone (see Chapter 13). Given its relatively large and well-developed industrial sector, much investment had concentrated on Egypt, but when Egypt was expelled from the Arab League this evaporated. Third, the Arab Fund established the Arab Authority for Agricultural Investment and Development (AAAID), allocating investments toward the Sudan in an attempt to reduce regional dependence on imported grain and sugar.

These activities did not work particularly well. At the same time, they had some impact, and until the Gulf War the political commitment to their long-range goals was unshaken. For example, AAAID mounted projects in the Sudan involving mechanized farming, poultry production, sorghum and oil seeds production, vegetable farming, and dairying. By its own account, these projects suffered from serious management problems and remained unprofitable. Public-sector managers and university experts initially oversaw operations—an unfortunate choice, since neither group had much experience in running enterprises that needed to show a profit. Plans to alter the situation were abruptly shelved when the Sudan supported Iraq against Kuwait and Saudi Arabia.

In summary, deliberate attempts to integrate the political economies of the region at the levels of the state, trade flows, and capital and investment have been relatively unsuccessful. Far more important has been the unplanned, market-driven integration of labor markets. Indeed, labor migration on a historically unprecedented scale has been a fundamental force in transforming national political economies even as it has integrated the most remote areas of the most backward countries into the regional economy.

LABOR MIGRATION: AN OVERVIEW

Most labor migration in the region has been driven by economics. With the politically crucial exception of the Palestinian refugees, most Middle Easterners have left home to make money rather than to flee political persecution.[5] The proximate cause of the migration is the huge gap in wages between sending and receiving countries. For example, during the late 1970s an unskilled rural Egyptian could earn *thirty times* more money working at a Saudi construction site than he could on an Egyptian farm. Jordanian engineers could double or triple their incomes by going to Kuwait. Migration was an excellent investment for workers from poorer countries. The low wages in the sending countries were caused by low productivity in agriculture and the failure of previous industrialization to absorb surplus labor. The cause of the upward spiral of wages in the oil countries was equally straightforward. The demand for labor shot up, while domestic labor supply was limited by economic, social, and political factors.

On the demand side, the explosion of oil prices in the 1970s flooded the treasuries of the oil-exporting states, which then launched ambitious development plans and investment projects. These implied huge increases in the demand for labor of all types, from construction laborers to computer programmers, from doctors to doormen. However, demography and sociopolitical factors constrained domestic labor supply. The Gulf States and Libya have small, young populations. Usually at least 40% of the indigenous population is less than fifteen years old and a majority is younger than twenty. Consequently, the economically active population and the domestic labor supply were limited. Limited female participation in the labor force further exacerbated the shortage of domestic workers in the oil-exporting states. Too often, males of working age were illiterate and unskilled, and those few who were skilled were often attracted to public-sector employment, especially in the armed forces. Finally, government subsidies of food, housing, medical care, and transportation reduced the incentives for local people to take unpleasant or difficult jobs. Meeting from domestic sources the huge demand for labor that the oil boom stimulated was simply impossible. Foreigners were needed, and they came in unprecedented numbers.

This is not to say that migration in the region began with the oil boom. The modern history of migration in the region may be roughly divided into five phases. During the first phase, prior to 1974, more than 80% of immigrating workers were Arabs, mainly Egyptians, Syrians, Yemenis, and Palestinians. The major characteristics of the Gulf labor market during this period were the relatively narrow wage differentials between sending and receiving countries and the high skill level of many migrant workers. Further, Iraq and Oman, which became major labor importers during the 1980s, were net exporters of manpower. The second phase began with the oil-price increase of 1974. During this period the absolute numbers of Arab immigrant workers rose dramatically, with immigration from poorer countries such as Egypt, the Sudan, and the Yemens being especially prominent. Some estimates of the size of these flows are shown in Tables 15.1–15.3. Such figures are and can only be approximations; existing data are often mutually inconsistent, and estimates of the numbers of migrant workers vary greatly.

The third phase occurred during the latter part of the 1970s and the early 1980s. Further oil-price increases in 1979 approximately doubled government revenues in a single year, stimulating still more ambitious development plans and projects and even more generous social-welfare programs. By 1980 an additional 1.8 million men were at work in Saudi Arabia and the other Gulf States alone (an increase of over 260% in five years) while the number of migrant workers in Iraq had increased more than ten times, to about 750,000. The number of expatriate workers in Libya had risen from just under 50,000 in 1973 to over 400,000 in 1980, by which time they constituted about one-third of that country's labor force (Sherbiny 1984a). As usual, there are sharply contrasting estimates of the total number of workers, but there seems little question that the most rapid expansion of labor migration in the Gulf occurred in the second half of the 1970s.

In addition to the increase in the total number of workers, two other trends stand out during this period. First, the share of Arab migrant workers in the total expatriate workforce declined from about 43% in 1975 to about 37% in 1980 as Indians, Pakistanis, Sri Lankans, and other Asian workers flocked to the region. Not only was the wage gap even greater for these countries than for some of the poorer Arab countries, but Gulf States often preferred these workers. As non-Arabs they were believed to be less likely to stay in the Gulf and perceived as politically safer than potentially recalcitrant Egyptians, Yemenis, Lebanese, and Palestinians. Second, the growth of demand for unskilled labor slowed as major infrastructural projects were completed, while that for skilled workers to operate the completed projects accelerated.

The fourth phase of decelerating migration began with the decline in oil prices in late 1982. The fall in oil revenues curtailed some development projects in the region. In turn, the demand for foreign workers decelerated in some countries, while the composition of demand continued to shift toward more skilled workers. The oil-price collapse of 1986 slashed the value of construction contracts in the region by 25% from 1986 to 1987 (*South*, September 1987, 65). As of 1985, however, only Iraq, fighting a major war, had actually reduced its labor imports.[6] By contrast, the stock of workers in Saudi Arabia rose by about 1 million from 1980 to 1985. This is not surprising; the kingdom's Third Development Plan of this period allocated even more funds for development projects than had the Second. Numbers for other countries are shown in Figure 15.3. The growth of immigration decelerated in the early 1980s (growing by about 8% per year in 1980–1985) and slowed further in the "oil crunch" of the late 1980s (growth of about 3% per year in 1985–1990), but by the end of the 1980s there were 2 million more foreign workers (a total of 5.2 million, some two-thirds of the labor force) in the Gulf than there had been in 1980.

The fifth phase began with the Iraqi invasion of Kuwait in August 1990. Operation Desert Storm tore asunder the web of intraregional labor and remittance flows—over 1.5 million people were directly affected by the crisis. Although, as usual, all numbers are approximations, about 750,000 Yemenis were expelled from Saudi Arabia and the Gulf, some 350,000 Egyptians fled Iraq, 300,000 Jordanians (of whom 60,000–70,000 were workers) were expelled from the Gulf, and another 150,000 Palestinians were expelled, along with nearly all of the Sudanese in Saudi Arabia. Countries such as Jordan, the Sudan, and Yemen, as well as the PLO, which backed Iraq, paid dearly. Egyptian emigration resumed quickly, bolstered by demand in Saudi Arabia and in Libya. In 1994, there were about 2.5 million Egyptians abroad, some 25% more than in 1987. Jordanians, Sudanese, Palestinians, and Yemenis have not been so fortunate, although there are reports that perhaps 200,000 Yemenis have been allowed to return to Saudi Arabia. The Gulf War transformed labor migration patterns as thoroughly as it did regional alliances.

All data refer to the stock of workers in a country at any one time. The total number of workers who have *ever* participated in work abroad is of course much larger than the stock in any one year. Data on the turnover of workers do not exist. However, if the average length of stay abroad is two to three years, the total number of workers who had ever emigrated for employment between 1974 and 1988 would have been four to seven times larger than the stock of workers in 1974, even assuming that the stock remained constant. By even our conservative estimates, however, the stock roughly tripled during this period. Most of the males of some countries, such as Yemen, have worked in Saudi Arabia at least once. A survey of over 1,000 rural Egyptian families found that one-third of all males had worked abroad, mainly in Iraq (Adams 1991). One direct estimate places the number of Egyptians who migrated at any time during 1973–1985 at 3.5 million, roughly one-third of the labor force (Fergany 1988). The socioeconomic consequences of migration are much larger and the benefits probably much more widely shared than the numbers in the tables would suggest.

In all countries the vast majority of these migrants are young adult males. For example, an ILO study of Sudanese migrants found that over 90% were men and over 60% were between eighteen and thirty years old (Berar-Awad 1984). A survey in Egypt found that the average age was thirty-two (Fergany 1988). Similar patterns have been observed in the former YAR and Jordan. By contrast, the educational and occupational composition of migrants varies markedly across countries. Emigrants

TABLE 15.1 Arab Migrant Workers in the Middle East, 1975

Country of Origin

Country of Employment	Egypt		YAR		Jordan/Palestine		PDRY		Syria		Lebanon	
	No.	%	No.	%	No.	%	No.	%	No.	%	No.	%
Bahrain	1,237	0.3	1,121	0.4	614	0.2	1,122	1.6	68	0.1	129	0.3
Iraq	7,000	1.8	–	–	5,000	1.9	–	–	–	–	3,000	6.0
Jordan	5,300	1.3	–	–	–	–	–	–	20,000	28.4	7,500	15.1
Kuwait	37,558	9.4	2,757	1.0	47,653	18.0	8,658	12.3	16,547	23.4	7,232	14.6
Libya	229,500	57.8	–	–	14,150	5.3	–	–	13,000	18.5	5,700	11.5
Saudi Arabia	95,000	23.9	280,400	96.6	175,000	66.1	55,000	77.9	15,000	21.3	20,000	40.3
Oman	4,600	1.2	100	0.0	1,600	0.6	100	0.1	400	0.6	1,100	2.2
Qatar	2,850	0.7	1,250	0.4	6,000	2.3	1,250	1.8	750	1.1	500	1.0
UAE	12,500	3.1	4,500	1.6	14,500	5.5	4,500	6.4	4,500	6.4	4,500	9.0
YAR	2,000	0.5	–	–	200	0.1	–	–	150	0.2	–	–
Total	397,545	100.0	290,128	100.0	264,717	100.0	70,630	100.0	70,415	100.0	49,661	100.0
All employing countries		30.7		22.4		20.4		5.5		5.4		3.8

Country of Origin

Country of Employment	Sudan		Tunisia		Oman		Iraq		Somalia		Morocco	
	No.	%	No.	%	No.	%	No.	%	No.	%	No.	%
Bahrain	400	0.9	–	–	1,383	3.6	126	0.6	–	–	–	–
Iraq	200	0.4	–	–	–	–	–	–	–	–	–	–
Jordan	–	–	–	–	–	–	–	–	–	–	–	–
Kuwait	873	1.9	49	0.1	3,660	9.5	17,999	87.3	247	3.8	47	1.8
Libya	7,000	15.3	38,500	99.6	–	–	–	–	–	–	2,500	98.2
Saudi Arabia	500	1.1	100	0.3	–	–	–	–	300	4.6	–	–
Oman	400	0.9	–	–	1,870	4.9	–	–	–	–	–	–
Qatar	35,000	76.3	–	–	17,500	45.6	2,000	9.7	5,000	76.4	–	–
UAE	1,500	3.2	–	–	14,000	36.4	500	2.4	1,000	15.2	–	–
YAR	–	–	–	–	–	–	–	–	–	–	–	–
Total	45,545	100.0	38,649	100.0	38,413	100.0	20,625	100.0	6,547	100.0	2,547	100.0
All employing countries		3.5		3.0		1.6		1.6		0.5		0.2

Source: Birks and Sinclair (1980).

TABLE 15.2   Arab Migrant Workers (Estimated) in Saudi Arabia and Other
Gulf States, Early 1980s

Country of Origin	Saudi Arabia	Other Gulf States
Egypt	800,000	1,150,000
Iraq[a]	3,250	44,760
Jordan/Palestine	140,000	227,850
Lebanon	33,200	54,850
Oman	10,000	33,450
Somalia	8,300	12,200
Sudan	55,600	65,470
Syria	24,600	67,150
Tunisia/Morocco	500	920
YAR	325,000	336,145
PDRY	65,000	83,845
Total	1,465,250	2,076,640

[a] In 1990 there were approximately 750,000 foreign workers in Iraq (*Quarterly Review of the Intergovernmental Committee for Migration,* January 1986).
Source: Owen (1985).

from the Sudan and Jordan are largely skilled. The ILO survey just cited found that only 11% of Sudanese migrants were illiterate, compared with a national illiteracy figure of over 75%; about 63% of the migrants in the sample possessed some skills (Berar-Awad 1984). Relatively skilled workers tend to predominate among non-Arab Asian labor, although there are many low-skilled service workers (cleaners, maids). However, emigrants from the former YAR were overwhelmingly unskilled and rural; the World Bank estimated that between two-thirds and three-fourths of the half-million Yemenis abroad in 1982 were from rural areas (World Bank 1986c). Still other countries occupy an intermediate position; a 1984 survey of Egyptian migrants found that although nearly half (49%) had at least a secondary education, another 31% (and 54% of rural migrants) were illiterate (al-Hanidi 1988).

THE IMPACT OF LABOR MIGRATION
ON SENDING COUNTRIES

The impact of labor migration on sending countries is much debated, and although the controversy is heated it is often unenlightening. Different analysts often have different values: what is "collapse of the national culture" to one may be "integration into the modern world" to another. Prejudices abound, as when from the comfort of their lavishly furnished living rooms rich officials decry peasant migrants' spending money on television sets and tape decks. These prejudices and value conflicts are difficult to

TABLE 15.3 Foreign Workers in Gulf States (Thousands), by Country of Origin, 1985

	Total		Egypt		Jordan		YAR		PDRY		Others	
	No.	%	No.	%	No.	%	No.	%	No.	%	No.	%
Bahrain	85	2.3	4	0.5	4	1.5	5	0.6	2	2.0	70	3.9
Kuwait	40	11.5	137	18.4	70	26.2	24	3.0	11	11.0	188	10.3
Oman	145	3.9	7	0.9	7	2.6	3	0.4	1	1.0	127	7.0
Qatar	108	2.9	16	2.2	8	3.0	8	1.0	3	3.0	73	4.0
Saudi Arabia	2,500	67.0	500	66.9	158	59.2	720	90.0	75	75.0	1,047	57.7
UAE	462	12.4	83	11.1	20	7.5	40	5.0	8	8.0	311	17.1
Total	3,730	100.0	747	100.0	267	100.0	800	100.0	100	100.0	1,816	100.0
% of total	100.0		20.0		7.2		2.4		2.7		48.7	

Source: Economic and Social Commission for Western Asia (1986).

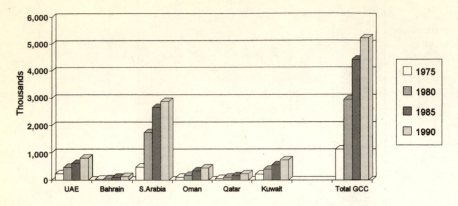

FIGURE 15.3   Foreign workers in the Gulf, 1975–1990. *Source:* Abdel-Jaber (1993).

confront or to clarify because the data are so poor. We do not really know how many people have been affected directly by migration, and still less is known about the indirect effects on localities. The debate on the impact of labor migration is too often a clash of ignorant armies in the night.

Few dispute the private benefits of emigration: if the benefits were not extensive, people would not go. The fundamental force driving the private decision to migrate is the huge gap between local and foreign wages. This gap is especially large for unskilled, rural workers who obtained construction jobs, as in the Egyptian example given above. It is also large for skilled and technical workers. For example, the average weekly pay in Jordan for professionals in 1979 was only 37% of weekly pay in Saudi Arabia, while Jordanian managers and administrators, when working in Jordan, earned only 20% of Saudi wages (World Bank 1986a). Although immigrant workers often have to finance travel abroad, these costs are reduced by labor contractors and by various informal information systems that typically involve whole villages and urban neighborhoods. Some analysts of labor migration stress that the appropriate unit of analysis is not the individual but the household: one or two members may be selected to seek work abroad while others remain behind to tend the store or the farm, to retain government jobs, and so forth (Stark 1983). This means that migrant workers can better afford an extended job search, thus reducing the riskiness of unemployment and increasing the incentive to migrate. This household strategy has been employed by millions of Middle Eastern families, and there is every reason to suppose that in most cases it has contributed to the welfare of the emigrant's family.

Assessing the social costs and benefits of labor migration is more contentious. This debate may be decomposed into a dispute about the net social benefits of three aspects of the migration process: "people out" (emigration), "money back" (remittances), and "people back" (return migration).

Emigration, or "People Out"

Perhaps the central question in debate over emigration is its impact on employment and its role in creating labor shortages. Those who applaud the migration phenomenon argue that emigration has acted as a safety valve for the sending countries' labor markets by providing jobs for the unemployed. The critics counter that most migrants were already employed and maintain that emigration has fostered labor shortages that have impeded development.

In assessing these arguments we must distinguish among different types of labor. Unquestionably, migration has been very beneficial for relatively unskilled workers, thereby reducing levels of unemployment and increasing wages for the underprivileged. Although some seasonal, short-term labor bottlenecks may have been created, there is little evidence that such phenomena reduced output at the peak of the boom. The fall of unskilled wages and the upsurge in poverty in Egypt after 1986 and in Jordan and Yemen after 1990 dramatically illustrate the importance of emigration in a context of rapid growth of labor supply (Chapter 4) and sluggish increases in domestic demand (Chapters 8 and 9). However, although emigration may also have helped to alleviate the chronic unemployment of university graduates, the "brain drain" made it very difficult for poorer countries' public sectors to find qualified skilled personnel. These shortages and the continual turnover of highly trained people contributed to the woes of the public sector.

Although it is often true that those who migrate were already employed, the departure of such workers creates new openings for those who remain behind. Emigration for work fueled the most dramatic growth of agricultural real wages in Egypt's modern history, with striking impacts on rural poverty. Similar ripple effects have been noted in Jordan and Morocco. Evidence of such benefits may also be seen in Tunisia and Yemen. In light of today's problems, the debate during the third phase (roughly, 1978–1982) on labor shortages due to migration is revealed for what it was: the conflation of a temporary disequilibrium with a long-run structural problem.[7]

This hardly means that large-scale emigration created no economic problems. For example, the growth of cereal production may have been slowed by the departure of labor. Cereals face strong competition from imports and sometimes significant taxation; it is difficult for local cereal farmers to pass on the increased cost of labor in the form of higher prices. This problem was probably most severe in marginal areas where some farms have simply been abandoned, as in the former YAR and Jordan. Because rural labor markets in the region are often poorly integrated and because labor migration tends to be selective, with some villages supplying many workers and others far fewer, local labor bottlenecks emerged.

In summary, although emigration of adult males from rural areas of the region created certain short- to medium-term adjustment problems, there is little evidence that it produced labor shortages sufficient to constrain the growth of agricultural production. The same point holds for the exit of unskilled urban workers; there is simply no evidence that unskilled-labor shortages have retarded industrial growth or the building of infrastructure in the region. The emigration of unskilled labor has created far more benefits than costs for the sending countries. The third-phase debate on unskilled labor shortages was really much ado about nothing.

The balance of social costs and benefits for the emigration of skilled manpower is somewhat more complicated. By definition, skills cannot be reproduced overnight. Accordingly, the supply of skilled workers is relatively inelastic. As a general rule, the greater the skill, the longer the period of necessary training and therefore the greater the interval of shortages induced by emigration. However, as conventional economic theory would predict, these shortages seem to have been fairly brief, as the ever-increasing number of new labor-force entrants replaced the departed migrants. Many teachers, engineers, computer programmers, and high-level managers went to work in the Gulf States. The domestic private sector could compete with Gulf State employment much more successfully than the public sector. There is little evidence that private construction activity in Egypt, for example, had difficulties attracting and retaining highly qualified professionals such as engineers and architects. By contrast, the public educational system of that country witnessed a massive outflow of teachers. Labor migration may also adversely affect higher education; some university faculties at Cairo University (e.g., economics, statistics, commerce) had up to one-third of their regular faculty abroad during the late 1970s. By the mid-1990s, however, all such effects had been swamped by the rising tide of job seekers.

In summary, the impact of emigration was on balance beneficial to the economies of the sending countries. Millions of unskilled workers and their families improved their living standards; there is little reason to suppose that economic growth would have been more rapid in these countries had these workers remained at home; with the exception of the emigration of the most skilled professionals, especially from the poorest countries such as the Sudan, the so-called labor shortages have been largely seasonal, short-run disequilibria. The "social experiment" of the Gulf War aimed a bright, cruel light on the benefits of emigration for social welfare in the sending countries.

Remittances, or "Money Back"

Workers go abroad to save money, which they hope to bring back home. They usually succeed. Some official estimates of the magnitude of remittances in selected countries of the region are shown in Table 15.4. Until the disaster of 1990, remittances were a crucial source of foreign exchange for many countries. Indeed, for Yemen and Egypt the value of remittances exceeded that of any commodity exports. Remittances often paid for a substantial fraction of imports, especially in Egypt, Jordan, Morocco, and Yemen (Table 15.5). Even in 1993, remittances were about US$90 per capita in Egypt, Jordan, and Yemen, accounting for 40% of exports and 10% of GDP (World Bank 1995a). They have risen and fallen with the price of oil, in turn the proximate determinant of spending booms in the Gulf.[8]

Official figures for remittances represent only the tip of the iceberg. Much money enters labor-exporting countries via unofficial channels (Choucri 1986). For exam-

TABLE 15.4 Official Remittances (US$ millions) of Migrant Labor in Selected Countries of Origin, 1973–1992

	1973	1974	1975	1976	1977	1978	1979
Egypt	123	310	455	842	988	1,824	2,269
Jordan	55.4	82	172	401.8	420.8	468	509
Morocco	211	299	480	499	546	702	891
Sudan	6.3	4.9	1.5	36.8	37	66.1	115.7
Tunisia	91	106	131	128	152	204	271
Turkey	1,234	1,466	1,398	1,104	1,068	1,086	1,799
YAR	–	135.5	270.2	675.9	987.1	910.1	936.7
PDRY	32.9	42.8	58.5	119.3	187.3	254.8	297.9

	1980	1981	1982	1983	1984	1985	1986
Egypt	2,791	2,230	2,481	3,688	3,981	–	–
Jordan	666.5	921.9	932.9	923.9	1,027.8	846.2	984.4
Morocco	209	322	1,071	245.8	276.8	248.6	89.3
Sudan	301	331	361	346	304	259	354
Tunisia	1,004	988	840	888	847	965	1,394
Turkey	2,153	2,559	2,189	1,549	1,855	1,762	1,703
YAR	1,069.5	777.4	911.4	1,084.4	995.5	763.2	527.4
PDRY	322.5	378.7	429.5	439.5	479.5	–	–

	1987	1988	1989	1990	1991	1992
Egypt	3,604	3,770	3,293	4,284	4,054	6,104
Jordan	742.9	79.8	565.4	457.4	408.1	781.3
Morocco	1,579	1,303	1,356	2,012	2,013	2,179
Sudan	133.7	216.3	412.4	59.8	45.2	123.7
Tunisia	481	548	485	591	574	570
Turkey	2,066	1,827	3,135	3,349	2,854	3,000
Yemen	1,010.3	566.5	414	977	340	125

Sources: International Financial Statistics (various years) and IMF *Country Tables* (line 77afd: Private Unregulated Transfers).

ple, only about 13% of remittances to the Sudan from Saudi Arabia and Kuwait in the early 1980s came through national banks; between half and three-fourths of the total value of remittances were simply carried by hand (Berar-Awad 1984). Applying this ratio to national figures would mean that total Sudanese remittances in 1985 were over US$1.9 billion rather than the official US$259 million. Although the extreme weakness of the Sudanese banking system and the gross overvaluation of the Sudanese pound in 1985 may make that country's experience special, a qualitatively

380

TABLE 15.5 Official Remittances as a Percentage of Imports and Exports in Selected Countries in the Middle East, 1973–1992

	1973 Imports	1973 Exports	1974 Imports	1974 Exports	1975 Imports	1975 Exports	1976 Imports	1976 Exports	1977 Imports	1977 Exports	1978 Imports	1978 Exports	1979 Imports	1979 Exports
Egypt	13.4	11.0	13.2	20.5	11.6	29.9	22.1	55.3	20.5	57.9	27.1	105.0	59.1	123.3
Jordan	18.4	23.2	15.7	17.5	18.8	31.2	19.1	39.2	17.1	41.9	23.6	46.6	24.2	45.5
Morocco	16.8	75.9	16.8	52.9	23.5	112.4	39.3	194.1	30.5	169.0	31.2	157.0	25.9	126.3
Sudan	1.4	1.5	0.7	1.4	0.2	0.3	3.8	6.6	3.4	5.6	5.5	12.8	10.4	21.6
Tunisia	13.3	21.6	9.4	11.5	9.2	15.3	8.4	16.2	8.3	16.4	9.5	18.1	9.5	15.1
Turkey	59.2	93.7	38.8	95.7	29.5	99.8	21.5	56.3	18.4	60.9	23.6	47.5	35.5	79.6
YAR	–	–	71.3	0	91.9	–	163.7	–	94.9	–	70.9	–	62.8	–
PDRY	19.2	32.9	10.2	18.8	18.2	34.2	29.0	67.4	34.4	103.5	44.3	132.7	32.2	63.9

	1980 Imports	1980 Exports	1981 Imports	1981 Exports	1982 Imports	1982 Exports	1983 Imports	1983 Exports	1984 Imports	1984 Exports	1985 Imports	1985 Exports	1986 Imports	1986 Exports
Egypt	57.4	91.6	25.4	69.0	27.3	79.5	35.9	114.8	37.0	126.8	–	–	–	–
Jordan	27.8	116.1	29.1	125.8	28.8	124.1	30.4	159.3	36.9	136.7	31.0	107.3	115.8	384.5
Morocco	23.6	41.1	22.5	41.4	19.5	40.7	24.7	44.3	21.7	39.0	25.1	44.2	–	–
Sudan	133.0	38.5	21.4	49.1	8.4	21.5	18.2	39.4	24.1	44.0	16.3	33.5	10.7	3.7
Tunisia	8.5	13.5	8.7	13.2	10.6	18.2	11.1	18.7	9.6	17.0	9.4	14.9	15.5	25.2
Turkey	27.2	74.0	28.7	54.4	24.8	38.1	16.8	27.0	17.5	26.4	16.0	22.1	15.4	22.8
YAR	57.7	–	44.2	–	59.9	–	68.1	–	–	–	29.3	–	–	–
PDRY	21.1	41.5	26.7	62.4	26.9	54.1	29.4	65.2	31.1	74.3	–	–	–	–

	1987		1988		1989		1990		1991		1992	
Egypt	24	91	17	29	22	65	36	130	56	120	73	195
Jordan	71	233	–	–	31	59	18	45	17	37	24	64
Morocco	38	58	28	37	24	40	30	48	39	46	31	57
Turkey	16	23	16	25	11	16	11	17	11	15	9	15
Tunisia	19	26	17	21	22	30	18	30	17	28	16	25
Yemen	62	848	30	107	23	58	51	127	25	67	10	31

Sources: International Financial Statistics (various years) and IMF *Country Tables* (line 77afd: Private Unregulated Transfers) for remittances, IMF *World Tables* (lines 70d and 71d) for imports and exports.

similar phenomenon has been observed in other countries (e.g., the former YAR, Jordan, Syria, and Egypt)—anywhere that national currencies were seriously overvalued.

Critics of remittances' effects at the macro level focus on their alleged tendency to be spent on imports rather than domestic production and their contribution to inflation. These two effects are mutually exclusive: If money is being spent on foreign goods, it should have no impact on domestic inflation. To the extent that domestic supply can respond to the increased demand, the result should be economic growth rather than simply inflation. Of course, as we have seen, there are numerous constraints to expanding the output of domestic goods and services in the economies of the region. But workers' remittances are hardly responsible for these constraints, often induced by inappropriate government policies. The way in which money enters the system may contribute to inflation. To the extent that remittances move outside of the banking system, the government may lose control of the money supply, as Egypt did until the spring of 1988.

The principal area of debate on the microeconomic effect of remittances concerns the division of the funds between consumption and investment and the types of investments that are selected. A substantial proportion of remittances is devoted to direct consumption. Given that a majority of migrants from most countries are from rural areas and that rural per capita incomes in the region are generally only half to one-third of urban ones, it would be surprising if this were not the case. However, detailed surveys tend to contradict the conventional wisdom. For example, Adams has shown that in Minya governorate in Egypt, one of the poorest areas of the country, migrants invested much of their earnings, particularly in housing and land (Adams 1991). An earlier estimate for Egypt, for 1980/81, calculated that some 25% of gross investment and fully 80% of private-sector investment were financed by remittances (Lesch 1985); others would question such high figures. Some criticize the form that such investment takes, faulting migrants for placing their savings in housing, consumer durables, dowries, and land rather than in productivity-enhancing investments such as machinery, small workshops, and improved agricultural techniques.

Remittances are indeed often spent on housing. One survey in Egypt found that over one-fifth of remittances were so used; a similar proportion was reported in a study of Sudanese migrants' spending (Berar-Awad 1984). Parallel patterns have been found in Turkey, Tunisia, and Morocco. Other priority items of expenditure include furniture and simple household articles (some 58% in one Egyptian case study [el-Dib, Ismail, and Gad 1984]). Few who have been inside the homes of Egyptian, Yemeni, or Moroccan manual workers would question this use of remittances, especially in rural areas. Substituting a brick home for a mud hut improves the quality of life of rural people and contributes directly to meeting basic human needs. To the extent that poorly ventilated, poorly heated, or excessively hot, vermin-ridden housing is a threat to human health, the spending of remittances on better housing may be viewed as an investment in human capital. Although building on irreplaceable agricultural land constitutes an Egyptian national disaster, faulty incentives may be more reasonably blamed than migration.

Remittances are also frequently invested in land. Since the supply of land is inelastic, the increased demand pushes land prices sharply upward. Of course, not all of the rise in land prices can be attributed to remittances. Land-price increases occurred primarily in the highly inflationary environment during the decade of the oil boom. From California to Kuwait, investors move into real estate in inflationary periods.

Some remittances have found their way into productive investments, such as irrigation equipment, small workshops and factories, and transportation equipment (trucks and cars), but these investments probably constitute a relatively small proportion of the total spending of remittances. This is hardly the fault of the migrants or of emigration. Instead, we should blame national policies for reducing the profitability of investments in productivity-enhancing technologies. For example, the ambivalence of many governments of the region toward private-sector manufacturing, combined with overvalued real exchange rates and other macromanagement problems, discourages the kind of industrial investment that critics of the observed pattern of remittance spending prefer.

The fact that so many remittances do not move through the banking system further reduces their use for productivity-enhancing investment. Weak and unstable financial systems have discouraged people from using banks. Returned migrants often keep their savings literally under the mattress; although they save, they cannot be expected to create their own investment opportunities. Banks have performed their function of financial intermediation between savers and investors rather poorly. Overvalued foreign exchange rates further dissuade migrants from forwarding their savings through official channels. Exchange-rate reforms in Egypt provide an example of what policy shifts can do; the realignment of exchange rates in the summer of 1987 increased bank deposits by perhaps US$750 million. Many of these funds were remittances of Egyptian workers abroad.

Although some charge that spending remittances on automobiles contributes to the monstrous urban congestion of cities like Cairo, subsidized motor fuel and the failure of urban management are more likely culprits. The diffusion of motor vehicles in the countryside is a healthy development. Immobile rural workers are typically poor; improved communication and transportation contribute to increased market integration. In some countries, for example, the Sudan, the transportation bottleneck is especially severe. In such cases it is desirable that a certain proportion of remittances be spent on transportation. The problem is that complementary public investment in roads and other infrastructure often lags. One challenge for policymakers is to determine how to channel remittances into needed public and semipublic goods and services, especially in rural areas. It is difficult to entice private funds into irrigation works, roads, public-health facilities, and schools. One promising attempt to solve this problem is the rural development associations of the former YAR, using *zakat* (Chapter 14) to finance spending on wells, schools, and roads (Cohen et al. 1981).

The combination of labor migration and remittances does undermine the potential for an export-led growth strategy. To the extent that wages in the oil countries contain an element of oil rent and these rents have seeped into the wage structure of the sending countries, the latter will find it difficult to compete in exporting labor-intensive products. Some critics of emigration have argued that labor exports were an alternative to the export of labor-intensive manufactured goods (Katanani 1981).

This was not, however, really a choice for most countries. The political policies, institutions, and entrepreneurial skills needed for successful export of manufactured goods were nowhere in sight in the region in 1973; even today, they are too often absent (Chapter 9). Imagine how many changes the Egyptian government of the early Sadat years would have had to undertake to begin to compete in the fiercely competitive international market for textiles! The exchange-rate regime, the tariff structure, and the domestic-communications infrastructure would all have had to be altered radically. Furthermore, the manufacturers of these products in Egypt were state-owned enterprises, infamous for their rigidity and indifference to consumer tastes. By contrast, all the government of Egypt had to do to facilitate labor exports was simply get out of the way. In the short run, there was really no choice. But the instability of labor exports and the absence of the numerous dynamic linkages that characterize the growth of manufactured exports suggest that, once again, history has not been kind to the political economies of the poorer, more crowded nations of the region.

Return Migration, or "People Back"

The vast majority of migrants want to return home. Neither they nor the receiving countries view labor migration as permanent resettlement. Most migrants do return home; the large majority come back at least temporarily, for major holidays or for important family events such as weddings. The more important question concerns the economic contribution of migrants who return home for good. How well did national labor markets absorb the return flow of workers in the wake of the Gulf War?

Many, perhaps most, migrants return to their village or urban neighborhood of origin (Amin and Taylor-Awny 1985). Whenever possible, formerly landless agricultural workers try to avoid agricultural work even if they come back to their villages. Returnees often set up small businesses, such as taxi services, shops, and, occasionally, small factories. Returnees may have acquired new skills (e.g., a farm laborer may have turned construction worker), although there is little direct evidence on this issue.

Return migration on a substantial scale had already become a major issue for many sending countries before the Gulf War. The fall in oil prices, the completion of major construction projects, and the increased competition of non-Arab Asian labor in the smaller Gulf States all contributed to the gradual reversal of labor flows. The declining importance of remittances as a source of foreign exchange was already evident in some countries. In the former YAR, remittances fell about 20% from 1983 to 1985. In just two years (1984 to 1986) Egyptian remittances plummeted 50%, from US$4 to US$2 billion, but exchange-rate overvaluation was the main culprit.

At the same time that the economic stimulus of remittances faltered, the numbers of young, first-time job seekers rose. These youths, not the returners themselves, were the ones most seriously affected by return migration. The returning migrants had often accumulated savings and acquired or sharpened skills abroad. They were relatively well placed to compete effectively in a tightening job market or to become successfully self-employed. But this was much less likely to be true for the semieducated youths who poured onto the job market in ever greater numbers.

The Gulf War heightened these problems. At first, returnees actually provided some economic stimulus, as they spent money on housing; this effect was particularly noticeable in Jordan. As the data in Table 15.4 show, however, remittances plummeted thereafter. Returnees tended to go back to urban areas, although in Yemen perhaps 50% returned to villages. They constituted an additional drag on already overburdened labor markets, driving the unemployment rate up to 25% in Yemen and 19% in Jordan. Jordan also lost its major export markets in Iraq and the Gulf, further compounding the economic crisis there.

Egypt was more fortunate. Although we are unaware of any detailed studies of returnees, anecdotal evidence suggests that emigration to Libya has increased considerably and that Egyptians have (to an unknown extent) supplanted other Arab expellees in Saudi Arabia. Certainly the estimated number of emigrants (now perhaps 2.5 million) and the numbers on remittances strongly suggest that for Egypt the Gulf War was mainly a blip in its experience of emigration. It is significant, however, that the additional 500,000 workers abroad constitutes roughly one year's annual addition to the labor force. It is also likely that the new emigrants and the expellees are often different people: certainly there is little evidence that the illiterate, rural emigrants (two-thirds of whom were in Iraq) have found new jobs abroad. Emigration may not have collapsed, but it can no longer act as the main source of new employment.

MIGRATION AND EQUITY

Generalizing about the equity consequences of migration is difficult. Not only are few reliable data available but also the spotty evidence suggests that the windfall gains of emigration have been fairly randomly distributed across society. Engineers and farm workers, doctors and drivers, teachers and mechanics have all participated. Migration offers a clear avenue of upward mobility for those able to emigrate. It may help small family farms to survive and strengthen some elements of the small urban entrepreneurial class. It leaves behind many white-collar workers, especially those employed by the state.

The impact on poverty is clearer than its effect on income distribution or on the class structure. Emigration and remittances reduced rural poverty, the worst poverty in the region. In Egypt, for example, emigration dramatically reduced the ranks of landless laborers, historically the poorest of the poor in that poor country. An ILO survey found that although 23% of all Egyptian villagers received remittances, 75% of the poorest 30% of villagers received them. For the absolutely poorest people, who are often disabled single persons, remittances constituted more than 75% of their (extremely meager) incomes. For the third-poorest income decile, 40% of their income came from remittances. The poorest fourth and fifth deciles obtained more than 30% of their incomes from agricultural wage labor; the real wages of farm workers more than doubled in the past decade, largely thanks to emigration (Radwan and Lee 1986; Richards and Martin 1983). Adams's survey in Minufiyya also showed a direct poverty-reducing impact of remittances (Adams 1991), and the largest impact on poverty was probably the indirect effect of raising farm wages for those left behind (Richards 1994). Similarly, emigration and remittances ameliorated the grinding rural poverty in the YAR. Researchers reported improved food and nutrition and better housing. The fact that sharecropping contracts now commonly allocate a higher percentage of the crop to the tenant is also evidence that poorer groups have benefited relatively as well as absolutely. In the Middle East, as everywhere, migrants often come from very poor and disadvantaged regions: from the western Sudan, from Upper Egypt, and from southern Tunisia. For poor Jordanians, Sudanese, and Yemenis, those opportunities vanished after August 1990.

It seems clear that migrants are usually not the very poorest rural inhabitants, simply because migration requires some money to finance the journey abroad. However, labor contractors and family networks can often bring these costs down within reach of quite poor Middle Easterners. Furthermore, the very poorest Egyptians do seem to benefit from migration via remittances, although survey evidence suggests that they benefit less than those with higher incomes (Radwan and Lee 1986; Adams 1991). Nevertheless, migration was unfortunately neither large enough nor stable enough to alter radically the serious problems of rural and urban poverty in the region. The deceleration (at best) or demise (at worst) of migration in 1990 is an important cause of the upsurge in poverty noted in Egypt, Jordan, and Yemen in the early 1990s.

THE IMPACT OF MIGRATION ON RECEIVING COUNTRIES

The economic benefits of migration to the receiving countries were clearly very large. The major oil exporters simply could not have undertaken their large-scale development projects without foreign workers, who made possible the rapid physical capital formation and infrastructure construction of the oil-boom period. Saudi nonoil GDP grew at 10.5%, 13%, and 8.9% for 1970–1975, 1975–1980, and 1980–1983, respectively; in the UAE nonoil GDP expanded at 14.1% per year from 1975 to 1980. Immigration of teachers also enabled the oil countries to embark on the rapid expansion of their educational systems. As has been explained above, the enormous increase in the demand for labor that such expansion implied could not have been met from domestic supply alone. By 1980, 53% of the Saudi labor force was foreign, while 78% of Kuwait's and 89% of the UAE's workforce came from abroad. Even in Iraq, with a much larger indigenous workforce than the other states, 14% of workers were foreign in 1980 (Sherbiny 1984). By 1990, nationalist rhetoric notwithstanding, this dependence had grown (Figure 15.4). The dependence of the Gulf States on foreigners for labor has no parallel in modern economic history.

The combination of such rapid economic growth with these massive influxes of foreign workers of all types had some unusual social and political consequences. To some extent, labor immigration has severed the "normal" link between economic growth and structural change, on the one hand, and class formation, on the other. Locals can and do avoid manual labor; they can continue to be merchants, soldiers, and bureaucrats. Some fear the long-run impact of the identification of hard work with foreigners—by implication, something that is less than perfect. To be sure, immigrants from poorer countries do the hard, dirty, and dangerous work in all rich countries, but only in the Gulf States do the foreign menials outnumber the indigenous leisured.

In the Gulf States, as everywhere, large-scale immigration has created political problems, violently illustrated by the Gulf War. Immigration posed a serious political challenge to the Saudi and Kuwaiti regimes. The legitimacy problem of denying citizenship rights and benefits to fellow Arabs and Muslims and the experiences of vast differences in wealth *and* effort between citizens of receiving countries and the workers from poorer Arab countries provided much of the animus against the Gulf States that was so visible in popular demonstrations from Morocco to Pakistan during the fall of 1990.[9] States that base their legitimacy on Arab nationalism (as in Iraq) or on Islam (as in Saudi Arabia) face contradictions when they deny other Arabs or Muslims the same treatment as nationals. However, ideological pronouncements notwithstanding, even the Iraqis (who require no visas from Arab migrants on the grounds that they are "citizens of the Arab Nation") treated their citizens differently from other Arab workers. Iraqi propagandists certainly got the better of the contest during the crisis, however.

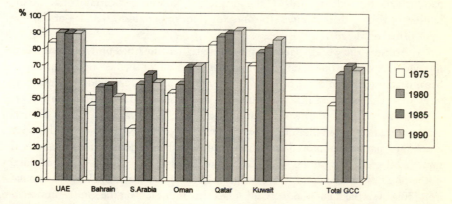

FIGURE 15.4   Foreigners as a percentage of Gulf State labor forces, 1975–1990. *Source:* Abdel-Jaber (1993).

Large-scale influxes of foreigners made national security agencies nervous before the Gulf crisis, which, of course, simply confirmed their worst fears. The disquiet in the Gulf was compounded by the volume of immigration, the political volatility of the region, and the relatively underdeveloped national-security apparatus in many Gulf States at the beginning of the 1970s when immigration soared. States handled these threats by implementing laws that insisted that all but a handful of immigrants be on short-term contracts, by forbidding job changes unless the original employer agreed, and by requiring all workers to leave the country for a specified period once their contracts had expired. They refused to allow the families of any but the most skilled professionals into the country. They mounted particular vigilance against special security threats such as Iranians after the Islamic revolution in Iran. The Saudis tightened security beginning in 1978 and with even more vigor after the Great Mosque incident of 1980. In particular, they sought to guarantee that *hajjis* (pilgrims) would return to their own countries and not use the pilgrimage as a means to slip into the country in search of work. Finally, the Gulf States resorted extensively to devices such as the use of turnkey construction contracts, in which the general contractor supplied the workers and guaranteed their subsequent departure.

Although the Gulf States tried to beef up enforcement by importing foreign police experts (and, in some cases, foreign soldiers and policemen such as the Pakistanis in Oman and Saudi Arabia) and by investing in expanded police equipment (e.g., computers), they continued to rely primarily on more traditional, personalized enforcement mechanisms. Effectively, the employer's right to hire and fire became the political prerogative to retain or expel a worker from the country. Not only could employers report workers to the Ministry of the Interior but also by simply dismissing them employers ensured that they would have legally irregular status. Employers usually took workers' passports upon arrival and would not return them until the contract had expired. But all of these mechanisms proved fruitless when Iraq invaded Kuwait. Despite the fact that many Jordanians, Palestinians, Sudanese, and Yemenis had little use for Saddam, disliked the invasion of Kuwait, and certainly had no intention of risking their families' fortunes for Iraqi imperialism, the sins of the few were visited on the many.

Nevertheless, the wealthy labor-importing states remain schizophrenic about labor immigration. On the one hand, they need these workers for their economies and have become accustomed to the benefits of greater money incomes and wider personal services that such migrants make possible. On the other hand, they fear being overwhelmed by the influx; they worry about losing their cultural values in a sea of foreigners and dread the possibility of political activism by the immigrants—who, however much they may have improved their status relative to their conditions at home, remain underprivileged in the context of the Gulf States themselves. Even the Gulf War could not resolve this contradiction. The percentage of foreign Arabs in the Kuwaiti population (30%) was the highest in the Gulf, a fact that is not lost on the Gulf States' security services.[10] The already pronounced tendency to rely on Asian labor in the lower Gulf may be spreading to Saudi Arabia and the upper Gulf. The Gulf States will remain dependent on immigrant labor for some time and will continue to loathe this dependence, even as their workers retain their own deep ambivalence.

CONCLUSION: THE RETURN OF SURPLUS LABOR

Labor migration has transformed the political economy of the region. Huge numbers of urban and rural citizens of the poorer countries of the region have left their homes, often for the first time, for extended stays abroad. Their departure, their remittances, and their return have transformed families, villages, neighborhoods, and national economies. Labor markets, if nothing else, have become thoroughly integrated across national boundaries. Although the Gulf War ruptured this network, political alliances shift and the structural features underpinning labor migration (wage gaps, reluctance of Gulf nationals to work in many jobs, etc.) remain. The citizens and governments of the oil states have acquired a taste for imported servants, and it will be some time before there are enough locals to staff the technical positions that the newly constructed petrochemical industries and infrastructure require. It is likely that foreigners will comprise a substantial proportion of the labor force of the Gulf States for many years to come.

However, the dynamism of labor migration as a force for raising wages and living standards in the poorer rural areas of the region is unlikely to be repeated. Migration will almost certainly never again boom as it did in the late 1970s or even the 1980s. Sluggish oil prices, completed infrastructure, memories of 1990, rising unemployment of Gulf State nationals, and shifting skill mixes all suggest that expatriate labor will, at best, remain stable in the coming years. At the same time, as a consequence of past fertility behavior the number of new job seekers rises inexorably (Chapter 4).

The oil boom's lasting legacy for labor exporters may have been a buying of time, which was largely squandered. Now the poorer countries of the region face a highly competitive international environment, with few of the policies in place to cope with mounting domestic political challenges and insufficient human-capital resources. Wage expectations have been affected by past migration experience, and such expectations change only slowly and with considerable social pain. Viewed from the mid-1990s, the legacy of migration to oil seems decidedly ambiguous.

NOTES

1. Cultural integration among the Arabs has been proceeding apace for several generations. We do not attempt to analyze this complex and vitally important phenomenon here.

2. Algeria, Egypt, Jordan, Morocco, Tunisia, and Syria.

3. In 1993, Saudi Arabian aid was 0.70% of GNP, while Norwegian aid was 0.038%. U.S. aid was 0.04% of GNP in that year (World Bank 1995a, 197).

4. Jordan, 58.2%; YAR, 27.1%; Syria, 237.8%; the Sudan, 36.2% (van den Boogaerde 1990).

5. However, the Lebanese, Sudanese, and Iraqi civil wars have also created large numbers of political refugees from those countries, and the authoritarianism of most countries of the region has guaranteed that nearly all of them have spawned at least some political exiles.

6. Official Iraqi data on labor imports do not exist, making all statements about that country even more speculative than for others. Many Egyptians remained in Iraq until the invasion of Kuwait. Indeed, in the early fall of 1989 there was a mini-crisis in Egyptian-Iraqi relations as demobilized Iraqi soldiers allegedly returned home to find that Egyptians had taken their jobs and (it was said) their wives. An unknown but sizable number of Egyptians were killed and their bodies sent home to Egypt.

7. As we argued in the first edition of this book (pp. 385–386 and Chapter 14, *passim*).

8. The elasticity of remittances with respect to oil prices is about 0.6 (World Bank 1995a).

9. These demonstrations are better understood as anti–Gulf monarchy and anti-Western demonstrations than as pro-Iraqi ones.

10. Compared with Saudi Arabia, 11%, Qatar, 11%, Oman <2%, the UAE, 10%, and Bahrain, <3% (CIA Atlas 1993).

16

CONCLUSION

There is an old paradox associated with the Nile. When one looks at its surface, churned by the prevailing northwest wind, it appears to be flowing south. Yet beneath the surface it is in fact flowing north, carried by the forces of gravity toward the Mediterranean. What we have laid out in these pages is a political and economic story that resembles the Nile paradox. With the exception of the Iranian revolution of 1978–1979, there have been no social upheavals of such scale as to bring about a change in regime. Instead, we have witnessed remarkable longevity, if not stability, in the regimes of the region. This, we would argue, is as real as the Nile's apparent southern flow. The real in the Middle East lies in the powerful countercurrent embodied by the spread of education, the growth of the middle classes, the shift of populations to urban centers, and the entry of women into the formal economy. These are destabilizing and hard to contain within authoritarian constraints.

These profound socioeconomic changes have been coupled, at least since the mid-1980s, with hard economic times: the collapse of the oil boom, the drying up of strategic rents, and the consequent necessity for profound structural shifts in the economy at a time when public resources are limited. A momentous side effect has been the exacerbation of unemployment or underemployment among the educated. That phenomenon may be temporary, but in political time "temporary" can be altogether too long.

Between the appearance of the first edition of this book in 1990 and the second edition, currents that we identified earlier have commingled and become more powerful. What was politically sustainable, albeit at the cost of heavy policing and repression, no longer is so. All regimes have begun to grapple with this reality, but because the great majority have been in power for many years the grappling is hesitant and inconsistent. It has begun, typically, with passes at economic reform and, less frequently, at political liberalization. With a few notable exceptions, the former steps have been hesitant and therefore not credible. In most cases, so far, states cannot and private investors will not provide the money needed better to manage the problems of jobs, water, food, education, urbanization, and so on.

Steps toward political liberalization have been halfhearted, as in Egypt or Tunisia, abortive, as in Algeria or Yemen, subverted, as in the Sudan, or carefully orchestrated, as in Jordan and Morocco. More aggressive moves toward electoral democracy have been stymied by the fear that the majority may vote for Islam, as Algeria's ill-fated experiment in 1991 revealed. Turkey shows that democracy and political Islam may be compatible, but its example has failed to impress other elites in the region. Incumbents are concerned not so much that elected Islamic parties may snuff out democracy altogether as that Islamists will use elections to drive the incumbents entirely from power.

Thus, while we can discern the sharpening of political and economic crises in the region, we cannot predict who or what will emerge from them politically dominant. The economic reform programs will be pursued, however hesitantly. Middle Eastern economies will open to international trade and capital movements, local private sectors will take on new life, and governments will reduce their direct management of the economy—but all this could take place under continued populist authoritarianism, electoral democracy, or Islamic government. All would have to bend to the realities of a world in which the socialist model has been discredited and establishing credibility with the sources of private investment is crucial. That such steps are essential does not mean, however, that they will be easy.

The middle classes in the Middle East want to be recognized as responsible and mature; they want direct responsibility for governance, not merely co-optation by praetorians and authoritarians. Many may, with greater or lesser degrees of sincerity or hypocrisy, seek empowerment through militant Islam. There is, in any case, no reason to expect them to be committed liberals. Authoritarianism of various kinds may find favor with them as long as they have a meaningful role in it. External conflict and martial law have kept the middle classes in an iron cage in countries such as Iraq and Syria. Civil war or Revolutionary Guards have driven them to migration or dissimulation, as in Lebanon and Iran. Curiously, however, in much of the Third World in the latter part of the twentieth century, the force for change is proving to be not the peasantry or the proletariat, as it was in the 1950s and 1960s, but the white-collar middle classes. Halpern (1963) said as much thirty years ago, but he was at least that many years premature.

The increasing engagement of governments with private wealth has at least one potent political consequence: it establishes a space for bargaining and negotiation that may constitute a kind of proto-accountability. This is quite new for paternalistic authoritarians who have regarded their citizens of all stripes as policy takers. Now certain citizens must be consulted in the formulation of policy, confidence in state adherence to laws and contracts must be established, and real legal recourse must be made available to aggrieved parties. It is possible that conceding the need to bargain with one set of economic actors will have a spillover effect for other sectors. This process of creeping accountability will take place not through sudden and highly visible shifts toward formal democracy but gradually, through legal reform and cumulative, reinforcing experiences. It will be helped along by the state's growing fiscal engagement with its citizens, resulting from diminished external rents and increasing direct and indirect taxes.

None of the above clearly distinguishes Middle Eastern nations from the rest of what is loosely called the Third World. The two major variables that do seem to characterize the Middle East are an unusually high incidence of regional conflict and violence, with attendant diversion of human and material resources to the pursuit of those conflicts, and the general spread of political Islam. It goes without saying that neither armed conflict nor religious fervor is exclusive to the Middle East, but their juxtaposition and, indeed, interrelationship do produce a peculiarly Middle Eastern phenomenon.

What is astonishing is that despite the investment of colossal resources and energies in the destruction of enemies, the region as a whole is more prosperous, its citizens better educated, its wealth more evenly distributed, and its nations more firmly rooted than forty years ago. Unquestionably for *most* of its inhabitants, the Middle East is a better place in which to live than it was even a couple of decades ago. The middle classes, largely urban and earning their living in the service sector and as professionals with advanced training, are both the cause and the major beneficiary of the general rise in standards of living. But we should not forget that in the countryside extensive road networks have been built, irrigation systems introduced to formerly arid areas, electricity brought to villages, and schools, dispensaries, veterinary services, agriculture extension services, and rural credit provided to much if not all of the rural population. And everywhere, far fewer infants and children die than even ten years ago. Some countries have pursued rural uplift and state welfare in general, with a strong egalitarian, populist, and occasionally socialist commitment. Others may have done so defensively, so as not to appear less caring than their populist neighbors. But whether one speaks of Jordan, Pahlavi Iran, and Morocco or Algeria, Syria, and Egypt, the overall distributional results are not very different.

Still, it should be abundantly clear from what has preceded that we believe that this new relative well-being is not built on firm foundations. There are several failings that are shared by many regimes in the region. No country has built an industrial base that can withstand international competition, although Turkey and Israel have made important strides in that direction. A great deal of industrialization has taken place, but it has been highly protected, often allowed to become technologically obsolete, and sustained by little indigenous research-and-development capacity. Moreover, to pay for this imperfect industrialization, several states have heavily taxed their agricultural sectors, thereby inhibiting more rapid agricultural growth, and borrowed heavily abroad. The new industries have rarely been able to earn foreign exchange to help service the external debt (Turkey again is the major exception), and only the oil exporters have kept themselves out of payments crises.

Middle Eastern states in recent decades have tried by and large to achieve high rates of growth *and* high levels of consumption. This is a very hard equation to solve over any extended period of time. Again, the oil exporters could afford to strive for both, but countries without petroleum increasingly have paid for investment by deficit financing and borrowing abroad. Countries such as Egypt were able in part to fill this resource gap—the difference between national savings and investment—through external rents: workers' remittances, Suez Canal fees, and tourism receipts. But in Egypt and elsewhere in the 1970s the big questions of raising the productivity of capital and labor, restructuring industrial production to compete abroad, and adjusting domestic prices to reflect real scarcities were largely avoided. Some countries hoped that their strategic significance would earn them financial support from the great powers, and for Morocco, Egypt, and Jordan, among others, that gamble paid off. For the Sudan it did not, and that country's economy has suffered profoundly. Even for the others, however, there are limits beyond which great powers or regional powers will not extend new lines of soft credit unless the borrowers do something to make their economies efficient. The Soviet Union, in its waning years, had already become much more exigent in its loan policies toward developing countries, but with its collapse and the end of the cold war MENA countries' ability to dissociate aid and credits from real economic reform has been greatly weakened.

Economic and societal development in the Middle East has too often consisted in educating and training new kinds of economic actors, not in increasing the productive capacity of economies. Engineers, accountants, schoolteachers, agronomists, stenographers, communications technicians, airline pilots, pharmacists, and computer experts are there in their tens and hundreds of thousands. In many instances they could have been better trained, but they are more than adequate for many of the challenges at hand. Yet they have been consistently misused and underemployed, assigned to positions more often than not where their talents and initiative are stifled and unrewarded and where seniority is the principal criterion by which one advances. The growth of the professional middle class, as Moore (1980) argued over a decade ago, became the surrogate for real economic development.

The middle classes in all their forms are better defined by their modes of consumption and styles of life than by their place in the mode of production. Because style of consumption is so crucial to the maintenance of middle-class status, regimes that rely on the middle classes for support are hard put to curb their consumption and reduce their standard of living. But this is precisely what many are doing now, in the mid-1990s, and it clearly poses the most momentous political challenge to incumbent regimes.

The nations of the Middle East have been economic underachievers. In aggregate the region showed relatively strong growth over the period 1960–1985, but that growth was rooted in high levels of protection and access to rents. Given its resource endowment, the Middle East should have entered more aggressively into world trade through encouraging private investment, deregulating national markets, and encouraging nontraditional exports. On all three counts Middle Eastern nations have, with the exceptions noted in Chapter 9, moved uncertainly. Hundreds of billions of dollars held by Middle Easterners abroad remain offshore because the governments of the region have yet to establish their credibility as supporters of private enterprise and market economies. At the same time, several nations of the region have joined the World Trade Organization, adhering to the international trade reforms specified by that new organization's charter. Unless very rapid structural adjustment is undertaken, the region will be left ill-prepared to face competition in world markets from the more dynamic economies of China, India, and Southeast Asia.

Yet the picture is by no means all gloomy. The period in which state-led ISI prevailed witnessed the building of national infrastructure in railroads, ports, and power generation. Many of the industries started may not have been appropriate, but production and managerial skills were built and a certain mastery of technology achieved. Several Middle Eastern societies are relatively well equipped to undertake new economic tasks, and the early phase, while creating many of the problems that must be addressed, has also provided their solutions. That Iran was able to conduct a war and manage an economy in a period of declining petroleum prices is a tribute not so much to Khomeini as to the cumulative impact of twenty-five years of rapid social and economic change.

Slow progress has been made in terms of education, literacy, infant mortality, and life expectancy. In most of the Middle East fertility rates are falling, albeit from very high levels. More could and should have been done in educating and providing for the health of Middle Eastern populations, but the trend lines are positive, and there is hopeful evidence of the acceleration of progress in the past decade.

Politically, it would have to be said, Middle Eastern countries have not been at all successful. If we judge several of the regimes by their own criteria, we see that they have failed to develop any coherent mass base to sustain their claims to populist support. Corporatist formulas, grouping citizens according to their functions and professions within single-party, single-ideology systems, have turned out to be little more than bureaucratic attempts to control the active population. The base has become increasingly divorced from the leadership, and as ideological commitment has failed to take hold, the police have become more prominent agents in the control process. Egypt under Nasser, Algeria, Syria, Iraq, and even Iran in the 1970s exemplify regimes that would not concede any real voice and responsibilities to the very people in whose name they spoke. Nor were they able to meet their own economic development goals or to build effective military forces; hence, they failed on all fronts. We have spoken frequently of regime exhaustion and the failure of secular ideologies, and both are perfectly apt terms. Most leaders in the Middle East can remember—and do not want to forget—better times.

The 1950s, it must be stressed, were a period of considerable optimism in the developing world. On the one hand, development economists and bilateral and multilateral sources of foreign assistance gave encouragement to activist states that set about the mobilization of national resources for the development effort. These external mentors, having themselves participated in state-guided efforts to pull Western economies out of the world depression and out of the wreckage of World War II, felt that Third World states could act with similar effectiveness. Moreover, a certain amount of central planning and price administration seemed perfectly appropriate. On the other hand, new regimes were confident that they could bring off the development task without relying on weak private sectors, market forces driven by monopoly and speculation, or foreign private investment, which appeared likely to compromise newly won independence. Leaders of these countries felt sustained by a reserve of nationalist goodwill and a willingness (though it was illusory) to sacrifice for and comply with the leaders' grand designs.

In this kind of atmosphere all good things were seen to go together. Resource utilization would be planned rationally, administrators would conscientiously carry out their duties, the citizens would actively support the development programs, both growth and rising incomes would result, all so that new resources would become available for new rounds of planned development. But, as we have seen, all this became reality only during very brief moments, and usually with attendant costs in foreign indebtedness or domestic price distortions that swamped the plans in subsequent phases. These were only a few of the unintended consequences we mentioned in Chapter 2.

Many things—sometimes all things—went wrong, and the combination of factors varied from country to country. The problem that no one addressed with much vigor was that of rapid population growth and the enormous demand that young populations created for the delivery of services and the expansion of job opportunities whether or not the jobs were truly needed. In addition, protection of import-substituting industries created gross inefficiencies at the same time that the industries themselves developed little capacity to earn foreign exchange in highly competitive external markets. Rather than leading to self-sustaining industrial growth, they became a net drain on public resources.

Bureaucrats behaved rationally, not altruistically. Regulations meant to rationalize economic activity created barriers, or gates, among public agencies and between them and client groups in the society. Those officials who guarded the gates began to collect fees for opening them, especially because their salaries, while predictable, were low, and their jobs, while stable, were dull. Nationalism was no antidote for officials trying to reach or sustain a middle-class way of life.

Concomitantly the citizenry, operating in centralized, top-down political structures, was given no effective means for calling its officials and leaders to account. There was taxation but little true representation. The strategically placed professional middle class was usually co-opted through material rewards and some real power. The rest could choose apathy, rioting, or the political equivalent of the parallel economy—local, informal politics in which vital resources were distributed in ways over which the state had little control. The Muslim political counterculture became the most positive and overt manifestation of the parallel political system, but in general the upshot was that the state found itself less and less in control of both economic and political life.

As the states renege on various parts of their social contracts, as cycles of inflation gnaw at everyday existence, as individuals and families are increasingly left to their own devices, people tend to respond by individualistic scrambling and by narrowly focused survival strategies with short time horizons. These constraints apply not only to the middle classes but also to virtually anyone seeking a livelihood in the urban environment or through migration. This serves the purposes of power wielders who are not unhappy to see potential adversaries caught up in the rat race. Some if not most people are able to stay even in this race, but only by taking on extra jobs and engaging in the informal, local-level politics of procuring the vital goods (licenses, credit, jobs) that are traded locally even if their ultimate source is the state itself. Not everyone makes it in the race, however, and even those who do are under enormous strain. A small elite visibly prospers in such times, living in a sense off the desperate scramble of the others, and that situation breeds anger, envy, and indignation. It literally exploded in Iran in 1978–1979 and nearly has in Egypt, Morocco, and Tunisia at various times since 1977.

It is a much more difficult time than thirty years ago, not merely because resources are so severely stretched against growing populations but also because so many experiments undertaken with confidence and enthusiasm have failed and an entire political generation is burdened with fatigue and self-doubt. Although the Islamic idiom seems to prevail, the countries in which it has been applied—principally Iran, Sudan, and Saudi Arabia—do not offer appealing models for the rest of the region. Thus, without tested models and without long-term strategies, the Middle East has entered a long period of austerity and restructuring. In part, it is some of the successes of the most recent decades, especially the establishment of a diverse middle class, that will make this restructuring particularly painful. At the same time, the talent upon which the effort depends is embodied in these classes and the new institutional arrangements that they will devise. A more peaceful regional environment may create an atmosphere in which bolder political experiments and more far-reaching economic reforms will be possible.

REFERENCES

The following abbreviations are used in the references: *MEJ, Middle East Journal,* and *IJMES, International Journal of Middle East Studies.*

'Abdalla, Ahmed (1985), *The Student Movement and National Politics in Egypt,* London, Zed Books.

Abdel-Fadil, Mahmoud (1980), *The Political Economy of Nasserism,* Cambridge, Cambridge University Press.

——— (1983), "Informal Sector Employment in Egypt," in R. Lobbon, ed., *Urban Research Strategies for Egypt,* Cairo Papers in Social Science, American University in Cairo, 6, 2 (June), 16–40.

Abdel-Jaber, Tayseer (1993), "Inter-Arab Labor Movements: Problems and Prospects," in Said El-Naggar, ed., *Economic Development of the Arab Countries: Selected Issues,* Washington, D.C., International Monetary Fund, 145–162.

Abdel-Khaleq, Gouda, and Tignor, Robert, eds. (1982), *The Political Economy of Income Distribution in Egypt,* New York, Holmes and Meier.

Abdel-Malek, Anouar (1968), *Egypt: Military Society,* New York, Vintage Books.

Abun-Nasr, Jamil M. (1971), *A History of the Magrib,* Cambridge, Cambridge University Press.

Adams, Richard H., Jr. (1986), *Development and Social Change in Rural Egypt,* Syracuse, N.Y., Syracuse University Press.

——— (1991), *The Effects of International Remittances on Poverty, Inequality, and Development in Rural Egypt,* Washington, D.C., International Food Policy Research Institute Research Report 86.

Addi, Lahouari (1995), *L'Algérie et la démocratie,* Paris, Editions de la Découverte.

Adelman, Irma (1984), "Beyond Export-Led Growth," *World Development* 12, 9 (September), 937–950.

Africa Watch (1990), *Denying the "Honor of Living": Sudan, a Human Rights Disaster,* New York.

Ahmad, Feroz (1981), "The Political Economy of Kemalism," in Kazancigil and Özbudun (1981).

Ahmad, Sadiq (1984), *Public Finance in Egypt, Its Structure and Trends,* World Bank Staff Working Papers no. 639.

Alderman, Harold (1993), "Food Preferences and Nutrition," in G. M. Craig, ed., *The Agriculture of Egypt,* Oxford, Oxford University Press, 114–127.

Alderman, Harold, and von Braun, J. (1984), *The Effects of the Egyptian Food Ration and Sub-sidy System on Income Distribution and Consumption,* Washington, D.C., IFPRI Research Report no. 45.

Algar, Hamid (1985), *Islam and Revolution: Imam Khomeini, Writings and Declarations,* London, KPI.

Amin, Galal (1980), *The Modernization of Poverty: A Study of the Political Economy of Growth in Nine Arab Countries, 1945–70,* Leiden, E. J. Brill.

——— (1995), *Egypt's Economic Predicament,* New York and Leiden, E. J. Brill.

Amin, Galal, and Taylor-Awny, Elizabeth (1985), *International Migration of Egyptian Labour: A Review of the State of the Art,* Ottawa, International Development Research Center (IDRC).

Amin, Samir (1982), *The Arab Economy Today,* London, Zed Press.

Amuzegar, Jahangir (1983), *Oil Exporters' Economic Development in an Interdependent World,* IMF Occasional Paper no. 18.

——— (1993), *Iran's Economy Under the Islamic Republic,* London and New York, I. B. Tauris.

Anderson, Lisa (1986), *The State and Social Transformation in Tunisia and Libya, 1930–1980,* Princeton, Princeton University Press.

Anderson, Perry (1980), *Lineages of the Absolutist State,* London, Verso Editions.

Annuaire statistique du Maroc (1984), Rabat, Kingdom of Morocco.

al-Ansari, Hamied (1986), *Egypt: The Stalled Society,* Albany, N.Y., State University of New York Press.

Arian, Asher (1985), *Politics in Israel: The Second Generation,* Chatham, N.J., Chatham House.

Assaad, Ragui (1994), "Kinship Ties, Social Networks, and Segmented Labor Markets: Evidence from the Construction Sector in Egypt," MS, University of Minnesota, November.

Ashraf, A., and Banuazizi, A. (1985), "The State, Classes, and Modes of Mobilization in the Iranian Revolution," *State, Culture, and Society* 1, 3, 3–40.

Atlantic Richfield (1994), "The Middle East: The New Economic Reality, Oil," talk by Anthony J. Finizza, Chief Economist, at the 1994 Southwest Asia Symposium of CENT-COM [U.S. Central Command], Tampa, Fla., May 18.

Axelrod, Robert (1984), *The Evolution of Cooperation,* New York, Basic Books.

Ayres, Ron (1983), "Arms Production as a Form of Import-Substituting Industrialization: The Turkish Case," *World Development* 11, 9, 813–823.

Ayubi, Nazih (1985), "Arab Bureaucracies: Expanding Size, Changing Roles," MS, Politics Department, University of Exeter.

——— (1989), *The Centralized State in Egypt* (in Arabic), Beirut, Center for Arab Unity Studies.

——— (1991a), *Political Islam: Religion and Politics in the Arab World,* London and New York, Routledge.

——— (1991b), *The State and Public Policies in Egypt Since Sadat,* Reading, UK, Ithaca Press.

Azzam, Henry (1994), "Development of Capital Markets in the Middle East," paper presented at the conference "The New Middle East: From Istanbul to Kabul . . . from Beirut to Cairo," The Brookings Institution and the U.S.-Arab Chamber of Commerce, October 19–21.

Baduel, Pierre-Robert (1983), "Le VIe plan tunisien: 1982–86," *Grand Maghreb,* March 21, 54–57.

Baer, Gabriel (1962), *A History of Landownership in Modern Egypt, 1800–1950,* London, Oxford University Press.

Bakhash, Shaul (1984), *The Reign of the Ayatollahs,* New York, Basic Books.

Barkey, Henri, ed. (1992), *The Politics of Economic Reform in the Middle East,* New York, St. Martin's Press.

Barnett, Michael (1992), *Confronting the Costs of War: Military Power, State, and Society in Egypt and Israel,* Princeton, Princeton University Press.

Batatu, Hanna (1978), *The Old Social Classes and the Revolutionary Movements of Iraq,* Princeton, Princeton University Press.

——— (1979), "Class Analysis and Iraqi Society," *Peuples Mediterranéens,* no. 8 (July-September), 101–116.

Bates, Robert (1981), *Markets and States in Tropical Africa,* Berkeley, University of California Press.

——— (1990), "Macropolitical Economy in the Field of Development," in James E. Alt and Kenneth A. Shepsle, eds., *Perspectives in Positive Political Economy,* Cambridge, Cambridge University Press.

Beblawi, Hazem (1984), *The Arab Gulf Economy in a Turbulent Age,* London, Croom Helm.

Ben-Dor, Gabriel (1983), *State and Conflict in the Middle East,* New York, Praeger.

Benissad, M. E. (1982), *Economie du développement de l'Algérie,* Paris, Economica.

Bennoune, Mahfoud (1988), *The Making of Contemporary Algeria, 1830–1987,* Cambridge, Cambridge University Press.

Ben-Porath, Yoram (1972), "Fertility in Israel, an Economist's Interpretation: Differentials and Trends, 1950–1970," in Cooper and Alexander (1972), 502–541.

Berar-Awad, Azita (1984), *Employment Planning in the Sudan: An Overview of Selected Issues,* Geneva, ILO.

Berger, Morroe (1964), *The Arab World Today,* New York, Doubleday.

Bianchi, Robert (1984), *Interest Groups and Political Development in Turkey,* Princeton, Princeton University Press.

——— (1986), "The Corporatization of the Egyptian Labor Movement," *MEJ* 4, 3 (Summer), 429–444.

Bienen, Henry S., and Gersovitz, M. (1985), "Economic Stabilization, Conditionality, and Political Stability," *International Organization* 39, 4 (Autumn), 729–754.

Bill, James A., and Springborg, Robert (1994), *Politics in the Middle East,* 4th ed. New York: Harper Collins.

Binder, Leonard (1957), "Prolegomena to the Comparative Study of Middle East Governments," *American Political Science Review* 51, 3, 651–668.

Binswanger, Hans (1989), "The Policy Response of Agriculture," *Proceedings of the World Bank Annual Conference on Development Economics,* 231–258.

Birks, J. S., and Sinclair, C. A. (1980), *International Migration and Development in the Arab Region,* Geneva, ILO.

Blair, John M. (1976), *The Control of Oil,* New York, Vintage Books.

Blake, Gerald, Dewdney, John, and Mitchell, Jonathan (1987), *The Cambridge Atlas of the Middle East and North Africa,* Cambridge, Cambridge University Press.

Bonnenfant, Paul (1982), *La péninsule arabique d'aujourd'hui,* vol. 1, Paris, Editions du CNRS.

Boratav, Korkut (1981), "Kemalist Economic Policies and Etatism," in Kazancigil and Özbudun (1981).

Braverman, Avishay (1989), "Comment," *Proceedings of the World Bank Annual Conference on Development Economics*, 259–262.

Brown, L. C., and Itzkowitz, N., eds. (1977), *Psychological Dimensions of Near Eastern Studies*, Princeton, Darwin Press.

Bujra, A. S. (1971), *The Politics of Stratification: A Study of Political Change in a South Arabian Town*, Oxford, Clarendon Press.

Bulatao, Rodolfo A., and Richardson, Gail (1994), *Fertility and Family Planning in Iran*, Middle East and North Africa Discussion Paper Series no. 13, Washington, D.C., World Bank, November.

Burgat, François (1993), *The Islamic Movement in North Africa*, Austin, University of Texas Press.

Caldwell, John C. (1986), "Routes to Low Mortality in Poor Countries," *Population and Development Review* 12, 2 (June), 171–220.

CAPMAS (Central Agency for Public Mobilization and Statistics) (1989), *Report of the Sample Census of 1986* (in Arabic), Cairo, Government of Egypt.

Celasun, Merih (1983), *Sources of Industrial Growth and Structural Change: The Case of Turkey*, Washington, D.C., World Bank Staff Working Papers no. 641.

Central Bank, Republic of Turkey (1984), *Annual Report, 1983*, Ankara.

Charmes, Jacques (1986), *Emploi et revenues dans le secteur non-structuré des pays du Maghreb et du Machrek*, New York, Social Science Research Council.

Chatelus, Michel (1982), "De la rente pétrolière au développement économique: Perspectives et contradictions de l'évolution économique dans la péninsule," in Bonnenfant (1982), 75–154.

———— (1984), "Attitudes Toward Public Sector Management and Reassertion of the Private Sector in the Arab World," paper presented at the Middle East Studies Association annual meeting, San Francisco, Calif., November 28–December 1.

Chaudhry, Kiren (1995), *The Price of Wealth: International Capital Flows and the Political Economy of Late Development*, Ithaca, Cornell University Press (forthcoming).

Choucri, Nazli (1986), "The Hidden Economy: A New View of Remittances in the Arab World," *World Development* 14, 6, 697–712.

CIA (Central Intelligence Agency) 1993, *Atlas of the Middle East*, Washington, D.C., Government Printing Office.

Clément, J. F. (1986), "Les révoltes urbaines de janvier 1984 au Maroc," *Bulletin du Réseau Villes Monde Arabe*, no. 5 (November), 3–46.

Cleaver, Kevin M. (1982), *The Agricultural Development Experience of Algeria, Morocco, and Tunisia*, World Bank Staff Working Papers no. 552.

Cohen, John M., et al. (1981), "Development from Below: Local Development Associations in the Yemen Arab Republic," *World Development* 9, 11/12, 1039–1061.

Colclough, Christopher (1982), "The Impact of Primary Schooling on Economic Development: A Review of the Evidence," *World Development* 10, 2/3, 1018–1035.

Collier, David, ed. (1979), *The New Authoritarianism in Latin America*, Princeton, Princeton University Press.

Commander, Simon, and Burgess, Simon (1988), *Labor Markets in N. Africa and the Near East: A Survey of Developments Since 1970*, Aleppo, Syria, International Center for Agricultural Research in Dry Areas (ICARDA).

Cooper, C., and Alexander, S., eds. (1972), *The Economic Development and Population Growth in the Middle East*, New York, American Elsevier.

Cremer, Jacques, and Salehi-Isfahani, Djavad (1991), *Models of the Oil Market,* Chur and London, Harwood Academic Publishers.

Crystal, Jill (1990), *Oil and Politics in the Gulf: Rulers and Merchants in Kuwait and Qatar,* New York, Cambridge University Press.

Danielson, Albert L. (1982), *The Evolution of OPEC,* New York, Harcourt Brace Jovanovich.

Danielson, Michael, and Keleş, Ruşen (1980), "Urbanization and Income Distribution in Turkey," in Özbudun and Ulusan (1980), 269–310.

——— (1985), *The Politics of Rapid Urbanization: Government and Growth in Modern Turkey,* New York, Holmes and Meier.

Dann, Uriel (1969), *Iraq Under Qassem: A Political History, 1958–1963,* Jerusalem, Israel Universities Press.

Danziger, Sheldon H., and Weinberg, Daniel H. (1994), "The Historical Record: Trends in Family Income, Inequality, and Poverty," in Sheldon H. Danziger, Gary D. Sandefur, and Daniel H. Weinberg, eds., *Confronting Poverty: Prescriptions for Change,* Cambridge, Harvard University Press, 18–50.

Davis, Eric (1983), *Challenging Colonialism: Bank Misr and Egyptian Industrialization, 1920–1941,* Princeton, Princeton University Press.

Deegan, Heather (1994), *The Middle East and Problems of Democracy,* Boulder, Colo.: Lynne Rienner.

Deger, Saadet (1992), "Military Expenditure and Economic Development: Issues and Debates," in Geoffrey Lamb and Valeriana Kallab, eds., *Military Expenditure and Economic Development,* Washington, D.C., World Bank, 35–52.

Denoeux, Guilain (1993), *Urban Unrest in the Middle East: A Comparative Study of Informal Networks in Egypt, Iran, and Lebanon,* Albany: State University of New York Press.

DERSA (1981), *L'Algérie en débat,* Paris, Maspero.

Derviş, Kemal, and Robinson, Sherman (1980), "The Structure of Income Inequality in Turkey, 1950–1973," in Özbudun and Ulusan (1980), 83–122.

Destanne de Bernis, G. (1971), "Industries industrialisantes et options algériennes," *Tiers Monde,* no. 47, 545–563.

Dethier, Jean-Jacques (1989), *Trade, Exchange Rate, and Agricultural Pricing Policies in Egypt,* Washington, D.C., World Bank.

——— (1991), "Egypt," in Anne O. Krueger, Maurice Schiff, and Alberto Valdes (1991), *The Political Economy of Agricultural Pricing Policy,* vol. 3, *Africa and the Mediterranean,* Baltimore, Johns Hopkins University Press for the World Bank, 15-78.

el-Dib, M.A.M., Ismail, S. M., and Gad, Osman (1984), "Economic Motivations and Impacts of External Migration of Agricultural Workers in an Egyptian Village" (in Arabic), *Population Studies* 11, 68, 27–46.

Diwan, Ishac, and Squire, Lyn (1993), *Economic Development and Cooperation in the Middle East and North Africa,* World Bank, Middle East and North Africa Discussion Paper Series no. 9, December.

Drysdale, Alasdair (1982), "The Asad Regime and Its Troubles," *MERIP Reports,* no. 110 (November-December), 3–11.

Drysdale, Alasdair, and Blake, Gerald (1985), *The Middle East: A Political Geography,* London and New York, Oxford University Press.

Duchac, René, ed. (1973), *La formation des elites politiques maghrébines,* Paris, Librairie Générale de Droit et de Jurisprudence.

Economic and Social Commission for Western Asia (1986), *Study on Impacts of Returning Migration in Selected Countries of the ECWA Region* (in Arabic) DPDI/86/14, United Nations, March.

Ehrlich, Paul (1968), *The Population Bomb,* New York, Ballantine.

Entelis, John P. (1980), *Comparative Politics of North Africa,* Syracuse, N.Y., Syracuse University Press.

Esman, Milton, and Rabinovich, Itamar, eds. (1988), *Ethnicity, Pluralism, and the State in the Middle East,* Ithaca, Cornell University Press.

FAO (Food and Agriculture Organization) (1983), "Agricultural Price Policies in the Near East: Lessons and Experience," 16th FAO Regional Conference for the Near East, Aden, PDRY, March 11–15.

———— (1986), *World-wide Estimates and Projections of the Agricultural and Non-Agricultural Population Segments, 1950–2025,* Statistical Division, Economic and Social Policy Department, Rome, December. *FAO Production Yearbook* (various years), Rome, FAO.

Falkenmark, Malin (1989), *Natural Resource Limits to Population Growth: The Water Perspective,* Gland, Switzerland, International Union for the Conservation of Nature.

Fargues, Philippe (1994), "Demographic Explosion or Social Upheaval?" in Salamé (1994), 156–179.

Fathaly, Omar, and Palmer, Monte (1980), *Political Development and Social Change in Libya,* Lexington, Mass., Lexington Books.

Fergany, Nader (1988), "Some Aspects of Return Migration in Egypt," MS, April.

———— (1991), "A Characterization of the Employment Problem in Egypt," in Handoussa and Porter (1991), 25–56.

Fitzgerald, E.V.K. (1977), "On State Accumulation in Latin America," in E.V.K. Fitzgerald et al., eds., *The State and Economic Development in Latin America,* Cambridge, Cambridge University Press.

Floyd, Robert H. (1984), "Some Topical Issues Concerning Public Enterprises," in Floyd, Gray, and Short (1984), 1–35.

Floyd, Robert, Gray, Clive S., and Short, R. P. (1984), *Public Enterprise in Mixed Economies: Some Macroeconomic Aspects,* Washington, D.C., IMF.

Fox, Robert (1995), *Cooperation and Security in the Western Mediterranean*, Ditchley Conference Report 94/11, Oxfordshire, England, Ditchley Foundation.

Fried, Edward R., and Trezise, Philip H. (1993), *Oil Security: Retrospect and Prospect,* Washington, D.C., Brookings Institution.

Garnham, David, and Tessler, Mark eds. (1995), *Democracy, War, and Peace in the Middle East,* Bloomington, Indiana University Press.

Gause, Gregory (1994), *Oil Monarchies: Domestic and Security Challenges in the Arab Gulf States,* New York, Council on Foreign Relations.

Gellner, E., and Micaud, C., eds. (1972), *Arabs and Berbers,* London, Duckworth.

el-Ghonemy, M. Riad (1984), *Economic Growth, Income Distribution, and Rural Poverty in the Near East,* Rome, FAO.

Gibbons, Diana C. (1986), *The Economic Value of Water*, Washington, D.C., Resources for the Future.

Gilbar, Gad (1992), "Population Growth and Family Planning in Egypt, 1985–92," *Middle East Contemporary Survey* 16, 335–348.

Gotheil, Fred (1981), "Iraqi and Syrian Socialism: An Economic Appraisal," *World Development* 9, 9/10 (September/October), 825–838.

Gutmann, E., and Landau, J. (1985), "The Political Elite and National Leadership in Israel," in G. Lenczowski, ed., *Political Elites in the Middle East,* Washington, D.C., American Enterprise Institute (AEI), 163–200.

Hale, William (1981), *The Political and Economic Development of Modern Turkey,* London, Croom Helm.

Halpern, Manfred (1963), *The Politics of Social Change in the Middle East and North Africa,* Princeton, Princeton University Press.

Handoussa, Heba (1989), "The Burden of Public Sector Employment and Remuneration: A Case Study of Egypt," MS, ILO, Geneva.

Handoussa, Heba, and Porter, Gillian, eds. (1991), *Employment and Structural Adjustment: Egypt in the 1990s,* Cairo: American University in Cairo Press for the ILO.

Al-Hanidi, Abdel-Latif Abdel-Muhid (1988), *Egyptians Resident Abroad (Size and Characteristics)* (in Arabic), Cairo, CAPMAS.

Hannoyer, Jean, and Seurat, Michel (1979), *Etat et secteur public industriel en Syrie,* Lyon, Centre des etudes et des recherches sur le Moyen Orient Contemporain (CERMOC), Presses Universitaires de Lyon.

Hansen, Bent (1985), *The Egyptian Labor Market: An Overview,* World Bank Discussion Paper, Report no. DRD/60.

——— (1991), "A Macro-Economic Framework for Economic Planning in Egypt," in Handoussa and Porter (1991).

——— (1992), *The Political Economy of Poverty, Equity, and Growth: Egypt and Turkey,* New York, Oxford University Press.

Hansen, Bent, and Radwan, Samir (1982), *Employment Opportunities and Equity in Egypt,* Geneva, ILO.

Harberger, A. C. (1971), "On Measuring the Social Opportunity Cost of Labor," *International Labor Review,* June.

——— (1984), "Basic Needs Versus Distributional Weights in Social Cost-Benefit Analysis," *Economic Development and Cultural Change,* 32, 4 (April), 455–477.

Harik, Ilya (1974), *The Political Mobilization of Peasants: A Study of an Egyptian Community,* Bloomington, Indiana University Press.

Harik, Ilya, and Sullivan, Denis, eds. (1992), *Privatization and Liberalization in the Middle East,* Bloomington, Indiana University Press.

Hazell, Peter et al. (1994), "Effects of Deregulating the Agricultural Production Sector on Food Availability and Resource Use in Egypt," Washington, D.C., International Food Policy Research Institute, September.

Heal, Geoffrey, and Chichilnisky, Graciela (1991), *Oil and the International Economy,* Oxford, Clarendon Press.

Helms, Christina (1984), *Iraq: Eastern Flank of the Arab World,* Washington, D.C., Brookings Institution.

Hemphill, Paul (1979), "The Formation of the Iraqi Army: 1921–23," in Kelidar (1979), 88–110.

Hermassi, Elbaki (1972), *Leadership and National Development in North Africa,* Berkeley, University of California Press.

Hershlag, Z. Y. (1968), *Turkey: The Challenge of Growth,* Leiden, E. J. Brill.

Heydemann, Steven (1992), "The Political Logic of Economic Rationality: Selective Stabilization in Syria," in Henri Barkey, ed., *The Politics of Economic Reform in the Middle East,* New York, St. Martin's Press, 11–39.

Heyneman, Stephen P. (1993), "Human Development in the Middle East and North Africa," in Said el-Naggar, ed., *Economic Development of the Arab Countries: Selected Issues,* Washington, D.C., IMF, 204–226.

Hinnebusch, Raymond (1979), "Party and Peasant in Syria," *Cairo Papers in Social Science* 3, 1 (November).

——— (1985), *Egyptian Politics Under Sadat,* Cambridge, Cambridge University Press.

Hodgson, Marshall G.S. (1974), *The Venture of Islam,* 3 vols., Chicago, University of Chicago Press.

Hooglund, Eric (1982), *Land and Revolution in Iran: 1960–1980,* Austin, University of Texas Press.

Hopkins, Nicholas (1983), "Social Aspects of Mechanization," in Richards and Martin (1983), 181–198.

Horton, Brendan (1990), *Morocco: Analysis and Reform of Economic Policy,* Washington, D.C., World Bank.

Hudson, Michael (1968), *The Precarious Republic: Modernization in Lebanon,* New York, Random House.

——— (1977), *Arab Politics,* New Haven, Yale University Press.

——— (1994), "Arab Regimes and Democratization: Responses to the Challenge of Political Islam," *International Spectator,* 29, 4, 3–28.

Huntington, Samuel P. (1968), *Political Order in Changing Societies,* New Haven, Yale University Press.

Hussein, 'Adil (1977), *The Bureaucratic Bourgeoisie: Between the Marxist Understanding and Marxising Slogans* (in Arabic), Beirut.

——— (1982), *The Egyptian Economy from Independence to Dependency: 1974–1979* (in Arabic), 2 vols., Cairo, Dar al-Mustaqbal al-'Arabi.

Hussein, Mahmoud (1971), *La lutte de classes en Egypte, 1945–70,* Paris, Maspero.

Ibrahim, Ibrahim, ed. (1983), *Arab Resources,* London, Croom Helm, for the Center for Contemporary Arab Studies.

Ibrahim, Saad Eddin (1980), "Anatomy of Egypt's Militant Islamic Groups: Methodological Note and Preliminary Findings," *IJMES* 12, 4, 423–453.

——— (1994), "Sociological Profile of Muslim Militants in Egypt," paper presented at Workshop on Egypt's Domestic Stability, National Defense University, United States Department of Defense, Ft. McNair, Washington, D.C., April 28–29.

IBRD (International Bank for Reconstruction and Development) (1983), *Arab Republic of Egypt: Issues of Trade Strategy and Investment Planning,* Washington, D.C.

IMF (International Monetary Fund) (various years), *International Financial Statistics,* Washington, D.C.

Islami, A. Reza, and Kavoussi, R. M. (1984), *The Political Economy of Saudi Arabia,* Near Eastern Studies no. 1, Seattle, University of Washington Press.

Islamoğlu, Huri Inan, and Keyder, Çağlar (1977), "Agenda for Ottoman History," *Review* 1, Summer, 31–55.

Issawi, Charles (1956), "Economic and Social Foundations of Democracy in the Middle East," *International Affairs,* January, 27–42.

——— (1969), "Economic Change and Urbanization in the Middle East," in Ira M. Lapidus, ed., *Middle Eastern Cities,* Berkeley, University of California Press, 102–121.

——— (1978), "The Iranian Economy 1925–1975: Fifty Years of Economic Development," in G. Lenczowski, ed., *Iran Under the Pahlevis,* Stanford, Calif., Hoover Institution, 129–166.

———— (1982), *An Economic History of the Middle East and North Africa,* New York, Columbia University Press.

Jacobson, Jodi (1994), *Family, Gender, and Population Policy: Views from the Middle East,* New York, Population Council.

Jamal, Abbashar (1991), "Funding Fundamentalism: The Political Economy of an Islamist State," *Middle East Report,* September-October, 15–17.

Jazairy, Idriss, Alamgir, Moniuddin, and Panuccio, Theresa (1992), *The State of World Rural Poverty: An Inquiry into Its Causes and Consequences,* New York, New York University Press for the International Fund for Agricultural Development.

Johnson, D. Gale (1950), "The Nature of the Supply Function for Agricultural Products," *Journal of Farm Economics,* 42, 2, 539–564.

Johnston, Bruce, and Kilby, Peter (1975), *Agriculture and Structural Transformation: Economic Strategies in Late-Developing Countries,* New York, Oxford University Press.

Kapil, Arun (1990), "L'évolution du régime autoritaire en Algérie: Le 5 Octobre et les réformes politiques de 1988–89," *Annuaire de l'Afrique du Nord,* 29, 499–534.

Karaspan, Omer (1987), "Turkey's Armaments Industries," *MERIP Reports,* January-February, 27–31.

Karpat, Kemal (1959), *Turkey's Politics,* Princeton, Princeton University Press.

Karshenas, Massoud, and Pesaran, M. Hashem (1995), "Economic Reform and Reconstruction of the Iranian Economy," *MEJ,* 49, 1 (Winter), 89–111.

Kasfir, Nelson (1979), "Explaining Ethnic Political Participation," *World Politics* 31, 3, 365–388.

Katanani, Ahmad K. (1981), "Economic Alternatives to Migration," paper presented to the Conference on International Migration in the Arab World, United Nations Economic Commission for West Africa (UNECWA), Nicosia, Cyprus, May.

Katouzian, Homa (1981), *The Political Economy of Modern Iran: Despotism and Pseudo-Modernism, 1926–79,* New York, New York University Press.

Kavalsky, Basil (1980), "Poverty and Human Development in the Middle East and North Africa," in *Poverty and the Development of Human Resources: Regional Perspectives,* World Bank Staff Working Papers no. 406.

Kazancigil, Ali, and Özbudun, Ergun, eds. (1981), *Atatürk: Founder of a Modern State,* Hamden, Conn., Archon Books.

Kazemi, Farhad (1980a), *Poverty and Revolution in Iran: The Migrant Poor, Urban Marginality, and Politics,* New York, New York University Press.

———— (1980b), "Urban Migrants and the Revolution," *Iranian Studies* 13, 1–4, 257–278.

Kazemi, F., and Abrahamian, E. (1978), "The Non-Revolutionary Peasantry of Modern Iran," *Iranian Studies* 11, 259–308.

Kazemi, Farhad, and Norton, Augustus Richard, eds. (1995), *Civil Society in the Middle East,* Leiden and New York, Brill.

Keen, David (1994), *The Benefits of Famine: A Political Economy of Famine and Relief in Southwestern Sudan, 1983–1989,* Princeton, Princeton University Press.

Kelidar, Abbas, ed. (1979), *The Integration of Modern Iraq,* London, Croom Helm.

Kelley, C., and Williamson, Jeffrey (1984), "Population Growth, Industrial Revolutions, and the Urban Transistion," *Population and Development Review* 10, 3 (September).

Kepel, Gilles (1986), *Muslim Extremism in Egypt: The Prophet and the Pharaoh,* Berkeley, University of California Press.

Kerr, Malcolm (1963), "Arab Radical Notions of Democracy," St. Anthony's Papers no. 16.

———— (1965), "Egypt," in James Coleman, ed., *Education and Political Development*, Princeton, Princeton University Press, 169–194.

Kerr, Malcolm, and el-Yassin, Sayed, eds. (1982), *Rich and Poor States in the Middle East*, Boulder, Colo., Westview Press/American University in Cairo.

Keyder, Çağlar (1979), "The Political Economy of Turkish Democracy," *New Left Review*, no. 115 (May-June), 3–45.

———— (1987), *State and Class in Turkey: A Study in Capitalist Development*, London and New York, Verso.

al-Khafaji, 'Issam (1983), *The State and the Evolution of Capitalism in Iraq: 1968–1978* (in Arabic), Cairo, Dar al-Mustaqbal al-Arabi.

al-Khalil, Samir (1989), *Republic of Fear*, New York, Pantheon Books.

Khoury, Philip (1983a), "Islamic Revival and the Crisis of the Secular State in the Arab World: An Historical Appraisal," in Ibrahim (1983), 213–236.

———— (1983b), *Urban Notables and Arab Nationalism: The Politics of Damascus 1860–1920*, New York, Columbia University Press.

Khoury, Philip, and Kostiner, Joseph eds. (1990), *Tribes and State Formation in the Middle East*, Berkeley, University of California Press.

Kimmerling, Baruch (1983), *Zionism and Economy*, Cambridge, Schenkman.

Korayem, Karima (1987), *The Impact of Economic Adjustment Policies on the Vulnerable Families and Children in Egypt*, Cairo, Third World Forum, Middle East Office.

———— (1994), *Poverty and Income Distribution in Egypt*, Cairo, Third World Forum Middle East Office.

Kravis, Irving, Heston, Alan, and Summers, Robert (1978), *International Comparisons of Real Product and Purchasing Power*, Baltimore, Johns Hopkins University Press.

Krimly, Rayed (1993), "The Political Economy of Rentier States: A Case Study of Saudi Arabia in the Oil Era, 1950–1990," Ph.D. diss., Department of Political Science, George Washington University.

Kubursi, Afif (1984), *Oil, Industrialization, and Development in the Arab Gulf States*, London, Croom Helm.

Kuran, Timur (1980), "Internal Migration: The Unorganized Urban Sector and Income Distribution in Turkey, 1963–73," in Özbudun and Ulusan (1980), 349–378.

———— (1992a), "The Economic System in Contemporary Islamic Thought," in K. S. Jomo, ed., *Islamic Economic Alternatives*, Kuala Lumpur, Iqraq.

———— (1992b), "Economic Justice in Contemporary Islamic Thought," in K. S. Jomo, ed., *Islamic Economic Alternatives*, Kuala Lumpur: Iqraq.

Lapham, R. J. (1983), "Background Notes and Illustrative Tables on Populations in the Middle East," paper prepared for the Conference on Population and Political Stability in the Near East and South Asia Region, Washington, D.C., March.

Lawless, Richard (1984), "Algeria: The Contradictions of Rapid Industrialization," in Lawless and Findlay (1984), 153–190.

Lawless, R., and Findlay, A., eds. (1984), *North Africa: Contemporary Politics and Economic Development*, London, Croom Helm.

Lazreg, Marnia (1976), *The Emergence of Classes in Algeria*, Boulder, Colo., Westview Press.

Leca, Jean (1975), "Algerian Socialism: Nationalism, Industrialization, and State-building," in Helen Desfosses and Jacques Levesque, eds., *Socialism in the Third World*, New York, Praeger.

Lerner, Daniel (1959), *The Passing of Traditional Society*, Glencoe, Ill., Free Press.

Lesch, Ann Mosely (1985), *Egyptian Labor Migration: Economic Trends and Government Policies,* University Field Services Institute Reports no. 38.

Leveau, Rémy (1985), *Le Fellah marocain: Défenseur du trone,* Paris, Presses de la FNSP.

———— (1993), *Le sabre et le turban: L'avenir du Maghrib,* Paris, Editions François Bourin.

Lewis, Bernard (1961), *The Emergence of Modern Turkey,* Oxford, Oxford University Press.

Lewis, W. Arthur (1954), "Economic Development with Unlimited Supplies of Labour," *Manchester School of Economic and Social Studies* 22, 139–191.

Lipton, Michael (1977), *Why Poor People Stay Poor: Urban Bias in World Development,* Cambridge, Harvard University Press.

Little, I.M.D., Scitovsky, Tibor, and Scott, Maurice (1970), *Industry and Trade in Some Developing Countries,* London, Oxford University Press.

Longuenesse, Elisabeth (1979), "The Class Nature of the State in Syria," *MERIP Reports* 9, 4 (May), 3–11.

———— (1985), "Syrie, secteur public industriel," *Maghreb-Machrek,* no. 109 (July-September), 5–24.

McClelland, David (1963), "National Character and Economic Growth in Turkey and Iran," in Lucian Pye, ed., *Communications and Political Development,* Princeton, Princeton University Press, 152–181.

el-Malki, Habib (1980), "Capitalisme d'état, Développement de la bourgeoisie et problématique de la transition—le cas du Maroc," *Revue Juridique, Politique et Économique du Maroc,* no. 8, 207–228.

———— (1982), *L'économie marocaine: Bilan d'une décennie, 1970–1980,* Paris, Editions du CNRS.

Mamdani, Mahmood (1972), *The Myth of Population Control: Family, Caste, and Class in an Indian Village,* New York, Monthly Review Press.

Margulies, Ronnie, and Yildizoğlu, Ergin (1984), "Trade Unions and Turkey's Working Class," *MERIP Reports* (February), 15–30, 31.

Meillassoux, Claude (1981), *Maidens, Meal, and Money,* Cambridge, Cambridge University Press.

Mellor, John (1976), *The New Economics of Growth: A Strategy for India and the Developing World,* Ithaca, Cornell University Press.

el-Midaoui, Ahmed (1981), *Les entreprises publiques au Maroc et leur participation au développement,* Casablanca, Editions Afrique-Orient.

Migdal, Joel (1987), "Strong States, Weak States: Power and Accommodation," in M. Weiner and S. P. Huntington, eds., *Understanding Political Development,* Boston, Little, Brown, 391–436.

Minority Rights Group (1983), *Lebanon: A Conflict of Minorities,* London.

Moghadem, Fatemah Etemad (1982), "Farm Size, Management, and Productivity: A Study of Four Iranian Villages," *Oxford Bulletin of Economics and Statistics* 44, 4 (November), 357–379.

Moghadem, Valentine (1993), *Modernizing Women: Gender and Social Change in the Middle East,* Boulder, Colo., Lynne Rienner.

Mohie el-Din, Amr (1982), *Income Distribution and Basic Needs in Urban Egypt,* Cairo Papers in Social Science 5, Monograph 3, November.

Moore, Barrington (1967), *Social Origins of Dictatorship and Democracy,* London, Allen Lane/Penguin Press.

Moore, C. H. (1965), *Tunisia Since Independence,* Berkeley, University of California Press.

——— (1970), *Politics in North Africa,* Boston, Little, Brown.

——— (1980), *Images of Development: Egyptian Engineers in Search of Industry,* Cambridge, MIT Press.

Morrison, Christian (1991), *Adjustment and Equity in Morocco,* Paris, OECD Development Centre.

Morocco, Kingdom of, Ministry of Economic and Social Affairs (1992), *Niveaux de vie des ménages, 1990/91,* Rabat.

Mosk, Carl (1983), *Patriarchy and Fertility: Japan and Sweden, 1880–1960,* New York, Academic Press.

Myint, Hla (1959), "The 'Classical Theory' of International Trade and the Underdeveloped Countries," *Economic Journal* 68, 2, 317–337.

el-Naggar, Said, and el-Erian, Mohamed (1993), "The Economic Implications of a Comprehensive Peace in the Middle East," in Stanley Fischer et al., eds., *The Economics of Middle East Peace,* Cambridge, MIT Press, 205–226.

Nasr, Salim (1985), "Roots of the Shi'i Movement," *MERIP Reports* (June), 10–16.

Nasr, Seyyed Vali Reza (1994), *The Vanguard of the Islamic Revolution: The Jama'at-i Islami of Pakistan,* Berkeley and Los Angeles, University of California Press.

al-Nasrawi, Abbas (1995), "Iraq's Economic Policies in a Transition Period," *Iraqi Issues,* 2, 3, 1–8.

National Academy of Sciences (1982), *The Estimation of Recent Trends in Fertility and Mortality in Egypt,* Washington, D.C., National Academy Press.

National Research Council (1986), *Population Growth and Economic Development: Policy Questions,* Washington, D.C., National Academy Press.

Nattagh, Nina (1986), *Agricultural and Regional Development in Iran, 1962–1978,* Cambridgeshire, Middle East and North African Studies Press.

Nellis, John (1977), "Socialist Management in Algeria," *Journal of Modern African Studies* 15, 4, 529–544.

——— (1980), "Maladministration: Cause or Result of Underdevelopment? The Algerian Example," *Canadian Journal of African Studies* 13, 3, 407–422.

——— (1983), "A Comparative Assessment of the Development Performances of Algeria and Tunisia," *MEJ* 37, 3, 370–393.

Nelson, Harold D., ed. (1979), *Tunisia: A Country Study,* Washington, D.C., Area Handbook Series, American University Press.

———, ed. (1985), *Algeria: A Country Study,* Washington, D.C., Area Handbook Series, American University Press.

Nelson, Joan (1979), *Access to Power: Politics and the Urban Poor in Developing Nations,* Princeton, Princeton University Press.

——— (1984), "The Political Economy of Stabilization Commitment, Capacity, and Public Response," *World Development* 12, 10, 983–1006.

Niblock, Tim, ed. (1982a), *Iraq: The Contemporary State,* London, Croom Helm.

———, ed. (1982b), *State, Society, and Economy in Saudi Arabia,* London, Croom Helm.

Noman, Omar (1988), *The Political Economy of Pakistan, 1947–85,* London and New York, KPI Press.

Nomani, Farhad, and Rahnema, Ali (1994), *Islamic Economic Systems,* London, Zed Press.

Nouschi, Andre (1970), "North Africa in the Period of Colonization," *Cambridge History of Islam,* vol. 1, *The Further Islamic Lands: Islamic Society and Civilization,* Cambridge, Cambridge University Press, 299–326.

Nyrop, Richard F., ed. (1982), *Egypt: A Country Study,* Washington D.C., Area Handbook Series, American University Press.

O'Brien, Patrick (1966), *The Revolution in Egypt's Economic System,* New York, Oxford University Press.

O'Donnell, Guillermo (1978), "Reflections on the Patterns of Change in the Bureaucratic-Authoritarian State," *Latin American Research Review* 12, 1, 3–38.

Olson, Mancur (1965), *The Logic of Collective Action: Public Goods and the Theory of Groups,* Cambridge, Harvard University Press.

Omran, Abdel R., and Roudi, Farzaneh (1993), *The Middle East Population Puzzle,* Population Bulletin 48, 1.

Öniş, Ziya, and Webb, Steven (1994), "Turkey: Democratization and Adjustment from Above," in Stephan Haggard and Steven B. Webb, *Voting for Reform: Democracy, Political Liberalization, and Economic Adjustment,* Washington, D.C., World Bank.

OPEC (1993), *Annual Statistical Bulletin,* Vienna.

Owen, Roger (1981), *The Middle East in the World Economy, 1800–1914,* London and New York, Methuen.

——— (1985), *Migrant Workers in the Gulf,* Minority Rights Group Report no. 68, September.

——— (1986), "Large Landowners, Agricultural Progress, and the State in Egypt, 1800–1970: An Overview," in Alan Richards, ed., *Food, States, and Peasants: Analyses of the Agrarian Question in the Middle East,* Boulder, Colo., Westview Press, 69–96.

——— (1992), *State, Power, and Politics in the Making of the Modern Middle East,* London and New York, Routledge.

Özbudun, Ergun (1981), "The Nature of the Kemalist Political Regime" in Kazancigil and Özbudun (1981), 79–102.

Özbudun, Ergun, and Ulusan, Aydin (1980), *The Political Economy of Income Distribution in Turkey,* New York, Holmes and Meier.

Özgediz, Selcuk (1980), "Education and Income Distribution in Turkey," in Özbudun and Ulusan (1980), 501–524.

Paulino, Leonardo (1986), *Food in the Third World: Past Trends and Projections to 2000,* IFPRI Research Report no. 52 (June).

Penrose, Edith, and Penrose, E. F. (1978), *Iraq: International Relations and National Development,* Boulder, Colo., Ernest Benn/Westview Press.

Piscatori, James, ed. (1983), *Islam in the Political Process,* Cambridge, Cambridge University Press.

Pissarides, Christopher A. (1993), *Labor Markets in the Middle East and North Africa,* World Bank Middle East and North Africa Discussion Paper Series no. 5 (February).

Przeworski, Adam (1991), *Democracy and the Market: Political and Economic Reforms in Eastern Europe and Latin America,* New York, Cambridge University Press.

Psacharopoulos, George (1980), "Returns to Education: An Updated International Comparison," in *Education and Income,* World Bank Staff Working Papers no. 402, 75–109.

——— (1994), "Returns to Investment in Education: A Global Update," *World Development* 22, 9 (September), 1325–1343.

Putnam, Robert (1993), *Making Democracy Work: Civic Traditions in Modern Italy*, Princeton, Princeton University Press.

Quandt, William B. (1981), *Saudi Arabia in the 1980s: Foreign Policy, Security, and Oil*, Washington, D.C., Brookings Institution.

al-Qudsi, Sulayman, Assaad, Ragui, and Shaban, Radwan (1993), "Labor Markets in the Arab Countries: A Survey," World Bank Initiative to Encourage Economic Research in the Middle East and North Africa, First Annual Conference on Development Economics, Cairo, Egypt (June 4–6).

Radwan, Samir (1977), *Agrarian Reform and Rural Poverty: Egypt, 1952–1975*, Geneva, ILO.

Radwan, S., and Lee, E. (1986), *Agrarian Change in Egypt: An Anatomy of Rural Poverty*, London, Croom Helm.

Radwan, Samir, Jamal, Vali, and Ghose, Ajit (1991), *Tunisia: Rural Labour and Structural Transformation*, London, Routledge.

Raffinot, Marc, and Jacquemot, Pierre (1977), *Le capitalisme d'état algérien*, Paris, Maspero.

Raymond, A., ed. (1980), *La Syrie d'aujourd'hui*, Paris, Editions du CNRS.

Razavi, H., and Vakil, F. (1984), *The Political Environment of Economic Planning in Iran, 1971–1983*, Boulder, Colo., Westview Press.

Reich, B., and Long, D., eds. (1986), *The Government and Politics of the Middle East and North Africa*, Boulder, Colo., Westview Press.

Riad, Hassan (1964), *L'Egypte nassérienne*, Paris, Editions de Minuit.

Richards, Alan (1982), *Egypt's Agricultural Development, 1800–1980: Technical and Social Change*, Boulder, Colo., Westview Press.

——— (1987), *Routes to Low Mortality in Low-Income Countries: Comment*, University of California, Santa Cruz, Applied Economics Working Paper no. 43.

——— (1991), "The Political Economy of Dilatory Reform: Egypt in the 1990s," *World Development* 19, 12 (December), 1721–1730.

——— (1992a), *Higher Education in Egypt*, World Bank Education and Employment Working Papers, WPS 862 (February).

——— (1994), "The Egyptian Farm Labor Market Revisited," *Journal of Development Economics* 43, 239–261.

——— (1996), "Arab Food Security in the 1980s: Stylized Facts and Lessons for the Future," in Michael Hudson, ed., *The Arab World in the New Middle East: Problems of Adaptation, Integration, and Interdependence*, Washington, D.C., Center for Contemporary Arab Studies.

Richards, Alan, and Martin, Philip, eds. (1983), *Migration, Mechanization, and Agricultural Labor Markets in Egypt*, Boulder, Colo., and Cairo, Westview Press/American University at Cairo.

Rivier, François (1980), *Croissance industrielle dans une économie assistée: Le cas Jordanien*, Lyon, CERMOC, Presses Universitaires de Lyon.

Roberts, Hugh (1982), "The Unforeseen Development of the Kabyle Question in Contemporary Algeria," *Government and Opposition* 17, 3, 312–334.

——— (1983), "The Economics of Berberism: The Kabyle Question in Contemporary Algeria," *Government and Opposition* 18, 2, 218–235.

——— (1984), "The Politics of Algerian Socialism," in Lawless and Findlay (1984), 5–49.

——— (1994), "Doctrinaire Economics and Political Opportunism in the Strategy of Algerian Islamism," in John Ruedy, ed., *Islamism and Secularism in North Africa*, New York, St. Martin's Press.

Rodrik, Dani (1994), "The Rush to Free Trade in the Developing World: Why So Late? Why Now? Will It Last?" in Haggard and Webb (1994), 61–88.

Rogers, Peter, and Lyndon, Peter, eds. (1994), *Water in the Arab World: Perspectives and Prognoses,* Cambridge, Harvard University Press.

Roos, Leslie, and Roos, Noralou (1971), *Managers of Modernization: Organization and Elites in Turkey (1950–1969),* Cambridge, Harvard University Press.

Rosegrant, Mark W., and Binswanger, Hans (1994), "Markets in Tradable Water Rights: Potential for Efficiency Gains in Developing Country Water Resource Allocation," *World Development,* 22, 11 (November), 1613–1625.

Rosenfeld, H., and Carmi, S. (1976), "The Privatization of Public Means, the State Made Middle Class, and the Realization of Family Value in Israel," in J. G. Peristiany, ed., *Kinship and Modernization in Mediterranean Society,* Rome, American Universities Field Staff, 131–153.

Roy, Olivier (1994), *The Failure of Political Islam,* Cambridge, Harvard University Press.

Rustow, Dankwart A., and Mugno, John F. (1976), *OPEC: Success and Prospects,* New York, New York University Press.

Sadik, Abdel-Karim, and Barghouti, Shawki (1994), "The Water Problems of the Arab World: Management of Scarce Resources," in Rogers and Lyndon (1994), 1–38.

Sadowski, Yahya (1985), "Cadres, Guns, and Money: The Eighth Regional Congress of the Syrian Ba'ath," *Middle East Report,* no. 134 (July-August), 3–8.

——— (1993), *Scuds or Butter? The Political Economy of Arms Control in the Middle East,* Washington, D.C., Brookings Institution.

Salamé, Ghassan, ed. (1994), *Democracy Without Democrats? The Renewal of Politics in the Muslim World,* London, I. B. Tauris.

Saloman Brothers (1992), *Morocco: An Oasis of Investment Opportunity,* New York.

Schmitter, P. C. (1974), "Still the Century of Corporatism?" *Review of Politics* 36, 85–132.

Schneider, Steven A. (1983), *The Oil Price Revolution,* Baltimore, Johns Hopkins University Press.

Schultz, T. W. (1981), *Investing in People: The Economics of Population Quality,* Berkeley, University of California Press.

Sen, Amartya (1981a), *Poverty and Famines: An Essay on Entitlement and Deprivation,* Oxford, Oxford University Press.

——— (1981b), "Public Action and the Quality of Life in Developing Countries," *Oxford Bulletin of Economics and Statistics* 43, 4 (November), 287–319.

Sethuramen, S. V., ed. (1981), *The Urban Informal Sector in Developing Countries: Employment, Poverty, and Environment,* Geneva, ILO.

Shafik, Nemat (1994a), *Learning from Doers: Lessons on Regional Integration for the Middle East,* Washington, D.C., World Bank.

——— (1994b), "Big Spending, Small Returns: The Paradox of Human Resource Development in the Middle East," MS, World Bank, MENA Region, December.

Sherbiny, Naiem A. (1984), "Expatriate Labor in Arab Oil Producing Countries," *Finance and Development* 21, 4 (December), 34–37.

Shlaes, Alfred (1994), "The End of the German Miracle," *Foreign Affairs* 73, 3 (May-June), 76–93.

Shorter, Frederic C. (1985), "Demographical Measures of Inequality and Development," in Shorter and Zurayk (1985).

Shorter, F. C., and Zurayk, Huda, eds. (1985), *Population Factors in Development Planning in the Middle East,* New York, Population Council.

Signoles, P., and Ben Romdane, M. (1983), "Les formes récentes de l'industrialisation tunisienne, 1979–1980," in GRESMO, *L'industrialisation du Bassin Méditerranéen,* Grenoble, Presses Universitaires de Grenoble, 109–150.

Simon, Julian (1982), *The Ultimate Resource,* Princeton, Princeton University Press.

Sivan, Emmanuel (1985), *Radical Islam: Medieval Theology and Modern Politics,* New Haven, Yale University Press.

Sluglett, Peter, and Sluglett, Marion Farouk (1984), "Modern Morocco: Political Immobilism, Economic Dependence," in Lawless and Findlay (1984), 50–100.

Smith, Tony (1975), "The Political and Economic Ambitions of Algerian Land Reform, 1962–1974," *MEJ* 29, 3 (Summer).

Soffer, Arnon (1986), "Lebanon—Where Demography Is the Core of Politics and Life," *Middle Eastern Studies* 22, 2 (April), 192–205.

Sousa, Alya (1982), "Eradication of Illiteracy in Iraq," in Niblock (1982a).

Springborg, Robert (1981), "Baathism in Practice: Agriculture, Politics, and Political Culture in Syria and Iraq," *Middle Eastern Studies* 17, 2 (April), 191–209.

——— (1987), "The President and the Field Marshal," *MERIP* Reports 17, 4 (July-August), 4–16.

Stark, Oded (1983), "A Note on Labor Migration Functions," *Journal of Development Studies* 19, 4 (July), 539–543.

Stauffer, Thomas R. (with Lennox, Frank H.) (1984), *Accounting for "Wasting Asset": Income Measurement for Oil and Mineral-Exporting Rentier States,* Vienna, OPEC Fund for International Development, November.

Stobaugh, Robert, and Yergin, Daniel (1979), *Energy Future,* New York, Random House.

Stork, Joe (1982), "State Power and Economic Structure: Class Determination and State Formation in Contemporary Iraq," in Niblock (1982a), 27–46.

——— (1987), "Arms Industries of the Middle East," *MERIP Reports* no. 144 (January-February), 12–16.

Swearingen, Will D. (1987), *Moroccan Mirages: Agrarian Dreams and Deceptions, 1912–1986,* Princeton, Princeton University Press.

Tachau, Frank, and Heper, Metin (1983), "The State, Politics, and the Military in Turkey," *Comparative Politics* 16 (October), 17–33.

Tignor, Robert L. (1984), *State, Private Enterprise and Economic Change in Egypt, 1918–1952,* Princeton, Princeton University Press.

Tilly, Charles, ed. (1975), *The Formation of National States in Europe,* Princeton, Princeton University Press.

Timmer, C. Peter, Falcon, Walter P., and Pearson, Scott (1983), *Food Policy Analysis,* Baltimore and London, Johns Hopkins University Press.

Todaro, Michael P. (1969), "A Model of Labor Migration and Urban Unemployment in Less Developed Countries," *American Economic Review* 59, 1, 138–148.

——— (1984), "Urbanization in Developing Nations: Trends, Prospects, and Policies," in Pradip K. Ghosh, ed., *Urban Development in the Third World,* Westport, Conn., Greenwood.

Trimberger, Ellen Kay (1978), *Revolution from Above: Military Bureaucrats and Development in Japan, Turkey, Egypt, and Peru,* New Brunswick, N.J., Transaction Books.

Tuluy, A. Hassan, and Salinger, B. Lynn (1991), "Morocco," in Anne O. Krueger, Maurice Schiff, and Alberto Valdes, eds., *The Political Economy of Agricultural Pricing Policy,* vol. 3,

Africa and the Mediterranean, Baltimore, Johns Hopkins University Press for the World Bank, 122–170.

Tuma, Elias (1978), "Bottlenecks and Constraints in Agrarian Reform in the Near East," background paper for the World Conference on Agrarian Reform and Rural Institutions, FAO, Rome.

——— (1987), *Economic and Political Change in the Middle East,* Palo Alto, Calif., Pacific Books.

Turner, John C. (1969), "Uncontrolled Urban Settlement: Problems and Policies," in Gerald Breese, ed., *The City in Newly Developing Countries,* Englewood Cliffs, N.J., Prentice-Hall, 507–534.

TÜSIAD (Turkish Businessmen and Manufacturers' Association) (1988), *The Turkish Economy, '88,* Istanbul.

Tyner, Wallace (1993), "Agricultural Sector Analysis and Adjustment: Recent Experiences in North Africa and the Baltics," Lecture at USAID, sponsored by Agricultural Policy Analysis Project-II, Washington, D.C., May 19.

UN (United Nations) (1991), *United Nations Demographic Yearbook,* New York.

——— (1992), *World Population Prospects: The 1992 Revision,* New York.

UNDP (United Nations Development Programme) (1994), *Human Development Report, 1994,* New York: Oxford University Press.

UNESCO (various years), *Statistical Yearbook,* Paris,

UNICEF (1986), *The State of the World's Children, 1984,* New York, Oxford University Press.

USAID (U.S. Agency for International Development) (1983), *Tunisia: The Wheat Development Program,* PN-AAL-022, October.

——— (1986), *Morocco Country Development Strategy Statement,* Rabat.

——— (1992), *Country Program Strategy, FY 1992–1996: Population,* MS, Cairo, May.

U.S. Arms Control and Disarmament Agency (1995), *World Military Expenditures and Arms Transfers,* Washington, D.C.

USDA (U.S. Department of Agriculture) (1987), *Middle East and North Africa: Situation and Outlook Report,* Washington, D.C., Economic Research Service.

U.S. Institute of Medicine (1979), "Health in Egypt: Recommendations for U.S. Assistance," prepared for USAID, Washington, D.C., January.

Valdes, Alberton (1989), "Comment on 'The Policy Response of Agriculture' by Binswanger," *Proceedings of the World Bank Annual Conference on Development Economics,* 263–268.

van den Boogaerde, Pierre (1990), *The Composition and Distribution of Financial Assistance from Arab Countries and Arab Regional Institutions,* IMF Middle East Department Working Paper WP/90/67 (July).

van der Kloet, Hendrik (1975), *Inégalités dans les milieux ruraux: Possibilités et problèmes de la modernisation agricole au Maroc,* Geneva, United Nations Research on International Social Development (UNRISD).

Vandewalle, D. (1992), "Breaking with Socialism in Algeria," in Harik and Sullivan (1992), 189–200.

Vatin, Jean-Claude, et al. (1992), *Démocratie et démocratisations dans le monde arabe,* Cairo, CEDEJ.

Vergès, Meriem (1993), "La casbah d'Alger: Chronique de survie dans un quartier en sursis," in Gilles Kepel, ed., *Exils et royaumes,* Paris, Presses de la FNSP, 69–88.

Volkan, V. D., and Itzkowitz, N. (1984), *The Immortal Atatürk,* Chicago, University of Chicago Press.

Walstedt, Bertil (1980), *State Manufacturing Enterprise in a Mixed Economy: The Turkish Case,* Baltimore and London, World Bank/Johns Hopkins University Press.

Ward, R. E., and Rustow, D., eds. (1964), *Political Modernization in Japan and Turkey,* Princeton, Princeton University Press.

Waterbury, John (1970), *The Commander of the Faithful: The Moroccan Political Elite, a Study in Segmented Politics,* New York, Columbia University Press.

——— (1973), *Land, Man, and Development in Algeria,* pt. 2, *Population, Employment, and Emigration,* American University Field Services Reports, North Africa Series, 17, 2.

——— (1978), *Egypt: Burdens of the Past, Options for the Future,* Bloomington, Indiana University Press.

——— (1979), *Hydropolitics of the Nile Valley,* Syracuse, N.Y., Syracuse University Press.

——— (1983), *The Egypt of Nasser and Sadat: The Political Economy of Two Regimes,* Princeton, Princeton University Press.

——— (1991), "Twilight of the State Bourgeoisie?" *International Journal of Middle East Studies* 23, 1–17.

——— (1992), "Export-Led Growth and the Center-Right Coalition in Turkey," *Comparative Politics* 24, 2.

Wikan, Unni (1980), *Life Among the Poor in Cairo,* London, Tavistock.

Wilson, Peter W., Graham, Douglas F. (1994), *Saudi Arabia: The Coming Storm,* New York, M. E. Sharpe.

World Bank (1979), *Yemen Arab Republic: Development of a Traditional Economy,* Washington, D.C.

——— (1981), *Morocco: Economic and Social Development Report,* Washington, D.C.

——— (1982), *Turkey: Industrialization and Trade Strategy,* Washington, D.C.

——— (1983), *Arab Republic of Egypt: Issues of Trade Strategy and Investment Planning,* Washington, D.C.

——— (1984), *World Development Report,* New York, Oxford University Press.

——— (1985), *Sudan: Prospects for Rehabilitation of the Sudanese Economy,* Report no. 5496-SU, October 7.

——— (1986a), *Jordan: Issues of Employment and Labor Market Imbalances,* Report no. 5117-JO, May.

——— (1986b), *Poverty and Hunger,* Washington, D.C.

——— (1986c), *YAR: Agricultural Strategy Paper,* Report no. 5574 YAR, May.

——— (1987), *World Development Report,* New York, Oxford University Press.

——— (1990a), *Egypt: Country Economic Memorandum,* Washington, D.C.

——— (1990b), *Poverty Alleviation and Adjustment in Egypt,* Washington, D.C.

——— (1990c), *Sudan: Reversing the Economic Decline,* Washington, D.C.

——— (1990d), *World Development Report, 1990: Poverty,* New York, Oxford University Press for the World Bank.

——— (1991), *Structural Adjustment Loan Document: Egypt,* Washington, D.C.

——— (1993a), *Arab Republic of Egypt: An Agricultural Strategy for the 1990s,* Washington, D.C.

——— (1993b), *Kingdom of Morocco: Poverty, Adjustment, and Growth,* Washington, D.C., July.

———— (1993c), *Republic of Tunisia: The Social Protection System,* Report no. 11376-TUN, April.

———— (1994a), *The Democratic and Popular Republic of Algeria: Country Economic Memorandum, the Transition to a Market Economy,* Washington, D.C.

———— (1994b), *Hashemite Kingdom of Jordan: Poverty Assessment,* vol. 1, *Main Report,* Washingston, D.C., October 28.

———— (1994c), *Islamic Republic of Iran: Country Economic Memorandum,* Report no. 13029 IRN June 8.

———— (1994d), *Kingdom of Morocco: Water Sector Review,* Washington, D.C.

———— (1994e), *A Population Perspective on Development: The Middle East and North Africa,* Washington, D.C.

———— (1994f). *A Strategy for Managing Water in the Middle East and North Africa,* Washington, D.C.

———— (1994g), *World Development Report, 1994,* Washington, D.C.

———— (1995a), *Claiming the Promise: A Long-Term Prospective Study for the Middle East and North Africa,* Washington, D.C.

———— (1995b), *Middle East and North Africa Environmental Strategy: Towards Sustainable Development,* Washington, D.C.

———— (1995c), *Will Arab Workers Prosper or Be Left Out in the 21st Century?* Washington, D.C.

———— (1995d), *World Development Report, 1995,* New York, Oxford University Press.

———— (1995e), *World Tables,* Baltimore, Johns Hopkins University Press.

Wrigley, E., and Schofield, R. (1981), *The Population History of England, 1541–1871: A Reconstruction,* Cambridge, Harvard University Press.

Yergin, Daniel (1991), *The Prize: The Epic Quest for Oil, Money, and Power,* New York: Simon and Schuster.

Zghal, Abdelkader (1977), "Pourquoi la réforme agraire ne mobilise-t-elle pas les paysans, Maghrebins?" in Bruno Etiènne, ed., *Problèmes Agraires au Maghreb,* Paris, Editions du CNRS, 295–312.

Zonis, Marvin (1991), *Majestic Failure: The Fall of the Shah,* Chicago, University of Chicago Press.

ABOUT THE BOOK
AND AUTHORS

This integrated, analytic text presents a comprehensive analysis of the transformation of the political economy of the entire contemporary Middle East region over the past several decades. As did the first edition, this new edition, extensively rewritten and revised, stresses how different development strategies have contributed to the creation of powerful interests that now often block needed change. The book also retains its focus on the interaction of economic development processes, state systems, and social actors. The revisions not only include much new data and evidence but also take into account emerging issues, such as youth unemployment, impending water shortages, the experience with structural adjustment, pressures for democratization, and the rise of political Islam. The authors also give special attention to the impact of such recent international events as the collapse of the oil boom, the end of the Cold War, and Operation Desert Storm.

Alan Richards is professor of economics at the University of California at Santa Cruz. **John Waterbury** is William Stewart Tod Professor of Politics and International Affairs at Princeton University.

INDEX

AAAID. *See* Arab Authority for Agricultural
   Investment and Development
Abboud, General Muhammed, 282
'Abd al'Aziz Al Saud (Saudi king), 300
'Abduh, Muhammed, 278
Absentee landlords, 154, 155(box)
Abu Ghazala (Egyptian field marshal), 341
Abu-Hanifa, 350
Accountability, 392
Accumulation, 201–202
Achour, Habib, 267, 317
Adams, Richard H., Jr., 382, 386
Addi, Lahouari, 288
Aden Protectorate, 26, 281, 293
Afghanistan, 74, 348
Aflaq, Michel, 129, 289
Africa, sub-Saharan, 110
Agriculture, 8, 10, 12–13, 15, 18, 27, 35,
   45, 64, 75, 83, 120, 172(n11), 174,
   175, 205, 213, 214, 215, 257, 273,
   280, 314, 348, 377
   aggregate farm output, 161
   arable land for, 48, 148, 155(box)
   development, 29–30, 353, 393
   European vs. Middle Eastern, 38–49
   exports, 21–23, 38, 40, 41, 159
   farm lobby, 154, 167
   growth rates of output, 151(fig. 6.7)
   import-substituting policies, 148
   labor force, 67–68, 76(n17), 134–135,
      148–149, 152(table), 384, 386
   public sector, 154, 156, 191
   taxation on, 19, 23, 26, 40, 147, 148,
      156, 157, 158(box), 159, 393
   unemployment in, 134–135

   variety of performance concerning,
      153(box)
   See also Food; Irrigation; *under* Water;
      individual countries
Ahmad, Kurshid, 363
Ahmad, Sa'ad Muhammed, 318
Aircraft, 337, 339, 340
Albania, 85
Al-Fatah, 295
Algeria, 1, 4, 23, 24–25, 26, 27, 31, 41, 43,
   49, 52, 71, 74, 92, 130, 214, 241,
   282, 305, 327
   agriculture, 15, 20, 148, 156, 157, 185,
      186, 230
   Algiers, 267
   Armed Islamic Group, 288, 327
   assistance to, 178
   Berbers in, 320
   bureaucracy, 286
   Charter of Algiers (1964), 285
   Charter of Socialist Management of
      Enterprise, 317
   civil war, 231, 232, 288, 326
   colonial, 155(box)
   constitution, 287
   cooperatives in, 156
   corporatism in, 316, 317
   debt, 70, 187, 231, 232
   earnings from petroleum exports, 20
   economic reforms, 225, 229–233, 249
   economy, fundamental weakness of, 228
   education/literacy in, 91, 112, 114, 115,
      117, 118, 122, 123, 126, 130, 131,
      144(n12), 287
   elections, 287–288, 308, 327, 392